What's New in This Edition!

Chapter 4, "Administering ColdFusion"

- Learn how to use all the new features in this valuable tool.

Chapter 10, "Introduction to ColdFusion Studio"

- Learn how to use the ColdFusion Studio editor.
- Use the tag chooser, expression builder, and other integrated tools.
- Read about remote development.

Chapter 14, "Using the SQL Query Builder"

- The new drag-and-drop interface can be used to write sophisticated SQL statements without any coding.

Chapter 17, "Debugging and Troubleshooting"

- The new ColdFusion Debugger is the first of its kind— a powerful remote debugger that supports breakpoints, variable watching, and more.

Chapter 18, "Working with Projects"

- Use Studio projects to manage your work.
- Read about one-step deployment.

Chapter 20, "Working with Stored Procedures"

- Learn how to write stored procedures for major database products.
- Use the three new ColdFusion stored procedure tags, which help you take advantage of the power of stored procedures within your applications.

Chapter 22, "Lists, Arrays, and Structures"

- Take advantage of the new ColdFusion data types for greater power and flexibility in data manipulation.

The ColdFusion 4.0 Web Application Construction Kit

The ColdFusion 4.0
Web Application
Construction Kit

Ben Forta
with Nate Weiss, Michael Dinowitz, Ashley King,
and David Crawford

201 West 103rd Street, Indianapolis, Indiana 46290

The ColdFusion 4.0 Web Application Construction Kit

Copyright © 1998 by Que

International Standard Book Number: 0-7897-1809-x

Library of Congress Catalog Card Number: 98-86969

Printed in the United States of America

First Printing: *December 1998*

00   99   4   3   2

Trademarks

Warning and Disclaimer

EXECUTIVE EDITOR
Bryan Gambrel

ACQUISITIONS EDITOR
Angela Kozlowski

MANAGING EDITOR
Patrick Kanouse

PROJECT EDITOR
Andrew Cupp

COPY EDITORS
Tonya Maddox
Chuck Hutchinson

PROOFREADER
Kim Cofer

TECHNICAL EDITORS
Jason Wright
Emily Kim
Ken Fricklas
Truman H. Esmond III

SOFTWARE DEVELOPMENT SPECIALIST
Todd Pfeffer

INTERIOR DESIGNER
Ruth Lewis

COVER DESIGNER
Dan Armstrong

LAYOUT TECHNICIAN
Ayanna Lacey

Contents at a Glance

V | Appendixes

Table of Contents

V Appendixes

About the Authors

Ben Forta is Allaire Corporation's product evangelist for the ColdFusion product line. Ben has over 15 years of experience in the computer industry, and spent 6 years as part of the development team responsible for creating OnTime, one of the most successful calendar and group-scheduling products, with over one million users worldwide. Ben is the author of the popular *ColdFusion Web Application Construction Kit* (now in its third edition), and the more recent *Advanced ColdFusion 4 Application Development Kit* (both published by Que). He coauthored the official Allaire ColdFusion training courses, writes a regular column on ColdFusion development, and now spends a considerable amount of time lecturing and speaking on ColdFusion and Internet application development worldwide. Born in London, England, and educated in London, New York, and Los Angeles, Ben now lives in Oak Park, Michigan, with his wife, Marcy, and their four children. Ben welcomes your email at ben@forta.com, and invites you to visit his own ColdFusion Web site at http://www.forta.com/cf.

Nate Weiss is the technical director at International Commerce Exchange Systems (ICES), a direct-marketing service for buyers and sellers. Nate used ColdFusion to design the Web, fax, and email services at the core of the company's suite of services, as well as the back-end system that serves as the the the company's worldwide account management, data-entry, and reporting mechanism. Visit the ICES Web site at http://www.icesinc.com, or Nate's own Web site at http://www.nateweiss.com. Nate can be reached via email at eponymous@nateweiss.com.

Michael Dinowitz is head of House of Fusion, a consulting firm specializing in ColdFusion-, dynamic-, and database-driven applications. His work focuses on merging ColdFusion with other technologies/languages and using them to their maximum potential. He has been with ColdFusion almost since its start and hosts the New York ColdFusion User Group. Michael has worked on sites ranging from the Publisher's Clearing House commerce engine to the Individual Investor financial site, with many other works in between. Many of his CFX tags, modules, and applications are available to help ColdFusion programmers everywhere. As a collector of information, he hosts a site at http://www.houseoffusion.com with lots of ColdFusion-related information.

Ashley King is a software engineer at Allaire Corporation and is the founder and former president of Aspx Interactive Media (CreatieAspect, Inc.), where he developed the MrPost! Web Messaging Server for ColdFusion. Ashley began his fateful foray into the programming world 13 years ago when he developed games and graphics software for Timex Sinclair 1000 and Commodore VIC-20 computers. He continued his programming career at BDM Corporation and as a contractor. Ashley later worked as a graphic artist, radio DJ, and touring musician, releasing a CD and founding one of the first Web-based music stores with his consulting company. Ashley now lives in Lexington, Massachusetts, after wandering from his native Albuquerque, New Mexico. When he's not too far behind schedule, Ashley formulates theories on paranormal experiences and writes music. He can be reached via email on the Internet at ashley@aspx.com or via the World Wide Web at http://www.trey.com.

Lieutenant Colonel **David Crawford**, CAP, is the Chief of Information Systems for National Headquarters, Civil Air Patrol, Maxwell AFB, Alabama (http://www.cap.af.mil), where he manages the day-to-day operations of a seven-person staff that provides computer support to the headquarters and 55,000 civilian volunteers of the United States Air Force Auxiliary. He holds an Associate of Arts degree in computer programming and a Bachelor of Arts in computer programming information systems from Northwest Nazarene College, is an Army Reserve officer, a long-time Civil Air Patrol member, and is active in amateur radio (KF4EQM).

Dedication

Nate Weiss

My contribution to this book is dedicated to the memory of Mr. Stanley C. Williams, a man whose voice whispers in my ear whenever I think about things like writing, chapters, outlines, and deadlines.

Michael Dinowitz

I want to thank my wife and editors for putting up with me while I wrote the black magic chapters.

Acknowledgments

Ben Forta

First and foremost, I'd like to thank the many hundreds of you who took the time to provide feedback and comments on the first two editions of this book. The numerous emails, phone calls, ICQ messages, online reviews, and impromptu meetings on tradeshow floors all helped shape this new edition. Once again, I welcome any and all comments on this book, and hope this new edition lives up to your expectations.

Thanks to everyone at Macmillan Computer Publishing for making this book a reality. In particular, special thanks to my Publisher, Joe Wikert, for recognizing the need for a book on ColdFusion, and for pushing me to work on this new edition, and to my Developer, Bryan Gambrel, for all his hard work and feedback (as well as for his help on both previous editions of this book).

Once again, a very special thank you to my Acquisitions Editor, Angela Kozlowski, for all her time, patience, advice, for not letting things fall through the cracks, and for keeping us authors on some semblance of a schedule (no easy task at all). I don't think I could have even considered updating this book had Angela not been involved.

Thanks once again to my coauthors, Ashley King, Mike Dinowitz, and Nate Weiss for their outstanding contributions. This book is as much theirs as it is mine.

Thanks to everyone at Allaire for all their hard work creating ColdFusion 4. The Internet application development community is indebted to you all. In particular, thanks to Jeremy Allaire, Jack Lull, Steve Penella, and Sim Simeonov for the support they gave the authors and editors as this book evolved.

This book's accompanying CD-ROM contains a collection of some of the best ColdFusion add-on tags and utilities that I have found. In addition to serving as examples of what ColdFusion can do, these tags will be of great value to all ColdFusion developers. A special thank you to all the developers who contributed tags. Unfortunately, there are too many of them to thank individually, but full credit is given in the documentation on the CD. If you find any of these tags or utilities useful, I urge you to email the developers directly to thank them.

A special thank you to my parents-in-law, Gerald and Eileen Borsand, for so many years of support and encouragement, and especially for helping Marcy and the kids cope with my often nightmareish travel schedule.

And most importantly, even though she insists there is no need for me to thank her publicly again, I must thank my wonderful wife Marcy. Anything I am, anything I have become, and anything I will be, is thanks to her. Marcy, for all your encouragement, sacrifices, support, love, and so much more, thank you.

Nate Weiss

A thousand thanks to Tanya Waldon for her thankless support while I was working on the original drafts of the chapters that appear here. Although my memory is generally poor, I remember your patience very clearly, Tanya. Thanks.

Tell Us What You Think!

As the reader of this book, *you* are our most important critic and commentator. We value your opinion and want to know what we're doing right, what we could do better, what areas you'd like to see us publish in, and any other words of wisdom you're willing to pass our way.

As the Executive Editor for the Client/Server Database team at Macmillan Computer Publishing, I welcome your comments. You can fax, email, or write me directly to let me know what you did or didn't like about this book—as well as what we can do to make our books stronger.

Please note that I cannot help you with technical problems related to the topic of this book, and that due to the high volume of mail I receive, I might not be able to reply to every message.

When you write, please be sure to include this book's title and author as well as your name and phone or fax number. I will carefully review your comments and share them with the author and editors who worked on the book.

Fax: 317-817-7070

Email: cs_db@mcp.com

Mail: Bryan Gambrel
         Client/Server Database
         Macmillan Computer Publishing
         201 West 103rd Street
         Indianapolis, IN 46290 USA

Introduction

In this chapter

Who Should Use This Book

This book is written for anyone who wants to create cutting-edge Web-based applications.

If you are a Webmaster or Web page designer and want to create dynamic data-driven Web pages, this book is for you. If you are an experienced database administrator who wants to take advantage of the Web to publish or collect data, this book is for you, too. If you are starting out creating your Web presence, but want to serve more than just static information, this book will help get you there. Even if you are an experienced ColdFusion user, this book provides you with invaluable tips and tricks, and also serves as the definitive ColdFusion developer's reference.

This book teaches you how to create real-world Web-based applications that solve real-world problems. Along the way you acquire all the skills you need to design, implement, test, and roll out world-class applications.

How to Use This Book

This book is designed to serve two different, but complementary, purposes.

First, it is a complete tutorial of everything you need to know to harness ColdFusion's power. As such, the book is divided into four sections, and each section introduces new topics building on what has been discussed in prior sections. Ideally, you will work through these sections in order, starting with ColdFusion basics and then moving on to advanced topics.

Second, this book is an invaluable desktop reference tool. The appendixes and the accompanying CD-ROM contain reference chapters that will be of use to you while dew{loping ColdFusion applications. Those reference chapters are cross-referenced to the appropriate tutorial sections, so that step-by-step information is always readily available to you.

N O T E ColdFusion has grown into a massive application in a very short time, and a single volume could not do justice to all its features. As such, this book is being released in conjunction with a second book: *Advanced ColdFusion 4 Application Development Kit* (Que, ISBN 0-7897-1810-3). Some of the advanced chapters that appear in prior editions of this book have been moved into that new book to facilitate better coverage of those topics. ■

Part I: Introduction

Part I of this book introduces ColdFusion and explains what exactly ColdFusion enables you to accomplish. Internet fundamentals are also introduced; a thorough understanding of these is a prerequisite to ColdFusion application development.

Chapter 1, "Why ColdFusion?," explains the concepts of data-driven World Wide Web sites and presents real-world examples of how this technology is being applied on some of the most popular sites on the Web. This chapter is not a technical overview of ColdFusion. Rather, it is a discussion of how ColdFusion can be used to enhance your Internet or intranet site.

In Chapter 2, "Introduction to ColdFusion," the core technologies that ColdFusion is built upon are introduced. The Internet and how it works are explained, as are DNS servers and URLs, Web servers and browsers, and Web server extensions such as CGI and server APIs. A good understanding of these technologies is a vital part of creating Web-based applications. This chapter also teaches you how ColdFusion works and explains the various components that comprise it.

Part II: Getting Up and Running

In Part II you learn how to install and configure ColdFusion, so that you can begin actual application development.

Chapter 3, "Installing ColdFusion and ColdFusion Studio," goes over ColdFusion's hardware and operating system prerequisites and walks you through the entire process of installing the ColdFusion Application Server and the ColdFusion Studio development environment.

Chapter 4, "Administering ColdFusion," introduces the ColdFusion Administrator. This Web-based program, written in ColdFusion itself, manages and maintains every aspect of your ColdFusion Application Server.

Part III: Getting Started with ColdFusion

Part III teaches the basics of Web-based application development, database design, and ColdFusion development. You learn how to create databases and tables, design relational databases, and create ODBC data sources that allow applications to interact with these tables. You also learn how to use ColdFusion Studio and begin creating live Web-based applications with ColdFusion.

Chapter 5, "Designing an Application," introduces fundamental concepts in application design and explains the process by which an application specification is created. Spending time up front on methodical application design pays great dividends later in the development process.

In Chapter 6, "Database Fundamentals," you are introduced to databases. Databases are mechanisms for storing and retrieving information, and almost every Web-based application you build will sit on top of a databases of some kind. Key database concepts such as tables, rows, columns, data types, keys, and indexes are taught, as are the basics of the relational database model. You also learn the differences between client-server– and shared-file–based databases, as well as the pros and cons of each.

Chapter 7, "Creating Databases and Tables," actually applies the lessons taught in Chapter 6. This chapter walks you through creating databases and tables for the sample application, with detailed step-by-step explanations of the entire process.

In Chapter 8, "Introduction to SQL," you learn the basics of the SQL language. SQL is a standard language for interacting with database applications, and all ColdFusion database manipulation is performed using SQL statements. The link between ColdFusion and your database itself is via ODBC, so this chapter introduces this technology and walks you through the process of creating ODBC data sources. Chapter 8 also teaches you how to use the SQL SELECT statement.

Chapter 9, "SQL Data Manipulation," introduces three other important SQL statements: INSERT, UPDATE, and DELETE.

Chapter 10, "Introduction to ColdFusion Studio," introduces ColdFusion's new development environment. ColdFusion Studio is a powerful HTML and CFML editor, and it is chock full of features designed to make Web page design and application development a whole lot easier. You learn how to use the editor, the tag chooser, and the expression builder, as well as how to configure the environment to work the way you do. You also learn how to use Studio for re-mote development.

Chapter 11, "ColdFusion Basics," is where you create your first ColdFusion application, albeit a very simple one. You also learn how to use <CFQUERY> to create queries that extract live data from your databases, and how to display query results using <CFOUTPUT>. Various formatting techniques, including using tables and lists, are taught as well. One method of displaying data on the Web is data drill down (which has become very popular), and this approach to data interaction is taught.

In Chapter 12, "ColdFusion Forms," you learn how to collect user-supplied data via HTML forms. This data may be used to build dynamic SQL statements that provide you with infinite flexibility in creating dynamic database queries. This chapter also teaches you how to create search screens that enable visitors to search on as many different fields as you allow.

Chapter 13, "Using Forms to Add or Change Data," teaches you how to use forms to add, up-date, and delete data in database tables. The ColdFusion tags <CFINSERT> and <CFUPDATE> are introduced, and you learn how <CFQUERY> can be used to insert, update, and delete data.

Chapter 14, "Using the SQL Query Builder," teaches you how to use the ColdFusion Studio SQL Query Builder to create complete SQL statements automatically. You learn how to create a JOIN, embed ColdFusion variables within your statements, how to test your statements within the environment, and about SQL statement reuse.

In Chapter 15, "Form Data Validation," you learn how to perform server-side and client-side validation. ColdFusion can generate JavaScript client-side validation code automatically, without you having to learn JavaScript. You learn how to use this feature, and how to provide your own validation rules.

Chapter 16, "The Report Writer," teaches the basics of using the Crystal Reports Professional report writer. The report writer allows you to create powerful data-driven reports that can be rendered into HTML on-the-fly using the ColdFusion <CFREPORT> tag.

Chapter 17, "Debugging and Troubleshooting," teaches you the kinds of things that can go wrong in ColdFusion application development and what you can do to rectify them. You learn how to use ColdFusion's debugging and logging features and the powerful integrated debugger; most importantly, you learn tips and techniques that can help you avoid problems in the first place.

Part IV: Advanced ColdFusion

Part IV teaches you advanced ColdFusion capabilities and techniques. The chapters in this section have been written with the assumption that you are familiar with basic SQL syntax and are comfortable creating ColdFusion templates.

Chapter 18, "Working with Projects," teaches you how to use the integrated ColdFusion Studio project tool. This time-saving feature allows you to work with entire applications at once, and one-step deployment simplifies the publishing process.

Chapter 19, "Advanced SQL," teaches you how to create powerful SQL statements using subqueries and joins and explains the advantages and disadvantages of each. You also learn how to calculate averages, totals, and counts, and how to use the EXISTS, NOT EXISTS, and DISTINCT keywords.

Chapter 20, "Working with Stored Procedures," takes advanced SQL one step further by teaching you how to create stored procedures and how to integrate them into your ColdFusion applications.

In Chapter 21, "Advanced ColdFusion Templates," you learn the tips and tricks needed to write powerful, scalable, and manageable applications. You learn how to comment your templates so that you, or other developers, will have an easier time maintaining the code in the future. You also see how ColdFusion facilitates code reuse with the <CFINCLUDE> tag and how to improve page processing time by using cached database queries. Finally, you learn how to create next N records-style interfaces—the same interface used by every major search engine and spider on the Internet!

Chapter 22, "Lists, Arrays, and Structures," teaches you how to use these advanced ColdFusion data types, enabling you to better manage and manipulate application data.

In Chapter 23, "Enhancing Forms with CFFORM," you learn how to take advantage of the ColdFusion-supplied Java form controls. These controls include a Windows Explorer–style tree control, an editable grid control, a slider control, and a highly configurable text input control. You also learn how to embed your own Java applets using the <CFAPPLET> tag.

Chapter 24, "Interacting with Email," introduces ColdFusion's email capabilities. ColdFusion allows you to create SMTP-based email messages using its <CFMAIL> tag. You learn how to send email messages containing user-submitted form fields, how to email the results of a database query, and how to do mass mailings to addresses derived from database tables. Additionally, you learn how to retrieve mail from POP mailboxes using the <CFPOP> tag.

Chapter 25, "Online Commerce," teaches you how to perform real-time electronic commerce, including credit card authorization via CyberCash. You build an entire working shopping cart application—one that you can use as a stepping stone when writing your own shopping applications.

In Chapter 26, "Web Application Framework," you learn how to take advantage of the ColdFusion Web Application Framework in order to add features to your Web application, including persistent client variables, sophisticated parameter and variable manipulation, and customized error message handling. You also learn how to use the application template to establish applicationwide settings and options.

Chapter 27, "Session Variables and Cookies," you learn how to use client, session, and application variables, as well as HTTP cookies. These special data types play an important part in creating a complete application that can track a client's state.

Chapter 28, "Working with Files and Directories," introduces the powerful and flexible ColdFusion <CFFILE> and <CFDIRECTORY> tags. You learn how to create, read, write, and append local files, manipulate directories, and even how to add file uploading features to your forms.

Chapter 29, "Full-Text Searching with Verity," introduces the Verity search engine. Verity provides a mechanism that does full-text searches against all sorts of data. The Verity engine is bundled with the ColdFusion Application Server, and the <CFINDEX> and <CFSEARCH> tags provide full access to Verity indexes from within your applications.

In Chapter 30, "Directory Services," you learn all about directory services and the LDAP protocol. You also learn how to use the powerful new <CFLDAP> tag that enables your applications to interact with directory services.

In Chapter 31, "Version Control," introduces version control and explains why it is such an important application development tool. You learn how to use ColdFusion's built-in version control system, as well as how to interface with existing version control systems of your own.

Chapter 32, "Event Scheduling," teaches you to create tasks that execute automatically and at timed intervals. You also learn how to dynamically generate static HTML pages using ColdFusion's scheduling technology.

Appendixes

Appendix A, "ColdFusion Tag Reference," is the definitive reference for every ColdFusion tag, with descriptive explanations, syntax tables, and examples for each. Topics are cross-referenced extensively to related topics and appropriate tutorial chapters in the book.

Appendix B, "ColdFusion Function Reference," is a complete reference of every ColdFusion function organized by category. Thorough descriptions and examples are given for every function, and extensive cross-references are provided.

Appendix C, "Verity Search Language Reference," is a complete guide to the Verity search language. Using the information provided here, you will be able to perform incredibly complex searches with minimal effort.

The CD-ROM

The accompanying CD-ROM contains everything you need to start writing ColdFusion applications, including:

- Evaluation versions of ColdFusion 4 (for Windows, Windows NT, and Solaris)
- Evaluation version of ColdFusion Studio 4

- Source code and databases for all the examples in this book
- Thirty add-on tags designed for use within your own applications
- A demonstration version of Synergy, a complete information management system, written entirely in ColdFusion
- Additional reference material and resources

Turn the page and start reading. In no time you'll be creating powerful Web-based applications using the ColdFusion Application Server.

Introduction

Why ColdFusion?

Introducing ColdFusion

The fact that you are reading this book suggests that you are interested in publishing information on the World Wide Web and that you are part of a growing number of developers interested in expanding the capabilities of their Web sites beyond simple publishing.

What kind of capabilities?

There are now over a half million Web sites that attract millions of visitors daily. Most Web sites are being used as electronic replacements for newspapers, magazines, brochures, and bulletin boards. The Web offers ways to enhance these publications using audio, images, animation, multimedia, and even virtual reality.

No one will dispute that these sites add value to the Net because information is knowledge, and knowledge is power. All this information is available at your fingertips—literally. Web sites, however, are capable of being much more than electronic versions of paper publications because of the underlying technology that makes the Web tick. Users can interact with you and your company, collect and process mission-critical information in real time, provide new levels of user support, and much more.

The Web is not merely the electronic equivalent of a newspaper or magazine—it is a communication medium that is limited only by the lack of innovation and creativity of Web site designers.

To help illustrate what ColdFusion is and where it fits into your Web site strategy, look at a few of the more impressive and innovative sites on the World Wide Web:

- Dell Computer Corporation (`http://www.dell.com`)

  Dell is a leading vendor of mail order computers. Its Web site, like many others, enables you to shop for a new computer online. The big difference is that you can customize the computer online. You are presented with a typical configuration with a price tag attached. You may click any of the components or peripherals to add or change them. Click the hard drive line item, for example, and you'll be presented with hard drive options and how they will affect the price. The price tag is dynamically recalculated when changes are made to the configuration. The Dell Web site now handles over $6,000,000 worth of business a day.

- Federal Express (`http://www.fedex.com`)

  The FedEx site hosts a whole array of impressive and innovative features. The most impressive is the online package tracking system. To test the system, I deposited a package (containing chapters that are now part of this book) in a drop box at 9:55 a.m. At 10:05 a.m. I checked the status of the package on the FedEx Web site. In less time than it took to click the Search button, I was informed that my package was picked up at 10:02 a.m. from the Southfield, MI, drop box. FedEx did not design a complete package tracking system for the Web, but cleverly linked its Web site to an already existing application. In doing so, it provides superior customer support and lowers real-time phone support costs.

- amazon.com (`http://www.amazon.com`)

  amazon.com is one of the major Internet success stories. With an online catalog of over 2.5 million books, a new online music store, and a loyal and committed user community, amazon.com is a retailer's dream come true. The biggest part of amazon.com's appeal is its sophisticated customization and personalization features. These allow amazon.com to learn a customer's buying habits and personal tastes so that the site can adapt itself during future visits. This type of customer service turns visitors into customers.

- Ticketmaster (`http://www.ticketmaster.com`)

  The Ticketmaster Web site is built around a massive database of every entertainment event in every city at every venue in the United States. The database can be searched by date, artist, event type, state, city, venue, category, and more. The site even contains seating maps of venues hosting events.

These selected sites are truly taking advantage of the World Wide Web.

What Is ColdFusion?

Initially, developing sites (like the ones mentioned earlier) was a difficult process. Writing custom Web-based applications was a job for experienced programmers only. A good working knowledge of UNIX was a prerequisite, and experience with traditional development or scripting languages was a must.

But all that has changed. Allaire's ColdFusion enables you to create sites every bit as powerful and capable as those listed earlier, without a long and painful learning curve.

What is ColdFusion? Simply put, ColdFusion is a rapid application development tool that enables the rapid creation of interactive, dynamic, and information-rich Web sites.

ColdFusion does not require coding in traditional programming languages (although traditional programming constructs and techniques are fully supported). Instead, you create applications by extending your standard HTML files with high-level formatting functions, conditional operators, and database commands. These commands are instructions to the ColdFusion processor and form the building blocks on which to build industrial-strength applications.

This method of creating Web applications has significant advantages over conventional application development.

- ColdFusion applications can be developed rapidly because no coding, other than use of simple HTML style tags, is required.

- ColdFusion applications are easy to test and roll out.

- The ColdFusion language contains all the processing and formatting functions you'll need (and the ability to create your own functions if you really run into a dead end).

- ColdFusion applications are easy to maintain because there is no compilation or linking step. The files you create are the files used by ColdFusion.

- ColdFusion provides all the tools you need to troubleshoot and debug applications, including a powerful remote interactive debugger.

- ColdFusion comes with all the hooks needed to link to almost any database application.

- ColdFusion is fast, thanks to its scalable, multithreaded, service-based architecture.

ColdFusion and Your Intranet or Extranet

Although all the examples mentioned so far have been Internet sites, the benefits of ColdFusion apply to intranets and extranets, too.

Most companies have masses of information stored in different systems. Users often don't know what information is available or how to access it even if they do.

ColdFusion bridges the gap between existing and legacy applications and your employees. It empowers employees with the tools to work more efficiently. See Chapter 2, "Introduction to ColdFusion," which discusses intranets and extranets in further detail.

The Dynamic Page Advantage

Linking your Web site to live data is a tremendous advantage, but the benefits of database interaction go beyond extending your site's capabilities.

With ColdFusion you can create dynamic, data-driven Web pages. Dynamic Web pages are becoming the norm for good reason. Consider the following:

- Static Web pages

  Static Web pages are made up of text, images, and HTML formatting tags. These pages are manually created and maintained so that when information changes, so must the page. This usually involves loading the page into an editor, making the changes, reformatting text if needed, and then saving the file. Of course, not everyone in the organization can make these changes. The Webmaster or Web design team is responsible for maintaining the site and implementing all changes and enhancements. This often means that by the time information finally makes it onto the Web site, it's out of date.

- Dynamic Web pages

  Dynamic Web pages contain very little text. Instead, they pull needed information from other applications. Dynamic Web pages communicate with databases to extract employee directory information, spreadsheets to display accounting figures, client/server database management systems to interact with order processing applications, and more. A database already exists. Why recreate it for Web page publication?

ColdFusion provides you with a full range of database interaction functions to create complete dynamic, data-driven Web pages. The features include the following capabilities:

- Query existing database applications for data
- Create dynamic queries facilitating more flexible data retrieval
- Execute stored procedures in databases that support them
- Execute conditional code on-the-fly to customize responses for specific situations
- Enhance the standard HTML form capabilities with data validation functions

- Dynamically populate form elements
- Customize the display of dates, times, and currency values with formatting functions
- Ease the creation of data entry and data drill-down applications with wizards

Powered by ColdFusion

You were probably planning to use ColdFusion to solve a particular problem or fill a specific need. While this book helps you do just that, I hope that your mind is now racing and beginning to envision just what else ColdFusion can do for your Web site.

In its relatively short life, ColdFusion has proven itself to be a solid, reliable, and scalable development platform. ColdFusion 4 is the fifth major release of this product, and with each release it becomes an even better and more useful tool. It is easy to learn, fun to use, and powerful enough to create real-world Web-based applications. With a minimal investment of your time, your Web site can be powered by ColdFusion. ●

Introduction to ColdFusion

Understanding the World Wide Web

The World Wide Web is the most talked about publishing medium. Recent statistics indicate that close to 40 million people browse the Web (with over 2,500,000 different Web sites) on a regular basis. Hembrecht & Quist, a leading investment firm, forecasts that by the year 2000 the number of regular Web users will grow to 200 million.

In August 1981, 213 hosts (computers) were connected to the Internet. By August 1997 that number had grown to almost 20 million! The number of Web sites on the Internet has grown at the same alarming rate. There were fewer than 25,000 Internet Web sites in June 1995, and exactly one year later there were 230,000.

What has made the World Wide Web so popular? That, of course, depends on who you ask. Most will agree that these are the two primary reasons:

- Ease of use. Publishing information on the Web and browsing for information are relatively easy tasks.
- Quantity of content. With hundreds of thousands of Web pages to choose from and thousands more being created each day, there are sites and pages to cater to almost every surfer's tastes.

A massive potential audience awaits your Web site and the services it offers. You could, and should, be offering much more than just static text and images. You need features like the following:

- Dynamic, data-driven Web pages
- Database connectivity
- Intelligent, user-customized pages
- Sophisticated data collection and processing
- Email interaction

ColdFusion enables you to do all this—and more.

You need to take a step back before starting ColdFusion development. Because ColdFusion takes advantage of existing Internet technologies, a prerequisite to ColdFusion development is a good understanding of the Internet, the World Wide Web, Web servers and browsers, and how all these pieces fit together.

The Internet

Much ambiguity and confusion surround the Internet, so you should start with a definition. Simply put, the Internet is the world's largest network.

The networks found in most offices today are local area networks, (LANs), comprised of a group of computers in relatively close proximity to each other and linked by special hardware and cabling (see Figure 2.1). Some computers are clients (more commonly known as *workstations*), others are servers (also known as *file servers*). All these computers can communicate with each other to share information.

FIGURE 2.1

A LAN is a group of computers in close proximity linked by special cabling.

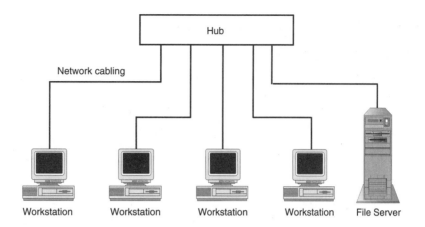

Now imagine a bigger network, one that spans multiple geographical locations. This type of network is typically used by larger companies with offices in multiple locations. Each location has its own LAN, which links the local computers together. All these LANs in turn are linked to each other via some communications medium. The linking can be anything from a 28.8 baud modem to high-speed T1 connections and fiber-optic links. The complete group of interconnected LANs, as shown in Figure 2.2, is called a WAN, or wide area network.

FIGURE 2.2

A WAN is made up of multiple, interconnected LANs.

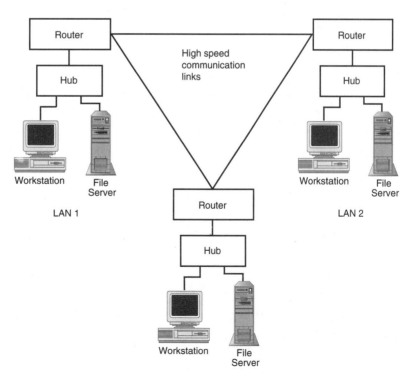

WANs are used to link multiple locations within a single company. Suppose that you need to create a massive network that links every computer everywhere. How would you do this?

You'd start by running high-speed *backbones*, connections capable of moving large amounts of data at once, between strategic locations—perhaps large cities or different countries. These backbones would be like high-speed, multi-lane, interstate highways connecting various locations.

You'd build in fault tolerance to make these backbones fully redundant so that if any connection broke, at least one other way to reach a specific destination would be available.

You'd then create thousands of local links that would connect every city to the backbones over slower connections—like state highways or city streets. You'd allow corporate WANs, LANs, and even individual users with dial-up modems to connect to these local access points. Some would stay connected at all times, whereas others would connect as needed.

You'd create a common communications language so that every computer connected to this network could communicate with every other computer.

Finally, you'd devise a scheme to uniquely identify every computer connected to the network. This would ensure that information sent to a given computer actually reached the correct destination.

Congratulations, you've just created the Internet!

Even though this is an oversimplification, it is exactly how the Internet works.

The high-speed backbones do exist. Many are owned and operated by the large telecommunications companies.

The local access points, more commonly known as POPs, or Points of Presence, are run by phone companies, online services, and local Internet service providers (also known as ISPs).

The common language is IP, the Internet protocol, except that the term *language* is a misnomer. A *protocol* is a set of rules governing behavior in certain situations. Foreign diplomats learn local protocol to ensure that they behave correctly in another country. The protocols ensure that there are no communication breakdowns or serious misunderstandings. Computers also need protocols, to ensure that they can communicate with each other correctly and that data is exchanged correctly. IP is the protocol used to communicate across the Internet, so every computer connected to the Internet must be running a copy of IP.

The unique identifiers are IP addresses. Every computer, or host, connected to the Internet has a unique IP address. These addresses are made up of four sets of numbers separated by periods—206.246.150.10, for example. Some hosts have *fixed* (or *static*) IP addresses, while others have dynamically assigned addresses. Regardless of how an IP address is obtained, no two hosts connected to the Internet can use the same IP address at any given time. That would be like two homes having the same phone number or street address. Information would end up in the wrong place all the time.

A Brief History of the Internet

The Internet has evolved over the past 25 years to become an incredibly important communications medium. What follows is a brief history of the Internet.

1969—The U.S. Department of Defense starts researching a new networking project. The first node in the network is established at UCLA and, soon after, nodes are set up at Stanford Research Institute, UCSB, and the University of Utah.

1971—The number of connected nodes reaches 15, as additional government and education institutions are brought online. The capability to send email over the Internet is introduced.

1972—Telnet is introduced to permit remote host access over the Internet.

1973—The U.S. Defense Advanced Research Projects Agency begins work on the "Internetting Project," researching ways to link different kinds of packet networks. File Transfer Protocol (FTP) is introduced.

1977—Email specifications are formalized.

1983—Name server technology is developed at the University of Wisconsin.

1984—Domain Name Service (DNS) is introduced.

1986—The U.S. National Science Foundation starts developing NFSNET, a major Internet backbone. Network News Transfer Protocol (NNTP) is introduced to enhance the performance of Usenet news.

1987—The number of hosts connected to the Internet tops 10,000.

1988—Internet worm cripples the Internet, affecting over 60,000 hosts. Internet Relay Chat (IRC) is introduced.

1989—The number of hosts connected to the Internet tops 100,000.

1991—Gopher is introduced. The World Wide Web is released by CERN, the European Laboratory for Particle Physics, located near Geneva, Switzerland.

1992—The number of hosts connected to the Internet tops 1,000,000.

1993—The InterNIC is created to handle directory and domain registration services.

1995—The World Wide Web becomes the service generating the most Internet traffic. InterNIC starts charging an annual fee for domain name registrations.

1996—The Java development language promises to usher in a new era of portable application development; VRML (Virtual Reality Markup Language) debuts; 30 more countries register their own top level domains and the number of hosts connected to the Internet tops 10,000,000.

1997—The two-thousandth RFC (Internet standards document) is published; human error at Network Solutions causes millions of hosts to be temporarily unreachable; 20 more countries register their own top level domains, and the number of hosts connected to the Internet reaches almost 20,000,000 (100% growth in a single year).

Part
I
Ch
2

Internet Applications

The Internet itself is simply a massive communications network and offers very little to most users, which is why it took 20 years for the Internet to become the phenomenon is it today.

The Internet has been dubbed the Information Superhighway, and that analogy is quite accurate. Highways themselves are not nearly as exciting as the places you can get to by traveling them—and the same is true of the Internet. What makes the Internet so exciting are the applications that run over it and what you can accomplish with them.

The most popular application now is the World Wide Web. It is the Web that single-handedly transformed the Internet into a household word. In fact, many people mistakenly think that the World Wide Web is the Internet. This is definitely not the case, and Table 2.1 lists some of the more popular Internet-based applications.

Table 2.1   Some Internet-Based Applications

Application	Description
Email	Simple Mail Transfer Protocol (SMTP) is the most popular email delivery mechanism.
FTP	File Transfer Protocol is used to transfer files between hosts.
Gopher	This menu-driven document retrieval system was very popular before the creation of the World Wide Web.
IRC	Internet Relay Chat allows real-time, text-based conferencing over the Internet.
NFS	Network File System is used to share files among different hosts.
Newsgroups	Newsgroups are threaded discussion lists, of which there are thousands.
Telnet	Telnet is used to log on to a host from a remote location.
WWW	The World Wide Web.

All these different applications—and many others—use IP to communicate across the Internet. The information transmitted by these applications is broken into *packets*, small blocks of data, which are sent to a destination IP address. The application at the receiving end processes the received information.

DNS—The Domain Name Service

IP addresses are the only way to uniquely specify a host. When you want to communicate with a host—a Web server for example—you need to specify the IP address of the Web server you are trying to contact.

As you know from browsing the Web, you rarely specify IP addresses directly. You do, however, specify a host name, like www.mcp.com (the Macmillan Computer Publishing Web site). If hosts are identified by IP address, how does your browser know which Web server to contact if you specify a host name?

The answer is the Domain Name Service. DNS is a mechanism that maps host names to IP addresses. When you specify the destination address www.mcp.com, your browser sends an address resolution request to a DNS server asking for the IP address of that host. The DNS server returns an actual IP address, in this case 204.95.236.226. Your browser can then use this address to communicate with the host directly.

If you've ever mistyped a host name, you've seen error messages telling you that the host could not be found, or that no DNS entry was found for the specified host. These error messages mean that the DNS server was unable to resolve the specified host name.

DNS is never needed. Users can always specify the name of a destination host by its IP address in order to connect to the host. There are, however, some very good reasons not to:

- IP addresses are hard to remember and easy to mistype. Users are more likely to find www.mcp.com than they are 204.95.236.226.

- IP addresses are subject to change. For example, if you switch service providers, you might be forced to use a new set of IP addresses for your hosts. If users only identified your site by its IP address, they'd never be able to reach your host if the IP address changed. Your DNS name stays the same, even if your IP address switches. You only need to change the mapping so the host name maps to the new, correct IP address.

- Multiple hosts, each with a unique IP address, can all have the same DNS name. This allows load balancing between servers, as well as the establishment of redundant servers.

- A single host, with a single IP address, can have multiple DNS names. This enables you to create aliases if needed. For example, ftp.mcp.com and www.mcp.com might point to the same IP address, and thus the same server.

DNS servers are special software programs. Your ISP will often host your DNS entries so that you don't need to install and maintain your own DNS server software.

You may host your own DNS server and gain more control over the domain mappings, but you inherit the responsibility of maintaining the server. If your DNS server is down, there won't be any way of resolving the host name to an IP address, and no one will be able to find your site.

Intranets and Extranets

Intranets and extranets are currently two of the industry's favorite buzzwords. It was not too long ago that most people thought *intranet* was a typo; but in a very short period of time, intranets and extranets became recognized as legitimate and powerful new business tools.

An *intranet* is nothing more than a private Internet. In other words, it is a private network, usually a LAN or WAN, that enables the use of Internet-based applications in a secure and private environment. As on the public Internet, intranets can host Web servers, FTP servers, and any other IP-based services.

Companies have been using private networks for years to share information. Traditionally, office networks have not been information friendly. Old private networks did not have consistent interfaces, standard ways to publish information, or client applications that were capable of accessing diverse data stores. The popularity in the public Internet has spawned a whole new generation of inexpensive and easy-to-use client applications. These applications are now making their way back into the private networks. The reason intranets are now gathering so much attention is that they are a new solution to an old problem.

Extranets take this new communication mechanism one step further. Extranets are intranet-style networks that link multiple sites or organizations using intranet-related technologies. Many extranets actually use the public Internet as their backbone and employ encryption techniques to ensure the security of the data being moved over the network.

The two things that distinguish intranets and extranets from the Internet is who can access them and from where they can be accessed. Don't be confused by hype surrounding applications that claim to be intranet ready. If an application can be used over the public Internet, it will work on private intranets and extranets too.

Web Servers

As mentioned earlier, the most commonly used Internet-based application is now the World Wide Web. The recent growth of interest in the Internet is the result of growing interest in the World Wide Web.

The World Wide Web is built upon a protocol called Hypertext Transport Protocol (HTTP). HTTP is designed to be a small, fast protocol that is well suited for distributed multimedia information systems and hypertext jumps between sites.

The Web consists of pages of information on hosts running Web-server software. The host is often referred to as the Web server, which is technically inaccurate. The Web server is software, not the computer itself. There are versions of Web server software that can run on almost all computers. There is nothing intrinsically special about a computer that hosts a Web server, and there are no rules dictating what hardware is appropriate for running a Web server.

The original World Wide Web development was all performed under different flavors of UNIX. The majority of Web servers still run on UNIX boxes, but this is changing. There are now Web server versions for almost every major operating system. Web servers hosted on high-performance operating systems, like Windows NT, are becoming more and more popular. This is because UNIX is still more expensive to run than Windows NT and is also more difficult for the average user to use. Windows NT has proven itself to be an efficient, reliable, and cost-effective platform for hosting Web servers. As a result, Windows NT's slice in the Web server operating system pie is growing.

What exactly is a Web server? A *Web server* is a program that serves Web pages upon request. Web servers typically don't know or care what they are serving. When a user at a specific IP address requests a specific file, the Web server tries to retrieve that file and send it back to the user. The requested file might be a Web page's HTML source code, a GIF image, VRML worlds, or AVI files. It is the Web browser that determines what should be requested, not the Web server. The server simply processes that request, as shown in Figure 2.3.

It is important to note that Web servers typically do not care about the contents of these files. HTML code in a Web page, for example, is markup that the Web browser—not the Web server—will process. The Web server returns the requested page as is, regardless of what the page is and what it contains. If there are HTML syntax errors in the file, those errors will be returned along with the rest of the page.

FIGURE 2.3

Web servers process requests made by Web browsers.

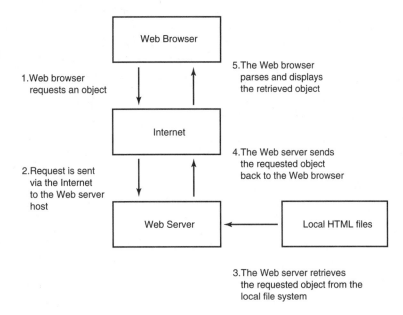

1. Web browser requests an object

2. Request is sent via the Internet to the Web server host

5. The Web browser parses and displays the retrieved object

4. The Web server sends the requested object back to the Web browser

3. The Web server retrieves the requested object from the local file system

N O T E   Some Web servers support advanced features so the servers can actually process Web pages themselves. For example, Netscape Enterprise Server has a feature called server-side includes, which enables you to instruct a Web server to include another URL in a specified location within a Web page.

You can expect to see more intelligent Web servers in the future. For now, however, these features are the exception rather than the norm. ▨

Connections to Web servers are made on an as-needed basis. If you request a page from a Web server, an IP connection is made over the Internet between your host and the host running the Web server. The requested Web page is sent over that connection, and the connection is broken as soon as the page is received. If the received page contains references to additional information to be downloaded (for example, GIF or JPG images), each would be retrieved using a new connection. Therefore, it takes at least six requests, or *hits*, to retrieve all of a Web page with five pictures in it.

This is why the number of hits is such a misleading measure of Web server activity. When you learn of Web servers that receive millions of hits in one day, it may not mean that there were millions of visitors. Hits do not equal the number of visitors or pages viewed. In fact, hits are only a useful measure of changes in server activity. Web servers are often not the only IP-based applications running on a single host. In fact, aside from performance issues, there is no reason a single host cannot run multiple services. For example, a Web server, an FTP server, a DNS server, and an SMTP POP3 mail server can run at the same time. Each server is assigned a port address to ensure that each server application only responds to requests and communications from appropriate clients. If IP addresses are like street addresses, ports can be thought of as apartment or suite numbers.

Most servers use a standard set of port mappings, and some of the more common ports are listed in Table 2.2. Most Web servers use port 80, but you can change that. If desired, Web servers can be installed on nonstandard ports to "hide" Web servers, as well as host multiple Web servers on a single computer by mapping each one to a different port. Remember that if you do use a nonstandard port mapping, users need to know the new port number.

Table 2.2   Common IP Port Numbers

Port	Use
20	FTP
21	FTP
23	Telnet
25	SMTP
53	DNS
70	Gopher
80	HTTP
107	Remote Telnet service
109	POP2
110	POP3
119	NNTP
143	IMAP4, Interactive Mail Access Protocol version 4 (previously used by IMAP2)
194	IRC
220	IMAP3
389	LDAP, Lightweight Directory Access Protocol
443	HTTPS, HTTP running over secure sockets
540	UUCP, UNIX to UNIX Copy

Web Pages

Information on the World Wide Web is stored in *pages*. A page can contain any of the following:

- Text
- Headers
- Lists
- Menus
- Tables
- Forms
- Graphics
- Multimedia

Web pages are plain text files constructed via HTML (Hypertext Markup Language). HTML is implemented as a series of easy-to-learn tags. Web page authors use these tags to mark up a page of text. Browsers then use these tags to render and display the information for viewing.

HTML is constantly being enhanced with new features and tags. To ensure backward compatibility, browsers must ignore tags they do not understand. For example, if you use the `<MARQUEE>` tag in an effort to create a scrolling text marquee, browsers that do not support this tag display the marquee text but do not scroll the text.

Web pages may also contain *hypertext jumps*, which are links to other pages or Web sites. Users may click links to either jump to other pages on the same site or any page on any site.

The word *Web* in World Wide Web refers to the capability to jump to any Web page on any Web server and back again.

Pages on a Web server are stored in different directories. When requesting a Web page, a user may provide a full path (directory and filename) to specify a particular document.

You can specify a *default* Web page, a page that is sent back to the user when only a directory is specified, with a Web server. These default pages are often called `index.html` or `default.htm`. If no default Web page exists in a particular directory, you either see an error message or a list of all the available files, depending on how the server is set up.

URLs

Every Web page on the World Wide Web has an address. This is what you type into your browser to instruct it to load a particular Web page.

These addresses are called *Uniform Resource Locators* (URLs). URLs are not just used to identify World Wide Web pages or objects. Files on an FTP server, for example, also have URL identifiers.

World Wide Web URLs consist of up to five parts:

- The protocol to retrieve the object. This is usually `http` for objects on the World Wide Web.
- The Web server from which to retrieve the object. This is specified as a DNS name or an IP address.
- The host machine port on which the Web server is running. If omitted, the specified protocol's default port is used; for Web servers this is port 80.
- The file to retrieve or the script to execute. You learn more about the script later in this chapter.
- Optional script parameters, also known as the *query string*.

Look at a few sample URLs:

- `http://www.mcp.com`

    This URL points to a Web page on the host `www.mcp.com`. Because no document or path was specified, the default document in the root directory is served.

■ http://www.mcp.com/que/

This URL also points to a Web page on the host www.mcp.com, but this time the directory /que/ is specified. Because no page name was provided, the default page in the /que/ directory is served.

■ http://206.246.150.10/que/

This URL points to the same file as the previous example, but this time the IP address is used instead of the DNS name.

■ http://www.mcp.com/que/topten.html

Once again, this URL points to a Web page on the www.mcp.com host. Both a directory and a filename are specified this time. This will retrieve the file topten.html from the /que/ directory, instead of the default file.

■ http://www.a2zbooks.com:81/catalog/internet.html

This is an example of an URL that points to a page on a Web server assigned to a nonstandard port. Because port 81 is not the standard port for Web servers, the port number must be provided.

■ http://www.a2zbooks.com/a2z/guestbook.cfm

This URL points to a specific page on a Web server, but not an HTML page. CFM files are ColdFusion templates, which are discussed later in this chapter.

■ http://www.a2zbooks.com/cgi/cfml.exe?template=/guestbook.cfm

This URL points to a script, rather than a Web page. /cgi/ is the directory name (or directory map) to the location where the cfml.exe script is located. Anything after the ? is parameters that are passed to the script. In this example, the Web server executes the script cfml.exe and passes the parameter template=/guestbook.cfm to it.

■ http://www.a2zbooks.com/cgi/cfml.exe?template=/ guestbook.cfm&src=10

This URL is the same as the previous example, with one additional parameter. A ? is always used to separate the URL itself (including the script to execute) from any parameter. Multiple parameters are separated by ampersands (the & character).

■ ftp://ftp.a2zbooks.com/pub/catalog.zip

This is an example of an URL that points to an object other than a Web page or script. The protocol ftp indicates that the object referred to is a file to be retrieved from an FTP server using the file transfer protocol. This file is catalog.zip in the /pub/ directory.

Links in Web pages are references to other URLs. When a user clicks a link, the browser processes whatever URL it references.

Web Browsers

Web browsers are client programs used to access Web sites and pages. The Web browser has the job of processing received Web pages, parsing the HTML code, and displaying the page to the user. The browser attempts to display graphics, tables, forms, formatted text, or whatever the page contains.

The most popular Web browsers now in use are Netscape Navigator, shown in Figure 2.4, and Microsoft Internet Explorer, shown in Figure 2.5. Both browsers are displaying the same Allaire home page, but the pages do not look the same in both browsers.

FIGURE 2.4

Netscape Navigator is the Web's most popular browser.

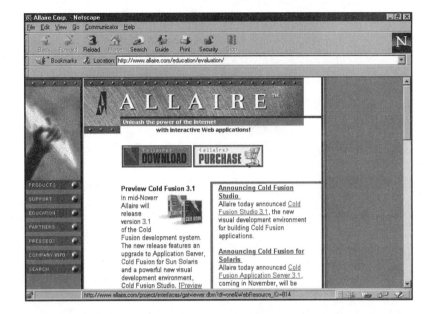

FIGURE 2.5

Microsoft Internet Explorer is gaining popularity, particularly among users running Windows 95 or Windows NT.

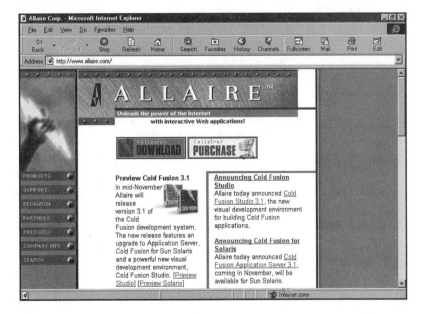

Part

I

Ch

2

Web page designers have to pay close attention to the differences between browsers because different Web browsers support different HTML tags. Unfortunately, there is not one single browser that supports every tag currently in use. Furthermore, the same Web page often looks different on two different browsers; every browser renders and displays Web page objects differently.

For this reason, most Web page designers use multiple Web browsers and test their pages in every one to ensure that the final output appears as intended. Without this testing, some Web site visitors will not see the pages you published correctly.

CGI

Web servers can do more than just serve static pages. As mentioned before, Web servers can execute scripts as well. When a Web server receives an URL request that references a script, it executes it and returns the script output instead of returning the script.

For example, suppose you had a Web site that reported stock quotes. Creating Web pages that listed all the stocks by exchange, along with their current values, would be close to impossible. It would be outdated as soon as you updated the page and saved it. What you could do instead is write a script that takes a stock symbol as a parameter and returns the current value. When a user requests a stock, the Web server executes the script referred to in the URL, passes the stock symbol as a parameter, connects the script to your designated system to obtain stock quotes, and generates HTML output containing the quote. This data flow is shown in Figure 2.6.

A standard script interface was created in order to make it easier to create scripts that work with multiple Web servers. Common Gateway Interface (CGI) is a Web server scripting standard. It is important to understand that CGI is not a program or script, but a mechanism that you can use to connect your script to your Web server.

When a CGI script executes, the following occurs:

1. The Web server creates a new session in which to execute the script.
2. A group of standard environment variables that contain information the script might need is set. This includes the remote host's IP address, the URL that was specified, server and browser version information, and so on.
3. The script is then executed within this session, and any parameters are passed to it.
4. The Web server captures any output generated by the script.
5. Once the script has completed running, the session is terminated and the captured output is sent to the requester's browser.

What exactly is a script? That depends on the Web server you are running.

In the past, most CGI programs were actually script files written in scripting languages like Perl, but current scripts can also be executable programs. You can write scripts in C and Visual Basic. Some Web servers even enable you to execute batch files as scripts. As long as your program can execute without any user intervention, it can be a script.

FIGURE 2.6

You can extend the publishing capabilities of your Web server with scripts.

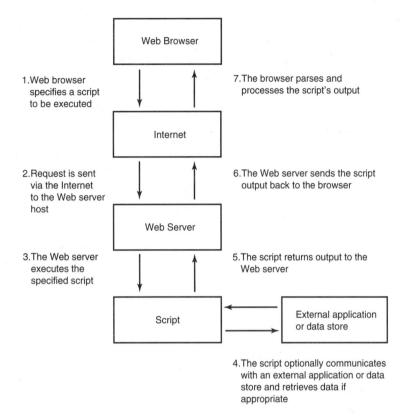

1. Web browser specifies a script to be executed

7. The browser parses and processes the script's output

2. Request is sent via the Internet to the Web server host

6. The Web server sends the script output back to the browser

3. The Web server executes the specified script

5. The script returns output to the Web server

4. The script optionally communicates with an external application or data store and retrieves data if appropriate

TIP The CGI specification has gone through several revisions. The best place to find up-to-date information on CGI is the W3 Consortium Web site, `http://www.w3.org`.

CGI scripts are a very powerful way to extend your Web server's capabilities, and you've probably used them without even realizing it. If you have ever used an Internet search engine or any intelligent forms, you've probably used CGI scripts. The beauty of CGI is that it is simple to implement, portable, and completely transparent to the end user.

Server APIs

As powerful as CGI is, it does have some shortcomings:

- The process of creating sessions and executing scripts is time consuming. Seconds and milliseconds might not sound like a lot of time, but these short delays add up when you have multiple requests running concurrently.

- CGI applications, by their very nature, must be loaded and unloaded each time they are used. There is no way to load a CGI script and keep it ready for future use.

- CGI applications are entities entirely separate from the Web server itself. CGI cannot be used to change the behavior of a Web server (perhaps to do URL redirection) or to implement your own security system.

To overcome these shortcomings, Web server developers have created interfaces to extend the capabilities of their Web servers. These interfaces are known as server APIs.

An API is an application programming interface. APIs are used by programmers to write applications that can interact with other applications. A server API is a published interface that enables software developers to write programs that become part of the Web server itself. These are usually Windows Dynamic Load Libraries (DLLs) that are loaded into memory and stay resident at all times. These DLLs hook directly into the guts of the Web server and enable you to extend or alter the server's capabilities as needed.

This power and capability does come with a price. Because server APIs are so closely tied to Web servers themselves, each is very server specific. In fact, four different ColdFusion server APIs are available for three different Web servers, as shown in Table 2.3. They are, of course, incompatible with each other.

Table 2.3   Server APIs and the Servers They Support

Server API	Supported Servers
APACHE	Apache HTTP Server on Windows NT and Solaris
ISAPI	Microsoft Internet Information Server
NSAPI	Netscape Commerce, Enterprise, and Fasttrack Servers
WSAPI	O'Reilly Web Site and Web Site Pro

Both CGI and server APIs have a place in the Web server arena. CGI is not as powerful or as fast as server APIs, but CGI scripts are simple to implement and can be portable across different computing platforms. Server APIs are not portable, but they are faster and more powerful.

Introducing ColdFusion

Now look at ColdFusion to see how it works its magic.

If you're wondering why you went through all this discussion about the Internet, Web servers, CGI, and server APIs, here's where it will all fit together.

ColdFusion Components

Back in the early ColdFusion days, ColdFusion was a CGI script. Every time a user would make a ColdFusion request (displaying data or inserting and updating records), the Web server executed the entire ColdFusion program. ColdFusion would process the user's request, perform whatever actions were necessary, and return HTML output to the user.

As ColdFusion's feature set grew, so did the application's response time. Because CGI programs are loaded and unloaded as needed, there is no way to maintain variables, settings, database connections, and file handles between each executed session. Performance was a serious problem.

The Allaire development team went back to the drawing board and developed a scaleable and elegant new design. They broke ColdFusion into multiple parts:

- The guts of ColdFusion, the engine that actually processes the user's requests, became a Windows NT service and a UNIX daemon. As a service, ColdFusion can remain running at all times, even when no one is logged on to the server. Under Windows 95, which does not support services, this engine is a separate application that remains running at all times.

- Web servers themselves have no idea how to communicate with a service or daemon, so server modules were written for the four different server APIs. These server modules are the glue that binds the Web server to the ColdFusion service.

- A CGI script (`cfml.exe`) was created for Web servers that don't support server APIs. This CGI script guarantees that any Web server that supports the CGI specification can be used with ColdFusion. Of course, the CGI script interface to ColdFusion is slower than the server API interfaces, so it should only be used when the server modules cannot.

The ColdFusion engine (the service on Windows NT, and the daemon on Solaris) is the program that actually parses and processes any supplied instructions. Instructions are passed to ColdFusion using templates.

A *template* looks much like any HTML file, with one big difference. Unlike HTML files, ColdFusion templates can contain special tags, which instruct ColdFusion to perform specific operations. Listing 2.1 contains a sample ColdFusion template; it is one that you'll use later in this book.

Listing 2.1 Sample ColdFusion Template

```
<CFQUERY
DATASOURCE=" A2Z"
>
INSERT INTO Employees(FirstName, LastName, PhoneExtension)
VALUES('#FirstName#', '#LastName#', '#PhoneExtension#')
</CFQUERY>

<HTML>

<HEAD>
<TITLE>Employee Added</TITLE>
</HEAD>

<BODY>

<H1>Employee Added</H1>

<CFOUTPUT>
Employee <B>#FirstName# #LastName#</B> added.
</CFOUTPUT>
```

continues

Listing 2.1   Continued

```
</BODY>

</HTML>
```

Earlier in this chapter it was stated that Web servers typically return the contents of a Web page without paying any attention to the file contents.

That's exactly what ColdFusion does not do. When ColdFusion receives a request, it parses through the template looking for special ColdFusion tags (they all begin with CF) or ColdFusion variables and functions (always surrounded by pound signs). Any HTML or plain text is left alone and is output to the Web server untouched. Any ColdFusion instructions are processed, and any existing results are sent to the Web server.

The Web server can then send the entire output back to the requester's browser.

CFML—The ColdFusion Markup Language

ColdFusion's power comes from its capable and flexible language. ColdFusion Markup Language (CFML) is modeled after HTML, which makes it very easy to learn.

CFML extends HTML by adding tags with the following capabilities:

- Read data from, and update data to, databases and tables
- Create dynamic data-driven pages
- Perform conditional processing
- Populate forms with live data
- Process form submissions
- Generate and retrieve email messages
- Interact with local files
- Perform HTTP and FTP operations
- Perform credit card verification and authorization
- Read and write client-side cookies

That's not even the complete list.

The majority of this book discusses ColdFusion templates and the use of CFML.

URLs

When accessing ColdFusion templates with your Web browser, you need a way to specify which template you want to execute. You do this by specifying the template name in the URL.

Because ColdFusion is both a CGI application and a server module, two different types of URL syntax are available for your use. As a general rule, you should use the server module syntax whenever you can.

ColdFusion CGI URL Syntax   Look at the CGI syntax first:

`http://www.a2zbooks.com/cgi/cfml.exe?template=/a2z/hello1.cfm`

This example instructs the Web server on host `www.a2zbooks.com` to execute `cfml.exe` (the ColdFusion CGI interface) and specifies that the template to process is `/a2z/hello1.cfm`.

ColdFusion Server Module URL Syntax   Now see how the same template executes using the server module's URL syntax:

`http://www.a2zbooks.com/hello1.cfm`

This URL is cleaner and simpler because it simply instructs the Web server to return the file `hello1.cfm`.

How does the Web server know to execute the template and return the results instead of returning the template itself? The answer is a technology called *document type mapping*. When ColdFusion is installed, it configures your Web server so that it knows that any file that has an extension of `.cfm` (or `.cfml`) is a ColdFusion file. Then, whenever a ColdFusion file is requested, the Web server knows to pass the file to ColdFusion for processing rather than returning it.

Of course, if you ever need to pass parameters to a ColdFusion template, you still have that option. The following example passes a parameter called `src` to the template for processing:

`http://www.a2zbooks.com/hello1.cfm?src=10`

TIP If you are using one of the Web servers for which ColdFusion has a server API module available, you should always use it instead of the CGI interface.

Linking to External Applications

One of ColdFusion's most powerful features is its capability to connect to data created and maintained in other applications. You can use ColdFusion to retrieve or update data in many applications, including the following:

- Corporate databases
- Client/server database systems (like Microsoft SQL Server and Oracle)
- Spreadsheets
- Contact management software
- ASCII delimited files

ColdFusion accesses these applications via ODBC. ODBC, which is discussed in detail later in this book, is a standard interface that applications can use to interact with a diverse set of external data stores.

The majority of Part II, "Getting Up and Running," and Part III, "Getting Started with ColdFusion," discusses ColdFusion's database interaction via ODBC. ●

Getting Up and Running

Installing ColdFusion and ColdFusion Studio

In this chapter

Preparing to Install ColdFusion

Before getting started, you need to know that ColdFusion is extremely easy to install and configure. As long as the basic hardware and software requirements are in place, installing ColdFusion should take just a few minutes.

N O T E   ColdFusion comes in two distinct versions, a *professional* version and an *enterprise* version. The enterprise version provides sophisticated scalability and security features, and additional high-end features. Everything taught in this book applies to both versions of the product. The evaluation version on this book's accompanying CD-ROM is the enterprise version of the ColdFusion Application Server. ■

Installing ColdFusion involves the following steps:

1. Verify that you have the correct hardware.
2. Select an operating system and ensure that it is configured correctly.
3. Select a Web server and ensure that it is installed and functions correctly.
4. Perform the actual installation.
5. Test the installation.

The first half of this chapter walks you through each of these steps.

Hardware Requirements

The ColdFusion Application Server runs on two different types of hardware: Intel-based hardware (capable of running 32-bit Windows), Sun SPARC hardware running Solaris, and HP boxes running HP/UX.

Intel-Based Hardware   ColdFusion runs under Windows 95 and Windows 98, and Windows NT (on Intel hardware only). The minimum recommended hardware is a Pentium class machine running at 100MHz.

If you'll be using Windows 95 or Windows 98, you should have no less than 32MB of RAM; 64MB of RAM is the minimum if you'll be using Windows NT. Additional memory enhances system performance, especially if you're running Windows NT.

Your computer should have 50MB of disk space available after the Web server is installed and configured. Obviously, as you create applications on the server, the amount of disk space needed will increase.

The computer also needs to be connected to a network. This is usually via a network interface card (NIC) installed into the computer on an Ethernet or Token Ring network. A modem can also be used to connect the computer to a network.

Sun SPARC Hardware   ColdFusion requires a minimum of 64MB of RAM, but 128MB is recommended.

Your computer should have 60MB of disk space available after the Web server is installed and configured. Again, the amount of disk space needed will increase as you create applications on the server.

The computer also needs to be connected to a network. Usually this is done via a NIC installed into the computer on an Ethernet or Token Ring network. A modem can also be used to connect the computer to a network.

Selecting a Hardware Platform   ColdFusion runs on two very different hardware platforms, each with its own advantages and disadvantages. Which is right for you? There is no right or wrong answer, but here are some points to consider when making this decision:

- Almost all of your ColdFusion code will run seamlessly on either platform. It is therefore possible to change your hardware platform at a later date without having to rewrite all of your code.
- Sun SPARC hardware is considerably more expensive than Intel hardware, and you do not have the selection of vendors and products that you have with Intel-based hardware.
- Intel-based hardware runs 32-bit Windows (Windows 95 or 98, or Windows NT), which is easier to install and manage.
- Intel hardware expertise is more readily available than is Sun SPARC hardware expertise.
- The hardware you have available, and any existing expertise, are primary factors to consider when selecting a hardware platform.
- Sun SPARC hardware generally performs better than Intel-based hardware, and it is more scalable.

Evaluation version of both the Windows and Solaris versions of the ColdFusion Application Server are on the accompanying CD-ROM. If you would like information on other versions, contact Allaire at 617-761-2000 or at http://www.allaire.com.

Selecting an Operating System

Once you have selected the hardware on which you will run your ColdFusion Application Server, the next step is to select an operating system. The choices available to you are going to be based on the hardware platform you select.

Operating Systems for Intel-Based Hardware   You have two operating system choices when running Intel-based hardware: Windows 95 or Windows 98 (from a ColdFusion perspective these are one and the same), and Windows NT. Windows 95 and Windows 98 does not come with a built-in Web server, Windows NT (version 4 or later) does.

Windows 95 and Windows 98 are a great testing and development platform, and could also be used for very low volume Web sites. Live production Web servers should run on Windows NT, not Windows 95 or Windows 98. Windows NT was designed to handle greater system loads, and is far more scalable than Windows 95 or Windows 98.

N O T E   ColdFusion runs under both Windows NT Server and Windows NT Workstation. The practical differences between using Server and Workstation are the number of concurrent connections that your Web server (and thus ColdFusion) will be able to handle. Windows NT Workstation limits the number of connections to 10; Windows NT Server does not have this limitation. ■

Your operating system must have the TCP/IP protocol installed in order to run Web services. You may do this either during operating system installation or after the operating system is installed. To verify that TCP/IP is installed (and to install it if not), do the following:

■ Windows 95 and Windows 98 users can right-click the Network Neighborhood icon on the desktop and select the Properties option to display the Network properties dialog box shown in Figure 3.1. The TCP/IP protocol should be shown in the Configuration tab. If it is not present, click the Add button to install it.

■ Windows NT users can right-click the Network Neighborhood icon and select Properties (select Network from the Control Panel if you are using Windows NT 3.5*x*) to display the Network properties dialog box, shown in Figure 3.2. If it is not present, click the Add button to install it.

FIGURE 3.1

The Windows 95 Control Panel applet shows all installed clients, protocols, and adapters.

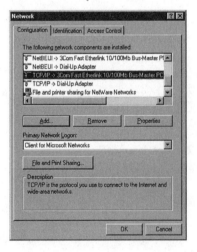

TCP/IP—as well as DNS and router settings—must be installed and configured properly for your Web server to function properly. Refer to your operating system documentation for details, or contact your network administrator or ISP. See Chapter 2, "Introduction to ColdFusion," for more information about TCP/IP and IP addresses.

To verify that TCP/IP is installed and operating properly, do the following:

1. Open an MS-DOS or Command Prompt window by selecting that option from the Start, Programs menu.

2. Type PING localhost or PING 127.0.0.1 at the DOS prompt. You should see a series of replies echoed onto the screen, as shown in Figure 3.3. If the replies are shown, TCP/IP is installed and working.

FIGURE 3.2

The Protocols tab in
Windows NT Control
Panel applet displays
the installed protocols.

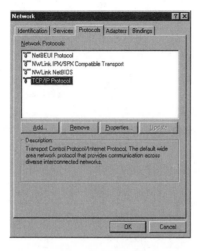

FIGURE 3.3

The Ping command
may be used to check
that the TCP/IP protocol
is installed and
running.

N O T E IP address 127.0.0.1 is a special address that always refers to your own computer,
regardless of what the actual IP address is. localhost is the host name for this special IP
address. ▥

Another good way to test that TCP/IP working is to install a Web browser on the server and
try to use it to access other Web sites and pages. TCP/IP is working properly if you can browse
the Web or access other intranet pages.

N O T E ColdFusion only supports Windows NT on Intel-based hardware. There is currently no
version of ColdFusion for Windows NT on other hardware, like DEC Alpha. ▥

Operating Systems for Sun SPARC Hardware   If you have opted to use Sun SPARC hardware,
you will use Sun's Solaris as your operating system. ColdFusion requires that you be running
Solaris version 2.5.1 or later, and that Solaris Patch 101242-11 or later be installed.

For more information about Sun's SPARC hardware and the Solaris operating system, visit the
Sun Internet site at http://www.sun.com.

Part

II

Ch

3

Selecting a Web Server

Your next task is to select a Web server. As explained in Chapter 2, Web servers are software programs and you must select a Web server that runs on the hardware platform and operating system that you selected.

ColdFusion supports several different Web servers, allowing you to choose the server that best suits your needs. Table 3.1 lists the supported Web servers and the platforms on which they are supported, as well as the address where you can obtain additional product information.

Table 3.1   ColdFusion-Supported Web Servers

Product	URL	Platforms
Apache	http://www.apache.org	Solaris
Microsoft IIS	http://www.microsoft.com/iis	Windows NT, Windows 95
Netscape Enterprise Server	http://www.netscape.com	Windows NT, Solaris
O'Reilly WebSite Pro	http://website.ora.com	Windows NT, Windows 95

Which Web server is right for you? There is no right or wrong answer here, and asking this question of a group of Webmasters is likely to elicit strong and differing opinions. If you already have a Web server installed or have experience with any particular product, you are best off starting with that product.

Here are some points to consider when picking your Web server:

- Microsoft IIS (and its Windows 95 counterpart, Microsoft Personal Web Server) are available from Microsoft at no charge. In fact, IIS comes bundled with Windows NT version 4 or later. IIS uses the user lists and security options in Windows NT itself, not requiring you to maintain yet another list of users' passwords and rights. This also means that IIS users must have a network login in order to have a Web server login.

- Netscape Enterprise Server is the latest addition to a long line of popular commercial Web servers. Evaluation versions are available from the Netscape Web site. Enterprise Server runs on both Windows NT and Sun Solaris, and the administration is all Web-based. Enterprise Server maintains its own user and rights list, and does not integrate its security with the operating system.

- O'Reilly WebSite Pro is extremely popular with ISPs and companies that offer hosting services. It is inexpensive and extremely easy to configure and maintain. An evaluation version is available on the O'Reilly Web site.

- Apache is the most popular Web server on the Internet. It has a solid and proven track record, and is available at no charge from the Apache Web site. It is, however, far more difficult to install and configure than any of the other servers listed here. It is supported online by the user community.

ColdFusion supports all of the servers listed here, and the code you write is portable among these servers. This means that you can choose one option now and then change your mind later. While this requires you to reconfigure your Web server itself, ColdFusion needs very little to be changed from a ColdFusion standpoint.

 T I P IIS version 2 is the version of Microsoft IIS bundled with Windows NT 4. If you have decided to use IIS as your Web server, it is worth your while to upgrade to IIS version 4. You will gain many new features, including the capability to use ColdFusion pages as default documents. To download the upgrade, visit the IIS page on Microsoft's Web site at `http://www.microsoft.com/iis`.

N O T E The list given only has the Web servers that ColdFusion supports using server APIs. Many other Web servers are supported via the ColdFusion CGI interface, but they are not listed here. As explained in Chapter 2, the CGI interface to ColdFusion should never be used if you can use the server APIs. ▒

Installation Checklist

You're about to install ColdFusion. Before doing so, run through this checklist to make sure your server is ready:

☐ Verify that the hardware you are installing ColdFusion onto meets the requirements previously listed.

☐ Verify that a supported operating system is installed and that the TCP/IP protocol is installed and working. (See the preceding section for details on how to test this.)

☐ Determine whether the operating system vendor has published patches or service packs. If any do exist, you might want to consider applying them before proceeding.

☐ Make sure you have installed a supported Web server. See Table 3.1 for servers supported by ColdFusion.

☐ Verify that the Web server is working. The simplest way to do this is load a browser on the server and go to `http://localhost`. The Web server is working if the default home page comes up.

☐ Make sure that you are logged in with administrative rights. (This step does not apply to Windows 95 machines.)

☐ Make sure that there is sufficient disk space following the Web server installation.

Once you have checked off the items in this list, you'll be ready to install ColdFusion.

Installing ColdFusion

The ColdFusion installation program walks you through the entire installation process. It usually even detects which Web server you have installed and configures ColdFusion accordingly.

Part
II
Ch
3

N O T E The installation instructions detailed here are for the Windows versions of ColdFusion only, as that is the only version bundled with this book. If you have downloaded the Solaris version of ColdFusion, refer to the documentation that came with it for installation instructions. ▪

Beginning the Installation Process

To start the installation program, run CF4EVAL.EXE found in the Evaluation directory on the accompanying CD-ROM. If you have downloaded ColdFusion from the Allaire Web site, run that executable instead. You should see a Welcome screen similar to the one shown in Figure 3.4.

N O T E All the installation instructions provided here apply to the live version of ColdFusion, not just to the evaluation version provided on the CD-ROM. The only difference between the two is that when installing the live version, you are prompted for a serial number that you will receive along with the software. ▪

FIGURE 3.4

The ColdFusion installation program walks you through the entire ColdFusion process.

Once you have agreed to the license conditions (and, if you are installing a live version of ColdFusion, entered your serial number), you are prompted for the installation directory; this is shown in Figure 3.5. The default directory is C:\CFUSION, but you may choose another directory if you so desire. It is strongly recommended that you keep the default directory if possible.

The installation program attempts to automatically detect which Web server is installed and then prompts you to verify the results (see Figure 3.6). If you have more than one Web server installed, you are prompted for the server with which ColdFusion will be used.

 T I P If you are using one of the servers listed in Table 3.1 and the installation program does not automatically detect it, cancel the installation. You might need to reinstall the Web server before proceeding.

Once ColdFusion knows which Web server you are using, it attempts to determine the location of the Web server's root directory. The ColdFusion examples, documentation, and Java applets are installed into this directory's subdirectories. The installation program displays the directory that it wants to use, as shown in Figure 3.7, and you may accept or change it.

FIGURE 3.5

To install ColdFusion on a directory other than the default, specify that directory during the installation process.

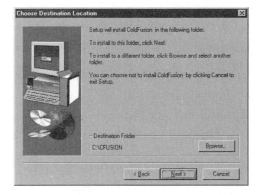

FIGURE 3.6

The ColdFusion installation program attempts to automatically detect which Web servers are installed.

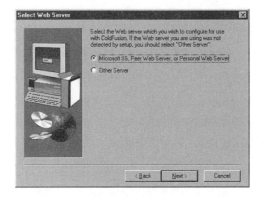

FIGURE 3.7

Select Web server document directory.

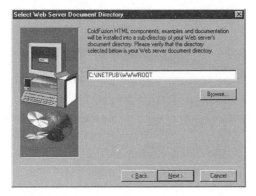

Part

II

Ch

3

Once you have specified the installation directories, you are prompted for the components to install. The components available to you will vary based on the operating system you are using. Figure 3.8 shows the Select Components dialog box that you'll see if using Windows 95. Figure 3.9 shows the Windows NT version. Table 3.2 lists the components and their descriptions, as well as the versions and platforms they are available on.

FIGURE 3.8

Only a subset of the ColdFusion Application Server components may be installed on Windows 95 and Windows 98.

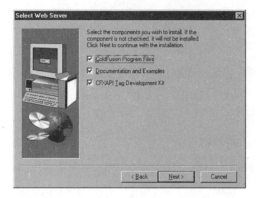

FIGURE 3.9

The entire set of components may be installed if using Windows NT.

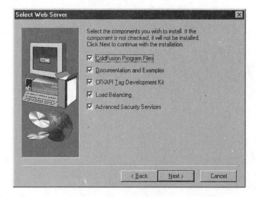

Table 3.2 ColdFusion Components

Component	Description
ColdFusion Program Files	ColdFusion itself. This component is the only one that must be present for ColdFusion to work. This option is available on all platforms.
Documentation and Examples	Complete online documentation and example applications. This option is available on all platforms.
CFXAPI Tag Development Kit	Everything you need to create your own tags in Microsoft Visual C++ version 4 or later. If you do not have MSVC installed, there is no need to install this component. If the installation program detects that MSVC is present, ColdFusion tag wizards are automatically added to it. This option is available on all platforms.
Load Balancing	Fault tolerance and load balancing features. This option is only available in the Enterprise version of the product, and only when installing on Windows NT or Solaris.

Component	Description
Advanced Security Services	Advanced security and server sandbox support. This option is only available in the Enterprise version of the product, and only when installing on Windows NT or Solaris.

 T I P If you omit a component that you want to install at a later date, you can rerun the installation program and just select that component.

Now you are prompted for two passwords, as seen in Figure 3.10 and Figure 3.11. The administrator password is the password that is required to administer and configure ColdFusion using the Web-based administration program. The ColdFusion Studio password is the one ColdFusion Studio users need in order to access directories, files, and data sources on the server machine.

N O T E If you are reinstalling ColdFusion, you are not prompted for the passwords—the existing passwords are used.

You must provide these passwords; they can be the same password if you prefer.

FIGURE 3.10

The ColdFusion Administrator password is used to configure and administer the ColdFusion Application Server.

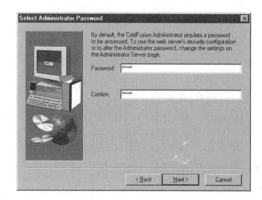

▶ **See** Chapter 4, "Administering ColdFusion," for more information about administering and configuring ColdFusion, **p. 57**.

▶ **See** Chapter 10, "Introduction to ColdFusion Studio," for more information about ColdFusion Studio, and using it to access server files and data sources, **p. 169**.

 T I P The passwords specified here may be changed at a later time using the ColdFusion Administrator described in Chapter 4.

Part
II

Ch
3

FIGURE 3.11

The ColdFusion Studio password is used by ColdFusion Studio users to access services on the ColdFusion Application Server.

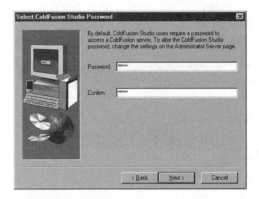

The installation program now prompts you for the name of the program group to create; then you are asked to verify all the options selected. Read through the settings, verify that they are correct, and then click the Next button to perform the actual installation.

You might be prompted to restart the server when you have finished installing ColdFusion.

Testing the Installation

Your next task is to test the installation using the provided test programs. As explained in Chapter 2, the ColdFusion Application Server must be running in order to process ColdFusion pages.

If you are running Windows NT, select the Services applet from the Control Panel. You will see a ColdFusion service listed, and the status should say Started. If the service is not Started, highlight it and click the Start button.

If you are running Windows 95 or Windows 98, an icon is displayed in the taskbar when ColdFusion is running, as shown in Figure 3.12. You may right click these icons to stop the server if needed. To manually start the ColdFusion Application Server (if it has been stopped, or if it is shown in the taskbar), select the ColdFusion menu option from the ColdFusion group beneath the Start button's Programs menu.

FIGURE 3.12

The Windows 95 and Windows 98 taskbar displays the ColdFusion Application Server icons when ColdFusion is running.

Once you have verified that ColdFusion is running, select the Welcome To ColdFusion option from the ColdFusion group, which is beneath the Start button's Programs menu. You should see a Getting Started screen similar to the one shown in Figure 3.13.

FIGURE 3.13

The ColdFusion Getting Started screen provides quick access to documentation, Help, testing tools, and links to Allaire.

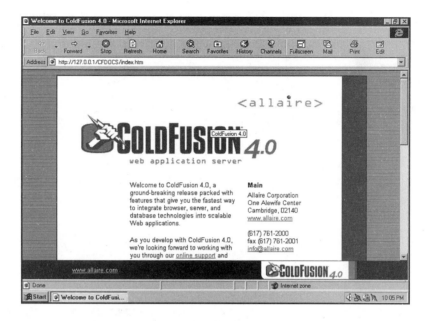

Select the Test Your ColdFusion Installation option from the Here's Where to Begin list. The Verify Installation and Configuration screen, shown in Figure 3.14, allows you to perform a databases lookup and display the results. You'll know that the installation was successful when this operation succeeds. Select a department from the Department drop-down list and then click the Verify Query button. If everything is working correctly, you'll see a results page like the one shown in Figure 3.15. If not, a series of suggestions is made to help you resolve the problem.

 The Installation Test page also contains links and instructions to other tests that you can perform to verify the operation of other ColdFusion features. You may use this page at any time to ensure that ColdFusion is running properly.

If you've made it this far—congratulations! You're ready to begin application development.

Preparing to Install ColdFusion Studio

ColdFusion Studio is a complete development environment designed especially for ColdFusion developers. You do not have to use Studio for your ColdFusion application development, but I strongly recommend that you do. Studio is full of features that will both simplify your application development and save you considerable amounts of time.

FIGURE 3.14

The Verify Installation and Configuration page contains a series of tests to ensure that ColdFusion is running properly.

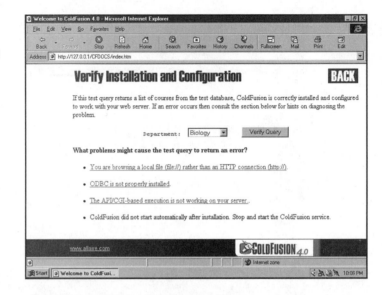

FIGURE 3.15

The Test Query Results page displays data retrieved from an Access database if ColdFusion is functioning properly.

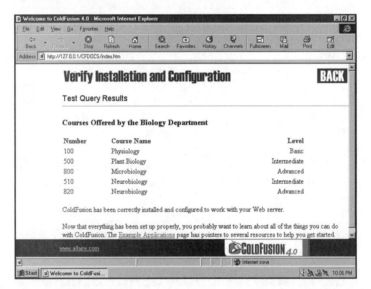

ColdFusion Studio comes bundled with a single user version of the ColdFusion Application Server. This is primarily of use when you are writing your code on a computer other than the one running the ColdFusion Application Server. The separate, local, single-user server allows you to test your applications locally.

 TIP   Studio is usually not installed on the Web server itself, but on any other computer on the same network. Studio can also be installed on a computer on a remote site, in which case it will communicate with the ColdFusion Application Server via any existing TCP/IP connection.

Hardware Requirements

Studio runs on Windows 95, Windows 98,and Windows NT only. There is no 16-bit version of Studio, nor is there a UNIX version. However, Studio running on Windows 95/98/NT can be used in conjunction with ColdFusion Application Server running on any platform, including Solaris and HP/UX.

Studio will run on any computer running Windows 95, Windows 98, or Windows NT (Intel only), but a minimum of 32MB of RAM is recommended; 15MB of disk space is also needed to install Studio.

What's on the CD-ROM

This book's accompanying CD-ROM contains a 30-day evaluation version of ColdFusion Studio. This is a complete version of Studio and it comes complete with all the documentation and Help. The only restriction is that it will only run for 30 days. This should be enough time for you to evaluate the product.

Once you have determined that Studio will work for you, you need to contact the Allaire Sales department at 617-761-2000 to order a live copy. You can install the live version directly over the evaluation version, and any options and settings will still be accessible to you.

The evaluation version of the ColdFusion Studio is saved in the ColdFusion directory on the CD-ROM as Setup.EXE.

Part
II
Ch
3

Installation Checklist

You're about to install Studio. Before doing so, run through this checklist to make sure your system is ready:

- [ ] Verify that the hardware you are installing ColdFusion Studio on meets the requirements previously listed.
- [ ] Make sure you have sufficient disk space.
- [ ] If you are planning on using Studio's remote access features, make sure that the TCP/IP protocol is installed and working. (See this chapter's previous details on how to test this.)
- [ ] Make sure that you are using the same version of both the ColdFusion Application Server and ColdFusion Studio.

You'll be ready to install Studio once you have checked off the items in this list.

Installing ColdFusion Studio

Just like ColdFusion itself, the Studio installation program makes installing ColdFusion Studio a very simple task.

N O T E All the installation instructions provided here apply to the live version of ColdFusion Studio, not just to the evaluation version provided on the CD-ROM. The only difference between the two is that when installing the live version, you are prompted for a serial number, which you will receive along with the software. ▪

Beginning the Installation Process

To start the installation program, run the CFSTUDIO4EVAL.EXE found in the Evaluation directory on the accompanying CD-ROM. If you have downloaded ColdFusion Studio from the Allaire Web site, run that executable instead. You should see a Welcome screen similar to the one shown in Figure 3.16.

FIGURE 3.16

The ColdFusion Studio installation program walks you through the entire Studio installation process.

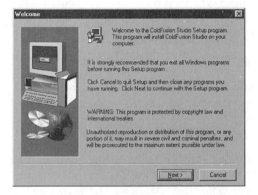

You are then prompted to agree to the license, as well as to enter a serial number (if you are installing a live copy of the software) and the destination directory. Once you have provided this information, you are prompted for the components to install, as shown in Figure 3.17. Unless you are suffering from the lack of disk space, it's recommended that you keep both components selected.

FIGURE 3.17

You may select any or all ColdFusion Studio components to be installed.

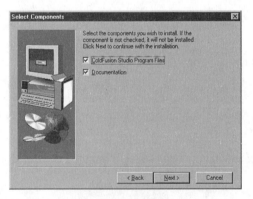

The installation program now prompts you for the name of the program group to create. Then you are asked to verify all the options selected. Read through the settings, verify that they are correct, and then click the Next button to perform the actual installation.

Testing the Installation

To test Studio, just run the program by selecting it from the Studio program group under the Start button's Programs menu. You are welcome to try it out right now. However, Studio is discussed in detail in Chapter 10. ●

Part

II

Ch

3

Administering ColdFusion

Using the ColdFusion Administrator

The ColdFusion Administrator manages and configures your ColdFusion Application Server. The Administrator is a Web-based management tool that lets you use your Web browser to manage all versions of ColdFusion, regardless of platform.

To use the Administrator, select ColdFusion Administrator from the ColdFusion program group beneath the Start button's Programs menu. If you have password protection enabled (it is enabled by default when ColdFusion is installed), then you are presented with a login screen like the one shown in Figure 4.1. Enter the password that you specified during the ColdFusion Application Server installation process to gain access to the Administrator for the first time.

FIGURE 4.1

The ColdFusion Administrator should be protected with a login password.

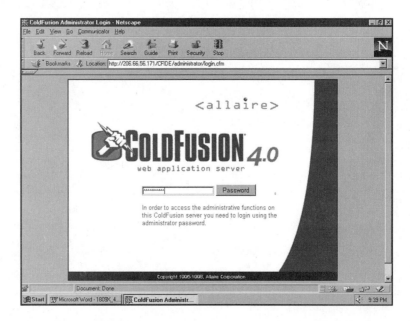

The ColdFusion Administrator uses a framed window interface. The left side of the screen contains a series of options divided into six sections, and clicking any option displays a relevant configuration screen on the right.

The rest of this chapter discusses each of these sections and options.

Using the Server Options

The Server options manage global settings and configuration parameters that effect the behavior of all ColdFusion applications running on this server. Many of these options can be overridden by application-specific settings specified using the <CFAPPLICATION> tag within your application.

Settings

The Server Settings screen (shown in Figure 4.2) allows you to configure the ColdFusion Application Server. When you have made your changes, click the Apply button to save them.

FIGURE 4.2

The Server Settings screen sets serverwide Application Server options.

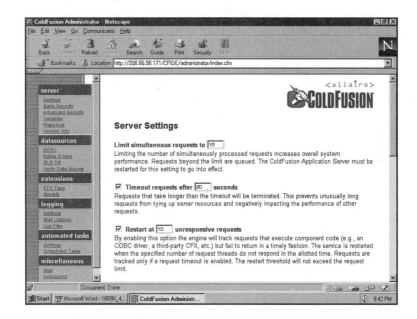

Part

II

Ch

4

Limit Simultaneous Requests To?　ColdFusion can process multiple requests simultaneously. The default number of requests that can be simultaneously processed is 15. If your applications are extremely load intensive or your server cannot handle the load because it is not powerful enough, lowering the number of simultaneous requests can help improve performance. Likewise, this number can be increased if your hardware supports it.

Of course, the downside of restricting requests is that additional requests will be queued; those requests that are being processed are processed quicker, but those that are queued to be processed actually take longer to complete.

Timeout Requests After *N* Seconds　This setting allows you to determine the maximum number of seconds that ColdFusion should allow for the processing of any particular request. Timing out requests can be disabled altogether, but this is generally not a good idea—it allows a badly behaved request (perhaps a slow database connection or a poorly written SQL statement) to tie up server resources.

The default value is 30 seconds. You should consider raising this value if you are working with large, complex templates or with complex database operations.

Restart at *N* Unresponsive Requests   ColdFusion monitors its own internal processes to ensure that they are responsive, automatically resetting them if needed. ColdFusion can also monitor the performance of external calls (ODBC requests, calls to a CFX tag, COM object requests, and so on). When you enable this option, the engine tracks the number of requests that execute component code but fail to return in a timely fashion. The service can then automatically be restarted when the specified number of requests fails. Requests are tracked only if a request timeout is enabled.

Enforce Strict Attribute Validation   ColdFusion supports two modes of syntax checking: strict and relaxed. The syntax checker does not allow extraneous or invalid attributes in strict mode; they are allowed in relaxed mode. Enforcing strict mode can boost system performance.

> **CAUTION**
>
> If you are upgrading to ColdFusion 4 from an older version, do not enable this option without first testing the pages thoroughly on a testing server. You will likely find that some of your existing code that worked under the older version (which only supported relaxed mode) does not work under ColdFusion 4.

Template Cache Size   This is the maximum amount of memory (in kilobytes) that ColdFusion can use to cache templates. The ideal number here is a little bigger than the total size of all templates within your applications. This allows for all templates to be cached, which improves system performance.

> **N O T E**   It is important to note that ColdFusion does not reserve this memory. Rather, it allocates it as needed, until the maximum size allowed has been reached. Therefore, there is no real risk in assigning a very high value. On the other hand, the performance penalty brought about by having too small a cache can be quite severe. ■

Trusted Cache   The Application Server does not need to read cached ColdFusion pages from the hard drive when they are requested. However, it does need to determine whether the page has been updated. It does this by comparing the date time stamp of the file with the copy stored in the cache. Checking this option forces ColdFusion to void checking for newer versions of files, always trusting that the copy in the cache is the newest copy. This can improve performance slightly on heavy volume sites.

 Enable this option to improve performance of sites that change infrequently. Do not enable this option for sites that change regularly or for sites that are under development.

Limit Database Connection Inactive Time to *N* Minutes   To improve database connection performance, ColdFusion caches and pools database connections. These connections are held open for up to 60 minutes by default, after which they are automatically closed. This value can be raised or lowered as needed. Enter 0 if you want inactive connections to be maintained as long as the ColdFusion server is executing.

> **N O T E**   Database connections are only cached and pooled when the maintain database connections attribute is checked for a data source. ■

Limit the Maximum Number of Cached Queries on the Server to *N* Queries   Do you want to improve performance of applications that make multiple database requests for the same data? Applications can cache query results. This option specifies the maximum number of cached queries that the server will maintain. Cached queries reside in memory on the server. This value should be lowered if memory usage is a concern. The maximum number of cached queries allowed at any given time is 100. When this value is exceeded, the oldest query is dropped from the cache and is replaced with the specified query.

Basic Security

The Basic Server Security screen (shown in Figure 4.3) defines the basic ColdFusion security options. The options specified here are used only if Advanced Security is not enabled. If Advanced Security is enabled, those settings override any Basic Security settings.

When you have made your changes, click the Apply button to save them.

Part

II

Ch

4

FIGURE 4.3

The Basic Server Security screen manages basic administration and ColdFusion Studio security options.

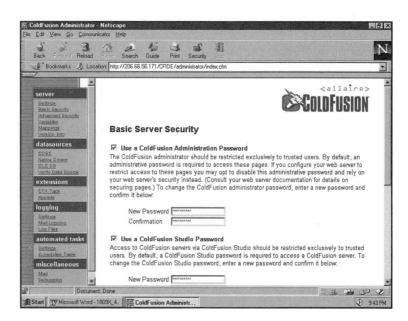

Use a ColdFusion Administration Password   As you can see, the ColdFusion Administrator manages and configures the ColdFusion Application Server. Any user with access to the Administrator can completely reconfigure the server, and could even render your application inoperable.

The ColdFusion Administrator is password protected by default. However, you may opt to remove the password protection. This is, however, not generally advisable. In fact, there are only two scenarios when you should even consider doing this:

- You are protecting the Administrator at the Web server level. (Refer to your Web server documentation for information on how to do this.)
- Your ColdFusion Server is on an isolated server (a test or demo server, for example) that is not connected to a network or the public Internet.

> **CAUTION**
>
> Your server's ColdFusion Administrator should always be password protected. Without password protection, any user can reconfigure the server or render your applications inoperable.

You may change the Administrator password. To do so, enter the new password in the New Password field and then reenter it in the Confirmation field.

N O T E   The ColdFusion Administration password is initially set during ColdFusion installation. This screen is primarily used to change the password. ■

Use a ColdFusion Studio Password   ColdFusion Studio users can remotely access server directories, files, and data sources. Therefore, Studio access should always be password protected.

ColdFusion Studio is password protected by default. However, you may opt to remove the password protection. This is not generally advisable—you'd be allowing unauthorized access to your hard disks, files, and databases.

> **CAUTION**
>
> ColdFusion Server access via ColdFusion Studio should always be password protected. Without password protection any user will have unlimited access to all of your server's hard drives, files, and databases.

You can change the ColdFusion Studio password. To do so, enter the new password in the New Password field and then reenter it in the Confirmation field.

N O T E   The ColdFusion Studio password is initially set during ColdFusion installation. This screen is primarily used to change the password. ■

Tag Restrictions Several ColdFusion tags could be misused, compromising system security. This is rarely a problem in typical installations, but there could be justification for restricting the use of these tags—in environments where the same ColdFusion Application Server is shared by multiple organizations, for instance. ISPs are an example. The aforementioned tags include <CFDIRECTORY>, <CFFILE>, <CFCONTENT>, and <CFOBJECT>. These tags are all enabled by default.

> **N O T E** Enabling these tags is not in itself a security risk. These tags can only be abused if users have the ability to save ColdFusion files on the server for execution. As long as users cannot save their own files on your server, there is no security risk. ■

 T I P For more granular control over the access to these tags, as well as all other ColdFusion features, use the Advanced Security settings instead of the basic Tag Restrictions.

Advanced Security

Advanced Security provides ColdFusion developers a powerful framework for building secure applications and development environments. Some of the Advanced Security features are as follows:

- Secure applications or parts thereof
- Use Windows NT domains or LDAP directory services for user list and password validation
- Control developer use of specific tags and specific tag action
- Control access to specific resources, including files, directories, and data sources
- Manage ColdFusion Administrator access, allowing different users different levels of ColdFusion administration
- Create and deploy server sandboxes

ColdFusion Advanced Security is beyond the scope of this book, but is covered in depth in *Advanced ColdFusion 4.0 Application Development* (also published by Que, ISBN 0-7897-1810-3).

Variables

The Client Variable Storage screen (shown in Figure 4.4) sets the storage for ColdFusion variables, as well as the default behavior of various variable types. When you have made your changes, click the Apply button to save them.

Part
II

Ch
4

FIGURE 4.4

This screen creates and manages client variable storage locations and establishes variable timeout defaults.

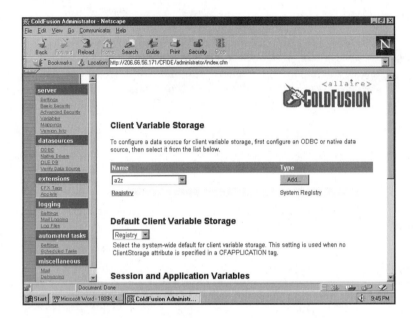

Client Variable Storage Client variables are usually stored in the system registry or in client cookies. To store client variables in a database, first create the data source, select it, and click the Add button to display the Create Client Variable Storage screen (shown in Figure 4.5).

FIGURE 4.5

The Create Client Variable Storage screen defines the life span of client variables and other options.

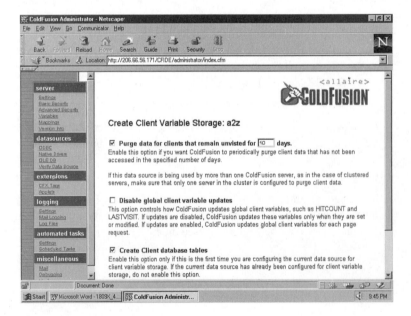

This screen lets you specify several things: the variable purge period (for how much time since the last visit should the variable be saved); whether to update global variables are updated in each page request; and whether to create the database tables to store client variable data.

> **CAUTION**
>
> Only select the Create Client Database Tables option when you first create a client variable storage location. Selecting this option for a data source that already has these tables created could result in the tables being overwritten and the client variable data being lost.

To share client variable data between different computers, create a data source on each computer pointing to the same external database and use that database for client variable storage.

Default Client Variable Storage   Client variable storage can be specified per application using the <CFAPPLICATION> tag. If no explicit storage is specified, the system default setting is used. The system default location is the system registry by default. To change the default location, select an option from the Default Client Variable Storage box.

To use a data source as the default storage location, first create a data source based storage location and then select it from the box.

Enable Application Variables   *Application variables* are applicationwide settings stored in memory on the ColdFusion Server. If you are not using application variables in any of your applications, you can save server memory by disabling them.

Enable Session Variables   *Session variables* are session-specific settings that are stored in memory on the ColdFusion server. If you are not using session variables in any of your application, you can save server memory by disabling them.

Application and Session Variable Timeouts   Application and session variables are stored in the server's memory until they timeout. This means they are deleted if they are not accessed for the specified amount of time. If support for these variables is enabled, you may specify the timeout interval. The default interval for application variables is two days; the default interval for session variables is 20 minutes.

The timeout values specified here are systemwide settings. Application and session variable timeouts can also be specified for specific applications using the <CFAPPLICATION> tag. However, in the event that invalid timeout values are specified at the application level, you can also specify maximum values that should be used instead. In practice, the default and the maximum values should usually be the same.

Mappings

The Add New Mappings screen (shown in Figure 4.6) creates ColdFusion-level directory mappings, which allow you to use directory aliases at a ColdFusion level.

To add a map, enter the alias name in the Logical Path field and enter the actual path in the Directory Path field; otherwise, click the Browse Server button to locate the directory.

Once the mapping is added, you can use it in all ColdFusion tags (<CFINCLUDE>, for example). However, you will be unable to use it in HTML paths (<A HREF> or <IMG> tags, for example).

To edit or delete an existing mapping, click it in the list of currently assigned mappings.

FIGURE 4.6

The Mapping tag allows you to configure ColdFusion-level alias mappings.

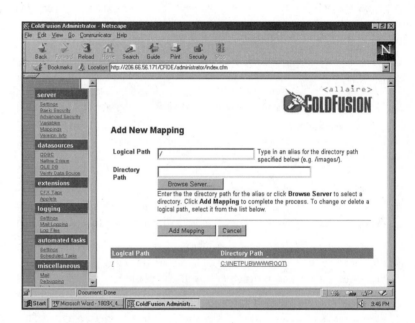

N O T E ColdFusion-level mappings should only be used for aliases needed within ColdFusion code. Mappings and aliases to be used at an HTML level should be defined within the Web server's own administration options. ■

Version Info

The Server Information area provides information about your ColdFusion Server and the environment it is running on. Make sure you have this information accessible if ever you need to contact Allaire Technical Support.

Using the Data Sources Options

ColdFusion uses data sources to interact with databases. ColdFusion supports ODBC and OLE-DB data sources, as well as native drivers for Sybase and Oracle. ODBC data sources are typically created and managed using the ODBC applet in the Windows Control Panel. However, as the Windows Control Panel is inaccessible from remote computers, the ColdFusion Administrator has its own interface for creating and configuring ODBC data sources.

ODBC

The screen displays a list of currently installed data sources. You can click any data source name to view or edit its settings. You can also add a new data sources by entering the data source name in the Data Source Name field, selecting the ODBC Driver from the drop-down list, and then clicking the Add button. This displays the ODBC Data Sources Available to ColdFusion screen, which is shown in Figure 4.7. Fill in the appropriate information and click the Create button to add the data source.

FIGURE 4.7

The Data Sources tab can be used to remotely add new ODBC data sources.

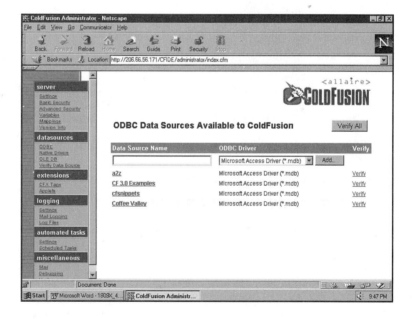

Part

II

Ch

4

N O T E If you are creating a data source to a client/server database such as Microsoft SQL Server, you must click the CF Settings button to expand the Create screen, where you specify the required database login information. ∎

Each data source has a Verify link associated with it; it verifies that the data source is working correctly. You can also click the Verify All button to ascertain whether all the listed data sources are operational.

Native Drivers

If you are using ColdFusion to connect to Sybase or Oracle databases, you can take advantage of ColdFusion's native data driver support for these products. The Native Database configuration screen is shown in Figure 4.8.

FIGURE 4.8

ColdFusion supports the use of native database drivers for Sybase and Oracle database servers.

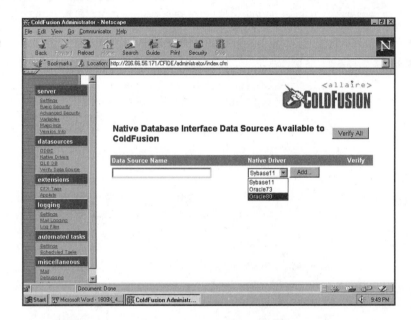

To set up a native data source, specify a unique data source name, select the driver, and click the Add button.

Each data source has a Verify link associated with it; it can be clicked to determine that the data source is working correctly. You can also click the Verify All button to verify that all the listed data sources are operational.

OLE-DB

You can take advantage of ColdFusion's OLE-DB support if you are using ColdFusion to connect to databases or products with OLE-DB support (Lotus Notes, Microsoft Exchange 5.5, and Microsoft SQL Server 7, for instance). The OLEDB configuration screen is shown in Figure 4.9.

To set up an OLE-DB data source, specify a unique data source name, specify the provider, and click the Add button.

Each data source has a Verify link and a Verify All button associated with it; the link and button perform the operations previously described.

FIGURE 4.9
ColdFusion's OLE-DB support can be used to connect to Lotus Notes, Microsoft Exchange, Microsoft SQL Server 7, and other systems.

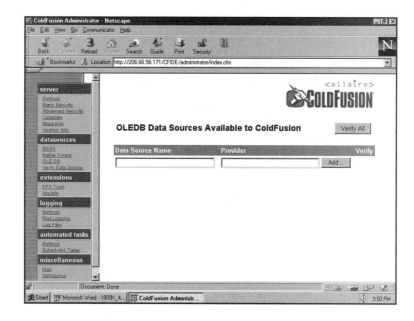

Verify Data Sources

In addition to verifying data sources within the screens used to create and manage them, this screen provides a single interface with which to verify any and all data sources, regardless of type.

To verify a single data source, simply click its name. If the database is functioning properly, you'll see a screen similar to the one shown in Figure 4.10. Click the Verify All button to verify all data sources. The screen will be updated to show the verification status (see Figure 4.11).

FIGURE 4.10
Verifying the operation of data sources is a vital part of application debugging and troubleshooting.

FIGURE 4.11

To verify the operation of all data sources (regardless of type), click the Verify All button.

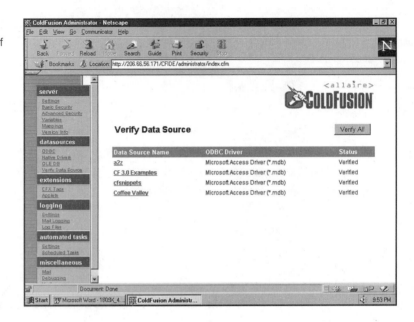

 Verifying data sources is an important debugging operation. If your application is having difficulty accessing or interacting with a database, the first thing you should do is use this screen to verify that the data source is functioning correctly.

Using the Extensions Options

The Extensions options configure ColdFusion's interaction with third-party tags and Java applets.

CFX Tags

CFX tags can be created as DLLs. In order to use DLL-based tags within ColdFusion they must first be registered. The list of installed CFX tags is displayed in the Registered CFX Tags page, as seen in Figure 4.12

In order to register your tag you must first copy the DLL onto your ColdFusion server, enter its name into the Tag Name field, and then click the Add button. The New CFX Tag screen shown in Figure 4.13 comes up.

In order to register the tag you must either specify the full path to the DLL in the Server Library field or click the Browse button to find the file in the server. The Procedure field should always be left with the default value ProcessTagRequest.

FIGURE 4.12

The Registered CFX Tags page can be used to install and manage CFX tags.

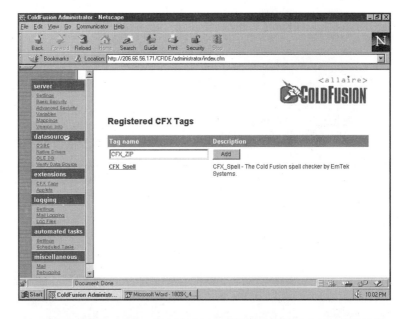

FIGURE 4.13

The New CFX Tag screen adds CFX tags to your ColdFusion server.

By default, CFX tag DLLs are loaded into memory when they are first used and kept there. This improves the performance of subsequent calls to the tag. However, resident tags take up server memory; you might want to disable the Keep Library Loaded option if the tag is infrequently used. The description is optional.

On the CD A collection of CFX tags is provided on the accompanying CD-ROM.

Applets

ColdFusion comes with a collection of Java applets that you can use to enhance your forms. These are accessed using the ColdFusion <CFFORM> tag. You can register your own Java applets, and add them to your <CFFORM> forms using the <CFAPPLET> tag.

Registered applets are listed in the Applets tab, which is shown in Figure 4.14. To register a new applet, enter its name in the Applet field and click the Register New Applet button to display the Register New Applet form (see Figure 4.15). Once you have filled in the form, click the Create button to register the applet.

You can also edit existing registered applets by clicking their names in the main Applet tab screen that's shown in Figure 4.14.

FIGURE 4.14

The Applet tab lists any registered Java applets.

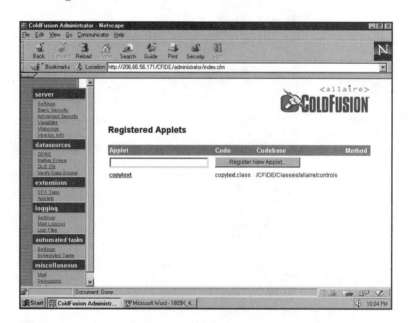

FIGURE 4.15

Use the Register New Applet form to register your own Java applets for use with the <CFAPPLET> tag.

Using the Logging Options

ColdFusion log files are used to log server activity, warnings, and error conditions. The Logging options allow you to manage and fine-tune the behavior of the logging capabilities.

Settings

The General Error Logging Settings screen (shown in Figure 4.16) manages ColdFusion logging and specifies exactly what should be logged. When you have made your changes, click the Apply button to save them.

Administrator Email   If an error occurs, ColdFusion displays a message that describes the error condition. If you enter an email address here, ColdFusion also displays it and instructs the visitor to notify that address of the error condition. You can override this address for a particular application by specifying an address in the APPLICATION.CFM file's <CFAPPLICATION> tag.

TIP

ColdFusion allows you to specify only a single email address for the mail administrator. To have messages sent to multiple recipients, create a mail group on your mail server and specify that group address in the Administrator E-Mail field.

FIGURE 4.16

The General Error Logging screen manages ColdFusion error and event logging.

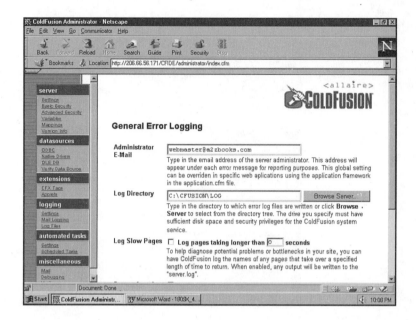

Log Directory   By default, ColdFusion log files are stored in a directory called LOG beneath the ColdFusion root directory (usually C:\CFUSION). You can specify an alternate directory if desired.

Log Slow Pages   To help diagnose potential problems or bottlenecks in your site, you can have ColdFusion log the names of any pages that take over a specified length of time to return. When enabled, any output will be written to the SERVER.LOG file. If you enable this option, a valid time value (in seconds) must be specified.

System Logging   In addition to writing error messages to the ColdFusion log files, ColdFusion can also log messages using whatever logging facilities your operating system provides. On Windows NT that is the event log. (You could use the Windows NT Event Viewer to browse these messages.) It is the syslog facility on UNIX.

Mail Logging

The Mail Logging screen (shown in Figure 4.17) manages the logging of outbound SMTP email generated within ColdFusion using the <CFMAIL> tag. When you have made your changes, click the Apply button to save them.

FIGURE 4.17

The Mail Logging screen manages the logging of outbound SMTP email transmissions.

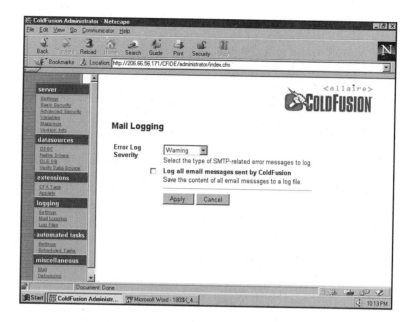

Error Log Severity   ColdFusion logs warnings and errors in the mail server log by default. You can raise the level to Error in order to log error messages only; lower it to Information to log informational messages in addition to all warnings and errors.

CAUTION

Set the mail error log severity to Information only if you absolutely need this information—set it back to Warning or Error when you have collected the information you need. Leaving the level at Information for an extended period of time causes the log file to grow rapidly and to consume lots of disk space.

Log All Email Messages Sent by ColdFusion   Enable this option to log the content of all outgoing mail messages. This can be useful when debugging mail delivery problems.

CAUTION

Only enable this option when debugging mail delivery problems; disable it when done. Leaving it enabled for an extended period of time causes the content of all outgoing messages to be saved, and that can consume large amounts of disk space.

Part
II
Ch
4

Log Files

You can view or download the ColdFusion log files directly from within the ColdFusion Administrator. The Log Files screen (shown in Figure 4.18) displays a list of all available log files, complete with filename, file size (in bytes), and the last modified date.

FIGURE 4.18

ColdFusion log files can be viewed or downloaded directly from within the ColdFusion Administrator.

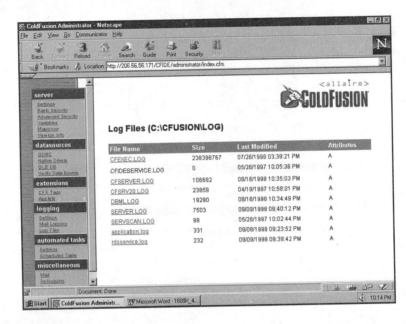

Click any log file to either view it within the administrator or to download it directly to your computer.

Using the Automated Tasks Options

ColdFusion can execute *automated tasks*, events that are scheduled to occur at a specific time or on a regular basis. The Automated Tasks options manage automated tasks and scheduled events.

Settings

The Scheduler Settings screen (shown in Figure 4.19) manages the behavior of the ColdFusion scheduling engine. When you have made your changes, click the Apply button to save them.

Scheduler Refresh Interval   This setting allows you to determine how often ColdFusion should check to see if new events have been added to the scheduled events list. Once events are on the list, ColdFusion checks them once every minute to determine which events need to be run. The default value is every 15 minutes.

FIGURE 4.19

The Scheduler Settings screen manages the ColdFusion Application Server scheduling engine.

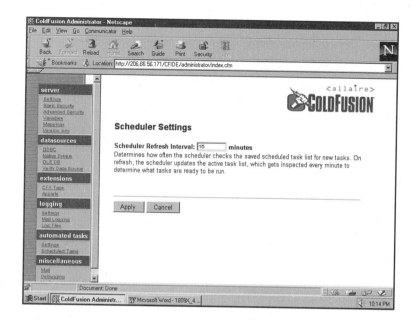

Scheduled Tasks

The ColdFusion Scheduler configures events that ColdFusion can automatically execute. The Scheduled Tasks screen, shown in Figure 4.20, creates and configures scheduled events.

FIGURE 4.20

The Scheduled Tasks screen configures timed events.

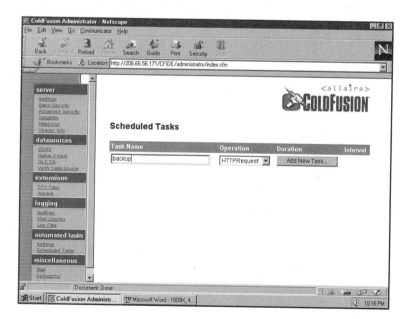

Part

II

Ch

4

To add a new scheduled event, enter the event name in the Task Name field and click the Add New Task button; the Add Scheduler Task screen appears (see Figure 4.21). Here you specify the duration and schedule, as well as the URL and publishing information, for the new task.

To edit a scheduled task, select it from the main Scheduled Tasks screen shown in Figure 4.20.

FIGURE 4.21

The Add Scheduler Task screen specifies the time, interval, and URL for the task to be scheduled.

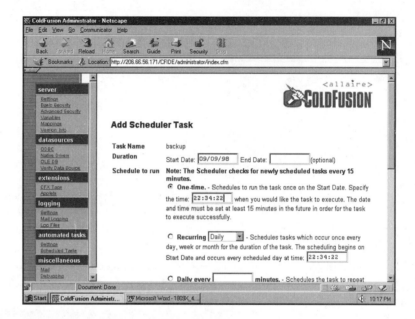

Using the Miscellaneous Options

The Miscellaneous options control ColdFusion email support, debugging features, and integration with the Verity engine.

Mail

Before you can use ColdFusion to generate SMTP-based email, you must configure the mail options in the Mail Server Connection Settings screen (shown in Figure 4.22). Once you have completed the fields, click the Apply button to save the changes. You can also click the Verify button to verify that ColdFusion is capable of communicating with the specified SMTP server.

> **CAUTION**
>
> If you try to use the ColdFusion <CFMAIL> tag without having configured a mail server in the Mail tab, your code fails and you will generate a ColdFusion error message.

FIGURE 4.22

Before using the
<CFMAIL> tag, email
settings must be
configured in the Mail
Server Connection
Settings screen.

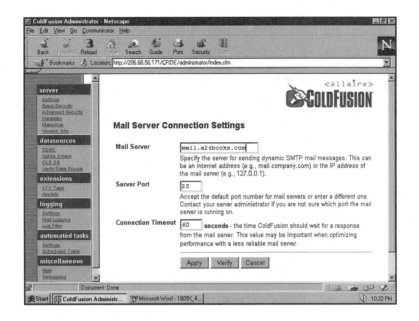

Mail Server   Enter the DNS name or IP address of your SMTP mail server here. If you do not know this information, contact your mail administrator or ISP.

Server Port   Enter the port number that your SMTP server is assigned to. This should remain at the default value of 25 unless instructed otherwise by your mail administrator or ISP.

Connection Timeout   Enter the amount of time ColdFusion should wait for the mail server to respond before timing out. This should only be raised from the default of 60 seconds if you are experiencing problems with an unreliable mail server.

 When debugging mail delivery problems, the first thing you should check is that ColdFusion can communicate with the specified SMTP server. You can do this by clicking the Verify button on this screen.

Debugging

The Debugging tab (shown in Figure 4.23) enables and disables the display of debug information, as well as specifies what debug information should be displayed and to whom. Select as many or as few options as you want and then click the Apply button to save your changes.

Part

II

Ch

4

FIGURE 4.23

The Debugging tab configures what debug information ColdFusion should display and to whom.

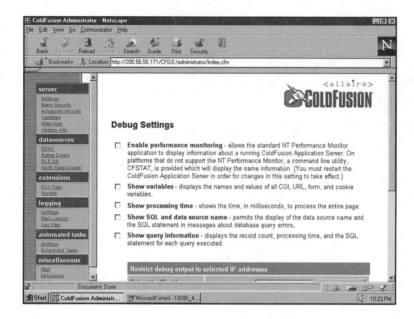

Enable Performance Monitoring

ColdFusion can publish real-time performance data for detailed analysis and monitoring of the ColdFusion services and their operation. The performance information is published to the Performance Monitor on Windows NT, as well as to a bundled software utility called CFSTAT on all other platforms.

N O T E Unlike all other configuration options, turning on and off the publishing of performance monitoring data requires restarting the ColdFusion Application Server. ■

CAUTION

Performance monitoring is a valuable debugging operation, but its use comes with a hefty price. Publishing performance monitoring data is resource intensive, and system performance will degrade when this option is checked. As such, this option should only be enabled when needed and should be disabled as soon as the monitoring is completed.

Show Variables

If this option is enabled, ColdFusion automatically appends a list of CGI variables, URL parameters, form fields, and HTTP cookies to the end of every ColdFusion page.

Show Processing Time

If this option is enabled, ColdFusion displays the total page processing time at the bottom of each page.

Show SQL and Data Source Name   If this option is enabled, the data source name and SQL statement are displayed in any error messages. This option should be disabled if you would rather your visitors not know the details of your underlying databases. However, during routine debugging sessions, the information provided by enabling this option is extremely useful.

Show Query Information   If this option is enabled, the SQL statement (retrieved record count) and query processing time are displayed at the end of each template. This option is useful in tracking down poorly performing database queries.

T I P   To determine how long ColdFusion is taking to process your code page itself without query processing, subtract the total amount of time spent processing all queries from the processing time option mentioned above.

Restrict Debug Output to Selected IP Addresses   By default, any and all debugging information is sent to every visitor to your site. To restrict the display of debugging information to specific users, you can enter their IP addresses here. To add an address, enter it into the IP Address field and click the Add button. The address is displayed in the list underneath. To delete an address from the list of addresses that are to receive debugging information, select the address from the list and click the Delete button.

N O T E   Debugging information will be sent to every one of your Web site visitors if debugging is enabled and no IP addresses are specified. It is therefore a good idea to always have at least one address in the list. You might want to add address 127.0.0.1, which refers to the local host (the server itself). ■

There is an add-on ColdFusion tag, CFX_Debug, on this book's accompanying CD-ROM. This tag allows you to enable and disable the display of debugging information from within a ColdFusion template without having to access the Administrator. This is very useful in environments that use dynamic IP addresses.

Verity

ColdFusion uses the Verity search engine to facilitate full-text searching. Verity stores its index information in collections, and the Verity tab (see Figure 4.24) manages these collections.

Verity Collections   To index, repair, optimize, purge, or delete a Verity collection, select the collection from the list and click the appropriate button.

Part
II

Ch
4

FIGURE 4.24

The Verity tab manages and creates Verity collections.

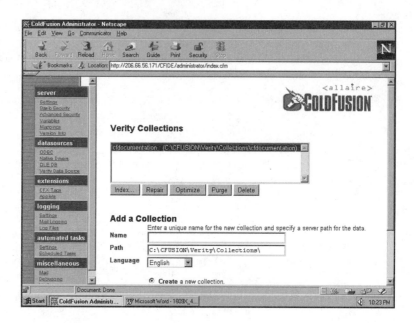

Add a Collection   To create a new Verity collection, enter the unique collection name, specify the path where the collection should be saved (the default path will most often be used), and choose the language of the data being indexed. Click the Create button when the information has been entered.

Getting Started with ColdFusion

Designing an Application

Introducing Application Design

The key to successful application development is careful application design. Like anything else, this design requires planning.

The design process has the following four basic steps:

- Educate yourself. Learn the business practices and processes that are currently in place. Find out what works, what doesn't, and what needs fixing.
- Build a high-level goal document based on the knowledge you have acquired, and verify that all goals are included in it.
- Determine what sets of information are needed to attain each of these goals successfully.
- List in detail the data that each of these data sets contains.

Through the rest of this chapter, I explain these steps in detail.

Introducing A2Z Books

A2Z Books is a small bookstore with big ideas. The company prides itself on top-notch customer service and goes out of its way to ensure complete customer satisfaction. A2Z Books is a mail- and phone-order company and, like many other small companies, A2Z Books is suffering from growing pains.

Just last week you were called into the boss's office and assigned a new project. "Orders are up," the boss said. "Way ahead of year-to-date projections. We've doubled our order processing staff to handle the load, but we can't seem to keep up. New titles are not being made available to our customers quickly enough, and orders are taking too long to ship out. Our customers have grown to expect better service than we can offer right now. We desperately need to find a way to streamline our operations and eliminate whatever is causing these bottlenecks. I want you to give this some thought and make recommendations. Oh, and I'll need them within the week."

And that is why you're sitting there, amidst piles of pads and sticky notes, trying to work out exactly what is wrong and how you're going to fix it. You know that the manual processes of order taking, shipping, accounting, and billing just cannot work anymore. Computers could, and should, be performing many of these tasks for you. But where do you start?

Educating Yourself

After reading and rereading your notes, you come to the conclusion that you just don't know enough about the individual processes and procedures that make up the day-to-day operations of the company. To design a computer system that will be both usable and useful, you really need to interview personnel around the company to learn just what they do, why they do it, and how the work gets done.

You start to compile a list of questions to ask during the interviews. Starting with the Accounting department, you create the following list:

How often are invoices processed?

How is order information provided to you?

How is client information provided to you?

What are the steps you take to create an invoice?

What happens to the invoices after they are printed?

What reports do you run after printing invoices?

Who gets these reports?

You also may want to observe some of these operations being performed. In this way, you can pick up details that you missed during the interview.

 TIP When you're conducting these interviews, ask very specific questions and try to obtain very specific answers. Remember, you're talking to someone who does a particular task regularly and who most likely takes many of the details involved for granted. The more explicit your questions are, the more useful the answers will be.

After you have this information in hand, creating a flowchart is often useful. It can depict the steps that make up a complete process, as shown in Figure 5.1. You also can have whoever gave you the information review the flowcharts for accuracy. This way, you can be sure that no steps have been overlooked.

This process might sound like a tedious and time-consuming task, but the more preparation you do up front, the more likely your computer program will work the first time and will be accepted. The acceptance, or lack thereof, usually determines the fate of any computer program.

NOTE Often, you may find that people have determined that their business needs computerizing, but they have no idea what they want or what the computer can actually do for them. Bear in mind that non-computer users usually know only what they want an application to do for them once they have seen the application and know what they don't like about it. ■

Too often, programs are designed and implemented by programmers working in a vacuum, without any real knowledge of the problems they are trying to solve. A program like this might be built around great business ideas and work models, but if it requires a change in the way employees go about their business, then employees will look for every excuse not to use it. Without mass acceptance, the new program is doomed to fail.

 TIP Computers are supposed to make our lives easier, not force us to relearn what we are already familiar with. A computer program that forces people to change the way they work will probably never be used.

The interview process should be conducted thoroughly and should include a diverse set of employees for another important reason. Often, employees view computerization and technology as a threat to their jobs instead of as a boon to their productivity. Although some of this fear might be justified, it is usually the result of computerphobia and horror stories of

Part
III

Ch
5

corporate downsizing. The interview and due-diligence process enables you to reassure employees and to persuade them to buy into your plans and suggestions instead of rejecting them. Making employees feel like they are a part of the application design rather than its victims can go a long way to boost mass acceptance.

FIGURE 5.1

Making flowcharts is an effective way to review and analyze business processes.

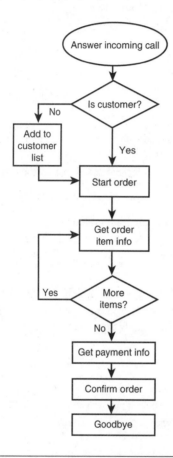

 Never rely on the input of a single individual. The more people you interview during the research project, the more likely you are to obtain information that is an accurate reflection of the way business is performed.

Putting It All Together

Armed with all this information, you now might be tempted to actually start application development, knowing that you can make educated suggestions and that you have the data to back them up. But don't run out to buy database applications and development tools just yet. You still have quite a bit more preparation to do.

Before you start actual development, you should document your application goals thoroughly. Include the various components of your application, what each component does, and how the components interact. You can use this document as your roadmap throughout the actual application development process.

What you should not be documenting at this point is databases, tables, and fields. Try not to get caught up in any technical details yet. This document is not a database schema; it is a high-level overview of what your program will do and how it will do it. What data will be stored in which tables and how that data will be stored are not considerations at this stage. You should make sure that the application design decisions you make are based on business needs and practices, not on features or peculiarities of any particular database system or development tool.

 Don't let the features of any database system or development tool influence your high-level application design. You know your business; the designers of the database systems do not. If a particular database system does not have the features you need, you can always pick another one. Switching databases is much easier than switching business practices.

The High-Level Design Document

You now can sift your way through the piles of data sitting in front of you and begin to formulate your application plan. The plan is initially broken down by department, so you can list the needs of each department based on the results of your interviews.

Human Resources Department   You start with the human resources needs and break down the requirements into an organized list, as follows:

- Human Resources needs an efficient way to manage employee information, including personal information.
- Some of this information, like lists of current employees and the phone extensions, should be made available to all employees. Other information is highly confidential and should be kept private.
- Human Resources wants a way to track employees' days off.

Accounting Department   The human resources list is relatively simple. So next, you try your Accounting department, as follows:

- Accounting needs to be able to automate the billing process so there are fewer manual steps between order taking and billing.
- They also have to run reports for upper management on a regular basis. Creating these reports is time consuming, so they need better reporting tools.
- Accounting wants a closer interaction with the Shipping and Receiving department so they can track when orders ship and, consequently, process returns more quickly.

Marketing Department   The Marketing department's chief complaint is that they cannot easily get information they need from other departments. Here's their list of requirements:

Part
III
Ch
5

- Marketing wants access to the Accounting department's customer lists.

- They also want customer histories so they can create targeted marketing programs.

- With the popularity of the Internet and the growing use of email, Marketing wants to be able to send email to notify interested customers when specific books become available.

- Marketing also wants to use the World Wide Web to interact with customers. Some of the ideas they want to pursue involve online surveys and communication among employees.

Sales Department   The sales team has the closest interaction with the customers. Therefore, you can safely assume that most of requests from the Sales department are customer driven. Here's their list of requirements:

- Sales needs a faster way to locate books for customers. A customer might know the title, author's name, publisher, book category, or any other information. The staff needs to locate the correct books no matter what information customer provides.

- Sales also needs a way to check item availability instantly.

- Sales wants to be able to refer to existing customer records when taking orders. This way they won't have to re-enter customer information unnecessarily.

- The sales manager wants to start selling books over the Internet. He wants to allow customers to browse through inventories, search for books, and place orders online.

Shipping and Receiving Department   Shipping and Receiving is where much of the bottle-neck occurs. Their requirements include:

- Receiving needs to be able to make new titles available rapidly.

- They also need to be able to track what books need to be reordered and when.

- To ship orders on the day they are received, Shipping wants to be notified automatically of orders waiting for shipment as soon as they are received.

- Shipping wants an easier way to notify Accounting when an order is shipped.

N O T E   The preceding lists are just examples demonstrating the kind of information to include in a high-level design document. The example lists have been simplified; they are by no means complete. Your own documents will typically be far more detailed than these.

Remember, the more detail you include, the more complete your design will be. Just make sure that it isn't so detailed that it is no longer a high-level document. ▥

You review the design document and refer back to your notes and scribbles to verify that all needs have been included. Just to make sure that you haven't omitted anything, circulate the design document to department heads for their approval.

Determining the Data Requirements

Now that you have your basic application goals documented, the next step is to determine what data sets you need to actually design the application. The goal-oriented design document im-plicitly lists all the sets of data you need to build the application. You just need to extract it.

Look through the design goals again and determine the data requirements for each.

- Human Resources needs to track employee information. The data needs here are simple.
- Accounting needs two different sets of data: customer data and accounting data.
- Marketing needs customer information and customer histories. Accounting already has both of these data sets.
- Sales needs order entry data, customer data, and inventory data. Two of these data sets—the order entry data and the customer data—are already documented as needs of the Accounting department.
- Shipping and Receiving needs order data and inventory data. Both of these data sets are already listed by other departments.

You can now summarize the data requirements for your entire application in one simple table, as shown in Table 5.1.

Table 5.1   Data Sets Required for A2Z Books

Data Set	Notes
Employee Information	Employee lists, personal information, vacation details
Customer Information	Customer details
Inventory Information	Lists of all book categories, book titles, number in stock, availability
Accounting Information	Invoicing, accounts receivable, financial reporting

This list is probably not as intimidating as you thought it would be. In fact, it's rather manageable. Just to make sure that you haven't missed anything, run through the goal list one more time. If you were to have these data sets in place and the tools with which to manipulate them, would you be able to meet all of the desired goals? If yes, then you're ready to move on to the final step.

Data Set Details

You're almost there. You have determined the goals for the application and what data sets you need to meet these goals—and all this without thinking about databases and tables. Well, that's not exactly true. Without even realizing it, you have started defining what your database and tables should look like. The data sets listed earlier roughly equate to database tables, and the relationships between these data sets can be translated into relationships between the tables.

Before you can create the tables, however, you need to list the details that make up each data set. Don't worry about how the data is stored and what information will go into which field. Those are table creation concerns, and you're not creating tables yet. Right now, you just want to ensure that you have all the data details you need so that you can complete your design documents.

TIP With most database applications, you can add columns or fields to your database tables after they have been created. However, restrictions that limit the types of columns you may add often exist. Therefore, you should make every effort to include all the needed data right now, before you create the application's first table.

The details for the first data set, the one for employee information, are listed in Table 5.2. The Notes column is useful for jotting down details you don't want to forget when you actually create your tables.

Table 5.2   Data to Be Included in the Employee Information Table

Data	Notes
Name	First name, middle initial, last name.
Address	Make sure that space is available for suite or apartment numbers.
City	
State	
Zip Code	
Home Phone	Also cellular phone and pager number.
Social Security	
Birth Date	
Date of Hire	
Title	
Department	
Phone Extension	
Email Address	

The details for the customer information data set are listed in Table 5.3.

Table 5.3   Data to Be Included in the Customer Information Table

Data	Notes
Name	First name, middle initial, last name.
Address	Make sure that space is available for suite or apartment numbers.
City	
State	
Zip Code	

Data	Notes
Phone	
Email Address	
Customer Since	

The details for the inventory information data set are listed in Table 5.4.

Table 5.4   Data to Be Included in the Inventory Information Table

Data	Notes
Category	Also need a category list.
ISBN	
Title	
Publisher	
Publication Date	
Author	
Pages	
Description	Brief title description.
Number in Stock	
Due Date	This data provides the date more copies are due in, especially if the number in stock is 0.
Location	To help Shipping locate the books, tracking where they are stored would be useful.

I'm not going to list all the sample application data sets and their details here. When you're creating your own application, however, make sure that you list every data set and all information details. ●

Database Fundamentals

In this chapter

Understanding Databases

Say that you have just been assigned a project. You must create and maintain a list of all employees in your company and their phone extensions. The list changes constantly because new employees start working for the company, others leave, and extensions and job titles change.

What do you use to maintain this list? Your first thought might be to use a word processor. You could create the list, one employee per line, and manually insert each employee's name so the list is alphabetical and usable. Your word processor provides you with sophisticated document-editing capabilities, so adding, removing, or updating employees is no more complicated than editing any other document.

Initially, you might think you have found the perfect solution—that is, until someone asks you to sort the list by department and then alphabetically within each department. Now you must recreate the entire list, again sorting the names manually and inserting them in the correct sequence. You end up with two lists to maintain. You must add new employees' names to both lists and remove names of employees leaving the company from both lists as well. You also discover that correcting mistakes or simply making changes to your list has become more complicated because you have to make every change twice. Still, the list is manageable. You have only the two word-processed documents to be concerned with, and you can even open them both at the same time and make edits simultaneously.

Okay, the word processor is not the perfect solution, but it is still a manageable solution—that is, until someone else asks for the list sorted by extension. As you fire up your word processor yet again, you review the entire list-management process in your mind. New names must now be added to three lists. Likewise, any deletions must be made to all three lists. If an extension changes, you need to change just the extension on two lists and re-sort the third as well.

And then, just as you think you have the entire process worked out, your face pales and you freeze. What if someone else wants the list sorted by first name? And then what if yet another department needs the list sorted by job title? You panic, break out in a sweat, and tell yourself, "There must be a better way!"

This example is a bit extreme, but the truth is that a better way really does exist. You need to use a database.

Databases: A Definition

Let's start with a definition. A database is simply a structured collection of similar data. The important words here are *structured* and *similar*, and the employee list is a perfect example of both.

Imagine the employee list as a two-dimensional grid or table, like that shown in Figure 6.1. Each horizontal row in the table contains information about a single employee. The rows are broken up by vertical columns. Each column contains a single part of the employee's record. The First Name column contains only employees' first names, and every employee's first name is listed in this column, one in each row. Similarly, the Last Name column contains only employees' last names.

FIGURE 6.1

Databases display data in an imaginary two-dimensional grid.

EMPLOYEES

First Name	Last Name
Adam	Stevens
Adrienne	Green
Dan	Johnson

The employee list contains similar data for all employees. Every employee's record, or row, contains the same type of information. Each has a first name, last name, phone extension, department, and job title. The data is also structured in that the data can be broken into logical columns, or fields, that contain a single part of the employee record.

Here's the rule of thumb: Any list of information that can be broken into similar records of structured fields should probably be maintained in a database. Product prices, phone directories, invoices, invoice line items, and vacation schedules are all database candidates.

Where Are Databases Used?

You probably use databases all the time, often without knowing it. If you use a software-based accounting program, you are using a database. All accounts payable, accounts receivable, vendor, and customer information is stored in databases. Scheduling programs use databases to store appointments and to-do lists. Even email programs use databases for directory lists and folders.

These databases are designed to be hidden from you, the end user. You never add accounts receivable invoice records into a database yourself. Rather, you enter information into your accounting program, and it adds records to the database.

Clarification of Database-Related Terms

Now that you understand what a database is, I must clarify some important database terms for you. In the SQL world (you learn about SQL in depth in Chapter 9, "SQL Data Manipulation"), this collection of data is called a *table*. The individual records in a table are called *rows*, and the fields that make up the rows are called *columns*. A collection of tables is called a *database*.

Picture a filing cabinet. The cabinet houses drawers, each of which contains groups of data. The cabinet is a means of keeping related but dissimilar information in one place. Each cabinet drawer contains a set of records. One drawer may contain employee records, whereas another drawer may contain sales records. The individual records within each drawer are different, but they all contain the same type of data, in fields.

The filing cabinet shown in Figure 6.2 is the database—a collection of drawers or tables, containing related but dissimilar information. Each drawer contains one or more records, or rows, made up of different fields, or columns.

FIGURE 6.2
Databases store information in tables, columns, and rows, similarly to how records are filed in a filing cabinet.

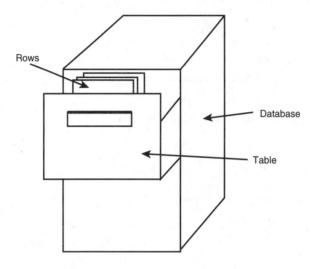

Rows

Database

Table

Data Types

Each row in a database table is made up of one or more columns. Each column contains a single piece of data, part of the complete record stored in the row. When a table is created, each of its columns needs to be defined. Defining columns involves specifying the column's name, size, and data type. The data type specifies what data may be stored in a column.

Data types specify the characteristics of a column and instruct the database as to what kind of data may be entered into it. Some data types allow the entry of free-form alphanumeric data. Others restrict data entry to specific data, like numbers, dates, or true or false flags. A list of common data types is shown in Table 6.1.

Table 6.1 Common Database Data Types and How They Are Used

Data Type	Restrictions	Typical Use
Character	Upper- and lowercase text, numbers, symbols	Names, addresses, descriptions
Numeric	Positive and negative numbers, decimal points	Quantities, numbers
Date	Dates, times	Dates, times

Data Type	Restrictions	Typical Use
Money	Positive and negative numbers, decimal points	Prices, billing amounts, invoice line items
Boolean	Yes and No or True and False	On/off flags, switches
Binary	Non-text data	Pictures, sound, and video data

Most database applications provide a graphic interface to database creation, enabling you to select data types from a list. Microsoft Access uses a drop-down list box, as shown in Figure 6.3, and provides a description of each data type.

FIGURE 6.3
Microsoft Access uses a drop-down list box to enable you to select data types easily.

You use data types for several reasons, instead of just entering all data into simple text fields. One of the main reasons is to control or restrict the data a user can enter into that field. A field that has to contain a person's age, for example, could be specified as a numeric field. This way, the user cannot enter characters into it—only the digits 0 through 9 would be allowed. This restriction helps ensure that no invalid data is entered into your database.

Different data types are also used to control how data is sorted. Data that is entered in a text field is sorted one character at a time, as if it were left justified. The digit 0 comes before 1, which comes before 9, which comes before *a*, and so on. As each character is evaluated individually, a text field containing the number 10 is listed after 1 but before 2 because 10 is greater than 1 but less than 2, just as a0 is greater than *a* but less than *b*. If the value being stored in this column is a person's age, correctly sorting the table by that column would be impossible. Data entered into a numeric field, however, is evaluated by looking at the complete value rather than a character at a time; 10 is considered greater than 2 instead of less than 2. Figure 6.4 shows how data is sorted if numbers are entered into a text field.

FIGURE 6.4
Unless you use the correct data type, data might not be sorted the way you want.

1000
2
248
39

The same is true for date fields. Dates in these fields are evaluated one character at a time, from left to right. The date 02/05/98 is considered less than the date 10/12/97 because the first character of the date 02/05/98—the digit 0—is less than the first character of the date 10/12/97—the digit 1. If the same data is entered in a date field, the database evaluates the date as a complete entity and therefore sorts the dates correctly.

The final reason for using different data types is the storage space that plain-text fields take up. A text field that is large enough to accommodate up to 10 characters takes up 10 bytes of storage. Even if only two characters are entered into the field, 10 bytes are still stored. The extra space is reserved for possible future updates to that field. Some types of data can be stored more efficiently when not treated as text. For example, a 4-byte numeric field can store numeric values from 0 to over 4 billion! Saving 4 billion in a text field requires 10 bytes of storage. Similarly, a 4-byte date/time field can store the date and time with accuracy to the minute. Storing that same information in a text field would take a minimum of 14 bytes or as many as 20 bytes, depending on how the data is formatted.

NOTE   Different database applications use different terms to describe the same data type. For example, Microsoft Access uses the term *text* to describe a data type that allows the entry of all alphanumeric data. Microsoft SQL Server calls this same data type char and uses text to describe variable-length text fields. After you determine the type of data you want a column to contain, refer to your database application's manuals to make sure you use the right term when making data type selections.

When you're designing a database, you should give careful consideration to data types. You usually cannot change the type of a field after the table is created. If you do have to change the type, you typically have to create a new table and write routines to convert the data from one table to the new one.

Planning the size of fields is equally important. With most databases, you cannot change the size of a field after the table is created. Getting the size right the first time and allowing some room for growth can save you much aggravation later.

CAUTION

When you're determining the size of data fields, always try to anticipate future growth. If you're defining a field for phone numbers, for example, realize that not all phone numbers follow the three-digit area code plus seven-digit phone number convention that is used in the United States. Paris, France, for example, has eight-digit phone numbers, and area codes in small towns in England can contain four or five digits.

Custom Data Types

With some databases, you can define your own data types. You can specify exactly what data is allowed and how it should be formatted.

Take a look at the employee list again. Suppose that you have to track your employees' social security numbers with their records. You can't use a numeric field here because you need to save the social security numbers with the dashes in their correct locations. You could create a text field that stores 11 characters—the length of a social security number with dashes—and require users to enter the data exactly as you want to save it. Doing so, however, requires that you ensure that only numbers are entered and that the dashes are in the correct places. The database does not do this validation automatically for you because as far as it is concerned, the field is a text field and all text is allowed.

A better solution is for you to create a data type specifically for social security numbers. Under the hood, this data type actually is an 11-character text field. Unlike a simple text field, this new data type has the dashes exactly where you want them—in positions four and seven—and allowed data would be limited to digits only.

After you define the new data type, you can use it whenever you need to store a social security number in a table. You can simply specify this as the column's data type without having to repeatedly detail the column's characteristics.

N O T E Not all database applications support custom data types, and no fixed set of rules governs those that do. Consult your database's manuals to determine whether custom data types are supported and, if so, how to use them. ■

Using a Database

Back to the example. At this point, you have determined that a database will make your job easier and might even help preserve your sanity. You create a table with columns for employee first name, employee last name, social security number, department, job title, and extension. You enter your employee list data into the table, one row at a time, and are careful to put the correct data in each column.

Next, you instruct the database application to sort the list by employee first name. The list is sorted in a second or less and you print it out. Impressed, you try additional sorts—by last name and by phone extension. The results of these sorts are shown in Figures 6.5, 6.6, and 6.7.

FIGURE 6.5

Data entered once into a Microsoft Access table can be sorted any way you want.

EmployeeID	FirstName	MiddleInit	LastName	PhoneExtension	Address1	Address2
1	Adam		Stevens	4878		
2	Adrienne		Green	4546		
3	Dan		Johnson	4824		
4	Jack		Smith	4545		
5	Jane		Smith	4876		
6	Jennifer		White	4345		
7	Kim		Black	4565		
8	Lynn		Wilson	4464		
9	Marcy		Gold	4912		
10	Steven		Jones	4311		
(AutoNumber)						

Part

III

Ch

6

You now have two or more lists, but you had to enter the information only once; because you were careful to break the employee records into multiple columns, you can sort or search the list in any way needed. You just need to reprint the lists whenever you add or delete employee names or make changes to employees' records. The new or changed data is automatically sorted for you.

FIGURE 6.6

Data sorted by last name.

EmployeeID	FirstName	MiddleInit	LastName	PhoneExtension	Address1	Address2
7	Kim		Black	4565		
9	Marcy		Gold	4912		
2	Adrienne		Green	4546		
3	Dan		Johnson	4824		
10	Steven		Jones	4311		
4	Jack		Smith	4545		
5	Jane		Smith	4876		
1	Adam		Stevens	4878		
6	Jennifer		White	4345		
8	Lynn		Wilson	4464		
(AutoNumber)						

FIGURE 6.7

Data sorted by phone extension.

EmployeeID	FirstName	MiddleInit	LastName	PhoneExtension	Address1	Address2
10	Steven		Jones	4311		
6	Jennifer		White	4345		
8	Lynn		Wilson	4464		
4	Jack		Smith	4545		
2	Adrienne		Green	4546		
7	Kim		Black	4565		
3	Dan		Johnson	4824		
5	Jane		Smith	4876		
1	Adam		Stevens	4878		
9	Marcy		Gold	4912		
(AutoNumber)						

"Yes," you think to yourself, "this really is a better way."

A Database Primer

You have just seen a practical use for a database. The employee list is a simple database that involves a single table and a small set of columns. Most well-designed database applications require many tables and ways to link them. You'll revisit the employee list when relational databases are introduced.

Your first table was a hit. You have been able to accommodate any list request, sorted any way anyone could need. But just as you are beginning to wonder what you're going to do with all your newfound spare time, your Human Resources department has a brainstorm. "Now that we have a database of all our employees, and it's so easy to manage and maintain, could we add their vacation schedules, too? That would be a real timesaver for us."

"No problem," you say. You open your database application and modify your table. You add two new columns, one called Vacation Start Date and one called Vacation End Date. Now, when an employee schedules a vacation, you can simply enter the dates in the appropriate columns. You even create a report of all upcoming scheduled vacations. Once again, you and your database have saved the day, and all is well.

Or so you think. Just when things are looking good, you get a call from an employee who wants to schedule two vacation dates, one in June and one in October. Your database has room for only one set of dates. Entering the October vacation dates will overwrite the June dates!

You think for a few moments and come up with two solutions to this new problem. The first solution is simply to add two more columns to your table: Vacation 2 Start Date and Vacation 2 End Date. You can enter the second set of vacation dates into these new columns.

This, you realize, is not a long-term solution at all. Inevitably, someone else will need space for three, four, or even more sets of dates. Adding all these extra columns, which will not be used by most records, is a tremendous waste of disk space. Furthermore, data manipulation becomes extremely complicated if data is stored in more than one column. If you need to search for who has booked vacation time on a specific date, you have to search multiple columns. This situation greatly increases the chance of incorrect results. It also makes sorting data impossible because databases sort data one column at a time, and you have data that must be sorted together spread over multiple columns.

N O T E An important rule in database design is that if columns are seldom used by most rows, they probably don't belong in the table. ▨

Your second solution is to create additional rows when an employee wants to book another set of dates. With this solution, you can add as many sets of dates as needed without creating extra columns.

This solution, though, is not workable. Although it does indeed solve the problem of handling more than a predetermined number of vacation dates, doing so introduces a far greater problem. Adding additional rows requires repeating the basic employee information—like Name and Phone Number fields—over and over, for each new row.

Not only does re-entering this information waste storage space, it also greatly increases the likelihood of your being faced with conflicting data. If an employee's extension changes, for example, you have to make sure to change every row that contains that employee's data. Failing to update all rows would result in queries and searches returning conflicting results. If you do a search for an employee and find two rows, both of which have different phone extensions, how do you know which is correct?

This problem is probably not overly serious if the conflicting data is phone extensions—but imagine that the problem is customer billing information. If you re-enter a customer's address with each order and then the customer moves, you could end up shipping orders to an incorrect address.

You should avoid maintaining multiple live copies of the same data whenever possible.

N O T E Another important rule in database design is that data should never be repeated unnecessarily. As you multiply the number of copies you have of the same data, the chance of data entry errors also multiplies. ▨

One point worth mentioning here is that the "never duplicate data" rule does not apply to backups of your data. Backing up data is incredibly important, and you can never have too many backup plans. The rule of never duplicating data applies only to *live data*—data to be used in a production environment on an ongoing basis.

Understanding Relational Databases

The solution to your problem is to break the employee list into two separate tables. The first table, the employee list, remains just that—an employee list. To link employees to other records, you add one new column to the list, a column containing a unique identifier for each employee. It might be an employee ID, a social security number, or a sequential value that is incremented as each new employee name is added to the list. The important thing is that no two employees have the same ID.

 TIP Never reusing record-unique identifiers is generally a good idea. If an employee with ID number 105 leaves the company, for example, that number should never be reassigned to a new employee. This policy guarantees that there is no chance of the new employee record getting linked to data that belonged to the old employee.

Next, you create a new table with just three columns: an Employee ID column, a Vacation Start Date column, and a Vacation End Date column. As long as no employees have vacations booked, the second table—the vacation table—remains empty. When an employee books vacation dates, you add a row to the vacation table. The row contains the employee ID that uniquely identifies this specific employee and the vacation start and end dates.

The point here is that no employee information is stored in the vacation table except for that employee ID, which is the same employee ID assigned in the employee list table. How do you know which employee the record is referring to when vacation dates are reported? The employee information is retrieved from the employee list table. When displaying rows from the vacation table, the database relates the row back to the employee list table and grabs the employee information from there. This relationship is shown in Figure 6.8.

This database design is called a *relational database*. With it you can store data in different tables and then define *links*, or *relationships*, to find associated data stored in other tables in the database. In this example, an employee who booked vacations in both June and October would have two rows in the employee vacation table. Both of these rows contain the same employee ID, and therefore both refer to the same employee record in the employee list table.

The process of breaking up data into multiple tables to ensure that data is never duplicated is called *normalization*.

Primary and Foreign Keys

Primary key is the database term for the column(s) that contains values which uniquely identify each row. A primary key is usually a single column, but doesn't have to be.

There are only two requirements for primary keys:

- Every row must have a value in the primary key. Empty fields, sometimes called *null fields*, are not allowed.
- Primary key values can never be duplicated. If two employees were to have the same ID, all relationships would fail. In fact, most database applications prevent you from entering duplicate values in primary key fields.

When your Human Resources department head asks for a list of all upcoming vacations sorted by employee, you can instruct the database to build the relationship and retrieve the required data. The employee list table is scanned in alphabetical order, and as each employee is retrieved, the database application checks the employee vacation table for any rows that have an employee ID matching the current primary key. You can even instruct the database to ignore the names of employees who have no vacation time booked at all and retrieve only those who have related rows in the employee vacation table.

N O T E   Not all data types can be used as primary keys. You cannot use columns with data types for storing binary data like sounds, images, variable-length records, or OLE links as primary keys. ■

The Employee ID column in the employee vacation table is not a primary key. The values in that column are not unique if any employee books more than one vacation. All records of a specific employee's vacations contain the same employee's ID. The employee ID is a primary key in a different table—the employee list table. This is a *foreign key*. A foreign key is a non-unique key whose values are contained within a primary key in another table.

To see how the foreign key is used, assume that you have been asked to run a report to see who will be out of the office during October. To do so, you instruct the database application to scan the employee vacation table for all rows that have vacation dates in October. The database application uses the value in the vacation table's Employee ID foreign key field to find the name of the employee; it's done so by using the employee table's primary key. This relationship is shown in Figure 6.8.

FIGURE 6.8

The foreign key values in one table are always primary key values in another table, allowing tables to be "related" to each other.

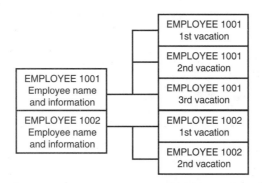

The relational database model helps overcome scalability problems. A database that can handle an ever-increasing amount of data without having to be redesigned is said to *scale well*. You should always take scalability into consideration when designing databases.

Now you've made a significant change to your original database, but what you've created is a manageable and scalable solution. Your Human Resources department is happy once again, and the employee booking two vacations at once (and who obviously has far less work to do than you) is happy, too. Once again, your database management skills save the day.

Part III Ch 6

Different Kinds of Relationships

The type of relationship discussed up to this point is called a *one-to-many* relationship. This kind of relationship allows an association between a single row in one table and multiple rows in another table. In the example, a single row in the employee list table may be associated with many rows in the employee vacation table. The one-to-many relationship is the most common type of relationship in a relational database.

Two other types of relational database relationships exist: the *one-to-one* relationship and the *many-to-many* relationship.

The one-to-one relationship allows a single row in one table to be associated with no more than one row in another table, as shown in Figure 6.9. This type of relationship is used infrequently. In practice, if you run into a situation in which a one-to-one relationship is called for, you should probably revisit the design. Most tables that are linked with one-to-one relationships can simply be combined into one large table.

FIGURE 6.9

One-to-one relation-
ships create links
between a single row in
one table and a single
row in another.

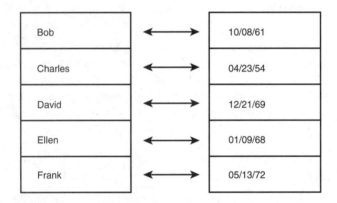

The many-to-many relationship is also used infrequently. The many-to-many relationship allows one or more rows in one table to be associated with one or more rows in another table. This kind of relationship is usually the result of bad design. Most many-to-many relationships can be more efficiently managed with multiple one-to-many relationships.

Indexes

Database applications make extensive use of a table's primary key whenever relationships are used. It is therefore vital that accessing a specific row by primary key value be a fast operation. When data is added to a table, you have no guarantee that the rows are stored in any specific order. A row with a higher primary key value could be stored before a row with a lower value. You should make no assumptions about the actual physical location of any rows within your table.

Now take another look at the relationship between the employee list table and the employee vacation table. You have the database scan the employee vacation table to learn who has vacation time booked in October; only rows in which October is between the vacation start and end dates are selected. This operation, however, returns only the employee ID—the foreign key value. To determine which employee this row is referring to, you have the database check the employee list table. A single row is selected—the row that has this employee ID as its primary key value.

To find a specific row by primary key value, you could have the database application sequentially read through the entire table. If the first row stored is the one needed, the sequential read would be terminated. If not, the next row is read, and then the next, until the desired primary key value is retrieved.

This process might work for small sets of data. Sequentially scanning hundreds, or even thousands, of rows is a relatively fast operation, particularly for a fast computer with plenty of available system memory. As the number of rows increases, however, so does the time it takes to find a specific row.

The problem of finding specific data quickly in an unsorted list is not limited to databases. Suppose that you're reading a book on mammals and are looking for information on cats. You could start on the first page of the book and read everything, looking for the word cat. This approach might work if you have just a few pages to search through, but as the number of pages grows, so does the difficulty of locating specific words and the likelihood that you will make mistakes and miss references.

To solve this problem, books have indexes. An index allows rapid access to specific words or topics spread throughout the book. Although the words or topics referred to in the index are not in any sorted order, the index itself is. Cat is guaranteed to appear in the index somewhere after bison, but before cow. To find all references to cat, you would first search the index. Searching the index is a quick process because the list is sorted. You don't have to read as far as dog if the word you're looking for is cat. When you find cat in the index list, you also find the page numbers where cats are discussed.

Databases use indexes in much the same way. Database indexes serve the same purpose as book indexes—allowing rapid access to unsorted data. Just as book indexes list words or topics alphabetically to facilitate the rapid location of data, so do database table indexes list the values indexed in a sorted order. Just as book indexes list page numbers for each index listing, database table indexes list the physical location of the matching rows, as shown in Figure 6.10. After the database application knows the physical location of a specific row, it can retrieve that row without having to scan every row in the table.

However, two important differences exist between an index at the back of a book and an index to a database table. First, an index to a database table is *dynamic*. This means that every time a row is added to a table, the index is automatically modified to reflect this change. Likewise, if a row is updated or deleted, the index is updated to reflect this change. As a result, the index is always up-to-date and always useful. Second, unlike a book index, the table index is never explicitly browsed by the end user. Instead, when the database application is instructed to retrieve data, it uses the index to determine how to complete the request quickly and efficiently.

The index is maintained by the database application and is used only by the database application. You never actually see the index in your database, and in fact, most modern database applications hide the actual physical storage location of the index altogether.

Part

III

Ch

6

FIGURE 6.10

Database indexes are lists of rows and where they appear in a table.

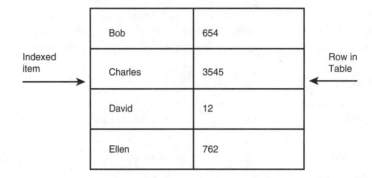

When you create a primary key for a table, it is automatically indexed. The database assumes the primary key will be used constantly for lookups and relationships and therefore does you the favor of creating that first index automatically.

When you run a report with the employee vacation list to determine who is off during October, the following process occurs. First, the database application scans the employee vacation table to find any rows that have vacation dates that fall anytime in October. This process returns the IDs of any employees with vacations booked for that time. Next, the database application retrieves the matching employee name for each vacation table row it has retrieved. It searches the primary key index to find the matching employee record in the employee list table. The index contains all employee IDs in order and, for each ID, lists the physical location of the required row. After the database application finds the correct index value, it obtains a row location from the index and then jumps directly to that location in the table. Although this process may look involved on paper, it actually happens very quickly and in less time than any sequential search would take.

Using Indexes

Now revisit your employee database. Your company has grown dramatically, and the number of employee names in your employee table has grown, too. Lately, you've noticed that operations are taking longer than they used to. The alphabetical employee list report takes considerably longer to run, and the performance drops even further as more names are added to the table. The database design was supposed to be a scalable solution, so why is the additional data bringing the system to its knees?

The solution here is the introduction of additional indexes. The database application automatically creates an index for the primary key. Any additional indexes have to be explicitly defined. To improve sorting and searching by last name, you just need an index on the Last Name column. With this index, the database application can instantly find the rows it is looking for without having to sequentially read through the entire table.

The maximum number of indexes a table can have varies from one database application to another. Some databases have no limit at all and allow every column to be indexed. That way, all searches or sorts can benefit from the faster response time.

> **CAUTION**
>
> Some database applications limit the number of indexes that any table can have. Before you create dozens of indexes, check to see whether you should be aware of any limitations.

Before you run off and create indexes for every column in your table, you have to realize the trade-off. As explained earlier, unlike an index at the end of a book, a database table index is dynamic. As data changes, so do the indexes, and updating indexes takes time. The more indexes a table has, the longer write operations take. Furthermore, each index takes up additional storage space, so unnecessary indexes waste valuable disk space.

When, then, should you create an index? The answer is entirely up to you. Adding indexes to a table makes read operations faster and write operations slower. You have to decide the number of indexes to create and which columns to index for each application. Applications that are used primarily for data entry have less need for indexes. Applications that are used heavily for searching and reporting can definitely benefit from additional indexes.

For example, you should index your employee list table by last name, as you will often be sorting and searching by employees' last names. You will seldom need to sort by employees' first names, so you don't have any justification for indexing the First Name column. You still can search or sort by first name if the need arises, but the search takes longer than a last name search. Likewise, the Phone Extension or Department column might be a candidate for indexing. Whether you add indexes is up to you and your determination of how the application will be used.

With some database applications, you can create and drop indexes as needed. You may decide that you want to create additional temporary indexes before running a batch of infrequently used reports. They enable you to run your reports faster. You can drop the new indexes after you finish running the reports, which restores the table to its previous state. The only downside to doing so is that write operations are slower while the additional indexes are present. This slowdown may or may not be a problem; again, the decision is entirely up to you.

Indexing on More Than One Column

Often, you may find yourself sorting data on more than one column; an example is indexing on last name plus first name. Your employee list table may have more than one employee with the same last name. To correctly display the names, you need to sort on last name plus first name. This way, Jack Smith always appears before Jane Smith, who always appears before John Smith, as shown in Figure 6.11.

Indexing on two columns—like Last Name plus First Name—is not the same as creating two separate indexes (one for Last Name and one for First Name). You have not created an index for the First Name column itself. The index is of use only when you're searching or sorting the Last Name column.

As with all indexes, indexing more than one column may often be beneficial, but this benefit comes with a cost. Indexes that span multiple columns take longer to maintain and take up more disk space. Here, too, you should be careful to create only indexes that are needed and justifiable.

FIGURE 6.11

Indexing data on more than one column is an effective way to achieve the sort order you need.

UNSORTED		SORTED BY LAST NAME		SORTED BY FIRST NAME		SORTED BY LAST NAME PLUS FIRST NAME	
Steve	Jones	Steve	Jones	Jack	Smith	Steve	Jones
John	Smith	John	Smith	Jane	Smith	Jack	Smith
Jane	Smith	Jane	Smith	John	Smith	Jane	Smith
Jack	Smith	Jack	Smith	Steve	Jones	John	Smith

Understanding the Different Types of Database Applications

All the information described to this point applies equally to all databases. The basic fundamentals of databases, tables, keys, and indexes are supported by all database applications. At some point, however, databases start to differ. They may differ in price, performance, features, security, scalability, and more.

One decision you should make very early in the process is whether to use a *shared-file–based* database, such as Microsoft Access, or a *client/server* database application, such as Microsoft SQL Server. Each has advantages and disadvantages, and the key to determining which will work best for you is understanding the difference between shared-file–based applications and client/server systems.

Shared-File–Based Databases

Databases such as Microsoft Access and Visual FoxPro and Borland dBASE are shared-file–based databases. They store their data in data files that are shared by multiple users. These data files are usually stored on network drives so they are easily accessible to all users who need them, as shown in Figure 6.12.

FIGURE 6.12

The data files in a shared-file–based database are accessed by all users directly.

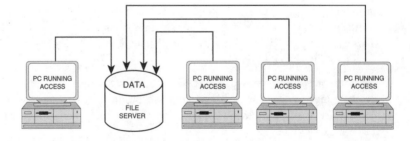

When you access data from a Microsoft Access table, for example, that data file is opened on your computer. Any data you read is read by Microsoft Access running on your computer. Likewise, any data changes are made locally by the copy of Access that is running on your computer.

Considering this point is very important when you're evaluating shared-file–based database applications. The fact that every running copy of Microsoft Access has the data files open locally has serious implications:

- *Shared data files are susceptible to data corruption.* Each user accessing the tables has the data files open locally. If the user fails to terminate the application correctly or the computer hangs, those files don't close gracefully. Abruptly closing data files like this can corrupt the file or cause garbage data to be written to it.

- *Shared data files create a great deal of unnecessary network traffic.* If you perform a search for the names of all employees who have vacation time booked in October, the search takes place on your own computer. The database application running on your computer has to determine which rows it wants and which it does not. The application has to know of all the records—including those that it will discard for this particular query—for this determination to occur. Those discarded records have to travel to your computer over a network connection. Because the data is discarded anyway, unnecessary network traffic is created.

- *Shared data files are insecure.* Because users have to open the actual data files they intend to work with, they must have full access to those files. This also means that users can delete, either intentionally or accidentally, the entire data file with all its tables.

This is not to say that you should never use shared-file–based databases. The following are some compelling reasons to use this type of database:

- Shared-file–based databases are inexpensive. The software itself costs far less than client/server database software. Furthermore, unlike client/server software, shared-file–based databases do not require dedicated hardware for database servers.

- Shared-file–based databases are easier to use and easier to learn than client/server–based databases.

Client/Server-Based Databases

Databases such as Microsoft SQL Server and Oracle are client/server–based databases. Client/server applications are split into two distinct parts. The *server* portion is a piece of software that is responsible for all data access and manipulation. This software runs on a computer called the *database server*. In the case of Microsoft SQL Server, it is a computer running Windows NT and the SQL Server software.

Only the server software interacts with the data files. All requests for data, data additions and deletions, and data updates are funneled through the server software. These requests or changes come from computers running client software. The *client* is the piece of software with which the user interacts. If you request a list of employees sorted by last name, for example, the client software submits that request over the network to the server software. The server software processes the request, filters, discards, and sorts data as needed, and sends the results back to your client software. This process is illustrated in Figure 6.13.

FIGURE 6.13

Client/server databases allow clients to perform database operations that are processed by the server software.

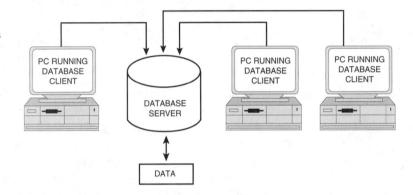

All this action happens transparently to you, the user. The fact that data is stored elsewhere or that a database server is even performing all this processing for you is hidden. You never need to access the data files directly. In fact, most networks are set up so that users have no access to the data, or even the drives on which it is stored.

Client/server–based database servers overcome the limitations of shared-file–based database applications in the following ways:

- Client/server–based data files are less susceptible to data corruption caused by incorrect application termination. If a user fails to exit a program gracefully, or if his or her computer locks up, the data files do not get damaged. That is because the files are never actually open on that user's computer.

- Client/server–based database servers use less network bandwidth. Because all data filtering occurs on the server side, all unneeded data is discarded before the results are sent back to the client software. Only the needed data is transmitted over the network.

- End users in a client/server database environment need never have access to the actual physical data files. This lack of access helps ensure that the files are not deleted or tampered with.

As you can see, client/server databases are more secure and more robust than shared-file databases—but all this extra power and security comes with a price.

- Running client/server databases is expensive. The software itself is far more expensive than shared-file database applications. In addition, you need a database server to run a client/server database. It must be a high-powered computer that is often dedicated for just this purpose.

- Client/server databases are more difficult to set up, configure, and administer. Many companies hire full-time database administrators to do this job.

Which Database Product to Use

Now that you have learned the various types of database systems you can use, how do you determine which is right for your application?

Unfortunately, this question has no simple answer. You really need to review your application needs, the investment you are willing to make in the system, and what systems you already have in place.

To get started, try to answer as many of the following questions as possible:

Do you have an existing database system in place? If yes, is it current technology that is still supported by the vendor? Do you need to link to data in this system, or are you embarking on a new project that can stand on its own feet?

Do you have any database expertise or experience? If yes, what database systems are you familiar with?

Do you have database programmers or administrators in-house? If yes, what systems are they familiar with?

How many users do you anticipate will use the system concurrently?

How many records do you anticipate your tables will contain?

How important is database uptime? What is the cost associated with your database being down for any amount of time?

Do you have existing hardware that can be used for a database server?

These questions are not easy to answer, but the effort is well worth your time. The more planning you do up front, the better chance you have of making the right decision. Getting the job done right the first time will save you time, money, and aggravation later.

Of course, there is no way you can anticipate all future needs. At some point you may, in fact, need to switch databases. If you ever do have to migrate from one database to another, contact the database vendor to determine what migration tools are available. As long as you pick known and established solutions from reputable vendors, you should be safe. ●

Part

III

Ch

6

Creating Databases and Tables

Creating Databases

The moment of truth has arrived. With your copy of the design document you created in Chapter 5, "Designing an Application," you can now create the A2Z Books database.

You can typically create databases and tables in two ways. You can use ODBC and the SQL CREATE TABLE command, or you can use the interactive tools provided with most database systems. Because ODBC and SQL are introduced in the next chapter, you'll create the databases and tables interactively here by using Microsoft Access.

> **N O T E** All the examples throughout this book use Microsoft Access and Access data files. To try the examples in this chapter, you need Microsoft Access installed on your computer.

If you don't have Microsoft Access, don't worry. In the next chapter, you'll begin working with the same Access data files via ODBC. You don't need Microsoft Access installed to access the data files via ODBC, and instead of creating the data files yourself, you can use the ones provided on the accompanying CD-ROM.

Two sets of data files are included on the CD-ROM. One is fully populated, thus allowing you to proceed directly with the examples in later chapters. The other, which is empty, is provided primarily for readers who do not have Microsoft Access installed. ■

Creating the A2Z Database

Each time you run Microsoft Access, you are prompted either to open an existing database or to create a new one, as shown in the dialog box in Figure 7.1. Select the Blank Database option, and then click OK.

FIGURE 7.1

When you start Microsoft Access, you are prompted to either open an existing database or create a new one.

You then are prompted to name your database. Microsoft Access databases have an .MDB extension. You don't need to supply this suffix; it is provided for you. Type **A2Z** in the File Name text box, and then choose Create. Microsoft Access creates the new database and then displays the Database window, as shown in Figure 7.2.

FIGURE 7.2

The Microsoft Access Database window displays all objects in a database and provides tools to manage these objects.

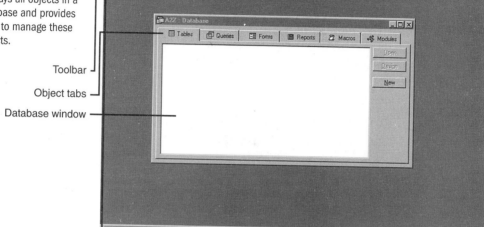

Toolbar

Object tabs

Database window

You have now created a new empty database. The database, you may recall, does not do very much itself. It is like a filing cabinet in which you place new folders to store information.

▶ **See** "Clarification of Database-Related Terms" for a more detailed discussion of the relationship between databases and tables, **p. 89**.

Creating Tables

Now that you have created your database, you need to create tables to store your different data sets, as detailed in the design document you created in Chapter 6, "Database Fundamentals." To create a table, select the Tables tab in the Microsoft Access Database window (shown in Figure 7.3), and then choose New.

You are prompted to select a view or wizard to create the new table from the New Table dialog box. Figure 7.4 shows the options from which you can choose. Select Design View and click OK.

Part

III

Ch

7

FIGURE 7.3
You must select the
Microsoft Access
Database window Tables
tab to create a new
table.

FIGURE 7.4
Microsoft Access
provides several views
and wizards to assist
you in creating tables.

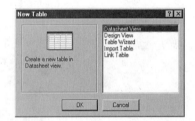

The Microsoft Access Table Wizard is an automated feature for creating tables. If you select the Table
Wizard option from the New Table dialog box, Microsoft Access prompts you to specify the type of data
you will store in this table, and then it suggests columns that you might need.

The Table Wizard is a useful tool that you will probably use extensively when creating tables. For this
example, however, choose Design View instead so that you can learn more about the table creation
process.

You then see the Microsoft Access Table Design View. The view is divided into three columns,
as shown in Figure 7.5. In the first column, Field Name, you specify the name of the column. In
the second column, Data Type, you select the column's data type. At the bottom of the view
window is the Field Properties section, where you can specify field length, default values, index
requirements, and more.

N O T E   Microsoft Access also provides a third column, Description, where you can save descriptive
notes about a particular column. Data you enter into this column appears on the Microsoft
Access status bar each time the field is accessed. Because this column is not used when you access
the database via ODBC, you should use it for these examples. ■

CAUTION

Microsoft Access uses the term *field* to describe an SQL table column and *record* to describe a row. Be
careful not to confuse these terms.

FIGURE 7.5
You use the Microsoft
Access Table Design
View to define the
columns in your table.

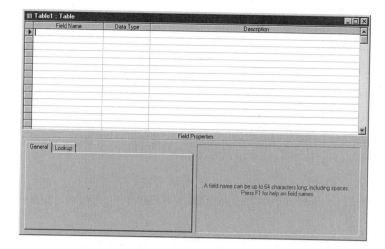

CAUTION

Many database systems, including Microsoft Access and Microsoft SQL Server, allow table names and column names to contain spaces. Although these names are valid, some ODBC drivers have difficulty using names with spaces in them. As a rule, never use spaces in table or column names.

Creating the Employees Tables

You now can specify all the columns that make up the first table, the employees list table. Fill in the first two columns in the database Design View with the values in the Field Name and Data Type columns in Table 7.1. Field Properties lists any properties you need to set for a specific column. For example, in the EmployeeID column, you should set the New Values option to Increment.

Table 7.1   Employees Table Columns

Field Name	Data Type	Field Properties
EmployeeID	AutoNumber	Select Increment from the drop-down list in New Values.
FirstName	Text	Type 30 in Field Size.
MiddleInit	Text	Type 1 in Field Size.
LastName	Text	Type 30 in Field Size.
Address1	Text	The default size is 50.
Address2	Text	The default size is 50.
City	Text	Type 40 in Field Size.

Part
III

Ch
7

continues

Table 7.1 Continued

Field Name	Data Type	Field Properties
State	Text	Type 5 in Field Size.
Zip	Text	Type 10 in Field Size.
PhoneHome	Text	Type 20 in Field Size.
PhoneCellular	Text	Type 20 in Field Size.
PhonePager	Text	Type 20 in Field Size.
SocialSecurity	Text	Type 11 in Field Size.
DateOfBirth	Date/Time	
DateOfHire	Date/Time	
Title	Text	Type 20 in Field Size.
DepartmentID	Number	Select Long Integer from the drop-down list in Field Size.
PhoneExtension	Text	Type 4 in Field Size.
Email	Text	Type 30 in Field Size.

Before you go any further, take a look at some of the data types and properties you defined.

▶ **See** "Data Types" for a detailed discussion of different data types and why they are used, **p. 90**.

The EmployeeID column has a data type of AutoNumber. AutoNumber is a special Microsoft Access data type that is automatically filled in each time you add a new row to your table. The value in an AutoNumber column is guaranteed to be unique for every row. By specifying Increment as the New Value option, you instruct that as each new employee is added to the table, the EmployeeID should be set to one higher than the last value used. Because the EmployeeID column is going to be used as a primary key, each employee must have an EmployeeID, and all IDs must be unique. The AutoNumber data type provides a simple way of accomplishing this task.

N O T E AutoNumber is a Microsoft Access-specific feature. Not all database systems have this feature, although many do. Those systems that do, however, may have a different name for it. With Microsoft SQL Server, for example, you can specify a column as an Identity column and specify how the identity value should be generated. ■

Almost has a data type of AutoNumber. AutoNumber is a special Microsofall text columns have a specified field size. The default field size in Microsoft Access is 50 characters. This number is more than is needed for name or zip code fields, so you can specify a size for each column that makes more sense. If you leave the field size at its default value, you waste lots of storage space.

The two date columns, DateOfBirth and DateOfHire, are specified as Date/Time columns. You do so to preserve disk space, as well as to ensure correct data sorting, as explained in detail in Chapter 6.

You might wonder why you specify the DepartmentID column as a number instead of text. This is a good example of data normalization. Remember that the rule in data normalization is to never repeat data. If you were to enter the complete department name for every employee into this table, you would have many occurrences of each department name. For every sales-person, you would see the word Sales in the department column. So you define the DepartmentID column as a number. Each department is assigned a number, a department ID, and that number is stored in the employee record. If Sales is department 4, then for every salesperson, you see the value 4 instead of the word Sales in the DepartmentID column.

The DepartmentID column has a size of Long Integer specified. With Microsoft Access, like many database systems, you can specify the width of numeric columns. A single-byte column can store 256 values (0–255). A two-byte column can store 65,536 values. Because it is unlikely that you'll have 60,000 departments in your company, a single byte is probably sufficient. How-ever, because this column is used to relate this table to the Departments table, it must have the same data type. The Microsoft Access AutoNumber data type is always a Long Integer, so you must use a Long Integer here.

The Employees Table's Primary Key   You have now defined all the columns in your employees list table. Before you save and name the table, however, you need to specify the primary key and any additional indexes you want to use.

▶ **See** "Primary and Foreign Keys" for a detailed discussion of primary keys and their purpose, **p. 96**.

To specify that the EmployeeID column should be used as the primary key, follow these steps:

1. Select the EmployeeID column by clicking EmployeeID in the Field Name column.
2. From the Edit menu, choose Primary Key to use the selected column as the table's primary key.

Microsoft Access then displays a key symbol in the row selector to the left of the EmployeeID field name, as shown in Figure 7.6. This symbol indicates that the column is the primary key.

As you learned in Chapter 6, a primary key is automatically indexed when it is created. In Figure 7.6, you can see that Field Properties for the EmployeeID column has been changed to show that this column is now indexed and does not allow duplicates.

The Employees Table's Indexes

▶ **See** "Indexes" for a detailed discussion of table indexes, **p. 98**.

Next, you can create the indexes you need to work with this table. One of the sort orders you anticipate using regularly is sorting by phone extensions, so the PhoneExtension column is a good candidate for indexing.

FIGURE 7.6

Microsoft Access indicates the primary key column with a key symbol.

Primary key indicator ┘

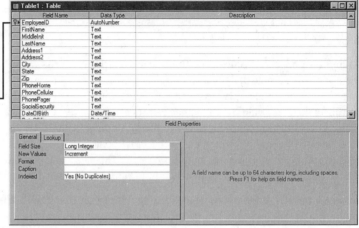

To create an index for a single column, follow these steps:

1. Select the desired column—in this case, PhoneExtension—by clicking its name in the Field Name column.

2. Select Yes (Duplicates OK) from the drop-down list in the Indexed field.

The other frequently used sort order is last name plus first name. To create an index for multiple columns, follow these steps:

1. From the View menu, choose Indexes to open the Indexes window. Any already defined indexes are listed.

2. In the Index Name column of a new blank row, enter a name for the index you want to create. For the example, type `EmployeeName`.

3. Select the first column you want to index from the drop-down list box in the Field Name column. For the example, select the LastName column.

4. Specify any additional columns to include in the row's index directly beneath the first column of the index. Again, for this example, select FirstName in the row directly beneath LastName, and select MiddleInit in the row beneath that. Your Indexes window should now look like the one shown in Figure 7.7.

5. From the View menu, choose Indexes again to close the Indexes window. (Alternatively, you can click the close button in the Indexes window to close the dialog box and return to the Design window.)

The last thing left to do is to save the table. From the File menu, choose Save to do so. You are prompted for a table name. Type `Employees` in Table Name, and click OK to save the table.

Congratulations, you have successfully created your first table.

The Departments Table   The Department field in the Employees table contains a single value that identifies an employee's department. Your next task then is to create the Departments table.

FIGURE 7.7

The Microsoft Access Indexes window displays or defines table indexes.

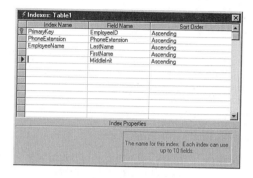

To create this new table, select the Tables tab in the Microsoft Access Database window, and then choose New. As before, you are prompted to select a wizard or a view. Select Design View and click OK.

The simple Departments table contains only two columns, as listed in Table 7.2. Enter the column information into the Design View window, and then select the ID field as the primary key. When it is completed, your window should look like the one shown in Figure 7.8.

Table 7.2 Departments Table Columns

Field Name	Data Type	Field Properties
ID	AutoNumber	Select Increment from the drop-down list in New Values.
Department	Text	Type 30 in Field Size.

FIGURE 7.8

You use the Departments table to map department IDs to department names.

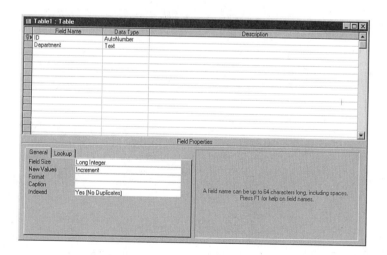

Because the Departments table will never have more than 256 rows, you don't need to create an index to sort by the Description column. Microsoft Access can sort that many rows quickly without having an index, and adding an index creates additional overhead.

Now that your table design is complete, you can save the table with the name Departments.

The Vacations Table One last table is needed to complete the employee data set as defined in Chapter 5. The Vacations table also is a simple table. Again, you create this new table using the Design view and enter the column information as shown in Table 7.3.

Table 7.3 Vacations Table Columns

Field Name	Data Type	Field Properties
EmployeeID	Number	Field Size must be Long Integer to match the EmployeeID field in the Employees table.
VacationStart	Date/Time	
VacationEnd	Date/Time	

The table does not have an incrementing field for a primary key. Instead, you'll use a combination of the EmployeeID and the VacationStart as the primary key. Because no employee can ever have two vacations that start on the same day, this assumption is safe. So, create a primary key on the EmployeeID field plus the VacationStart field. To do so, select both columns and then click the Primary Key button. The EmployeeID column must relate back to the Employees table and therefore should be indexed too. Set the EmployeeID Indexed property to Yes (Duplicates OK). You must select the Duplicates OK option; otherwise, no one can book more than one vacation, and that prospect is likely to make you very unpopular.

Next, save the table as Vacations, which should look like the screen shown in Figure 7.9.

FIGURE 7.9

The Vacations table has a primary key comprised of two different columns.

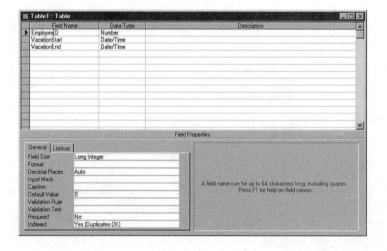

Creating the Inventory Table

The Employees table and all its supporting tables are now ready for use. Next, you need to create the Inventory table. Like the department information in the Employees table, the Inventory table uses a category ID to identify title categories. This way, you can prevent the category information from being duplicated. Create the Inventory table with the information listed in Table 7.4.

Table 7.4 Inventory Table Columns

Field Name	Data Type	Field Properties
BookID	AutoNumber	Select Increment from the drop-down list in New Values.
CategoryID	Number	Select Long Integer from the drop-down list in Field Size.
ISBN	Text	Type 13 in Field Size.
Title	Text	Type 50 in Field Size.
Publisher	Text	Type 50 in Field Size.
PublicationDate	Date/Time	
AuthorFirstName	Text	Type 30 in Field Size.
AuthorLastName	Text	Type 30 in Field Size.
Pages	Number	Select Integer from the drop-down list in Field Size.
Description	Memo	
NumberInStock	Number	Select Integer from the drop-down list in Field Size.
DueDate	Date/Time	
Location	Text	Type 80 in Field Size.

Again, every book needs a way for you to uniquely identify it, so you create a BookID field with a data type of AutoNumber.

The CategoryID column contains the ID number that identifies a book category. This number relates this book to its appropriate category in the Category table.

The ISBN column has a data type of Text, even though ISBN numbers are usually all digits. Even if your ISBN numbers were all numeric, you would want to make the ISBN value a text field for two reasons. First, ISBNs are usually formatted with hyphens in them, such as 0-7897-1414-0. If you save the ISBN as a number, formatting it correctly for display would be difficult. Second, if you treat it as a real number, ISBNs that start with 0, as this book's does, lose that 0 when the value is saved. The number 0789714140 is saved as 789714140. Obviously, you don't want this result, so sometimes you need to save numbers as text.

Part
III

Ch
7

The Pages n `Integer`. Once again, the range of values of a byte is not enough; most books have more than 256 pages. Therefore, `Integer`, which can store numbers greater than 60,000, is a more realistic choice.

The Description column uses a data type you have not seen yet. `Memo` is a variable-length data type. This means that you do not define a field size; instead, space is allocated as needed. If you enter 3KB of data (about 3,000 bytes) into the field, then 3KB of space is used. If you enter 64KB (about 64,000 bytes), then 64KB of space is used. `Memo` is often used for notes that might vary dramatically in size from one row to the next.

CAUTION

Variable-length columns have one very important limitation. They cannot be indexed. Only columns with a fixed, known length can be indexed. If you're going to need indexed access to a column, do not use a variable-length data type.

N O T E Different database systems use different terms to refer to variable-length columns. Microsoft Access and Borland dBASE use the term *memo*, whereas Microsoft SQL Server uses the term *text*.

In addition, the maximum size of data you can store in a variable-length field varies from one database application to the next. Microsoft Access can store up to 64KB (about 64,000 bytes) in a memo field. Microsoft SQL Server can store up to 2GB (over 2 billion bytes) in a text field. ■

The NumberInStock column is also defined as a `Number` with an `Integer` for its field size. Again, 256 might not be a large enough range of values.

Your table should now look like the one shown in Figure 7.10.

FIGURE 7.10

The Inventory table uses a Memo data type to store variable-length data.

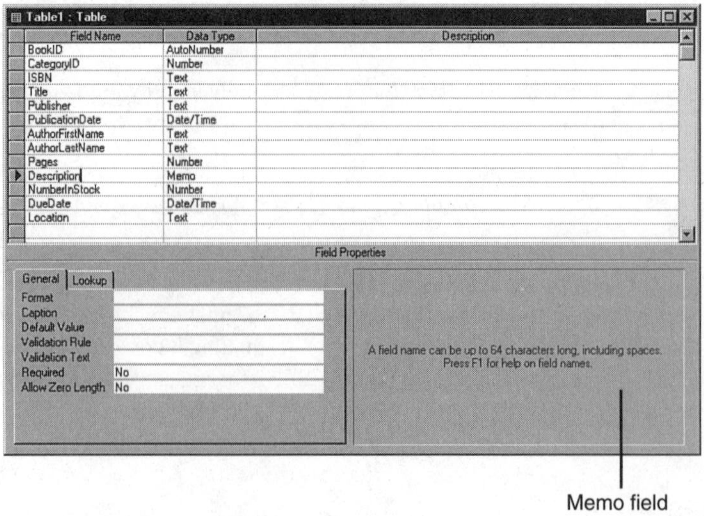

Memo field

The Inventory Table's Indexes   The Inventory table has six indexes you should now create:

Create a primary key on the BookID column.

Create a Duplicates OK index on the CategoryID column.

Create a Duplicates OK index on the ISBN column.

Create a Duplicates OK index on the Title column.

Create a Duplicates OK index on the Publisher column.

Create a Duplicates OK index called Author that indexes the AuthorLastName column plus the AuthorFirstName column.

After you define the indexes, your Indexes window should look like the one shown in Figure 7.11.

FIGURE 7.11

The Inventory table uses both single-column indexes and multiple-column indexes.

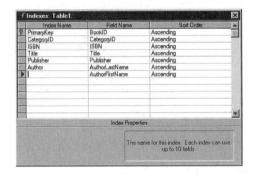

Finally, save the table as Inventory.

The Category Table   The Category table stores category IDs instead of categories, just like the department IDs in the Employees table. Now create the Category table as detailed in Table 7.5.

Table 7.5   Category Table Columns

Field Name	Data Type	Field Properties
ID	AutoNumber	Select Increment from the drop-down list in New Values.
Category	Text	Type 30 in Field Size.

Next, create a primary key on the ID column. Your Table Design View window should look like the one shown in Figure 7.12.

Creating the Customer Table

The Customer table is similar to the Employees table. Create this new table using the columns listed in Table 7.6.

Part

III

Ch

7

FIGURE 7.12

You use the Category table to map category IDs into category names.

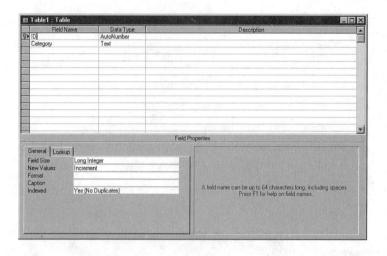

Table 7.6 Customer Table Columns

Field Name	Data Type	Field Properties
CustomerID	AutoNumber	Select Increment from the drop-down list in New Values.
Company	Text	Type 40 in Field Size.
FirstName	Text	Type 30 in Field Size.
MiddleInit	Text	Type 1 in Field Size.
LastName	Text	Type 30 in Field Size.
Address1	Text	Accept the default size of 50.
Address2	Text	Accept the default size of 50.
City	Text	Type 40 in Field Size.
State	Text	Type 5 in Field Size.
Zip	Text	Type 10 in Field Size.
Phone	Text	Type 20 in Field Size.
Email	Text	Type 30 in Field Size.
CustomerSince	Date/Time	

The Customer table will likely be searched in many different ways; when a customer is waiting on the phone, you want rapid responses to your searches. As you learned in Chapter 6, using indexes creates some trade-offs. More indexes can improve the performance of searches and queries but can also slow down data inserts and updates, so you must make the decision of how many indexes to create for each table individually. Because of your need to respond quickly to the customer on the phone, the Customer table is a prime candidate for extra indexes.

Create the Customer table indexes listed here:

Create a primary key on the CustomerID column.

Create a Duplicates OK index on the Company column.

Create a Duplicates OK index on the Phone column.

Create a Duplicates OK index called Name that indexes the LastName column plus the FirstName column plus the MiddleInit column.

Create a Duplicates OK index called Location that indexes the City column plus State column.

With all these indexes, you and your sales people should have no trouble locating customer information. If a customer's name is misspelled, for example, your staff can search by company name, phone number, or even city and state to locate the required record.

Figure 7.13 shows what your completed Indexes window should look like. After you verify that the indexes are correct, save the table as `Customers`.

FIGURE 7.13

The Customer table is heavily indexed to improve the performance of data retrieval.

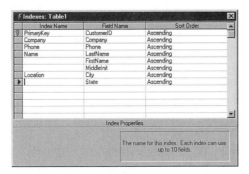

Creating the Order Tables

Order entry is a good example of a type of data that must be normalized. Some order information pertains to the entire order, and other information pertains to individual line items within the order.

To process order entry correctly, you need to create two new tables. The first, the Order table, will store information that is relevant to the entire order. The second, the OrderItems table, will list the individual line items that make up the order. Figure 7.14 shows the relationship between these two tables. As you can see, only one entry appears per order in the Order table. The related OrderItems table, however, contains multiple entries per order, one for each item ordered.

The Order Table   Create the Order table with the information shown in Table 7.7.

Part

III

Ch

7

FIGURE 7.14

Order entry provides a good example of how data should be normalized.

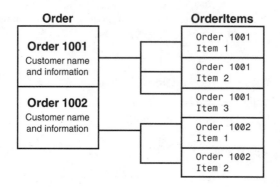

Order

Order 1001
Customer name and information

Order 1002
Customer name and information

OrderItems

Order 1001
Item 1

Order 1001
Item 2

Order 1001
Item 3

Order 1002
Item 1

Order 1002
Item 2

Table 7.7 Order Table Columns

Field Name	Data Type	Field Properties
OrderID	AutoNumber	Select Increment from the drop-down list in New Values.
CustomerID	Number	Select Long Integer from the drop-down list in Field Size.
OrderDate	Date/Time	
PurchaseOrder	Text	Type 30 in Field Size.
ShipTo	Text	Type 50 in Field Size.
ShipCompany	Text	Type 40 in Field Size.
ShipAddress1	Text	
ShipAddress2	Text	
ShipCity	Text	Type 40 in Field Size.
ShipState	Text	Type 5 in Field Size.
ShipZip	Text	Type 10 in Field Size.
ShipMethodID	Number	Select Long Integer from the drop-down list in Field Size.
ShippingCharge	Currency	
Taxable	Yes/No	

The OrderID column stores the unique order ID. You should designate this column as the primary key.

The CustomerID column stores the `CustomerID` value from the Customer table, linking an order to the appropriate customer. If a customer has more than one order, then all those orders have the same CustomerID and are linked to the same Customer row.

ShipMethodID is another column that has been normalized. It contains the ID to relate an order with the ShippingMethod table.

ShippingCharge introduces a new data type, the Currency type. As its name implies, this data type is used to store amounts of money.

N O T E   Almost all database systems have a Currency data type, but they are not all called *Currency*. Microsoft SQL Server uses the term *Money* for a similar data type. ▨

Taxable is defined as having a Yes/No data type. A column that has a Yes/No data type can accept only two values: Yes and No. This data type is useful for storing flags (a value that indicates whether an option is selected). Whenever a column can have only one of two responses—Yes or No—then you can use this data type.

N O T E   Microsoft Access uses the term Yes/No to describe a data type that has only two states: Yes (On, True) and No (Off, False). Other database systems use different terms to describe this data type. Microsoft SQL Server calls this a Bit data type. ▨

The Order Table's Indexes   For the Order table, you should create four indexes:

Create a primary key on the OrderID column.

Create a Duplicates OK index on the CustomerID column.

Create a Duplicates OK index on the OrderDate column.

Create a Duplicates OK index on the ShipMethodID column.

You index the OrderDate column so orders can be sorted by order date, a sort order that you anticipate will be used often. You index the ShipMethodID column so Shipping can easily find all orders that need to be shipped via the same method.

After you define the indexes, your Indexes window should look like the one shown in Figure 7.15.

FIGURE 7.15

The Order table contains IDs to relate it to three other tables.

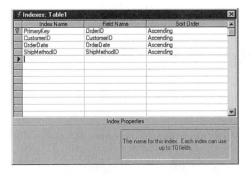

The OrderItems Table   Create the OrderItems table with the information shown in Table 7.8.

The OrderID column must be a Long Integer because it is the data type of the OrderID in the Order table. The OrderID column in each table relates an order to the order items.

Part

III

Ch

7

Table 7.8 OrderItems Table Columns

Field Name	Data Type	Field Properties
OrderID	Number	Select Long Integer from the drop-down list in New Values.
OrderLine	Number	Select Byte from the drop-down list in New Values.
BookID	Number	Select Long Integer from the drop-down list in New Values.
Quantity	Number	Select Integer from the drop-down list in New Values.
UnitPrice	Currency	
SalePrice	Currency	

OrderLine is the line number within a specific order. You will not have more than 256 line items in each order (your invoices can't even print that many items on a single order), so a byte is adequate.

Create a primary key on OrderID plus OrderLine.

BookID contains the ID of the title ordered and relates back to the Inventory table you created earlier.

The OrderItems Table's Indexes   The OrderItems table has just two indexes you should create:

> Create a unique index called Order that indexes the OrderID column plus the OrderLine column. To specify that this index is unique (a Duplicates No index), select Yes from the drop-down list box in the Unique field in the Index Properties area, as shown in Figure 7.16.

> Create a Duplicates OK index on the BookID column.

FIGURE 7.16

To create a unique index that spans more than one column, you must use the Indexes window.

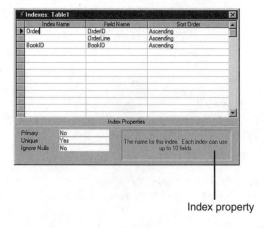

Index property

The ShippingMethod Table   The Order table stores shipping method IDs instead of shipping details. These IDs relate the order record to the shipping method in the ShippingMethod table. Create the ShippingMethod table as detailed in Table 7.9.

Table 7.9   ShippingMethod Table Columns

Field Name	Data Type	Field Properties
ID	AutoNumber	Select Increment from the drop-down list in New Values.
ShippingMethod	Text	Type 20 in Field Size.

Create a primary key on the ID column, and save the table as ShippingMethod.

Understanding Table Relationships

You have now created nine tables, and almost every one of these tables is related. When an order is placed, for example, the following steps must occur:

1. Every customer must have a record in the Customer table. If the customer is new, then you have to add a new row. If it is an existing customer, then you must locate the appropriate row.

2. You create a new order by adding the order information to the Order table. This process generates a new order number.

3. You select the shipping method from the ShippingMethod table, and it is stored in the order record.

4. You enter the items to be ordered. Each item is added to the OrderItems table, one row per item. The rows are related to the order by their OrderIDs.

5. You select the titles from the Inventory table, and the BookID is stored in the OrderItems table. Multiple copies of the same title are entered only once; the Quantity column indicates the number ordered.

If this process sounds rather complex, don't worry about it. As soon as you start building an application that uses these tables, you'll find that it all makes perfect sense. In the meantime, you may find that drawing a flowchart to describe the relationships between tables is worthwhile. The flowchart in Figure 7.17 shows the relationships between some of the tables created in this chapter.

Adding Data with Microsoft Access

In the next chapter you learn how to create SQL statements to query your tables for data. To do so, you need sample data in your tables. You can use Microsoft Access, and indeed whatever front-end application you use to create your tables, to add that data.

Part

III

Ch

7

FIGURE 7.17

Almost all the tables created in this chapter are related.

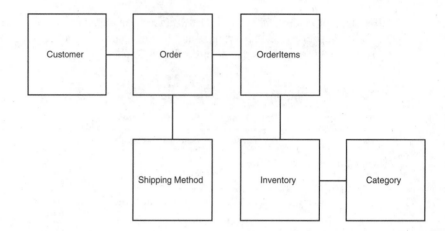

For your immediate needs, though, you need to add data to the Employees tables. You should add 2 rows to the Departments table and 10 rows to the Employees table.

Adding Data to the Departments Table

First, if Access is not currently running, load the program. Then open the A2Z database. You are presented with a list of the available tables. Click the Departments table to select it, and then choose Open. The table then opens so that you can add and edit data, as shown in Figure 7.18.

FIGURE 7.18

Microsoft Access opens tables in a grid in which you can add or edit data.

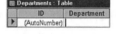

FIGURE 7.19

When a table has a column of type AutoNumber, Microsoft Access assigns numbers automatically as new rows are entered.

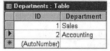

The ID column is an AutoNumber column; you don't enter a value in it because Microsoft Access does that job for you automatically.

In the Department column, type **Sales**. Sales is the first department to create, and Access assigns ID 1 to it. Now click the empty Department field beneath the Sales field, and type Accounting. Access assigns ID 2 to this record. Your completed window should look like the one shown in Figure 7.19.

Adding Data to the Employees Table

Now you're going to add rows to the Employees table. First, save the Departments table by clicking the Save button (the one with the picture of the disk). Then, from the File menu, choose Close to close the table.

Next, open the Employees table by selecting it and double-clicking, or by clicking the Open button. You are now going to put values in all the columns. The values you need to enter are listed in Table 7.10. Enter the data for all 10 rows. Note that you have to scroll the window to get to the DepartmentID and PhoneExtension columns.

Table 7.10 Sample Data for the Employees Table

FirstName	LastName	DepartmentID	PhoneExtension
Adam	Stevens	1	4878
Adrienne	Green	2	4546
Dan	Johnson	2	4824
Jack	Smith	1	4545
Jane	Smith	2	4876
Jennifer	White	1	4345
Kim	Black	1	4565
Lynn	Wilson	1	4464
Marcy	Gold	1	4912
Steven	Jones	1	4311

After you enter the data, click the Save button and close the window. You're now ready to start learning SQL. ●

CHAPTER 8

Introduction to SQL

Introducing SQL, the Structured Query Language

SQL, pronounced *sequel*, is an acronym for Structured Query Language. SQL is a language you use to access and manipulate data in a relational database. It is designed to be both easy to learn and extremely powerful, and its mass acceptance by so many database vendors proves that it has succeeded in both.

In 1970, Dr. E. F. Codd, the man credited with being the father of the relational database, described a universal language for data access. In 1974, engineers at IBM's San Jose Research Center created the Structured English Query Language, or SEQUEL, built on Codd's ideas. This language was incorporated into System R, IBM's pioneering relational database system.

Toward the end of the 1980s, two of the most important standards bodies, the American National Standards Institute (ANSI) and the International Standards Organization (ISO), published SQL standards, opening the door to mass acceptance. With these standards in place, SQL was poised to become the de facto standard used by every major database vendor.

Although SQL has evolved a great deal since its early SEQUEL days, the basic language concepts and its founding premises have remained the same. The beauty of SQL is its simplicity. But don't let that simplicity deceive you. SQL is a powerful language, and it encourages you to be creative in your problem solving. You can almost always find more than one way to perform a complex query or to extract desired data. Each solution has pros and cons, and no solution is explicitly right or wrong.

Before you panic at the thought of learning a new language, let me reassure you that SQL really is easy to learn. In fact, you need to learn only four statements to be able to perform almost all the data manipulation you will need on a regular basis. Table 8.1 lists these statements.

Table 8.1 SQL-Based Data Manipulation Statements

Statement	Description
SELECT	Query a table for specific data.
INSERT	Add new data to a table.
UPDATE	Update existing data in a table.
DELETE	Remove data from a table.

Each of these statements takes one or more keywords as parameters. By combining different statements and keywords, you can manipulate your data in as many different ways as you can imagine.

ColdFusion provides you with all the tools you need to add Web-based interaction to your databases. ColdFusion itself, though, has no built-in database. Instead, it communicates with whatever database you select, passing updates and requests and returning query results.

Introducing ODBC

The communication between ColdFusion and the database takes place via a database interface called Open Database Connectivity, or ODBC. ODBC is a standard Application Programming Interface (API) for accessing information from different database systems and different storage formats.

Working with Database System Differences

The purpose of ODBC is to enable you to access a diverse selection of databases and data formats without having to learn the features and peculiarities of each. ODBC provides a layer of abstraction, accomplished using database drivers, between your client application and the underlying database. The database drivers create a database-independent environment, as illustrated in Figure 8.1. This way, you can write one program and have it work with almost any major database system.

FIGURE 8.1
ODBC creates a database-independent development environment.

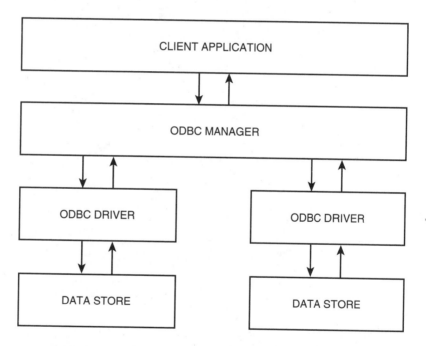

Of course, differences exist between database systems. Microsoft SQL Server, for example, requires you to log in to the database server before you are able to manipulate any data. Based on your login, you are granted or denied access to specific tables or other objects. Microsoft Access, on the other hand, has no concept of login-based security. If you have access to the data file (the MDB file), then you have full access to all data in it.

You will find other differences, too. To access Microsoft SQL Server, your client application must know the address of the server. It might be an IP address or an NT server name. To use Microsoft Access data files, you just need to know the drive and path to the data file.

Part of the job of ODBC is to hide these differences from your client application. To accomplish this feat, each ODBC driver has its own configuration options. When you select the SQL Server ODBC driver, you are asked for a server name, a server login name, and a password, as shown in Figure 8.2. When you select the Access ODBC driver, you are prompted for a file path, as shown in Figure 8.3.

FIGURE 8.2

The Microsoft SQL Server ODBC driver prompts you for login information.

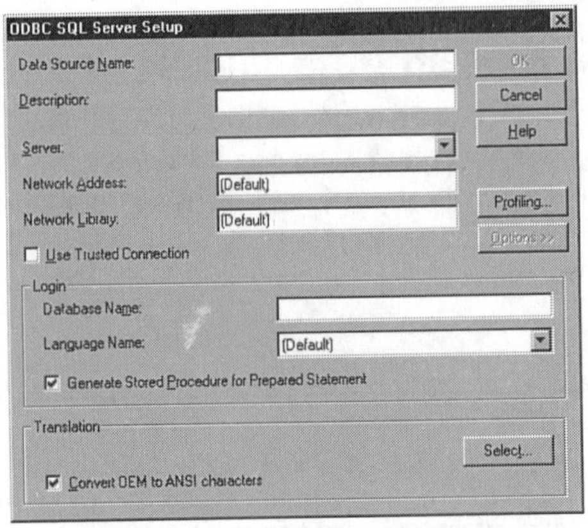

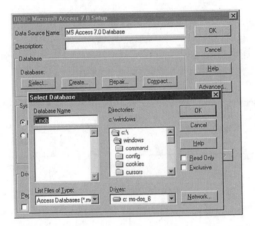

FIGURE 8.3

The Microsoft Access ODBC driver prompts you for the file path to the Access data file.

This way, your client software can load any ODBC driver and connect to a database. The ODBC driver you select will handle opening the database, whether it's opening a network file or logging in to a server. All your client software knows is that it must connect to a database; the details of how this process occurs are all hidden.

The ODBC Story

ODBC was created in an effort to allow Microsoft Excel, Microsoft's popular spreadsheet program, to access diverse data stores.

In April 1988, Microsoft's Kyle Geiger proposed a model that used database drivers to isolate the native data types of different database applications. This model, in conjunction with a standard application interface, would allow client software to communicate with any message store. To access a particular data store, all that would be required was a driver designed specifically for that data store.

While Geiger worked on his proposal, engineers at DEC, Lotus, and Sybase were working on much the same idea. The four companies joined forces, and between 1988 and 1992 they helped shape the specification.

The original name for this project was Microsoft Data Access API. In early 1989, the effort was renamed Open SQL, and then in the summer of 1989, it was renamed again to SQL Connectivity. Finally, in the winter of 1992, the name was changed one last time to Open Database Connectivity, or ODBC.

The beta version of ODBC 1.0 was released in March 1992, and in September 1992, version 1.0 finally was released. Shortly thereafter, in October 1992, the specification was reviewed and accepted by the ANSI SQL committee.

ODBC itself is not a language; the language used by ODBC is SQL. Part of the magic of the ODBC database driver is that it understands SQL and converts it to whatever is appropriate for any specific database. This way, you can use SQL commands to work with xBASE-based databases, such as Microsoft FoxPro and Borland dBASE, even though they have an entirely different native language.

Herein lies the power of ODBC. The combination of database independence and a common standard language grants ODBC clients a tremendous level of freedom—freedom to use any database they want, freedom to use different databases for different tasks seamlessly and simultaneously, and the freedom to concentrate on application development without having to learn database-specific languages and APIs.

Understanding ODBC and ColdFusion

ColdFusion is an ODBC client. ODBC enables you to use ColdFusion with whatever database you choose. If you're using Microsoft Access, then ColdFusion uses the Access driver; if you're using Oracle, then the Oracle ODBC driver is used instead. You can even use ODBC to read and write plain-text files. As long as you have the correct ODBC driver, ColdFusion will support that data store.

Because ColdFusion is an ODBC client, the database language used by ColdFusion is SQL. To truly exploit the power of ColdFusion, you must have a thorough understanding of SQL. Fortunately, by the end of this chapter, you should be enough of a SQL expert to start generating world-class ColdFusion applications.

Creating an ODBC Data Source

ODBC client applications do not directly load ODBC drivers. In fact, they have no knowledge of what driver to use with any specific database. Rather, the application connects to a data source. A data source appears to your application as a virtual database. Within the data source, all the ODBC settings are configured, including specifying which ODBC driver to use.

Before your application can use an ODBC driver, you must create a data source. Doing so involves the following steps:

1. Select the ODBC driver that is appropriate for the database you plan to use. You have to install the driver if it is not already present on your computer.

2. Name your data source with a unique and descriptive name.

3. Configure the driver-specific settings via the ODBC driver's configuration options.

After you create your data source, any ODBC client application can use it to access or manipulate the database with which it is associated.

N O T E The ODBC Control Panel applet and basic ODBC drivers are installed by many applications. If you have Microsoft Office installed, then you should have the applet and half dozen drivers installed, too. (If you do not have the drivers installed, run the Office setup again, select Custom Install, and then select the drivers manually.)

If you need to obtain the applet, new ODBC drivers, or updated versions of existing drivers, the best place to start is the Microsoft FTP server at `ftp.microsoft.com`. ■

Configuring the ODBC Data Source Control Panel Applet

You configure ODBC data sources from within the ODBC applet in the Windows Control Panel. Try bringing up the Windows Control Panel now. You should see an applet called ODBC or 32bit ODBC. Double-click the ODBC applet to open the ODBC Data Sources dialog box, as shown in Figure 8.4.

FIGURE 8.4

You can create and configure data sources and obtain driver version information in the ODBC Data Sources dialog box.

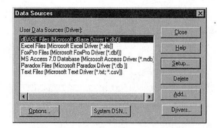

The User Data Sources box shows the currently installed ODBC data sources, including generic data sources for accessing Microsoft Excel, Microsoft FoxPro, and text files. Double-clicking any data source opens the ODBC Setup window for the driver associated with that data source.

N O T E Different versions of the ODBC Manager and the ODBC drivers could have different user interfaces. If the dialog boxes you see on your machine look different from the ones shown here, don't worry. ColdFusion, and all the code and examples in this book, will still run properly. ■

Figures 8.5, 8.6, and 8.7 show the Microsoft Excel Setup window, the dBASE Setup window, and the Microsoft SQL Server Setup window, respectively. Each setup window has a required

Data Source Name field and an optional Description field. All other options are driver specific and, therefore, vary from one driver to the next.

FIGURE 8.5

The Microsoft Excel ODBC driver setup prompts for Excel-specific information, including the version of Excel and worksheet-related options.

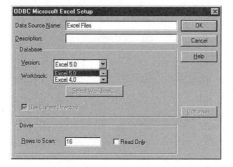

FIGURE 8.6

The dBASE ODBC driver setup prompts for dBASE-specific information, including the dBASE version.

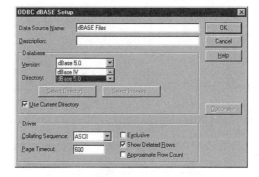

FIGURE 8.7

The Microsoft SQL Server ODBC driver setup prompts for network login and address information.

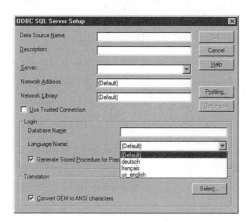

The ODBC Data Sources dialog box is also used to configure systemwide ODBC options. These options are all accessed via the buttons listed in Table 8.2.

Table 8.2 ODBC Data Source Buttons

Button	Description
Options	Configure systemwide ODBC options, such as tracing.
System DSN	Set up data sources that the system, or any user, can use, rather than the local user.
Close	Close the ODBC Data Sources dialog box.
Help	Obtain help.
Setup	Configure the selected data source, which is the same as double-clicking a data source.
Delete	Permanently remove the selected data source.
Add	Add a new data source using an existing ODBC driver.
Drivers	Display a list of available ODBC drivers.

Try clicking the Drivers button now. A Drivers dialog box similar to the one shown in Figure 8.8 should appear. In this dialog box, select any driver by clicking it, and then click the About button. An About dialog box like the one shown in Figure 8.9 should then appear.

FIGURE 8.8

You can see what ODBC drivers are installed on your system by clicking the Data Source dialog box's Drivers button.

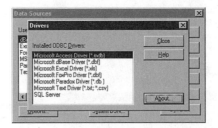

FIGURE 8.9

ODBC drivers include descriptions of themselves, vendor information, the release date, and a version number.

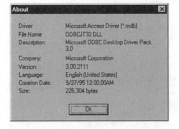

N O T E   If you look at the About information for the Access, dBASE, Excel, FoxPro, Paradox, and Text drivers, you may notice that they are all, in fact, the same driver. Microsoft supplies all these drivers as part of its ODBC Desktop Driver Pack, and they are installed automatically with the ODBC applet. ■

Creating a Data Source for the A2Z Books Database

Now that you've learned about data sources, you're ready to put all this newly acquired knowledge to use. In Chapter 7, "Creating Databases and Tables," you created a Microsoft Access database called A2Z. Now you're going to create an ODBC data source for this data file. Here are the steps:

1. Select the ODBC applet from the Windows Control Panel.

2. Click the Add button to open the Add Data Source dialog box. If your Control Panel applet has a tabbed dialog that lets you select data source types, make sure DSN or System DSN is selected.

3. Select Microsoft Access Driver from the Installed ODBC Drivers list, and click OK to open the ODBC Microsoft Access Setup dialog box.

4. Name the data source by typing A2Z in the Data Source Name field.

5. Click the Select button to locate the A2Z.MDB file.

6. Click OK to save your new data source.

That's all there is to it. The ODBC Data Sources dialog box now shows the new data source, A2Z, in the list of available User Data Sources, as shown in Figure 8.10.

FIGURE 8.10

When you add new data sources, they appear in the list of available User Data Sources.

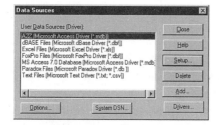

N O T E Don't confuse ODBC data sources and ODBC drivers. ODBC drivers are dynamic link libraries, or DLLs, that communicate with a specific data store type. A data source is a complete database configuration that uses an ODBC driver to communicate with a specific database.

A data source communicates with only one database. To use an ODBC driver to communicate with two or more of the same types of databases, you need to create multiple data sources that all use the same ODBC driver. ■

 You just created a data source using the ODBC Control Panel applet. The ColdFusion Administrator provides an alternate way to create data sources using a Web-based interface (and a ColdFusion application, of course). Regardless of how you create the data source, it will be available to all applications, not just ColdFusion. Use whatever method is more convenient for you.

Using Microsoft Query

Now that you have a data source, all you need is a client application with which to access the data. Ultimately, the client you will use is ColdFusion; after all, that is why you're reading this book. But to start learning SQL without having to learn ColdFusion, you need to start with Microsoft Query.

Microsoft Query is a SQL query utility. It is a simple ODBC database front end that Microsoft supplies with many of its other applications, including Microsoft Office. With Microsoft Query, you can test ODBC connectivity, interactively build SQL statements, and view the results of SQL queries, all in an easy-to-use environment. Microsoft Query is therefore a useful development and prototyping tool, and one well worth learning.

NOTE   If you set up Microsoft Office using the minimum setup, then you might not have Microsoft Query installed. If this is the case, run the Office setup program again and select Microsoft Query from the Database Tools option.

 TIP   As you start developing ColdFusion applications, you will find that most data-retrieval problems are caused by incorrect SQL statements. Microsoft Query is a useful debugging tool because it enables you to test SQL statements interactively. Using Microsoft Query is a powerful way to validate SQL queries and to isolate data-retrieval problems.

Now run Microsoft Query. When the program loads, you should see a screen similar to the one shown in Figure 8.11. Along the top of the screen is the toolbar that gives you quick access to commonly used functions. The toolbar buttons are described in Table 8.3.

FIGURE 8.11

Microsoft Query is a multiple document interface (MDI) application. Using it, you can open multiple documents, or in this case queries, at once.

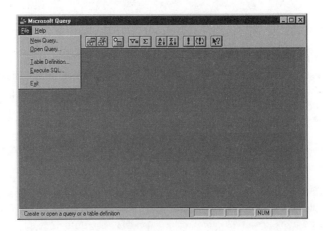

Table 8.3   The Microsoft Query Toolbar

Button	Effect
	Create a new query.
	Open a saved query.
	Save the currently selected query.
	View or edit a query's SQL statement directly.
	Show or hide the available tables pane.
	Show or hide the selection criteria pane.
	Include additional tables in the currently selected query.
	Show only records that match the value of the selection.
	Cycle through totals for the currently selected column.
	Sort the table via the currently selected column in ascending order.
	Sort the table via the currently selected column in descending order.
	Execute the query immediately.
	Automatically execute the query as it is created and changed, and show results immediately.
	Display Microsoft Query online help.

TIP The toolbar buttons in MS Query have ToolTips assigned to them. Just hold your mouse cursor over any button to display a pop-up title and a description in the status bar below.

Preparing to Create Queries

You are now ready to create your first query. Click the New Query button to open the Select Data Source dialog box, as shown in Figure 8.12.

FIGURE 8.12

In the Microsoft Query Select Data Source dialog box, you can select the data source for your new query.

The first time Microsoft Query uses a data source, you need to add it to the Select Data Source dialog box. To do so, click the Other button to view the currently available data sources; then select the A2Z data source you just created, and click OK.

The A2Z data source then appears in the Select Data Source dialog box, as shown in Figure 8.13. At this point, select the A2Z data source and then click Use.

FIGURE 8.13

The first time Microsoft Query uses a data source, you need to add it to the Select Data Source dialog box.

Creating Queries

With all the preliminaries taken care of, you can roll up your sleeves and start writing SQL. The SQL statement that you will use most is the SELECT statement. You use SELECT, as its name implies, to select data from a table.

Most SELECT statements require at least the following two parameters:

- What data you want to select, known as the select list. If you specify more than one item, you must separate each with a comma.
- The table (or tables) to select the data from, specified with the FROM keyword.

When you click Use in the Select Data Source dialog box to open a data source in a new query, Microsoft Query prompts you for the tables to include in this query. This feature is useful for interactively building queries. But, because you're going to learn how to create queries by writing SQL statements yourself, don't select any tables now. Just click the Close button.

After you select your data source, Microsoft Query displays the Query window, as shown in Figure 8.14. The top half is used by Microsoft Query to show tables in use and to display their relationships graphically, if any are defined. In the bottom half of the screen, the results of your query are displayed.

FIGURE 8.14

The Microsoft Query window is split into a table pane and a data pane.

Toolbar

Table pane

Data pane

Current record indicator

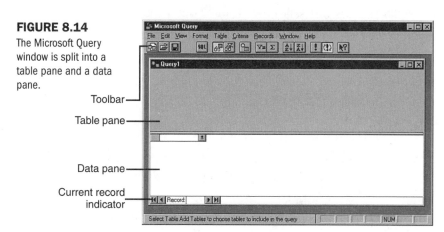

Click the View SQL button (or choose SQL from the View menu) to open the SQL window. Here, you can view the SQL statement that produced the query results shown, and you also can create and modify SQL statements directly.

The first SQL SELECT you will create is a query for a list of employees' last names and phone extensions. Type the code in Listing 8.1 into the SQL Statement box, shown in Figure 8.15, and then click OK.

Listing 8.1   Simple SELECT Statement

```
SELECT
Employees.LastName,
Employees.FirstName,
Employees.PhoneExtension
FROM A2Z.Employees
```

FIGURE 8.15

You can view generated SQL or enter SQL statements directly into the SQL window.

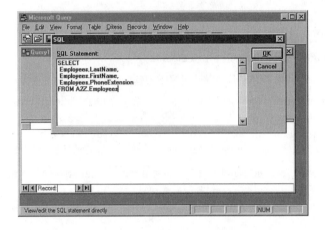

That's it! You've written your first SQL statement. Microsoft Query shows the table you are using in the top half of the screen, and the results of your query appear in the bottom half. You should have 10 records listed, the same 10 records you entered into Microsoft Access directly, shown in Figure 8.16.

FIGURE 8.16

Microsoft Query displays query results in the data pane, the bottom part of the Query window.

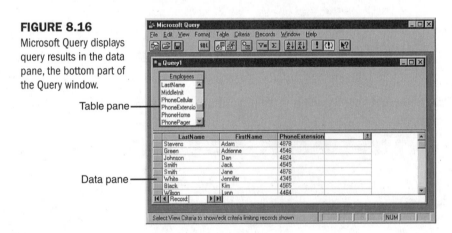

NOTE You can enter SQL statements on one long line or break them up over multiple lines. All whitespace characters (spaces, tabs, newline characters) are ignored when the command is processed. If you break a statement into multiple lines and indent parameters, you make the statement easier to read and debug. ■

Before you go any further, take a closer look at the SQL code you entered. The first parameter you pass to the SELECT statement is a list of the three columns you want to see. A column is specified as *table.column*, such as Employees.LastName, where Employees is the table name and LastName is the column name.

Because you want to specify three columns, you have to separate them with commas. No comma appears after the last column name, so if you have only one column in your select list, you don't need a comma.

Right after the select list, you specify the table on which you want to perform the query. You always precede the table name with the keyword FROM. The table name itself is fully qualified, meaning it is specified as *database.table*, or in this case A2Z.Employees.

N O T E SQL statements are not case sensitive; that is, you can specify the SELECT statement as SELECT, select, Select, or however you want. Common practice, however, is to enter all SQL keywords in uppercase and parameters in lowercase or mixed case. This way, you can read the SQL code and spot typos more easily.

Now modify the SELECT statement so it looks like the code in Listing 8.2. Click the SQL button to make the code changes and then click OK.

Listing 8.2 SELECT All Columns

```
SELECT
Employees.*
FROM A2Z.Employees
```

This time, instead of specifying explicit columns to select, you use an asterisk (*). The asterisk is a special select list option that represents all columns. The data pane now shows all the columns in the table in the order in which they appear in the table itself.

CAUTION

Generally, you should not use an asterisk in the select list unless you really need every column. Each column you select requires its own processing, and retrieving unnecessary columns can dramatically affect retrieval times as your tables get larger.

Sorting Query Results

When you use the SELECT statement, the results are returned to you in the order in which they appear in the table. This is usually the order in which the rows were added to the table, typically not a sort order that is of much use to you. More often than not, when you retrieve data by using a SELECT statement, you want to sort the query results. To sort rows, you need to add the ORDER BY clause. ORDER BY always comes after the table name; if you try to use it before, you generate a SQL error.

Now click the SQL button, enter the SQL code shown in Listing 8.3, and then click OK.

Listing 8.3 **SELECT** with Sorted Output

```
SELECT
Employees.LastName,
Employees.FirstName,
Employees.PhoneExtension
FROM A2Z.Employees
ORDER BY PhoneExtension
```

Your output is then sorted by the PhoneExtension column, as shown in Figure 8.17.

FIGURE 8.17

You use the ORDER BY clause to sort SELECT output.

Sorted by phone extension

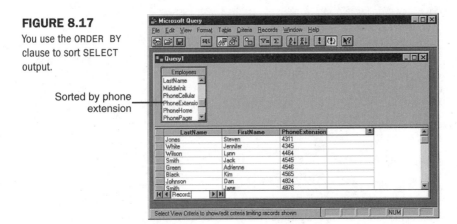

What if you need to sort by more than one column, as you did in the beginning of Chapter 7? No problem. You can pass multiple columns to the ORDER BY clause. And once again, if you have multiple columns listed, you need to separate them with commas. The SQL code in Listing 8.4 demonstrates how to sort on more than one column by sorting the employee list by last name plus first name. The sorted output is shown in Figure 8.18.

Listing 8.4 **SELECT** with Output Sorted on More Than One Column

```
SELECT
Employees.LastName,
Employees.FirstName,
Employees.PhoneExtension
FROM A2Z.Employees
ORDER BY LastName, FirstName
```

You also can use ORDER BY to sort data in descending order (from Z to A). To sort a column in descending order, just use the DESC (short for descending) parameter. Listing 8.5 retrieves all the employee records and sorts them by extension in reverse order. Figure 8.19 shows the output that this SQL SELECT statement generates.

FIGURE 8.18
You can sort output by
more than one column
via the ORDER BY
clause.

Sorted by last name
plus first name

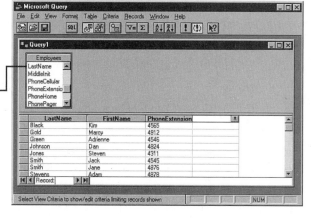

Listing 8.5 SELECT with Output Sorted in Reverse Order

```
SELECT
Employees.LastName,
Employees.FirstName,
Employees.PhoneExtension
FROM A2Z.Employees
ORDER BY PhoneExtension DESC
```

FIGURE 8.19
Using the ORDER BY
clause, you can sort
data in a descending
sort sequence.

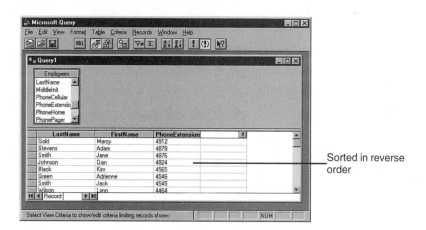

Sorted in reverse
order

Filtering Data

So far, all your queries have retrieved all the rows in the table. You also can use the SELECT
statement to retrieve only data that matches specific search criteria. To do so, you must use the
WHERE clause and provide a restricting condition. If a WHERE clause is present, when the SQL
SELECT statement is processed, every row is evaluated against the condition. Only rows that
pass the restriction are selected.

If you use a WHERE clause, it must appear after the table name. If you use both the ORDER BY and WHERE clauses, the WHERE clause must appear after the table name but before the ORDER BY.

Filtering on a Single Column

To demonstrate filtering, modify the SELECT statement to retrieve only employees whose last name is Smith. Listing 8.6 contains the SELECT statement, and the resulting output is shown in Figure 8.20.

Listing 8.6 SELECT **with** WHERE **Clause**

```
SELECT
Employees.LastName,
Employees.FirstName,
Employees.PhoneExtension
FROM A2Z.Employees
WHERE LastName = 'Smith'
```

FIGURE 8.20

Using the WHERE clause, you can restrict the scope of a SELECT search.

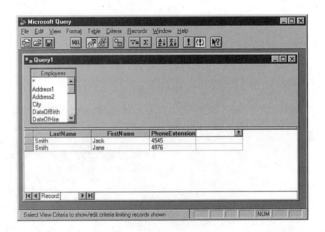

N O T E Text passed to a SQL query must be enclosed within quotation marks. If you omit the quotes, the SQL parser thinks that the text you specified is the name of a column, and you receive an error because that column does not exist. Pure SQL allows strings to be enclosed within single quotation marks ('like this') or within double quotation marks ("like this"). When passing text in a SQL statement to an ODBC driver, you *must* use single quotation marks. If you use double quotation marks, the ODBC parser treats the first double quote as a statement terminator, ignoring all text after it. ∎

Filtering on Multiple Columns

The WHERE clause also can take multiple conditions. To search for Jack Smith, you can specify a search condition in which the last name is Smith and the first name is Jack, as shown in Listing 8.7. As Figure 8.21 shows, only Jack Smith is retrieved.

Listing 8.7 SELECT with Multiple WHERE Clauses

```
SELECT
Employees.LastName,
Employees.FirstName,
Employees.PhoneExtension
FROM A2Z.Employees
WHERE LastName = 'Smith' AND FirstName = 'Jack'
```

Part
III

Ch
8

FIGURE 8.21

You can narrow your search with multiple WHERE clauses.

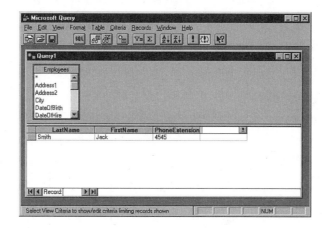

The AND and OR Operators

Multiple WHERE clauses can be evaluated as AND conditions or OR conditions. The example in Listing 8.7 is an AND condition. Only rows in which both the last name is Smith and the first name is Jack will be retrieved. If you change the clause to the following, other employees with a last name of Smith are retrieved no matter what the first name is:

```
WHERE LastName = 'Smith' OR FirstName = 'Jack'
```

Similarly, any employee named Jack is retrieved, regardless of the last name.

You can combine the AND and OR operators to create any search condition you need. Listings 8.8 and 8.9 show two different WHERE clauses that seem to accomplish the exact same thing—specifically, retrieving only Jack Smith and Kim Black.

Listing 8.8 Combining WHERE Clauses with AND and OR Operators

```
SELECT
Employees.LastName,
Employees.FirstName,
Employees.PhoneExtension
FROM A2Z.Employees
WHERE (LastName = 'Smith' AND FirstName = 'Jack')
OR (LastName = 'Black' AND FirstName = 'Kim')
```

Listing 8.9 Combining WHERE Clauses with AND and OR Operators

```
SELECT
Employees.LastName,
Employees.FirstName,
Employees.PhoneExtension
FROM A2Z.Employees
WHERE (LastName = 'Smith' OR LastName = 'Black')
AND (FirstName = 'Jack' OR FirstName = 'Kim')
```

Although both Listings 8.8 and 8.9 would work with this limited data, Listing 8.9 is actually wrong. If an employee were named Kim Smith, Listing 8.8 would correctly ignore that record and not retrieve it. Listing 8.9 would retrieve it, however.

Evaluation Precedence

When a WHERE clause is processed, the operators are evaluated in the following order of precedence:

- Parentheses have the highest precedence.
- The AND operator has the next level of precedence.
- The OR operator has the lowest level of precedence.

What does this mean? Well, look at the WHERE clause in Listing 8.9. (Even though I just said that Listing 8.9 could retrieve invalid data, it's still a good example with which to understand evaluation precedence.) The clause reads WHERE (LastName = 'Smith' OR LastName = 'Black') AND (FirstName = 'Jack' OR FirstName = 'Kim'). This clause evaluates to the following:

(LastName = 'Smith' OR LastName = 'Black')—This clause retrieves only people whose last name is Smith or Black.

AND (FirstName = 'Jack' OR FirstName = 'Kim')—Of the names retrieved, this clause keeps only those whose first name is Jack or Kim. The rest are discarded.

The results of this query are shown in Figure 8.22. As you can see, only Jack Smith and Kim Black are retrieved, which is exactly the result you want.

Without the parentheses, the clause would read WHERE LastName = 'Smith' OR LastName = 'Black' AND FirstName = 'Jack' OR FirstName = 'Kim'. Because the AND operator takes precedence over the OR operator, this clause would be evaluated as follows:

WHERE LastName = 'Smith'—This clause retrieves anyone whose last name is Smith, regardless of first name.

OR LastName = 'Black' AND FirstName = 'Jack'—This clause also retrieves anyone whose last name is Black and whose first name is Jack.

OR FirstName = 'Kim'—And finally, this clause also retrieves anyone whose first name is Kim.

FIGURE 8.22

With parentheses, you can control the precedence with which operators are evaluated.

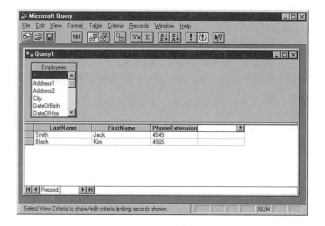

The results of this query are shown in Figure 8.23. As you can see, Jane Smith is also retrieved. Because no parentheses bind the Smith restriction with the Jack restriction, the Smith restriction is evaluated by itself. Jane Smith is therefore a valid match.

FIGURE 8.23

Without parentheses, the default order of precedence is used; the results might not be what you expect.

This row should not have been retrieved

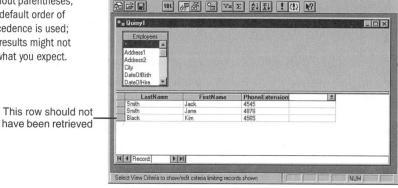

Obviously, this result is not what you want. To force the correct evaluation precedence for your operators, you must use parentheses. This way, there is no doubt as to what you are trying to retrieve.

 TIP Always using parentheses whenever you have more than one WHERE clause is good practice. They make the SQL statement easier to read and easier to debug.

WHERE Conditions

For theexamples to this point, you have used only the = (equal) operator. You filtered rows based on their being equal to a specific value. Many other operators and conditions can be used with the WHERE clause; they're listed in Table 8.4.

Table 8.4 WHERE Clause Search Conditions

Condition	Description
=	Equal to. Tests for equality.
<>	Not equal to. Tests for inequality.
<	Less than. Tests that the value on the left is less than the value on the right.
<=	Less than or equal to. Tests that the value on the left is less than or equal to the value on the right.
>	Greater than. Tests that the value on the left is greater than the value on the right.
>=	Greater than or equal to. Tests that the value on the left is greater than or equal to the value on the right.
BETWEEN	Tests that a value is in the range between two values; the range is inclusive.
EXISTS	Tests for the existence of rows returned by a subquery.
IN	Tests to see whether a value is contained within a list of values.
IS NULL	Tests to see whether a column contains a NULL value.
IS NOT NULL	Tests to see whether a column contains a non-NULL value.
LIKE	Tests to see whether a value matches a specified pattern.
NOT	Negates any test.

Testing for Equality: =

You use the = operator to test for value inequality. The following example retrieves only employees whose last name is Smith:

```
WHERE LastName = 'Smith'
```

Testing for Inequality: < >

You use the < > operator to test for value inequality. The following example retrieves only employees whose first name is not Kim:

```
WHERE FirstName < > 'Kim'
```

Testing for Less Than: <

By using the < operator, you can test that the value on the left is less than the value on the right. The following example retrieves only employees whose last name is less than *C*, meaning that their last name begins with an *A* or a *B*:

```
WHERE LastName < 'C'
```

Testing for Less Than or Equal To: <=

By using the <= operator, you can test that the value on the left is less than or equal to the value on the right. The following example retrieves only employees whose phone extension is 4500 or less:

```
WHERE PhoneExtension <= '4500'
```

Testing for Greater Than: >

You use the > operator to test that the value on the left is greater than the value on the right. The following example retrieves only employees whose phone extension is greater than 4800:

```
WHERE PhoneExtension > '4800'
```

Testing for Greater Than or Equal To: >=

You use the >= operator to test that the value on the left is greater than or equal to the value on the right. The following example retrieves only employees whose first name begins with the letter *J* or higher:

```
WHERE FirstName >= 'J'
```

BETWEEN

Using the BETWEEN condition, you can test whether a value falls into the range between two other values. The following example retrieves only employees whose phone extensions are between 4500 and 4600. Because the test is inclusive, extensions 4500 and 4600 are also retrieved:

```
WHERE PhoneExtension BETWEEN '4500' AND '4600'
```

The BETWEEN condition is actually nothing more than a convenient way of combining >= and <= conditions. You also could specify the preceding example as follows:

```
WHERE PhoneExtension >= '4500' AND PhoneExtension <= '4600'
```

The advantage of using the BETWEEN condition is that it makes the statement easier to read.

EXISTS

Using the EXISTS condition, you can check whether a subquery returns any rows. Subqueries are explained in Chapter 19, "Advanced SQL."

IN

You can use the IN condition to test whether a value is part of a specific set. The set of values must be surrounded by parentheses and separated by commas. The following example retrieves employees whose last name is Black, Jones, or Smith:

```
WHERE LastName IN ('Black', 'Jones', 'Smith')
```

The preceding example is actually the same as the following:

```
WHERE LastName = 'Black' OR LastName = 'Jones' OR LastName = 'Smith'
```

Using the IN condition does provide two advantages. First, it makes the statement easier to read. Second, and more important, you can use the IN condition to test whether a value is within the results of another SELECT statement.

IS NULL and IS NOT NULL

A NULL value is the value of a column that is empty. The IS NULL condition tests for rows that have a NULL value; that is, the rows have no value at all in the specified column. IS NOT NULL tests for rows that have a value in a specified column.

The following example retrieves all employees whose PhoneExtension column is left empty:

```
WHERE PhoneExtension IS NULL
```

To retrieve only the employees who do have a phone extension, use the following example:

```
WHERE PhoneExtension IS NOT NULL
```

LIKE

Using the LIKE condition, you can test for string pattern matches using wildcards. Two wildcard types are supported. The % character means that anything from that position on is considered a match. You also can use [ ] to create a wildcard for a specific character.

The following example retrieves employees whose last name begins with the letter *S*. To match the pattern, a last name must have an *S* as the first character, and anything at all after it:

```
WHERE LastName LIKE 'S%'
```

To retrieve employees with an *S* anywhere in their last names, you can use the following:

```
WHERE LastName LIKE '%S%'
```

You also can retrieve just employees whose last name ends with *S*, as follows:

```
WHERE LastName LIKE '%S'
```

The LIKE condition can be negated with the NOT operator. The following example retrieves only employees whose last name does not begin with *S*:

```
WHERE LastName NOT LIKE 'S%'
```

Using the LIKE condition, you also can specify a wildcard on a single character. If you want to find all employees named Smith but are not sure if the one you want spells his or her name Smyth, you can use the following:

```
WHERE LastName LIKE 'Sm[iy]th'
```

This example retrieves only names that start with *Sm*, then have an *i* or *y*, and then a final *th*. With this example, as long as the first two characters are *Sm* and the last two are *th*, and as long as the middle character is *i* or *y*, the name is considered a match.

TIP Using the powerful LIKE condition, you can retrieve data in many different ways. But everything comes with a price, and the price here is performance. Generally, LIKE conditions take far longer to process than other search conditions, especially if you use wildcards at the beginning of the pattern. As a rule, use LIKE and wildcards only when absolutely necessary.

SQL Data Manipulation

Adding Data

All the queries you created in Chapter 8, "Introduction to SQL," were using data that you directly entered into Microsoft Access. Direct data entry is useful in prototyping and testing queries and applications.

In real-world applications, however, data must often be added via an ODBC client application. ColdFusion has to add data to your table if you're going to collect data via a Web-browser form and then have ColdFusion process the data.

Using the INSERT Statement

You use the INSERT statement to add data to an ODBC table. INSERT is usually made up of three parts:

- The table into which you want to insert data, specified with the INTO keyword.
- The column(s) into which you want to insert values. If you specify more than one item, each must be separated by a comma.
- The values to insert, which are specified with the VALUES keyword.

When you created the Departments table in Chapter 7, "Creating Databases and Tables," you inserted two departments directly into the table using Microsoft Access. The Departments table is made up of just two columns—ID and Department. The ID column is an AutoNumber column, meaning that its value is assigned automatically each time a row is added. The Department column, on the other hand, must be specified manually.

Your first task is to add two more departments to that table: Administration and Shipping & Receiving.

Again, you use Microsoft Query to do this, but this time you'll use the Execute SQL feature.

◊ **See** "Creating Tables" for a discussion of the use of different data types and AutoNumber columns, **p. 109**.

◊ **See** "Using Microsoft Query" for an introduction to using Microsoft Query to enter SQL statements, **p. 138**.

Run Microsoft Query and select File, Execute SQL to display the Execute SQL window shown in Figure 9.1. You'll notice that the Data Sources option is set to <none>, so you need to select the A2Z data source.

◊ **See** "Creating a Data Source for the A2Z Books Database" if you need instructions on creating the data source, **p. 137**.

Click Data Sources to display the Select Data Source dialog box, shown in Figure 9.2. Select the A2Z data source and then select Use. The Execute SQL window now shows the selected data source; you can see it in Figure 9.3.

Now you're ready to add the department. Listing 9.1 contains the SQL INSERT statement. Enter the statement, exactly as it appears in Listing 9.1, into the SQL Statement box. That box is in the Execute SQL window, which is shown in Figure 9.4, and then select Execute. Microsoft Query submits your SQL statement to the Access ODBC driver for insertion and then notifies you that the operation was successful. If the insertion fails, the ODBC driver will display an error message describing the reason for the failure (see Figure 9.5).

FIGURE 9.1

The Microsoft Query Execute SQL window is used to directly enter and execute any SQL statement.

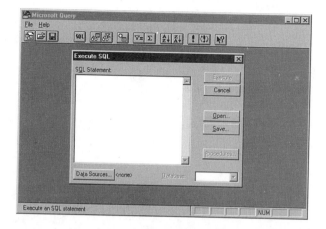

FIGURE 9.2

To execute a SQL statement, you must first select an ODBC data source.

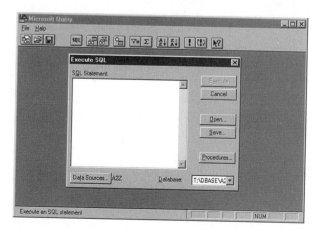

FIGURE 9.3

The Execute SQL window always shows you which data source has been opened.

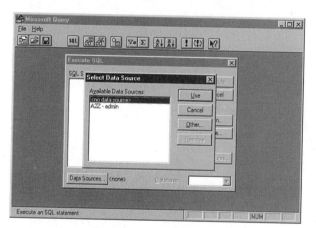

Listing 9.1 SQL INSERT Statement to Add a Department

```
INSERT INTO Departments(Department)
VALUES('Administration')
```

FIGURE 9.4

Type the statement into the SQL Statement box and then click Execute.

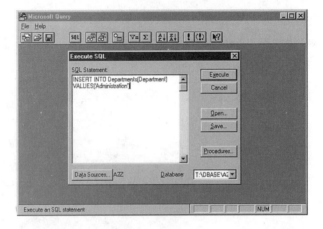

FIGURE 9.5

Microsoft Query notifies you regarding your SQL statements' successful execution.

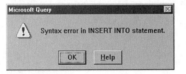

Understanding INSERT

Now that you've successfully inserted a row using the SQL INSERT statement, take a minute to look at the statement's syntax.

The first line of your statement reads as follows:

```
INSERT INTO Departments(Department)
```

The text immediately following the INTO keyword is the name of the table into which the new row is being inserted. In this case, it is the Departments table.

Next, the columns being added are specified. The columns are listed within parentheses, and if multiple columns are specified, each must be separated by a comma. You need to provide only one column to the Departments table because the ID column is automatically filled in for you. Your INSERT statement specifies only one column—the Department column, which contains the department name.

> **N O T E** When you insert a row into a table, you may provide values for as many (or as few)
> columns as you prefer. The only restriction is that any columns defined as NOT NULL
> columns—meaning they may not be left empty—must have values specified. If you do not set a value
> for a NOT NULL column, the ODBC driver returns an error message and the row is not inserted. ■

The next line reads as follows:

```
VALUES('Administration')
```

A value must be specified for every column listed whenever you insert a row. Values are passed to the VALUES keyword; all values are contained within parentheses, just like their column names. Here you specified a single column, so that a single value is passed to the VALUES keyword.

N O T E When inserting rows into a table, columns may be specified in any order. Make sure that the order of the values in the VALUES keyword exactly matches the order of the columns after the table name.

Now add the next department. Modify the SQL statement so that it looks like the one shown in Listing 9.2 and then choose Execute to perform the insertion.

Listing 9.2 SQL INSERT Statement to Add a Department

```
INSERT INTO Departments(Department)
VALUES('Shipping & Receiving')
```

You now have four departments in the Departments table. To verify this, use Microsoft Query to select all the rows in the Departments table.

Enter the following SELECT statement in the Execute SQL window and then select Execute:

```
SELECT * FROM Departments
```

As explained in Chapter 8, SELECT * means select all columns. As you can see in Figure 9.6, the two new departments were correctly added and Microsoft Access automatically assigned new ID numbers to them.

FIGURE 9.6

You can use Microsoft Query to execute SQL statements and verify the results of those statements.

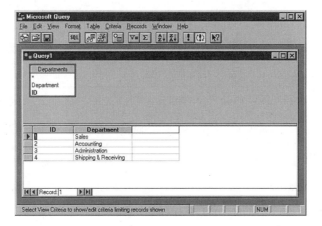

Inserting and Setting Values for Multiple Columns

You've now seen and used the INSERT statement to add a row and specify a value for one column. Setting values for multiple columns is just as simple.

One of your employees, Kim Black, has booked a vacation for two weeks in the summer. You need to add that information to the Vacations table. The Vacations table has three columns—the first is the employee ID, which uniquely identifies each employee, and the next two are the vacation start and end dates.

Kim's employee ID is 7, so you enter the SQL statement shown in Listing 9.3 into the Execute SQL window and then select Execute. The Execute SQL window is shown in Figure 9.7. You should receive a confirmation message telling you that the operation was successful and that the row was inserted.

Listing 9.3   Adding a Vacation Record Requires That Three Columns Be Specified

```
INSERT INTO Vacations(EmployeeId, VacationStart, VacationEnd)
VALUES(7, 'Aug 1 1997', 'Aug 15 1997')
```

FIGURE 9.7

When multiple columns are passed to SQL INSERT, each must be separated by a comma.

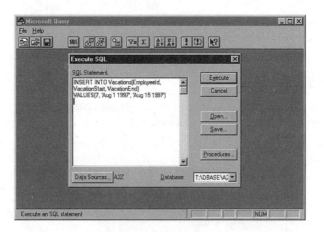

 The exact format of the ODBC Date/Time data type is a little tricky to remember, so most ODBC drivers allow you to specify dates and times as simple strings that they interpret. The parser is not perfect, however, because 'Aug 1st 1997', for example, fails with many ODBC drivers. On the other hand, 'Aug 1 1997' is usually supported. There are no hard and fast rules governing what is and what is not supported, so to minimize incompatibilities, remember to keep the strings as simple as possible.

Verify that the row was correctly added. Use Microsoft Query to select all rows and column in the Vacations table. Your output should look like that shown in Figure 9.8.

FIGURE 9.8
Microsoft Query
displays columns in
their native format
without any special
output formatting.

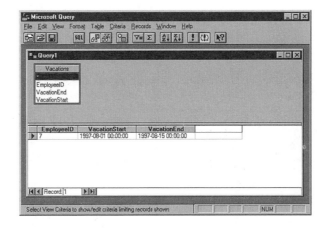

Part
III

Ch
9

The row is there, but look at the date columns. They contain both a date and a time. The time
is `0:00:00` because no time was specified. Why is there a time here at all? The Microsoft Access `Date/Time` data type is a date and time data type. If you use just one part of the data type,
the other sets to `0`. This is perfectly valid and is an acceptable practice.

Adding Multiple Rows

All the `INSERT` statements you have used so far add single rows to a table. When you need to add
multiple rows, you can use an `INSERT` statement to add them in a single executed statement.

The `INSERT` statement cannot specify multiple `VALUES` keywords. To add multiple rows, you
must create a `SELECT` statement that retrieves the values to be inserted and then pass that
`SELECT` statement to the `INSERT` statement instead of the `VALUES` keyword.

Don't panic, this is not as confusing as it sounds. To clarify how you could use this functionality,
look at an example.

The Shipping and Receiving department manager has just notified you that his entire department is taking the first week of February off, so you need to add a vacation record to the Vacations table for each employee in that department.

You could do this all manually. The steps would look something like this:

1. Find the department ID for the Shipping and Receiving department.
2. Search for all employees that have a department ID that matches the Shipping and
   Receiving department ID in order to retrieve the employee IDs.
3. Add a row to the Vacations table for each employee ID to set the vacation dates.

While this manual process will work, it is both time consuming and highly error prone. A better solution is to perform the entire operation in one step. To do this, you need to create an
`INSERT` statement that inserts values retrieved by a `SELECT` statement. The `SELECT` statement
produces a set of values for each row to be inserted.

To try this, enter the SQL statement shown in Listing 9.4 into the Execute SQL window and then select Execute. The Execute SQL window is shown in Figure 9.9.

Listing 9.4 SELECT **Statement Using** INSERT

```
INSERT INTO Vacations(EmployeeID, VacationStart, VacationEnd)
SELECT
EmployeeID,
'Feb 1 1997',
'Feb 7 1997'
FROM Employees
WHERE DepartmentID =
(SELECT id FROM Departments
 WHERE Department = 'Accounting')
```

FIGURE 9.9

A SELECT statement can be passed to an INSERT statement to place multiple rows in one operation.

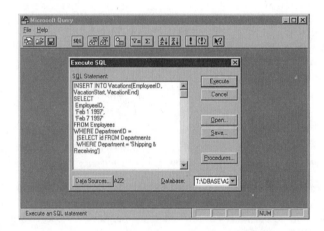

This book is not going to cover all the details that make up Listing 9.4 right now. Nested queries (SELECT statements within SELECT statements) are discussed in Chapter 19, "Advanced SQL." A couple of points are worth noting here, however.

Like all INSERT statements, you started by specifying the destination table and the columns that are to be populated. The code INSERT INTO Vacations(EmployeeID, VacationStart, VacationEnd) instructs the ODBC driver that three columns in the Vacations table will be populated with each row added.

Unlike all of your INSERT statements until now, the INSERT statement in Listing 9.4 does not have a VALUES keyword. There is a SELECT statement instead, which returns three columns that correspond to the three columns that were specified after the destination table. This is shown in the following code line:

```
SELECT EmployeeID, 'Feb 1 1997', 'Feb 7 1997'
```

EmployeeID, which is retrieved from the Employees table, is the first value returned by the SELECT statement. The second and third values are static dates, so the same value returns with every row that was retrieved.

If you select the Vacations table, you'll see that three rows were inserted by this operation with the execution of one SQL statement.

```
INSERT INTO Vacations(EmployeeID, VacationStart, VacationEnd)
SELECT
EmployeeID,
'Feb 1 1997',
'Feb 7 1997'
FROM Employees
WHERE DepartmentID =
(SELECT id FROM Departments
WHERE Department = 'Accounting')
```

Modifying Data

You use the SQL UPDATE statement to update one or more columns. This usually involves specifying the following:

- The table containing the data you want to update.
- The column or columns you want to update, preceded by the SET keyword. If you specify more than one item, each must be separated by a comma.
- An optional WHERE clause to specify which rows to update. If no WHERE clause is provided, all rows are updated.

Try updating a row. Open the Execute SQL window and enter the SQL statement shown in Listing 9.5. Your code should look like the example shown in Figure 9.10. Select Execute to perform the update. Microsoft Query displays a confirmation dialog indicating that the operation completed successfully.

If you now select the contents of the Employees table, you see that Kim Black has the title Senior Account Rep.

Listing 9.5   The SQL UPDATE Statement Updates One or More Rows in a Table

```
UPDATE Employees
SET Title='Senior Account Rep'
WHERE EmployeeID = 7
```

Understanding UPDATE

Now take a closer look at the SQL statement in Listing 9.5. The first line issued the UPDATE statement and specified the name of the table to update. As with the INSERT and DELETE statements, the table name is required.

You next specified the column you wanted to change and its new value:

```
SET Title='Senior Account Rep'
```

This is an instruction to update the Title column with the text `'Senior Account Rep'`. The SET keyword is required for an UPDATE operation because it would make little sense to update rows without specifying what to update.

FIGURE 9.10

The SQL UPDATE statement is most often used with a WHERE clause.

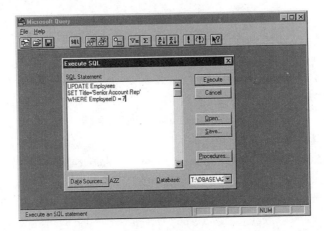

The SET keyword can only be used once in an UPDATE statement. If you are updating multiple rows—for example, to change Kim to Kimberly and to set her title to Senior Account Rep in one operation—the SET keyword would look like this:

```
SET FirstName='Kimberly', Title='Senior Account Rep'
```

When updating multiple columns, each column must be separated by a comma.

The last line of Listing 9.5 specifies a WHERE clause. The WHERE clause is optional in an UPDATE statement. Without it, all rows will be updated. The following code uses the primary key column to ensure that only a single row gets updated:

```
WHERE EmployeeID = 7
```

◊ **See** "Primary and Foreign Keys" for an explanation of primary keys. **p. 96**.

CAUTION

Be sure to provide a WHERE clause when using the SQL UPDATE statement, or all rows will be updated.

Making Global Updates

You will occasionally want to update all rows in a table.

For example, none of the employees in the A2Z Books Employees table have their email address listed. You could update every employee one at a time, but there is a better way. A2Z Books instituted a standard for email addresses to make them easier to remember. All email addresses are made up of the first letter of the first name, plus the entire last name. Of course, all email addresses are @a2zbooks.com.

To perform this update easily, you could update the EMail column with a calculated column, a value that is dynamically built for each employee. Look at this code:

```
LEFT(FirstName, 1)+LastName+'@a2zbooks.com'
```

This is a SQL statement that builds a value based on several other values. The first portion, `LEFT(FirstName, 1)`, extracts the first character from the FirstName column. `LEFT()` is a function that returns the requested leftmost characters of a string. `LEFT(FirstName, 1)` means to extract the first character of the `FirstName` value. `LEFT(FirstName, 5)` extracts the first five characters of the `FirstName` value.

Part
III
Ch
9

Next, you concatenate the entire `LastName` value and the string `@a2zbooks.com` to the first character of the FirstName column. Strings are *concatenated* (added together to make a longer string) with the + operator.

With this statement, you can generate email addresses for every employee in the Employees table. Before you update the table, however, it's a good idea to test the statement. The best way to test this statement, and indeed every SQL statement, is to first use it in a SELECT statement.

To test `LEFT(FirstName,1)+LastName+'@a2zbooks.com'`, enter the code shown in Listing 9.6 into the Execute SQL window. Select the Execute button to display the statement results.

Listing 9.6   Testing SQL Statements with a SELECT Statement

```
SELECT
LEFT(FirstName, 1)+LastName+'@a2zbooks.com'
FROM Employees
```

As shown in Figure 9.11, Microsoft Query displays the calculated column, which contains the correct email address for every employee. Because the column has no name, the statement used to build it is shown as the column title instead.

FIGURE 9.11

Microsoft Query displays calculated values just as it does any other columns.

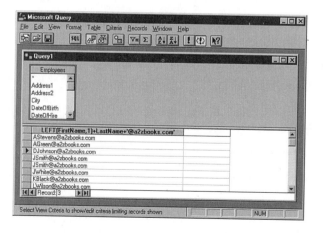

You now know that the statement works correctly and that the calculated value it creates is exactly what you wanted. Now update all the rows in the Employees table. Enter the SQL UPDATE statement shown in Listing 9.7 (see Figure 9.12). Select Execute to update the entire table; Microsoft Query displays a success notification.

TIP Before executing INSERT, UPDATE, or DELETE operations that contain complex statements or WHERE conditions, you should test the statement or condition by using it in a SELECT statement. If SELECT returns incorrect statement results or an incorrect subset of data filtered by the WHERE clause, you'll know that the statement or condition is incorrect.

The SELECT statement never changes any data, unlike INSERT, UPDATE, and DELETE, so if there is an error in the statement or condition, you'll find out about it before any damage is done.

FIGURE 9.12

Table columns may be updated with calculated values.

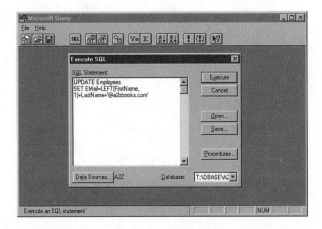

Listing 9.7 Updating All Rows in a Table with a Calculated Value

```
UPDATE Employees
SET EMail=LEFT(FirstName, 1)+LastName+'@a2zbooks.com'
```

To verify that the operation was successful, try selecting the FirstName, LastName, and EMail columns from the Employees table. Your results should look like those shown in Figure 9.13.

Deleting Data

Deleting data from a table is even easier than adding or updating data—perhaps too easy.

You use the SQL DELETE statement to delete data. The statement takes only two parameters—one required and one optional.

FIGURE 9.13

Always verify any tablewide changes by displaying the resulting data.

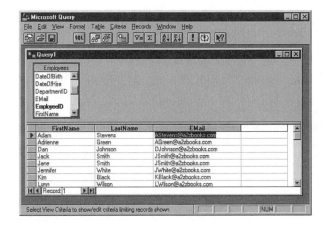

- The name of the table from which to delete the data must be specified immediately following the words DELETE FROM.
- An optional WHERE clause can be used to restrict the scope of the deletion process.

The DELETE statement is dangerously easy to use. Look at the following line of code (but don't execute it):

```
DELETE FROM Employees
```

This statement removes all employee records from the Employees table without any warnings or confirmation.

 TIP Some databases, client/server databases like Microsoft SQL Server in particular, offer safeguards against accidental (or malicious) deletions. There are generally two approaches to preventing mass deletion.

One is to create a *trigger* (a piece of code that runs on the server when specific operations occur) that verifies every DELETE statement and blocks any DELETE without a WHERE clause.

Another popular option is to restrict the use of DELETE without a WHERE clause based on login name. Only certain users, usually those with administrative rights, are granted permission to execute DELETE without a WHERE clause. Any other user attempting a mass DELETE will receive an error message, and the operation will abort.

Not all database systems support these techniques. Consult the database administrator's manuals to ascertain what safeguards are available to you.

The DELETE statement is most often used with a WHERE clause. For example, the SQL statement shown in Listing 9.8 deletes a single employee's record from the Employees table.

Listing 9.8 The DELETE Statement Used with a WHERE Clause

```
DELETE FROM Employees
WHERE EmployeeID = 10
```

As with all WHERE clauses, the DELETE statement's WHERE clause can be a SELECT statement that retrieves the list of rows to delete. If you do use a SELECT statement for a WHERE clause, be careful to test the SELECT statement first to ensure that it retrieves all the values you want, and only those values you want. ●

Introduction to ColdFusion Studio

Understanding ColdFusion Studio

It is impossible to cover every aspect of Studio in this single chapter, but I'll attempt to demonstrate some of the most important features to get you up and running. You are encouraged to experiment on your own. There is nothing in Studio that you can break by tinkering; the more you play with it, the more you'll discover, and the more useful a tool it will be.

To understand what ColdFusion Studio is and how it can simplify your application development, you first need to understand what it is not.

ColdFusion Studio (referred to as Studio from this point on) is not a WYSIWYG HTML generator. Nor is it an HTML authoring tool. It will not let you drag and drop page elements onto a page to generate the underlying HTML. In fact, it makes no effort to try to conceal HTML from you.

Quite the opposite. In fact, Studio tries very hard to expose all of the underlying code to you, ensuring that you, the developer, have full control over it.

So what exactly is ColdFusion Studio?

ColdFusion Studio is an editor, much like Windows Notepad (or DOS's EDIT). With Studio you create and open files, write your code, and save files, just as you would in any other editor. That's where the similarity ends. Unlike typical editors, Studio was designed from the ground up as a programmer's editor. It is based on HomeSite, the award-winning HTML editor used by over 100,000 Web page designers, and boasts a feature set that not one other editor can match:

- Menus and toolbars provide shortcuts to the most common tags and functions.
- Multiple document interface.
- Automatic color coding of HTML, CFML, and other languages.
- Wizards and templates.
- Drag-and-drop editing, and context-sensitive right mouse-click options.
- Design mode to simplify the creation of some HTML elements (like tables).
- Integrated image and thumbnail viewer.
- Edit dialog for most HTML and CFML tags (and you can even create your own dialog for your own tags).
- Pop-up help for all HTML and CFML tags.
- Automatic tag completion.
- Built-in expression builder.
- Built-in SQL query builder.
- Integrated project management.
- Built-in HTML validation.
- Open and save files over an Internet connection (using HTTP or FTP).
- Built-in support for version control systems.

The bottom line is that if you are serious about Web application development and serious about development with ColdFusion, ColdFusion Studio is a must.

Running ColdFusion Studio

If you haven't already done so, start Studio by selecting ColdFusion Studio from your Programs menu (which is usually in a group called ColdFusion Studio followed by a version number).

N O T E   If you have not yet installed ColdFusion Studio, now is a good time to do so. Refer to Chapter 3, "Installing ColdFusion and ColdFusion Studio," for installation instructions. ■

Introducing ColdFusion Studio

Start with a quick guided tour of the Studio environment shown in Figure 10.1.

FIGURE 10.1
The Studio environment is divided into multiple windows and tabs.

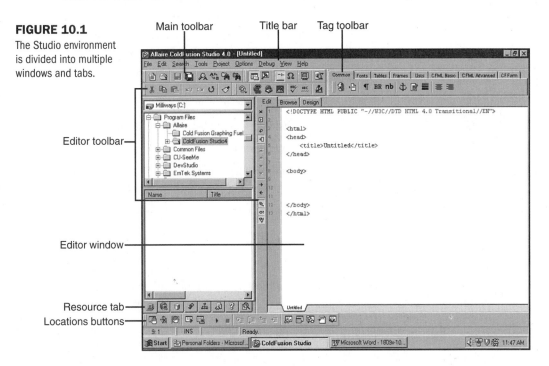

The top of the screen has two toolbars. The main toolbar on the left contains buttons for opening and saving files, performing searches, cut, copy, and paste operations, undo and redo, search, and more. The tag toolbar on the right is actually a collection of tabbed toolbars containing dozens of tag shortcuts and wizards. Table 10.1 lists the tabs of the tag toolbar and what each one contains. The exact layout and the placement of tabs is highly configurable. If your screen does not exactly match the one shown in Figure 10.1 it is because some tabs have been changed or relocated.

Table 10.1 ColdFusion Studio Tag Toolbars

Tab	Description
ASP	Options useful to ASP developers
CFFORM	ColdFusion CFFORM tags, including the ColdFusion Java controls
CFML Advanced	Advanced ColdFusion tags, including CFCOOKIE, CFMAIL, CFPOP, CFLDAP, CFHTP, CFFTP, and the Verity interface tags
CFML Basic	Basic ColdFusion tags, including CFQUERY, CFOUTPUT, CFIF, CFSET, and CFINCLUDE
Common	Commonly used tags (paragraph and line breaks, bold, links, horizontal rules), and quick start options for creating header and body tags
Debug	Options to manage the debugger, including setting breakpoints, trace options, and setting debugger options
Edit	Copy, cut, paste, undo, redo, and related editing options
Fonts	Font face, color, and size control, and the heading tags
Forms	Forms and all form field types
Frames	Frame wizard, and all the frame related tags
Lists	Menus, ordered lists, unordered lists, and list items
Standard	File open, save, search, replace, and similar options
Tables	Table wizard, all the table tags, and a Quick Table button that creates a basic table for you based on the size you select
Tools	Color palette, link verification, spell checker, and other tools
View	Enable and disable tabs and views

You may select a button from any of these toolbars to automatically insert HTML or CFML tags into the document you are editing. Some buttons insert text and others bring up dialog boxes, prompting you for additional information, inserting the text after you fill in the fields and click Apply.

To the left of the screen is the Resource tab. This is a multi-purpose tab that actually contains six different tabs. Table 10.2 lists the tabs and what each is used for. You select the tab you want by clicking the tab selectors at the bottom of the Resource tab.

Table 10.2 ColdFusion Studio Resource Tabs

Tab	Description
Local Files	Local files and directories in a Windows Explorer-style window.

Tab	Description
Remote Files	Access for files and directories on a remote server (which is discussed later in this chapter).
Database	Access to ODBC (and other) data sources on either a local or remote server (which is discussed later).
Projects	Project management, create and work with entire projects rather than one file at a time.
Site View	Site management features.
Snippets	Create your own code snippets that you can insert into any page.
Help	Help library.
Tag Inspector	Tag drill-down view of pages.

 Hold your mouse over any button to display a pop-up description of what that button does.

The right side of the screen is the ColdFusion editor itself. This highly customizable editor is where you actually write your Web pages. If you click buttons on any of the tag toolbars, the code is inserted right where the flashing cursor is.

To the left of the Editor window is the editor toolbar, which contains 10 buttons you can use to control the editor itself. For example, clicking the top button closes the currently active file, and clicking the second option displays a pop-up list of all files currently open. Other buttons are used to turn on or off word wrap, text indentation, and pop-up help.

 The Resource tab is a very important part of ColdFusion Studio, and you will probably want access to it at all times. However, it does take up a significant amount of screen space. To save space you can hide and display the entire Resource tab by toggling the F9 key, thus displaying it only when needed.

Working with Files

Studio is an editor, and most of your time using Studio will be spent working with files. These will usually be plain HTML Web pages or ColdFusion application pages. Studio gives you several ways to create, open, and manipulate files:

- The File menu contains the standard file manipulation options, like New, Open, Save, and Close.
- The main toolbar contains buttons for creating and opening files.
- Double-clicking any file in the Resource tab's local window opens that file for editing.

The Studio title bar shows the name of the file currently open and active in the editor. There is no limit to the number of files that you can open at one time, but there's more on that when the multiple document interface is discussed later in this chapter.

N O T E If the active file has never been saved, it is named Untitled and that is the name displayed in Studio's title bar. ■

Using the Editor

The heart of ColdFusion Studio is its editor. This is obviously where you do most of your work, and thus, this is where the Studio feature set shines.

This has been said before, but it bears repeating—Studio is not an HTML authoring tool, and it won't write HTML or CFML for you. Studio assumes that you, the developer, want to be in complete control of the application development effort. At the same time, Studio attempts to simplify the development process without getting in your way.

To demonstrate the Studio editor, open any HTML or CFML file. Use the File, Open menu option, the Main Toolbar Open button, or just browse through the local files in the Resource tab and double-click any file to open it.

Using Color Coding

The first thing you'll notice is that the text in the editor window is color-coded. Color coding is used to highlight specific tags or text, and Studio performs all color coding automatically. There are two primary reasons to use color-coding:

- ■ Color-coded text makes it easy to quickly find specific tags or tag types. For example, all table-related tags are shown in one color, while all ColdFusion tags are shown in another.

- ■ Color coding makes it easier to find mistakes in your code. If a tag or block of text does not display in the correct color, you'll know right away that you've made a typo there. If you do something as simple as missing the > symbol from the end of the tag, you'll immediately see that the text after the tag is incorrectly color-coded.

Color coding can be turned off by choosing Color Coding from the Setting dialog in the Options menu, but there is seldom a reason to do so unless you are working with massive files (so large that Studio takes a significant amount of time to perform the color coding). As a rule, you should always keep color coding turned on.

 T I P You can change the colors that Studio uses for color coding by selecting the Color Coding tab from the Options Settings dialog box (or by pressing F8).

Using Toolbars

As mentioned earlier, the tag toolbars provide shortcuts to commonly used HTML and CFML tags. Clicking any button on any tag toolbar either inserts tag text or displays a dialog box that prompts you for tag options. To try this out, follow these steps:

1. Close any files you have opened. (You can simply right-click the file in the Editor window and select Close.)

2. Type the text My first page written in Studio in the Editor window.

3. Highlight the text you just typed with your mouse.

4. Click the Bold button (the one with the big bold B on it) on the Fonts toolbar.

Studio automatically applied the HTML bold tags (<B> and </B>) to the highlighted text, as shown in Figure 10.2.

FIGURE 10.2

Studio allows you to highlight text and select a Tag Toolbar button to apply tags to that text.

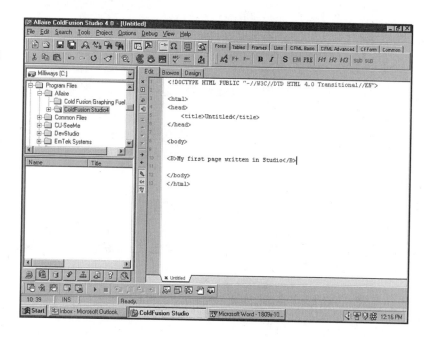

Part
III

Ch
10

Try another example. This time you create an HTML table:

1. Close any files you have opened. (You can simply right- click the file in the Editor window and select Close.)

2. Select the Tables Toolbar tag.

3. Click the Table Sizer button (the one on the right) to display a table selection box, as shown in Figure 10.3.

4. Move your mouse down and to the right to select the number of rows and columns you'd like in your HTML table.

5. When you have highlighted the number of desired rows and columns, click your mouse to make the selection.

FIGURE 10.3

The Table Sizer button allows you to quickly generate code to create HTML tables.

As shown in Figure 10.4, Studio generated the HTML code for your table, and it even indented the cells to make working with your table easier.

FIGURE 10.4

Studio automatically indents generated HTML table code to make working with tables easier.

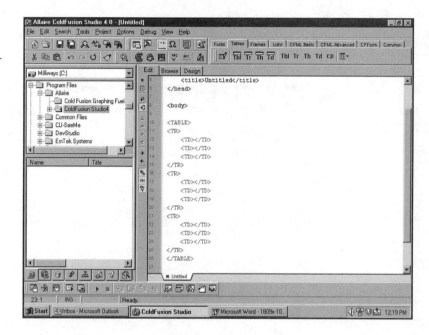

As you can see, the tag toolbar buttons are both a tremendous time saver and a way to help ensure that you don't mistype tags or tag attributes.

CAUTION

When clicking tag toolbar buttons, pay close attention to where you editor cursor is. Studio inserts the selected tag at the current cursor position. If the cursor is in the wrong place (in the middle of another tag, for example), that's where the text is inserted.

Browsing Your Web Pages

Because Studio is not a WYSIWYG authoring tool, what you see in the editor is code, not the generated output. To view the page that your code creates, you need to browse that page.

If you have Microsoft Internet Explorer (version 3 or later) installed on your computer, Studio can use it internally to display your page, as shown in Figure 10.5. To browse a page this way, just click the Browse tab above the Editor window. You can also use the F12 key to toggle between edit and browse modes.

Web developers often need to view their pages in more than one browser. This is generally good practice because of browser incompatibilities and differences. Studio lets you configure external browsers, which can be spawned from within Studio as needed. To set up external browsers, choose Configure External Browsers from the Options menu.

FIGURE 10.5

Studio can use Microsoft Internet Explorer as its internal browser if it is installed.

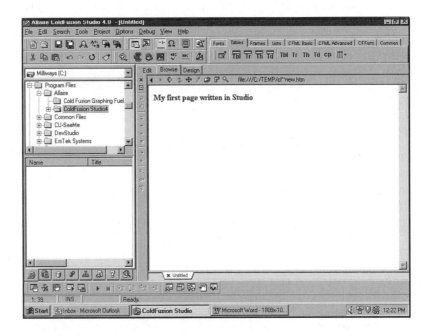

N O T E The internal browser can be used to view HTML files, but not ColdFusion files—ColdFusion files need to be preprocessed by the ColdFusion Application Server. If you attempt to browse a CFM or CFML file, Studio will likely display an error message. ■

Using the Multiple Document Interface

Studio allows you to open multiple files at once. When you open multiple files, each one has a tab at the bottom of the Editor window, as shown in Figure 10.6. You may click these tabs to switch between files. The tab belonging to the file that is actually open is shown brighter and in the foreground, so that you'll always know which file you are looking at. In addition, the Studio title bar also shows the name of the currently active file.

The file tabs at the bottom of the Editor window have another important use. They indicate which files have been saved and which have not. The text in the tab changes to blue and an X is displayed to the left of the filename as soon as any changes are made to that file. Once the file is saved, the text is displayed in black and the X is removed. This makes it easy to see which files have not been saved yet.

Using the Right Mouse Button

Right-clicking is probably the most important tip to remember when using Studio. Studio makes extensive use of the right mouse button, particularly in the Editor window. Studio's right mouse button support is *context sensitive*, which means that the options displayed vary, based upon where you right-click. Try right-clicking any tag. You'll see a pop-up menu similar to the one shown in Figure 10.7. You can select the Edit Tag option to display a context-sensitive tag dialog box, like the one shown in Figure 10.8.

FIGURE 10.6

The ColdFusion Editor window displays a tab for each open document.

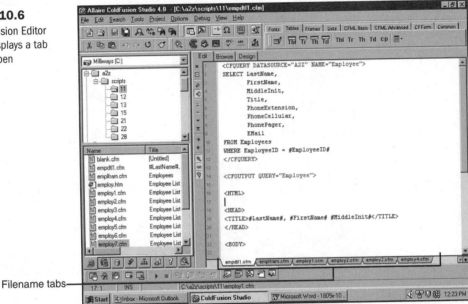

Filename tabs—

FIGURE 10.7

Clicking the right mouse button in Studio displays a pop-up, context-sensitive options menu.

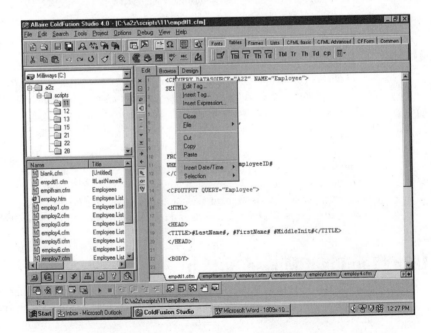

FIGURE 10.8

Selecting Edit Tag from the right mouse button menu displays a tag-specific editing dialog box.

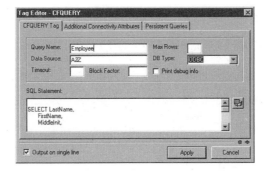

Other right mouse button options include Insert Expression and Insert SQL Statement. These options are explored later in this chapter.

The right mouse button can also be used in the Resource tab. Right-click any file or directory to display a pop-up menu of relevant options.

 TIP Use the right mouse button extensively. Because it is context sensitive, you are always presented with a list of useful options.

Getting Help

ColdFusion developers have to remember the HTML language, CFML tags and functions, SQL interfaces, and communication with many other protocols and standards. That's a lot of information to remember, and most developers keep a selection of reference books and manuals close by at all times.

Studio greatly simplifies the process of finding the help you need. It boasts an extensive array of help-related features, all designed to give you immediate, useful, and relevant help. The following sections look at some of these features.

Using Tag Completion

Tag Completion is a feature that lets Studio automatically finish writing tags for you. This is an invaluable feature for two reasons:

- Tag Completion helps ensure that you don't mistakenly miss a tag's required ending tag.
- Tag Completion writes end tags for you, helping prevent typos.

To try out Tag Completion, do the following:

1. Close any files you have opened. (You can simply right-click the file in the Editor window and select Close.)
2. In the Editor window, type <CENTER>.

As soon as you type the > at the end of <CENTER>, Studio automatically inserts the matching </CENTER> tag and places your cursor in between them so you can continue typing.

Part

III

Ch

10

TIP Tag Completion can be disabled by clicking the Tag Completion button in the editor toolbar, or in the Tag Help tab in the Options, Settings dialog box.

 TIP You can add tags to the list of tags to be completed in the Tag Help tab in the Options, Settings dialog box.

Using Tag Tips

Tag Tips are inline, pop-up help dialog boxes shown right in your Editor window. Tag Tips pop up if you press the F2 key while the typing cursor is on a tag. The Tag Tips for the <BODY> tag are shown in Figure 10.9.

FIGURE 10.9

Tag Tips appear right in the Editor window to provide tag-specific help.

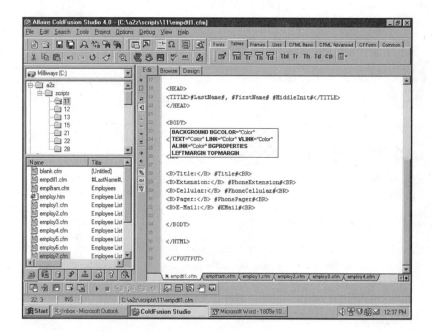

Using Tag Insight

Tag Insight takes online help to the next level by providing pop-up, interactive, tag-specific help, as shown in Figure 10.10. To try this out, do the following:

1. Close any files you have opened. (You can simply right-click the file in the Editor window and select Close.)

2. In the Editor window, type **<BODY** and then wait a second or two.

3. Studio displays a pop-up selectable menu of all the attributes appropriate for the tag you are editing—the <BODY> tag in this case.

4. Select any attribute in order to insert it into your tag.

FIGURE 10.10
Tag Insight can be used to display interactive, tag-specific help.

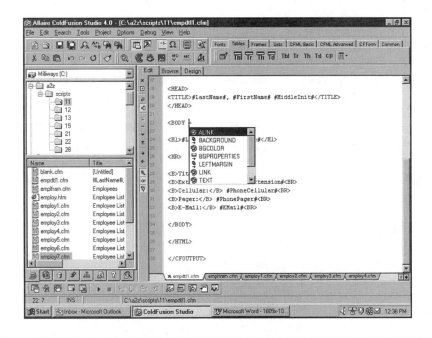

 TIP Tag Insight can be disabled by clicking the Tag Insight button in the editor toolbar, or in the Tag Help tab in the Options, Settings dialog box. You can also adjust the *delay* (the number of seconds Studio should wait before displaying the menu).

Using Edit Dialog Box Help

Studio can display tag-specific edit dialog boxes to help you create and edit tags. Any options you select or fill in are added as tag attributes to the tag when you click the Apply button.

Many of these edit dialog boxes, those for ColdFusion tags in particular, have optional syntax help built right into them. If help is available for a specific tag, two little buttons are displayed at the bottom right of the dialog box, as shown in Figure 10.11. These buttons toggle on and off the help display, in either the dialog box itself or in a separate window.

FIGURE 10.11
Many tag edit dialog boxes have built-in, embedded syntax help.

Using Online Help

In addition to all the help options just discussed, Studio also has a complete online searchable help library. To access the help, click the Help tab in the Resource tab (the one with the yellow question mark). You'll see a list of Help References that you may browse or search, as shown in Figure 10.12.

FIGURE 10.12

Studio comes with a complete searchable reference library.

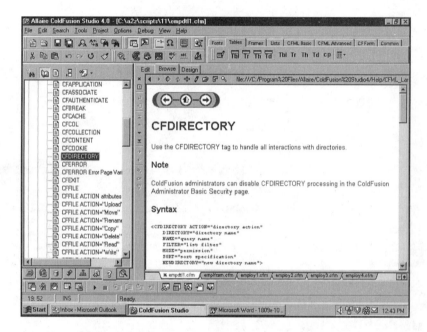

To search for a specific topic, click the Search button (the one with the binoculars on it). This displays a Help Search dialog box, where you can type in any search text.

Using Tags and Expressions

ColdFusion developers spend much of their time working with tags and expressions, and so Studio provides interactive utilities to make both of these operations easier.

We'll explore two of these interactive utilities: the Tag Chooser and the Expression Builder. Both of these tools, as well as other useful tools, are available as menu selections and as right-click options.

Using the Tag Chooser

The Tag Chooser is a drill-down tree interface to HTML and CFML tags, as well as other tag types such as HDML and VTML, and even to custom tags. It is accessible via the right-click menu in the Editor window, or by choosing Tag Chooser from the Tools menu.

The Tag Chooser's primary purpose is to help you find the tag you are looking for by context or category. To try the Tag Chooser, do the following:

1. Close any files you have opened. (You can simply right-click the file in the Editor window and select Close.)

2. Right-click in the Editor window and select Insert Tag to display the Tag Chooser dialog box, as shown in Figure 10.13.

3. Expand the HTML tag list by double-clicking HTML tags, or by clicking the + items symbol.

4. Select Tables to display the list of table related tags.

5. Double-click the TABLE item to display the Table dialog box.

6. Click the Apply button to insert the tag into your document.

FIGURE 10.13

The Studio Tag Chooser lets you drill down through a list of tags to find what you are looking for.

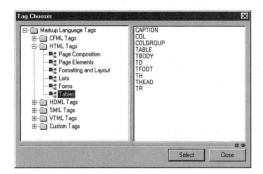

Part

III

Ch

10

 T I P The Tag Chooser dialog box can also display tag-specific help by clicking either of the help buttons on the bottom right of the dialog box.

Using the Expression Builder

ColdFusion *expressions* are collections of references, ColdFusion functions, variables, and operators. Expressions are an important part of ColdFusion application development, and so Studio provides an Expression Builder to help you construct and edit expressions. It is accessible via the right-click menu in the Editor window, or by choosing Expression Builder from the Tools menu.

N O T E Don't worry if you are unfamiliar with expressions; they are covered extensively throughout this book. For now, you are shown how to use the builder so that you can take advantage of it later.

The Expression Builder, shown in Figure 10.14, works much like the Tag Chooser. You select the element type you want (function, constant, operator, or variable), and then drill down to find the specific expression element you are seeking. As you select elements, they are displayed at the top of the Expression Builder dialog box so that you can see and edit the complete expression.

FIGURE 10.14

The Studio Expression Builder can be used to simplify creating and editing ColdFusion expressions.

Once you have finished creating or editing an expression, clicking the Insert button places the expression into your document in the Editor window.

 TIP The Expression Builder dialog box can also display element-specific help by clicking either of the help buttons on the bottom right of the dialog box.

Accessing ColdFusion Application Server Services

Unlike Web page development, ColdFusion application development usually involves a high level of integration with services on the ColdFusion Application Server machine. At a minimum, this integration involves ODBC data sources, as well as files and directories on the server.

Studio can be used to open and work with these services over any Internet connection. This allows developers to work from a computer located anywhere, and still gain full access to the file system as well as to the ODBC data sources.

Connecting to a ColdFusion Server

In order to access these services, you might first tell Studio about your ColdFusion server and how to get to it. To do this, select the Remote tab on the Resource tab (the one with the picture of the computer in front of a globe).

Studio supports two forms of remote server connection, direct connection to ColdFusion servers, and FTP server connections. These are described in Table 10.3.

Table 10.3   Server Types Supported by ColdFusion Studio

Server	Description
RDS	Connecting to a ColdFusion server using the RDS (Remote Development Services) gives you access to the server's file system and all system ODBC data sources. The connection is made via HTTP. Use this option to connect to a ColdFusion server.

Server	Description
FTP	Connecting to an FTP server gives you access to the file system on a remote host. Use this connection to transfer files to and from FTP servers.

To add a ColdFusion Server via RDS, follow these steps:

1. Select the Remote tab from the Resource tab.

2. Right-click in the Tab window and select Add RDS Server to display the server properties dialog box shown in Figure 10.15.

3. Enter any descriptive name in the Description field.

4. Specify the host name or IP address of the server to connect to. Use localhost or 127.0.0.1 to connect to a local server.

5. Enter the Studio server password in the Password field, or leave it blank to be prompted for it each time you access the server. (If you do enter the password, you are not prompted for it again to gain server access; therefore, anyone who has access to Studio on your computer also has server access.)

6. Click OK to add the server.

Part
III

Ch
10

FIGURE 10.15
The Configure RDS Server dialog box is used to add a ColdFusion Server to the Studio remote server list.

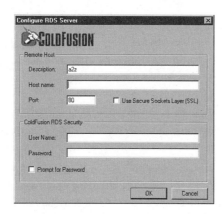

You'll now see the server you added appear in the list of remote servers.

See Chapter 3 for more about setting up the Studio password ColdFusion installation.

Accessing Server Files

To browse files on a remote server (either a ColdFusion or an FTP server), just expand the server name by clicking the + to its left. You are prompted for a password if you did not specify one when setting up the server, and then Studio attempts to connect to the server. If the connection is successful, you see a tree control that lets you browse drives and directories available on the server, as shown in Figure 10.16. Click any directory to display its contents in the file pane.

FIGURE 10.16

The Resource Tab Remote tab shows files and directories on the ColdFusion server machine.

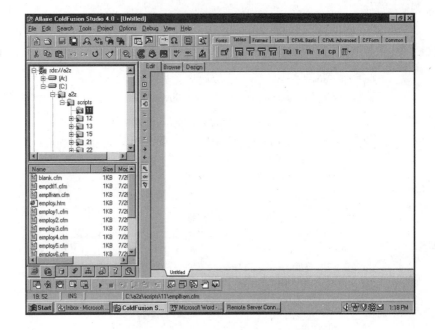

You may double-click any file to open it for editing, just as you would a local file. Studio automatically handles the retrieving of files from the server (using either HTTP or FTP) and saving the files back to the server.

Access Server Data Sources

Accessing server data sources is much the same as accessing files and directories. To access server data sources you must first have configured a ColdFusion Server for remote access within Studio. You cannot use FTP server connections for data source interaction.

To browse your server's data sources, select the Database tab in the Resource tab (the one with the yellow cylinder on it). You'll see the same ColdFusion servers that you set up in the Remote tab. Select a server from the drop-down list to display a list of data sources available on the server, as shown in Figure 10.17.

There are lots of things you can do with this list:

- Expand any data source to view the tables, views, and queries within it (as seen in Figure 10.18).

- Expand any table to see the list of columns and the column data types within it.

- Double-click a table or view to browse the data contained in it.

- Drag and drop any table, view, or field name into the Editor window.

- Access the SQL Query Builder (discussed in detail in the next chapter).

FIGURE 10.17
The Resource Tab gives you remote access to the ODBC data sources on the ColdFusion Server machine.

FIGURE 10.18
The Resource Tab allows you to drill down into remote data sources to see table and view names, as well as column data types and sizes.

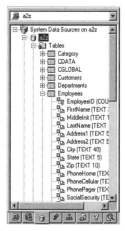

Part
III

Ch
10

Configuring Studio

Studio is a powerful and flexible editor, and the more you use it, the more you'll want to customize it. Fortunately, this is easy to do. The Options menu lists the most frequently used options, several of which you have already utilized in this chapter.

The Studio Settings dialog box is where you can customize most of Studio's features and options. To display the dialog box shown in Figure 10.19, choose Settings from the Options menu, or press the F8 key. The Settings dialog box has nine tabs, which are described in Table 10.4.

FIGURE 10.19

The Settings dialog box is used to configure Studio.

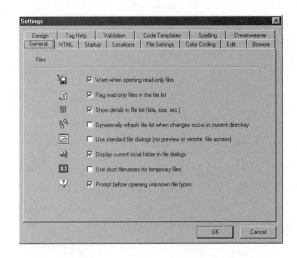

Table 10.4   Settings Dialog Box Tabs

Tab	Description
General	All sorts of editor options, including whether colors are inserted using text or RGB values, and whether or not to lowercase all inserted tags.
HTML	HTML-related options, including whether to match <P> tags with </P>, whether tags should be inserted in uppercase, whether to insert empty ALT attributes in IMG tags, and related options.
Startup	Configure how Studio behaves at startup, what files should be opened, and the initial directory.
Locations	Location of help files, snippets, and the default template.
File Settings	The list of extensions that Studio should treat as editable files, the default extension for any new files, and file format options.
Color Coding	Changes or creates color schemes used for the color coding.
Edit	Editor font and size, text and background color, indentation, drag-and-drop support, and other editor options.
Browse	Specify whether to use Microsoft Internet Explorer as the internal browser, and debugger development mappings.
Design	Hide or enable design mode and CodeSweeper settings.
Tag Help	Enables or disables Tag Insight and Tag Validation; customizes Tag Completion.
Validation	Manage validator settings and enable and disable specific validation levels.
Code Templates	Create and manage code shortcuts (*aliases*).

Tab	Description
Spelling	Spell-checking options and which dictionaries to use.
Dreamweaver	Macromedia Dreameaver integration options.

When you click OK after making any settings changes, Studio automatically saves the changes, ensuring that they are there for future sessions.

ColdFusion Studio is a powerful and flexible editor designed with ColdFusion developers in mind. As such, it does much more then edit files. The integrated Tag Chooser, Expression Builder, and SQL Query Builder (discussed in detail in the next chapter) all serve to simplify the application development process. With extensive built-in help options and support for re-mote development, Studio is an invaluable tool. Start using it and you'll wonder how you man-aged without it. ●

Part
III

Ch
10

ColdFusion Basics

Using Templates

As explained in Chapter 2, "Introduction to ColdFusion," all ColdFusion interaction is via templates rather than HTML files. Templates can contain HTML, ColdFusion tags and functions, or both.

ColdFusion templates are plain text files, just like HTML files are. Unlike HTML files, which are sent to the user's browser, templates are first processed by ColdFusion. This allows you to embed instructions to ColdFusion within your templates. If, for example, you wanted to process user-passed parameters, retrieve data from a database, or conditionally display certain information, you could instruct ColdFusion to do so.

Instead of just reading about templates, why don't we create one?

The first template you create will just say hello to you. You can do that with any HTML file, but along with saying hello, this template also identifies your IP address and the browser you are using. You can't do that with plain HTML.

Create a text file containing the code in Listing 11.1 and save it in your C:\A2Z\SCRIPTS\11 directory as HELLO1.CFM.

Listing 11.1 HELLO1.CFM—Hello ColdFusion Template

```
<HTML>

<HEAD>
<TITLE>Hello!</TITLE>
</HEAD>

<BODY>

<CFOUTPUT>

Hello,<BR>
Your IP address is: <B>#REMOTE_ADDR#</B><BR>
Your browser is: <B>#HTTP_USER_AGENT#</B><P>

</CFOUTPUT>

</BODY>

</HTML>
```

N O T E The instructions here (and throughout this book) assume that source files are saved in a directory structure named C:\A2Z\SCRIPTS, with a subdirectory for each chapter in the book. If you have not already done so, create a directory to store the files that you create as you work through these chapters.

You also need to create a Web server mapping (or *alias*) to map the virtual path a2z to the physical directory C:\A2Z\SCRIPTS. Refer to you Web server documentation for instructions on how to do this.

If you are using Microsoft IIS or Personal Web Server, you must also ensure that the a2z alias has execute privileges. ■

Once you have created and saved the file, load your browser and enter **http://yourserver.com/a2z/11/hello1.cfm** in the URL field (replacing *yourserver.com* with your own server name or IP address).

TIP If you are running ColdFusion on the same machine that you are developing on, you can use the address *localhost* to refer to your own computer. *localhost* is a special host name (which maps to the IP address 127.0.0.1) that always points to itself. In an environment where you are using dynamic IP address (dialing up to your ISP or using DHCP on a company network, for example) this is the only host name that always works, regardless of the IP address actually assigned.

Your browser will display a page that should look similar to the one shown in Figure 11.1; of course, your IP address and browser information could be different.

FIGURE 11.1
ColdFusion templates allow you to display dynamic data in your Web pages.

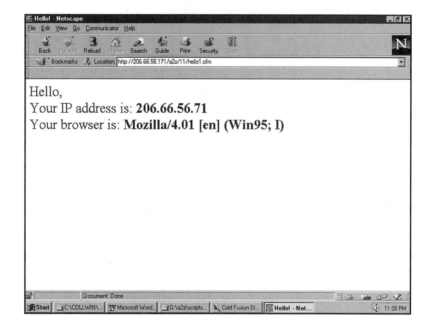

Understanding ColdFusion Templates

Now take a look at the code in Listing 11.1. Most of the code should be familiar to you as standard HTML. The tags for head, title, line breaks, and bold text are the HTML that you'd use in any other Web page.

What is not standard HTML? The <CFOUTOUT> tag and fields surrounded by pound signs (#).

All ColdFusion-specific tags begin with CF, and <CFOUTPUT> is a ColdFusion-specific tag. <CFOUTPUT> (or ColdFusion output) is used to mark a block of code that ColdFusion should itself process prior to submitting it to the Web server for sending to your browser. When

ColdFusion encounters a <CFOUTPUT> tag it scans all the text until the next </CFOUTPUT> for ColdFusion functions or fields delimited by pound signs.

There are two fields used in Listing 11.1: #REMOTE_ADDR# and #HTTP_USER_AGENT#. They are CGI variables that HTTP servers make available to CGI applications like ColdFusion. #REMOTE_ADDR# contains your browser's IP address, and #HTTP_USER_AGENT# contains the string that your browser identified itself with. When ColdFusion encountered the text #REMOTE_ADDR# in the CFOUTPUT block, it replaced it with the value in the REMOTE_ADDR CGI variable. When it encountered #HTTP_USER_AGENT# on the next line, it replaced that with the appropriate CGI variable. Instead of sending the text you entered back to your browser, ColdFusion replaced the field names with the field values, and sent that back to you instead.

Why did we need the CFOUTPUT block? Take a look at what ColdFusion would have done without it. Listing 11.2 contains a modified version of the code used earlier, this time twice—once within a CFOUPUT block and once without.

Listing 11.2   HELLO2.CFM—CFOUTPUT **Use**

```
<HTML>

<HEAD>
<TITLE>Hello!</TITLE>
</HEAD>

<BODY>

<I>The next 3 lines <B>are not</B> within a CFOUTPUT block.</I><BR>
Hello,<BR>
Your IP address is: <B>#REMOTE_ADDR#</B><BR>
Your browser is: <B>#HTTP_USER_AGENT#</B><P>

<CFOUTPUT>

<I>The next 3 lines <B>are</B> within a CFOUTPUT block.</I><BR>
Hello,<BR>
Your IP address is: <B>#REMOTE_ADDR#</B><BR>
Your browser is: <B>#HTTP_USER_AGENT#</B><P>

</CFOUTPUT>

</BODY>

</HTML>
```

If you use fields outside of a CFOUTPUT block, ColdFusion displays the field name as you entered it, complete with the delimiting characters. You can see this in Figure 11.2. More often than not, this is not the result you'll want.

FIGURE 11.2

Fields not contained within a CFOUTPUT block will be output as is, and not replaced with their values.

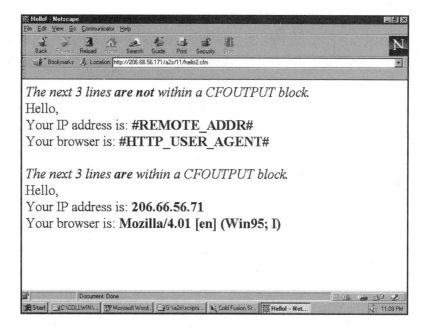

*The next 3 lines **are not** within a CFOUTPUT block.*
Hello,
Your IP address is: **#REMOTE_ADDR#**
Your browser is: **#HTTP_USER_AGENT#**

*The next 3 lines **are** within a CFOUTPUT block.*
Hello,
Your IP address is: **206.66.56.71**
Your browser is: **Mozilla/4.01 [en] (Win95; I)**

 TIP Every `<CFOUTPUT>` tag must have a corresponding `</CFOUTPUT>` tag, and vice versa. ColdFusion returns a syntax error if you omit either tag.

Part
III

Ch

11

Passing Parameters to Templates

In the first example you used ColdFusion to display dynamic data by specifying the field names for two CGI variables. ColdFusion can be used to display process parameters passed to an URL in exactly the same way.

To pass a parameter to a template, the parameter name and value are specified within the URL. For example, to pass a parameter NAME with a value of BEN, add ?NAME=BEN to the URL. If you specify multiple URL parameters, each one must be separated by a ampersand character (&).

Try this yourself. Listing 11.3 contains a template that displays—if it exists—the value of a parameter called NAME. To do so, it uses the `<CFIF>` tag to create a condition, and a ColdFusion function called IsDefined(). If the parameter NAME exists, its value is displayed; otherwise, the user is notified that the parameter was not passed.

Once you have created and saved the file as **HELLO3.CFM** in the C:\A2Z\SCRIPTS\11 directory, load your browser and type **http://*yourserver.com*/a2z/11/hello3.cfm?NAME=BEN**. (You don't have to use my name, any name will do.) Your browser display should look like the one shown in Figure 11.3. Now try it again without any NAME parameter. This time you should see a display like the one shown in Figure 11.4.

Listing 11.3 HELLO3.CFM—**Demonstration of URL Parameter Passing**

```
<HTML>

<HEAD>
<TITLE>Hello!</TITLE>
</HEAD>

<BODY>

Hello,<BR>

<CFIF IsDefined("name")>
 <CFOUTPUT>
 The name you entered is <B>#name#</B>
 </CFOUTPUT>
<CFELSE>
 You did not pass a parameter called NAME
</CFIF>

</BODY>

</HTML>
```

Why did we bother testing for IsDefined("name")? Try removing the <CFIF> statement (you have to remove the <CFELSE> and </CFIF> lines too) and then enter **http://*yourserver.com*/a2z/11/ hello3.cfm** without any NAME parameter. You'll see an error screen similar to the one shown in Figure 11.5. ColdFusion returns an error message because it has no idea what #name# is. You instructed ColdFusion to process a field that did not exist, and so it rightfully complained.

FIGURE 11.3

ColdFusion converts parameters passed to an URL into fields that you can use within your template.

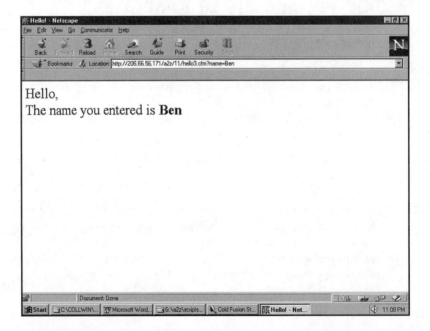

FIGURE 11.4
Whenever fields are optional, you should verify that they exist before using them.

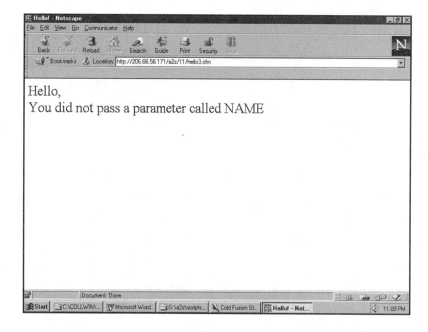

FIGURE 11.5
ColdFusion displays an error message if you refer to a variable or field that does not exist.

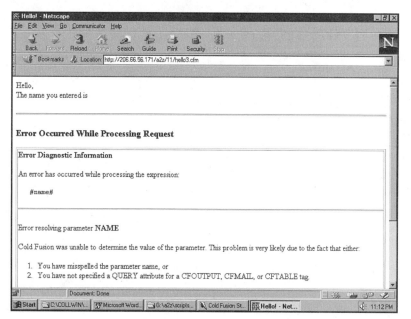

Creating Data-Driven Templates

Now that you've seen what ColdFusion templates look like, and know how to create, save, and test them, return to A2Z Books.

Your employee database is set up and populated with data, and so your next task is to publish this information on your intranet. This way your users can use an up-to-date employee list at all times and won't need any special software to do so. All they need to access the data is a Web browser.

Static Web Pages

Before we create the ColdFusion template, first take a look at how not to create this page.

Listing 11.4 contains the HTML code for the employee list Web page. The HTML code is relatively simple; it contains header information and then a list of employees in an HTML unordered list (<UL>).

Listing 11.4   EMPLOY.HTM—HTML Code for Employee List

```
<HTML>
<HEAD>
<TITLE>Employee List</TITLE>
</HEAD>
<BODY>
<H1>Employees</H1>
<UL>
 <LI>Black, Kim - Ext. 4565
 <LI>Brown, William - Ext. 4443
 <LI>Forta, Ben - Ext. 4615
 <LI>Gold, Marcy - Ext. 4912
 <LI>Green, Adrienne - Ext. 4546
 <LI>Johnson, Dan - Ext. 4824
 <LI>Jones, Steven - Ext. 4311
 <LI>Smith, Jack - Ext. 4545
 <LI>Smith, Jane - Ext. 4876
 <LI>Stevens, Adam - Ext. 4878
 <LI>White, Jennifer - Ext. 4345
 <LI>Wilson, Lynn - Ext. 4464
</UL>
</BODY>
</HTML>
```

Figure 11.6 shows the output that this code listing generates.

Dynamic Web Pages

Why is a static HTML file not the way to create the Web page? What would you do when a new employee is hired, or when an employee leaves the company? What would you do if phone extensions changed?

FIGURE 11.6

You can create the employee Web page as a static HTML file.

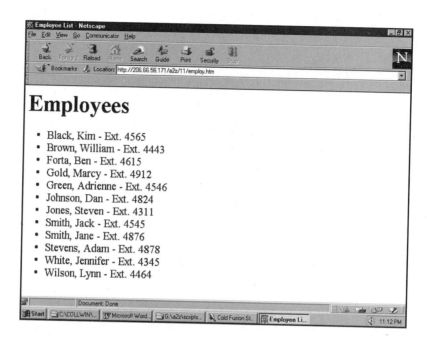

You could directly modify the HTML code to reflect these changes, but you already have all this information in a database. Why would you want to have to enter it all again? You'd run the risk of making mistakes—names being misspelled, entries out of order, and possibly missing names altogether. As the number of names in the list grows, so will the potential for errors occurring. In addition, employees will be looking at inaccurate information during the period between updating the table and updating the Web page.

A much easier and more reliable solution is to have the Web page display the contents of your Employees table; this way any table changes are immediately available to all employees. The Web page would be dynamically built based on the contents of the Employee table.

To create your first ColdFusion template, enter the code as it appears in Listing 11.5 and save it in the C:\A2Z\SCRIPTS\11 as EMPLOY1.CFM. (Don't worry if the ColdFusion code does not make much sense yet; I explain it in detail in just a moment.)

Listing 11.5 EMPLOY1.CFM—**The Employee List**

```
<CFQUERY DATASOURCE="A2Z" NAME="Employees">
  SELECT FirstName, LastName, PhoneExtension
  FROM Employees
  ORDER BY LastName, FirstName
</CFQUERY>

<HTML>

<HEAD>
```

continues

Part

III

Ch

11

Listing 11.5 Continued

```
<TITLE>Employee List</TITLE>
</HEAD>

<BODY>

<H1>Employees</H1>

<UL>

<CFOUTPUT QUERY="Employees">
 <LI>#LastName#, #FirstName# - Ext. #PhoneExtension#
</CFOUTPUT>

</UL>

</BODY>

</HTML>
```

Now load your browser and type **http://*yourserver.com*/11/a2z/employ1.cfm** in the URL field (replacing *yourserver.com* with your own server name). The results are shown in Figure 11.7.

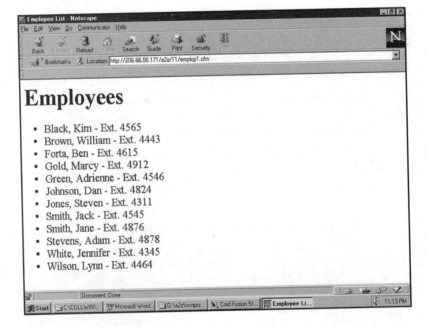

FIGURE 11.7
Ideally, the employee Web page should be generated dynamically, based on live data.

Understanding Data-Driven Templates

Now compare Figure 11.6 to Figure 11.7. Can you see the difference between them? Look carefully.

Give up? The truth is that there is no difference at all. The screen shots are identical, and if you looked at the HTML source that generated Figure 11.7, you'd see that aside from lots of extra whitespace, the dynamically generated code is exactly the same as the static code you entered in Listing 11.4, and nothing like the dynamic code you entered in Listing 11.5.

How did the code in Listing 11.5 become the HTML source code that generated Figure 11.7? Review the code listing carefully.

The CFQUERY Tag

The first lines in Listing 11.5 include a ColdFusion tag called `<CFQUERY>`, which submits any SQL statement to an ODBC data source. The SQL statement is usually a SQL `SELECT` statement, but could also be an `INSERT`, `UPDATE`, `DELETE`, a stored procedure call, or any other SQL statement.

▶ **See** "Creating an ODBC Data Source" for a more detailed discussion of ODBC data sources, **p. 133**.

▶ **See** "Creating Queries" for a detailed discussion of SQL statements, specifically the SQL `SELECT` statement, **p. 140**.

The `<CFQUERY>` tag has several attributes, or parameters, that are passed to it when used. The `<CFQUERY>` in Listing 11.5 uses only two attributes:

- The `NAME` attribute is used to name the query and any returned data.
- The `DATASOURCE` attribute contains the name of the ODBC data source to be used.

The query `NAME` we specified is Employees. This name will be used later when we process the results generated by the query.

> **N O T E** Query names passed to `<CFQUERY>` need not be unique to each query within your page. If you do reuse query names, subsequent `<CFQUERY>` calls will overwrite the results retrieved by the earlier query. ▨

We specified A2Z for the `DATASOURCE` attribute, which is the name of the data source we created in Chapter 9, "Introduction to SQL."

`SELECT FirstName, LastName, PhoneExtension FROM Employees ORDER BY LastName, FirstName` was the SQL statement used. This statement selects the columns we need from the Employees table and sorts them by last name plus first name.

T I P The SQL statement in Listing 11.5 is broken up over many lines to make the code more readable. While it is perfectly legal to write a long SQL statement that is wider than the width of your browser, these generally should be broken up over as many lines as needed.

When ColdFusion processes the template, the first item it finds is the ColdFusion tag <CFQUERY>. ColdFusion knows which tags it itself must process, and which it must pass to the server directly. <CFQUERY> is a ColdFusion tag, and therefore must be processed by ColdFusion.

When ColdFusion encounters a <CFQUERY> tag, it creates an ODBC request and submits it to the specified data source. The results, if there are any, are stored in a temporary buffer and are identified by the name specified in the NAME attribute. All this happens before ColdFusion processes the next line in the template.

The <CFQUERY> code, and indeed all ColdFusion markup code, never gets sent on to the server for transmission to the browser. Unlike HTML tags, which are browser instructions, CFML tags are ColdFusion instructions.

It is important to note that at this point no data has been displayed. <CFQUERY> retrieves data from a database table, but it does not display that data. Actually, it does nothing at all with the data—that's your job.

The next lines in the template are standard HTML tags, headers, title, and headings. Because these are not ColdFusion tags, they are sent to the Web server and then on to the client browser.

Displaying Query Results with the CFOUTPUT Tag

Next we created an HTML unordered list using the <UL> tag. The list is terminated a few lines later with a </UL> tag.

The list of employees itself goes between the <UL> and </UL> tags. Each name is a separate list item, and therefore begins with an HTML <LI> tag. Instead of listing the employees as shown in Figure 11.6, we used a <CFOUTPUT> tag.

<CFOUTPUT> is the same ColdFusion output tag we used earlier. This time, however, we are using it to create a code block that is used to output the results of a <CFQUERY>. In order for ColdFusion to know which query results to output, the query name is passed to <CFOUTPUT> in the QUERY attribute. The name provided is the same that was assigned to the <CFQUERY> tag's NAME attribute. In this case, the NAME is Employees.

The code between the <CFOUTPUT QUERY="Employees"> and </CFOUTPUT> is the output code block. ColdFusion uses this code once for every row that was retrieved. Because there are currently 12 rows in the Employees table, the <CFOUPUT> code is looped through 12 times. And any HTML or CFML tags within that block are repeated as well, once for each row.

◊ This chapter teaches you how to use the CFOUTPUT tag and only introduces the features needed for the examples presented here. For a detailed discussion of this tag, with examples showing the use of all attributes, **see** the "CFOUTPUT" section, **p. 830**.

Using Table Columns

As explained earlier, ColdFusion uses # to delimit fields. In addition to CGI variables and URL parameters, which we used at the beginning of this chapter, ColdFusion fields can also be columns retrieved by a `<CFQUERY>`. Whatever field is used, ColdFusion replaces the field name with the actual value. When ColdFusion processed the output block, it replaced #LastName# with the contents of the LastName column that was retrieved in the Employees query. Each time the output code block is used, that row's LastName value is inserted into the HTML code.

ColdFusion fields can be treated as any other text in an HTML document; any of the HTML formatting tags can be applied to them. In our example the query results need to be displayed in an unordered list. Each employee's name and phone extension is a list item, and is therefore preceded by the `<LI>` tag. Because the `<LI>` tag is included within the CFOUTPUT block, ColdFusion outputs it along with every row.

Look at the following line of code:

```
<LI> #LastName#, #FirstName# - Ext. #PhoneExtension#
```

That code becomes the following for employee Kim Black at extension 4565:

```
<LI> Black, Kim - Ext. 4565.
```

Only the `<LI>` tag is within the CFOUPUT block—not the `<UL>` and `</UL>`—because you want only one list, not many. If the `<UL>` and `</UL>` were within the CFOUPUT block, you would have a new list created for each employee—definitely not the desired result at all.

Figure 11.7 shows the browser display that this template creates. It is exactly the same result as Figure 11.6, but without any new data entry whatsoever.

Welcome to ColdFusion, and the wonderful world of dynamic data-driven Web pages!

Using Drill-Down Applications

The nature of the World Wide Web places certain restrictions on data interaction. Every time a Web browser makes a request, a connection is made to a Web server, and that connection is maintained only for as long as it takes to retrieve the Web page. Subsequent selections and Web requests create yet another connection; again, for the specific request.

Simple user interfaces that we take for granted in most commercial software, such as scrolling through previous or next records with the cursor keys, become quite complex within the constraints of Web pages and how they interact with Web servers.

One very elegant and popular form of Web-based data interaction is the drill-down approach. *Drill down* is designed to break up data and display only what is needed on a single page. Selecting an item in that page causes details about that item to be displayed. The process is called drilling down because you drill through the data layer by layer to find the information you need.

The employee page you just created, for example, displays a simple list of employees and extensions. What if you want to display more information such as title, department, and email address? You could select more columns in `<CFQUERY>` and display them in the `<CFOUTPUT>` code, but that would clutter the screen and make it hard to use.

A better approach is to display less information on a page, and allow the user to click an employee's name in order to display more information about that employee. This approach—gradually digging deeper into a data set to find the information you want—is known as drilling down.

Building Dynamic SQL Statements

Creating a drill-down application in ColdFusion involves creating multiple templates. In our example, one template lists the employees, and a second template displays an employee's details.

First create the detail template. The SQL query in this template has to select detailed user information for a specific user. Obviously you don't want to create a template for every employee in your database. Doing so would totally defeat the purpose of using templates in the first place. Rather, the template needs to be passed a parameter, a value that uniquely identifies an employee. Fortunately, when we created the Employees table, we created a column called EmployeeID, which contains a unique employee ID for each employee in the table. The code in Listing 11.6 demonstrates how this is done.

Listing 11.6 `EMPDTL1.CFM`—**Passing URL Parameters**

```
<CFQUERY DATASOURCE="A2Z" NAME="Employee">
SELECT LastName,
       FirstName,
       MiddleInit,
       Title,
       PhoneExtension,
       PhoneCellular,
       PhonePager,
       EMail
FROM Employees
WHERE EmployeeID = #EmployeeID#
</CFQUERY>

<CFOUTPUT QUERY="Employee">

<HTML>

<HEAD>
<TITLE>#LastName#, #FirstName# #MiddleInit#</TITLE>
</HEAD>

<BODY>

<H1>#LastName#, #FirstName#</H1>

<HR>

<B>Title:</B> #Title#<BR>
<B>Extension:</B> #PhoneExtension#<BR>
<B>Cellular:</B> #PhoneCellular#<BR>
<B>Pager:</B> #PhonePager#<BR>
<B>E-Mail:</B> #EMail#<BR>
```

```
</BODY>

</HTML>

</CFOUTPUT>
```

Before you look at the Web page produced by this code, take a look at the SQL statement in this <CFQUERY> tag.

The SQL SELECT statement selects the columns needed and uses a WHERE clause to specify which row to select. The WHERE clause cannot be hard-coded for any particular employee ID and therefore uses a passed field: #EmployeeID#. The #EmployeeID# field is passed to the template as part of the URL.

Therefore, if an EmployeeID of 7 were passed with the URL, the WHERE clause (WHERE EmployeeID = #EmployeeID#) would become exactly what you need to select the correct row:

```
WHERE EmployeeID = 7
```

As seen earlier, parameters are passed to URLs after the template name, and each parameter is separated by an ampersand character. To specify employee ID 7, you'd add ?EmployeeID=7 to the URL.

Now try this out. Type the URL **http://*yourserver.com*/a2z/11/empdtl1.cfm?EmployeeID=7** in the URL field (replacing *yourserver.com* with your own server name) in your browser. The resulting output is shown in Figure 11.8.

FIGURE 11.8

If you want to create truly dynamic pages, parameters can be passed to ColdFusion templates and used to create dynamic SQL statements.

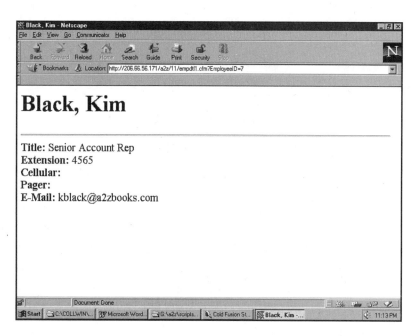

To display the details for another employee, all you need to do is change the value passed to the URL EmployeeID parameter. Try replacing EmployeeID=7 with EmployeeID=5, which displays information on a different employee. The same template can now be used to display details for any employee in the database because the Web page is data driven.

Implementing Data Drill Down

To complete the drill-down application, you need to modify the employee list page to include links to the employee details page.

The code for the updated template is in Listing 11.7.

Listing 11.7 EMPLOY2.CFM—ColdFusion Fields Can Be Used to Build

```
<CFQUERY DATASOURCE="A2Z" NAME="Employees">
 SELECT FirstName, LastName, PhoneExtension, EmployeeID
 FROM Employees
 ORDER BY LastName, FirstName
</CFQUERY>

<HTML>

<HEAD>
<TITLE>Employee List</TITLE>
</HEAD>

<BODY>

<H1>Employees</H1>

<UL>

<CFOUTPUT QUERY="Employees">

<LI><A HREF="empdtl1.cfm?EmployeeID=#EmployeeID#">#LastName#, #FirstName#</A>
➥ - Ext. #PhoneExtension#

</CFOUTPUT>

</UL>

</BODY>

</HTML>
```

Listing 11.7 is the same as Listing 11.5, with two exceptions. Firstly, you now need the EmployeeID value, and so the SQL SELECT statement in the <CFQUERY> has been changed to also include this column. Secondly, the employee's name in the <CFOUTPUT> code block has been modified so that it is a hyperlink to the employee detail page.

The new employee name code reads as follows:

```
<LI> <A HREF="empdtl1.cfm?EmployeeID=#EmployeeID#">#LastName#, #FirstName#</A>
➡ - Ext. #PhoneExtension#
```

When ColdFusion processes employee 7, this line becomes the following:

```
<LI> <A HREF="empdtl1.cfm?EmployeeID=7">Black, Kim</A> - Ext. 4565.
```

This way, the URL needed for the hyperlink is also dynamic. The URL built for each employee will contain the correct employee ID, which can be passed to the employee detail template.

Now try this example. Type the URL **http://*yourserver.com*/a2z/11/employ2.cfm** (replacing *yourserver.com* with your own server name). Figure 11.9 shows what the output looks like. The only difference between this display and the one in Figure 11.7 is that now the employee names are hyperlinks. You can click any one of these links to display employee details, as seen in Figure 11.10.

Using Frames to Implement Data Drill Down

One problem with the drill-down templates just created is that every time you view an employee's details you have to click your browser's Back button to return to the employee list page. A more useable approach is to display the employee list and details at the same time.

Fortunately you can easily do this via a browser feature called frames. *Frames* allow you split your browser window in two or more windows and control what gets displayed within each.

ColdFusion templates are very well suited for use within frames.

Creating frames involves creating multiple templates (or HTML pages). Each window in a frame typically displays a different template; you need two templates if you have two windows. In addition, there is always one more page that is used to lay out and create the frames.

Part
III

Ch
11

FIGURE 11.9

You can build hyperlink URL's dynamically to create even more dynamic Web pages.

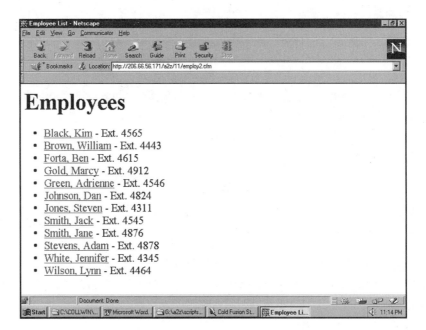

FIGURE 11.10

By passing parameters to a ColdFusion template, you can use the same template to display different records and bypass requiring a different HTML page for each.

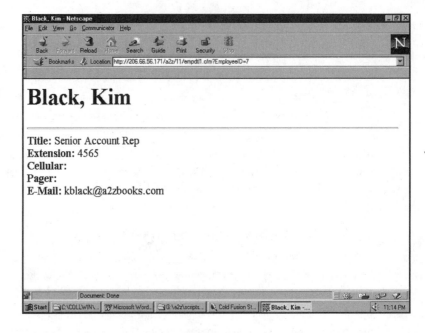

When the frames are created, each window is titled with a unique name. In a non-framed window, the new page is opened in the same window every time you select a hyperlink, replacing whatever contents were there previously. In a framed window you can use the window name to control the destination for any output.

Creating Frames for Use with ColdFusion

Now that you know how frames work, the first thing you need to do is create the template to define and create the frames. The code for template EMPLFRAM.CFM is shown in Listing 11.8.

Listing 11.8   EMPLFRAM.CFM—Employee Frame Definition and Creation

```
<HTML>

<HEAD>
<TITLE>Employees</TITLE>
</HEAD>

<FRAMESET COLS="50%,50%">
 <FRAME SRC="employ3.cfm" NAME="employees">
 <FRAME SRC="blank.cfm" NAME="details">
</FRAMESET>

</HTML>
```

This template first defines the frames. `<FRAMESET COLS="50%,50%">` creates two columns (or windows), each that take up 50% of the width of the browser window.

The two columns are then defined: `<FRAME SRC="employ3.cfm" NAME="employees">` creates the left frame; the NAME attribute names the window; and the SRC attribute specifies the name of the template to initially display within the window when the frame is first displayed.

There is no employee selected when the frame is first displayed, and therefore there is no information to display in the details window (the right frame). You obviously can't display employee information in that frame before the user selects the employee to view, and so instead we display an empty page. `SRC="blank.cfm"` loads a blank page, the source for which is shown in Listing 11.9.

Listing 11.9 `BLANK.CFM`—**Blank Files Are Used to Fill Empty Frames**

```
<BODY>
</BODY>
```

The next thing to do is create the employee list template. Actually, it is the same as the one in Listing 11.7, with one important difference. The URL to display the employee detail must include a TARGET attribute to designate which window to display the URL in. If the TARGET is omitted, the new data is displayed in the frame that it was selected from.

The modified code is shown in Listing 11.10. As you can see, the URL has been modified to include the attribute `TARGET="details"`. This specifies that the new URL should be displayed in the frame we named Details, the right window.

Part III

Ch 11

Listing 11.10 `EMPLOY3.CFM`—**To Load an URL in Another Frame You Need to Specify the Name of the Target Frame**

```
<CFQUERY DATASOURCE="A2Z" NAME="Employees">
 SELECT FirstName, LastName, PhoneExtension, EmployeeID
 FROM Employees
 ORDER BY LastName, FirstName
</CFQUERY>

<HTML>

<HEAD>
<TITLE>Employee List</TITLE>
</HEAD>

<BODY>

<H1>Employees</H1>

<UL>
```

continues

Listing 11.10 Continued

```
<CFOUTPUT QUERY="Employees">
 <LI><A HREF="empdtl1.cfm?EmployeeID=#EmployeeID#" TARGET="details">
    #LastName#, #FirstName#</A> - Ext. #PhoneExtension#
</CFOUTPUT>

</UL>

</BODY>

</HTML>
```

That's all there is to it.

To try it out, go to http://yourserver.com/a2z/scripts/11/emplfram.cfm. Figure 11.11 shows the output as it appears in framed windows. Try clicking any employee's name in the left window; the right window will display employee details.

FIGURE 11.11
ColdFusion is very well suited for use within HTML frames.

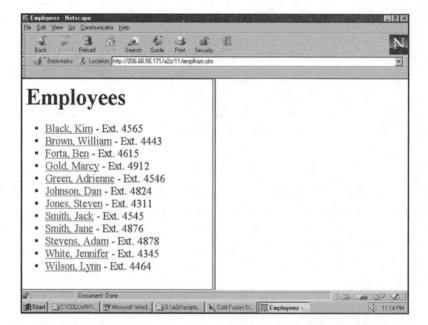

Displaying Results in Tables

Most Web browsers support tables. The HTML <TABLE> tag enables you to display data in a two-dimensional grid. Tables are very useful for presenting lists in a clean columnar display.

As HTML tables are used so often to display query results in data-driven pages, and the <TABLE> syntax can be a little confusing at times, the makers of ColdFusion created a ColdFusion tag called <CFTABLE>. The <CFTABLE> tag is designed to conceal the details involved in creating HTML tables. All you have to do is tell ColdFusion what data to put in each column; ColdFusion generates the <TABLE> markup code for you.

The <CFTABLE> tag has another important advantage. It allows you to create tables that can be viewed by all browsers, even those that do not support HTML tables. To do this, ColdFusion renders the output in a non-proportional font and pads fields with spaces so that they line up in columns. While the resulting table might not look as good as a true HTML table, it is functional and is supported by all browsers.

N O T E   While <CFTABLE> can simplify the process of creating dynamic data-driven HTML tables, it does so at a price. <CFTABLE> does not provide much control over table formatting. For more detailed table layout, you need to create the HTML table manually using <CFOUTPUT> and <TABLE>. ▨

◊ This chapter teaches you the basic use of CFTABLE and only introduces the features needed for the examples presented here. For a detailed discussion of this tag, with examples showing the use of all attributes and how it can be used, **see** the "CFTABLE" section, **p. 851**.

Creating Non-HTML Tables with CFTABLE

For an example of where <CFTABLE> can be used, look at the browser output shown in Figure 11.9. Notice how the phone extension is right next to the name, and in a different location on the screen depending on how long the employee's name is? If the employees were listed in a table, the data could be presented in a cleaner and more organized fashion.

Part III
Ch 11

Listing 11.11 is based on Listing 11.4, but instead of using an unordered list and presenting each employee as a list item, the list is displayed in a table.

Listing 11.11   EMPLOY4.CFM—Using <CFTABLE> to Create Non-HTML Tables

```
<CFQUERY DATASOURCE="A2Z" NAME="Employees">
SELECT FirstName, LastName, PhoneExtension, EmployeeID
FROM Employees
ORDER BY LastName, FirstName
</CFQUERY>

<HTML>

<HEAD>
<TITLE>Employee List</TITLE>
</HEAD>

<BODY>

<H1>Employees</H1>

<CFTABLE QUERY="Employees" COLHEADERS>
<CFCOL
  HEADER="Employee"
```

continues

Listing 11.11   Continued

```
TEXT="<A HREF=""empdtl1.cfm?EmployeeID=#EmployeeID#"">#LastName#, #FirstName#
  ➥</A>"
>
<CFCOL
 HEADER="Extension"
 TEXT="Ext. #PhoneExtension#"
>
</CFTABLE>

</BODY>

</HTML>
```

You use the tag <CFTABLE QUERY="Employees" COLHEADERS> to create the table. The <CFTABLE> tag is a special type of <CFOUTPUT>, and therefore requires that you specify a QUERY attribute, just like the one you'd provide to <CFOUTPUT>. <CFTABLE> is only used to display query results, and the QUERY attribute specifies which result set to process.

The COLHEADERS attribute is used to instruct ColdFusion to create optional column headers for each column in the table.

ColdFusion needs to know what columns you want to include in your table. Each column is specified using the <CFCOL> tag. You specify two columns here, one for the employee name and one for the phone extension.

The code for the phone extension column is <CFCOL HEADER="Extension" TEXT="Ext. #PhoneExtension#">. The HEADER attribute specifies the text to use in the column header. This column has a header with the text Extension in it. The TEXT attribute is required; every <CFCOL> tag must have one. It tells ColdFusion what you want to display in this column. The TEXT attribute here contains the expression "Ext. #PhoneExtension#". As ColdFusion processes each row, it replaces the #PhoneExtension# field with the value of the retrieved PhoneExtension column.

The employee name column may look more complicated, but it really isn't at all. This is the source for the column:

```
<CFCOL HEADER="Employee" TEXT="<A HREF=""empdtl1.cfm?EmployeeID=#EmployeeID#"">
➥#LastName#, #FirstName#</A>">.
```

Again, you first specify the text for the optional header in the HEADER attribute. The TEXT attribute contains the text to display, and because the name has to be a hyperlink, you must also specify the A HREF link tag.

In fact, the contents of the TEXT attribute are almost the same as the hyperlink tag used in Listing 11.7, with one notable exception. You'll notice that the link tag has double quotation marks around the URL, instead of the usual single set. You need the double quotation marks to tell ColdFusion to treat this as a quote, and not as the end of the TEXT attribute. If you had entered a single quotation mark, ColdFusion would have thought that the TEXT attribute ended right after the HREF=. Because it would not know what to do with the text after the quotation mark, ColdFusion would have reported a syntax error.

Now that you understand the code listing, run the template by typing **http://yourserver.com/a2z/11/employ4.cfm**.

As you can see in Figure 11.12, the employee names and phone extensions are now displayed in clearly labeled columns.

FIGURE 11.12

ColdFusion can generate non-HTML tables using the <CFTABLE> tag.

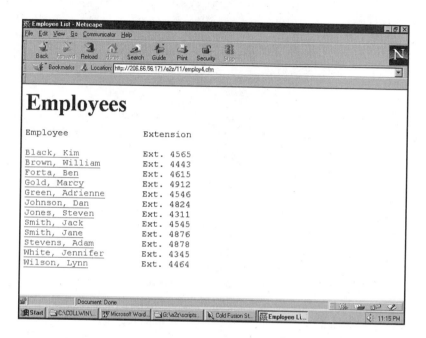

How is this table created without using the HTML <TABLE> tag? Look at the source code generated by ColdFusion to find out.

Select the View Source option in your browser. (In Netscape, select Page Source from the View menu; in Microsoft Internet Explorer, select Source from the View menu.)

As you can see in Figure 11.13, ColdFusion used the HTML <PRE> tag, which displays text exactly as it appears in the source code. Web browsers usually ignore whitespace characters such as spaces and line feeds. The <PRE> tag instructs the browser to maintain all spacing and line feeds, allowing ColdFusion to lay out the data exactly as it wants the browser to display it.

TIP

Viewing the source code generated by ColdFusion is very useful when debugging template problems. When you view the source, you are looking at the complete output as it was sent to your browser. If you ever need to ascertain why a Web page does not look like what you intended it to be, a good place to start is comparing your template with the source code it generated.

Part

III

Ch

11

FIGURE 11.13
To see how ColdFusion interprets your template, view the generated markup language code with your browser's view source option.

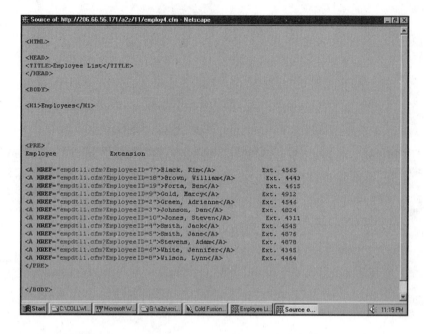

Creating HTML Tables with CFTABLE

Tables created with the HTML <TABLE> tag, of course, look much better, so ColdFusion also supports HTML tables. As you can see in Listing 11.12, to create HTML tables all you need to do is specify the HTMLTABLE attribute in the <CFTABLE> tag.

Figure 11.14 shows the same employee list screen rendered in an HTML table. Note that standard fonts are used when displaying data in an HTML table; the fixed font used when the <PRE> tag is specified is not used. Therefore, it is safe to use any other HTML formatting options in the CFCOL TEXT attribute if required. Therefore, if you wanted the name in bold, for example, you could have specified this:

```
TEXT="<A HREF=""empdtl1.cfm?EmployeeID=#EmployeeID#"">
➥<B>#LastName#, #FirstName#</B></A>"
```

ColdFusion would still have been able to display the table correctly. The <B> and </B> tags are HTML tags, not CFML tags; therefore, ColdFusion passes them through to the Web server to be sent to your Web browser.

Listing 11.12 EMPLOY5.CFM—**Creating HTML Tables with** <CFTABLE>

```
<CFQUERY DATASOURCE="A2Z" NAME="Employees">
SELECT FirstName, LastName, PhoneExtension, EmployeeID
FROM Employees
ORDER BY LastName, FirstName
</CFQUERY>
```

```
<HTML>

<HEAD>
<TITLE>Employee List</TITLE>
</HEAD>

<BODY>

<H1>Employees</H1>

<CFTABLE QUERY="Employees" COLHEADERS HTMLTABLE>
<CFCOL
 HEADER="Employee"
 TEXT="<A HREF=""empdtl1.cfm?EmployeeID=#EmployeeID#"">#LastName#, #FirstName#
 ➥</A>"
>
<CFCOL
 HEADER="Extension"
 TEXT="Ext. #PhoneExtension#"
>
</CFTABLE>

</BODY>

</HTML>
```

To create this table, ColdFusion generated HTML table code. This source code, as displayed by the browser's view source function, is shown in Figure 11.15.

FIGURE 11.14

You can use the
<CFTABLE> tag to
create HTML tables.

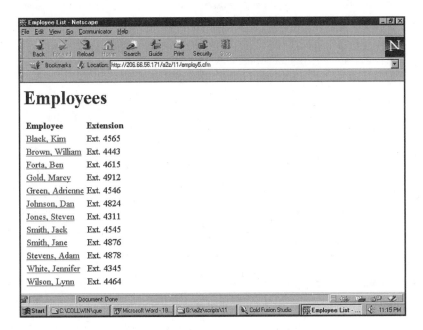

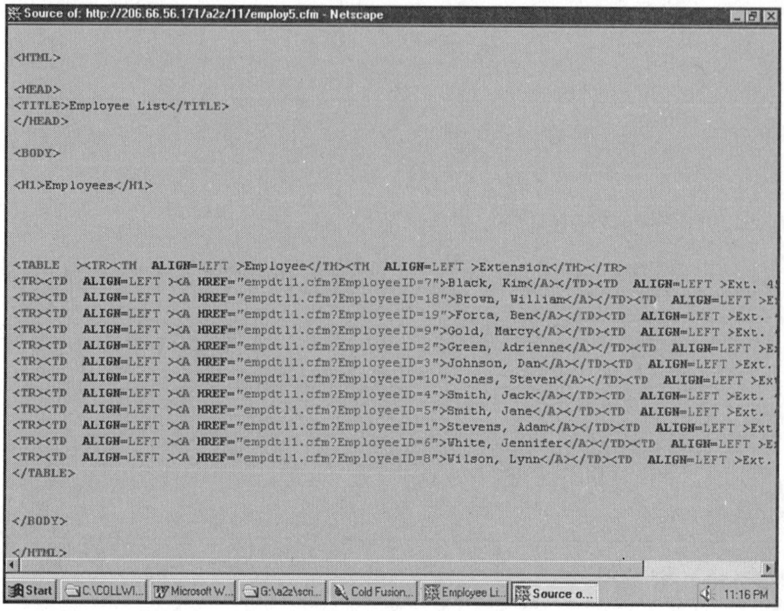

FIGURE 11.15

ColdFusion can generate all the required code to create HTML tables.

Creating HTML Tables Manually

As good as the ColdFusion `<CFTABLE>` tag is, it is very limited. HTML tables support many advanced features, including table headers, cells that span multiple rows or columns, borders and border colors, background colors and images, and more. If you really want to control how your tables are displayed, you must resort to creating your tables manually.

Listing 11.13 demonstrates how to manually create a bordered table for our employee list, and Figure 11.16 shows what the output looks like.

Listing 11.13 EMPLOY6.CFM—**Creating Tables Manually**

```
<CFQUERY DATASOURCE="A2Z" NAME="Employees">
SELECT FirstName, LastName, PhoneExtension, EmployeeID
FROM Employees
ORDER BY LastName, FirstName
</CFQUERY>

<HTML>

<HEAD>
<TITLE>Employee List</TITLE>
</HEAD>

<BODY>

<CENTER>
```

```
<TABLE BORDER=5>

<TR>
 <TH COLSPAN=2>
  <H1>Employees</H1>
 </TH>
</TR>

<CFOUTPUT QUERY="Employees">
 <TR>
  <TD>
   <A HREF="empdtl1.cfm?EmployeeID=#EmployeeID#">#LastName#, #FirstName#</A>
  </TD>
  <TD>
   Ext. #PhoneExtension#
  </TD>
 </TR>
</CFOUTPUT>

</TABLE>

</CENTER>

</BODY>

</HTML>
```

Part
III

Ch
11

FIGURE 11.16
Creating tables
manually allows a
greater degree of
control over table
appearance.

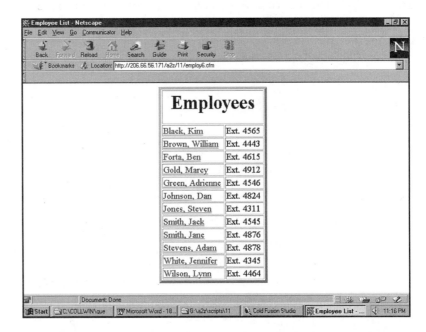

Look at the code in Listing 11.13. First we created the table with the <TABLE> tag and specified an optional border. HTML tables can have borders of varying thicknesses, and the BORDER attribute specifies the border to use; then we created a table title and placed it in a header cell (specified with the <TH> tag) that spans two columns.

Next comes <CFOUTOUT>. A new table row is created as each query row is output. This is why there is a complete table row (<TR>) and cells (<TD>) within the <CFOUTPUT> code block.

Finally, you close the table with </TABLE>.

TIP Pay close attention to what code you place within and without the <CFOUTPUT> block. Misplacing a <TR> or </TD> could result in a badly formatted HTML table, and some browsers may opt to not even display that table.

As you can see, manually creating tables requires a little more effort and a better understanding of HTML tables, but the rewards are well worth it.

N O T E HTML tables are a very useful way to format data, but there is a cost associated with using tables. In order for a browser to correctly display a table, it cannot display any part of that table until it has received the entire table from the Web server. This is because any row, even one near the end of the table, could affect the width of columns and how the table will be formatted. Therefore, if you display data in a table, the user will see no data at all until all the data is present. If you were to use another type of display, a list for example, the data would be displayed as it was received. The reality of it is that the page will likely take as long to fully load with or without tables. The downside of using tables is that it takes longer for any data to appear. This does not apply to tables created without the <TABLE> tag. ▨

Grouping Query Results

Before a new level of complexity is introduced, review how ColdFusion processes queries.

In ColdFusion data queries are created using the <CFQUERY> tag. <CFQUERY> performs a SQL operation and retrieves results if there are any. Results are stored temporarily by ColdFusion and remain around only for the duration of the processing of the template that contained the query.

The <CFOUTPUT> tag is used to output query results. <CFOUTPUT> takes a query name as an attribute and then loops through all the rows that were retrieved by the query. The code block between the <CFOUTPUT> and the </CFOUTPUT> is repeated once for every row retrieved.

All the examples created until now displayed results in a single list or a single table.

What would you do if you wanted to process the results in subsets? For example, suppose you wanted to list the employees by department. You could change the SQL statement in the <CFQUERY> to set the sort order to be department, and then perhaps by name within each department.

This would retrieve the data in the correct order, but how would you display it? If you used <CFOUTPUT> as we have until now, every row created by the <CFOUTPUT> block would have to be the same. If one had a department name, all would have to, because every row that is processed is processed with the same block of code.

How would you create the output shown in Figure 11.17?

FIGURE 11.17
You can use the <CFOUTPUT> tag to group query results and display them accordingly.

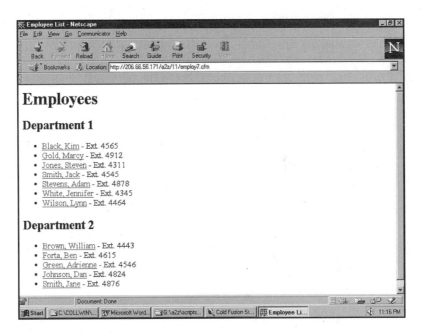

The solution is to group the data results. Grouping allows you to have more than one <CFOUTPUT> loop. To understand how grouping works, look at the template in Listing 11.14.

Listing 11.14 EMPLOY7.CFM—Employee List Grouped by Department

```
<CFQUERY DATASOURCE="A2Z" NAME="Employees">
SELECT DepartmentID, FirstName, LastName, PhoneExtension, EmployeeID
FROM Employees
ORDER BY DepartmentID, LastName, FirstName
</CFQUERY>

<HTML>

<HEAD>
<TITLE>Employee List</TITLE>
</HEAD>

<BODY>

<H1>Employees</H1>
```

continues

Listing 11.14 Continued

```
<CFOUTPUT QUERY="Employees" GROUP="DepartmentID">
 <H2>Department #DepartmentID#</H2>

 <UL>

  <CFOUTPUT>
   <LI><A HREF="empdtl1.cfm?EmployeeID=#EmployeeID#">
➥#LastName#, #FirstName#</A> - Ext. #PhoneExtension#
  </CFOUTPUT>

 </UL>

</CFOUTPUT>

</BODY>

</HTML>
```

The first change you made was adding the DepartmentID column to the SQL SELECT statement, and modifying the sort sequence with ORDER BY DepartmentID, LastName, FirstName. To group results by a column, that column must be the first in the sort sequence. Because we want to sort by DepartmentID, that column is now the first in the ORDER BY list.

The big change, however, is the <CFOUTPUT> block. There are now two of them, one nested inside the other. The outer <CFOUTPUT> tag has a new attribute: GROUP="DepartmentID".

Don't panic—this is explained right now.

A <CFOUTPUT> tag creates a loop that executes once for each row retrieved by a query. When you add the GROUP attribute, you instruct ColdFusion to only execute the <CFOUPUT> block when the group value (the field specified in the GROUP attribute) changes.

If you had seven employees all with the same DepartmentID, the GROUP <CFOUTPUT> block would be executed just once. In our list we have 12 employees who work in 2 departments. The outer <CFOUPUT> block only gets executed twice, once for each department. The first row processed has a DepartmentID of 1, so the <CFOUTPUT> block is executed. The next six rows processed also have a DepartmentID of 1, and so the <CFOUTPUT> block is not executed for them. The eighth row has a different DepartmentID, the value is 2, and so the <CFOUTPUT> block is executed. The next two rows also have a DepartmentID of 2, so no <CFOUTPUT> block is executed for them.

That's just the outer <CFOUTPUT> block. The inner block gets executed for every row, just like the <CFOUTPUT> blocks used earlier.

Now look at the output code in Listing 11.14. The outer <CFOUTPUT> creates a header for each new group and then starts a new unordered list. The inner <CFOUTPUT> populates that list until the group is completed; then the outer <CFOUTPUT> terminates the list and the process loops to the next DepartmentID.

The results are shown in Figure 11.17.

N O T E There is no limit to the number of groupings you can create; you may nest as many CFOUTOUT tags as you need. The only restrictions are in using groups. Firstly, every group must be part of the sort sequence used to retrieve the data. Secondly, the order that the columns appear in the ORDER BY clause must match the order of the groupings. ■

Now you can see why the column you want to group on must be the *first* in the ORDER BY list. For grouping to work, all rows with the same value in the grouping column must be processed as a group. If the group is broken up, as could happen if you did not sort by the grouping column, ColdFusion would execute the outer block at the wrong times, and the resulting groups would fragmented.

Specifying Field Types

You have now used two different types of fields: CGI variables and URL parameters. ColdFusion supports several field types, as shown in Table 11.1, as well as fields that are database table columns retrieved with a <CFQUERY>.

Table 11.1 ColdFusion Field Types

Field	Description
Application	Application scope variables
Attributes	Attributes passed to custom tags
Caller	Caller scope variables
CGI	HTTP CGI variables
Client	Client variables
Cookie	HTTP client-side cookies
Form	HTML form fields
Server	Server scope variables
Session	Session variables
URL	Parameters passed to an URL
Variables	ColdFusion variables

Part
III

Ch
11

In this chapter you use two of these field types and <CFQUERY> results. By the time you have finished reading this book you'll be using them all regularly.

Sooner or later you are going to run into a name collision. For example, you'll have a form field with the same name as a table column, or a variable with the same name as an URL parameter. How does ColdFusion know which one to use when this happens?

ColdFusion doesn't know, but it can make a best guess by using a known order of precedence; either that or you can specify it. You specify this by qualifying the field name with the field type.

Listing 11.15 is the same template you created in Listing 11.15 with one difference. The references to field Name are fully qualified as URL.name. This way, even if you had any other field called Name, ColdFusion would still know which field you were referring to.

Listing 11.15   HELL04.CFM—Avoiding Variable Name Conflicts

```
<HTML>

<HEAD>
<TITLE>Hello!</TITLE>
</HEAD>

<BODY>

Hello,<BR>

<CFIF IsDefined("URL.name")>
 <CFOUTPUT>
 The name you entered is <B>#URL.name#</B>
 </CFOUTPUT>
<CFELSE>
 You did not pass a parameter called NAME
</CFIF>


</BODY>

</HTML>
```

Use your browser to view this template. The resulting display should be exactly the same as the one shown in Figure 11.3. ●

ColdFusion Forms

Using Forms

In Chapter 11, "ColdFusion Basics," you learned how to create ColdFusion templates that dynamically display data retrieved from ODBC data sources. The A2Z Employees table has just 10 rows, so the data fits easily within a Web browser window.

What do you do if you have hundreds or thousands of rows? Displaying all that data in one long list is impractical. Scrolling through lists of names to find the one you want just doesn't work well. The solution is to enable users to search for names by specifying what they are looking for. You can allow them to enter a first name, a last name, or part of a name, and then you can display only the employee records that meet the search criteria.

To accomplish this solution, you need to do two things. First, you need to create your search form using the HTML form tags. Second, you need to create a template that builds SQL SELECT statements dynamically based on the data collected and submitted by the form.

▶ **See** "Creating Queries" for a detailed discussion of SQL statements—specifically the SQL SELECT statement, **p. 140**.

Creating Forms

Before you can create a search form, you need to learn how ColdFusion interacts with HTML forms. Listing 12.1 contains the code for a sample form that prompts for a first and last name. Create this template and save it in the C:\A2Z\SCRIPTS\12 directory as FORM1.CFM.

On the CD

Listing 12.1   FORMS1.CFM—HTML Forms Can Be Used to Collect and Submit Data to ColdFusion for Processing

```
<HTML>

<HEAD>
<TITLE>Learning ColdFusion Forms 1</TITLE>
</HEAD>

<BODY>

<FORM ACTION="forms2.cfm" METHOD="POST">

Please enter your name and then click <B>Process</B>.
<P>
First name:
<INPUT TYPE="text" NAME="FirstName">
<BR>
Last name:
<INPUT TYPE="text" NAME="LastName">
<BR>
<INPUT TYPE="submit" VALUE="Process">

</FORM>

</BODY>

</HTML>
```

In your browser, type **http://*yourserver.com*/a2z/12/FORMS1.cfm** to display the form as shown in Figure 12.1.

This form is simple, with just two data entry fields and a submit button, but it clearly demonstrates how forms are used to submit data to ColdFusion.

FIGURE 12.1

You can use HTML forms to collect data to be submitted to ColdFusion.

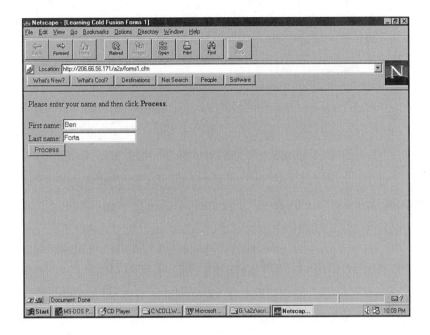

Using HTML Form Tags

You create HTML forms by using the <FORM> tag. <FORM> usually takes two parameters passed as tag attributes. The ACTION attribute specifies the name of the script or program that the Web server should execute in response to the form's submission. To submit a form to ColdFusion, you simply specify the name of the ColdFusion template that will process the form. The following example specifies that the template forms2.cfm should process the submitted form:

```
ACTION="forms2.cfm"
```

The METHOD attribute specifies how data is sent back to the Web server. All ColdFusion forms must be submitted as type POST.

CAUTION

The default submission type is not POST; it is usually GET. If you omit the METHOD="POST" attribute from your form tag, you run the risk of losing form data—particularly in long forms or forms with TEXTAREA controls.

Your form has only two data entry fields: `<INPUT TYPE="text" NAME="FirstName">` and `<INPUT TYPE="text" NAME="LastName">`. Both create simple text fields. The `NAME` attribute in the `<INPUT>` tag specifies the name of the field, and ColdFusion uses this name to refer to the field when it is processed.

Each form in a field is typically given a unique name. If two fields have the same name, both sets of values are returned to be processed and are separated by a comma. You usually want to be able to validate and manipulate each field individually, so each field should have its own name. The notable exceptions are the check box and radio button input types, which are described later in this chapter.

The last item in the form is an `INPUT` submit type. The submit input type creates a button that, when clicked, submits the form contents to the Web server for processing. Almost every form has a submit button (or a graphic image that acts like a submit button). The `VALUE` attribute specifies the text to display within the button, so `<INPUT TYPE="submit" VALUE="Process">` creates a submit button with the text `Process` in it.

TIP When you're using an `INPUT` type of submit, you should always specify button text by using the `VALUE` attribute. If you don't, the default text `Submit Query` (or something similar) is displayed, and this text is likely to confuse your users.

Understanding ColdFusion Error Messages

If you enter your name into the fields and submit the form right now, you receive a ColdFusion error message like the one shown in Figure 12.2. This error says that template `C:\A2Z\SCRIPTS\12\FORMS2.CFM` cannot be found.

FIGURE 12.2

ColdFusion returns an error message when it cannot process your request.

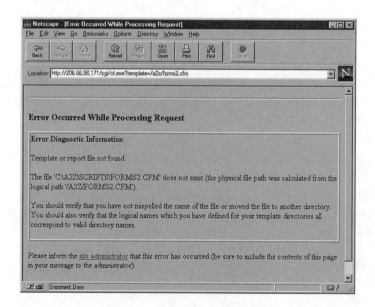

This error message, of course, is perfectly valid. You submitted a form to be passed to ColdFusion and processed with a template, but you have not created that template yet. Your next task, then, is to create a template to process the form submission.

Processing Form Submissions

To demonstrate how to process returned forms, you need to create a simple template that echoes the name you enter. The template is shown in Listing 12.2.

On the CD

Listing 12.2 FORMS2.CFM—Processing Form Fields

```
<HTML>

<HEAD>
<TITLE>Learning ColdFusion Forms 2</TITLE>
</HEAD>

<BODY>

<CFOUTPUT>

Hello #FirstName# #LastName#

</CFOUTPUT>

</BODY>

</HTML>
```

Processing Text Submissions

By now the CFOUTPUT tag should be familiar to you; you use it to mark a block of code that ColdFusion should parse and process. The line Hello #FirstName# #LastName# is processed by ColdFusion. #FirstName# is replaced with the value you entered into the FirstName field, and #LastName# is replaced with the value in the LastName field in Form 1. See Chapter 11 for a detailed discussion of the ColdFusion CFOUTPUT tag.

Create a template called FORMS2.CFM that contains the code in Listing 12.2 and save it in the C:\A2Z\SCRIPTS\12 directory. Resubmit your name by clicking the form's submit button once again. This time you should see a browser display similar to the one shown in Figure 12.3. Whatever name you enter into the First Name and Last Name fields in Form 1 is displayed.

Processing Check Boxes and Option Buttons

Other input types that you will frequently use are check boxes and option buttons. *Check boxes* are used to select options that have one of two states: on or off, yes or no, and true or false. To ask a user if he wants to be notified of book availability via email, for example, you would create a check box field. If the user selects the box, his name is added to the mailing list; if the user does not select the box, his name is not added.

FIGURE 12.3
Submitted form fields may be displayed simply by referring to the field name.

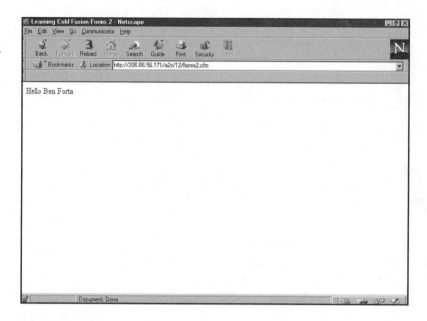

Option buttons are used to select one of at least two mutually exclusive options. You can implement a field prompting for payment type with options such as Cash, Check, Credit card, or P.O., for example, as an option button field.

The code example in Listing 12.3 creates a form that uses both option buttons and check box fields.

On the CD

Listing 12.3   FORMS3.CFM—Using Option Buttons and Check Boxes

```
<HTML>

<HEAD>
<TITLE>Learning ColdFusion Forms 3</TITLE>
</HEAD>

<BODY>

<FORM ACTION="forms4.cfm" METHOD="POST">

Please fill in this form and then click <B>Process</B>.
<P>
Payment type:<BR>
<INPUT TYPE="radio" NAME="PaymentType" VALUE="Cash">Cash<BR>
<INPUT TYPE="radio" NAME="PaymentType" VALUE="Check">Check<BR>
<INPUT TYPE="radio" NAME="PaymentType" VALUE="Credit card">Credit card<BR>
<INPUT TYPE="radio" NAME="PaymentType" VALUE="P.O.">P.O.
<P>
Would you like to be added to our mailing list?
<INPUT TYPE="checkbox" NAME="MailingList" VALUE="Yes">
<P>
```

```
<INPUT TYPE="submit" VALUE="Process">

</FORM>

</BODY>

</HTML>
```

Figure 12.4 shows how this form appears in your browser.

FIGURE 12.4

You can use input types of option buttons and check boxes to facilitate the selection of options.

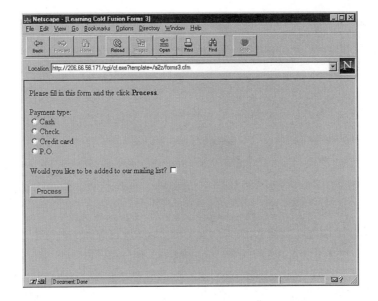

Before you create FORMS4.CFM to process this form, you should note a couple of important points. First look at the four lines of code that make up the Payment Type option button selection. Each one contains the exact same NAME attribute—NAME="PaymentType". The four input fields clearly have the same name, so your browser knows that they are part of the same field. If each option button has a separate name, the browser does not know that these buttons are mutually exclusive and thus allows the selection of more than one button.

Another important point is that, unlike INPUT type text, option buttons have no associated text or data entry area. Therefore, you must use the VALUE attribute in order for the browser to associate a particular value with each option button. The code VALUE="Cash" instructs the browser to return the value Cash in the PaymentType field if that button is selected.

Now that you can accept option button and check box fields, you're ready to create a template to process them. Create a template called FORMS4.CFM in the C:\A2Z\SCRIPTS\12 directory using the template code in Listing 12.4.

Part
III

Ch
12

Listing 12.4 `FORMS4.CFM`—**Processing Option Buttons and Check Boxes**

```
<HTML>

<HEAD>
<TITLE>Learning ColdFusion Forms 4</TITLE>
</HEAD>

<BODY>

<CFOUTPUT>

Hello,<BR>
You selected <B># PaymentType#</B> as your payment type.<BR>
<CFIF #MailingList# IS "Yes">
You will be added to our mailing list.
<CFELSE>
You will not be added to our mailing list.
</CFIF>
</CFOUTPUT>

</BODY>

</HTML>
```

The form processing code in Listing 12.4 displays the payment type you select. The field PaymentType is fully qualified with the FORM field type to prevent name collisions.

▶ **See** "Specifying Field Types" for an explanation of name collisions and how to avoid them, **p. 221**.

When the check box is selected, the value specified in the VALUE attribute is returned; in this case the value is Yes. If the VALUE attribute is omitted, the default value of on is returned.

▶ **See** " Using CFIF to Create Conditional Code" for a complete explanation of the <CFIF> tag and its use, **p. 291**.

Now load form FORMS3.CFM on your browser, select a payment option, and then select the check box. Click the Process button. Your browser display should look like the one shown in Figure 12.5.

That process worked exactly as intended, so now get ready to complicate things a little. Reload template FORMS3.CFM and submit it without selecting a payment type or with the MailingList field not selected. As a result, ColdFusion generates an error message, as shown in Figure 12.6. The field you do not select generates a "Form Field Not Found" error.

Check the code in Listing 12.3 to verify that the form fields do in fact exist. Why does ColdFusion report that the form field does not exist? That is one of the quirks of HTML forms. If you select a check box, the on value is submitted; nothing is submitted if you do not select the check box—not even an empty field. The same is true of option buttons: if you make no selection, the field is not submitted at all. (This behavior is the exact opposite of the text INPUT type, which returns empty fields as opposed to no field.)

FIGURE 12.5
You can use ColdFusion templates to process user-selected options.

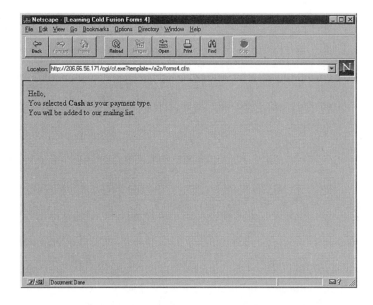

FIGURE 12.6
Option buttons or check boxes that are submitted with no value generate a ColdFusion error.

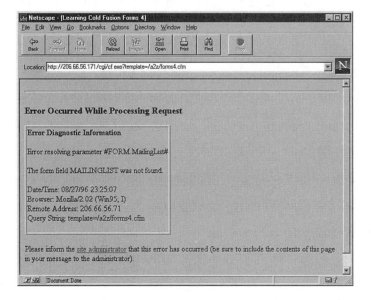

How do you work around this limitation? You can choose from two solutions. The first: Modify your form processing script to check which fields exist by using the #ParameterExists()# function and, if the field exists, process it.

The second: The simpler solution is to prevent the browser from omitting fields that are not selected. You can modify the option button field so that one option is preselected. The users cannot avoid making a option button selection, so they have to make a selection or use the preselected options. To preselect an option button, just add the attribute CHECKED to one of the buttons.

Check boxes are trickier because by their nature they have to be able to be turned off. Check boxes are used for on/off states, and, when the check box is off, there is no value to submit. The solution is to set a default value in the action template. This is done using a ColdFusion tag called <CFPARAM>, which allows you to create variables on-the-fly if they do not already exist. Look at this code:

```
<CFPARAM NAME="MailingList" DEFAULT="No">
```

When ColdFusion encounters this line, it checks to see if a variable named MailingList exists. If yes, processing continues. If it does not exist, ColdFusion creates the variable and sets the value to whatever is specified in the DEFAULT attribute. The key here is that either way—whether the variable existed or not—the variable does exist once the <CFPARAM> tag is processed. It is therefore safe to refer to that variable further down the template code.

The updated form is shown in Listing 12.5. The first option button in the PaymentType field is modified to read <INPUT TYPE="radio" NAME="PaymentType" VALUE="Cash" CHECKED>. The CHECKED attribute ensures that a button is checked. The MailingList check box has a VALUE of Yes when it is checked, and the <CFPARAM> in the action page ensures that if MailingList is not checked, the value will automatically be set to No.

On the CD

Listing 12.5 FORMS5.CFM—**Using Hidden Fields to Set Default Form Values**

```
<HTML>

<HEAD>
<TITLE>Learning ColdFusion Forms 5</TITLE>
</HEAD>

<BODY>

<FORM ACTION="forms4.cfm" METHOD="POST">

Please fill in this form and then click <B>Process</B>.
<P>
Payment type:<BR>
<INPUT TYPE="radio" NAME="PaymentType" VALUE="Cash" CHECKED>Cash<BR>
<INPUT TYPE="radio" NAME="PaymentType" VALUE="Check">Check<BR>
<INPUT TYPE="radio" NAME="PaymentType" VALUE="Credit card">Credit card<BR>
<INPUT TYPE="radio" NAME="PaymentType" VALUE="P.O.">P.O.
<P>
Would you like to be added to our mailing list?
<INPUT TYPE="checkbox" NAME="MailingList" VALUE="Yes">
<P>
<INPUT TYPE="submit" VALUE="Process">

</FORM>

</BODY>

</HTML>
```

Create and save this template as `C:\A2Z\SCRIPTS\12\FORMS5.CFM` and then add the following code to the top of `FORMS4.CFM`:

```
<CFPARAM NAME="MailingList" DEFAULT="No">
```

Try using it and experiment with the two fields. You'll find that this form is reliable and robust, and it does not generate ColdFusion error messages.

Processing List Boxes

Another field type you will frequently use is the list box. Using list boxes is an efficient way to enable users to select one or more options. If a list box is created to accept only a single selection, you can be guaranteed that a value is always returned. If you don't set one of the options to be preselected, the first one in the list is selected. An option always has to be selected.

List boxes that allow multiple selections also allow no selections at all. If you use a multiple selection list box, you once again have to find a way to ensure that ColdFusion does not generate "Form Field Not Found" errors.

Listing 12.6 contains the same data entry form you just created but replaces the option buttons with a list box. Save this template as `C:\A2Z\SCRIPTS\12\FORMS6.CFM` and then test it with your browser.

On the CD

Listing 12.6 FORMS6.CFM—Using a SELECT List Box for User Options

```
<HTML>

<HEAD>
<TITLE>Learning ColdFusion Forms 6</TITLE>
</HEAD>

<BODY>

<FORM ACTION="forms4.cfm" METHOD="POST">

Please fill in this form and then click <B>Process</B>.
<P>
Payment type:
<SELECT NAME="PaymentType">
<OPTION>Cash
<OPTION>Check
<OPTION>Credit card
<OPTION>P.O.
</SELECT>
<P>
Would you like to be added to our mailing list?
<INPUT TYPE="checkbox" NAME="MailingList" VALUE="Yes">
<P>
<INPUT TYPE="submit" VALUE="Process">

</FORM>

</BODY>

</HTML>
```

Part
III

Ch
12

For this particular form, the browser display shown in Figure 12.7 is probably a better user interface. The choice of whether to use option buttons or list boxes is yours, and no hard and fast rules exist as to when to use one versus the other. The following guidelines, however, may help you determine which to use:

- If you need to allow the selection of multiple items or of no items at all, use a list box.
- List boxes take up less screen space. With a list box, one hundred options take up no more precious real estate than a single option.
- Option buttons present all the options to the users without requiring mouse clicks.

FIGURE 12.7
You can use HTML list boxes to select one or more options.

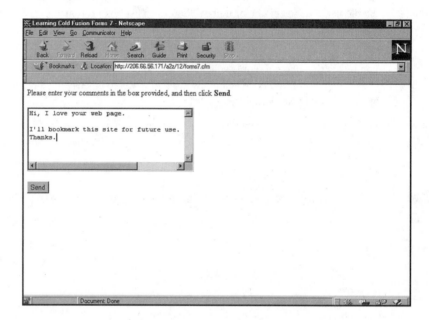

Processing Text Areas

Text area fields are boxes in which the users can enter free-form text. When you create a text area field, you specify the number of rows and columns of screen space it should occupy. This area, however, does not restrict the amount of text that users can enter. The field scrolls both horizontally and vertically to enable the users to enter more text.

Listing 12.7 creates an HTML form with a text area field for user comments. The field's *width* is specified as a number of characters that can be typed on a single line; the *height* is the number of lines that are displayed without scrolling.

The TEXTAREA COLS attribute is specified as a number of characters that can fit on a single line. This setting is dependent on the font in which the text is displayed, and the font is browser specific. Make sure that you test any TEXTAREA fields in more than one browser because a field that fits nicely in one might not fit at all in another.

Listing 12.7   `FORMS7.CFM`—**Using a Text Area Field**

```
<HTML>

<HEAD>
<TITLE>Learning ColdFusion Forms 7</TITLE>
</HEAD>

<BODY>

<FORM ACTION="forms8.cfm" METHOD="POST">

Please enter your comments in the box provided, and then click <B>Send</B>.
<P>
<TEXTAREA NAME="Comments" ROWS="6" COLS="40"></TEXTAREA>
<P>
<INPUT TYPE="submit" VALUE="Send">

</FORM>

</BODY>

</HTML>
```

Listing 12.8 contains ColdFusion code that displays the contents of a TEXTAREA field.

Listing 12.8   `FORMS8.CFM`—**Processing Free-Form Text Area Fields**

```
<HTML>

<HEAD>
<TITLE>Learning ColdFusion Forms 8</TITLE>
</HEAD>

<BODY>

<CFOUTPUT>

Thank you for your comments. You entered:

<P>

<B>#FORM.Comments#</B>

</CFOUTPUT>

</BODY>

</HTML>
```

Figure 12.8 shows the TEXTAREA field you created, and Figure 12.9 shows how ColdFusion displays the field.

Part

III

Ch

12

FIGURE 12.8

The HTML TEXTAREA field is a means by which you can accept free-form text input from users.

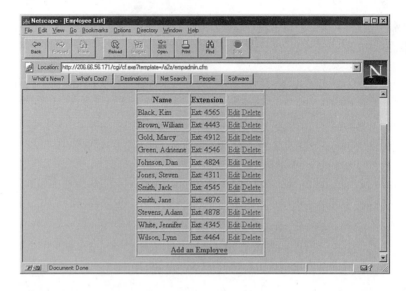

Try entering line breaks (by pressing the Enter key) in the text field and then submit it. What happens to the line breaks? Line break characters are considered whitespace characters, just like spaces, by your browser, and all whitespace is ignored by browsers. "WHITESPACE IS IGNORED" is displayed no differently than "WHITESPACE   IS   IGNORED."

FIGURE 12.9

Without ColdFusion output functions, TEXTAREA fields are not displayed with line breaks preserved.

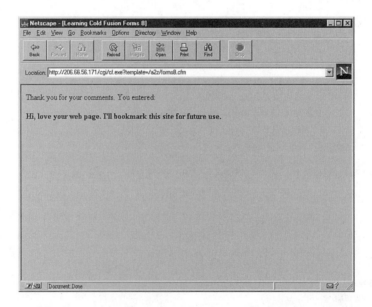

The only way to display line breaks is to replace the line break with an HTML paragraph tag: <P>. You therefore have to parse through the entire field text and insert <P> tags wherever needed. Fortunately, ColdFusion makes this task a simple one. The ColdFusion

`#ParagraphFormat()#` function automatically replaces every double line break with a `<P>` tag. (Single line breaks are not replaced because ColdFusion has no way of knowing if the next line is a new paragraph or part of the previous one.)

TIP The ColdFusion `Replace()` and `ReplaceList()` functions may be used instead of `ParagraphFormat()` in order to have greater control over the paragraph formatting. These functions are explained in Appendix A "ColdFusion Tag Reference."

The code in Listing 12.9 contains the same comments form as the one in Listing 12.7, with two differences. First, default field text is provided. Unlike other INPUT types, `<TEXTAREA>` default text is specified between `<TEXTAREA>` and `</TEXTAREA>` tags—not in a VALUE attribute.

Second, you use the WRAP attribute to wrap text entered into the field automatically. `WRAP="VIRTUAL"` instructs the browser to wrap to the next line automatically, just as most word processors and editors do.

On the CD

Listing 12.9 FORMS9.CFM—**The HTML** TEXTAREA **Field with Wrapping Enabled**

```
<HTML>

<HEAD>
<TITLE>Learning ColdFusion Forms 9</TITLE>
</HEAD>

<BODY>

<FORM ACTION="forms10.cfm" METHOD="POST">

Please enter your comments in the box provided, and then click <B>Send</B>.
<P>
<TEXTAREA NAME="Comments" ROWS="6" COLS="40" WRAP="VIRTUAL">
Replace this text with your comments.
</TEXTAREA>
<P>
<INPUT TYPE="submit" VALUE="Send">

</FORM>

</BODY>

</HTML>
```

N O T E Many browsers do not support the TEXTAREA WRAP attribute. These browsers ignore the attribute and require the users to enter line breaks manually. Because the attribute is ignored when not supported, you can safely use this option when necessary; your forms do not become incompatible with older browsers. ■

Part

III

Ch

12

Listing 12.10 shows the template to display the user-supplied comments. The Comments field code is changed to #ParagraphFormat(FORM.Comments)#, ensuring that all line breaks are maintained and displayed correctly, as shown in Figure 12.10.

On the CD

Listing 12.10   FORMS10.CFM—Using the `ParagraphFormat` Function to Preserve Line Breaks

```
<HTML>

<HEAD>
<TITLE>Learning ColdFusion Forms 10</TITLE>
</HEAD>

<BODY>

<CFOUTPUT>

Thank you for your comments. You entered:

<P>

<B>#ParagraphFormat(FORM.Comments)#</B>

</CFOUTPUT>

</BODY>

</HTML>
```

FIGURE 12.10

You should use the ColdFusion ParagraphFormat() function to display TEXTAREA fields with their line breaks preserved.

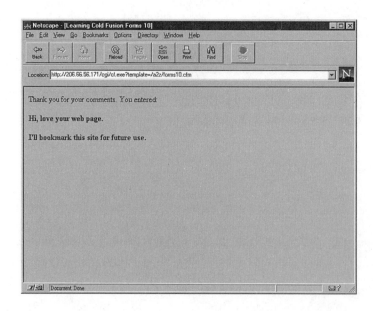

Processing Buttons

The HTML forms specification supports only two types of buttons. Almost all forms, including all the forms that you create in this chapter, have a submit button. Submit, as its name implies, instructs the browser to submit the form fields to a Web server.

The second supported button type is reset. *Reset* clears all form entries and restores default values if any existed. Any text entered into INPUT TYPE="text" or TEXTAREA fields is cleared, as are any check box, list box, and option button selections. Many forms have reset buttons, but you never need more than one.

On the other hand, you may want more than one submit button. For example, if you're using a form to modify a record, you could have two submit buttons: one for Update and one for Delete. (Of course, you also could use two forms to accomplish this task.) If you create multiple submit buttons, you must name the button with the NAME attribute and make sure to assign a different VALUE attribute for each. The code in Listing 12.11 contains a reset button and two submit buttons.

On the CD

Listing 12.11 FORMS12.CFM—Template with a Reset Button and Multiple Submit Buttons

```
<HTML>

<HEAD>
<TITLE>Learning ColdFusion Forms 11</TITLE>
</HEAD>

<BODY>

<FORM ACTION="forms12.cfm" METHOD="POST">

<P>

First name:
<INPUT TYPE="text" NAME="FirstName">
<BR>
Last name:
<INPUT TYPE="text" NAME="LastName">

<P>
<INPUT TYPE="submit" NAME="Operation" VALUE="Update">
<INPUT TYPE="submit" NAME="Operation" VALUE="Delete">
<INPUT TYPE="reset" VALUE="Clear">

</FORM>

</BODY>

</HTML>
```

The result of this code is shown in Figure 12.11.

Part
III

Ch
12

FIGURE 12.11

When you're using multiple submit buttons, you must assign a different value to each button.

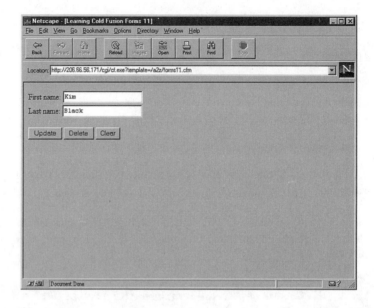

When you name submit buttons, you treat them as any other form field. Listing 12.12 demonstrates how to determine which submit button was clicked. The code `<CFIF FORM.Operation IS "Update">` checks to see if the Update button was clicked, and `<CFELSEIF FORM.Operation IS "Delete">` checks to see if Delete was clicked, but only if Update was not clicked.

Listing 12.12 FORMS12.CFM—**ColdFusion Example of Multiple Submit Button Processing**

```
<HTML>

<HEAD>
<TITLE>Learning ColdFusion Forms 12</TITLE>
</HEAD>

<BODY>

<CFOUTPUT>

<CFIF FORM.Operation IS "Update">
You opted to <B>update</B> #FirstName# #LastName#
<CFELSEIF FORM.Operation IS "Delete">
You opted to <B>delete</B> #FirstName# #LastName#
</CFIF>

</CFOUTPUT>

</BODY>

</HTML>
```

Creating Dynamic SQL Statements

Now that you're familiar with forms and how ColdFusion processes them, you can return to creating an employee search screen. The first screen enables users to search for an employee by last name. To begin, you need an INPUT field of type text. The field name can be anything you want, but using the same name as the table column to which you're comparing the value is generally a good idea.

> **TIP**
>
> When you're creating search screens, you can name your form fields with any descriptive name you want. When you're creating insert and update forms, however, the field name must match the table column names so that ColdFusion knows which field to save with each column. For this reason, you should get into the habit of always naming form fields with the appropriate table column name.

The code in Listing 12.13 contains a simple HTML form, not unlike the test forms you created earlier in this chapter. The form contains a single text field called LastName and a submit button.

On the CD

Listing 12.13 EMPSRCH1.CFM—Code Listing for Employee Search Screen

```
<HTML>

<HEAD>
<TITLE>Employee Search</TITLE>
</HEAD>

<BODY>

<H2>Please enter the last name to search for.</H2>

<FORM ACTION="empsrch2.cfm" METHOD="POST">

Last name: <INPUT TYPE="text" NAME="LastName"><BR>
<P>
<INPUT TYPE="submit" VALUE="Search">

</FORM>

</BODY>

</HTML>
```

Part
III

Ch
12

Save this form as C:\A2Z\SCRIPTS\12\EMPSRCH1.CFM and then go to it with your browser. Your display should look like the one shown in Figure 12.12.

The FORM ACTION attribute specifies which ColdFusion template should be used to process this search. The code ACTION="empsrch2.cfm" instructs ColdFusion to use the template EMPSRCH2.CFM, which is shown in Listing 12.14. Create this template and save it as C:\A2Z\SCRIPTS\12\EMPSRCH2.CFM.

FIGURE 12.12

On the employee search screen, users can search for employees by last name only.

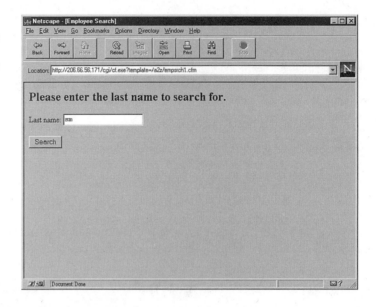

Listing 12.14 `EMPSRCH2.CFM`—**Using a Passed Form Field in a SQL**
WHERE Clause

```
<
CFQUERY
DATASOURCE="A2Z"
NAME="Employees"
>
SELECT FirstName, LastName, PhoneExtension, EmployeeID
FROM Employees
WHERE LastName LIKE '#LastName#%'
ORDER BY LastName, FirstName
</CFQUERY>

<HTML>

<HEAD>
<TITLE>Employee List</TITLE>
</HEAD>

<BODY>

<CENTER>

<TABLE BORDER=5>

<CFOUTPUT QUERY="Employees">
<TR>
<TD>
<A HREF="empdtl2.cfm?EmployeeID=#EmployeeID#">#LastName#, #FirstName#</A>
</TD>
```

```
<TD>
Ext. #PhoneExtension#
</TD>
</TR>
</CFOUTPUT>

</TABLE>

</CENTER>

</BODY>

</HTML>
```

The template begins with a CFQUERY tag that specifies the ODBC data source, the SQL statement to execute, and the name ColdFusion should use to refer to the results set.

The WHERE clause in Listing 12.14 contains a ColdFusion field rather than a static value. When ColdFusion parses templates, it replaces field names with the value contained within the field. If you search for all last names beginning with Sm, the code WHERE LastName LIKE '#LastName#%' becomes WHERE LastName LIKE 'Sm%'. If no search text is specified at all, the clause becomes WHERE LastName LIKE '%'—a wildcard search that finds all records.

▶ **See** "Creating Queries" for a detailed discussion of SQL statements, and specifically the SQL SELECT statement, **p. 140**.

▶ **See** "Creating an ODBC Data Source" for a complete discussion of ODBC data sources and how to create and maintain them, **p. 133**.

▶ **See** "The CFQUERY Tag" for an explanation of the use of the ColdFusion CFQUERY tag, **p. 201**.

You use a LIKE clause to enable users to enter partial names. The clause WHERE LastName = 'Sm' finds only employees whose last names are Sm; users with a last name of Smith are not retrieved. Using a wildcard, as in WHERE LastName LIKE 'Sm%', enables users to also search on partial names.

Try experimenting with different search strings. The sample output should look like the output shown in Figure 12.13. Of course, depending on the search criteria you specify, you'll see different search results.

Listing 12.15 contains the code for template C:\A2Z\SCRIPTS\EMPDTL2.CFM, which is an updated version of the employee detail template you created in the preceding chapter. The template is changed to enable users to send email directly to an employee by clicking his or her email address. You make this action possible by using the mailto identifier, which instructs the browser to open an email window so that the users can enter messages to be sent to the selected address. Look at the following code:

```
<A HREF="mailto:#EMail#">#EMail#</A>
```

Assume employee Kim Black is selected; the code expands into this:

```
<A HREF="mailto:kblack@a2zbooks.com">kblack@a2zbooks.com</A>
```

Part
III

Ch
12

FIGURE 12.13

By building WHERE clauses dynamically, you can create different search conditions on-the-fly.

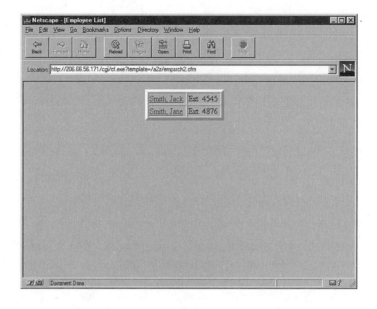

Anyone can click that address to send Kim email. In order to prevent errors, the code is conditional, based on an email address being present. `<CFIF EMail IS NOT "">` evaluates to true only if the EMail field is not empty.

On the CD

Listing 12.15 `EMPDTL2.CFM`—**Passing Parameters to Templates**

```
<
CFQUERY
DATASOURCE="A2Z"
NAME="Employee"
>
 SELECT LastName,
 FirstName,
 MiddleInit,
 Title,
 PhoneExtension,
 PhoneCellular,
 PhonePager,
 EMail
 FROM Employees
 WHERE EmployeeID = #EmployeeID#
</CFQUERY>

<HTML>

<CFOUTPUT QUERY="Employee">

<HEAD>
<TITLE>#LastName#, #FirstName# #MiddleInit#</TITLE>
</HEAD>
```

```
<BODY>

<H1>#LastName#, #FirstName#</H1>

<HR>

Title: #Title#
<BR>
Extension: #PhoneExtension#
<BR>
Cellular: #PhoneCellular#
<BR>
Pager: #PhonePager#
<BR>
E-Mail: <CFIF EMail IS NOT ""><A HREF="mailto:#EMail#">#EMail#</A></CFIF>

</BODY>

</CFOUTPUT>

</HTML>
```

Building Truly Dynamic Statements

When you roll out your employee search screen, you are immediately inundated with requests. "Searching by last name is great, but what about first name or phone extension?" your users ask. Now that you have introduced the ability to search for data, your users want to be able to search on several different fields.

Adding fields to your search screen is simple enough. Add two fields: one for first name and one for phone extension. The code for the updated employee search screen is shown in Listing 12.16.

On the CD

Listing 12.16 EMPSRCH3.CFM—**Employee Search Screen**

```
<HTML>

<HEAD>
<TITLE>Employee Search</TITLE>
</HEAD>

<BODY>

<H2>Please enter your search text below</H2>

<FORM ACTION="empsrch4.cfm" METHOD="POST">

First name: <INPUT TYPE="text" NAME="FirstName"><BR>
Last name: <INPUT TYPE="text" NAME="LastName"><BR>
Extension: <INPUT TYPE="text" NAME="PhoneExtension">
```

continues

Part

III

Ch

12

Listing 12.16 Continued

```
<P>
<INPUT TYPE="submit" VALUE="Search">
<INPUT TYPE="reset" VALUE="Clear">

</FORM>

</BODY>

</HTML>
```

This form enables the users to specify text in one of three different fields, as shown in Figure 12.14.

FIGURE 12.14

The employee search screen is used to locate employee records by name or a part thereof.

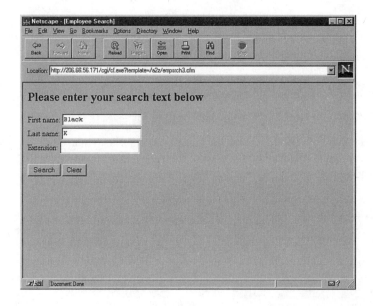

You need to create a search template before you can actually perform a search. The complete search code is shown in Listing 12.17.

Listing 12.17 EMPSRCH4.CFM—Building SQL Statements Dynamically

```
<
CFQUERY
DATASOURCE="A2Z"
NAME="Employees"
>
 SELECT FirstName, LastName, PhoneExtension, EmployeeID
 FROM Employees
```

```
<CFIF FirstName IS NOT "">
 WHERE FirstName LIKE '#FirstName#%'
<CFELSEIF LastName IS NOT "">
 WHERE LastName LIKE '#LastName#%'
<CFELSEIF PhoneExtension IS NOT "">
 WHERE PhoneExtension LIKE '#PhoneExtension#%'
</CFIF>

 ORDER BY LastName, FirstName

</CFQUERY>

<HTML>

<HEAD>
<TITLE>Employee List</TITLE>
</HEAD>

<BODY>

<CENTER>

<TABLE BORDER=5>

<CFOUTPUT>
<TR>
<TH COLSPAN=2>
<H3>Found #Employees.RecordCount# Employees</H3>
</TH>
</TR>
</CFOUTPUT>

<CFOUTPUT QUERY="Employees">
<TR>
<TD>
<A HREF="empdtl2.cfm?EmployeeID=#EmployeeID#">#LastName#, #FirstName#</A>
</TD>
<TD>
Ext. #PhoneExtension#
</TD>
</TR>
</CFOUTPUT>

</TABLE>

</CENTER>

</BODY>

</HTML>
```

Part
III

Ch
12

Understanding Dynamic SQL

Before you actually perform a search, take a closer look at the template in Listing 12.17. The CFQUERY tag is similar to the one you used in the previous search template, but in this one the SQL SELECT statement in the SQL attribute is incomplete. It does not specify a WHERE clause with which to perform a search, nor does it specify a search order. No WHERE clause is specified because the search screen has to support not one, but four search types, as follows:

- If none of the three search fields is specified, no WHERE clause should be used so that all employees can be retrieved.

- If a first name is specified, the WHERE clause needs to filter data to find only employees whose first name starts with the specified text. For example, if John is specified as the search text, the WHERE clause has to be WHERE FirstName LIKE 'John%'.

- If a last name is specified, the WHERE clause needs to filter data to find only employees whose last name starts with the specified search text. If you specify Sm as the last name, the WHERE clause must be WHERE LastName LIKE 'Sm%'.

- If you're searching by phone extension and specify 45 as the search text, a WHERE clause of WHERE PhoneExtension LIKE '45%' is needed.

How can a single search template handle all these search conditions? The answer is dynamic SQL.

When you're creating dynamic SQL statements, you break the statement into separate common SQL and specific SQL. The common SQL is the part of the SQL statement that you always want. The sample SQL statement has two: the SELECT FirstName, LastName, PhoneExtension, EmployeeID FROM Employees and the ORDER BY LastName, FirstName.

The common text is all the SQL statement you need if no search criteria is provided. If, however, search text is specified, the number of possible WHERE clauses is endless.

Take another look at Listing 12.17 to understand the process of creating dynamic SQL statements. The code <CFIF #FirstName# IS NOT ""> checks to see that the FirstName form field is not blank. This condition fails if no text is entered into the FirstName field in the search form, and any code until the next <CFELSE> <CFELSEIF> or </CFIF> is ignored.

▶ **See** "Using CFIF to Create Conditional Code" for a complete explanation of the CFIF tag and its use, **p. 291**.

If a value does appear in the FirstName field, the code WHERE FirstName LIKE '#FirstName#%' is processed and appended to the SQL statement. #FirstName# is a field and is replaced with whatever text is entered into the FirstName field. If John is specified as the first name to search for, this statement translates to WHERE FirstName LIKE 'John%'. This text is appended to the previous SQL statement, which now becomes the following:

```
SELECT FirstName, LastName, PhoneExtension, EmployeeID
FROM Employees WHERE FirstName LIKE 'John%'
```

All you need now is the ORDER BY clause. Even though ORDER BY is fixed and does not change with different searches, it has to be built dynamically because the ORDER BY clause must come after the WHERE clause, if one exists. After ColdFusion processes the code ORDER BY LastName, FirstName, the finished SQL statement reads as follows:

```
SELECT FirstName, LastName, PhoneExtension, EmployeeID
FROM Employees WHERE FirstName LIKE 'John%'
ORDER BY LastName, FirstName
```

▶ **See** "LIKE" for an explanation of the LIKE condition and the % wildcard character, **p. 152**.

N O T E You cannot use double quotation marks in a SQL statement. When ColdFusion encounters a double quotation mark, it thinks it has reached the end of the SQL statement. It then generates an error message because extra text appears where ColdFusion thinks there should be none. To include text strings with the SQL statement, use only single quotation marks. ▪

Similarly, if a last name of Sm is specified as the search text, the complete SQL statement reads as follows:

```
SELECT FirstName, LastName, PhoneExtension, EmployeeID
FROM Employees WHERE LastName LIKE 'Sm%'
ORDER BY LastName, FirstName
```

The code <CFIF FirstName IS NOT ""> evaluates to false because #FirstName# is actually empty; ColdFusion therefore checks the next condition—<CFELSEIF LastName IS NOT "">. This condition evaluates to true because a last name value is provided. ColdFusion then processes the next line, the CFSQL statement, and builds the required SELECT statement.

Processing Search Results

Now that the template is complete and all the code to build dynamic SQL is in place, try performing a search. First try a search without specifying any search criteria at all. Your browser display should look like the one shown in Figure 12.15.

Notice that the number of employees found is displayed at the top of the table. ColdFusion stores the number of rows retrieved with a query in a field called RecordCount. To determine how many rows the Employees query retrieves, you use the code Found #Employees.RecordCount# Employees; just like any other field, ColdFusion replaces it with the actual value.

The RecordCount field is also useful for returning messages or options if a search returns no data at all. For example, the following code displays a message that states that no records are retrieved:

```
<CFIF Employees.RecordCount IS 0>
No employees located, try changing your search criteria.
</CFIF>
```

Try performing different searches via the search form. You can search on any of the fields to retrieve specific records.

FIGURE 12.15

You can use a single template with dynamic SQL to perform an infinite number of searches.

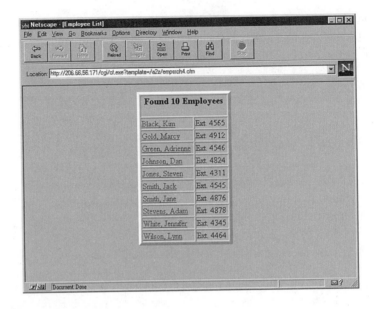

Concatenating SQL Clauses

Now try entering text in both the first name and last name fields. What happens? The answer is not much at all. The dynamic SQL code processes only the first search criteria it encounters. If it finds text in the First Name field, it does not even check the Last Name and Extension fields. If you follow the flow of the <CFIF> statement, you see that as soon as any condition is true, either a <CFIF> or a <CFELSEIF>, ColdFusion ceases processing the condition and jumps to the </CFIF> tag.

How can you search on more than one field? Creating a WHERE clause with an unknown number of conditions is more complicated than the WHERE clauses you created earlier. If a particular condition is the first condition in the clause, you need to precede it with WHERE. If it is not the first condition, you need to precede it with an AND. Of course, you have no idea if any fields will be specified, nor do you know which fields will be specified, if any. How do you construct a dynamic SQL statement like this?

One solution is shown in Listing 12.18. The SQL SELECT statement has a dummy WHERE clause—WHERE EmployeeID = EmployeeID. This condition checks to see if the EmployeeID in a retrieved record matches itself, which, of course, it always does. For example, when the employee with ID 6 is retrieved, the database checks to see if 6=6. Because only one column is being checked and the condition involves no complicated arithmetic or subqueries, the check has almost no performance penalty. If no search criteria is specified, the WHERE clause remains WHERE EmployeeID = EmployeeID and all records are retrieved.

There are three sets of <CFIF> conditions immediately after CFQUERY. Each one determines whether a specific search field is provided; if so, it is appended to the SQL SELECT statement. If

Kim is entered into the first name field, the new WHERE clause is WHERE EmployeeID = EmployeeID AND FirstName LIKE 'Kim%'. This clause correctly filters out only employees whose first name begins with Kim.

Now see what happens if a second field is specified. This example assumes B is entered in the Last Name field. The <CFIF LastName IS NOT ""> evaluates to true because LastName is not empty, and the AND LastName LIKE '#LastName#%' code is added from the LastName filter to the WHERE clause. The new WHERE clause reads WHERE EmployeeID = EmployeeID AND FirstName LIKE 'Kim%' AND LastName LIKE 'B%'. If you execute this search, only Kim Black is found.

To try this code example, save Listing 12.18 as C:\A2Z\SCRIPTS\12\EMPSRCH5.CFM. You also need to modify the FORM ACTION attribute in template EMPSRCH3.CFM so that it specifies EMPSRCH5.CFM as the destination template instead of EMPSRCH4.CFM.

On the CD

Listing 12.18 EMPSRCH5.CFM—**Employee Search Template That Concatenates WHERE Clauses**

```
<
CFQUERY
DATASOURCE="A2Z"
NAME="Employees"
>
SELECT FirstName, LastName, PhoneExtension, EmployeeID
FROM Employees
WHERE EmployeeID = EmployeeID

<CFIF FirstName IS NOT "">
AND FirstName LIKE '#FirstName#%'
</CFIF>

<CFIF LastName IS NOT "">
AND LastName LIKE '#LastName#%'
</CFIF>

<CFIF PhoneExtension IS NOT "">
AND PhoneExtension LIKE '#PhoneExtension#%'
</CFIF>

ORDER BY LastName, FirstName

</CFQUERY>

<HTML>

<HEAD>
<TITLE>Employee List</TITLE>
</HEAD>

<BODY>

<CENTER>
```

Part

III

Ch

12

continues

Listing 12.18 Continued

```
<TABLE BORDER=5>

<CFOUTPUT>
<TR>
<TH COLSPAN=2>
<H3>Found #Employees.RecordCount# Employees</H3>
</TH>
</TR>
</CFOUTPUT>

<CFOUTPUT QUERY="Employees">
<TR>
<TD>
<A HREF="empdtl2.cfm?EmployeeID=#EmployeeID#">#LastName#, #FirstName#</A>
</TD>
<TD>
Ext. #PhoneExtension#
</TD>
</TR>
</CFOUTPUT>

</TABLE>

</CENTER>

</BODY>

</HTML>
```

After you create the template, use your browser to try performing different combinations of searches. You'll find that this new search template is both powerful and flexible. Indeed, this technique for creating truly dynamic SQL SELECT statements will likely be the basis for some sophisticated database interaction in real-world applications.

Creating Dynamic Search Screens

The more power and flexibility you give your users, the more they want. Now they want to search by department, too. For example, they may want to display all the Sales department personnel or find a particular employee by specifying a name within a specific department.

The search screen is simple enough to create. A list of departments is the perfect place to use a list box. You can create a list box with the HTML <SELECT> tag and then list all the departments as <OPTION> tags within.

Before you modify the search template, however, remember that you're creating data-driven applications. You don't want to have to enter the departments manually in the list box. Rather, you want the list box to be driven by the data in the Departments table. This way, you can acquire changes automatically when departments are added or if a department name changes.

The code in Listing 12.19 demonstrates a data-driven form. The CFQUERY at the top of the template should be familiar to you by now. It creates a result set called Departments, which contains the ID and name of each department in the database.

The body of the form is essentially the same as the one you created in Listing 12.16, with the exception of the new DepartmentID field. DepartmentID is a list box that displays the names of all the departments. The <SELECT> tag creates the list box, and it is terminated with the </SELECT> tag. The individual entries in the list box are specified with the <OPTION> tag, but here that tag is within a CFOUTPUT block. This block is executed once for each row retrieved by the CFQUERY, creating an <OPTION> entry for each one.

The code in Listing 12.19 demonstrates the process of building data-driven forms. The SELECT NAME attribute (don't confuse it with the SQL SELECT statement) contains the name of the field, which is the same as the column in the Employees table that you need to compare against. The CFQUERY block creates the individual options, using the ID field as the VALUE and the department name as the description. When ColdFusion processes department 2, the Sales department, the code <OPTION VALUE="#id#">#Department# is translated into <OPTION VALUE="2">Sales.

Also notice that you need to include a blank <OPTION> line in the list box. Remember that list boxes always must have a selection. Save Listing 12.19 as C:\A2Z\SCRIPTS\12\EMPSRCH6.CFM.

On the CD

Listing 12.19 EMPSRCH6.CFM—**Data-Driven Employee Search Template**

```
<
CFQUERY
DATASOURCE="A2Z"
NAME="Departments"
>
SELECT ID, Department
FROM Departments
ORDER BY Department
</CFQUERY>

<HTML>

<HEAD>
<TITLE>Employee Search</TITLE>
</HEAD>

<BODY>

<H2>Please enter your search text below</H2>

<FORM ACTION="empsrch7.cfm" METHOD="POST">

First name: <INPUT TYPE="text" NAME="FirstName"><BR>

Last name: <INPUT TYPE="text" NAME="LastName"><BR>

Extension: <INPUT TYPE="text" NAME="PhoneExtension"><BR>
```

Part

III

Ch

12

continues

Listing 12.19   Continued

```
Department:
<SELECT NAME="DepartmentID">
<OPTION>
<CFOUTPUT QUERY="Departments">
<OPTION VALUE="#id#">#Department#
</CFOUTPUT>
</SELECT>

<P>
<INPUT TYPE="submit" VALUE="Search">
<INPUT TYPE="reset" VALUE="Clear">

</FORM>

</BODY>

</HTML>
```

The completed search screen is shown in Figure 12.16.

FIGURE 12.16

Search forms should use a mixture of input types to create a user-friendly interface.

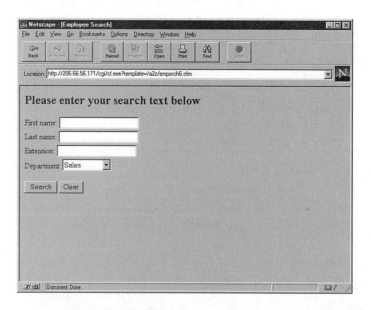

Now you have one last thing left to do: You need to modify the search template to include the new DepartmentID field. The code in Listing 12.20 is updated to include one more possible WHERE condition. The code AND DepartmentID = #DepartmentID# adds the DepartmentID field only if it is specified in the search screen, thereby enabling users to search on as many or as few fields as they want.

Listing 12.20 `EMPSRCH7.CFM`—**Final Employee Search Template**

```
<
CFQUERY
DATASOURCE="A2Z"
NAME="Employees"
>
SELECT FirstName, LastName, PhoneExtension, EmployeeID
FROM Employees
WHERE EmployeeID = EmployeeID


<CFIF FirstName IS NOT "">
AND FirstName LIKE '#FirstName#%'
</CFIF>

<CFIF LastName IS NOT "">
AND LastName LIKE '#LastName#%'
</CFIF>

<CFIF PhoneExtension IS NOT "">
AND PhoneExtension LIKE '#PhoneExtension#%'
</CFIF>

<CFIF DepartmentID IS NOT "">
AND DepartmentID = #DepartmentID#
</CFIF>

ORDER BY LastName, FirstName

</CFQUERY>

<HTML>

<HEAD>
<TITLE>Employee List</TITLE>
</HEAD>

<BODY>

<CENTER>

<TABLE BORDER=5>

<CFOUTPUT>
<TR>
<TH COLSPAN=2>
<H3>Found #Employees.RecordCount# Employees</H3>
</TH>
</TR>
</CFOUTPUT>

<CFOUTPUT QUERY="Employees">
<TR>
<TD>
```

continues

Part
III

Ch
12

Listing 12.20 Continued

```
<A HREF="empdtl2.cfm?EmployeeID=#EmployeeID#">#LastName#, #FirstName#</A>
</TD>
<TD>
Ext. #PhoneExtension#
</TD>
</TR>
</CFOUTPUT>

</TABLE>

</CENTER>

</BODY>

</HTML>
```

The final WHERE condition in Listing 12.20 is different from the prior listing in two ways. First, the condition checks for equality instead of LIKE. The value you're comparing is an ID value—a number—and numbers either match or don't match. Wildcards don't apply to numbers.

Second, no quotation marks appear around the field identifier. The prior three fields all require quotation marks because they are text values. DepartmentID is a number, and numbers don't need quotation marks around them. In fact, if you do put quotation marks around the number, you generate an ODBC error because you're comparing a numeric field to a string. ●

Using Forms to Add or Change Data

Using a Web Browser as a Universal Client

Your online employee list was well received. Everyone has access to up-to-date employee lists and they can search for employees by name, department, or phone extension.

You and your users discover that a Web browser can be used as a front end to access almost any type of data. Using the same front end, a Web browser, makes it easier for people to switch between applications, and greatly lowers the learning curve that each new application introduces. Why? Because there is only one application to learn—the Web browser itself.

The popular term that describes this type of front-end application is *universal client*. This means that the same client application, your Web browser, is used as a front end to multiple applications.

Adding Data with ColdFusion

When you created the employee search forms in Chapter 12, "ColdFusion Forms," you had to create two templates for each search. One created the user search screen that contains the search form, and the other performs the actual search using the ColdFusion <CFQUERY> tag.

Breaking an operation into more than one template is typical of ColdFusion, as well as all Web-based data interaction. As explained in Chapter 2, "Introduction to ColdFusion," a browser's connection to a Web server is made and broken as needed. An HTTP connection is made to a Web server whenever a Web page is retrieved. That connection is broken as soon as that page is retrieved. Any subsequent pages are retrieved with a new connection that is used just to retrieve that page.

There is no way to keep a connection alive for the duration of a complete process—when searching for data, for example. Therefore, the process must be broken up into steps, as you read in Chapter 12, and each step is a separate template.

Adding data via your Web browser is no different. You need at least two templates to perform the insertion. One displays the form that you use to collect the data, and the other processes the data and inserts the record.

Adding data to a table involves the following steps:

1. Display a form to collect the data. The names of any input fields should match the names of the columns in the destination table.
2. Submit the form to ColdFusion for processing. ColdFusion adds the row via the ODBC driver using a SQL statement.

Creating an Add Record Form

Forms used to add data are no different from the forms you created to search for data. The form is created using the standard HTML <FORM> and <INPUT> tags, as shown in Listing 13.1.

Listing 13.1 EMPADD1.CFM—**Template That Adds an Employee**

```
<HTML>

<HEAD>
<TITLE>Add an Employee</TITLE>
</HEAD>

<BODY>

<H1>Add an Employee</H1>

<FORM ACTION="empadd2.cfm" METHOD="POST">

<P>

First name:
<INPUT TYPE="text" NAME="FirstName" SIZE="30" MAXLENGTH="30">
<BR>
Last name:
<INPUT TYPE="text" NAME="LastName" SIZE="30" MAXLENGTH="30">
<BR>
Phone Extension:
<INPUT TYPE="text" NAME="PhoneExtension" SIZE="4" MAXLENGTH="4">

<P>
<INPUT TYPE="submit" VALUE="Add Employee">
<INPUT TYPE="reset" VALUE="Clear">

</FORM>

</BODY>

</HTML>
```

The <FORM> ACTION attribute specifies the name of the template to be used to process the insertion; in this case it's EMPADD2.CFM.

Each <INPUT> field has a field name specified in the NAME attribute. These names correspond to the names of the appropriate columns in the Employees table.

Studio users can take advantage of the built-in drag-and-drop features when using table and column names within your code. Simply open the Resource Tab's Database tab, select the server you are using, open the data source, and expand the tables item to display the list of tables within the data source. You can then drag the table name into your source code. Similarly, expanding the table name displays a list of the fields within that table, and those too can be dragged into your source code.

You also specified the SIZE and MAXLENGTH attributes in each of the text fields. SIZE is used to specify the size of the text box within the browser window. Without the SIZE attribute, the browser uses its default size, which varies from one browser to the next.

The SIZE attribute does not restrict the number of characters that can entered into the field. SIZE="30" creates a text field that occupies the space of 30 characters, but the text scrolls within the field if you enter more than 30 characters. In order to restrict the number of characters that can be entered, you must use the MAXLENGTH attribute. MAXLENGTH="30" instructs the browser to allow no more than 30 characters in the field.

The SIZE attribute is primarily used for aesthetics and the control of screen appearance. MAXLENGTH is used to ensure that only data that can be handled is entered into a field. Without MAXLENGTH, users could enter more data than would fit in a field, and that data would be truncated upon insertion.

You do not have to specify the same SIZE and MAXLENGTH values. The following example only allocates 20 characters of screen space for the field, but allows 30 characters to be entered. Once 20 characters have been entered into the field, the text scrolls to accommodate the extra characters.

```
<INPUT TYPE="text" NAME="FirstName" SIZE="20" MAXLENGTH="30">
```

T I P You should always use both the SIZE and MAXLENGTH attributes for maximum control over form appearance and data entry. Without them, the browser will use its defaults—and there are no rules governing what these defaults should be.

The add employee form is shown in Figure 13.1.

FIGURE 13.1

HTML forms can be used as a front end for data insertion.

Processing Additions

The next thing you need is a template to process the actual data insertion. Use the SQL INSERT statement to add the row.

▶ **See** "Adding Data" for a detailed discussion of the SQL INSERT statement, **p. 156**.

As shown in Listing 13.2, the <CFQUERY> tag can be used to pass any SQL statement—not just SELECT statements. The SQL statement here is INSERT, which adds a row to the Employees table and sets the FirstName, LastName, and PhoneExtension columns to the form values passed by the browser.

Listing 13.2 EMPADD2.CFM—Adding Data with the SQL INSERT Statement

```
<CFQUERY DATASOURCE="A2Z">
INSERT INTO Employees(FirstName, LastName, PhoneExtension)
VALUES('#FirstName#', '#LastName#', '#PhoneExtension#')
</CFQUERY>

<HTML>

<HEAD>
<TITLE>Employee Added</TITLE>
</HEAD>

<BODY>

<H1>Employee Added</H1>

<CFOUTPUT>
Employee <B>#FirstName# #LastName#</B> added.
</CFOUTPUT>

</BODY>

</HTML>
```

N O T E Notice that the <CFQUERY> in Listing 13.2 has no NAME attribute. NAME is an optional attribute and is only necessary if you need to manipulate the data returned by <CFQUERY>. Because the operation here is an INSERT, no data is returned; the NAME attribute is unnecessary. ▪

Save this template as **C:\A2Z\SCRIPTS\13\EMPADD2.CFM** and then execute the EMPADD1.CFM template with your browser. Try adding an employee to the table; your browser display should look like the one shown in Figure 13.2.

You can verify that the employee was added by browsing the table with Microsoft Access, Microsoft Query, or any of the employee search templates that you created in the previous chapter.

FIGURE 13.2

Data can be adding via
ColdFusion using the
SQL INSERT statement.

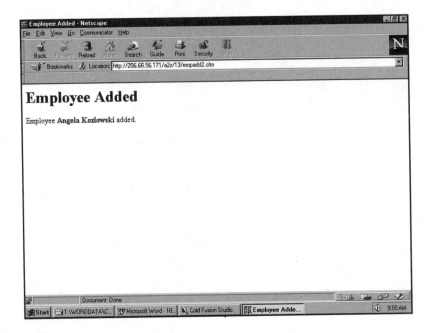

Introducing <CFINSERT>

The example in Listing 13.2 demonstrates how to add data to a table using the standard SQL INSERT command. This works very well if you only have to provide data for a few columns, and if those columns are always provided. If the number of columns can vary, using SQL INSERT gets rather complicated.

For example, assume you have two or more data entry forms for similar data. One might collect a minimal number of fields, while another collects a more complete record. How would you create a SQL INSERT statement to handle both sets of data?

You could create two separate templates, with a different SQL INSERT statement in each, but that's a situation you should always try to avoid. As a rule, you should try to avoid having more than one template perform a given operation. That way you don't run the risk of future changes and revisions being applied incorrectly. If a table name or column name changes, for example, you won't have to worry about forgetting one of the templates that references the changed column.

TIP As a rule, you should never create more than one template to perform a specific operation. This helps prevent introducing errors into your templates when updates or revisions are made. You are almost always better off creating one template with conditional code than creating two separate templates.

Another solution is to use dynamic SQL. You could write a basic INSERT statement and then gradually construct a complete statement by using a series of <CFIF> statements.

While this might be a workable solution, it is not a very efficient one. The conditional SQL INSERT code is far more complex than conditional SQL SELECT. The INSERT statement requires that both the list of columns and the values be dynamic. In addition, the INSERT syntax requires that you separate all column names and values by commas. This means that every column name and value must be followed by a comma—except the last one in the list. Your conditional SQL has to accommodate these syntactical requirements when the statement is constructed.

A better solution is to use `<CFINSERT>`, which is a special ColdFusion tag that hides the complexity of building dynamic SQL INSERT statements. `<CFINSERT>` takes the following parameters as attributes:

- DATASOURCE is the name of the ODBC data source that contains the table to which the data is to be inserted.
- TABLENAME is the name of the destination table.
- FORMFIELDS is an optional comma-separated list of fields to be inserted. If this attribute is not provided, all the fields in the submitted form are used.

Look at the following ColdFusion tag:

```
<CFINSERT DATASOURCE="A2Z" TABLENAME="Employees">
```

This code does exactly the same thing as the `<CFQUERY>` tag in Listing 13.2. When ColdFusion processes a `<CFINSERT>` tag it builds a dynamic SQL INSERT statement under the hood. If a FORMFIELDS attribute is provided, the specified field names are used. No FORMFIELDS attribute was specified in this example, so ColdFusion automatically uses the form fields that were submitted, building the list of columns and the values dynamically (see Listing 13.3).

Listing 13.3 `C:\A2Z\SCRIPTS\13\EMPADD3.CFM`—**Adding Data with the `<CFINSERT>` Tag**

```
<CFINSERT DATASOURCE="A2Z" TABLENAME="Employees">

<HTML>

<HEAD>
<TITLE>Employee Added</TITLE>
</HEAD>

<BODY>

<H1>Employee Added</H1>

<CFOUTPUT>
Employee <B>#FirstName# #LastName#</B> added.
</CFOUTPUT>

</BODY>

</HTML>
```

Try modifying the form in template EMPADD1.CFM so that it submits the form to template EMPADD3.CFM instead of EMPADD2.CFM; then add a record. You'll see the code in Listing 13.3 does exactly the same thing as the code in Listing 13.2, but with a much simpler syntax and interface.

Of course, because <CFINSERT> builds its SQL statements dynamically, EMPADD3.CFM can be used even if you add fields to the data entry form. Listing 13.4 contains an updated template that adds several fields to the Add an Employee form. Even so, it submits data to the same template that you just created. Using <CFINSERT> allows for a cleaner action template—one that does not require changing every time the form itself changes.

Listing 13.4 EMPADD4.CFM—Template That Adds an Employee

```
<HTML>

<HEAD>
<TITLE>Add an Employee</TITLE>
</HEAD>

<BODY>

<H1>Add an Employee</H1>

<FORM ACTION="empadd3.cfm" METHOD="POST">

<P>

First name:
<INPUT TYPE="text" NAME="FirstName" SIZE="30" MAXLENGTH="30">
Middle Initial:
<INPUT TYPE="text" NAME="MiddleInit" SIZE="1" MAXLENGTH="1">
<BR>
Last name:
<INPUT TYPE="text" NAME="LastName" SIZE="30" MAXLENGTH="30">
<BR>
Title:
<INPUT TYPE="text" NAME="Title" SIZE="20" MAXLENGTH="20">
<BR>
Phone Extension:
<INPUT TYPE="text" NAME="PhoneExtension" SIZE="4" MAXLENGTH="4">
<BR>
E-Mail:
<INPUT TYPE="text" NAME="EMail" SIZE="30" MAXLENGTH="30">

<P>
<INPUT TYPE="submit" VALUE="Add Employee">
<INPUT TYPE="reset" VALUE="Clear">

</FORM>

</BODY>

</HTML>
```

Try adding an employee using this new form, your browser display should look no different than it did before.

When to Use <CFINSERT> Form Fields

<CFINSERT> instructs ColdFusion to build SQL INSERT statements dynamically. ColdFusion automatically uses all submitted form fields when building this statement.

Sometimes you might want ColdFusion to not include certain fields. For example, you might have hidden fields in your form that are not table columns, like the hidden field shown in Listing 13.5. That field might be there as part of a security system you have implemented; it is not a column in the table. If you try to pass this field to <CFINSERT>, ColdFusion passes the hidden Login field as a column. Obviously this generates an ODBC error, as seen in Figure 13.3.

Listing 13.5 EMPADD5.CFM—Template That Adds an Employee

```
<HTML>

<HEAD>
<TITLE>Add an Employee</TITLE>
</HEAD>

<BODY>

<H1>Add an Employee</H1>

<FORM ACTION="empadd3.cfm" METHOD="POST">

<INPUT TYPE="hidden" NAME="Login" VALUE="Bob">

<P>

First name:
<INPUT TYPE="text" NAME="FirstName" SIZE="30" MAXLENGTH="30">
Middle Initial:
<INPUT TYPE="text" NAME="MiddleInit" SIZE="1" MAXLENGTH="1">
<BR>
Last name:
<INPUT TYPE="text" NAME="LastName" SIZE="30" MAXLENGTH="30">
<BR>
Title:
<INPUT TYPE="text" NAME="Title" SIZE="20" MAXLENGTH="20">
<BR>
Phone Extension:
<INPUT TYPE="text" NAME="PhoneExtension" SIZE="4" MAXLENGTH="4">
<BR>
E-Mail:
<INPUT TYPE="text" NAME="EMail" SIZE="30" MAXLENGTH="30">

<P>
<INPUT TYPE="submit" VALUE="Add Employee">
<INPUT TYPE="reset" VALUE="Clear">

</FORM>

</BODY>

</HTML>
```

Part
III

Ch
13

FIGURE 13.3

A ODBC error message is generated if ColdFusion tries to insert fields that are not table columns.

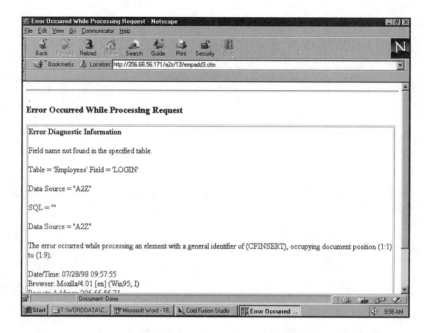

In order to solve this problem you must use the FORMFIELDS attribute. FORMFIELDS instructs ColdFusion to only process form fields that are in the list. Any other fields are ignored.

It is important to note that FORMFIELDS is not used to specify which fields ColdFusion should process. Rather, it specifies which fields should not be processed. The difference is subtle. Not all fields listed in the FORMFIELDS value need be present. They are processed if they are present; if they are not present, they are not processed. Any fields that are not listed in the FORMFIELDS list are ignored.

Listing 13.6 contains an updated data insertion template. The <CFINSERT> tag now has a FORMFIELDS attribute, and so now ColdFusion knows to ignore the hidden Login field in EMPADD5.CFM. The following code ensures that only these fields are processed, and that any others are ignored:

```
FORMFIELDS="FirstName, MiddleInit, LastName, Title, PhoneExtension, EMail"
```

Listing 13.6   EMPADD6.CFM—**Using the** CFINSERT FORMFIELDS **Attribute to Specify Which Fields to Avoid Processing**

```
<CFINSERT
 DATASOURCE="A2Z"
 TABLENAME="Employees"
 FORMFIELDS="FirstName, MiddleInit, LastName, Title, PhoneExtension, EMail"
>

<HTML>
```

```
<HEAD>
<TITLE>Employee Added</TITLE>
</HEAD>

<BODY>

<H1>Employee Added</H1>

<CFOUTPUT>
Employee <B>#FirstName# #LastName#</B> added.
</CFOUTPUT>

</BODY>

</HTML>
```

Collecting Data for More Than One INSERT

Another situation in which <CFINSERT> FORMFIELDS can be used is when a form collects data that needs to be added to more than one table. You can create a template that has two or more <CFINSERT> statements by using FORMFIELDS.

As long as each <CFINSERT> statement has a FORMFIELDS attribute that specifies which fields are to be used with each INSERT, ColdFusion correctly executes each <CFINSERT> with its appropriate fields.

<CFINSERT> Versus SQL INSERT

Adding data to tables using the ColdFusion <CFINSERT> tag is both simpler and helps prevent the creation of multiple similar templates.

Why would you ever avoid using <CFINSERT>? Is there ever a reason to use SQL INSERT instead of <CFINSERT>?

The truth is that both are needed. <CFINSERT> can only be used for simple data insertion to a single table. If you want to insert the results of a SELECT statement, you could not use <CFINSERT>. Similarly, if you want to insert values other than FORM fields—perhaps variables or URL parameters—you'd be unable to use <CFINSERT>.

Here are some guidelines to help you decide when to use each method:

1. Whenever possible, use <CFINSERT> to add data to ODBC tables.
2. If you find that you need to add specific form fields—and not all that were submitted—use the <CFINSERT> tag with the FORMFIELDS attribute.
3. If <CFINSERT> cannot be used because you need a complex INSERT statement or are using fields that are not form fields, use SQL INSERT.

Part
III

Ch
13

Updating Data with ColdFusion

Updating data with ColdFusion is very similar to inserting data. You need two templates to update a row—a data entry form template and a data update template. The big difference between a form used for data addition and one used for data modification is that the latter needs to be populated with existing values, like the screen shown in Figure 13.4.

FIGURE 13.4

When using forms to update data, the form fields usually need to populated with existing values.

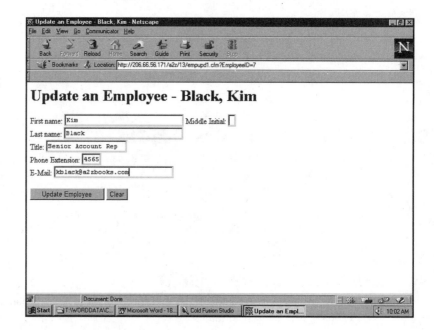

Building a Data Update Form

Populating an HTML form is a very simple process. First you need to retrieve the row to be updated from the table. You do this with a standard <CFQUERY>; the retrieved values are then passed as attributes to the HTML form.

▶ **See** "The CFQUERY Tag" for a detailed discussion of the ColdFusion CFQUERY tag and how it is used, **p. 201**.

Listing 13.7 contains the code for EMPUPD1.CFM, a template that updates an employee record. You must specify an employee ID to test this template. Without it, ColdFusion would not know what row to retrieve. To ensure that an employee ID is passed, the first thing you do is check for the existence of the EmployeeID parameter. The following code returns TRUE only if EmployeeID was not passed, in which case an error message is sent back to the user and template processing is halted with the <CFABORT> tag:

```
<CFIF IsDefined("EmployeeID") IS "No">
```

Without the <CFABORT> tag, ColdFusion continues processing the template. An error message is generated when the <CFQUERY> statement is processed because the WHERE clause WHERE EmployeeID = #EmployeeID# references a nonexistent field.

Test the EMPUPD1.CFM template, passing ?EmployeeID=7 as an URL parameter. Your screen should look like the one shown in Figure 13.4.

Listing 13.7 EMPUPD1.CFM—**Template That Updates an Employee**

```
<CFIF IsDefined("EmployeeID") IS "No">
 Error! No EmployeeID was specified!
 <CFABORT>
</CFIF>

<CFQUERY DATASOURCE="A2Z" NAME="Employee">
 SELECT FirstName,
        MiddleInit,
        LastName,
        Title,
        PhoneExtension,
        EMail
 FROM Employees
 WHERE EmployeeID = #EmployeeID#
</CFQUERY>

<CFOUTPUT QUERY="Employee">

<HTML>

<HEAD>
<TITLE>Update an Employee - #LastName#, #FirstName#</TITLE>
</HEAD>

<BODY>

<H1> Update an Employee - #LastName#, #FirstName#</H1>

<FORM ACTION="empupd2.cfm" METHOD="POST">

<INPUT TYPE="hidden" NAME="EmployeeID" VALUE="#EmployeeID#">

<P>

First name:
<INPUT TYPE="text" NAME="FirstName" SIZE="30" MAXLENGTH="30"
➥ VALUE="#Trim(FirstName)#">
Middle Initial:
<INPUT TYPE="text" NAME="MiddleInit" SIZE="1" MAXLENGTH="1"
➥ VALUE="#Trim(MiddleInit)#">
<BR>
Last name:
<INPUT TYPE="text" NAME="LastName" SIZE="30" MAXLENGTH="30"
➥ VALUE="#Trim(LastName)#">
<BR>
Title:
<INPUT TYPE="text" NAME="Title" SIZE="20" MAXLENGTH="20" VALUE="#Trim(Title)#">
<BR>
Phone Extension:
```

Part
III

Ch
13

continues

Listing 13.7   Continued

```
<INPUT TYPE="text" NAME="PhoneExtension" SIZE="4" MAXLENGTH="4"
➥ VALUE="#Trim(PhoneExtension)#">
<BR>
E-Mail:
<INPUT TYPE="text" NAME="EMail" SIZE="30" MAXLENGTH="30" VALUE="#Trim(EMail)#">

<P>
<INPUT TYPE="submit" VALUE="Update Employee">
<INPUT TYPE="reset" VALUE="Clear">

</FORM>

</BODY>

</HTML>

</CFOUTPUT>
```

Before you create the data update template, take a closer look at Listing 13.7. The template is similar to the Add an Employee template, but has some important differences.

The first thing you do is verify that the primary key, EmployeeID, is present. ColdFusion can then retrieve the employee data with the <CFQUERY> tag. The WHERE clause WHERE EmployeeID = #EmployeeID# selects data by the primary key value, ensuring that no more than one row will ever be retrieved. The rest of the template is contained with a <CFOUTPUT> tag, allowing you to use any of the retrieved columns within the page body.

▶ **See** "Primary and Foreign Keys" for a detailed discussion of table keys and how they uniquely identify every row in a table, **p. 96**.

▶ **See** "Displaying Query Results with the CFOUTPUT Tag" for an explanation of that particular tag, **p. 202**.

The retrieved data is used throughout the template. Even the page title is dynamically created with the code <TITLE>Update an Employee - #LastName#, #FirstName#</TITLE>.

To populate the data entry fields, the current field value is passed to the <INPUT> VALUE attribute. For employee 7, Kim Black, this code

```
<INPUT TYPE="text" NAME="FirstName" SIZE="30" MAXLENGTH="30"
VALUE="#Trim(FirstName)#">
```

becomes this

```
<INPUT TYPE="text" NAME="FirstName" SIZE="30" MAXLENGTH="30" VALUE="Kim">
```

When the FirstName field is displayed, the name Kim appears in it.

To ensure that there are no blank spaces after the retrieved value, the fields are trimmed with the ColdFusion Trim() function before they are displayed. Why would you do this? Some databases, such as Microsoft SQL Server, pad text fields with spaces so that they take up the full column width in the table. The FirstName field is a 30-character–wide column, and so the name

Kim is retrieved with 27 spaces after it! The extra space can be very annoying when you try to edit the field. To append text to a field, you'd first have to backspace or delete all of those extra characters.

 TIP

When populating forms with table column values, it is a good idea to always trim the field first. Unlike standard browser output, spaces in form fields are not ignored. Removing them allows easier editing. The ColdFusion Trim() function removes spaces at the beginning and end of the value. If you want to only trim trailing spaces, you could use the RTrim() function instead. See Appendix A, "ColdFusion Tag Reference," for a complete explanation of the ColdFusion Trim() functions.

There is one hidden field in the FORM. The following code creates a hidden field called EmployeeID, which contains the ID of the employee being updated:

```
<INPUT TYPE="hidden" NAME="EmployeeID" VALUE="#EmployeeID#">
```

This hidden field must be present. Without it, ColdFusion has no idea what row you were updating when the form was actually submitted.

Remember that HTTP sessions are created and broken as needed, and every session stands on its own two feet. ColdFusion retrieved a specific row of data for you in one session, but it does not know that in the next session. Therefore, when you update a row, you must specify the primary key so that ColdFusion knows which row to update.

Processing Updates

Just as with adding data, there are two ways to update rows in a table. The code in Listing 13.8 demonstrates a row update using the SQL UPDATE statement.

◊ **See** "Modifying Data" for a detailed discussion of the SQL UPDATE statement, **p. 163**.

> **Listing 13.8** EMPUPD2.CFM—**Updating Table with the SQL UPDATE Statement**

```
<CFQUERY DATASOURCE="A2Z">
 UPDATE Employees
 SET FirstName='#FirstName#',
     MiddleInit='#MiddleInit#',
     LastName='#LastName#',
     Title='#Title#',
     PhoneExtension='#PhoneExtension#',
     EMail='#EMail#'
 WHERE EmployeeID = #EmployeeID#
</CFQUERY>

<CFOUTPUT>

<HTML>

<HEAD>
<TITLE>Employee #LastName#, #FirstName# Updated</TITLE>
</HEAD>
```

Part III

Ch 13

continues

Listing 13.8   Continued

```
<BODY>

<H1> Employee #LastName#, #FirstName# Updated </H1>

</BODY>

</HTML>

</CFOUTPUT>
```

This SQL statement updates the six specified rows for the employee whose ID is the passed EmployeeID.

To test this update template, try executing template EMPUPD1.CFM with different EmployeeID values (pass as URL parameters), and then submit your changes.

Introducing <CFUPDATE>

Just as you saw earlier in regards to inserting data, hard-coded SQL statements are neither flexible nor easy to maintain. ColdFusion provides a simpler way to update rows in database tables.

The <CFUPDATE> tag is very similar to the <CFINSERT> tag discussed earlier in this chapter. <CFUPDATE> requires just two attributes: the ODBC data source and the name of the table to update.

Just like <CFINSERT>, the following attributes are available to you:

■ DATASOURCE is the name of the ODBC data source that contains the table to which the data is to be updated.

■ TABLENAME is the name of the destination table.

■ FORMFIELDS is an optional comma-separated list of fields to be updated. If this attribute is not provided, all the fields in the submitted form are used.

When using <CFUPDATE>, ColdFusion automatically locates the row you want to update by looking at the table to ascertain its primary key. All you have to do is make sure that primary key value is passed, as you did in Listing 13.7 using a hidden field.

The code in Listing 13.9 performs the same update as that in Listing 13.8, but uses the <CFUPDATE> tag rather than the SQL UPDATE tag. Obviously this code is both more readable, reusable, and accommodating of form field changes you might make in the future.

Listing 13.9   EMPUPD3.CFM—Updating Data with the CFUPDATE Tag

```
<CFUPDATE DATASOURCE="A2Z" TABLENAME="Employees">

<CFOUTPUT>
```

```
<HTML>

<HEAD>
<TITLE>Employee #LastName#, #FirstName# Updated</TITLE>
</HEAD>

<BODY>

<H1> Employee #LastName#, #FirstName# Updated </H1>

</BODY>

</HTML>

</CFOUTPUT>
```

You have to change the <FORM> ACTION attribute in EMPUPD1.CFM in order to use EMPUP3.CFM to test this form. Make this change and try updating several employee records.

CFUPDATE Versus SQL UPDATE

Just as with adding data, the choice to use <CFUPDATE> or SQL UPDATE is yours. The guidelines as to when to use each option are similar as well.

The following are some guidelines that help you decide when to use each method:

1. Whenever possible, use <CFUPDATE> to update data to ODBC tables.

2. If you find that you need to update specific form fields—not all that were submitted—use the <CFUPDATE> tag with the FORMFIELDS attribute.

3. If <CFUPDATE> cannot be used because you need a complex UPDATE statement or you are using fields that are not form fields, use SQL UPDATE.

4. If you ever need to update all rows in a table, you must use SQL UPDATE.

Deleting Data with ColdFusion

Unlike adding and updating data, ColdFusion provides no efficient way to delete data. DELETE is always a dangerous operation, and ColdFusion developers didn't want to make it too easy to get rid of the wrong data.

To delete data in a ColdFusion template you must use the SQL DELETE statement, as shown in Listing 13.10. The code first checks to ensure that an employee ID was passed; it terminates if the EmployeeID field is not present. If an employee ID is passed, a <CFQUERY> is used to pass a SQL DELETE statement to the ODBC data source.

▶ **See** "Deleting Data" for a detailed discussion of the SQL DELETE statement, **p. 166**.

Part
III

Ch
13

Listing 13.10   EMPDEL1.CFM—Deleting Table Data with the SQL DELETE Statement

```
<CFIF IsDefined("EmployeeID") IS "No">
 Error! No EmployeeID was specified!
 <CFABORT>
</CFIF>

<CFQUERY DATASOURCE="A2Z">
 DELETE FROM Employees
 WHERE EmployeeID = #EmployeeID#
</CFQUERY>

<HTML>

<HEAD>
<TITLE>Employee Deleted</TITLE>
</HEAD>

<BODY>

<H1>Employee Deleted</H1>

</BODY>

</HTML>
```

The following code deletes the record for the employee ID passed:

```
DELETE Employees WHERE EmployeeID = #EmployeeID#
```

If EmployeeID were 7, the code would translate to the following and the employee with an employee ID of 7 would be deleted from the Employees table:

```
DELETE Employees WHERE EmployeeID = 7
```

Reusing Forms

You can now add to as well as update and delete from your Employees table—but nothing lasts. Just when you thought you could relax and take a day off, Human Resources needs you to provide access to additional table columns.

You start to modify both the Employee Add and the Employee Update forms. You make sure that the additional five fields are added to both templates and that they are in the same order, spelled the same way, and are the exact same length.

Then you realize that you are doing everything twice! There is really very little difference between the Add and Update forms, except that one needs existing values pre-filled for updating. The form itself is identical.

With all the effort you have gone to in the past few chapters to prevent any duplication of effort, this seems counterproductive.

Indeed it is.

The big difference between an Add and an Update form is whether the fields are pre-filled to show current values. Using ColdFusion conditional expressions, you can create a single form that can be used for both adding and updating data.

A new and improved Add and Update form is shown in Listing 13.11.

Listing 13.11 EMPAU1.CFM—**Template That Displays an Employee Add or an Employee Update Form**

```
<CFIF IsDefined("EmployeeID")>
 <CFSET NewRecord = "No">
<CFELSE>
 <CFSET NewRecord = "Yes">
</CFIF>

<CFIF NewRecord IS "No">
 <CFQUERY DATASOURCE="A2Z" NAME="Employee">
  SELECT FirstName,
         MiddleInit,
         LastName,
         Address1,
         Address2,
         City,
         State,
         Zip,
         Title,
         PhoneExtension,
         EMail
  FROM Employees
  WHERE EmployeeID = #EmployeeID#
 </CFQUERY>
</CFIF>

<HTML>

<HEAD>

<CFIF NewRecord IS "Yes">
 <TITLE>Add an Employee</TITLE>
<CFELSE>
 <CFOUTPUT QUERY="Employee">
  <TITLE>Update an Employee - #LastName#, #FirstName#</TITLE>
 </CFOUTPUT>
</CFIF>

</HEAD>

<BODY>

<H1>
<CFIF NewRecord IS "Yes">
```

Part

III

Ch

13

continues

Listing 13.11   Continued

```
 Add an Employee
<CFELSE>
 <CFOUTPUT QUERY="Employee">
  Update an Employee - #LastName#, #FirstName#
 </CFOUTPUT>
</CFIF>
</H1>

<FORM ACTION="empau2.cfm" METHOD="POST">

<CFIF NewRecord IS "No">
 <CFOUTPUT QUERY="Employee">
  <INPUT TYPE="hidden" NAME="EmployeeID" VALUE="#EmployeeID#">
 </CFOUTPUT>
</CFIF>

<P>

First name:
<INPUT TYPE="text" NAME="FirstName" SIZE="30" MAXLENGTH="30"
 <CFIF NewRecord IS "No">
  <CFOUTPUT QUERY="Employee">VALUE="#Trim(FirstName)#"</CFOUTPUT>
 </CFIF>
>
Middle Initial:
<INPUT TYPE="text" NAME="MiddleInit" SIZE="1" MAXLENGTH="1"
 <CFIF NewRecord IS "No">
  <CFOUTPUT QUERY="Employee">VALUE="#Trim(MiddleInit)#"</CFOUTPUT>
 </CFIF>
>
<BR>
Last name:
<INPUT TYPE="text" NAME="LastName" SIZE="30" MAXLENGTH="30"
 <CFIF NewRecord IS "No">
  <CFOUTPUT QUERY="Employee">VALUE="#Trim(LastName)#"</CFOUTPUT>
 </CFIF>
>
<BR>
Address:
<INPUT TYPE="text" NAME="Address1" SIZE="50" MAXLENGTH="50"
 <CFIF NewRecord IS "No">
  <CFOUTPUT QUERY="Employee">VALUE="#Trim(Address1)#"</CFOUTPUT>
 </CFIF>
>
<BR>
<INPUT TYPE="text" NAME="Address2" SIZE="50" MAXLENGTH="50"
 <CFIF NewRecord IS "No">
  <CFOUTPUT QUERY="Employee">VALUE="#Trim(Address2)#"</CFOUTPUT>
 </CFIF>
>
<BR>
City:
<INPUT TYPE="text" NAME="Address1" SIZE="40" MAXLENGTH="40"
```

```
   <CFIF NewRecord IS "No">
    <CFOUTPUT QUERY="Employee">VALUE="#Trim(City)#"</CFOUTPUT>
   </CFIF>
>
<BR>
State:
<INPUT TYPE="text" NAME="State" SIZE="5" MAXLENGTH="5"
   <CFIF NewRecord IS "No">
    <CFOUTPUT QUERY="Employee">VALUE="#Trim(State)#"</CFOUTPUT>
   </CFIF>
>
<BR>
Zip:
<INPUT TYPE="text" NAME="Zip" SIZE="10" MAXLENGTH="10"
   <CFIF NewRecord IS "No">
    <CFOUTPUT QUERY="Employee">VALUE="#Trim(Zip)#"</CFOUTPUT>
   </CFIF>
>
<BR>
Title:
<INPUT TYPE="text" NAME="Title" SIZE="20" MAXLENGTH="20"
   <CFIF NewRecord IS "No">
    <CFOUTPUT QUERY="Employee">VALUE="#Trim(Title)#"</CFOUTPUT>
   </CFIF>
>
<BR>
Phone Extension:
<INPUT TYPE="text" NAME="PhoneExtension" SIZE="4" MAXLENGTH="4"
   <CFIF NewRecord IS "No">
    <CFOUTPUT QUERY="Employee">VALUE="#Trim(PhoneExtension)#"</CFOUTPUT>
   </CFIF>
>
<BR>
E-Mail:
<INPUT TYPE="text" NAME="EMail" SIZE="30" MAXLENGTH="30"
   <CFIF NewRecord IS "No">
    <CFOUTPUT QUERY="Employee">VALUE="#Trim(EMail)#"</CFOUTPUT>
   </CFIF>
>

<P>
<CFIF NewRecord IS "Yes">
 <INPUT TYPE="submit" VALUE="Add Employee">
<CFELSE>
 <INPUT TYPE="submit" VALUE="Update Employee">
</CFIF>
<INPUT TYPE="reset" VALUE="Clear">

</FORM>

</BODY>

</HTML>
```

Understanding Conditional Forms

Now analyze Listing 13.11. The first thing you do in it is determine if an insert or an update is required. How can you know that? An employee ID must be passed in order for a record to be updated; otherwise ColdFusion would have no idea which record needs updating. It makes no sense to pass an employee ID when adding a row; the new employee's ID will be assigned when the data is actually inserted into the table.

You can therefore make a safe assumption that this is an update operation if a employee ID is present; if not, it's an addition.

The first line in the template checks to see if EmployeeID was specified:

```
<CFIF IsDefined("EmployeeID") >
```

This code sets a variable called NewRecord to Yes or No based on its existence. The following code sets NewRecord to No because the IsDefined("EmployeeID") test returned TRUE.

```
<CFSET NewRecord = "No">
```

If IsDefined("EmployeeID") returns FALSE, the following code sets NewRecord to Yes:

```
<CFSET NewRecord = "Yes">
```

Either way, once the first five lines of the template have been processed, you'll have a new variable called NewRecord, which indicates whether a new record is being added. You can then use this variable throughout the template wherever different code is needed for insertions or updates. Of course, you could have named this variable with some other name as well; the actual variable name is not that important, as long as it is descriptive.

N O T E   ColdFusion *variables* are special fields that you can create at any time; they can contain any values. Once a variable is created during the processing of a template, it is available for use until that processing is complete. Variables are assigned using the CFSET tag and can be reassigned using that same tag. ▪

The <CFQUERY> that retrieves the record of the employee you want updated is conditional. It would make no sense to try to retrieve a record that does not yet exist in the table. Therefore, the entire <CFQUERY> statement is enclosed in a <CFIF> statement. The code <CFIF NewRecord IS "No"> ensures that everything until the matching </CFIF> is processed only if this is an update.

The page title is also conditional; that way it accurately reflects the operation that is being performed, and if the operation is an update, the name of the employee being updated is displayed. Of course, displaying the employee name requires displaying dynamic data; the title is therefore enclosed within a <CFOUTPUT> block if the operation is an update:

```
<CFOUTPUT QUERY="Employee">
<TITLE>Update an Employee - #LastName#, FirstName#</TITLE>
</CFOUTPUT>
```

The very first field in the form itself is a hidden field. The following code creates a hidden field containing the primary key of the record to be updated:

```
<INPUT TYPE="hidden" NAME="EmployeeID" VALUE="#EmployeeID#">
```

This is required for the <CFUPDATE> tag to work, as explained earlier in this chapter.

This hidden field is only wanted if the operation is an update. A new employee ID is generated automatically at the time of data insertion for insert operations, so the entire <INPUT> tag is conditional and is only processed if the <CFIF NewRecord IS "No"> condition returns TRUE. If NewRecord is Yes, all the code until the matching </CFIF> tag is ignored.

Conditional INPUT Fields

Next comes all the fields themselves, starting with the FirstName field. When adding a new record, the FirstName input field needs to look like this:

```
<INPUT TYPE="text" NAME="FirstName" SIZE="30" MAXLENGTH="30">
```

When updating a record, the same field needs one additional attribute: VALUE. The parameter passed to the VALUE attribute is the FirstName column as retrieved by the <CFQUERY> tag. The complete field for an update operation, therefore, looks like this:

```
<INPUT TYPE="text" NAME="FirstName" SIZE="30" MAXLENGTH="30"
 Â VALUE="#Trim(FirstName)#">
```

Because the only difference between the two is the VALUE attribute, you can also make that conditional. This typically involves breaking the <INPUT> field over multiple lines, but that is allowed. The basic <INPUT> tag is first defined in the following code, but no terminating > is provided yet. Instead, you test to see if this is an update; if yes, the VALUE attribute is included within a <CFOUTPUT> block so that it can be populated with the current value. The terminating > appears after the condition, ensuring that the VALUE attribute will be contained within the <INPUT> tag if it is needed.

```
<INPUT TYPE="text" NAME="FirstName" SIZE="30" MAXLENGTH="30"
 <CFIF NewRecord IS "No">
  <CFOUTPUT QUERY="Employee">VALUE="#Trim(FirstName)#"</CFOUTPUT>
 </CFIF>
>
```

That's all you need to create a conditional <INPUT> tag. The tag is a little more complicated to read—and the generated HTML source code will likely contain multiple lines and blank lines in the middle of the tag—but the benefit here is that you'd only have to make any necessary tag attributes changes once. Similarly, if you needed to add input fields, you'd only have to make changes to a single template.

The final conditional code in Listing 13.11 is the submit button. Again, check the value of the NewRecord variable so you can specify an appropriate value for the submit button text.

You can now try this form. If you specify an EmployeeID parameter such as ?EmployeeID=7 in the URL, you'll be presented with an update form. Executing the same template without an EmployeeID parameter displays an add form. Both forms are shown in Figure 13.5 and Figure 13.6.

But don't submit the form yet. Now you have to create a template that can conditionally perform the actual insert or update.

Part
III

Ch
13

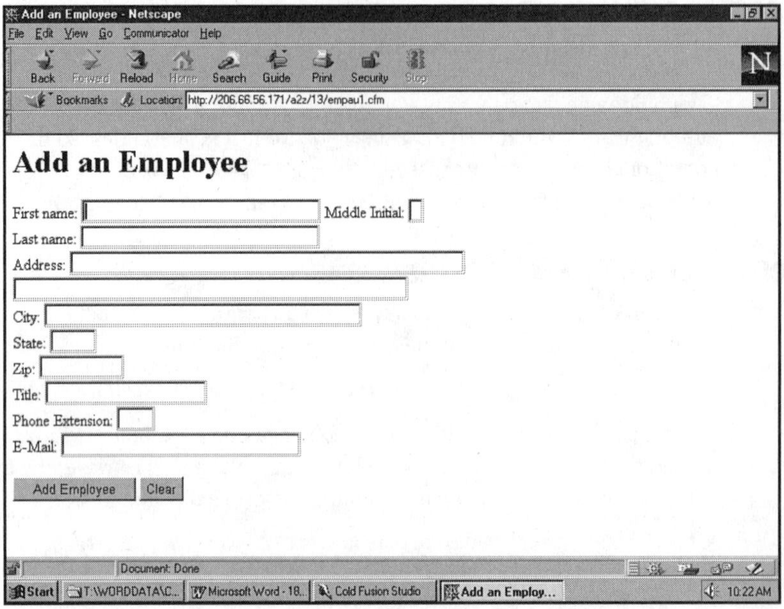

FIGURE 13.5

Templates can be reused when using conditional code; this Add form is also an Update form.

FIGURE 13.6

Templates can be reused when using conditional code; and this Update form is also an Add form.

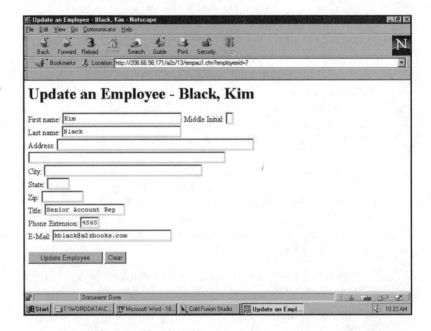

Processing Conditional Forms

Processing a conditional form requires that the destination template ascertain which operation needs to be performed, and there are many ways to do this:

- Embedding a hidden field in the form that specifies the operation
- Checking for the existence of a specific field, or the lack thereof (similar to what you did in Listing 13.11)
- Checking the value of a known entity (the submit button for example), which could have a different value based on the operation being performed

> **CAUTION**
>
> In order to submit the value of a button you must name the field with the `<INPUT>` NAME attribute. This way the browser can submit a name=value pair for the submit button.
>
> Some older browsers do not support naming submit buttons, and they might ignore the attribute altogether.

For this example you do the same thing you did in the form template itself—check for the existence of an `EmployeeID`. The hidden EmployeeID field is only present if the operation is an update.

Listing 13.12 `EMPAU2.CFM`—**Template That Conditionally Inserts or Updates an Employee Record**

```
<CFIF IsDefined("FORM.EmployeeID")>
 <CFSET Operation="Updated">
 <CFUPDATE DATASOURCE="A2Z" TABLENAME="Employees">
<CFELSE>
 <CFSET Operation="Inserted">
 <CFINSERT DATASOURCE="A2Z" TABLENAME="Employees">
</CFIF>

<CFOUTPUT>

<HTML>

<HEAD>
<TITLE>Employee #LastName#, #FirstName# #Operation#</TITLE>
</HEAD>

<BODY>
<H1>Employee #LastName#, #FirstName# #Operation#</H1>
</BODY>

<HTML>

</CFOUTPUT>
```

Part

III

Ch

13

The conditional insert and update template is shown in Listing 13.12. Just as in Listing 13.11's form, the first thing you do is check for the presence of the EmployeeID field, but this time we explicitly check for an EmployeeID field within a FORM. The primary key form field must be present for an update to work. Chances are that there would not be any other EmployeeID field present, but just to make sure, you preface the field name with the FORM identifier, as follows:

```
<CFIF IsDefined("FORM.EmployeeID")>
```

You execute a <CFUPDATE> if the EmployeeID exists; otherwise you execute a <CFINSERT>—it's that simple. You now have a single template that can both insert and update employee records.

Unlike Listing 13.11, here you did not set a variable to indicate which operation to perform. Why not? There were many conditional elements within the code in Listing 13.11, and so you don't have to repeatedly check for parameter existence, you created a variable you could check instead. There is only one conditional code block here, and so you might as well perform the insert or update operations right there, within the conditional block.

The other thing you did in the conditional code is set a variable called Operation, which is either set to Inserted and Updated. You then used this variable twice later, in the title and in the body. This way you did not need to create two more conditional code blocks. The variable contains the appropriate text to be displayed automatically, wherever it is used.

Try to update EmployeeID 7. Your browser should look like the one shown in Figure 13.7.

N O T E   There are an unlimited number of ways to structure your conditional code, and no single approach is right or wrong. The examples in this chapter demonstrate several different techniques, and you will undoubtedly develop several of your own. The only rule to remember is to make your code readable, manageable, and wherever possible, reusable. ■

FIGURE 13.7

All the elements in a page can be created dynamically using ColdFusion variables and fields, including the HTML <TITLE>.

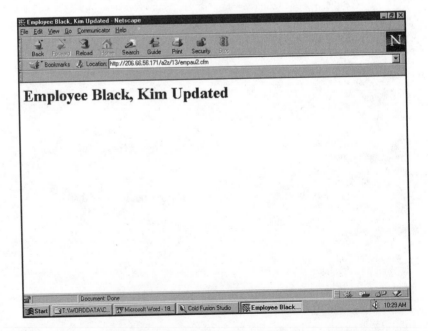

Additional Code Reuse Techniques

While we're on the subject of code reuse, look at another useful way to create reusable forms.

The combination Insert and Update form you created in Listing 13.11 works very well. The only problem with it is one of manageability. With so many `<CFIF>` statements you run the risk of introducing mismatched tags or typos, especially if you were to modify the form at a later date.

As a rule, programmers like to keep all conditional code in one place, creating a simpler program flow. The code in Listing 13.13 shows how to do this.

Listing 13.13 `EMPAU3.CFM`—**Alternate Combination Insert and Update Form**

```
<CFIF IsDefined("EmployeeID")>
 <CFSET NewRecord="No">
<CFELSE>
 <CFSET NewRecord="Yes">
</CFIF>

<CFIF NewRecord>
 <CFSET PageTitle = "Add an Employee">
 <CFSET ButtonText = "Add Employee">
 <CFSET FirstName = "">
 <CFSET MiddleInit = "">
 <CFSET LastName = "">
 <CFSET Address1 = "">
 <CFSET Address2 = "">
 <CFSET City = "">
 <CFSET State = "">
 <CFSET Zip = "">
 <CFSET Title = "">
 <CFSET PhoneExtension = "">
 <CFSET EMail = "">
<CFELSE>
 <CFQUERY DATASOURCE="A2Z" NAME="Employee">
  SELECT FirstName,
         MiddleInit,
         LastName,
         Address1,
         Address2,
         City,
         State,
         Zip,
         Title,
         PhoneExtension,
         EMail
  FROM Employees
  WHERE EmployeeID = #EmployeeID#
 </CFQUERY>
 <CFSET PageTitle =
➥"Update an Employee - " & Employee.LastName & ", " & Employee.FirstName>
 <CFSET ButtonText = "Update Employee">
 <CFSET FirstName = Trim(Employee.FirstName)>
 <CFSET MiddleInit = Trim(Employee.MiddleInit)>
```

continues

Part

III

Ch

13

Listing 13.13   Continued

```
 <CFSET LastName = Trim(Employee.LastName)>
 <CFSET Address1 = Trim(Employee.Address1)>
 <CFSET Address2 = Trim(Employee.Address2)>
 <CFSET City = Trim(Employee.City)>
 <CFSET State = Trim(Employee.State)>
 <CFSET Zip = Trim(Employee.Zip)>
 <CFSET Title = Trim(Employee.Title)>
 <CFSET PhoneExtension = Trim(Employee.PhoneExtension)>
 <CFSET EMail = Trim(Employee.EMail)>
</CFIF>

<CFOUTPUT>

<HTML>

<HEAD>
<TITLE>#PageTitle#</TITLE>
</HEAD>

<BODY>

<H1>#PageTitle#</H1>

<FORM ACTION="empau2.cfm" METHOD="POST">

<CFIF NewRecord IS "No">
 <INPUT TYPE="hidden" NAME="EmployeeID" VALUE="#EmployeeID#">
</CFIF>

<P>

First name:
<INPUT TYPE="text" NAME="FirstName" SIZE="30" MAXLENGTH="30"
VALUE="#FirstName#">
Middle Initial:
<INPUT TYPE="text" NAME="MiddleInit" SIZE="1" MAXLENGTH="1"
VALUE="#MiddleInit#">
<BR>
Last name:
<INPUT TYPE="text" NAME="LastName" SIZE="30" MAXLENGTH="30" VALUE="#LastName#">
<BR>
Address:
<INPUT TYPE="text" NAME="Address1" SIZE="50" MAXLENGTH="50" VALUE="#Address1#">
<BR>
<INPUT TYPE="text" NAME="Address2" SIZE="50" MAXLENGTH="50" VALUE="#Address2#">
<BR>
City:
<INPUT TYPE="text" NAME="Address1" SIZE="40" MAXLENGTH="40" VALUE="#City#">
<BR>
State:
<INPUT TYPE="text" NAME="State" SIZE="5" MAXLENGTH="5" VALUE="#State#">
<BR>
Zip:
<INPUT TYPE="text" NAME="Zip" SIZE="10" MAXLENGTH="10" VALUE="#Zip#">
```

```
<BR>
Title:
<INPUT TYPE="text" NAME="Title" SIZE="20" MAXLENGTH="20" VALUE="#Title#">
<BR>
Phone Extension:
<INPUT TYPE="text" NAME="PhoneExtension" SIZE="4" MAXLENGTH="4"
➥ VALUE="#PhoneExtension#">
<BR>
E-Mail:
<INPUT TYPE="text" NAME="EMail" SIZE="30" MAXLENGTH="30" VALUE="#EMail#">

<P>
<INPUT TYPE="submit" VALUE="#ButtonText#">
<INPUT TYPE="reset" VALUE="Clear">

</FORM>

</BODY>

</HTML>

</CFOUTPUT>
```

This template first determines whether this is an insert or an update operation. If it is an update, a <CFQUERY> is used to retrieve the current values. The fields retrieved by that <CFQUERY> are saved into local variables using multiple <CFSET> tags. There's no <CFQUERY> used if it is an insert operation, but <CFSET> is used to create empty variables.

Now look at the <INPUT> fields themselves. You'll notice that there is no conditional code within them as there was before. Instead, every <INPUT> tag has a VALUE attribute regardless of whether this is an insert or an update. The value in the VALUE attribute is a ColdFusion variable, a variable that is set at the top of the template, not a database field.

Regardless of the operation, a set of variables will exist once that conditional code has been processed. The variables are empty if the operation is an insert, although they could also contain default values. If it is an update operation, the variables will contain the current values. Either way, there is a valid set of variables to work with.

If an insert form is being displayed, the FirstName variable is empty. (The variable would exist, it would just have "" as its value). The following code:

```
<INPUT TYPE="text" NAME="FirstName" SIZE="30" MAXLENGTH="30" VALUE="#FirstName#">
```

translates into this:

```
<INPUT TYPE="text" NAME="FirstName" SIZE="30" MAXLENGTH="30" VALUE="">
```

If an update form is being displayed for EmployeeID 7, the FirstName variable would contain the text Kim. The following code:

```
<INPUT TYPE="text" NAME="FirstName" SIZE="30" MAXLENGTH="30" VALUE="#FirstName#">
```

translates into this:

```
<INPUT TYPE="text" NAME="FirstName" SIZE="30" MAXLENGTH="30" VALUE="Kim">
```

Part III

Ch 13

The rest of the code in the template uses these variables, without needing any conditional processing. Even the page title and submit button text can be initialized in variables this way, so <CFIF> tags are not needed for them, either.

Obviously this is a far more elegant and manageable form than the one you saw before. You may use either technique or a combination thereof—whatever suits you and your application.

Creating a Complete Application

Now that you've created add, modify, and delete templates, put it all together and create a finished application.

The following templates are a combination of all that you have learned in both this and the previous chapter.

The template shown in Listing 13.14 is the main employee administration page. It displays all the employees in the Employees table and provides links to edit and delete them (using the data drill-down techniques discussed in the previous chapter); the links also enable you to add a new employee. The administration page is shown in Figure 13.8.

Listing 13.14   EMPADMIN.CFM—**Employee Administration Template**

```
<CFQUERY DATASOURCE="A2Z" NAME="Employees">
 SELECT FirstName, LastName, PhoneExtension, EmployeeID
 FROM Employees
 ORDER BY LastName, FirstName
</CFQUERY>

<HTML>

<HEAD>
<TITLE>Employee List</TITLE>
</HEAD>

<BODY>

<CENTER>

<TABLE BORDER>
 <TR>
  <TH COLSPAN=3>
   <H1>Employees</H1>
  </TH>
 </TR>
 <TR>
  <TH>
   Name
  </TH>
  <TH>
   Extension
  </TH>
 </TR>
```

```
<CFOUTPUT QUERY="Employees">
 <TR>
  <TD>
   #LastName#, #FirstName#
  </TD>
  <TD>
   Ext: #PhoneExtension#
  </TD>
  <TD>
   <A HREF="empau4.cfm?EmployeeID=#EmployeeID#">Edit</A>
   <A HREF="empdel2.cfm?EmployeeID=#EmployeeID#">Delete</A>
  </TD>
 </TR>
</CFOUTPUT>

<TR>
 <TH COLSPAN=3>
  <A HREF="empau3.cfm">Add an Employee</A>
 </TH>
</TR>

</TABLE>

</CENTER>

</BODY>

</HTML>
```

▶ **See** "Displaying Results in Tables" for details on how to create table containing dynamic data, **p. 210**.

FIGURE 13.8

The employee administration page is used to add, edit, and delete employee records.

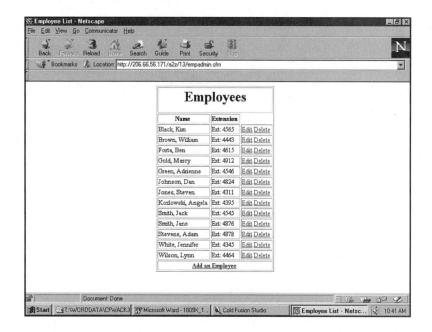

Listing 13.15 is essentially the same reusable Add and Update form you created earlier. The only significant change is that the `<FORM>` ACTION has been changed so that template EMPAU5.CFM processes the responses.

Listing 13.15 EMPAU4.CFM—**Employee Add and Update Form**

```
<CFIF IsDefined("EmployeeID")>
 <CFSET NewRecord="No">.
<CFELSE>
 <CFSET NewRecord="Yes">
</CFIF>

<CFIF NewRecord>
 <CFSET PageTitle = "Add an Employee">
 <CFSET ButtonText = "Add Employee">
 <CFSET FirstName = "">
 <CFSET MiddleInit = "">
 <CFSET LastName = "">
 <CFSET Address1 = "">
 <CFSET Address2 = "">
 <CFSET City = "">
 <CFSET State = "">
 <CFSET Zip = "">
 <CFSET Title = "">
 <CFSET PhoneExtension = "">
 <CFSET EMail = "">
<CFELSE>
 <CFQUERY DATASOURCE="A2Z" NAME="Employee">
  SELECT FirstName,
         MiddleInit,
         LastName,
         Address1,
         Address2,
         City,
         State,
         Zip,
         Title,
         PhoneExtension,
         EMail
  FROM Employees
  WHERE EmployeeID = #EmployeeID#
 </CFQUERY>
 <CFSET PageTitle =
➥ "Update an Employee - " & Employee.LastName & ", " & Employee.FirstName>
 <CFSET ButtonText = "Update Employee">
 <CFSET FirstName = Trim(Employee.FirstName)>
 <CFSET MiddleInit = Trim(Employee.MiddleInit)>
 <CFSET LastName = Trim(Employee.LastName)>
 <CFSET Address1 = Trim(Employee.Address1)>
 <CFSET Address2 = Trim(Employee.Address2)>
 <CFSET City = Trim(Employee.City)>
 <CFSET State = Trim(Employee.State)>
 <CFSET Zip = Trim(Employee.Zip)>
 <CFSET Title = Trim(Employee.Title)>
```

```
  <CFSET PhoneExtension = Trim(Employee.PhoneExtension)>
  <CFSET EMail = Trim(Employee.EMail)>
</CFIF>

<CFOUTPUT>

<HTML>

<HEAD>
<TITLE>#PageTitle#</TITLE>
</HEAD>

<BODY>

<H1>#PageTitle#</H1>

<FORM ACTION="empau5.cfm" METHOD="POST">

<CFIF NewRecord IS "No">
  <INPUT TYPE="hidden" NAME="EmployeeID" VALUE="#EmployeeID#">
</CFIF>

<P>

First name:
<INPUT TYPE="text" NAME="FirstName" SIZE="30" MAXLENGTH="30"
VALUE="#FirstName#">
Middle Initial:
<INPUT TYPE="text" NAME="MiddleInit" SIZE="1" MAXLENGTH="1"
VALUE="#MiddleInit#">
<BR>
Last name:
<INPUT TYPE="text" NAME="LastName" SIZE="30" MAXLENGTH="30" VALUE="#LastName#">
<BR>
Address:
<INPUT TYPE="text" NAME="Address1" SIZE="50" MAXLENGTH="50" VALUE="#Address1#">
<BR>
<INPUT TYPE="text" NAME="Address2" SIZE="50" MAXLENGTH="50" VALUE="#Address2#">
<BR>
City:
<INPUT TYPE="text" NAME="Address1" SIZE="40" MAXLENGTH="40" VALUE="#City#">
<BR>
State:
<INPUT TYPE="text" NAME="State" SIZE="5" MAXLENGTH="5" VALUE="#State#">
<BR>
Zip:
<INPUT TYPE="text" NAME="Zip" SIZE="10" MAXLENGTH="10" VALUE="#Zip#">
<BR>
Title:
<INPUT TYPE="text" NAME="Title" SIZE="20" MAXLENGTH="20" VALUE="#Title#">
<BR>
Phone Extension:
<INPUT TYPE="text" NAME="PhoneExtension" SIZE="4" MAXLENGTH="4"
➥ VALUE="#PhoneExtension#">
<BR>
```

Part

III

Ch

13

continues

Listing 13.15 Continued

```
E-Mail:
<INPUT TYPE="text" NAME="EMail" SIZE="30" MAXLENGTH="30" VALUE="#EMail#">

<P>
<INPUT TYPE="submit" VALUE="#ButtonText#">
<INPUT TYPE="reset" VALUE="Clear">

</FORM>

</BODY>

</HTML>

</CFOUTPUT>
```

Listings 13.16 and 13.17 perform the actual data insertions, updates, and deletions. The big change in these templates is that they themselves provide no user feedback at all. Instead, they return to the administration screen using the <CFLOCATION> tag as soon as they finish processing the database changes. <CFLOCATION> is used to switch from the current template being processed to any other URL, including another ColdFusion template. The following example code instructs ColdFusion to switch to the EMPADMIN.CFM template.

```
<CFLOCATION URL="empadmin.cfm">
```

This way, the updated employee list is displayed ready for further processing as soon as any change is completed.

Listing 13.16 EMPAU5.CFM—**Employee Insert and Update Processing**

```
<CFIF IsDefined("FORM.EmployeeID")>
 <CFUPDATE DATASOURCE="A2Z" TABLENAME="Employees">
<CFELSE>
 <CFINSERT DATASOURCE="A2Z" TABLENAME="Employees">
</CFIF>

<CFLOCATION URL="empadmin.cfm">
```

Listing 13.17 EMPDEL2.CFM—**Employee Delete Processing**

```
<CFIF IsDefined("EmployeeID") IS "No">
 Error! No EmployeeID was specified!
 <CFABORT>
</CFIF>

<CFQUERY DATASOURCE="A2Z">
 DELETE FROM Employees
 WHERE EmployeeID = #EmployeeID#
</CFQUERY>

<CFLOCATION URL="empadmin.cfm">
```

Using CFIF to Create Conditional Code

The conditions you have created so far have all tested for equality or inequality; they determine if a field or value equals another value or does not equal it—but you are not limited to testing for equality. ColdFusion provides a complete set of conditional operators, and you can also combine conditions with AND and OR operators.

The complete list of operators is shown in Table 13.1. Many of the operators have alternate syntax, and you may use whatever syntax you are comfortable with. The syntax GREATER THAN OR EQUAL TO is very descriptive, but is also very wordy and takes up additional screen space, which might force you to have to scroll or wrap text over multiple lines. The abbreviated syntax GTE accomplishes the exact same thing and takes far less space, but is also less intuitive.

Table 13.1 ColdFusion Conditional Operators

Operator	Alternate	Description
IS	EQUAL, EQ	Check that the right value is equal to the left value.
IS NOT	NOT EQUAL, NEQ	Check that the right value is not equal to the left value.
CONTAINS		Check that the right value is contained within the left value.
DOES NOT CONTAIN		Check that the right value is not contained within the left value.
GREATER THAN	GT	Check that the left value is greater than the right value.
LESS THAN	LT	Check that the left value is less than the right value.
GREATER THAN OR EQUAL	GTE	Check that the left value is greater than or equal to the right value.
LESS THAN OR EQUAL	LTE	Check that the left value is less than or equal to the right value.

The Boolean operators available to you are shown in Table 13.2.

Table 13.2 ColdFusion Boolean Operators

Operator	Description
AND	Conjunction; returns TRUE only if both expressions are true.
OR	Disjunction; returns TRUE if either expression is true.
NOT	Negation.

Part
III

Ch
13

When combining conditions, each condition must be contained within a set of parentheses. The following example checks to see if both the FirstName and LastName fields exist:

```
<CFIF (IsDefined("FirstName")) AND (IsDefined("LastName"))>
```

To check for either a first name or a last name, you could use the following:

```
<CFIF (IsDefined("FirstName")) OR (IsDefined("LastName"))>
```

Often you will want to verify that a field is not empty and that it does not contain blank spaces. The following condition demonstrates how this can be accomplished:

```
<CFIF Trim(LastName) IS NOT "">
```

You can use the CONTAINS operator (used in these two examples) to check whether a value is within a range of values:

```
<CFIF "KY,MI,MN,OH,WI" CONTAINS State>
```

```
<CFIF TaxableStates CONTAINS State>
```

More complex expressions can be created by combining conditions within parentheses. For example, the following condition determines whether payment is by check or credit card; if payment is by credit card, it checks to ensure that there is an approval code:

```
<CFIF (PaymentType IS "Check") OR ((PaymentType IS "Credit")
➥ AND (ApprovalCode IS NOT ""))>
```

As you can see, the ColdFusion conditional support is both extensive and powerful. You'll make much more use of the <CFIF> tag in upcoming chapters. ●

Using the SQL Query Builder

Understanding the SQL Query Builder

Almost every ColdFusion application uses some sort of database integration. While database integration is probably the most commonly used ColdFusion feature, learning SQL—the language used to interact with these databases—remains the single biggest hurdle facing ColdFusion developers.

Allaire added a graphical SQL generation tool to ColdFusion Studio for this reason. This too, the SQL Query Builder, helps ColdFusion developers construct powerful SQL statements without actually writing a single line of SQL code.

Some of the features built in to the Query Builder include the following:

- Drag-and-drop interface simplifies fields selection.
- Simple drop-down list boxes for filter and sort selection.
- Full support for relational queries and all JOIN types.
- Capability to generate SELECT, INSERT, DELETE, and UPDATE statements.
- Generated SQL shown in real time.
- SQL statements may be executed and any results displayed.
- Generates <CFQUERY> read code.

Unlike other query builders built into database client applications, the ColdFusion Studio SQL Query Builder has been designed from scratch with the ColdFusion developer in mind. As such, learning to effectively use the Query Builder can dramatically improve the rate at which you roll out applications, and it can help you get the code right on the first try.

N O T E As good as the SQL Query Builder is, it is no substitute for a good working knowledge of SQL. The Query Builder can help with your most common SQL statements, but at some point you will need to write SQL code directly. Whether it is to fine-tune the SQL code or to write statements not supported by the Query Builder, you must learn SQL if you are serious about ColdFusion development.

Navigating the SQL Query Builder

First of all, let's take a look at the Query Builder screen. To start the SQL Query Builder, do one of the following:

- Select Insert SQL Statement from the Tools menu. Select a server from the drop-down list box, select a table, and click New Query.
- Right-click in the Editor window and select Insert SQL Statement. Select a server from the drop-down list box, select a table, and click New Query.
- Within the <CFQUERY> Tag Editor dialog box, click the SQL Query Builder button (to the right of the SQL Statement field); select a server from the drop-down list box, select a table, and click New Query.
- Right-click any table in the Database tab in the Resource windows and select New Query.

This opens the Query Builder, as seen in Figure 14.1.

FIGURE 14.1

The SQL Query Builder window is used to interactively construct SQL statements.

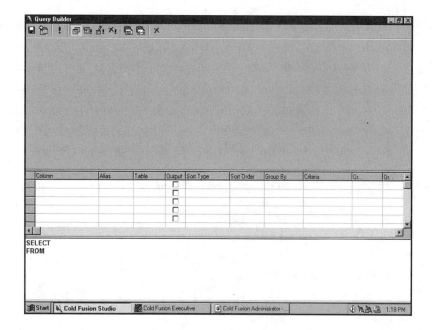

N O T E The SQL Query Builder is password protected to prevent unauthorized access to the databases. If you are not already logged into the ColdFusion Remote Development Server, you are prompted for a password at this point. Enter the ColdFusion Studio password as specified during system installation (or in the ColdFusion Administrator). ▒

The Query Builder window is divided into three sections, with a standard Windows toolbars at the top.

The top portion of the window is the Table pane. This is where you are presented with a graphical representation of the tables in your SQL query. You can add and remove tables, define relationships between tables, and select the columns you want included in the query.

The middle portion of the window is the Selection pane. This is where the list of currently selected columns is displayed. You may add and remove columns, attach criteria to perform data filtering, specify search orders and grouping, and pass subqueries.

The bottom portion of the window is the SQL pane. This is where the Query Builder shows you the SQL code being constructed. As you make changes in the two upper panes, the SQL code in the SQL pane changes in real time. The final code, as it appears in this pane, is what gets pasted into your application.

Part

III

Ch

14

Using the Toolbar

The SQL Query Builder window has no menus. All selections are made using the items in the two panes and the toolbar. The toolbar buttons are described in Table 14.1.

Table 14.1 SQL Query Builder Toolbar Buttons

Button	Effect
	Save Query allows you to save the query for reuse. Queries are saved on the ColdFusion server, allowing queries to be shared by multiple users.
	Add Tables is used to add tables to a query.
	Run Query executes the SQL code appearing in the SQL pane. Results are displayed in a pop-up window.
	Select Query puts the Query Builder in SELECT mode, allowing you to create a SQL SELECT statement.
	Insert Query puts the Query Builder in INSERT mode, allowing you to create a SQL INSERT statement.
	Update Query puts the Query Builder in UPDATE mode, allowing you to create a SQL UPDATE statement.
	Delete Query puts the Query Builder in DELETE mode, allowing you to create a SQL DELETE statement.
	Copy SQL to Clipboard copies the SQL code from the SQL pane to the Windows Clipboard so that you can paste into other applications.
	Copy CFQUERY to Clipboard copies the SQL code formatted as a complete <CFQUERY> tag from the SQL Pane to the Windows Clipboard.
	Close Query Builder quits the Query Builder.

The majority of SQL statements that you write are SQL SELECT statements, and so the Query Builder window opens in the default SELECT mode. To generate SQL code for INSERT, UPDATE, or DELETE operations, you must switch the mode using the toolbar buttons shown in Table 14.1.

Generating SQL SELECT Statements

Before you can start creating your SQL statement, you must select at least one database table. If you open the Query Builder while a database table is selected, that table will be pre-selected in the Table pane (see Figure 14.2). If no database table is highlighted, the Query Builder will prompt you for the initial table to use (see Figure 14.3).

FIGURE 14.2
By default, the table that was highlighted when you opened the Query Builder will be opened for selection in the Table pane.

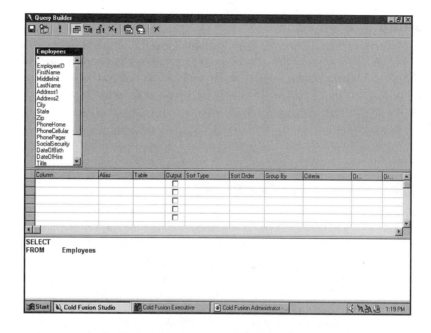

FIGURE 14.3
If no table was highlighted when the Query Builder was opened, you are prompted for the database table to use.

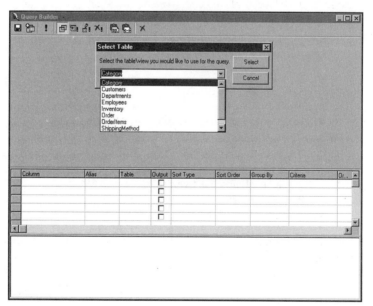

The Query Builder begins constructing your SQL statement as soon as a table is selected; this is shown in the SQL pane in Figure 14.2. For more information on the SQL SELECT statement, see Chapter 8, "Introduction to SQL."

Creating a JOIN

If your SQL statement is going to need to join two or more tables, the first thing you should do is create those relationships. You create relationships by adding all the desired tables into the Table pane and then dragging the related columns to each other. For more information on the SQL JOIN and relational databases, see Chapter 6, "Database Fundamentals."

To demonstrate this, you create a SQL statement that retrieves the employees from the A2Z Employees table. As you probably recall, the Employees table is related to the Departments table in that the Employees table stores a department ID that maps to a department name in the Departments table.

To create the join, follow these steps:

1. If you have not already done so, select the A2Z data source and open the Query Builder window (using any of the methods described earlier). Highlight the Employees table before you click the New Query button so that that table is pre-selected.

2. Click the Add Table button (or right-click in the Table pane and select Add Tables) to display the Add Tables or Views to Query dialog box.

3. Select the Departments table and click the Add button to add the table to the Table pane.

4. Click the Done button to close the Add Tables or Views to Query dialog box. You now have two tables displayed in the Table pane. If they overlap, drag one of them out of the way by clicking its title bar and dragging it with your mouse.

5. To define the relationship between the tables, simply click the DepartmentID field in the Employees table and drag it to the ID field in the Departments table.

Your screen should now look like the one shown in Figure 14.4. The Table pane shows relationships by drawing a line connecting the related tables.

As seen in Figure 14.4, the SQL pane now shows the SQL code creating the JOIN between the two tables.

N O T E   The Query Builder supports several JOIN types, including OUTER and FULL OUTER JOINs. To specify the JOIN type, right-click the box in the middle of the line joining the tables and check the appropriate options. ■

T I P   To remove a relationship, right-click the box in the middle of the line joining the tables and then select the Remove Join option.

To remove tables from the Table pane, right-click the table and select the Remove Table option.

Selecting Table Columns

The SQL in the SQL pane is not yet a valid SQL statement. The next thing you need to do is select the columns to be retrieved. There are several ways to add columns to your statement:

■ Double-click any column in any of the tables in the Table pane to add that column to the Selection pane.

FIGURE 14.4

Creating a JOIN in the Query Builder is simply a matter of selecting the tables and dragging the related columns to each other.

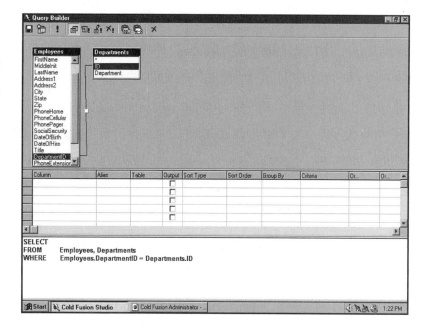

- Drag a column from the Table pane and drop it into the Columns area, which is in the Selection pane grid.

- Click any line in the Columns area to display a drop-down list box of all the columns that may be added to the selection; click any one to select it.

Select the Department column from the Departments table and the FirstName and LastName columns from the Employees table.

Notice how as you select each column, the SQL statement in the SQL pane reflects that change. Your screen should now look like the one in Figure 14.5.

Testing SQL Statements

Now that you have a valid SQL statement, the next step is to test that it works as intended. To test your SQL statement, simply click the Run Query button in the toolbar.

The Query Builder will open a results grid that displays the retrieved data for browsing. The results window's title bar displays the SQL code executed, like the example shown in Figure 14.6.

To close the results window, just click the Close Window button (on the right with an X).

CAUTION

The Query Builder lets you execute any valid SQL statement. When you execute a SQL statement, the Query Builder submits the statement over the TCP/IP connection to the ColdFusion server for processing; the returned data is then displayed. Be careful not to execute a statement that could return very large result sets, as this could take a very long time to return, giving you the impression that Studio has hung.

Part

III

Ch

14

FIGURE 14.5

The SQL Query Builder allows you to add columns to your table in three different ways.

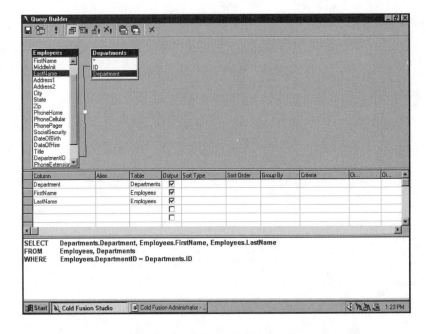

FIGURE 14.6

SQL statements can be tested directly in the Query Builder, and results are displayed in a results grid.

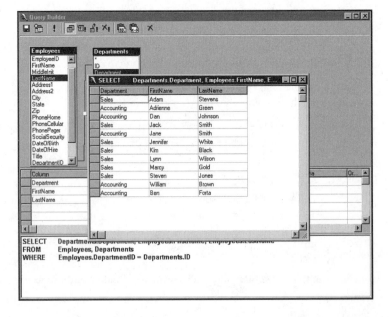

Sorting Results

Now sort the returned data. SQL results are sorted by columns in the retrieved columns list. Multiple columns may be selected, in which case the data is sorted by the first column and then by the second.

You're going to sort the data by DepartmentName, LastName, and then by FirstName. Here's how to do that:

1. In the Selection Pane grid, click the Sort Type column on the DepartmentName row. Select Ascending from the drop-down list.
2. Click the Sort Type column on the LastName row and set it to Ascending as well.
3. Repeat this step for the FirstName column.

The SQL pane now shows an ORDER BY clause, which sorts the retrieved data. Data is now sorted by department name; within each department it's sorted by last name and then first name. To verify that this worked, try running the query using the Run Query button.

TIP To reorder the sequence within the ORDER BY clause, click the Sort Order column in the Selection pane and change the position as required.

Filtering Data

So far you have retrieved all the data in the tables. Next you add SQL WHERE clauses using the Query Builder filtering tools.

To apply filtering within Query Builder, all you do is specify a search criteria in the Criteria column for the required row. For example, to find all employees whose first name is Kim, type the following into the FirstName row's Criteria box:

```
='Kim'
```

As soon as you click anywhere outside that Criteria box, the SQL code in the SQL pane is updated to include your WHERE clause. You can test this query to verify that it returns the required data.

When you typed that criteria, you might have noticed that the Criteria box has a built in drop-down list box with a selection of common criteria types, as shown in Figure 14.7. You may select any of this to help you construct your SQL WHERE clauses.

Many of the selections in the drop-down list box contain the text value or #CFvariable#. These are designed to be placeholders. You replace the word value with an actual value (as you did with the word Kim), and the word #CFvariable# with the name of a ColdFusion variable to be used within your WHERE clause.

N O T E There are two versions of each value and #CFvariable# in the Criteria drop-down list box. One is enclosed within single quotation marks, and the other is not. Because SQL is not typeless, it is your responsibility to enclose values and variables within single quotation marks when constructing WHERE clauses. Selecting the correct option from this list can help ensure that you do not inadvertently omit this. ▪

Part

III

Ch

14

FIGURE 14.7

The Criteria drop-down list box contains common WHERE clause conditions for selection.

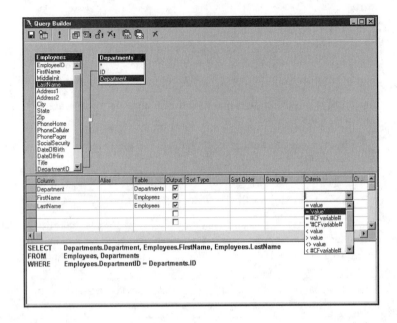

<CFQUERY> SQL SELECT statements often contain ColdFusion variables within their WHERE clauses. For example, you might be retrieving all employees whose last name is whatever value was specified in a form field. This kind of WHERE clause cannot easily be tested outside the ColdFusion environment because the variables used do not exist until the submitted form is processed by ColdFusion.

Fortunately, the SQL Query Builder has a very elegant solution to this problem. To demonstrate it, perform the following steps:

1. Click in the Criteria box for the LastName field.

2. Select ='#CFvariable#' from the drop-down list box.

3. Replace the text CFvariable with the text FORM.LastName. (Make sure to leave the single quotation marks and pound signs intact.)

4. Click any box other than the Criteria box you are editing, so that the SQL pane sees the changes.

5. Click the Run Query button.

The SQL code you are trying to run is invalid. The SQL was not processed under ColdFusion control, and therefore the variables that it refers to do not exist yet. To compensate for this, and to simulate ColdFusion processing, the Query Builder prompts you to enter the query parameters as seen in Figure 14.8.

You can provide a value here for each field in your query (there is one in the example), and the Query Builder will then process the SQL as if ColdFusion itself were processing it. For more information on the SQL WHERE clause, see Chapter 6, "Database Fundamentals."

FIGURE 14.8

Manually setting query parameters allows you to simulate ColdFusion processing dynamic SQL statements.

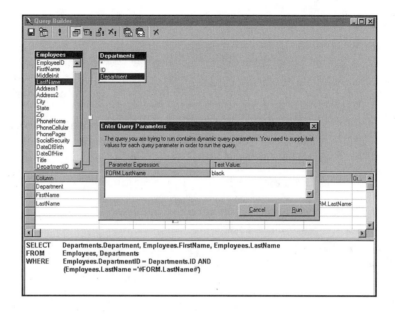

Advanced Data Filtering

The filter you just created is a simple SQL WHERE clause, with a single criterion. The Query Builder can also be used to build more complex WHERE clauses, including AND and OR clauses, and any combination thereof.

AND clauses are created by making multiple selections of the fields to be filtered on, once for each condition. To create an AND clause, perform the following steps:

1. Follow the steps selecting columns as explained in the "Selecting Table Columns" section.

2. Enter the first condition in the Criteria column as explained in the "Filtering Data" section.

3. Select the field to be included in the AND clause again. (There are two occurrences of this field in the selection grid now.)

4. Uncheck the Output box on the second occurrence of the column; this prevents this second occurrence from being retrieved as a selected column in the SQL statement, while allowing filtering criteria to be attached to it.

5. Enter the next condition in the new Criteria column as explained in "Filtering Data."

6. Repeat steps 4 and 5 for each AND clause.

N O T E There is no limit to the number of AND clauses that may be included in a WHERE clause. ▪

To create an OR clause, perform the following steps:

Part

III

Ch

14

1. Follow the steps for selecting columns as explained in the "Selecting Table Columns" section.

2. Enter the first condition in the Criteria column as explained in "Filtering Data."

3. Specify up to three additional conditions in any of the Or columns to the right of the Criteria column, using the same techniques for filtering data explained earlier.

N O T E   The SQL Query Builder supports up to four OR conditions per column in the WHERE clause. ■

 T I P   Depending on the SQL code needed and the filter criteria used, it is often possible to use a single criterion with an IN operator instead of creating multiple OR clauses.

Using Query Builder SQL Statements

Once you have created and tested your SQL statements in the SQL Query Builder, you have several options. You can execute it as is, copy and paste the SQL code, or save the code for reuse. Use the Copy SQL to Clipboard toolbar button to copy and paste the SQL code from the SQL pane.

Populating <CFQUERY> Tags

If you launched the Query Builder from within the <CFOUTPUT> Tag Editor dialog, you have the option of pasting the SQL code back into that dialog. To do this follow these steps:

1. Click the Close Query Builder button.

2. You are prompted to save the query. Select Yes if you plan to use this query again; otherwise, select No.

3. You are then prompted to reinsert the query into your code; select Yes.

4. The <CFQUERY> Tag Editor displays the final SQL code, and automatically sets the data source correctly, as seen in Figure 14.9.

For more information on the <CFQUERY> tag, see Chapter 11, "ColdFusion Basics."

Reusing Queries

As mentioned earlier, SQL statements created with the Query Builder can be saved for future use. ColdFusion Studio saves generated queries on the ColdFusion server. This allows anyone connected to that ColdFusion server to reuse existing queries.

Perform the following steps to reuse a saved query:

1. Open the Database tab in the ColdFusion Studio Resource tab.

2. Connect to the desired ColdFusion server (providing the password if required).

3. Expand the desired data source to display a Queries selection.

FIGURE 14.9
The Query Builder can insert generated SQL directly into the <CFQUERY> Tag Editor.

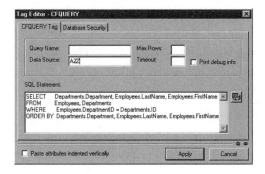

4. Expand the Queries option to display the list of saved queries.

5. Drag the desired query from the list to the Editor window. As shown in Figure 14.10, ColdFusion Studio creates a complete <CFQUERY> tag at the location that the query was dropped.

FIGURE 14.10
Drag and drop an existing database query to create a fully populated <CFQUERY> tag containing the query's SQL statement.

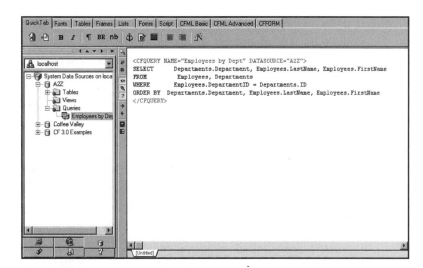

Generating Other SQL Statements

More often than not, you'll find yourself using the Query Builder to construct SQL SELECT statements—but that is not all the Query Builder can do. To assist you in writing SQL INSERT, UPDATE, and DELETE statements, these are also supported by the Query Builder.

Generating SQL INSERT Statements

The SQL Query Builder cannot be used to generate simple SQL INSERT statements like this:

```
INSERT INTO Employees(FirstName, LastName)
VALUES('Ben', 'Forta')
```

The Query Builder can only be used to build SQL INSERT SELECT statements, which are used to insert the results of a SELECT statement into another table.

To generate a SQL INSERT statement, you must switch SQL Query Builder to Insert mode by clicking the INSERT Query button in the toolbar. The Query Builder then prompts you for the name of the table into which you will be inserting data.

To create an INSERT statement, follow these steps:

1. Select the table into which data is to be inserted.
2. Right-click the table and select Remove Table. This removes it from the Table pane, but retains the table as the destination for the inserted data in the SQL pane.
3. Click the Add Tables (or right-click in the Table pane and select Add Table) to select the tables from which data is to be selected for insertion.
4. Select the columns to be inserted using any of the selection methods described in the "Selecting Table Columns" section.
5. Click the Append To column for the first row in the columns grid and select the field into which the data is to be inserted from the drop-down list box.
6. Repeat step 5 for every column listed in Columns.
7. If they are not already chosen, select the columns to be used for the SELECT WHERE clause.
8. Specify the criteria for the SELECT WHERE clause as explained in "Filtering Data" and "Advanced Data Filtering."

The completed insert screen is shown in Figure 14.11.

FIGURE 14.11

Insert mode is used to generate SQL INSERT SELECT statements.

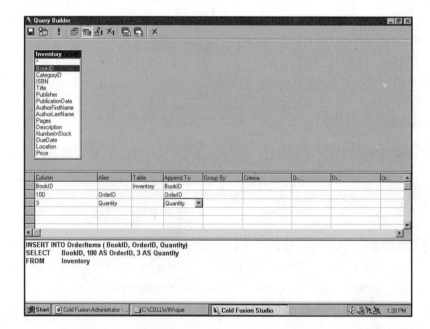

> **CAUTION**
>
> Make sure you always specify a WHERE clause criteria. Otherwise you will insert every selected row into the destination table.

For more information on the SQL INSERT statement, see Chapter 9, "SQL Data Manipulation."

Generating SQL UPDATE Statements

To generate a SQL UPDATE statement, you must switch the SQL Query Builder to Update mode by clicking the UPDATE Query button in the toolbar. The Query Builder then prompts you for the name of the table whose data you will be updating.

To create an UPDATE statement, follow these steps:

1. Select the table to be updated.
2. Select the columns to be updated using any of the selection methods described in the "Selecting Table Columns" section.
3. Specify the new value for each field in that field's New Value box. You may specify either a literal value or a ColdFusion variable.
4. If they are not already chosen, select the columns to be used for the WHERE clause.
5. Specify the criteria for the UPDATE WHERE clause as explained in "Filtering Data" and "Advanced Data Filtering."

The completed update screen is shown in Figure 14.12.

FIGURE 14.12
Update mode is used to generate SQL UPDATE statements.

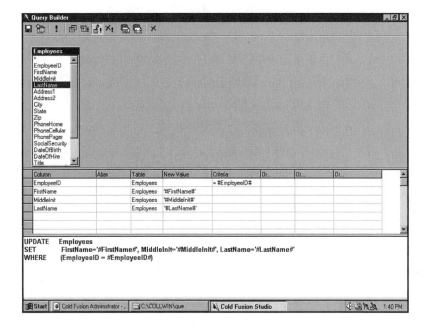

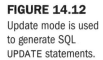

Part

III

Ch

14

> **CAUTION**
>
> Make sure you always specify a WHERE clause criteria. Otherwise you will update every row in the table with the new values.

N O T E   It is your responsibility to put single quotation marks around values or variables in the New Value column if they are needed. ■

For more information on the SQL UPDATE statement, see Chapter 9.

Generating SQL DELETE Statements

To generate a SQL DELETE statement, you must switch the SQL Query Builder to Delete mode by clicking the DELETE Query button in the toolbar. The Query Builder then prompts you for the name of the table whose data you will be deleting.

To create a DELETE statement, follow these steps:

1. Select the table from which to delete data.

2. Select the columns to be used for the WHERE clause using any of the selection methods described in the "Selecting Table Columns" section.

3. Specify the criteria for the DELETE WHERE clause as explained in "Filtering Data" and "Advanced Data Filtering."

The completed delete screen is shown in Figure 14.13.

FIGURE 14.13

Delete mode is used to generate SQL DELETE statements.

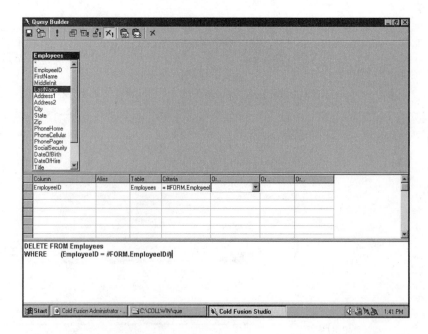

CAUTION

Make sure you always specify a WHERE clause criteria. Otherwise, you will delete every row in the table with the new values.

For more information on the SQL DELETE statement, see Chapter 9. ●

Part

III

Ch

14

CHAPTER 15

Form Data Validation

In this chapter

Understanding Form Validation

HTML forms are used to collect data from users by using several different field types. Forms are used for data entry, as front-end search engines, for filling out orders, signing guest books, and much more. While forms have become one of the most important features in HTML, these forms provide almost no data validation tools.

This becomes a real problem when developing Web-based applications. As a developer you need to be able to control what data users may enter into what fields. Without that, your programs will constantly be breaking due to mismatched or unanticipated data.

Thankfully, ColdFusion provides a complete and robust set of tools with which to implement form data validation, both client-side and server-side.

Since its inception, HTML has always provided Web page developers with a variety of ways to format and display data. With each revision to the HTML specification, additional data display mechanisms have been made available. As a result, HTML is a powerful data-publishing tool.

While its data presentation options continue to improve, HTML's data collection capabilities leave much to be desired. In fact, they have barely changed at all since the language's very early days.

HTML data collection is performed using forms. (See Chapter 12, "ColdFusion Forms," for more information about HTML forms and using them with ColdFusion.) HTML forms support the following field types:

- Free-form text fields
- Select box (or drop-down list boxes)
- Radio buttons
- Check boxes
- Multi-line text boxes
- Password (hidden input) boxes

So what's wrong with this list? Nothing at all. These field types are all the standard fields you would expect to be available to you in any development language. What is wrong, however, is that these fields have very limited capabilities. There are two primary limitations:

- Inability to mark fields as required.
- Inability to define data types or filters—only accepting digits, a zip code, or a phone number, for instance.

What this means is that there is no simple way to tell HTML to disallow form submission if certain fields are left empty. Similarly, HTML cannot be instructed to only accept certain values or types of data in specific fields.

HTML itself has exactly one validation option, the MAXLENGTH attribute, which can be used to specify the maximum number of characters that may be entered in a text field. But that's it. There are no other validation options.

To work around these limitations, HTML developers have typically adopted two forms of validation options:

■ Server-side validation
■ Client-side validation

Comparing Server-Side and Client-Side Validation

Server-side validation involves checking for required fields or invalid values after a form has been submitted. The script on the server first validates the form and then continues processing only if all validation requirements are met. An error message is sent back to the user's browser if validation fails; the user then makes the corrections and resubmits the form. Of course, the form submission has to be validated again upon resubmission, and the process has to be repeated if the validation fails again.

Client-side scripting allows the developer to embed instructions to the browser within the HTML code. As HTML itself provides no mechanism for doing this, developers have resorted to using scripting languages like JavaScript (supported by both Netscape Navigator and Microsoft Internet Explorer) or VBScript (supported by Microsoft Internet Explorer alone). These interpreted languages support basic data manipulation and user feedback, and are thus well suited for form validation. To validate a form, the page author would create a function to be executed as soon as a Submit button is clicked. This function would perform any necessary validation, and only allow the submission to proceed if the validation checked was successful. The advantage of this approach is that the user does not have to submit a form to find out there was an error in it. Notification of any errors occurs prior to form submission.

Understanding the Pros and Cons of Each Option

Neither of these options are perfect, and they are thus often used together, complimenting each other. Table 15.1 lists the pros and cons of each option.

Table 15.1 The Pros and Cons of Client and Server Form Validation

Validation Type	Pros	Cons
Server-side	Most flexible form of validation. Validation is browser-independent.	User must submit data before validation occurs, any errors require correction and resubmission.
Client-side	Validation occurs prior to form submission, allowing for a more intuitive and less aggravating user interface.	Not all browsers support scripting languages. Languages have high learning curves.

From a user's perspective, client-side validation is preferable. Obviously, users would like to know what is wrong with the data they entered *before* they submit the form for processing. From a developer's perspective, however, server-side validation is simpler to code, and less likely to fall victim to browser incompatibilities.

Using Server-Side Validation

As mentioned earlier, server side validation involves adding code to your application that performs form field validation *after* the form is submitted. In ColdFusion this is usually achieved with a series of <CFIF> statements that check each field's value and data types. If any validation steps fail, processing can be terminated with the <CFABORT> function.

There are two ways to perform server-side validation in ColdFusion. You'll look at basic server-side validation first, and then you'll use embedded validation codes to automate the validation where possible.

Using Basic Server-Side Validation

The code shown in Listing 15.1 is a simple login prompt used to gain access to a secure site. The user is prompted for a user id and password. The form itself is shown in Figure 15.1.

On the CD

Listing 15.1 PROMPT1.CFM—HTML Code for the Simple Login Screen Shown in Figure 15.1

```
<FORM ACTION="login1.cfm" METHOD="POST">

<CENTER>
<TABLE BORDER>
 <TR>
  <TH ALIGN="RIGHT">
   ID:
  </TH>
  <TD>
   <INPUT TYPE="text" NAME="login_id" SIZE="5" MAXLENGTH="5">
  </TD>
 </TR>
 <TR>
  <TH ALIGN="RIGHT">
   Password:
  </TH>
  <TD>
   <INPUT TYPE="password" NAME="login_password" SIZE="20" MAXLENGTH="20">
  </TD>
 </TR>
 <TR>
  <TH COLSPAN="2">
   <INPUT TYPE="submit" VALUE="Login">
  </TH>
 </TR>
</TABLE>
```

```
    </CENTER>

    </FORM>
```

FIGURE 15.1

HTML forms supports basic field types, like text and password boxes.

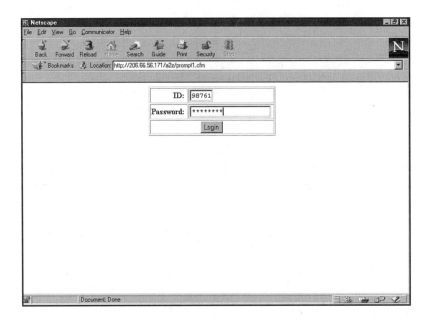

This particular form gets submitted to a template named login1.cfm. That template is responsible for validating the user input, and processing the login only if all the validation rules passed. The validation rules here are:

Login id is required

Login must be numeric

Login password is required

To perform this validation, three <CFIF> statements are used, as shown in Listing 15.2. The first <CFIF> checks the length of login_id after trimming it with the Trim() function. The Trim() function is necessary to trap space characters which are technically valid characters in a text field, but are not valid here. If the Len() function returns 0, an error message is displayed, and the <CFABORT> statements halts further processing.

On the CD

Listing 15.2 LOGIN1.CFM—**Basic Validation Code**

```
<!-- Make sure login_id is not empty -->
<CFIF Len(Trim(login_id)) IS 0>
 <H1>ERROR! ID cannot be left blank!</H1>
 <CFABORT>
</CFIF>
```

continues

Listing 15.2 Continued

```
<!-- Make sure login_id is a number -->
<CFIF IsNumeric(login_id) IS "No">
 <H1>ERROR! Invalid ID specified!</H1>
 <CFABORT>
</CFIF>

<!-- Make sure password is not empty -->
<CFIF Len(Trim(login_password)) IS 0>
 <H1>ERROR! Password cannot be left blank!</H1>
 <CFABORT>
</CFIF>
```

The second `<CFIF>` statement checks the data type. The `IsNumeric()` function returns `Yes` if the passed value was numeric (contained only digits, for example), or `No` if not. Once again, if the `<CFIF>` check fails, then an error is displayed and `<CFABORT>` halts further processing, as shown in Figure 15.2.

FIGURE 15.2

`<CFIF>` statements can be used to perform validation checks and then display error messages if the checks fail.

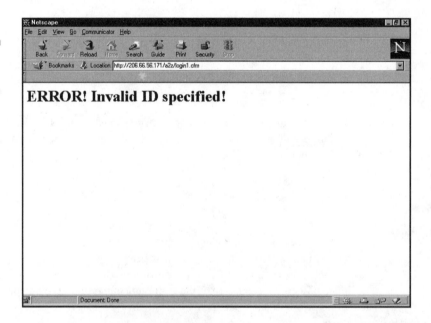

This form of validation is the most powerful and flexible of all the validation options available to you. There is no limit to the number of `<CFIF>` statements you can use, and there is no limit to the number of functions or tags that you can use within them. You can even perform database operations (perhaps to check that a password matches) and use the results in comparisons.

▶ **See** Appendix B, "ColdFusion Function Reference," for a complete list of functions that may be used for form field validation, **p. 865**.

> **TIP**
>
> <CFIF> statements can be combined using AND and OR operators if needed. For example, the first two <CFIF> statements shown in Listing 15.2 could be combined to read
>
> `<CFIF (Len(Trim(login_id)) IS 0) OR (IsNumeric(login_id) IS "No")>`

The big downside here, however, is that this type of validation code is neither clean nor manageable. If you were to add or rename a field for example, you'd have to remember to update the destination form (the form that the fields get submitted to, as specified in the <FORM> ACTION attribute), as well as the form itself. As your forms grow in complexity, so does the likelihood of your forms and their validation rules getting out of synch.

Using ColdFusion Embedded Form Validation

To work around this problem, ColdFusion enables developers to embed basic form validation instructions within an HTML form. These instructions are embedded as hidden form fields. They get sent to the user's browser along with the rest of the form fields, but they are not displayed to the user. Nonetheless, when the user submits the form back to the Web server, those hidden fields are submitted too. ColdFusion can then use them to perform automatic field validation.

To add a validation rule, you add a hidden field to the form. The field name must be the name of the field to validate, followed by the validation rule, for example, _required to flag a field as required. The field's VALUE attribute can be used to specify the error message to be displayed if the validation fails. This next line of code tells ColdFusion that the login_id field is required, and that the error message ID is required! should be displayed if it not present.

`<INPUT TYPE="hidden" NAME="login_id_required" VALUE="ID is required!">`

ColdFusion supports seven basic validation rules, as listed in Table 15.2. It is important to remember that even though the validation rules are being sent to the browser as hidden form fields, the actual validation still occurs on the server after the form has been submitted.

Table 15.2   HTML Validation Rule Suffixes

Suffix	Description
_date	Date in most common date formats like MM/DD/YY and MM/DD/YYYY (year is optional, and will default to the current year if omitted)
_eurodate	Same as _date, but with day before year (European format)
_float	Numeric data, decimal point allowed
_integer	Numeric data, decimal point not allowed
_range	Range of values, the minimum and maximum values (or just one of them) must be specified in the VALUE attribute as MIN= and MAX=, for example, "MIN=5 MAX=10"
_required	Field is required and may not be left blank
_time	Time in most common time formats

N O T E There is no limit to the number of validation rules that you can embed in a form. The only restriction is that every validation rule must be embedded as a separate hidden field. So to flag a field as required and numeric, you'd need two embedded rules, as shown in Listing 15.3. ■

To demonstrate using these validation rules, update the login prompt screen you looked at earlier. Listing 15.3 shows the updated form, to which you've added three lines of code.

Listing 15.3 `PROMPT2.CFM`—**Code for Login Prompt Screen with Embedded Field Validation Rules**

```
<FORM ACTION="login1.cfm" METHOD="POST">

<CENTER>
<TABLE BORDER>
 <TR>
  <TH ALIGN="RIGHT">
   ID:
  </TH>
  <TD>
   <INPUT TYPE="text" NAME="login_id" SIZE="5" MAXLENGTH="5">
   <INPUT TYPE="hidden" NAME="login_id_required" VALUE="ID is required!">
   <INPUT TYPE="hidden" NAME="login_id_integer"
   ➥VALUE="Invalid ID specified!">
  </TD>
 </TR>
 <TR>
  <TH ALIGN="RIGHT">
   Password:
  </TH>
  <TD>
   <INPUT TYPE="password" NAME="login_password" SIZE="20" MAXLENGTH="20">
   <INPUT TYPE="hidden" NAME="login_password_required" VALUE="Password is
   ➥required!">
  </TD>
 </TR>
 <TR>
  <TH COLSPAN="2">
   <INPUT TYPE="submit" VALUE="Login">
  </TH>
 </TR>
</TABLE>
</CENTER>

</FORM>
```

The first rule you added specified that the `"login_id"` field is a required field. The second rule further specifies that only numeric data may be entered into the `"login_id"` field. And finally, the third rule flags the `"login_password"` field as required too.

So, what happens if the validation rules fail? The screen shown in Figure 15.3 is what gets displayed if non-numeric data was entered into the login field and the password field was left blank.

FIGURE 15.3

When using embedded form field validation, ColdFusion automatically displays an error message listing what checks failed.

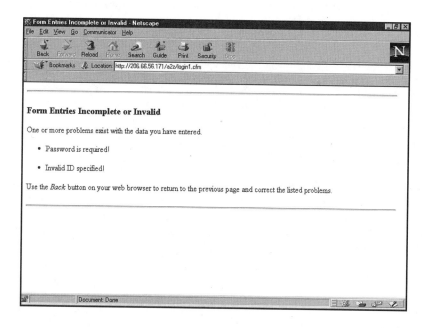

▶ **See** Chapter 26, "Web Application Framework," for information about using <CFERROR>, **p. 637**.

As you can see, the ColdFusion validation rules are both simple and effective. And best of all, because the validation rules are embedded into the form itself, it is less likely that your forms and their rules will get out of synch.

T I P

Validation rules can be embedded anywhere in your form, either before or after the field being validated. To make maintaining your code easier, you should establish guidelines governing rule placement. Two popular standards are grouping all the rules together at the very top of the form, or listing validation rules right after the field that they validate.

Using Client-Side Validation

The biggest drawback in using server-side validation is that the validation occurs after form submission. This means that if any validation rules fail, the user will have to go back to the form, make the corrections, and resubmit it again to the server. To make matters worse, many browsers lose the data in the form fields when the back button is pressed, forcing the user to reenter all the data.

Obviously this is not a user-friendly interface. Too many good Web sites have lost visitors because their forms were too aggravating to work with.

Fortunately there is an alternative, client-side validation.

Understanding Client-Side Validation

To perform client-side validation, you add a series of browser instructions to your Web page. The browser interprets these instructions, and executes them right on the client (the user's computer) before the form ever gets submitted to the server.

These instructions are written in scripting languages, like JavaScript (supported by both Netscape Navigator and Microsoft Internet Explorer) or VBScript (based on Visual Basic, and supported by Microsoft Internet Explorer alone). These are interpreted languages that allow you to control browser behavior.

> **N O T E**   Don't confuse JavaScript with Java. Java is a true compiled object-oriented application development language, one that can be used to write entire programs. JavaScript (including JScript, which is a variant of JavaScript) is an interpreted language design to control Web browsers. Unlike Java, JavaScript cannot access anything on your computer other than your Web browser. ■

To validate a form you would write a script that would trap the form submission, and only allow it to proceed if a series of validation checks passed. If any checks failed, you would display an error message and prevent the form from being submitted.

Of course, to do this, you'd have to learn JavaScript or VBScript.

Using <CFFORM>

To simplify the process of embedding client-side validation scripting code into your forms, ColdFusion includes a tag called <CFFORM>. <CFFORM> is an extremely powerful tag that actually has several distinct functions. The function that you are most interested in here is its support for client-side JavaScript.

> ▶ **See** Chapter 23, "Enhancing Forms with CFFORM," for more information about <CFFORM> and how to use its Java applets to extend your forms, **p. 525**.

So, what can <CFFORM> do for you here? Simply put, <CFFORM> can *automatically* generate JavaScript code to handle most forms of data validation. And the best part of it is that you don't even have to know or learn JavaScript.

To see <CFFORM> in action, once again modify your login screen.

The code in Listing 15.4 is essentially the same code as your original form (see Listing 15.1). The only thing you've changed is replacing <FORM> with <CFFORM> and </FORM> with </CFFORM>.

Listing 15.4   PROMPT3.CFM—Code for <CFFORM>- Driven Login Form

```
<CFFORM ACTION="login1.cfm">

<CENTER>
<TABLE BORDER>
 <TR>
  <TH ALIGN="RIGHT">
```

```
      ID:
     </TH>
     <TD>
      <INPUT TYPE="text" NAME="login_id" SIZE="5" MAXLENGTH="5">
     </TD>
    </TR>
    <TR>
     <TH ALIGN="RIGHT">
      Password:
     </TH>
     <TD>
      <INPUT TYPE="password" NAME="login_password" SIZE="20" MAXLENGTH="20">
     </TD>
    </TR>
    <TR>
     <TH COLSPAN="2">
      <INPUT TYPE="submit" VALUE="Login">
     </TH>
    </TR>
   </TABLE>
   </CENTER>

   </CFFORM>
```

So what happens when ColdFusion processes this form? The best way to understand it is to look at the code that this template generated. You can do this by selecting the View Source option in your browser. The code you see should like something like this:

```
<script LANGUAGE=JAVASCRIPT>
<!--
function _CF_checkCFForm_1(_CF_this)
    {
    return true;
    }
//-->
</script>
<FORM NAME="CFForm_1" ACTION="login1.cfm" METHOD=POST onSubmit=
➥"return _CF_checkCFForm_1(this)">

<CENTER>
<TABLE BORDER>
 <TR>
  <TH ALIGN="RIGHT">
   ID:
  </TH>
  <TD>
   <INPUT TYPE="text" NAME="login_id" SIZE="5" MAXLENGTH="5">
  </TD>
 </TR>
 <TR>
  <TH ALIGN="RIGHT">
   Password:
  </TH>
  <TD>
```

```
  <INPUT TYPE="password" NAME="login_password" SIZE="20" MAXLENGTH="20">
 </TD>
</TR>
<TR>
 <TH COLSPAN="2">
  <INPUT TYPE="submit" VALUE="Login">
 </TH>
</TR>
</TABLE>
</CENTER>

</FORM>
```

The first thing you'll notice is that a JavaScript function has been added to the top of the page. The function currently always returns true, because no validation rules have been set up yet. As you add validation rules to <CFFORM>, this function will automatically be expanded.

The <CFFORM> and </CFFORM> tags in your code (Listing 15.2) have been replaced with standard HTML <FORM> and </FORM> tags.

The <FORM> tag itself now has a NAME attribute with a unique value that was assigned by ColdFusion. You could provide a name yourself, in which case ColdFusion would use your own name instead of generating one for you. If you do specify your own name, make sure that each form on your page is uniquely named.

And finally, an onSubmit attribute was added. This is the JavaScript instruction to your browser that tells it to execute the JavaScript function specified prior to submitting the form to the server. If the specified function returns true, the form submission will continue. If the function returns false, the submission will be canceled.

Using <CFINPUT>

<CFFORM> creates the foundation on which to build JavaScript validation. To specify the validation rules themselves, you have to use the <CFINPUT> tag. <CFINPUT> does the same thing as the standard HTML <INPUT> tag, and takes the same attributes as parameters. But it also takes additional optional attributes, attributes that you can use to specify validation rules.

Look at this code sample:

```
<CFINPUT TYPE="text" NAME="login_id" SIZE="5" MAXLENGTH="5" REQUIRED="Yes">
```

It looks just like a standard <INPUT> tag. The only differences are <CFINPUT> instead of <IN-PUT>, and the extra REQUIRED attribute which has a value of Yes.

And yet this code does so much more than <INPUT>. This <CFINPUT> tag instructs ColdFusion to generate the JavaScript code required to flag this field as required.

So, update your login screen once again.

Listing 15.5 is yet another updated version of your login screen. This time you've replaced the "login_id" field's <INPUT> tag with a <CFINPUT> tag.

On the CD

Listing 15.5 PROMPT4.CFM—**Code for Login Prompt Screen with** <CFINPUT> **Used to Flag Required Field**

```
<CFFORM ACTION="login1.cfm">

<CENTER>
<TABLE BORDER>
 <TR>
  <TH ALIGN="RIGHT">
   ID:
  </TH>
  <TD>
   <CFINPUT TYPE="text" NAME="login_id" SIZE="5"
   ➟MAXLENGTH="5" REQUIRED="Yes">
  </TD>
 </TR>
 <TR>
  <TH ALIGN="RIGHT">
   Password:
  </TH>
  <TD>
   <INPUT TYPE="password" NAME="login_password" SIZE="20" MAXLENGTH="20">
  </TD>
 </TR>
 <TR>
  <TH COLSPAN="2">
   <INPUT TYPE="submit" VALUE="Login">
  </TH>
 </TR>
</TABLE>
</CENTER>

</CFFORM>
```

When ColdFusion processes this new form, it generates no fewer than 50 lines of JavaScript code (as shown here), and all automatically.

```
<script LANGUAGE=JAVASCRIPT>
<!--
function _CF_onError(form_object, input_object, object_value,
➟error_message)
    {
        alert(error_message);
        return false;
    }
function _CF_hasValue(obj, obj_type)
    {
    if (obj_type == "TEXT" || obj_type == "PASSWORD")
        {
        if (obj.value.length == 0)
                return false;
        else
                return true;
        }
    else if (obj_type == "SELECT")
```

```
             {
             for (i=0; i < obj.length; i++)
                     {
                     if (obj.options[i].selected)
                             return true;
                     }
             return false;
             }
         else if (obj_type == "RADIO" || obj_type == "CHECKBOX")
             {

             for (i=0; i < obj.length; i++)
                     {
                     if (obj[i].checked)
                             return true;
                     }
             return false;
             }
         }
 function  _CF_checkCFForm_1(_CF_this)
     {
     if  (!_CF_hasValue(_CF_this.login_id, "TEXT" ))
         {
         if  (!_CF_onError(_CF_this, _CF_this.login_id, _CF_this.login
         ➥id.value, "Error in login_id text."))
             {
             return false;
             }
         }
     return true;
     }
 //-->
 </script>

 <FORM NAME="CFForm_1" ACTION="login1.cfm" METHOD=POST onSubmit=
 ➥"return _CF_checkCFForm_1(this)">

 <CENTER>
 <TABLE BORDER>
  <TR>
   <TH ALIGN="RIGHT">
    ID:
   </TH>
   <TD>
    <INPUT TYPE="TEXT" NAME="login_id" SIZE=5 MAXLENGTH=5>
   </TD>
  </TR>
  <TR>
   <TH ALIGN="RIGHT">
    Password:
   </TH>
   <TD>
    <INPUT TYPE="password" NAME="login_password" SIZE="20" MAXLENGTH="20">
   </TD>
  </TR>
  <TR>
   <TH COLSPAN="2">
```

```
    <INPUT TYPE="submit" VALUE="Login">
   </TH>
  </TR>
 </TABLE>
 </CENTER>

 </FORM>
```

As you can see, the <CFINPUT> tag has been replaced by a standard HTML <INPUT> tag. In fact, the generated tag looks exactly the same as the <INPUT> tag looked before you added the <CFINPUT> attributes. Those attributes were used by ColdFusion to generate the JavaScript code, which ensures that a blank "login_id" field cannot be submitted. If the user tries to submit the form, the JavaScript will pop up an error message box as shown in Figure 15.4.

FIGURE 15.4

Unless otherwise specified, a default error message is used when JavaScript validation rules fail.

N O T E The pop-up error box is a standard browser dialog box that varies from browser to browser, and there is no way to change what it looks like. The only thing you can change is the actual error message itself.

Using <CFINPUT> Validation Options

So far you have used <CFINPUT> to flag fields as required. And if you were impressed with that, wait, there's more. <CFINPUT> also lets you specify data type validation rules, as well as customized error messages.

To provide these capabilities, <CFINPUT> supports all the attributes supported by HTML <INPUT>, as well as some additional ones. These are listed in Table 15.3.

Table 15.3 <CFINPUT> Attributes

Attribute	Description
MESSAGE	Error message text to pop up if this field's validation fails.
ONERROR	The name of a JavaScript function to execute if a validation rule fails, overriding the default error function.
ONVALIDATE	To override the default JavaScript validation code, and to use your own JavaScript, specify the JavaScript function name here.
RANGE	Range of valid values (for numeric data only) specified as "minimum;maximum".

continues

Table 15.3 Continued

Attribute	Description
REQUIRED	Set to `"Yes"` to flag field as required, default is `"No"`.
VALIDATE	One of the nine supported data validation types, as listed in Table 15.4.

The `<CFINPUT>` VALIDATE attribute takes a data type as a value. The supported data types are listed in Table 15.4.

Table 15.4 `<CFINPUT>` Data Validation Types

Type	Description
Creditcard	Blanks and dashes are stripped and the number is verified using the mod10 algorithm
date	Verifies U.S. date entry in the form mm/dd/yyyy
eurodate	Verifies valid European date entry in the form dd/mm/yyyy
float	Verifies a floating point entry
integer	Verifies an integer entry
social_security_number	Social Security Number in the form ###-##-#### (the hyphen separator can be replaced with a blank)
telephone	Verifies a telephone entry, telephone data must be entered as ###-###-#### (the hyphen separator can be replaced with a blank), the area code and exchange must begin with a digit between 1 and 9
time	Verifies a time entry in the form hh:mm:ss
zipcode	(U.S. formats only) Number can be a 5-digit or 9-digit zip in the form #####-#### (the hyphen separator can be replaced with a blank)

Now that you've seen what `<CFINPUT>` can do, update your login screen one final time. The code shown in Listing 15.6 uses `<CFINPUT>` tags for both input fields, and flags both of them as required fields. In addition, the `"login_id"` has a validation type of `"integer"` which will prevent the user from entering non-numeric data in it. And finally, both fields have custom error messages specified using the MESSAGE attribute. If validation fails, then the specified error message will be displayed as shown in Figure 15.5.

On the CD

Listing 15.6 PROMPT5.CFM—The Completed Prompt Form, with JavaScript Validation

```
<CFFORM ACTION="login1.cfm">

<CENTER>
<TABLE BORDER>
 <TR>
  <TH ALIGN="RIGHT">
   ID:
  </TH>
  <TD>
   <CFINPUT TYPE="text" NAME="login_id" SIZE="5" MAXLENGTH="5"
   ➡REQUIRED="Yes" VALIDATE="integer" MESSAGE="Numeric ID is required!">
  </TD>
 </TR>
 <TR>
  <TH ALIGN="RIGHT">
   Password:
  </TH>
  <TD>
   <CFINPUT TYPE="password" NAME="login_password" SIZE="20" MAXLENGTH="20"
   ➡REQUIRED="Yes" MESSAGE="Password is required!">
  </TD>
 </TR>
 <TR>
  <TH COLSPAN="2">
   <INPUT TYPE="submit" VALUE="Login">
  </TH>
 </TR>
</TABLE>
</CENTER>

</CFFORM>
```

FIGURE 15.5
The <CFINPUT>
MESSAGE attribute can
be used to customize
the displayed error
message.

Putting It All Together

Before you run off and plug in <CFFORM> and <CFINPUT> into all your templates, there are some other details that you should know.

- Not all browsers support JavaScript, and those that don't will ignore it, allowing your forms to be submitted without being validated.

- It is a good idea to combine the use of JavaScript validation with server-side validation using embedded fields. These will never fail validation if the browser does support JavaScript, and if the browser does not, at least you have some form of validation.

- Older browsers (including some versions of Netscape 3) might have trouble with some of the generated JavaScript, so make sure you test your forms in as many different browsers as possible.

- The JavaScript code can be quite lengthy, and this will increase the size of your Web page and thus the time it takes to download it from your Web server.

The Report Writer

Introducing Crystal Reports Professional

Crystal Reports Professional has long been recognized as one of the most powerful and easy-to-use report writers available. This is why so many software vendors, including Allaire, have chosen it as the report writer to be bundled with their applications.

Crystal Reports Professional is popular because

- It is easy to use, and even provides *experts* (essentially wizards with a different name) that step you through the process of creating reports.
- It supports all major databases, including SQL Server, Oracle, and all ODBC drivers.
- It can create reports based on Web-server logs and Windows NT system logs.
- It enables you to create reports, charts, graphs, mailing labels, forms, cross-tab reports, and more.
- It provides you with flexible formatting and display options.
- It displays previews of how your report will look using live data.
- It can convert reports into HTML on-the-fly.

It is the last feature in this list that makes Crystal Reports Professional so appealing to ColdFusion developers.

N O T E Crystal Reports does not have to be installed on the computer running your Web server and ColdFusion. All the files that ColdFusion uses to interact with Crystal Reports' RPT files are installed during the ColdFusion installation. ■

A Note from the Author

Crystal Reports Professional version 5 is an extremely powerful and capable report writer. Complete coverage of all of its features is beyond the scope of this book.

This chapter does not teach you everything there is to know about Crystal Reports Professional. Instead, it teaches you how to create a basic report with the report writer and how to execute that report from within your ColdFusion templates.

Crystal Reports Professional comes with complete online help and step-by-step tutorials. If you are planning on using the report writer, I strongly urge you to use these tools.

Crystal Reports Professional only reads your data files, it does not write to them. Therefore, there is nothing that you can do within the report writer that will corrupt or damage any data, so don't be afraid to experiment.

Creating Reports with Crystal Reports Professional

To learn how to use the report writer, start by creating a simple report—an employee directory.

T I P You can use Crystal Reports on any computer, not just on the Web server machine. Make sure, however, that the ODBC data source you use is set up exactly the same way it is on the Web server machine. That way you can be sure that reports created on one computer will work on another.

For starters, load the Crystal Reports program. Click its icon to display the welcome screen shown in Figure 16.1. You are presented with two options: one to create a new report and the other to open an existing report. Select the New Report option to display the Report Gallery, which is shown in Figure 16.2. The Report Gallery displays eight popular report types from which you can select, but also allows you to create your own type.

Part III

Ch 16

FIGURE 16.1

The Crystal Reports Professional welcome screen prompts you to either create a new report or open an existing one.

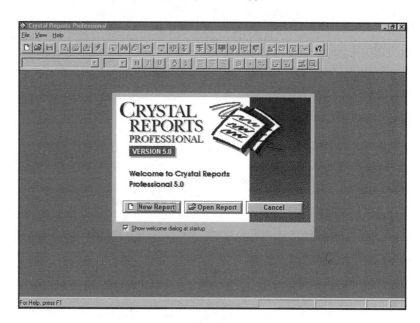

FIGURE 16.2

The Report Gallery allows you to pick a report type or create a custom type.

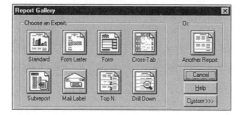

You're going to create a standard report, so select the Standard button to display the

The *experts* are interactive tools that walk you through much of the report design process. Crystal Reports' experts are made up of multiple screens in a tabbed dialog box, as shown in Figure 16.3. You may jump to any screen by clicking a tab at the top. Alternatively, you may use the Back and Next buttons to walk through the screens while building your report.

FIGURE 16.3

The Create Report Expert walks you through the process of creating a report.

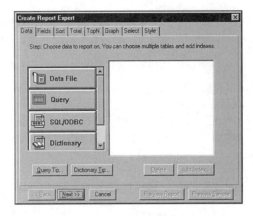

To build your report, follow these steps:

1. The first thing you need to do is specify the tables to be used in this report. You use data from an ODBC data source, so select the SQL/ODBC option from the list of data types.

2. You are prompted for a server type. Servers are what Crystal Reports calls any data source, including ODBC data source. The list of servers includes both ODBC data sources (they all have the prefix *ODBC*) and other sources available to you. You use the A2Z ODBC data source, so select ODBC-A2Z from the list and then choose OK.

3. Now that you have specified a data source, Crystal Reports can prompt you for the tables to include in the report. Select the Employees table and the Departments table for your first report, and then choose Add. Once you have selected both files, choose Done.

4. Because you selected more than one table for your report, the expert now wants to know how these tables are related. To set relationships between tables, you must locate the related columns in each table and then drag one to the other in order to link them. The columns that link your two tables are the DepartmentID column in the Employees table, and the ID column in the Departments table. Scroll down the list of columns in the Employees table until you find the DepartmentID column; click it. Drag it to the ID column in the Departments table. The Expert draws a white line that shows the link between the two tables (see Figure 16.4). (You can choose Arrange to arrange the tables to clearly see the links.) When you have finished creating the link, choose Next.

5. Now the expert needs to know which fields to include in the report. The left list is Database Fields, which contains all the available fields sorted by table and fields within a table. The right list is Report Fields, which contains any selected fields. To include fields in a report, select them from the left list and click the Add button. Select these fields in this order: Employees.LastName, Employees.FirstName, Departments.Department, Employees.PhoneExtension.

6. Unless you specify alternative text, Crystal Reports uses the field name as the column heading when displaying your data in the final report. To specify column heading text, select a field from the Report Fields list and enter the desired text into the Column Heading field. Set the Employees.LastName field to Last Name, Employees.FirstName to First Name, leave the Departments.Department field as is, and set the

Employees.PhoneExtension field to Extension. Choose Next when you have completed this step.

7. Now you can specify a sort order. You want the list sorted by last name plus first name. Select Employees.LastName from the Report Fields list and click the Add button to select that field. Now do the same for the Employees.LastName field. The selected fields are shown in the Group Fields list.

8. Your basic report does not require any of the options in the other expert screens, so click Preview Report to see what the finished report will look like. As shown in Figure 16.5, the report writer displays a preview of the finished report using live data retrieved from the specified tables.

9. There are two tabs, Design and Preview, above the display area in Figure 16.6. The Preview tab allows you to preview the finished report at any time. The Design tab is where you can modify the report layout. Choose the Design tab to show the Design screen, which is divided into groups (also called *bands*). The top group, Page Header, contains information that appears at the top of every page in the report. The bottom group, Page Footer, contains information that appears at the bottom of each page. The middle group is Details, which contains the fields that appear in the body of the report. The Details group is repeated once for every row selected in the final report.

10. To format or change any field or text, you need to right-click it. This action displays a context-sensitive menu containing options applicable to the selected field. Change the format of the column headers by selecting all four column headers at once by clicking your mouse above the first column and then dragging the box outline over all four fields. When you release the mouse button, all four fields are selected. Now right-click any of the selected fields and select the Format Objects option. Select the Font page and set the Font to Arial, the Size to 12, and turn off Underline; then choose OK. The Design view immediately reflects the changes you just made. (You can also switch to the Preview view at any time to see how the change affects the final report.)

11. The Page Footer group contains a page number field. This is a very useful field for printed reports, but is useless for reports that display as Web pages. When a report is output as a Web page, it is formatted as a single page, so you should remove that field. To remove it, click the field to select it and press the Delete key.

12. Save and name the report. Crystal Reports saves its reports in RPT files and each RPT file contains a single report. Select the Save option from the File menu and save the report as EMPLIST.RPT in the C:\A2Z\SCRIPTS directory.

You've just created a complete report using the Crystal Reports report writer. You may print this report at any time by selecting Print from the File menu.

N O T E Many of the report writer's formatting features cannot be supported by HTML, so some advanced formatting is lost when the report output displays in a Web page. For example, Crystal Reports allows you to specify single, double, or mixed borders around text, all of which are rendered into HTML as standard TABLE borders. Before rolling out your reports for public use, make sure you test them thoroughly to ensure that the output is acceptable.

Part

III

Ch

16

FIGURE 16.4

The Expert graphically displays any links established between different tables.

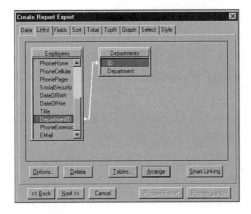

FIGURE 16.5

Crystal Reports Professional previews reports using live data that enables you to see exactly how a finished report will look.

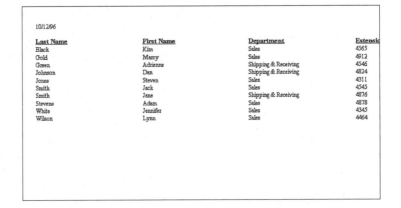

Embedding Reports into ColdFusion Templates

Reports created with Crystal Reports Professional can easily be printed. Your interest is in its HTML publishing capabilities because Crystal Reports is most often used for printing.

Reports are embedded into ColdFusion Templates using the <CFREPORT> tag. When ColdFusion processes a template and encounters a <CFREPORT> tag, it executes a Crystal Reports engine, which processes the report and creates an HTML version of the report output.

N O T E ColdFusion returns an error message if you try to process a report that is already open in Crystal Reports. You must close any reports in the report writer before using them with ColdFusion. ▓

Now create a template to process the report you just created. Listing 16.1 contains the code to process report EMPLIST.RPT. As you can see, the code listing is standard HTML, except for the <CFREPORT> tag. <CFREPORT> requires a single attribute, REPORT, which contains the name and fully qualified path of the report to execute. Create a template containing the code in Listing 16.1 and save it as EMPLIST.CFM in the C:\A2Z\SCRIPTS directory.

FIGURE 16.6
Use the Design screen to make any changes to a report.

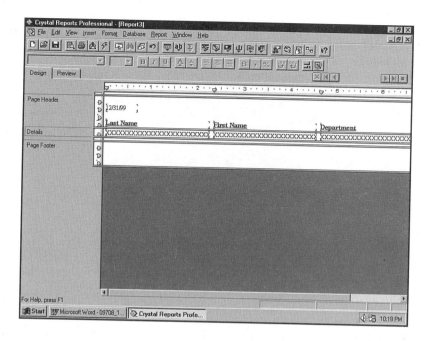

On the CD

Listing 16.1 EMPLIST.CFM—**Employee List Displayed Using a Crystal Reports Professional Report**

```
<HTML>

<HEAD>
<TITLE>Employee List</TITLE>
<HEAD>

<BODY>

<CFREPORT REPORT="emplist.rpt" >
</CFREPORT>

</BODY>

</HTML>
```

Now test the report. Load your Web browser and go to http://*yourservername*/a2z/ emplist.cfm. After a few seconds of processing, your browser display should look like the one shown in Figure 16.7.

Customizing Reports On-The-Fly

Crystal Reports Professional enables you to interactively create powerful reports that you can easily embed into ColdFusion.

FIGURE 16.7

ColdFusion executes a
Crystal Reports
Professional engine to
process embedded
reports.

10/12/96			
Last Name	**First Name**	**Department**	**Extension**
Stevens	Adam	Sales	4878
Smith	Jack	Sales	4545
White	Jennifer	Sales	4345
Black	Kim	Sales	4565
Wilson	Lynn	Sales	4464
Gold	Marcy	Sales	4912
Jones	Steven	Sales	4311

ColdFusion also allows you to pass parameters to the Crystal Reports processing engine, enabling you to customize the reports on-the-fly.

For example, the phone list report you created earlier displays all employees in all departments. How could you create a report to display the employees in a single department?

You could create multiple reports and specify a filter condition in each one. One report would filter only the Sales department employees, another would filter just the Shipping and Receiving department employees, and so on.

It can be done, but it is definitely not a scalable or manageable solution. A better alternative is to use the same report and modify it on-the-fly by passing additional information to it.

The code in Listing 16.2 shows how this is done. The <CFREPORT> tag is the same, but you add a line between the <CFREPORT> and </CFREPORT> tags. The code {Departments.Department} = "Sales" is passed to the Crystal Reports engine as a selection filter. In this case, only employees who have a Departments.Department value of " Sales" are included in the report.

Listing 16.2 EMPSALES.CFM—**Crystal Reports with Passed Filter Condition**

```
<HTML>

<HEAD>
<TITLE>Employee List</TITLE>
<HEAD>

<BODY>

<CFREPORT REPORT="emplist.rpt">
{Departments.Department} = "Sales"
</CFREPORT>

</BODY>

</HTML>
```

N O T E   Field names passed to Crystal Reports must be fully qualified with the table name and must be enclosed within curly braces.

The selection criteria may even be made up of ColdFusion tags, functions, and fields. For example, instead of hard coding the filter to a department called Sales, you could have compared it to a passed field name. In fact, the entire filter condition could be contained with a `<CFIF>` conditional statement so that the same template could display as many different employee lists as needed.

▶ **See** "`<CFREPORT>`" for more details about how the ColdFusion interface to the Crystal Reports Engine enables you to specify options and attributes other than the ones discussed in this chapter, **p. 838**.

Part

III

Ch

16

Debugging and Troubleshooting

Debugging ColdFusion Applications

As with any development tool, sooner or later you're going to find yourself debugging or troubleshooting a ColdFusion problem. Many different applications and interfaces have to work seamlessly in order for a ColdFusion application to function correctly. The key to quickly isolating and correcting problems is a thorough understanding of ColdFusion, ODBC data sources, SQL syntax, the CGI interface, URL syntax, and your Web server.

If the prospect of debugging an application sounds overly bleak, don't panic. Thankfully, ColdFusion has powerful built-in debugging and error-reporting features. These capabilities, coupled with logical and systematic evaluation of trouble spots, enable you to diagnose and correct all sorts of problems.

This chapter teaches you how to use the ColdFusion debugging tools and introduces techniques that help you quickly locate the source of a problem. More importantly, because an ounce of prevention is worth a pound of cure, guidelines and techniques that help prevent common errors from occurring in the first place are introduced.

Understanding What Can Go Wrong

As an application developer, sooner or later you are going to have to diagnose, or *debug*, a ColdFusion application problem. Because ColdFusion relies on so many other software components to work its magic, there are a lot of places where things can go wrong.

As you are reading this chapter, the following assumptions are made:

- You are familiar with basic ColdFusion concepts.
- You understand how ColdFusion uses ODBC for all database interaction.
- You are familiar with basic SQL syntax and use.

If you are not familiar with any of these topics, it is strongly recommended that you read the chapters on them before proceeding.

▶ **See** Chapter 2, "Introduction to ColdFusion," for more information on how ColdFusion works, and how all the pieces fit together to create a complete application, **p. 17**.

▶ **See** Chapter 6, "Database Fundamentals," for a detailed explanation of databases, tables, rows, columns, keys, and other database-related terms, **p. 87**.

▶ **See** Chapter 8, "Introduction to SQL," for more information about ODBC drivers and data sources, and how ColdFusion uses them for all database interaction, **p. 129**.

Almost all ColdFusion problems fall into one of the following categories:

- Web server configuration problems
- ODBC driver errors
- SQL statement syntax or logic errors
- ColdFusion syntax errors
- URL and path problems

Now look at each of these potential problem areas to learn what can go wrong in each.

Debugging Web Server Configuration Problems

You should almost never encounter ColdFusion problems during routine, day-to-day operation of your Web server that are caused by Web server configuration problems. These kinds of problems almost always occur either during the initial ColdFusion setup or while testing ColdFusion for the first time.

You receive a "ColdFusion Application Server not currently running" error when attempting to execute a ColdFusion script. This error, shown in Figure 17.1, is generated by both the ColdFusion server modules and the CGI when they cannot communicate with the ColdFusion Application Server.

FIGURE 17.1

The ColdFusion Application Server must be running or else all ColdFusion requests will generate an error message.

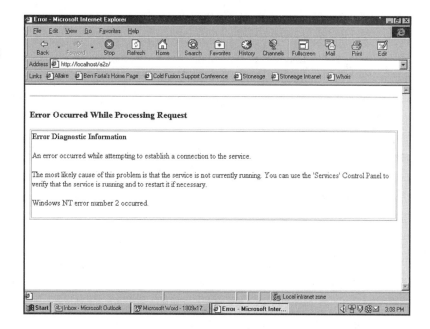

The Application Server must be running for ColdFusion to process templates. Steps to verifying that the server is running, and starting it if it is not, differ based on your operating system.

If you are running ColdFusion on a Windows NT machine, you should run the Service applet in the Window NT Control Panel. It will determine whether the service is running and start it if is not.

If you are running Windows 95 or Windows 98, you'll see the ColdFusion icon on the taskbar (near the clock) when the Application Server is running. If it is not running, select ColdFusion from the ColdFusion program groups under your Start button menu.

Windows NT services can be started automatically every time the server is restarted. The service Startup option must be set to Automatic in order for a service to start automatically. Windows 95 and Windows 98 users can automatically start ColdFusion by ensuring that the ColdFusion Application Server is in the Programs, Startup group. This setting is turned on by the ColdFusion installation procedure, and typically should be left on at all times. However, if the service does not automatically start, check these options.

Every time you try to execute a ColdFusion script, your browser prompts you to save a file. If you are using ColdFusion via CGI, the most common Web server configuration problem is the Web server not being able to find the CGI script—the CFML.EXE file. If you are using the Web server modules, this is not an issue.

As explained in Chapter 2, a Web server has to know that the script is a CGI script that needs to be executed—not just a file to be served when requested—in order to correctly execute a CGI script.

Different Web servers use different mechanisms to achieve this. Table 17.1 lists the configuration requirements of some of the more popular Web servers.

Table 17.1 Web Server CGI Configuration Requirements

Web Server	Configuration
Microsoft IIS and	The default CGI directory is a directory Personal Web Server called SCRIPTS mapped as SCRIPTS in the server properties. You may map another CGI directory to wherever CFML.EXE is installed, or copy CFML.EXE into the SCRIPTS directory. If you do map another directory, make sure the Execute option is enabled in the mapping properties.
Netscape Commerce	Netscape servers do not enable CGI support or Enterprise by default when installed. You need to use the administration server to enable CGI support and then create a mapping to the directory that contains CFML.EXE. You then use that mapping in every ColdFusion URL.
O'Reilly WebSite	The default mapping and directory for CGI scripts is the CGI-SHL directory. Assuming you have not changed this default, just copy the CFML.EXE file into that directory. Of course, you may change the mapped directory, or add another, if you so desire.

If your Web server does not know that the CFML.EXE file is a script, it will try to send you the file every time you make a ColdFusion request, instead of executing the script and returning the response.

If you are being prompted to save a file, one of the following two things is wrong:

■ You did not set up the script mapping on the Web server, and as a result, the server is trying to serve the script rather than execute it. To fix this, make sure the CFML.EXE file is in a CGI or SCRIPTS directory (see Table 17.1).

■ Your Web server allows you to create multiple maps to the same directory, and you are using the wrong directory mapping.

You can verify that the CGI file is being executed and not served: Use your browser to go to an URL that specifies the CFML.EXE CGI script, but does not specify a ColdFusion template. If ColdFusion is installed correctly and you are using a correct script mapping, you receive an error message telling you that no template was specified. If you are prompted to save a file, refer to Table 17.1.

N O T E This section only affects users who are using ColdFusion with its CGI interface. As explained in Chapter 2, this is a practice that should generally be avoided. ■

Part

III

Ch

17

Debugging ODBC Driver Errors

ColdFusion relies on ODBC for all its database interaction. You receive ODBC error messages if ColdFusion cannot communicate with the appropriate ODBC driver, or the driver cannot communicate with the database.

ODBC error messages are always generated by an ODBC driver, not by ColdFusion. ColdFusion merely displays whatever error message it received from the ODBC driver. However, ColdFusion often adds its own suggestions to the error screen to help you diagnose the problem, as shown in Figure 17.2.

FIGURE 17.2

ColdFusion attempts to display useful information along with ODBC error messages.

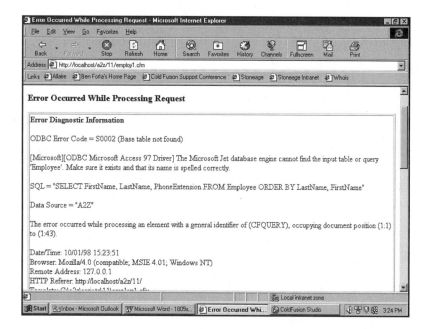

> ▶ **See** "Introducing ODBC" or more information about ODBC drivers and what they are used for, **p. 131**.

ODBC error messages always contain an error number, which by itself is pretty useless. A text message that describes the problem follows the error number, however. The text of these messages varies from driver to driver, and so it would be pointless to list all the possible error messages here. Instead, the more common symptoms and how to fix the problems that cause them are listed.

 You can use the ColdFusion Administrator to verify that an ODBC data source is correctly set up, and that it is attached to the appropriate data file correctly. To do this, run the ColdFusion Administrator and select the Verify Data Sources option from the menu on the left. Then select the data source from the displayed list. ColdFusion attempts to connect to the data source, and notifies you of its success or failure.

Receiving the ODBC Error Message "Data Source Not Found"

Cold Fusion communicates with databases via ODBC drivers. These drivers access data sources—external data files. If the ODBC driver reports that the data source could not be found, check the following:

- Make sure you have created the ODBC data source.
- Verify that the data source name is spelled correctly. ODBC data source names are not case sensitive, so don't worry about that.
- Under Windows NT, ODBC data sources are *user login-specific*. If you create a data source from within the ODBC Control Panel applet while logged in as a user without administrator privileges, then only that user will have access to that ODBC data source. To prevent this situation from occurring, always create ColdFusion's ODBC data sources from within the ColdFusion Administrator program.

Receiving the ODBC Error Message "File Not Found"

You may get the error message "File not found" when trying to use a data source you have created. This error message only applies to data sources that access data files directly (like Microsoft Access, Microsoft Excel, and Borland dBASE), and not to client/server database systems (like Microsoft SQL Server and Oracle).

"File not found" simply means that the ODBC driver could not locate the data file in the location it was expecting to find it. To diagnose this problem, perform the following steps:

1. Data files must be created before ODBC data sources can use them. If you have not yet created the data file, you must do so before proceeding.
2. Check the ODBC data source settings, verify that the file name is spelled correctly, and ensure that the file exists.
3. If you have moved the location of a data file, you must manually update any ODBC data sources that reference it.

Receiving Login or Permission Errors When Trying to Access a Data Store

Some database systems, like Microsoft SQL Server, Sybase, and Oracle, require that you log on to a database before you can access it. When setting up an ODBC data source to this kind of database, you must specify the login name and password that the driver should use to gain access.

The following steps will help you locate the source of this problem:

1. Verify that the login name and password are spelled correctly. (You will not be able to see the password, only asterisks are displayed in the password field.)

2. On some database systems, passwords are case sensitive. Make sure that you have not left the Caps Lock key on by mistake.

3. Verify that the name and password you are using do indeed have access to the database to which you are trying to connect. You can do this using a client application that came with your database system. (For example, if you are using Microsoft SQL Server you can use the iSQL/w utility to try to connect with the database via the suspect name and password.)

Receiving the ODBC Error Message "Unknown Table"

After verifying that the data source name and table names are correct, you may still get "unknown table" errors. A very common problem, especially with client/server databases like Microsoft SQL Server, is forgetting to provide a fully qualified table name. There are two ways you can do this:

■ Explicitly provide the fully qualified table name whenever it is passed to a SQL statement. Fully qualified table names are usually made up of three parts, separated by periods. The first is the name of the database containing the table; the second is the owner name (usually specified as dbo); the third is the actual table name itself.

■ Some ODBC drivers, like the Microsoft SQL Server driver, allow you to specify a default database to be used if none is explicitly provided. If this option is set, its value is used whenever a fully qualified name is not provided.

 TIP If your ODBC driver allows you to specify a default database name, use that feature. This allows you to write fewer and simpler hard-coded SQL statements.

Debugging SQL Statement or Logic Errors

Debugging SQL Statements is one of the two types of troubleshooting that you'll spend most of your debugging time doing (the other is debugging ColdFusion syntax errors, which you get to next). You will find yourself debugging SQL statements if you run into either of these situations:

■ ColdFusion reports SQL syntax errors. Figure 17.3, for example, is an error caused by misspelling a table name in a SQL statement.

■ No syntax errors are reported, but the specified SQL statement did not achieve the expected results.

FIGURE 17.3

ColdFusion displays the SQL error reported by ODBC and often attempts to provide hints of its own.

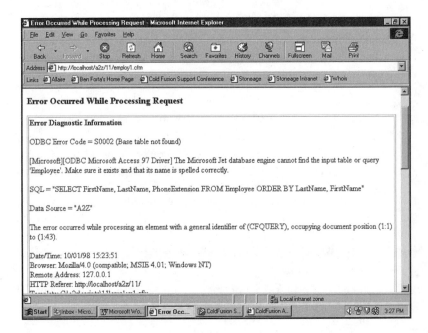

Obviously, a prerequisite to debugging SQL statements is a good working knowledge of the SQL language. I'm assuming that you are already familiar with the basic SQL statements and are comfortable using them. See Chapter 9, "SQL Data Manipulation," for information about basic SQL statements and examples of their use.

The keys to successfully debugging SQL statements are as follows:

1. Isolate the problem. Debugging SQL statements inside ColdFusion templates can be tricky, especially when creating dynamic SQL statements. Try executing the same statement from within another ODBC client, like Microsoft Query or ColdFusion Studio, replacing dynamic parameters with fixed values if appropriate.

2. The big difference between ColdFusion SQL statements and statements entered into any other ODBC client, is the use of ColdFusion fields. If you are using ColdFusion fields within your statement, verify that you are enclosing them within quotation marks when needed. If the value is a string, it must be enclosed in single quotation marks. If it is a number, it must not be enclosed in quotation marks.

3. Look at the bigger picture. Dynamic SQL statements are one of ColdFusion's most powerful features, but this power comes with a price. When you create a dynamic SQL statement, you are effectively relinquishing direct control over the statement itself, and

are allowing it to changed based on other conditions. This means that the code for a single ColdFusion query can be used to generate an infinite number of queries. Because some of these queries might work—and others might not—debugging dynamic SQL requires that you be able to determine exactly what the dynamically created SQL statement looks like. Thankfully, ColdFusion makes this an easy task, as you will see a little later in the "Using the ColdFusion Debugging Options" section.

4. Break complex SQL statements into smaller, simpler statements. If you are debugging a query that contains subqueries, verify that the subqueries properly work independently of the outer query.

Whenever a SQL syntax error occurs, ColdFusion displays the SQL statement it submitted. The fully constructed statement is displayed if your SQL statement was constructed dynamically.

The field names are displayed as submitted if the error occurred during an INSERT or UPDATE operation, but the values are replaced with question marks (except for NULL values, which are displayed as NULL).

▶ **See** "Creating Dynamic SQL Statements" for more information about ColdFusion's dynamic SQL statement support, **p. 241**.

Part
III

Ch
17

  If you are using ColdFusion Studio (and you should be), then you can completely avoid typos in table and column names by using the Studio database drag-and-drop support. To do this, open the database tab in the Resource Tab, select the desired data source, and expand the tables to find the table and column you need. You can then click on the table or column name and just drag it to the Editor window where it will be inserted when you release the mouse key.

Debugging ColdFusion Syntax Errors

Debugging ColdFusion syntax errors is the other type of troubleshooting you'll find yourself doing. Thankfully, and largely as a result of the superb ColdFusion error reporting and debugging capabilities, these are usually the easiest bugs to find.

ColdFusion syntax errors are usually one of the following:

- Mismatched pound signs or quotation marks
- Mismatched begin and end tags; a <CFIF> without a matching </CFIF>, for example
- A tag with a missing or incorrectly spelled attribute
- Missing quotation marks around tag attributes
- Using double quotation marks instead of single to delimit strings when building SQL statements
- Illegal use of tags

If any of these errors occur, ColdFusion generates a descriptive error message, as shown in Figure 17.4. The error message lists the problematic code (and a few lines before and after it) and identifies exactly what the problem was.

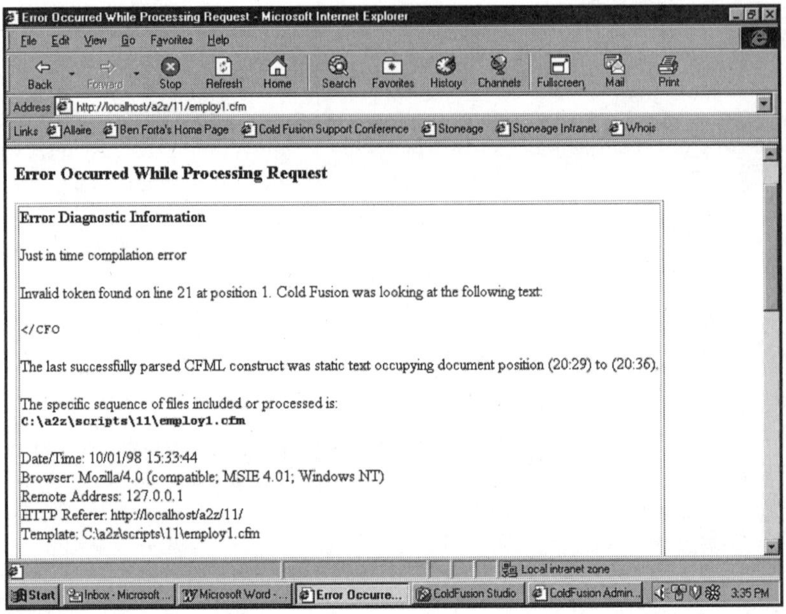

FIGURE 17.4
ColdFusion generates descriptive error messages when syntax errors occur.

CAUTION

If your template contains HTML forms, frames, or tables, you might have trouble viewing generated error messages. If an error occurs in the middle of a table, for example, that table will never be terminated and there is no way to know how the browser will attempt to render the partial table. If the table is not rendered and displayed properly, you will not see the error message.

TIP If you think that an error has occurred but no error message is displayed, you may view the source in the browser. The generated source will contain any error messages that were included in the Web page but not displayed.

One of the most common ColdFusion errors is missing or mismatched tags. Indenting your code, as shown in Listing 17.1, is a good way to ensure that all tags are correctly matched.

Listing 17.1 Nesting Conditional Code Makes Debugging Mismatched Tags Much Easier

```
<CFIF some condition here>
 <CFOUTPUT>
  Output code here
  <CFIF another condition>
   Some other output code here
  </CFIF>
 </CFOUTPUT>
<CFELSE>
```

```
Some action here
</CFIF>
```

 TIP You can use <CFABORT> anywhere in the middle of your template to force ColdFusion to halt further processing. You can move the <CFABORT> tag farther down the template as you verify that lines of code work.

ColdFusion Studio users should take advantage of Studio's Tag Insight, Tag Tips, and Tag Completion features to avoid common mismatching problems. The right-click menu's Edit Tag option is also useful in helping prevent typos in tags and their attributes. See Chapter 10, "Introduction to ColdFusion Studio," for more information about ColdFusion Studio and its tag options.

 You can use a custom tag called CF_Log, which can be found on this book's CD-ROM. The tag simplifies the process of writing debugging log files.

On the CD

Part

III

Ch

17

Using the Document Validator

To help you catch syntax errors before your site goes live, ColdFusion Studio has an integrated Validator. The Validator can be used to check for mismatched tags, unknown variables, missing pound signs, and other common errors.

To use the Validator, open the file to be checked in Studio and then select Validate Document from the Tools menu. ColdFusion Studio validates your code and lists any errors in a Results window at the bottom of the screen as seen in Figure 17.5.

To quickly jump to the problematic code, just double-click the error message in the Results window. As seen in Figure 17.6, the Studio Validator displays the same error message as ColdFusion itself does at runtime, and even highlights the trouble spot in the Editor window. This enables you to fix errors before you roll out your application.

TIP To quickly validate the current document while you are editing it, press Shift+F6.

N O T E You can customize the behavior of the Validator, including specifying what gets validated, and what tags to validate. To do this, select Settings from the Options menu, and then select the Validate tab. ▪

Debugging URL and Path Problems

URL and path problems are less of an issue when using server module-style URLs than they are when using CGI-style URLs. If you are using ColdFusion's CGI interface, ColdFusion has to maintain its own mappings and the Web server mappings are not used. This is yet another reason why you should always use the server modules if possible.

FIGURE 17.5

The ColdFusion Studio Validator lists any errors in a Results window.

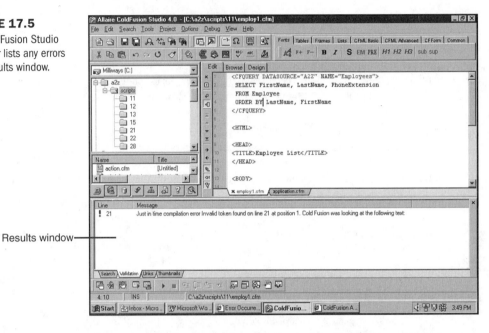

Results window——

FIGURE 17.6

The error message highlighted in the Studio Validator.

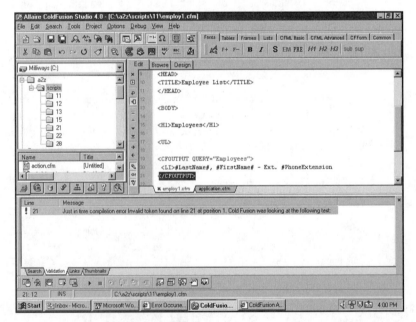

Referencing Files That Are Not Displayed

Image files (and other files) are not always displayed when you reference them from within ColdFusion. If you are using CGI-style URLs, you may not use relative paths to images or files.

Relative paths (paths to files without a full path from the server root) are treated by the browser as being relative to the current page. Because the current page is the result of a CGI script and not an actual file, the relative paths will be incorrect.

As a rule, if you are using CGI-style URLs, any included files (like images) must be somewhere beneath the server root—not in the template directory.

Passing Parameters That Are Not Processed

Parameters that you pass to an URL may not be processed by ColdFusion, even though you see them present in the URL. URLs are finicky little beasts, and you have to abide by the following rules:

- URLs may only have one question mark character in them. The question mark separates the URL itself from the query.
- Each parameter must be separated by an ampersand (&) in order to pass multiple parameters in the URL query section.
- URLs must not have spaces in them. If you are generating URLs dynamically based on table column data, you must be sure to trim any spaces from those values. If you must use spaces, replace them with plus signs. ColdFusion correctly converts the plus signs to spaces when used. Use the ColdFusion URLEncodedFormat() function to convert text to URL-safe text.

Debugging Form Problems

If a form is submitted without data, it can cause an error. There are two ways in which Web browsers submit data to Web servers. These are called GET and POST, and the submission method for use is specified in the FORM METHOD attribute.

As a rule, forms being submitted to ColdFusion should always be submitted using the POST method. The default method is GET, so if you omit or misspell METHOD = "POST", ColdFusion will be unable to process your forms correctly.

You can occasionally get an "Unknown variable" error message when referring to form fields in the action template. Radio buttons, checkboxes, and list boxes are not submitted if no option was selected. It is important to remember this when referring to form fields in an action template. If you refer to a checkbox without first checking for its existence (and then selecting it), you'll generate an error message.

The solution is to always check for the existence of any fields or variable before using them. Alternatively, you can use the <CFPARAM> function to assign default values to fields, thereby ensuring that they always exist.

See Chapter 12, "ColdFusion Forms," for more information about working with form fields and working with specific form controls.

How can you check what form fields were actually submitted and what their values are? Enable ColdFusion debugging—any time you submit a form, its action page contains a debugging section that describes the submitted form. This is shown in Figure 17.7. There is a field named FORMFIELDS, which contains a comma-delimited list of all the submitted fields, as well as a list of the submitted fields and their values.

FIGURE 17.7

ColdFusion displays form-specific debugging information if debugging is enabled.

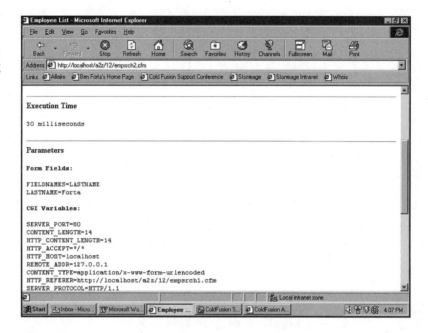

Using the ColdFusion Debugging Options

The ColdFusion debugging options are enabled or disabled via the ColdFusion Administrator program. To enable debugging, check the debugging options you want to monitor in the Administrator's Debugging tab; that tag is shown in Figure 17.8. You should also specify the IP addresses to which you'd like to send debugging information. At a minimum, the local host IP address (127.0.0.1) should be specified. If no IP address is in the list, debugging information will be sent to anyone who browses any ColdFusion page.

▶ **See** Chapter 4, "Administering ColdFusion," for more information about the ColdFusion Administrator program, **p. 57**.

The ColdFusion debugging options work by appending debugging information to the end of any generated Web pages, as shown in Figure 17.9. The exact information that is displayed varies, based on the options you selected and the contents of your template.

TIP You may restrict the display of debugging information to specific IP addresses. If you enable debugging, you should generally use this feature to prevent debugging screens from being displayed to your site's visitors.

FIGURE 17.8

The ColdFusion Administrator's Debugging tab allows you to enable debugging options, as well as specify the IP address.

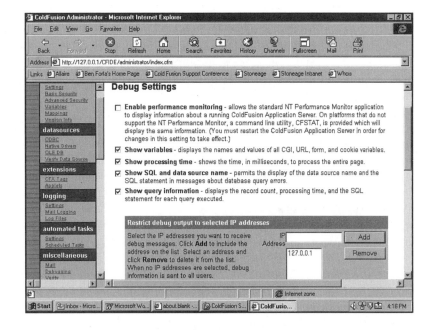

FIGURE 17.9

ColdFusion can append debugging information to any generated Web page.

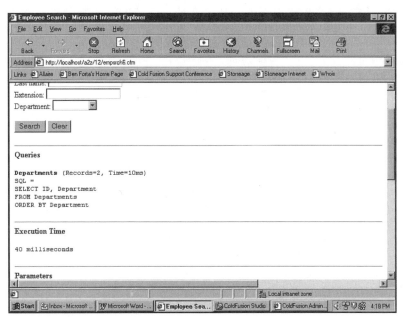

You will often find yourself needing temporary access to debug information for specific IP addresses. You'll find a CFX tag, CFX_Debug, on the CD-ROM. The tag enables you to simply turn on and off debug information without having to access the ColdFusion Administrator.

Using the Studio Remote Debugger

ColdFusion Studio (version 4 or later only) features a complete integrated remote debugger. Key features of the Debugger include the following:

- Debug applications running on any server, local, or across any IP connection
- Create breakpoints to examine code where needed
- Examine variables and expressions mid-execution
- Analyze query results in real time
- Browse the tag stack dynamically
- Monitor output generation

Full coverage of all the features of this powerful tool are beyond the scope of this chapter. What follows, however, should be enough information to get you up and running using the Debugger.

N O T E   The Debugger can only be used to debug code on a server configured as a remote RDS server within ColdFusion Studio. To debug local files you must have a local RDS server configured. For more information on configuring RDS servers, see Chapter 10. ■

The ColdFusion Debugger is controlled using the Debug toolbar. This is usually at the bottom of the Studio window, as seen in Figure 17.10.

FIGURE 17.10

The ColdFusion Studio Debugger is controlled using the Debug toolbar.

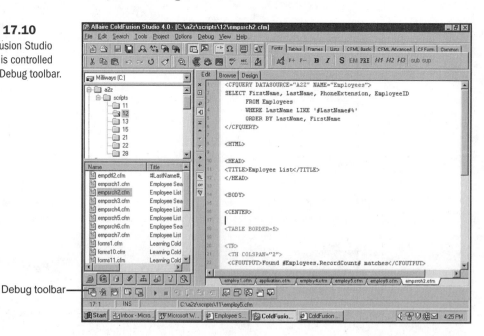

The Debug toolbar contains the following buttons:

🖐	Display list of breakpoints
✂	Clear all breakpoints
🖐	Toggle the current breakpoint
➡	Debugger settings
🗔	Debugger mappings
▶	Start Debugger
■	Stop Debugger
⬇	Step into code
⬇	Step over code
⬆	Step out of current code block
➡	Run to cursor
🔍	Display watches
▦	Display record sets
🗂	Display tag stack
📄	Display output
🔍	Display variables

N O T E The following examples use files from Chapter 11 of this book. They can be found in the
`\A2Z\SCRIPT\11` directory. ▨

To use the Debugger, open the page to be debugged in the Editor window. You can set breakpoints (points in your code where the Debugger should stop and wait for your input) by clicking on the line number in the gray bar to the left of the Editor window. You can only put breakpoints on CFML code. Figure 17.11 shows a breakpoint on a `<CFOUTPUT>` tag. When a breakpoint is set the line of code is displayed with a red background.

FIGURE 17.11

The ColdFusion Studio Debugger is controlled using the Debug toolbar.

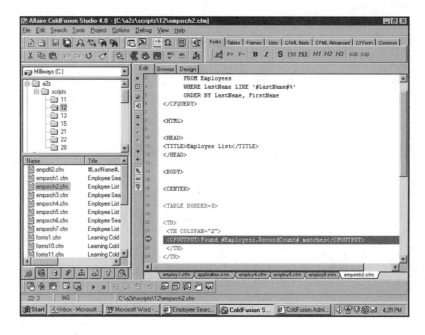

 TIP To remove a single breakpoint, click on the line number again twice. To remove all breakpoints click on the Clear All Breakpoints button in the Debug Toolbar.

To use the Debugger, simply click the Start Debugging button in the Debug Toolbar, or select Start from the Debug menu. You will be prompted with a Remote Development Settings dialog box, as shown in Figure 17.12.

FIGURE 17.12

Debugger settings, including the initial file to load, are specified in the Remote Development Settings dialog box.

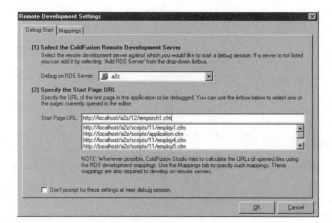

In the Debug on RDS Server field specify the server to debug against. The default value here should be correct.

In the Start Page URL specify the URL to start the Debugger in. By default, Studio will construct a URL for the currently selected file. If you are debugging a page that must be called from another page (for example, a form action page), then you must specify that initial page URL in this field.

Once you have entered the information into these two fields, click the OK button to start the Debugger. This will display the Debug window as seen in Figure 17.13.

FIGURE 17.13

The Debug window hovers over the Studio window, allowing you to browse your files and access debug options at the same time.

Once the Debugger has started, you typically will want to execute the program until the first breakpoint has been reached. To do this, use the program in the Studio Browse window. You might have to move the Debug window out of the way to get to the page.

As soon as a breakpoint is reached, the Debugger will stop execution and highlight the breakpoint with a blue background. In Figure 17.14 the Debug window displays the breakpoint that was reached.

FIGURE 17.14

The Breakpoints pane in the Debug window shows all breakpoints, and allows adding, editing, and deleting of breakpoints.

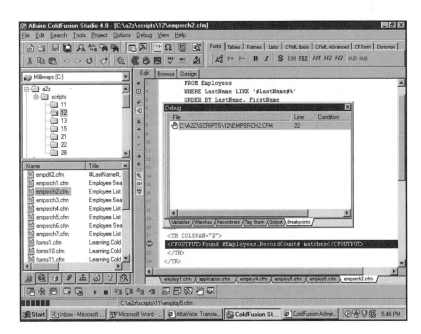

Part

III

Ch

17

Once code execution has stopped, you may use any of the debugging options by selecting the tabs in the Debug window. To display a list of all variables and their values, click on the Variables tab. The variables are categorized by type as seen in Figure 17.15, and each type can be expanded or closed as needed.

FIGURE 17.15

The Variables pane shows the current value all variables, categorized by type.

The Watches tab lets you enter variables or expressions that you can monitor, as seen in Figure 17.16. As they change, their values are updated in this window. To evaluate an expression once, type it in the expression field and click the Evaluate button. To watch (*monitor*) an expression, type it in the Expression field and click the Watch button.

FIGURE 17.16

The Watches pane shows the all expressions being watched, and allows for the real type evaluation of expressions.

The Recordset tab displays a list of all queries that have been executed up to the breakpoint. As seen in Figure 17.17, the query name, number of rows retrieved, and the SQL statement are listed in this tab.

FIGURE 17.17

The Recordset pane shows all executed queries and their details.

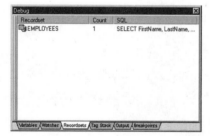

The Tag Stack pane as seen in Figure 17.18 shows you the current page being executed and the calling tag stack if there is one. If you are debugging a page that has been called or included from any other page, those pages will be listed in descending order.

FIGURE 17.18

The Recordset pane shows all executed queries and their details.

The Output pane, shown in Figure 17.19, displays the HTML output as it is being generated. The data shown here is post-processing data, the same data that will be sent back to the client browser.

FIGURE 17.19

The Output pane shows generated client output as it is being generated.

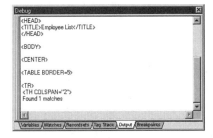

The Debug pane can be opened, closed, moved, and broken out into multiple panes. Each of the panes can be undocked and repositioned as needed, as seen in Figure 17.20. To move a pane, select and drag it by clicking the double vertical lines to the left of the pane.

As you can see, the remote Debugger provides you with industrial-strength tools to aid you in pinpointing code trouble spots—the kind of tool never yet seen in the Internet application development space.

Part
III

Ch

17

FIGURE 17.20

The Output pane shows generated client output as it is being generated.

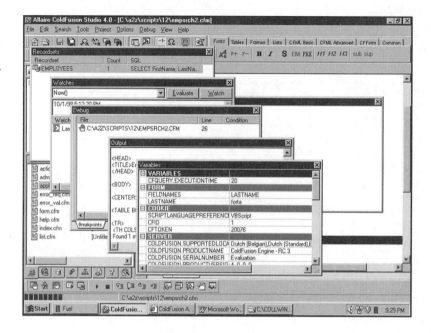

Using the ColdFusion Log Files

ColdFusion logs all warnings and errors to log files, which aids you and Allaire Technical Support in troubleshooting problems. ColdFusion log files are created when the ColdFusion service starts. You may delete these log files if they get too large, or move them to another directory for processing. If you do move or delete the log files, ColdFusion will create new ones automatically.

 TIP   If you are having trouble locating the ColdFusion log files, check the Debugging screen in the ColdFusion Administrator program. That is where the location of the log files is specified.

All of the ColdFusion log files are plain-text, comma-delimited files. You may import these files into a database or spreadsheet application of your choice for analysis.

ColdFusion creates several log files:

- APPLICATION.LOG logs every ColdFusion error reported to a user. All template errors, including ColdFusion syntax errors, ODBC errors, and SQL errors, are written to this log file. This is the log file you will typically want to monitor so that you'll know of any problems that are occurring. Every error message displayed on a visitor's browser is logged here, along with the visitor's IP address and browser information, if possible.

- CFSLTRACE.LOG logs trace messages from ColdFusion script code within <CFSCRIPT> tags.

- CLIENT.LOG logs error messages logged by the COM objects used in the ColdFusion Studio client environment.

■ EXECUTIVE.LOG logs problems with the ColdFusion Executive service.

■ PERFMON.LOG logs errors returned by the Performance Monitor module CFPERF.DLL.

■ RDSSERVICE.LOG logs problems with the ColdFusion Remote Development Service.

■ REMOTE.LOG logs messages and error returned by the CFDIST listener module.

■ SCHEDULER.LOG logs ColdFusion scheduled events scheduled using the Administrator or the <CFSCHEDULE> tag.

■ SERVER.LOG logs system failure messages. If the SMTP mailer cannot be initialized, it is logged to this file.

■ UNKNOWN.LOG is a catch-all for any messages from parts of ColdFusion that the logging systems cannot identify.

■ WEBSERVER.LOG logs errors that occurred in the communication between Cold Fusion and your Web server.

See Chapter 32, "Event Scheduling," for more information about scheduled events.

The ColdFusion Administrator provides Web-based access to all the system log files. Select the Log Files options from the menu on the left to display a list of log files. Select a log file to display buttons that allow you to view or download the file as seen in Figure 17.21. To view a file online, as shown in Figure 17.22, click the View the File button.

FIGURE 17.21

ColdFusion Administrator allows you to view or download log files from any browser.

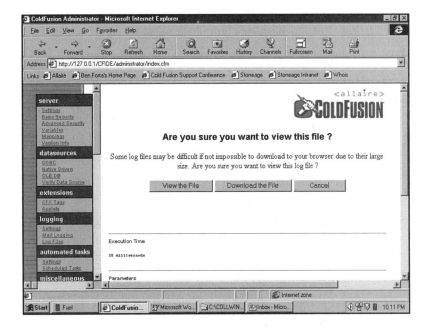

You should definitely get into the habit of inspecting the contents of the APPLICATION.LOG file on a regular basis. To make this easier, you'll find a CFX tag on the CD-ROM called CFX_ViewCFLog. This tag allows you to display and filter the APPLICATION.LOG log file, as well as view it within your Web browser.

FIGURE 17.22

Log files may be viewed within the Administrator window directly.

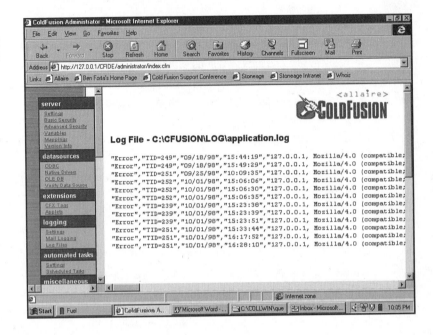

Some errors are browser-related. If you are having a hard time reproducing reported error messages, try to determine which version of which browser the user was running and on what platform. You may find that you have run into browser bugs (yes, some versions of popular browsers are very buggy). The APPLICATION.LOG file logs any identification information provided by a browser, along with the error message.

End users are notorious for reporting that "an error occurred" without specifying what the error message was, what screen they were on, and what they were doing when the error was generated. The log files, the APPLICATION.LOG file in particular, can help you find an error message if you know roughly when it occurred and who it was sent to.

Preventing Problems

As mentioned earlier, the best approach to troubleshooting ColdFusion problems (and indeed any development problems) is to prevent them from ever occurring in the first place.

Bugs are inevitable. As the size of an application grows, so does the likelihood of a bug being introduced. As an application developer, you need to have two goals in mind:

1. Develop 100% bug-free code.
2. In the event that your code is not 100% bug-free, make sure that it is easy to debug.

As an application developer myself, I know that these are lofty goals. The reality of it is that application development almost always takes longer than planned, and sacrifices have to be made if release dates are to be met. Code quality is usually the first thing that gets sacrificed.

Of course, sooner or later these sacrifices come back to haunt you. Then come the long debugging sessions, rapid code fixes, software upgrades, and possibly even data conversion. Then, as the rapidly patched code often introduces bugs of its own, the whole cycle restarts.

While there is no surefire way of preventing all bugs, there are guidelines and coding practices that both help prevent many of them and make finding them easier when they do occur. Here are my 10 Commandments of ColdFusion development:

I. **Functionality first, then features.** This might seem like an obvious one, but it is one of the most common beginner mistakes. Implementing fancy interface ideas is much more fun than perfecting or optimizing search routines, but the search routines are more important. The fancy outputting techniques will clutter the important code and make it even harder to debug.

II. **Never develop applications on a live server.** Another obvious but often ignored rule. That "safe little cosmetic enhancement" might not be as safe or as little as it seems. No enhancement is ever worth bringing an existing working application down to its knees.

III. **Test each piece of code individually.** Trying to find a bug amidst a several-hundred[nd]line template is like looking for a needle in a haystack. The best way to test code is to isolate it. After you have verified that a SQL statement works properly, plug it into your template—never before.

IV. **Write code with reuse in mind.** Anything worth doing is worth doing properly, and application development is no exception. When designing a piece of code, it's worth putting in a little extra effort up front to ensure that the code is neither task specific nor hard coded unless it has to be. Always try to keep the big picture in mind.

V. **Break long source files into shorter, more manageable ones.** ColdFusion lets you include templates within other templates. There is a very slight performance penalty in doing this, but the degradation is never enough to warrant long, unmanageable templates. Smaller, more focused templates are easier to maintain, and they lend themselves very well to code reuse.

VI. **Comment your code.** You're going to have to revisit it one day, and descriptive template headers and embedded comments will help you remember why you did what you did. This also helps prevent you from making changes without realizing what else they will impact.

VII. **Use descriptive variable names.** Six months from now you will not remember what `ord` or `var` were used for. A variable name like `order_number` or `OrderNumber` takes a little longer to type, but you will remember what it stored.

VIII. **Don't be scared to waste space.** The "don't kill trees" rule does not apply to software development. Be a little wordier if necessary, space your code properly to make it more readable, and don't cram so much text onto one line that you have to scroll your editor to read it. Yes, the extra whitespace might make your source files a little bigger; yes, every character counts when the generated output is transmitted over a slow modem connection—but be a little selfish sometimes. You have to maintain the code, and your time is worth preserving too.

IX. **Set coding standards.** There are no right or wrong ways to present your code. Any coding style is good if it helps make your code easier to read and more maintainable. This becomes even more important if more than one developer is working on a project. If you are part of a team of developers, try to agree on what style of variable names to use, when to indent code, what should be capitalized and what should not, and so on.

X. **Implement a version control system.** ColdFusion applications, by their very nature, are made up of many different source files; these files change regularly. Version control lets you keep tabs of all changes to each source file and allows you to restore all files to the state they were in at any prior time. Both of these capabilities will become vital to you as your application grows. Version-control applications, like PVCS or Microsoft SourceSafe, are inexpensive and are an investment well worth making. ColdFusion Studio supports both client and server side version control management, so there is no excuse for not using this invaluable tool.

Advanced ColdFusion

Working with Projects

Understanding Projects

By now you have learned that ColdFusion applications are made up of file sets of many different types. As the complexity and depth of your applications grows, so will the number of files that you find yourself regularly working with. Some of the most common types of files are as follows:

- ColdFusion application pages (.CFM files)
- Static HTML pages (usually .HTM or .HTML files)
- Images (GIF and JPEG files, for example)
- Imagemaps

More often than not, you will find yourself having to read, edit, update, and manipulate more than one file at a time when working on your Web application. This typically requires opening multiple files and manually determining which files belong with which.

Introducing ColdFusion Studio Projects

ColdFusion Studio allows you to group sets of files in a single unit. These units are called projects. A *project* is simply a container for one or more other files. You can add files (or entire directories) into a project, you can open and close entire projects with one selection, and you can even upload projects to remote servers in one step.

Project support is fully integrated into ColdFusion Studio. All of Studio's standard features can be used with project files. The only difference is that instead of working with specific files, you are working with sets of files.

Where to Use Projects

How projects are defined, and what files are put into them, is entirely up to you. You may create projects that contain entire applications, small subsets of an application, or any combination thereof.

Here are some guidelines that you can use to determine how to define your projects:

- Start off with one project for your entire application (including all subdirectories). This project will be too big for use most of the time, but it is still useful for making global changes or searches.
- Create multiple projects for logical subsets of the application. These subsets could be directories, specific menu options and associated files, related functions, or any other grouping that makes sense.
- A single file may be part of multiple projects. You can therefore create multiple projects for an application with overlapping files if needed.
- Consider grouping files and their included file (or related custom tags) in projects together; this makes them easier to work with.

TIP If you do remote development (via the ColdFusion Remote Development Services), you should definitely create multiple smaller projects in addition to any larger projects. Opening a smaller project over a remote connection is much quicker than opening a large project. Remote projects are described at the end of this chapter.

N O T E ColdFusion Studio projects cannot span multiple file servers. Once a project has been created, you will only be able to add files if they are within the directory structure defined when the project was first created. ■

Using Projects

ColdFusion projects are created and maintained within ColdFusion Studio. The projects themselves are stored as plain text files within the directory the project was created in. These files have an extension of APJ, and double-clicking them (in Windows Explorer) directly opens Studio and with the entire project loaded.

N O T E ColdFusion projects are only available within the ColdFusion Studio environment. Individual project components may be accessed with any other tools, but the project itself can only be accessed and manipulated using ColdFusion Studio. ■

There are two ways to access projects within ColdFusion Studio:

■ Most project manipulation occurs in the Projects tab in the Resource tab within ColdFusion Studio.

■ Specific project manipulation functions are accessible via the Project menu option.

The options in both of these locations are discussed in detail in this chapter.

The Studio Project Tab

The Project tab, seen in Figure 18.1, is in the Studio Resource tab; it is split into two panes. The upper pane shows directories within a project, and the lower pane shows files within a selected directory.

TIP If you are having trouble locating the Project tab, hold your mouse over each of the tabs at the bottom of the Resource tab until the name pops up.

There are a series of controls above the upper pane. These can be used as shortcut option to open a recent project, create a new project, or upload a project to a remote server. See Figure 18.2 for the exact position of each of these controls.

Part
IV

Ch

18

FIGURE 18.1

The Project tab is used to manage and interact with ColdFusion Studio projects.

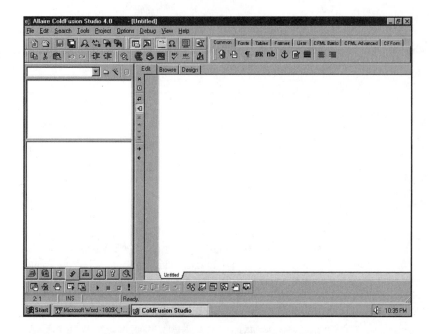

FIGURE 18.2

The Project tab features shortcut controls for some of the more commonly used project manipulation functions.

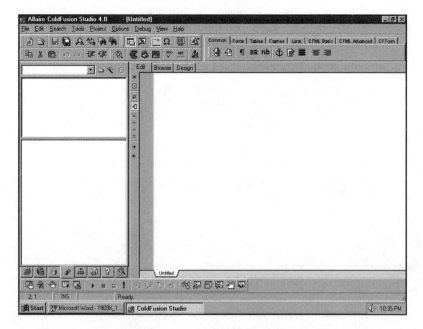

As with all the screens and tabs in Studio, the panes in the Projects tab feature context-sensitive right mouse button support. You can right-click in either pane for options related to that pane.

Creating Projects

There are several ways to create a new project:

- Select New Project from the Project menu.
- Click the New Project button (above the upper Project tab pane).
- Right-click in the upper pane and select New Project.

Any of these options will display the New Project dialog box shown in Figure 18.3.

FIGURE 18.3
The New Project dialog box is used to create new ColdFusion Studio projects.

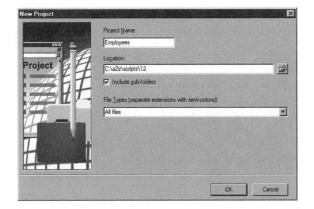

The steps to create a local project are as follows:

1. Display the New Project dialog box.
2. Specify a unique name for the project in the Project Name field. Be as descriptive as possible, using punctuation or whatever special characters you need.
3. In the Location field specify the root directory that contains the files to be included in the project. The APJ file is created in this directory. The directory may be any locally accessed directory (with a full or UNC path).
4. By default, all subdirectories in the specified directory are included in the project. To prevent this, uncheck the Include Subfolders check box.
5. Specify the files to be included in the File Types field. You can select the default All Types selection, any selection from the drop-down list box, or enter the extensions of specific files you want.

TIP For simple graphics manipulation, you might want to create a project called Graphics that contains all the GIF and JPEG images throughout your entire application (including files in all subdirectories).

Once the project has been created it will automatically be opened as seen in Figure 18.4. The upper pane shows the directories in your project, and the lower pane shows the files within a specified directory.

FIGURE 18.4

Open projects are displayed in the Project tab, with directories in the upper pane and files in the lower pane.

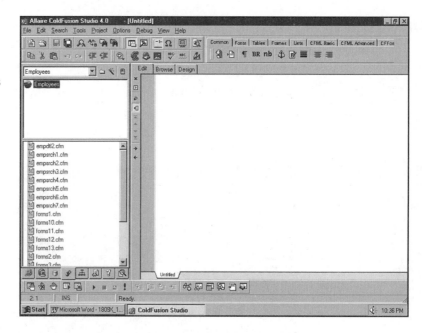

Opening Existing Projects

To open an existing local project, do any of the following:

- Select Open Project from the Project menu.
- Click the Open Project button (above the upper Project tab pane).
- Right-click in the upper pane and select Open Project.

Any of these options will display the Open dialog box shown in Figure 18.5.

FIGURE 18.5

The Open dialog box is used to open existing project files.

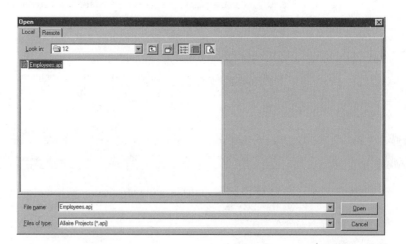

To open a *local* project (a project to which you have direct access via your PC), select the Local tab and locate the required APJ file. Once you have found the APJ file, click the Open button.

T I P To reopen a recently used project, select that project name from the Recent Projects drop-down list box above the upper pane. You can also select the project name by selecting Reopen Project from the Projects menu.

Manipulating Project Files

ColdFusion Studio makes it very easy to manipulate or edit files in an open project. You may open individual files, all files, or files in a selected directory.

- To open a single file, double-click it in the Project tab's lower pane. This opens the file for editing, just like any other file in Studio.
- To open all files, right-click in the upper pane; make sure that pane has focus by ensuring that a directory is selected. Select the Open All Documents in Project option. This opens every file in your project for editing.
- To open the files in a specific directory within a project, select that directory in the upper pane, right-click it, and select the Open All Documents in This Folder option. (The option is labeled Open All Documents in Root Folder if you select the project's root directory.)

You can then edit these files directly in Studio.

Modifying Projects

Once a project is created its contents remain the same unless you explicitly change them.

To add files to a project, click the directory that contains the files to be added, right-click, and select the Add Files to Project option. This displays the Add Files to Project dialog box as shown in Figure 18.6. This dialog box only displays the files that are not currently in the project. Select as many files as needed and then click the OK button.

FIGURE 18.6
Files may be added to existing projects using the Add Files to Project dialog box.

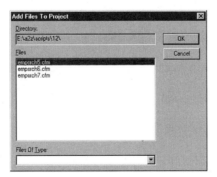

To remove a file from a project, select the file in the lower pane, right-click it, and select Remove from Project.

Part

IV

Ch

18

TIP To refresh a specific directory or to add or remove files from a specific directory, click the directory in the upper pane, right-click, and select the Refresh option.

Performing Global Searches and Changes

In addition to grouping files together for opening and editing, ColdFusion allows you to perform global searches and changes to projects with a single action. These operations are accessed via the Extended Find and Extended Replace selections in the Search menu.

Extended Find is used to search for text in one or more files. Extended Find supports case-sensitive and non–case-sensitive searches, as well as regular expression searches. The Extended Find dialog box is shown in Figure 18.7.

FIGURE 18.7

Extended Find can be used to perform searches across entire projects.

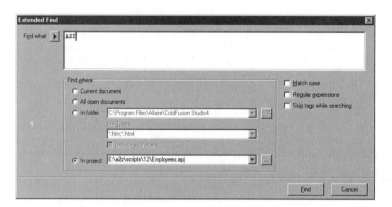

For more information about regular expressions, see Chapter 20, "Regular Expressions," in *Advanced ColdFusion 4.0 Application Development* (Que, 1999).

Extended Replace is used to find and replace text in one or more files. Like Extended Find, Extended Replace supports case-sensitive and non–case-sensitive replacements, as well as regular expression replacements. The Extended Replace dialog box is shown in Figure 18.8.

Both the Extended Find and Extended Replace dialog boxes allow you to select a project on which to perform this operation. In order to use projects you must set the Find Where option to In Project. You may select the project from a drop-down list of recently used projects, or find the project directly by clicking the ellipsis button.

NOTE Projects do not have to be open to perform Extended Find and Extended Replace operations. ■

Closing Projects

To close a project, select the Close Project option from the Project menu. Any project files that are open in the Studio Editor window are closed, too. If you have not saved any files, you are prompted to save them before they are closed.

FIGURE 18.8

Extended Replace can be used to make text replacements across entire projects.

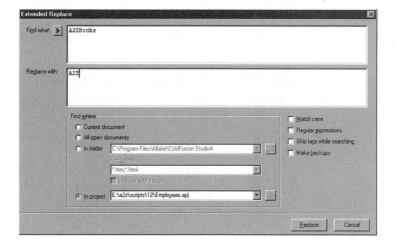

Using Remote Projects

As mentioned earlier in this chapter, ColdFusion Studio fully supports the use of remote projects. *Remote* projects are those that are accessed over a TCP/IP connection via a ColdFusion server running on a remote site.

In order to use remote projects, you must have already configured the remote server within ColdFusion Studio. If you have not yet set up your remote servers, click the Resource tab's Remote Files tab.

For more information about ColdFusion Studio remote servers, see Chapter 10, "Introduction to ColdFusion Studio."

Creating Remote Projects

The steps to create a remote project are as follows:

1. Make sure that the desired remote server has already been set up within ColdFusion Studio.

2. Display the New Project dialog box as explained in "Creating Projects."

3. Specify a unique name for the project in the Project Name field. Be as descriptive as possible, using punctuation or whatever special characters you need.

4. To set the location, click the folder button to the right of the Location field; this displays the Select Directory dialog box. Select the Remote tab to show the remote server selector as shown in Figure 18.9. Expand the servers and directories to find the desired project's root directory. The APJ file is created in this directory.

5. By default, all subdirectories of the specified directory are included in the project. To prevent this, uncheck the Include Subfolders checkbox.

Part
IV

Ch
18

6. Specify the files to be included in the File Types field. You may select the default All Types selection, any selection from the drop-down list box, or enter the extensions of specific files you want.

FIGURE 18.9

The Create Project dialog box's Select Directory Remote tab is used to create projects on a remote ColdFusion server.

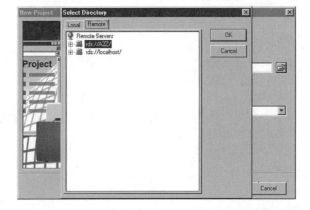

Opening Remote Projects

To open an existing remote project, do any of the following:

- Select Open Project from the Project menu.
- Click the Open Project button (above the upper Project tab pane).
- Right-click in the upper pane and select Open Project.

Any of these options will display the Open Project dialog box. Select the Remote tab, as shown in Figure 18.10, to select the appropriate remote server. You need to expand the servers and directories to locate the required APJ file.

FIGURE 18.10

The Open Project dialog box's Remote tab is used to open projects that reside on a remote ColdFusion server.

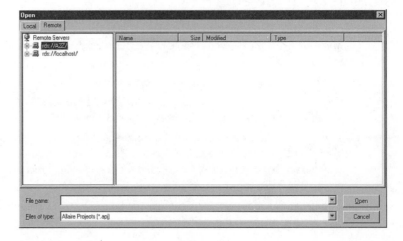

Click the Open button when you find the APJ file.

TIP The reopen options (described in the tip in "Opening Existing Projects") can also be used to open remote projects.

Uploading Projects

Projects are especially useful when working remotely. The capability to open sets of files for editing saves time, particularly over slower connections.

Projects can also be used to simplify deploying applications developed locally. For example, imagine an ISP situation. If an ISP hosts your ColdFusion application, you will likely be doing all development on a local host and only deploying the finished application to the ISP's site once the application is complete.

The traditional way to do this is to develop the application locally and then FTP the files one by one (each to their appropriate directories) over an FTP connection. While this is workable, it is not an ideal solution. Manually sending files over an FTP connection involves creating individual directories, selecting the local files and the appropriate remote directories for each, checking which files have been changed (you wouldn't want to upload files that had not changed as that would take extra time unnecessarily), and then transferring them one at a time. Obviously this is both tedious and highly error prone. Files can get easily missed or placed in incorrect directories.

ColdFusion Studio can fully automate the process of uploading applications to remote servers. Studio's project-uploading feature allows you to create a project locally (complete with any directory structure needed) and then deploy the entire project to a server with the click of a button.

Part

IV

Ch

18

TIP Even though I am discussing Web applications here, the same techniques can also be used for traditional Web sites hosted by an ISP; those sites can benefit from Studio's project-uploading feature as well.

To deploy a project to a remote server, do the following:

1. Make sure a connection to the remote server has been configured in ColdFusion Studio.
2. If the project to be uploaded is not open, open it as described in "Opening Existing Projects."
3. Click the Upload Project button (above the Project tab in the upper pane). This brings up the Upload Project dialog box as shown in Figure 18.11.
4. Select the remote server to upload the project in the Upload Locations server tree.
5. Expand the selected server to select the root directory into which the project should be saved.

6. Some operating systems (Sun's Solaris, for example) have case-sensitive file systems. If you are uploading the project to a server hosted on a computer with a case-sensitive file system, you might need to force all file and directory names to lowercase. To do this automatically, check the Force File and Folder Names to Lowercase check box.

7. To save transfer time, ColdFusion Studio automatically checks the date and timestamp of files being uploaded so that only newer (changed) files are transmitted to the remote server. To force an upload of all files (to perform a complete refresh), uncheck the Only Upload New or Modified Files check box.

8. Click the OK button to transfer the files.

FIGURE 18.11

The Upload Project dialog box can be used to upload entire projects to a remote ColdFusion server in a single operation.

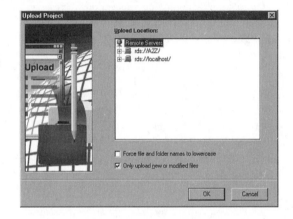

N O T E Only local projects can be uploaded using the Upload Project option. To upload projects to a remote server, you must have already created a project locally and placed all the desired files and directories into it. ▪

Advanced SQL

Using the DISTINCT Keyword

In Chapter 8, "Introduction to SQL," you learned how to use the SELECT statement to get information from your database tables. You can add DISTINCT to these SELECT statements in situations where you don't want to get any duplicate information from your tables.

For instance, if you want to find all of the unique last names of your employees—that is, without any repeats—you execute the SQL statement shown in Listing 19.1. The results are shown in Figure 19.1.

On the CD

Listing 19.1 DISTINCT.CFM—**Using DISTINCT to Eliminate Duplicates**

```
<CFQUERY NAME="Report" DATASOURCE="A2Z">
  SELECT DISTINCT LastName
  FROM Employees
</CFQUERY>

<HTML>

<HEAD>
<TITLE>Last Names</TITLE>
</HEAD>

<BODY>

<H1>Last Names</H1>

<CFTABLE QUERY="Report" COLHEADERS HTMLTABLE BORDER>
  <CFCOL HEADER="LastName" TEXT="#LastName#">
</CFTABLE>

</BODY>

</HTML>
```

If you look at the actual data in our Employees table, you see that there are two employees by the name of Smith (employee number 4, Jack, and employee number 5, Jane). The inclusion of DISTINCT in the SQL code has kept the last name from appearing twice. This is a particularly helpful technique when dealing with information such as states, area codes, and the like.

Using Column Aliases

As you work through the rest of this chapter, you need to make use of column aliases in your code. Providing a *column alias* gives you a way to "rename" a column in the query's results. Nothing about the actual table changes in any way; the column simply appears to have a different name for this one specific query.

You can go back to any SELECT statement that you've already worked with and add column aliases so that your columns present themselves under different names. For instance, Listing 19.2 revises Listing 11.5, the Employ1.cfm template from Chapter 11, "ColdFusion Basics." The code is almost exactly the same. All that's changed is that column aliases have been added—the FirstName column is presented to ColdFusion as NameF, and LastName is presented as NameL.

FIGURE 19.1

The value `Smith`, which appears several times in the database, only shows up once here.

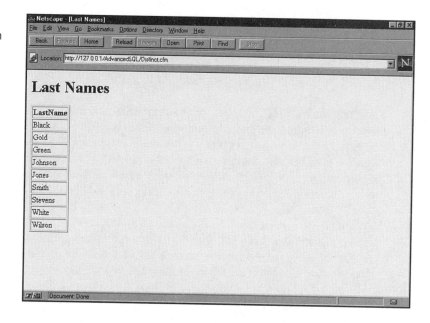

Listing 19.2 `EMPLOY1A.CFM`—**Using AS to Create Column Aliases**

```
<
CFQUERY
DATASOURCE="A2Z"
NAME="Employees"
>
 SELECT FirstName AS NameF, LastName AS NameL, PhoneExtension
 FROM Employees
 ORDER BY LastName, FirstName
</CFQUERY>

<HTML>

<HEAD>
<TITLE>Employee List</TITLE>
</HEAD>

<BODY>

<H1>Employees</H1>

<UL>

<CFOUTPUT QUERY="Employees">
```

Part

IV

Ch

19

continues

Listing 19.2   Continued

```
 <LI>#NameL#, #NameF# - Ext. #PhoneExtension#
</CFOUTPUT>

</UL>

</BODY>

</HTML>
```

Note that you use `NameL` and `NameF` after `AS` in the SQL statement, and you also use `#NameL#` and `#NameF#` to refer to the code in the template itself. If you had left `#LastName#` in the template code, you would have gotten a "column not found" error from ColdFusion because it is now convinced that the only relevant column names are NameL and NameF. This illustrates the important concept that ColdFusion is not really aware of what your table and column names are—it "believes" whatever your SQL statements tell it to believe.

> **NOTE**   Even though you provided a column alias for the LastName field, you still used the real column name (LastName) in the `ORDER BY` part of the query. In other words, use column aliases to change the column names that are presented to ColdFusion, but refer to the columns normally in the `WHERE`, `ORDER BY`, and other parts of the query statement itself. ∎

You may be asking yourself what the point of all this is. Why would you care whether the column appears under its rightful name of LastName, or masquerades under the "aliased" name of `NameL`? In reality, of course, you probably don't care. But here's a much more useful reason for column aliases: using table columns whose rightful names ColdFusion considers illegal.

Pretend for a moment that when the Employees table was first created, the designer of the table used the column names Last-Name and First Name instead of LastName and FirstName. ColdFusion doesn't allow spaces or dashes in column names, so errors occur if you try to use the columns in your templates. All is not lost, however. You can use column aliases to present ColdFusion with perfectly respectable column names.

As a quick example, look back at Listing 11.5 in Chapter 11. Now look at Listing 19.3. Listing 19.3 is what you need to use in order to get the same results as Listing 11.5 if your database had the illegal column names Last-Name and First Name. The `AS` keyword presents Last-Name to ColdFusion as LastName, and First Name as FirstName.

Listing 19.3   Using Column Aliases to Work Around Illegal Column Names

```
SELECT `First Name` AS FirstName, `Last-Name` AS LastName, PhoneExtension
  FROM Employees
  ORDER BY `Last-Name`, `First Name`
```

Notice the backtick character around the column names. The backtick character is used by ODBC to indicate that the characters between the backticks are to be treated "literally." For instance, the backticks around First Name make it clear to ODBC that you're talking about a single column named First Name, rather than two different columns. Different database drivers may not have had a problem with the space in the column name, so backticks were used just to be safe.

In short, you had two obstacles to overcome. You had to use AS to prevent an error message from ColdFusion. You also needed to use backticks to prevent potential error messages from the ODBC driver itself.

You can also use backticks to work around situations where a column name is perfectly legal to ColdFusion, but is considered illegal to the ODBC driver. For instance, people often make the mistake of creating a column named Date.

Referring to this Date column can cause syntax error messages from the ODBC driver if the particular ODBC driver considers Date a reserved word. In such a case, you can use backticks around the column name to avoid the error. It is not necessary to create a column alias with AS in such a case, however, because ColdFusion has no problem with Date being used as a column name.

You can now go ahead and refer to #LastName# and #FirstName# in your CFML without errors, and you didn't have to resort to renaming the actual columns (which could have caused problems if the database was also being used by an application other than ColdFusion).

Using Aggregate Functions to Report on Your Data

SQL supplies a number of *functions* for your use. There are basically two types of functions in SQL:

- Scalar functions—They ask questions about individual rows in your database tables. You probably won't use these terribly often because ColdFusion's own built-in functions are generally easier to use and more flexible.
- Aggregate functions—They are used to *crunch* information from any number of rows at once into a *summarized* overview of your data. You will find yourself using these functions whenever you want to provide report-style summaries or overviews in your ColdFusion applications. (Sometimes aggregate functions are referred to as *set functions*.)

There are a total of five aggregate functions in all. Table 19.1 explains what each function does and the types of columns that each function can be used on. Note that Count(*) and Count(Column) behave differently, and in some ways can be considered two different functions.

Table 19.1   Aggregate Functions

Function	On Numeric Columns	On Date Columns	On Character Columns
COUNT(*)	Counts the number of rows in a table	Same	Same

continues

Table 19.1 Continued

Function	On Numeric Columns	On Date Columns	On Character Columns
COUNT(Column)	Counts the actual values found in a column	Same	Same
SUM(Column)	Adds the total of the values found in a column	n/a	n/a
AVG(Column)	Computes the average of values found in a column	n/a	n/a
MIN(Column)	Finds the smallest value in a column	Earliest date in a column	First value (alphabetically) in a column
MAX	Finds the largest number in a column	Latest date in a column	Last value (alphabetically) in a column

N O T E Not every aggregate function can be used with every type of column. For instance, a mathematical concept such as "average" makes perfect sense in the context of a column full of numbers, like the Pages column of the Inventory table. However, the mathematical concept of averaging doesn't really make sense in the context of a character-type column like the Title column of that same table. While the average of two numbers like 10 and 20 is clearly 15, there's really no way to express an average of *Moby Dick* and *The Hitchhiker's Guide to the Galaxy*. For this reason, the AVG(Column) function is not allowed on character-type columns. ■

The SQL syntax for using the various aggregate functions is identical and can easily be combined into one SQL statement for a single CFQUERY.

Listing 19.4 demonstrates the functionality of each aggregate function. Note that you can make up any name you want for the computed column that each function returns. I recommend using the column name or part of the column name, an underscore, and then the name of the function you're using. It's easier to keep things straight this way.

Listing 19.4 INVRPT1.CFM—Code That Uses All of the Aggregate Functions

```
<CFQUERY NAME="Report" DATASOURCE="A2Z">
  SELECT
    COUNT(*)                AS Book_Count,
    COUNT(Publisher)        AS Pub_Count,
    MIN(PublicationDate)    AS PubDate_Min,
    MAX(PublicationDate)    AS PubDate_Max,
```

```
    SUM(NumberInStock)        AS InStock_Sum,
    AVG(Pages)                AS Pages_Avg
  FROM Inventory
</CFQUERY>

<HTML>

<HEAD>
<TITLE>Inventory Report</TITLE>
</HEAD>

<BODY>

<H1>Inventory Report</H1>

<UL>

<CFOUTPUT>
  <LI>Number of different books:      #Report.Book_Count#
  <LI>Number of publishers:           #Report.Pub_Count#
  <LI>First book published on:        #DateFormat(Report.PubDate_Min)#
  <LI>Last book published on:         #DateFormat(Report.PubDate_Max)#
  <LI>Total number of copies in stock: #NumberFormat(Report.InStock_Sum)#
  <LI>Average number of pages:        #Report.Pages_Avg#
</CFOUTPUT>

</UL>

</BODY>

</HTML>
```

Take note that in Figure 19.2, Book_Count and Pub_Count indicate the same value of 6. However, most people probably think that Pub_Count is 4 because there are only four different publishers represented. Unfortunately, with most desktop database drivers such as the Access driver, Count(Publisher) doesn't behave the way you'd expect. It simply counts the number of rows found in the Publishers column that have values, not the number of unique publishers.

Most server-based database systems allow you to use the DISTINCT keyword with the Count function, which gives the information that you probably expect. For instance, Microsoft SQL Server allows you to use the SQL code in Listing 19.5. Unfortunately, it won't work with the Access, FoxPro, and other file-based database drivers that ship with ColdFusion.

Listing 19.5 Using DISTINCT with Count

```
SELECT
    COUNT(*)                  AS Book_Count,
    COUNT(DISTINCT Publisher) AS Pub_Count,
    MIN(PublicationDate)      AS PubDate_Min,
    MAX(PublicationDate)      AS PubDate_Max,
    SUM(NumberInStock)        AS InStock_Sum,
    AVG(Pages)                AS Pages_Avg
  FROM Inventory
```

FIGURE 19.2

Book_Count and Pub_Count appear to be the same.

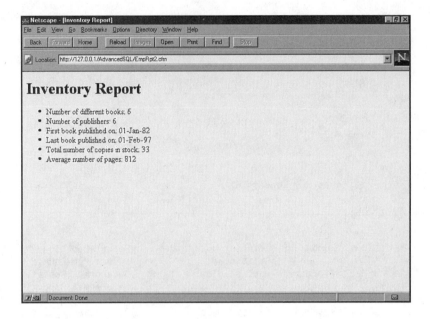

The introduction of the DISTINCT keyword causes Pub_Count to reflect the value of 4 that you'd expect. Book_Count remains 6 because Count(*) counts the number of physical rows without regard to their contents.

Counting Rows with COUNT(*)

The simplest aggregate function is COUNT(*), which simply counts the number of rows found by a query statement. You include the COUNT(*) function in the SELECT part of a query, as if it were a column in your table. Indeed, the value that the function returns is presented to ColdFusion as if it were a column in a table. This means that you can go ahead and use the value in your ColdFusion templates in the same ways you're already familiar with.

The code in Listing 19.6 queries the data source for the number of rows in the Employees table. The value calculated by Count(*) is returned to the template as a column named Emp_Count. The actual table is not changed in any way.

Listing 19.6 EMPRPT1.CFM—**Counting the Number of Rows with COUNT(*)**

```
<CFQUERY NAME="Report" DATASOURCE="A2Z">
  SELECT COUNT(*) AS Emp_Count
  FROM Employees
</CFQUERY>

<HTML>

<HEAD>
<TITLE>Employee Report</TITLE>
</HEAD>
```

```
<BODY>

<H1>Employee Report</H1>

<CFOUTPUT QUERY="Report">
  Total Number Of Employees: #Emp_Count#
</CFOUTPUT>

</BODY>

</HTML>
```

Note that you used your newfound column-aliasing skills to create the column alias of Emp_Count with AS. This is optional as far as SQL is concerned, but it's required for using the value in your ColdFusion code. People often think that the name of the computed column will be Employees by default, but it's not—the column remains unnamed unless you use AS. That's fine in many environments, but not ColdFusion—CFML requires you to refer to columns by name.

The SQL statement generates a new result set that contains just one column: Emp_Count. There is also just one row in this result set and it contains the integer 10, which is the number of rows in the Employees table. When this template is run, it should look like Figure 19.3.

FIGURE 19.3

Using the computed column's alias in your CFML code.

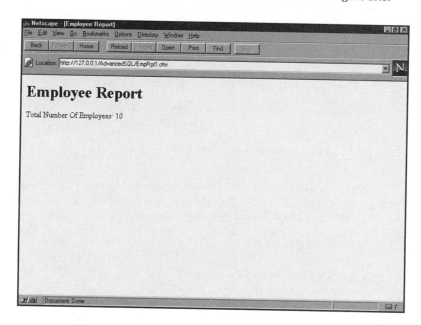

Part
IV

Ch
19

Making Aggregate Functions More Selective with WHERE

You can easily make your functions perform their computations only on certain rows by using the WHERE clause, as covered in Chapter 8. For instance, to have the report in Figure 19.3 computed only for books in category number 2 (Humor), change the SQL statement in Listing 19.5 to the statement in Listing 19.7.

Listing 19.7 Limiting an Aggregate Function's Scope with WHERE

```
SELECT
    COUNT(*)              AS Book_Count,
    COUNT(Publisher)      AS Pub_Count,
    MIN(PublicationDate)  AS PubDate_Min,
    MAX(PublicationDate)  AS PubDate_Max,
    SUM(NumberInStock)    AS InStock_Sum,
    AVG(Pages)            AS Pages_Avg
  FROM Inventory
  WHERE CategoryID = 2
```

The addition of the WHERE clause tells the database driver that only those rows that meet the criteria specified in the WHERE clause should be considered by the aggregate functions.

You're free to use WHERE in just about any way you would normally. For instance, you could easily make the report operate on more than one category by using OR in the WHERE part of the query, as shown in Listing 19.8. Refer to Chapter 8 for more information on using WHERE.

Listing 19.8 Using WHERE, OR, and Aggregate Functions Together

```
SELECT
    COUNT(*)              AS Book_Count,
    COUNT(Publisher)      AS Pub_Count,
    MIN(PublicationDate)  AS PubDate_Min,
    MAX(PublicationDate)  AS PubDate_Max,
    SUM(NumberInStock)    AS InStock_Sum,
    AVG(Pages)            AS Pages_Avg
  FROM Inventory
  WHERE (CategoryID = 2 OR CategoryID = 3)
```

If you're using ColdFusion Studio (see Figure 19.4), you can create queries that use aggregate functions in Studio's Query Builder. Start by right-clicking the A2Z database's Inventory table from the Resource Tab's Database tab, then selecting New Query from the pop-up menu.

Now you can click the column names at the top of the Query Builder. For each column name, select the aggregate function you want from the Group By column at the bottom of the Query Builder; also provide the alias by typing in the Alias column. A few clicks later, you've built virtually the same query that you came up with in Listing 19.8, without having to concentrate on the SQL syntax involved.

Providing Broken Down Detail with GROUP BY

So far you've used aggregate functions to run simple computations that return only one row of data. You'll often want to construct queries that apply the function to every value in a given column. You can get this effect by including a GROUP BY clause in your query.

FIGURE 19.4
ColdFusion Studio's
query-building facilities
support aggregate
functions.

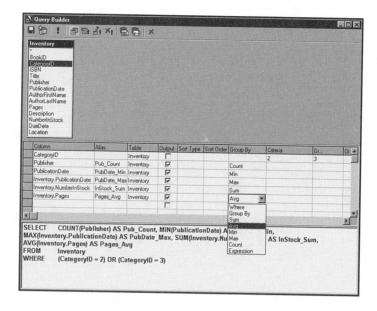

GROUP BY *column* causes an aggregate function to be computed for each unique value encountered in the column. For instance, say you wanted to find the number of books you had in stock for each category. The query in Listing 19.9 returns a result set with two columns: Category and InStock_Sum. The result set contains a row for each category, with the corresponding total of copies from each category.

Listing 19.9 INVRPT2.CFM—Computing a SUM for Each Category

```
<CFQUERY NAME="Report" DATASOURCE="A2Z">
  SELECT Publisher, SUM(NumberInStock) AS InStock_Sum
  FROM Inventory
  GROUP BY Publisher
</CFQUERY>

<HTML>

<HEAD>
<TITLE>Inventory Report</TITLE>
</HEAD>

<BODY>

<H1>Inventory Report</H1>

<UL>

<CFOUTPUT QUERY="Report">
  <LI>#Publisher#:  #NumberFormat(InStock_Sum)#
</CFOUTPUT>
```

continues

Part

IV

Ch

19

Listing 19.9 Continued

```
</UL>

</BODY>

</HTML>
```

Behind the scenes, this query causes your database system to find all the unique values in the Publisher column. It then moves through each of the publishers and applies whatever aggregate functions you've specified—the SUM function in this case—to all of that publisher's rows. Figure 19.5 shows the results.

FIGURE 19.5

The SUM gets computed for each publisher.

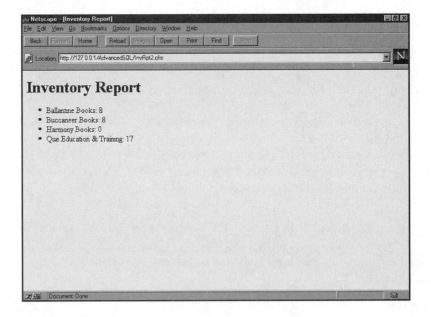

You can use more than one column in the GROUP BY clause. For instance, you could specify both the Publisher and Category columns. This is done by replacing the query in Listing 19.9 with the following query:

```
<CFQUERY NAME="Report" DATASOURCE="A2Z">
  SELECT Publisher, AuthorFirstName, AuthorLastName, SUM(NumberInStock)
 AS InStock_Sum
  FROM Inventory
  GROUP BY Publisher, AuthorFirstName, AuthorLastName
</CFQUERY>
```

Now, instead of merely finding all the unique publishers in the table, your database system finds all the unique combinations of Publisher and Category and applies the SUM function to all of each publisher's rows for each category. Then all you have to do is refer to AuthorFirstName and AuthorLastName in the CFOUTPUT block, along with Publisher and InStock_Sum. Figure 19.6 shows the results that you might come up with.

FIGURE 19.6

The aggregate function is calculated for every combination of values in the GROUP BY clause.

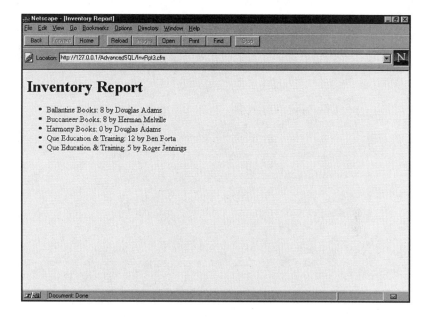

N O T E If you're using ColdFusion Studio, you can specify a GROUP BY clause by choosing Group By from the drop-down list in the Group By column for a particular field. ■

Comparing GROUP BY in SQL and GROUP in CFOUTPUT

Don't get confused between GROUP BY in SQL and the GROUP parameter that can be used with the CFOUTPUT tag. As you've just seen, GROUP BY in a query is a standard SQL construct that asks your database about sets of rows. It's usually used along with aggregate functions to get a summarized version of your data.

Using GROUP with CFOUTPUT, on the other hand, is a ColdFusion-specific feature that has nothing specifically to do with aggregate functions. GROUP asks ColdFusion to process certain parts of a template—for instance, to display a category heading—only when a new value is encountered in a particular column. It's generally used to avoid a "repeating" effect on your ColdFusion pages. For instance, you could add a GROUP parameter to your code to eliminate the visual repetition of Que Education & Training on the page. Listing 19.10 shows the code that accomplishes this.

Part IV

Ch 19

Listing 19.10 INVRPT4.CFM—Adding GROUP (as Opposed to GROUP BY) to the CFOUTPUT Tag

```
<CFQUERY NAME="Report" DATASOURCE="A2Z">
  SELECT Publisher, AuthorFirstName, AuthorLastName, SUM(NumberInStock)
 AS InStock_Sum
  FROM Inventory
  GROUP BY Publisher, AuthorFirstName, AuthorLastName
```

continues

Listing 19.10 Continued

```
</CFQUERY>

<HTML>

<HEAD>
<TITLE>Inventory Report</TITLE>
</HEAD>

<BODY>

<H1>Inventory Report</H1>


<CFOUTPUT QUERY="Report" GROUP="Publisher">
  <P>#Publisher#:
  <UL>
  <CFOUTPUT>
    <LI>#AuthorFirstName# #AuthorLastName#: #NumberFormat(InStock_Sum)#
  </CFOUTPUT>
  </UL>
</CFOUTPUT>


</BODY>

</HTML>
```

Figure 19.7 shows the results of Listing 19.10.

◊ **See** "Grouping Query Results" for more information on CFOUTPUT's GROUP parameter, **p. 218**.

FIGURE 19.7

SQL's GROUP BY and CFOUTPUT's GROUP can be used together.

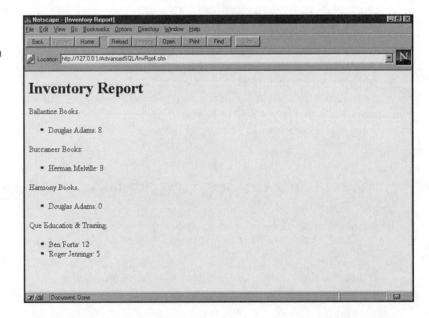

Displaying the "Top n" Records   Sooner or later, nearly every company president will make a request of her tech people for a report that shows the top 10 clients, the top 100 products, or what have you.

In most cases, you take care of this quite easily by grabbing an existing template and adding an ORDER BY clause to the SQL statement and a MAXROWS parameter to the CFQUERY tag. As you learned in Chapter 8, using ORDER BY with DESC sorts a query's results—largest values first—according to the column you specify. The MAXROWS parameter causes the query to return a certain number of rows. Therefore, by adding a MAXROWS=2 parameter to a query that's been sorted with DESC, you end up with the two top values.

For instance, the Listing 19.11 is a "Top 2" version of the report you put together in Listing 19.9. Figure 19.8 shows the results of Listing 19.11.

Listing 19.11   **INVRPT2A.CFM—Adding MAXROWS and Reversing the Sort Order**

```
<CFQUERY NAME="Report" DATASOURCE="A2Z" MAXROWS=2>
  SELECT Publisher, SUM(NumberInStock) AS InStock_Sum
  FROM Inventory
  GROUP BY Publisher
  ORDER BY SUM(NumberInStock) DESC
</CFQUERY>

<HTML>

<HEAD>
<TITLE>Inventory Report</TITLE>
</HEAD>

<BODY>

<H1>Top 2 Publishers</H1>

<UL>

<CFOUTPUT QUERY="Report">
  <LI>#Publisher#:  #NumberFormat(InStock_Sum)#
</CFOUTPUT>

</UL>

</BODY>

</HTML>
```

Part

IV

Ch

19

Note that you are able to use aggregate functions in the ORDER BY part of the query. In general, just about any function or expression that is allowed in the SELECT part can also be used in the other parts of a query, such as the WHERE or ORDER BY parts.

FIGURE 19.8

You can use MAXROWS and ORDER BY to create "Top n" types of reports.

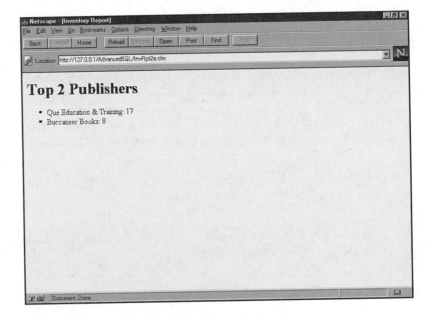

Selecting Certain Aggregated Values with HAVING

You've seen how you can use WHERE to cause the aggregate functions to run their computations on certain rows. The aggregate functions are calculated on only those rows that pass the tests called for in the WHERE clause. What if you wanted to choose which rows are returned in a different way—based not on what the values are *before* the aggregate functions do their work, but *after*?

You guessed it: You use the HAVING keyword. Compared to everything else you're learning in this chapter, HAVING is relatively obscure, and you probably won't use it much. It is important to know that it's there if you need it.

For instance, what if you wanted to adapt the SQL in Listing 19.10 so that it only showed the counts for the authors for which there are more than five copies in stock? By adding a HAVING clause to the SQL in Listing 19.10, you tell your database system to do all the same computations as before—but then to only return the computed rows that pass the tests in the HAVING clause. Listing 19.12 shows the modified SQL statement.

Listing 19.12 Adding HAVING to Choose Which GROUP BY Rows You Want

```
SELECT Publisher, AuthorFirstName, AuthorLastName,
➥SUM(NumberInStock) AS InStock_Sum
  FROM Inventory
  GROUP BY Publisher, AuthorFirstName, AuthorLastName
  HAVING SUM(NumberInStock) > 5
```

Figure 19.9 shows the result of replacing the SQL statement in Listing 19.10 with the SQL statement in Listing 19.12.

FIGURE 19.9

This template uses SUM, GROUP BY, HAVING, and GROUP together.

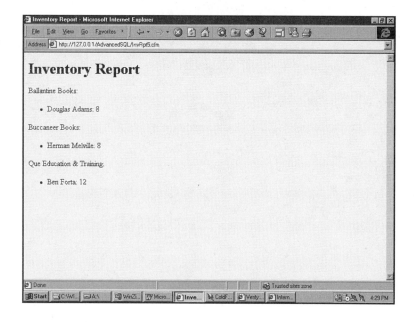

Selecting Data from Two Tables Using Joins

The design of the tables in your A2Z database calls for a number of relationships between the various tables. Concentrate for a little while on the Customer, Order, and OrderItems tables. Recall from Chapter 7, "Creating Databases and Tables," that when you created these tables, you were also implicitly creating conceptual relationships between them:

- There is a one-to-many relationship between the Customer and Orders tables. In other words, any one customer can make any number of orders.

- There is also a one-to-many relationship between the Orders and OrderItems tables. In other words, any one order can consist of any number of items.

Refer to Chapter 6, "Database Fundamentals," to refresh your memory about one-to-many and other types of table relationships.

In order for this three-table design to be useful, you obviously need to be able to use the SE-LECT statement to get data from more than one table. SQL makes this simple, relying on a simple concept called a *join*.

You specify a join by using special SQL syntax that "links" two tables together to get the desired results. Of course, you already know in your head what the relationship between the two tables is. *Join syntax* is what you use to describe the relationship between the tables that you're using in a particular query.

Part
IV

Ch
19

Take a look at Listing 19.13. In some ways, it looks like the simple SELECT queries you've already explored. There are three big differences:

- There are two tables listed in the FROM part.
- The = sign is used to join the two tables in the WHERE part.
- Because there is more than one table involved, simple "dot notation" in the form Tablename.Columnname is used to refer to the columns.

Listing 19.13 ORDERRPT1—**Joining Tables with WHERE**

```
<CFQUERY NAME="Report" DATASOURCE="A2Z">
  SELECT
    Customers.CustomerID, Customers.Company,
    Orders.OrderID, Orders.OrderDate
  FROM Customers, Orders
  WHERE Customers.CustomerID = Orders.CustomerID
</CFQUERY>

<HTML>

<HEAD>
<TITLE>Order Report</TITLE>
</HEAD>

<BODY>

<H1>Order Report</H1>

<CFTABLE QUERY="Report" COLHEADERS HTMLTABLE BORDER>
  <CFCOL HEADER="CustomerID" TEXT="#CustomerID#">
  <CFCOL HEADER="Company" TEXT="#Company#">
  <CFCOL HEADER="OrderID" TEXT="#OrderID#">
  <CFCOL HEADER="Date" TEXT="#DateFormat(OrderDate)#">
</CFTABLE>

</BODY>

</HTML>
```

The WHERE keyword is clearly being used in a new way here. Rather than merely specifying selection criteria as you've seen previously, it is used here to "bind" the Customers and Order tables together. Translated into plain English, this statement might read "Using the CustomerID as a guide, show me the company name for each row in the Customers table, along with the corresponding dates for each order from the Order table." Figure 19.10 shows the results of joining these tables to build an orders report.

That WHERE clause is critical to understand. You know that the conceptual relationship between the two tables hinges on the fact that the rows of the Order table where the CustomerID column is 1 "match up" with the row in the Customers table where CustomerID is 1, and so on. The WHERE clause "explains" this fact to your ODBC driver.

FIGURE 19.10

Here you see the results of your first join.

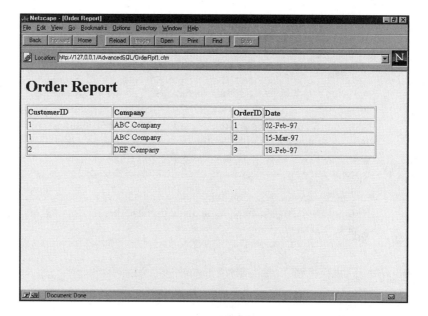

It's recommended that you specify the table name for every column. However, it is only required when the column name exists in more than one table. You may simply refer to Company instead of Customers.Company if you like, but you cannot omit the table name when referring to the CustomerID column because a column by that name exists in both tables.

The columns in the join don't have to be named the same. If for some reason the relevant column in the Order table was called Customer_Number instead of CustomerID, you could just use WHERE Customers.CustomerID = Orders.Customer_Number.

However, the data types of the columns do have to match. An error would occur, for instance, if you tried to create a join using Customers.CustomerID = Orders.CustomerID if for some foolish reason you had defined the CustomerID column of the Orders table to be a text-type column. Since the column on the left side of the = is not of the same data type as the column on the right side, an error would occur and the join would fail.

TIP

If you absolutely need to join columns of different data types, you may be able to use the CONVERT scalar function (see Table 19.1) on one of the columns as an emergency workaround.

Part

IV

Ch

19

I just can't stress the importance of Listing 19.13 enough. If there is a single listing in this chapter that you shouldn't skim past, this is it. Joins are a critical concept to get your head around. Once you "get it" conceptually, you're well on your way to creating sophisticated relational database applications.

Improving Readability via Table Aliases   SQL allows you to use *table aliases* when using multiple tables in an SQL statement. It is a good idea to use them when joining tables, mainly to make your SQL statements more readable. The syntax is quite simple—just make up an alias for the table and put it right after the table name in the FROM part. Use that alias instead of the table name everywhere else, such as in the SELECT and the WHERE parts. You can make the alias anything you want—simply using the first letter of the table name is suggested as a convention.

You can change the SQL statement in Listing 19.13 to the statement in Listing 19.14. No other changes to the template need to be made because the query is still delivering the exact same result set to ColdFusion.

Listing 19.14   Adding c and o as Table Aliases

```
SELECT
    c.CustomerID, c.Company,
    o.OrderID, o.OrderDate
  FROM Customers c, Order o
  WHERE c.CustomerID = o.CustomerID
```

Joining Three or More Tables   So far so good. Now what if you wanted to see which books were included with each order? That involves using the SELECT statement with three tables. The syntax for your first three-table join should come as no great surprise. You just add the OrderItems table to the SQL statement in Listing 19.14 and join it to the Order table in the WHERE part. Listing 19.15 shows the new SQL statement that includes the OrderItems table.

Listing 19.15   ORDERRPT2.CFM—A Three-Table Join

```
<CFQUERY NAME="Report" DATASOURCE="A2Z">
  SELECT
    c.CustomerID, c.Company,
    o.OrderID, o.OrderDate,
    oi.OrderLine, oi.BookID
  FROM Customers c, Orders o, OrderItems oi
  WHERE c.CustomerID = o.CustomerID
    AND oi.OrderID = o.OrderID
</CFQUERY>

<HTML>

<HEAD>
<TITLE>Order Report</TITLE>
</HEAD>

<BODY>
```

```
<H1>Order Report</H1>

<CFTABLE QUERY="Report" COLHEADERS HTMLTABLE BORDER>
  <CFCOL HEADER="CustomerID" WIDTH="" ALIGN="" TEXT="#CustomerID#">
  <CFCOL HEADER="Company" WIDTH="" ALIGN="" TEXT="#Company#">
  <CFCOL HEADER="OrderID" WIDTH="" ALIGN="" TEXT="#OrderID#">
  <CFCOL HEADER="Date" WIDTH="" ALIGN="" TEXT="#DateFormat(OrderDate)#">
  <CFCOL HEADER="Line" WIDTH="" ALIGN="" TEXT="#OrderLine#">
  <CFCOL HEADER="BookID" WIDTH="" ALIGN="" TEXT="#BookID#">
</CFTABLE>

</BODY>

</HTML>
```

Note that because both table joins have to be specified in the same WHERE clause, you use the AND keyword between them. This is consistent with specifying multiple criteria in simpler queries (such as Listing 8.7 in Chapter 8). SQL is designed to allow you to think of a table join as just another piece of filtering criteria.

T I P A four-table join is about as far as you would want to go under most circumstances. Queries that involve more than four or five tables are certainly possible, but you may start to notice that performance will degrade, especially with file-based databases such as Access tables.

Joining Tables with INNER JOIN ON   So far you've done all of your joining using the WHERE part of your queries to describe the relationship between your tables. SQL offers an alternate syntax that could be used to create any of the joins you've done so far. Instead of specifying the join in the WHERE part of the query, the join is specified in the FROM part of the query with the INNER JOIN and ON keywords.

As you are listing the table names in the FROM part of the query, the words INNER JOIN are placed between the table names. The ON keyword is then used to indicate the column names to be used in the join. Some developers find the resulting statements more readable because the syntax seems to describe the relationship in something closer to plain English. Listing 19.16 demonstrates the INNER JOIN syntax.

Part IV

Ch 19

Listing 19.16   Joining Tables with INNER JOIN Instead of WHERE

```
SELECT
    c.CustomerID, c.Company,
    o.OrderID, o.OrderDate
  FROM Customers c INNER JOIN Orders o
      ON c.CustomerID = o.CustomerID
```

The statements in Listing 19.14 and 19.16 are synonymous. Both tell your database driver to do the same thing, so use the syntax you prefer. You'll probably find that you have a personal preference; I happen to find the WHERE syntax more intuitive. Whatever your preference, it's important to at least be aware that both syntaxes exist, since you are likely to encounter both as a developer.

N O T E   To use three or more tables using the INNER JOIN syntax, you "nest" the join statements using parentheses. The structure would be:

```
SELECT * FROM (table1 INNER JOIN table2
ON table1.columnA = table2.columnA)
INNER JOIN table3 ON table1.columnB = table3.columnB
```

Joining to Display All Records from the Master Table   So far you've used the word *join* as a fairly general term. There are actually two main types of joins that you need to use as a ColdFusion developer:

- An *inner join* is the "default" type of join. Inner joins are used when you are interested in values that exist in both tables in a relationship. Only when rows in both tables "sync up" does the query return anything. All of the joins you have explored so far have been inner joins.

- An outer join is used when you are interested in all values from one of the tables, even when there are no corresponding values in the other table. For instance, you might want to create a "Book Order Report" that shows how many times each book has been ordered—even those books that have not gotten any orders at all.

Say you wanted to display a little report that showed how many copies of each book had been ordered. Using the Count aggregate function and a join, you might come up with the code in Listing 19.17.

Listing 19.17   BOOKRPT1—The Inner Join Version of Your Book Order Report

```
<CFQUERY NAME="Report" DATASOURCE="A2Z">
  SELECT  i.BookID, i.Title, SUM(oi.Quantity) AS CopiesOrdered
  FROM Inventory i INNER JOIN OrderItems oi
                   ON i.BookID = oi.BookID
  GROUP BY i.BookID, i.Title
</CFQUERY>

<HTML>

<HEAD>
<TITLE>Book Order Report</TITLE>
</HEAD>

<BODY>

<H1>Book Order Report</H1>

<CFTABLE QUERY="Report" COLHEADERS HTMLTABLE BORDER>
  <CFCOL HEADER="BookID" TEXT="#BookID#">
  <CFCOL HEADER="Title" TEXT="#Title#">
  <CFCOL HEADER="Orders" TEXT="#NumberFormat(CopiesOrdered)#">
</CFTABLE>
```

```
</BODY>

</HTML>
```

Figure 19.11 shows the results of Listing 19.17.

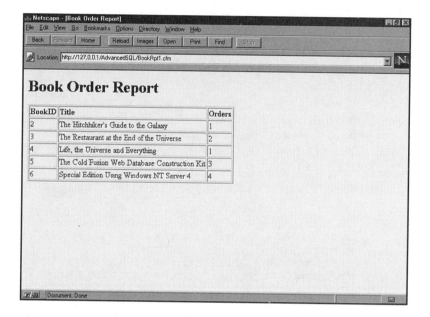

The browser display shown in Figure 19.11 looks fine, depending on what the user expects from the application. Notice that *Moby Dick* does not appear in the display at all. Technically speaking, there is nothing wrong. SQL has done exactly what it was asked to do. One of your application's users, however, would probably expect *Moby Dick* to be included in the display, with 0 shown for the number of copies ordered. *Moby Dick's* absence in the list may cause the user to make incorrect assumptions about books that have never been ordered (namely, that they don't exist).

Fortunately, SQL provides a way to deal with this situation through the use of an outer join. Unlike the simple inner joins that you've used so far—where all the tables involved carry the same conceptual weight—writing your SQL statements with outer join syntax tells your database engine that certain tables are more important than others, and thus should be represented in the results no matter what. Specifically, here you want to see all of the appropriate records from one of the tables (the outer table), even if there are no matching records from the second table.

Listing 19.18 revises the query from Listing 19.17, using outer join syntax. As you can see, not too much has changed. The word INNER has been changed to OUTER, the word LEFT was added to indicate that the table to the left of the word JOIN is to be considered the outer table—in other words, Inventory is the table that should have all rows returned no matter what. In general, you usually want the LEFT to point to the one table in a one-to-many relationship.

Listing 19.18   BOOKRPT2.CFM—**Changing the Book Order Report to Use Outer Join Syntax**

```
<CFQUERY NAME="Report" DATASOURCE="A2Z">
  SELECT  i.BookID, i.Title, SUM(oi.Quantity) AS CopiesOrdered
  FROM Inventory i LEFT OUTER JOIN OrderItems oi
                 ON i.BookID = oi.BookID
  GROUP BY i.BookID, i.Title
</CFQUERY>

<HTML>

<HEAD>
<TITLE>Book Order Report</TITLE>
</HEAD>

<BODY>

<H1>Book Order Report</H1>

<CFTABLE QUERY="Report" COLHEADERS HTMLTABLE BORDER>
  <CFCOL HEADER="BookID" TEXT="#BookID#">
  <CFCOL HEADER="Title" TEXT="#Title#">
  <CFCOL HEADER="Orders" TEXT="#NumberFormat(CopiesOrdered)#">
</CFTABLE>

</BODY>

</HTML>
```

Now the report works the way a user expects—all books are listed. A book that has gotten orders shows the number of copies that have been ordered. A book that has not gotten any orders—like Moby Dick—still appears on the list. Figure 19.12 shows the new results.

N O T E   If you are using ColdFusion Studio, the Query Builder makes it a snap to change an ordinary join to an outer join. Simply right-click the small square on the line that represents the join and choose the Select All Rows From option for the appropriate table from the pop-up menu. ■

Depending on the database you are using, there may be other syntax that you can use to specify an outer join. For instance, Microsoft SQL Server 6.5 allows you to use *= or =* instead of LEFT OUTER JOIN or RIGHT OUTER JOIN, respectively.

In fact, you'll find that ColdFusion Studio uses a slight variant on the pure OUTER JOIN syntax previously outlined. Studio is using the ODBC standard's oj command, which is designed to get around the fact that some databases want you to construct outer joins slightly differently. Consult your database documentation for discussions of such alternate syntax.

FIGURE 19.12

The outer join version of your report shows all master records, even if there are no detail records.

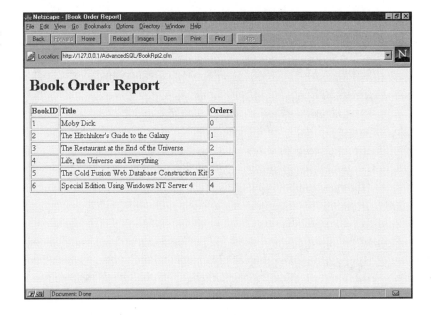

Gaining Extra Flexibility with Subqueries

SQL allows you to nest complete SQL statements within other SQL statements for various purposes. These nested queries are called *subqueries*. Subqueries provide great flexibility and allow the language to get into those "hard-to-reach" places. Subqueries can be introduced into a SQL statement in two basic ways:

- In the WHERE part of your SQL statement, to correlate data in different tables. Either IN or EXISTS is used to indicate the subquery's role.

- In the SELECT part of your SQL statement, to create an extra computed column.

In either case, the subquery itself is put inside parentheses and can contain just about any valid SELECT statement. The subquery can use dot notation to refer to tables outside the parentheses, but not vice-versa. (The main statement cannot reach in and refer to tables inside the parentheses, but the subquery can reach out and refer to tables outside the parentheses.)

You can insert a subquery into a larger SQL statement to cause the whole unit to find only certain records. Generally, you do this when the logic to select the records is fairly complex or involves other tables. You include the subquery by using either the equal (=) sign or the IN or EXISTS keywords.

Including a Subquery with the Equal Sign   The simplest way to include a subquery in your SQL statements is with the = sign. Suppose you wanted to create an account summary page for individual customers that shows the orders they've placed and so on.

In Chapter 8 you learned how to use WHERE to find particular rows in your tables. For instance, you could use WHERE OrderID = 3 to find all the rows for order number 3. What if your template doesn't know the OrderID and only has a CustomerID to go on? You can put a subquery in

Part
IV

Ch
19

the place of the 3. The subquery's job is to look up the relevant OrderID and supply it to the main query. Take a look at Listing 19.19.

Listing 19.19 CUSTRPT1.CFM—Customer Report Page That Uses a Subquery

```
<CFQUERY NAME="Report" DATASOURCE="A2Z">
  SELECT OrderID, BookID, Quantity
  FROM OrderItems
  WHERE OrderID = (SELECT OrderID FROM Orders
                   WHERE CustomerID = #URL.CustomerID#)
  ORDER BY OrderID, BookID
</CFQUERY>

<HTML>

<HEAD>
<TITLE>Orders By Customer</TITLE>
</HEAD>

<BODY>

<H1>Customer No.  <CFOUTPUT>#URL.CustomerID#</CFOUTPUT></H1>

<CFTABLE QUERY="Report" COLHEADERS HTMLTABLE BORDER>
  <CFCOL HEADER="OrderID" TEXT="#OrderID#">
  <CFCOL HEADER="BookID" TEXT="#BookID#">
  <CFCOL HEADER="Quantity" TEXT="#Quantity#">
</CFTABLE>

</BODY>

</HTML>
```

If you pull the CustRpt1.cfm page (see Listing 19.19) up in your browser, passing it a CustomerID parameter of 2 in the URL, you get the results shown in Figure 19.13.

The template seems to work correctly. Your database system starts from inside the parentheses and works its way out, so it evaluates the subquery first. The subquery uses the CustomerID of 2 to find a relevant OrderID number, which turns out to be 3. Your database system then plugs the number 3 into the main query, so the main query behaves just as if WHERE OrderID = 3 had been hard-coded into the template in the first place.

CAUTION

Whenever you use a subquery with the = sign, make sure that only one record will ever be found by the subquery. For instance, more than one OrderID would be found for CustomerID number 1, which would cause an error message to appear. Your code really should use the IN keyword instead, which is discussed next.

FIGURE 19.13

This template uses a subquery to look up the `OrderID` number.

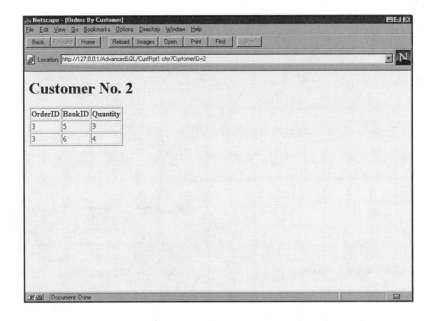

Including a Subquery with the IN Keyword   Replace the = sign with the IN keyword to allow subqueries to return more than one value. By using IN instead of =, your database system is expecting any number of values from the subquery, rather than just one. Listing 19.20 introduces IN as the method of including the subquery.

Listing 19.20   CUSTRPT2.CFM—Including the Subquery with IN Instead of the = Sign

```
<CFQUERY NAME="Report" DATASOURCE="A2Z">
  SELECT OrderID, BookID, Quantity
  FROM OrderItems
  WHERE OrderID IN (SELECT OrderID FROM Orders
                    WHERE CustomerID = #URL.CustomerID#)
  ORDER BY OrderID, BookID
</CFQUERY>

<HTML>

<HEAD>
<TITLE>Orders By Customer</TITLE>
</HEAD>

<BODY>

<H1>Customer No. <CFOUTPUT>#URL.CustomerID#</CFOUTPUT></H1>

<CFTABLE QUERY="Report" COLHEADERS HTMLTABLE BORDER>
  <CFCOL HEADER="OrderID" TEXT="#OrderID#">
```

continues

Part
IV
Ch
19

Listing 19.20 Continued

```
  <CFCOL HEADER="BookID" TEXT="#BookID#">
  <CFCOL HEADER="Quantity" TEXT="#Quantity#">
</CFTABLE>

</BODY>

</HTML>
```

Now bring up your revised report using `CustomerID` number 1. As you can see in Figure 19.14, two `OrderID` numbers are represented.

FIGURE 19.14

When you introduce a subquery with `IN` instead of the = sign, it's okay for it to return multiple values.

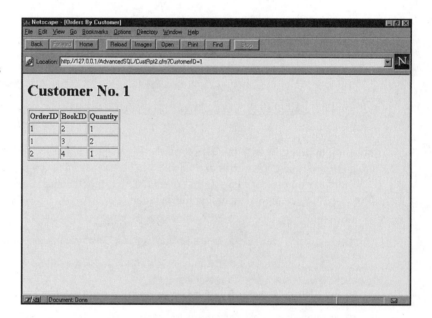

NOTE You can also include a subquery with `EXISTS` instead of `IN`. The `EXISTS` query causes the database system to consider the main query first. Conceptually, you are asking your database system to move through all rows returned by the main query statement, testing to see if the subquery statement is true for each row as it goes. The following could be used in place of the SQL statement in Listing 19.20:

```
SELECT OrderID, BookID, Quantity
  FROM OrderItems o
  WHERE EXISTS (SELECT * FROM Orders
                WHERE CustomerID = #URL.CustomerID#
                AND OrderID = o.OrderID)
  ORDER BY OrderID, BookID ■
```

Choosing the Opposite Set of Records with NOT IN or NOT EXISTS You may be thinking that subqueries look like a clunky alternative to joins, but using subqueries with IN or EXISTS gets more interesting when you use the NOT operator. The NOT operator does pretty much what you'd think—it causes the records that don't comply with the subquery to be affected.

The query in Listing 19.21 returns the titles of all books that the customer has not ordered. Figure 19.15 shows the results.

Listing 19.21   CUSTRPT4.CFM—Getting the Non-Matches with NOT IN

```
<CFQUERY NAME="Report" DATASOURCE="A2Z">
  SELECT BookID, Title
  FROM Inventory o
  WHERE BookID NOT IN (SELECT BookID
                       FROM OrderItems
                       WHERE OrderID IN (SELECT OrderID
                                         FROM Orders
                                         WHERE CustomerID = #URL.CustomerID#) )
  ORDER BY BookID
</CFQUERY>

<HTML>

<HEAD>
<TITLE>Orders By Customer</TITLE>
</HEAD>

<BODY>

<H1>Customer No. <CFOUTPUT>#URL.CustomerID#</CFOUTPUT></H1>

<CFTABLE QUERY="Report" COLHEADERS HTMLTABLE BORDER>
  <CFCOL HEADER="BookID" TEXT="#BookID#">
  <CFCOL HEADER="Title" TEXT="#Title#">
</CFTABLE>

</BODY>

</HTML>
```

Part

IV

Ch

19

Note, also, that you're nesting your subqueries two levels deep here. Your database system starts at the innermost subquery and works its way out. First it performs the SELECT OrderID subquery and passes the results to the SELECT BookID subquery, which passes its results to the main query, which finally passes its results to ColdFusion.

TIP You can also use the NOT keyword with EXISTS.

Using a Subquery to Create a New Calculated Value   Up to now, you've only used subqueries in the WHERE part of the main SQL statement. Subqueries can also be used in the SELECT part of the statement to produce a new, calculated value. Just like the aggregate functions you learned about at the beginning of this chapter, the values from subqueries included in the SELECT part of a query appear to ColdFusion as if they were table columns. The name of the subqueried column is whatever name you make up with the AS keyword. (You should recognize this use of AS from your work with aggregate functions as well.)

FIGURE 19.15

Now you see the opposite list of books— the ones the customer has not ordered.

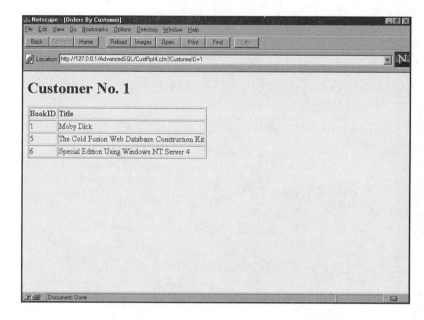

For instance, you could use the syntax in Listing 19.22 to find the total amount of money collected from the sale of each book. Figure 19.16 shows the results.

Listing 19.22 CUSTRPT5.CFM—Using a Subquery in the SELECT List to Generate a New, Computed Column

```
<CFQUERY NAME="Report" DATASOURCE="A2Z">
  SELECT OrderID, OrderDate, (SELECT SUM(SalePrice)
                              FROM OrderItems
                              WHERE OrderID = o.OrderID) AS SalePrice_SUM
  FROM Orders o
  WHERE CustomerID = #URL.CustomerID#
</CFQUERY>

<HTML>

<HEAD>
<TITLE>Orders By Customer</TITLE>
</HEAD>

<BODY>

<H1>Customer No. <CFOUTPUT>#URL.CustomerID#</CFOUTPUT></H1>

<CFTABLE QUERY="Report" COLHEADERS HTMLTABLE BORDER>
  <CFCOL HEADER="OrderID" TEXT="#OrderID#">
```

```
    <CFCOL HEADER="Date" TEXT="#DateFormat(OrderDate)#">
    <CFCOL HEADER="Total Of Order" TEXT="#DollarFormat(SalePrice_SUM)#">
</CFTABLE>

</BODY>

</HTML>
```

FIGURE 19.16

The value computed by the subquery is included as a new column for each row from the main query.

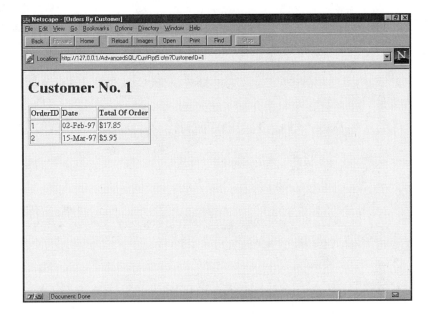

Using a Subquery Instead of a Table Join   As you can see, it's often possible to write a subquery that returns the same results as a table join. When should you use which syntax? Unfortunately, there's no easy answer to this question.

In my opinion, using a table join is generally recommended over the equivalent subquery syntax, which is why joins were discussed first in this chapter. Joins generally provide better performance in the majority of situations—especially as the number of values returned by the subquery increases over time as your database tables come to hold more and more data.

However, there are situations where a subquery will provide equal or better performance, especially if the number of values returned by the inner query is consistently going to be very small.

You may also encounter situations where the table join syntax turns out to be very messy and convoluted, but the equivalent subquery syntax is comparatively intuitive and straightforward.

Simple lookups—like getting one ID number based on another ID number as you did in Listing 19.20—are usually better left to subqueries. When you actually need to get information from more than one table at once, a table join is the way to go.

Part
IV

Ch
19

TIP Deciding on using a join or a subquery is definitely a judgment call and it may often be best to consider (or try) both alternatives when in doubt. Keep in mind that the difference in performance, if any, may be so slight that either method could be used without any noticeable difference in how your application behaves overall.

In general, a sensible rule of thumb might be to use table joins unless your knowledge of your tables, indexes, and data allow you to construct a subquery that you know will run very quickly, and which returns relatively few rows in comparison to the outer query into which it is placed.

Also try to think about what you are actually asking SQL to do for you. How hard is that going to be? Does one syntax take advantage of indexes that another does not?

Combining SQL Statements

Sometimes you'll want to write compound SQL statements that rely on one another to get something done. This section discusses using SELECT, INSERT, UPDATE, and DELETE statements together in various ways.

It is generally unnecessary to use these statements in your ColdFusion applications because it is usually possible to get the same results using some kind of looping constructs in your ColdFusion templates. The techniques discussed in these sections can often get things done more efficiently.

Making Multiple a SELECT Behave as One with UNION

You can use SQL's UNION operator to combine the results from two different queries. Compared to joins and subqueries, UNION is pretty simple because it doesn't have anything to do with relationships between tables. It's simply about combining the results of two different SELECT statements. The SELECTs can be based on the same table or on different tables.

Say you are planning a holiday party and want to display the names of all employees and customers. You want them in alphabetical order by first name, which means that the employees will be freely intermixed with the customers. Listing 19.23 shows the code used to accomplish this, and Figure 19.17 shows the results.

Listing 19.23 EVERYONE.CFM—**Using UNION to Combine Two Result Sets**

```
<CFQUERY NAME="Report" DATASOURCE="A2Z">
  SELECT FirstName, LastName, Phone
  FROM Customers
  UNION
  SELECT FirstName, LastName, PhoneExtension
  FROM Employees
  ORDER BY FirstName, LastName
</CFQUERY>

<HTML>
```

```
<HEAD>
<TITLE>Invitation List</TITLE>
</HEAD>

<BODY>

<H1>Invitation List</H1>

<CFOUTPUT QUERY="Report">
  #FirstName# #LastName# - #Phone#<BR>
</CFOUTPUT>

</BODY>

</HTML>
```

FIGURE 19.17

The ORDER BY sorts the results of both SELECT statements as one unit.

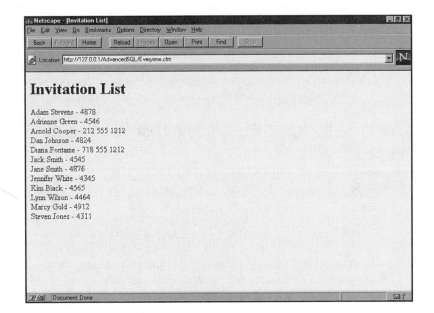

The first SELECT gets the names and phone numbers from the Customers table. The second SELECT gets the name and phone extensions from the Employees table. These two tables are then stacked on top of each other, with the first employee right after the last customer. Finally, this new mass of rows is sorted according to the ORDER BY clause and returned to ColdFusion. The column names FirstName, LastName, and Phone are available for use in your ColdFusion code.

N O T E   Even though the phone numbers come from columns that have different names, the name from the first SELECT is the one that's available to ColdFusion. You'd get an error message if you were to try to refer to the #PhoneExtension# column in your code. ▪

Part
IV

Ch
19

When you are using UNION in your queries, the following rules apply:

- You can use more than one UNION in an SQL statement, so you can use more than two tables together.

- All the SELECT statements have to specify the same number of columns, even though the underlying column names and data don't have to be the same.

- The columns' data types—Text, Numeric, Date, and so on—have to match. However, the text width or numeric precision of the columns may not need to match, depending on the type of database you're using. See your database documentation for details on this rule.

- The column names in the SELECT statements don't have to match. If they don't, the column names from the first SELECT become the column names that appear in the combined output.

- You can't use the DISTINCT keyword at all.

- BLOB columns—like Memo columns in Access—can't be used.

- There should only be one ORDER BY statement (at the end) and it must only refer to column names from the first SELECT statement.

- Duplicate rows (rows that are the same from more than one of the SELECTs) are automatically eliminated, unless you use UNION ALL in the place of UNION.

Using INSERT and SELECT Together to Move Data Between Tables

With many databases, it is possible to use a special kind of INSERT statement that gets its data from a correlated SELECT statement instead of a VALUES clause. This technique is particularly useful when you want to insert many rows at once.

Pretend that you've just received a list of names from some other source. These new names exist in your database, under the table name CustomersToImport. CustomersToImport has the same column structure as the Customers table. The task at hand is to add the names to the Customers table, so that they'll be assigned CustomerID numbers and be available to our application. This is done in Listing 19.24.

Listing 19.24 IMPORT.CFM—Using an INSERT with SELECT

```
<CFQUERY NAME="Report" DATASOURCE="A2Z">
  INSERT INTO Customers (Company, FirstName, MiddleInit, LastName,
Address1, Address2, City, State, ZIP, Phone, EMail, CustomerSince)
    SELECT Company, FirstName, MiddleInit, LastName, Address1, Address2,
City, State, ZIP, Phone, EMail, #CreateODBCDateTime(Now())#
    FROM CustomersToImport
</CFQUERY>

<HTML>

<HEAD>
<TITLE>Import</TITLE>
</HEAD>
```

```
<BODY>

<H1>Import</H1>

Import complete.

</BODY>

</HTML>
```

The SELECT part of the statement gets the data and then feeds its results—however many rows that may be—directly into the INSERT part. Note that you don't specify the CustomerID number in either the INSERT or the SELECT parts because you want your AutoNumber column to kick in and assign the next available CustomerID numbers to these new customers. (See Chapter 7, "Creating Databases and Tables," for information about Access's AutoNumber columns.)

Also note that the SELECT part can supply constant values as well as table columns. In this example the CustomerSince column is supplied with the current date, courtesy of ColdFusion's Now() function.

The INSERT SELECT syntax in Listing 19.24 is a welcome alternative to retrieving all the data with a CFQUERY, and then inserting it row-by-row into the new table with a CFLOOP. Because SQL's SELECT statement is so flexible, you can use the INSERT SELECT technique in more complex ways as well. All that's required is that the number of values called for by the INSERT part match the number of columns supplied by the SELECT part, and that the data types match up. The SELECT part can contain joins or subqueries, so you can fairly easily create a query where correlated rows from two or more tables are inserted into another table. Listing 9.4 in Chapter 9, "SQL Data Manipulation," provides an example of this.

Using UPDATE or DELETE with Subqueries

As you learned in Chapter 8, the UPDATE statement can be used to change the values of particular columns in a database table.

SQL allows you to make correlated updates by including a subquery in the WHERE part of an UPDATE query. Only the rows found by the subquery are updated. The rules for including the subquery in an UPDATE statement's WHERE clause are the same as for including one in a SELECT statement's WHERE clause—you can use IN, EXISTS, or = to include the subquery.

Listing 19.25 shows such a UPDATE / subquery combination in action. First the subquery finds the relevant rows; then the UPDATE fires on those rows, increasing the Pages column by 1 for each book that has been ordered by customer number 2. Figure 19.18 shows the results.

Part

IV

Ch

19

Listing 19.25 ADJUST.CFM—**Using** UPDATE **with a Subquery**

```
<!-- GET THE "BEFORE" INFORMATION -->
<CFQUERY NAME="Before" DATASOURCE="A2Z">
  SELECT * FROM Inventory
</CFQUERY>
```

continues

Listing 19.25 Continued

```
<!-- MAKE THE CHANGE -->
<CFQUERY NAME="Report" DATASOURCE="A2Z">
  UPDATE Inventory
  SET Pages = Pages + 1
  WHERE BookID IN (SELECT BookID
                   FROM OrderItems
                   WHERE OrderID IN (SELECT OrderID
                                     FROM Orders
                                     WHERE CustomerID = 2))
</CFQUERY>

<!-- GET THE "AFTER" INFORMATION -->
<CFQUERY NAME="After" DATASOURCE="A2Z">
  SELECT * FROM Inventory
</CFQUERY>

<HTML>

<HEAD>
<TITLE>Inventory Adjustment</TITLE>
</HEAD>

<BODY>

<B>Before</B><BR>

<CFTABLE QUERY="Before" COLHEADERS HTMLTABLE BORDER>
  <CFCOL HEADER="BookID" TEXT="#BookID#">
  <CFCOL HEADER="Title" TEXT="#Title#">
  <CFCOL HEADER="Pages" TEXT="#Pages#">
</CFTABLE>

<BR><B>After</B><BR>

<CFTABLE QUERY="After" COLHEADERS HTMLTABLE BORDER>
  <CFCOL HEADER="BookID" TEXT="#BookID#">
  <CFCOL HEADER="Title" TEXT="#Title#">
  <CFCOL HEADER="Pages" TEXT="#Pages#">
</CFTABLE>

</BODY>

</HTML>
```

Similarly, you can also create a DELETE statement that uses a subquery to choose the rows that get deleted. For instance, by replacing the SQL code in the report CFQUERY from Listing 19.25 with the SQL in Listing 19.26, you would cause the code to delete all the rows that had been ordered by customer number 2.

FIGURE 19.18

Subqueries can be used to drive updates.

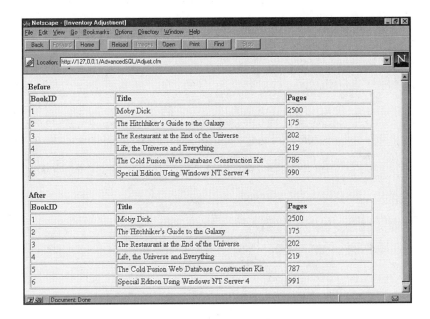

Listing 19.26 Using DELETE with a Subquery

```
DELETE FROM Inventory
   WHERE BookID IN (SELECT BookID
                    FROM OrderItems
                    WHERE OrderID IN (SELECT OrderID
                                      FROM Orders
                                      WHERE CustomerID = 2))
```

Part
IV

Ch

19

Working with Null Values

One of the most confusing concepts in SQL is the idea of a null value. A null value indicates that there is literally nothing recorded in the table for that row and column. For instance, consider the Customers table's CustomerSince column. Obviously, if you know this information, you'll record it here. If you don't, you probably want to leave the column blank; you set it to NULL.

To indicate that you want to set a column to a null value, use the keyword NULL where you would normally provide the value. To update your records, you might use the SQL statement in Listing 19.27. Note that quotation marks should never be used around the NULL keyword, even when dealing with a character-type field. The only time you'd want to put quotation marks around the word NULL is if you literally want to store the word NULL in your database, which is very unlikely.

Listing 19.27   Setting Columns to NULL

```
UPDATE Customers SET
  CustomerSince = NULL,
  MiddleInit = NULL
WHERE CustID = 3
```

If you need to record a null value when a form field has been left blank, ColdFusion's CFIF and CFELSE tags come in handy. For instance, imagine a form with BookID and CategoryID fields on it. The code in Listing 19.28 sets the CategoryID column to NULL if the user leaves the CategoryID field blank. Otherwise, the CategoryID column is set to whatever the user typed in.

Listing 19.28   CHANGE.CFM—Using CFIF and CFELSE to Allow for Setting of NULLs Conditionally

```
<CFQUERY DATASOURCE="A2Z">
  UPDATE Inventory
  SET CategoryID = <CFIF Trim(Form.CategoryID) is "">NULL
➥<CFELSE>#Form.CategoryID#</CFIF>
  WHERE BookID = #Form.BookID#
</CFQUERY>

<HTML>

<HEAD>
<TITLE>Record Updated</TITLE>
</HEAD>

<BODY>

<H2>Record Updated.</H2>

</BODY>

</HTML>
```

SQL statements that deal with null values can give unexpected results because a null value is not equal to anything. Pretend for a moment that there is a row in your Inventory table that has NULL for the CategoryID and NULL for the Title. None of the SQL statements in Listing 19.29 will find such a row. You'd probably expect this from the first one, but the rest may surprise you.

Listing 19.29   None of These Find the Row You Updated in Listing 19.28

```
SELECT * FROM Inventory
WHERE CategoryID > 1
```

```
SELECT * FROM Inventory
WHERE CategoryID < 1

SELECT * FROM Inventory
WHERE Title = ""

SELECT * FROM Inventory
WHERE Title <> "Moby Dick"
```

Note that NULL is not less than or greater than any number. It's also not the same thing as an empty string (""). Perhaps most surprising, it is not even unequal to anything, as the last of the four examples illustrates. Null values are also excluded from the calculations that aggregate functions like Count(column) make. In short, a NULL fails any test.

In fact, with database systems that handle nulls absolutely correctly (such as Microsoft SQL Server 6.5), even the following SQL statement will not find the record. That's because a null value by definition must fail any equality test, even against another null value:

```
SELECT * FROM Inventory
WHERE Title = NULL
```

Instead, you need to use the following SQL Statement, which would find the record:

```
SELECT * FROM Inventory
WHERE Title IS NULL
```

Therefore, to get all books except *Moby Dick*, you need to use the tedious and counter-intuitive SQL statement shown here:

```
SELECT * FROM Inventory
WHERE (Title <> 'Moby Dick' OR Title IS NULL)
```

The lesson? If possible, try to avoid null values in your tables, unless you specifically want to represent the fact that a piece of data hasn't been recorded. When in doubt, consider that it often makes sense to allow null values in numeric columns (there is a difference between a CategoryID of 0 and no CategoryID at all), but with text-type columns they almost always lead to trouble. (Rarely would you encounter a real-world difference between a book that has no title and a book whose title has not been recorded.) Keep in mind that when you add a new column to a table, all of the rows in that new column probably hold null values. Just be careful if you must allow null values, especially with character-type columns, and especially when using such a column in a WHERE clause.

The situation is further complicated by the fact that ColdFusion doesn't have the concept of a null value—only SQL does. If you refer to a column that happens to be NULL once a SQL statement runs in a ColdFusion template, ColdFusion treats it just like an empty string (""). That means the following CFIF code works, even if the Title column is NULL in the actual table:

```
<CFIF #Title# is "">
  The value is either null, or just set to an empty string ("").
  We can't tell which from a ColdFusion template.
</CFIF>
```

Part
IV

Ch
19

Using Views to Simplify and Reuse Your Queries

Many database systems support views. A *view* is a SELECT statement that is given a name and stored as a permanent part of your database, just as your tables are a permanent part of your database. Once a view has been created, it can be thought of as a virtual table that can be used in most of the same ways a normal table can.

The syntax for creating a view is quite simple: just type CREATE VIEW *viewname* AS, followed by virtually any SELECT statement.

TIP While the name of the view can be anything you want, you may want to follow my lead and use a lowercase v as the first letter; that way you can easily distinguish your views from your tables.

Listing 19.30 shows a SQL statement that creates a view of the entire Customers table. This is not a statement that you would likely want to include in a ColdFusion template—it only needs to be executed once. Instead, you would execute it from your database natively, such as from Microsoft Access itself, or from a tool like Microsoft Query, ColdFusion Studio, or Microsoft SQL Enterprise Manager.

Listing 19.30   Creating a Simple View

```
CREATE VIEW vInventory AS
SELECT * FROM Inventory
```

Now that the vInventory view has been defined, you can use it in your ColdFusion application in the same way as the Inventory table. You could do a search-and-replace, changing Inventory to vInventory in all of your templates, and everything should continue to work. In short, Inventory and vInventory have essentially become synonyms. Why would you do such a thing? You probably wouldn't. The example in Listing 19.31 makes a little more sense.

Listing 19.31   Creating a More Practical View

```
CREATE VIEW vCompInventory AS
SELECT * FROM Inventory
WHERE CategoryID = 3
```

Now you can refer to vCompInventory in your ColdFusion templates and you'll automatically only be talking about the books in category number 3 (the computer books). SELECT statements only return rows about computer books, and INSERT statements do not work if the CategoryID of the new row is not 3. In addition, UPDATE statements only affect computer books. For instance, you could show that all computer books had sold out with the SQL statement in Listing 19.32, which would only change the NumberInStock column for the computer books, even though there is no WHERE clause.

Listing 19.32 Running an Update Against a View

```
UPDATE vCompInventory
SET NumberInStock = 0
```

By using `vCompInventory` in your application, you do more than merely save yourself from having to type `WHERE CategoryID = 3` over and over again; you have also allowed the whole issue of the `CategoryID` to become irrelevant as you build your application. In fact, if the database tables you're using are administered by another person, `vCompInventory` may be all you have to develop with. You may not even know that the Inventory table exists at all. This might make lots of sense if your project were to develop a shopping cart system for computer books only. You could rest easy knowing that there is no chance for any other types of books to be revealed just because of a programming oversight on your part.

 TIP

If you're working with Microsoft Access, you will notice that after you use CREATE VIEW, the new view becomes visible in the actual Access program as a query. The reverse is also true. If you create a query from within Access, it is available as a view to ColdFusion.

This strategy really pays off later if the business decides to change its categorizing system. For instance, the books handled by the entire application could be changed just by changing the definition of the view. Listing 19.33 shows a SQL statement that creates an alternative `vCompInventory` view.

Listing 19.33 Changing the Scope of the Application by Editing the View

```
CREATE VIEW vCompInventory AS
SELECT * FROM Inventory
WHERE (CategoryID = 3 OR
       Title LIKE '%Active Server Pages%')
```

Part
IV

Ch
19

This changes the scope of the entire ColdFusion application without editing a single line of ColdFusion code. As far as your application is concerned, nothing has changed. However, books about active server pages would suddenly be included, even if they were in category number 2 (Humor) instead of category number 3 (Computers).

By using views to separate your programming tasks from real-world business rules whenever possible, you can save yourself a lot of time and make your code much more abstract and reusable.

Restricting the View to Certain Columns

You can also create views with more complex `SELECT` statements. The SQL statement in Listing 19.34 makes only the BookID and Title available in the view. The rating, pricing, and other columns are inaccessible.

Listing 19.34   View that Accesses Certain Columns of the Base Table

```
CREATE VIEW vCompInventory AS
SELECT BookID, Title FROM Inventory
WHERE CategoryID = 3
```

Using More Than One Table

Because a view can be based on just about any SELECT statement, you can create views that are based on more than one table by using the various join and subquery techniques you've learned in this chapter.

For instance, the SQL statement in Listing 19.35 creates a view that allows you to see how many orders a customer has placed without having to bother joining the tables in each query.

Listing 19.35   Creating a View Based on More Than One Table

```
CREATE VIEW vCustomers AS
SELECT CustomerID, Company,
  (SELECT COUNT(*) FROM Orders
   WHERE CustomerID = c.CustomerID) AS OrdersPlaced
FROM Customers c
```

SELECT statements issued against the view will now automatically contain an OrdersPlaced column that always reflects the correct number of orders that each customer has made, even though there is no such column in Customers and you are not manually incrementing any kind of counter column anywhere in your application. Listing 19.36 shows the ColdFusion code that uses the vCustomers view created by Listing 19.35. Figure 19.19 shows the results.

Listing 19.36   CUSTRPT6—Putting the vCustomers View to Use

```
<CFQUERY NAME="Report" DATASOURCE="A2Z">
  SELECT * FROM vCustomers
</CFQUERY>

<HTML>

<HEAD>
<TITLE>Orders By Customer</TITLE>
</HEAD>

<BODY>

<H1>New York</H1>

<CFTABLE QUERY="Report" COLHEADERS HTMLTABLE BORDER>
  <CFCOL HEADER="CustomerID" TEXT="#CustomerID#">
  <CFCOL HEADER="Company" TEXT="#Company#">
  <CFCOL HEADER="Orders Made" TEXT="#NumberFormat(OrdersPlaced)#">
</CFTABLE>
```

```
</BODY>

</HTML>
```

FIGURE 19.19

Once a multi-table view is created, using SELECT is a simple task.

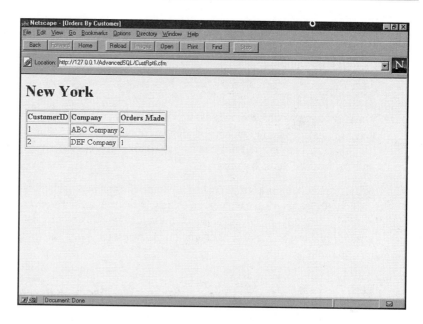

N O T E As you can see, views based on more than one table can be quite useful, but the view is considered read-only by most database systems. SELECT statements are allowed, but INSERT and UPDATE statements generate error messages (which means that CFINSERT and CFUPDATE tags will also fail). ▨

Using Scalar Functions to Manipulate Data Row-by-Row

You may want to create queries that do things like manipulate dates or perform arithmetic on your data. The ODBC standard defines a number of date, time, numeric, and string functions for your use. These are called *scalar functions*. Unfortunately, not all are supported by every type of database.

ODBC says that if the database supports a function *natively*, it should be mapped to the appropriate ODBC function to provide some common ground between systems, but nothing's required here. Most databases support only a subset of the complete list. A complete reference on scalar function syntax can be found in Appendix E of the *Microsoft ODBC SDK Programmer's Reference*. (Visit http://www.microsoft.com/odbc to get the reference.)

Part
IV

Ch
19

N O T E   There are many more scalar functions than those listed in this book. The number of scalar functions supported varies from one driver to another. Consult the documentation of the person who supplies your ODBC driver for a complete list of supported functionality. ■

Using Scalar Functions in the SELECT List and the WHERE Clause

You can use scalar functions to create computed columns on-the-fly for each row that your query returns. Use the following syntax to use these functions in your queries:

```
{ fn function-name(parameter, parameter ... ) }
```

The curly braces indicate that this is an ODBC command (as opposed to native SQL). The fn indicates that a scalar function is to follow. A list of parameters follows, in parentheses. Finally, just as with the aggregate functions covered earlier, you must use the AS keyword to give the new, computed column a name.

Say you wanted to list all of your company names. Your boss has told you that she only wants the first 10 characters of each person's name to be displayed. The example in Listing 19.37 demonstrates the use of the LEFT scalar function to get this accomplished. For each row of the Inventory table, just the first 10 characters of the Title column are returned with the column name of TitlePart.

Listing 19.37   SCALAR1.CFM—Using a Scalar Function in the SELECT List

```
<CFQUERY NAME="Report" DATASOURCE="A2Z">
  SELECT BookID, { fn LEFT(Title, 10) } AS TitlePart
  FROM Inventory
</CFQUERY>

<HTML>

<HEAD>
<TITLE>Scalar Functions</TITLE>
</HEAD>

<BODY>

<H1>SUBSTRING Scalar Function</H1>

<CFTABLE QUERY="Report" COLHEADERS HTMLTABLE BORDER>
  <CFCOL HEADER="BookID" TEXT="#BookID#">
  <CFCOL HEADER="Title" TEXT="#TitlePart#">
</CFTABLE>

</BODY>

</HTML>
```

Other scalar functions are used in the same way. Figure 19.20 shows the results.

FIGURE 19.20

ODBC's scalar functions provide basic text-manipulation capabilities.

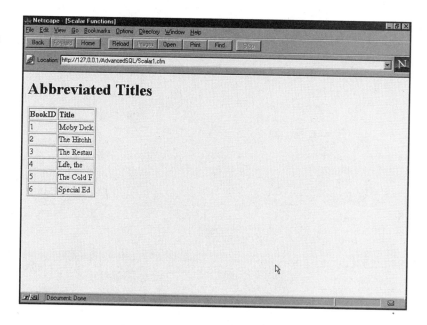

You can also use scalar functions in the WHERE part of your query to select rows based on a calculated condition.

Say you need to display all the books that were published during the month of November—any November, regardless of the year. Listing 19.38 shows how to accomplish this with the MONTH scalar function. Conceptually, the MONTH function asks every row what the month part of the value in the PublicationDate column is. Only the rows that answer with the number 11 are returned to ColdFusion, as shown in Figure 19.21.

Listing 19.38 SCALAR2.CFM—Using a Scalar Function in the WHERE Part of a Query

```
<CFQUERY NAME="Report" DATASOURCE="A2Z">
  SELECT BookID, Title, PublicationDate
  FROM Inventory
  WHERE { fn MONTH(PublicationDate) } = 11
</CFQUERY>

<HTML>

<HEAD>
<TITLE>Scalar Functions</TITLE>
</HEAD>

<BODY>

<H1>Published in the month of November</H1>
```

Part
IV
Ch
19

continues

Listing 19.38   Continued

```
<TABLE BORDER>
  <TR><TH>BookID</TH><TH>Title</TH><TH>Publication Date</TH></TR>
  <CFOUTPUT QUERY="Report">
    <TR>
      <TD>#BookID#</TD>
      <TD>#Title#</TD>
      <TD>#DateFormat(PublicationDate, 'mmmm, yyyy')#</TD>
    </TR>
  </CFOUTPUT>
</TABLE>

</BODY>

</HTML>
```

FIGURE 19.21

Scalar functions can be very useful in the WHERE part of a query.

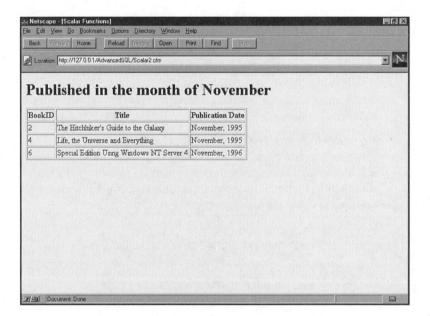

Using Scalar Functions Instead of ColdFusion Functions

In general, I recommend using ColdFusion's functions rather than scalar functions in your queries. They're often more versatile and easier to understand. In addition, you won't run into incompatibilities between differing types of databases when using ColdFusion functions. It's just that much less to learn and think about. Who wants to memorize the parameters for both sets of functions?

Sometimes you'll want to use scalar functions, though. To demonstrate when it's a good idea and when it's not, consider the two examples given so far.

The first example (see Listing 19.37) used a scalar function in the SELECT list to return a truncated version of the Title column. It would be just as easy—if not easier—to retrieve the Title column with ordinary SELECT syntax. ColdFusion's LEFT function could then be used to get the first 10 characters, as shown in Listing 19.39.

Listing 19.39 SCALAR1A.CFM—**Getting the Same Results Without Scalar Functions**

```
<CFQUERY NAME="Report" DATASOURCE="A2Z">
  SELECT BookID, Title
  FROM Inventory
</CFQUERY>

<HTML>

<HEAD>
<TITLE>Without Scalar Functions</TITLE>
</HEAD>

<BODY>

<H1>Abbreviated Titles</H1>

<CFTABLE QUERY="Report" COLHEADERS HTMLTABLE BORDER>
  <CFCOL HEADER="BookID" TEXT="#BookID#">
  <CFCOL HEADER="Title" TEXT="#Left(Title, 10)#">
</CFTABLE>

</BODY>

</HTML>
```

This ColdFusion function approach produces the same results in the browser as the scalar function approach did (see Figure 19.20). The only difference? When the titles are truncated. The scalar function approach does it at the ODBC level, before ColdFusion ever gets the data. If there are tons of rows, the scalar function approach may be slightly more efficient—particularly if the data resides on a different machine than ColdFusion—because the full text of the titles never has to be retrieved from the data source. The real lesson is that you can—and in most cases should—use ColdFusion functions instead of scalar functions in SELECT lists. As a general practice, they're more flexible and database-independent.

In contrast, the second scalar function example (see Listing 19.38) is quite different. The scalar function is in the WHERE part of the query and is doing something that ColdFusion really can't do so efficiently. Rather than altering the way the rows are returned, it's making decisions about which rows to return—without sending the "bad rows" back to ColdFusion.

To get the same effect without the use of scalar functions, SELECT all of the rows and then test each row, one at a time, in a CFOUTPUT block, as shown in Listing 19.40.

Listing 19.40 SCALAR2A.CFM—**Compare This with Listing 19.38**

```
<CFQUERY NAME="Report" DATASOURCE="A2Z">
  SELECT BookID, Title, PublicationDate
  FROM Inventory
</CFQUERY>

<HTML>

<HEAD>
<TITLE>Scalar Functions</TITLE>
</HEAD>

<BODY>

<H1>Published in the month of November</H1>

<TABLE BORDER>
  <TR><TH>BookID</TH><TH>Title</TH><TH>Publication Date</TH></TR>
  <CFOUTPUT QUERY="Report">
  <CFIF Month(PublicationDate) is 11>
    <TR>
      <TD>#BookID#</TD>
      <TD>#Title#</TD>
      <TD>#DateFormat(PublicationDate, 'mmmm, yyyy')#</TD>
    </TR>
  </CFIF>
  </CFOUTPUT>
</TABLE>

</BODY>

</HTML>
```

In this second case, the ColdFusion function approach is less efficient—you're making your application do a lot of extra work. First off, you have to collect every single row in the table—even though you know, as a developer, that only around one-twelfth of the rows are going to be displayed in the end. Then you have ColdFusion test every row in the table individually to see if it passes the test. It works, but it's much less efficient than letting the scalar function do all the work for you in the WHERE clause.

In general, scalar functions aren't generally needed in your SELECT lists. However, do consider using them in a WHERE clause if you need to retrieve data based on some kind of calculation that needs to be performed on each row individually.

A Short List of Scalar Functions

Table 19.2 summarizes scalar functions supported by the Microsoft desktop family of ODBC drivers that ships with ColdFusion (Access, Paradox, FoxPro, Text, dBASE, Excel). These are not the only scalar functions defined by ODBC—just those supported by the desktop drivers. Drivers for other database systems—and drivers from third-party vendors like Visigenic and Intersolv—may provide support for more (or different) functions.

Table 19.2   Scalar Function Quick Reference

Scalar Function	What It Returns	Similar to CF Expression
CONVERT (value, datatype)	Value converted to data type†	n/a
CONCAT (string1, string)	string1 concatenated to string2	string1 and string2
LCASE(string)	String converted to lowercase	LCase(string)
LEFT(string, count)	First count characters of string	Left(string, count)
LENGTH(string)	Number of characters in string	Len(string)
LOCATE(substring, [, start])	Position of substring in string after start	Find (substring, string string [, start])
LTRIM(string)	String without leading	LTrim(string)
RIGHT(string, count)	Last count characters of string	Right(string, count)
RTRIM(string)	String without trailing spaces	RTrim(string)
SUBSTRING(string, start, count)	Count characters of string after start	Mid(string, start, count)
UCASE(string)	String converted to uppercase	UCase(string)
CURDATE()	The current date	DateFormat(Now())
CURTIME()	The current time	TimeFormat(Now())
DAYOFMONTH(date)	The day (between 1 and 31)	Day(date)
DAYOFWEEK(date)	The day (between 1 and 7)	DayOfWeek(date)
MONTH(date)	The month (between 1 and 12)	Month(date)
YEAR(date)	The year	Year(date)
MOD(integer1, integer2)	Remainder of integer1	integer1 MOD

Part

IV

Ch

19

†The following are the keywords for use as the data type for the CONVERT *function listed earlier:* SQL_BIGINT, SQL_INTERVAL_HOUR_TO_MINUTE, SQL_BINARY, SQL_INTERVAL_HOUR_TO_SECOND, SQL_BIT, SQL_INTERVAL_MINUTE_TO_SECOND, SQL_CHAR, SQL_LONGVARBINARY, SQL_DECIMAL, SQL_LONGVARCHAR, SQL_DOUBLE, SQL_NUMERIC, SQL_FLOAT, SQL_REAL, SQL_INTEGER, SQL_SMALLINT, SQL_INTERVAL_MONTH, SQL_TYPE_DATE, SQL_INTERVAL_YEAR, SQL_TYPE_TIME, SQL_INTERVAL_YEAR_TO_MONTH, SQL_TYPE_TIMESTAMP, SQL_INTERVAL_DAY, SQL_TINYINT, SQL_INTERVAL_HOUR, SQL_VARBINARY, SQL_INTERVAL_MINUTE, SQL_VARCHAR, SQL_INTERVAL_SECOND, SQL_WCHAR, SQL_INTERVAL_DAY_TO_HOUR, SQL_WLONGVARCHAR, SQL_INTERVAL_DAY_TO_MINUTE, SQL_WVARCHAR, *and* SQL_INTERVAL_DAY_TO_SECOND. *Do not use quotation marks around these keywords. You will probably need to experiment a little to figure out which of these corresponds to the desired data type that your database system supports natively.*

N O T E The functions described in this section are provided by Microsoft's ODBC specification, rather than by your database system itself. This means that you can only use these functions with data sources that have been set up as ODBC data sources or OLE-DB data sources in the ColdFusion Administrator. You cannot use them with the native Oracle and Sybase drivers that ship with the Enterprise version of ColdFusion. ■

CHAPTER 20

Working with Stored Procedures

Most server-based database systems—SQL Server, Oracle, and Sybase—support stored procedures. A *stored procedure* is a chunk of SQL code that's given a name and stored as a part of your database, along with your actual data tables. Once the stored procedure has been created, you can invoke it in your ColdFusion templates using the CFSTOREDPROC tag.

TIP The use of stored procedures in database applications is a relatively advanced topic. As the saying goes, it's not exactly rocket science, but it probably makes sense to start working with stored procedures only after you have become pretty familiar with the SQL concepts introduced in the previous chapter, or have a specific reason for using stored procedures in a particular ColdFusion application.

N O T E At the time of this writing, stored procedures are supported by most server-based database systems (such as SQL Server, Oracle, and Sybase), but are not supported by any file-based databases like Access, FoxPro, Paradox, dBASE, and the like. If you are not using a server-based database system, you can skip this chapter without missing out on anything essential. ▪

Why Use Stored Procedures?

Stored procedures provide a way to consolidate any number of SQL statements—such as SELECT, INSERT, UPDATE, and so on—into a little package that encapsulates a complete operation to be carried out in your application.

For instance, consider a book-ordering system for a bookstore. To place an order for a book, your application might need to first make sure that the book is in stock, ensure that the customer's account is in good standing, carry out an INSERT or two to record the actual order itself and, finally, update the number of books in stock to reflect the fact that one less copy of the book is now sitting on the shelves. If the order cannot be placed because there are no more copies in stock, the application needs to display some kind of "sorry, out of stock" message for the user, and may need to update another table somewhere else to indicate that more copies need to be purchased from the publisher.

This kind of complex, causally related set of checks and record-keeping is often referred to generally as a *business rule* or *business process*. Using the techniques you've learned so far in this book, you already know that you could accomplish the steps with several CFQUERY tags and some conditional processing using CFIF and CFELSE tags. In this chapter you see that it is possible to wrap up all of the steps listed into a single stored procedure called PlaceOrder, thus encapsulating the entire business process into one smart routine that your ColdFusion templates need only refer to.

This shifts the responsibility for making sure that the steps are followed properly away from your ColdFusion code and places that responsibility in the hands of the database server itself. This shift generally requires a little bit of extra work on your part up front, but offers some real advantages later.

Advantages of Using Stored Procedures

Depending on the situation, there are a number of possible advantages to using a stored procedure in your application (rather than a series of CFQUERY and CFIF tags). Some of the most important advantages are outlined in this chapter. You may want to consult your database server documentation for further details and remarks on the advantages of using stored procedures.

Modularity Is a Good Thing   When developing any type of application, it generally pays to keep pieces of code—whether it be CFML code, SQL statements, or some other type of code—broken into little self-explanatory modules that know how to perform a specific task on their own. This kind of practice keeps your code readable, easier to maintain, and easier to reuse in other applications that you might need to write later on.

It can also make it easier for several people to work on the same project at the same time without stepping on each other's toes. Developer A might say to Developer B, "Make me a stored procedure that does such-and-such. Meanwhile, I'll be putting together the ColdFusion templates that use the procedure." Since the procedure runs independently of the templates and vice versa, neither developer needs to wait for the other to get started. The result can be an application that gets up and running more quickly.

Sharing Code Between Applications   Once a stored procedure has been created, it allows you to share code between different types of applications, even applications written with different development tools. For instance, a ColdFusion template, a Visual Basic program, and a PowerBuilder application might all refer to the same stored procedure on your server. Clearly, this cuts down on development time and ensures that all three applications enforce the various business rules in exactly the same way.

This kind of consistent enforcement of business rules may be particularly important if the three applications are being developed by different teams or developers. In addition, if the business rules change for order-taking in the future, it's likely that only the stored procedure would need to be adapted, rather than having to revise the code in all three applications.

Increasing Performance   Depending on the situation, using stored procedures can often cause an application to perform better. There are two basic reasons the use of stored procedures will speed your application. Firstly, most database systems do some kind of precompilation of the stored procedure so that it runs faster when it is actually used. For instance, Microsoft SQL Server makes all of its performance-optimizing decisions (like what indexes and what join algorithms to use) the first time a stored procedure is run. Subsequent executions of the stored procedure do not need to be parsed and analyzed, which causes the procedure to run somewhat faster than if you executed its SQL statements in an ad hoc fashion every time. Generally, the more steps the procedure represents, the more of a difference this precompilation makes.

Part
IV

Ch
20

Secondly, if you compare the idea of having one stored procedure versus several CFQUERY and CFIF tags in a template, the stored procedure approach is often more efficient because there is much less communication needed between ColdFusion and the database server. Instead of sending the information about the number of books in stock and customer account status back and forth between the ColdFusion server and the database server, all of the querying and decision-making steps are kept in one place. Because less data needs to move between the two systems, and because the database drivers aren't really involved at all until the very end, you are likely to have a slightly faster process in the end if you use the stored procedure approach. Generally, the more data that needs to be examined to enforce the various business rules, the more of a difference the use of stored procedures on the situation, using stored procedures can often cause makes.

N O T E In general, the performance increases mentioned here are going to be relatively modest. Of course, your mileage is going to vary from application to application and from database to database, but it probably makes sense to expect speed increases of 10% or so as a ballpark figure in your mind. In other words, don't expect your application to work 20 times faster just because you put all of your SQL code into stored procedures. ▪

Making Table Schemas Irrelevant Since a stored procedure is invoked simply by referring to it by name, it is possible for a database administrator to shield whoever is actually using a stored procedure from having to be familiar with the database tables' underlying structure. In fact, in a team environment, it's easy to imagine a situation where you are developing a ColdFusion application but don't even know the names of the tables that the various data are being stored in.

You can get your work done faster if whoever designed the database provides you with a number of stored procedures that you can use to get your job done without having to learn the various table and column names involved. In return, the database designer can be comforted by the knowledge that if the relationships between the tables change at some point in the future, only the stored procedure will need to be changed, rather than the ColdFusion code that you're working on.

Addressing Security Concerns Depending on the type of database server you're using, stored procedures can provide advantages in terms of security. For instance, you might have some very confidential data in some of your database tables, so the database administrator may not have granted SELECT or INSERT privileges to whatever database username ColdFusion uses to interact with the database server. It is impossible to display information on ColdFusion pages without stored procedures. By creating a few stored procedures, however, it may be quite possible to get the needed information to ColdFusion without granting more general privileges than are necessary.

By only granting privileges to the stored procedures rather than allowing the actual tables to be queried or updated, the database administrator can be confident that the data in the tables does not become compromised or lose its real-world meaning. Since all database servers allow the administrator to grant SELECT, UPDATE, DELETE, and INSERT privileges separately, the administrator could allow your ColdFusion application to retrieve data, but only make changes via stored procedures. That gives the administrator a lot of control and keeps you from worrying about harming the organization's data because of some mistake in your code.

That is a policy that would allow the ColdFusion developer, the database administrator, and the company in general to feel very confident about the development of a ColdFusion application.

Everyone involved can see that nothing crazy is going to happen as the company shifts toward Web-based applications.

Comparing Stored Procedures to CFML Custom Tags

It's worth noting that stored procedures are similar in many conceptual ways to custom tags (also known as *modules*) written in CFML. You can think about a stored procedure as the database server equivalent of a custom tag, which might help you get a handle on when you should consider writing a stored procedure.

Here are some of the ways stored procedures are like custom tags:

- Both stored procedures and custom tags allow you to take a bunch of code, wrap it up, slap a name on it, and use it as you develop your applications almost as if it were part of the language all along.
- Both encourage code reuse, cutting development times and costs in the long run.
- Both can accept parameters as input.
- Both can set ColdFusion variables in the calling template that can be used in subsequent CFML code.
- Both can generate one or more query result sets for the calling template.
- Both make it easier to integrate other people's work into your own.

Calling Stored Procedures from ColdFusion Templates

Now that you have an idea about what kinds of things stored procedures can be used for, this is a good time to see how to integrate them into your ColdFusion templates. For the moment, assume that several stored procedures have already been created and are ready for use within your ColdFusion application. Perhaps you put the stored procedures together yourself, or maybe they were created by another developer or by the database administrator (DBA). At this point, all you care about is what the name of the stored procedure is and what it does. You learn how to actually create the stored procedures later in this chapter.

> **N O T E** The CFSTOREDPROC and related tags explained during the course of this chapter are new for ColdFusion 4. If you are using an earlier version of ColdFusion, or must maintain backward compatibility with version 3.1 or earlier, skip ahead to the section titled "Calling Procedures with CFQUERY Instead of CFSTOREDPROC," later in this chapter. ∎

Using the CFSTOREDPROC Tag

To call an existing stored procedure from a ColdFusion template, you refer to the procedure by name using the CFSTOREDPROC tag. The CFSTOREDPROC tag is kind of like the CFQUERY tag in that it knows how to interact with data sources you've defined in the ColdFusion Administrator.

Part

IV

Ch

20

However, rather than accepting ad hoc SQL query statements (such as SELECT and DELETE), CFSTOREDPROC is very structured, optimized specifically for dealing with stored procedures.

The CFSTOREDPROC tag takes a number of relatively simple parameters. For simple stored procedures, you just need to include the tag in a ColdFusion template. When the template is executed in a Web browser, the stored procedure executes on the database server, accomplishing whatever it was designed to accomplish as it goes.

For instance, suppose that you have access to a stored procedure called ImportCustomers. It's been explained to you that the stored procedure takes any customers listed in the database's CustomersToImport table and imports them into the Customers table. Now you want to create a Web page on which someone can cause this stored procedure to be executed at the click of a button. Listing 20.1 shows a simple ColdFusion template called ProcImportCustomers.cfm, which does exactly that.

N O T E The code listings in this chapter refer to a data source called A2Z Server in order to indicate a copy of the A2Z example database sitting on a SQL Server, Sybase, Oracle, or some other database server. You cannot work though the examples in this chapter using the Access version of the A2Z database used elsewhere in this book. SQL Server, Oracle, and Sybase each provide a tool that can import the Access version of the A2Z database into the database server. See the section titled "Creating Stored Procedures" later in this chapter for instructions on how to start the import tool for your database server. ■

Listing 20.1 `ProcImportCustomers.cfm`—**Calling a Stored Procedure with CFSTOREDPROC**

```
<!DOCTYPE HTML PUBLIC "-//W3C//DTD HTML 4.0 Transitional//EN">

<HTML>
<HEAD>
    <TITLE>Customer Import</TITLE>
</HEAD>

<BODY>
<H2>Customer Import</H2>


<!--- If the ImportNow button was not just pressed, display form --->
<CFIF NOT ParameterExists(Form.ImportNow)>

  <FORM ACTION="ProcImportCustomers.cfm" METHOD="POST">
    <INPUT TYPE="SUBMIT" NAME="ImportNow" VALUE="Import Customers Now">
  </FORM>


<!--- If the user just clicked the "Import" button --->
<CFELSE>

  <P>Executing stored procedure...</P>
```

```
<!--- Go ahead and execute the stored procedure --->
<CFSTOREDPROC
  PROCEDURE="ImportCustomers"
  DATASOURCE="A2Z Server">


<P>Done executing stored procedure!</P>


</CFIF>


</BODY>
</HTML>
```

As you can see, the code to execute the stored procedure is extremely simple. You see in a moment how to use stored procedures that receive input and respond by providing output back to you. This particular stored procedure doesn't require any information to be provided to it, so the only things you need to specify in the CFSTOREDPROC tag are the PROCEDURE and DATASOURCE parameters. As you can see, the PROCEDURE parameter tells ColdFusion what the name of the stored procedure is. The DATASOURCE parameter works just like it does for the CFQUERY tag; it must be the name of the appropriate ODBC, OLE-DB, or native-driver data source as defined in the ColdFusion Administrator.

N O T E   Listing 20.1 uses a simple piece of CFIF logic that tests to see if a form parameter called ImportNow exists. Assuming that it does not exist, the template puts a simple form, with a single submit button, on the page. Since the submit button is named ImportNow, the CFIF logic executes the second part of the template when the form is submitted; the second part contains the CFSTOREDPROC tag that executes the stored procedure. The template is put together this way so you can see the form code and the form-processing code in one listing. See the section titled "Understanding Conditional Forms" in Chapter 13, "Using Forms to Add or Change Data," for further discussion of this type of single template technique. ■

T I P   If you are using ColdFusion Studio 4 to edit your templates, you can use the Tag Inspector or the CFSTOREDPROC Tag Editor to help you add the CFSTOREDPROC tag to your code (see Figure 20.1).

FIGURE 20.1

You can use ColdFusion Studio to help you code your CFSTOREDPROC tags.

When the `ProcImportCustomers.cfm` template from Listing 20.1 is first brought up in a Web browser, it displays the simple form shown in Figure 20.2. When the Import Customers Now button is clicked, the procedure is executed and a simple message is displayed to the user to indicate that the work has been done. Figure 20.3 shows what the user will see after the procedure runs.

FIGURE 20.2

The `ProcImportCustomers.cfm` template first displays a simple form.

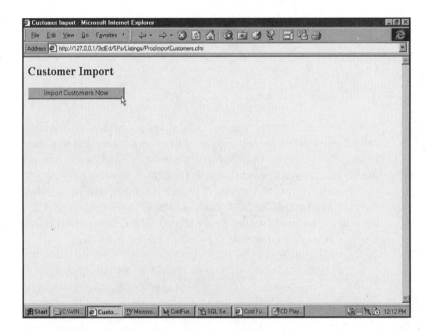

FIGURE 20.3

The stored procedure executes when the form is submitted.

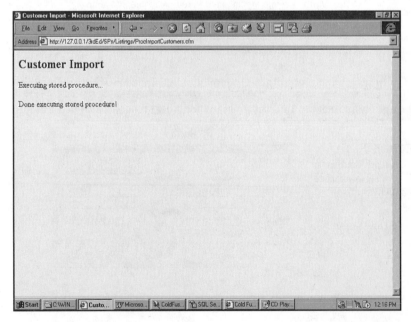

Getting a Return Value from a Stored Procedure

With most database server software, stored procedures can return something called a return value. The *return value* is simply a value that the calling application (in this case, your ColdFusion template) can look at after the stored procedure runs, so that the application can understand what actually happened as the procedure did its work. Whoever designs the stored procedure can decide what the return value should be, depending on the real-world conditions that the procedure encounters as it runs. With most database systems, the only requirement is that the return value needs to be an integer. Often, the stored procedure is written so that the return value returns a positive integer to indicate success, or one of several negative integers to indicate an error of some kind. With most database systems, all stored procedures automatically generate a return value of 0 by default.

> **N O T E** Oracle return values work differently. They can be of any data type, and are not set to 0 by default. However, you cannot use return values from Oracle stored procedures in ColdFusion 4. See the section titled "Creating Stored Procedures with Oracle" later in this chapter for details. · ■

For instance, what if you wanted to be able to indicate to the user how many customers were actually "imported" by the ImportCustomers stored procedure? This could be accomplished by having whoever wrote the stored procedure adapt it a little so that the return value gets set to the number of customer records actually processed by the procedure.

Listing 20.2 shows how to get the return value from a stored procedure. As you can see, all you need to do is add a RETURNCODE="YES" parameter to the CFSTOREDPROC tag, which tells ColdFusion to capture the return code from the stored procedure and put its value into the #CFSTOREDPROC.StatusCode# variable. You can then do whatever you want with the variable.

Listing 20.2 `ProcImportCustomers2.cfm`—**Displaying a Procedure's Return Value**

```
<!DOCTYPE HTML PUBLIC "-//W3C//DTD HTML 4.0 Transitional//EN">

<HTML>
<HEAD>
    <TITLE>Customer Import</TITLE>
</HEAD>

<BODY>
<H2>Customer Import</H2>


<!--- If the ImportNow button was not just pressed, display form --->
<CFIF NOT ParameterExists(Form.ImportNow)>

  <FORM ACTION="ProcImportCustomers2.cfm" METHOD="POST">
    <INPUT TYPE="SUBMIT" NAME="ImportNow" VALUE="Import Customers Now">
  </FORM>
```

Part IV Ch 20

continues

Listing 20.2   Continued

```
<!--- If the user just clicked the "Import" button --->
<CFELSE>

  <P>Executing stored procedure...</P>

  <!--- Go ahead and execute the stored procedure --->
  <CFSTOREDPROC
    PROCEDURE="ImportCustomers"
    DATASOURCE="A2Z Server"
    RETURNCODE="YES">

  <!--- Set #ImportCount# variable to value of return code --->
  <CFSET ImportCount = CFSTOREDPROC.STATUSCODE>


  <P>Done executing stored procedure!</P>

  <CFIF ImportCount IS 0>
    Sorry, there were no customers to import at this time.

  <CFELSE>
    <CFOUTPUT>#ImportCount# customer records were imported.</CFOUTPUT>

  </CFIF>

</CFIF>


</BODY>
</HTML>
```

Here, a CFSET tag is used to set the return code to the #ImportCount# variable, which is then displayed to the user in a ordinary CFOUTPUT block. If the stored procedure generates a return code of 0, the user gets a message saying that there are no customers available to import at this time. Figure 20.4 shows what the user would see if the procedure generated a return code of 2.

Stored Procedures That Take Parameters

So far you've been working with stored procedures that always work the same exact way each time they are called. The ImportCustomers procedure used in the first two examples doesn't accept any input from the calling application (in this case, a ColdFusion template) to do its work.

Most stored procedures, however, will take input parameters. *Input parameters* are values that you supply by name when you execute a stored procedure, kind of like providing parameters to a ColdFusion tag. The stored procedure can then use the values of the input parameters internally, like variables.

FIGURE 20.4

It's easy to capture and display a stored procedure's return code.

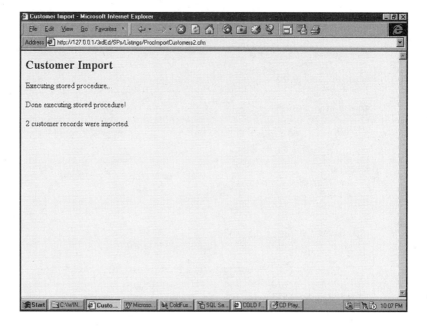

For instance, consider a new stored procedure called AddNewBook that allows the user to add a new book to the A2Z bookstore's Inventory table. Whoever created the stored procedure set it up to require three input parameters: @CategoryID, which is an integer value that represents which category the new book belongs in; @ISBN, which is the ISBN number for the new book; and @Title, which passes the title for the new book. The stored procedure has also been designed to perform a few "sanity checks" before blindly recording the new book:

- First, it makes sure that the book doesn't already exist in the Inventory table; you can do so by checking the ISBN number. If the book is already in the table, the procedure stops with a return value of -1.

- It makes sure that the category number provided by the @CategoryID parameter is valid, by ensuring that there is a corresponding entry in the Category table. If the category number is invalid, the procedure stops with a return value of -2.

- Provided that both of the tests are okay, the procedure inserts a new row in the Inventory table using the values of the supplied parameters. Finally, it sends a return value of 1 to indicate success.

Providing Parameters with CFPROCPARAM ColdFusion 4 makes it easy to supply input parameters to a stored procedure by providing the CFPROCPARAM tag. For instance, to provide values for the @CategoryID, @ISBN, and @Title input parameters, three CFPROCPARAM tags need to be included in your template, between paired CFSTOREDPROC tags.

ProcAddNewBook.cfm, shown in Listing 20.3, creates a simple form that a user can use to fill in the category number, ISBN number, and title for a new book. The form collects the information

Part
IV

Ch
20

from the user and posts it to the `ProcAddNewBookGo.cfm` template, which will execute the stored procedure. Figure 20.5 shows what the form will look like when one of your users fills in some data for a new entry.

Listing 20.3   `ProcAddNewBook.cfm`—A Simple Form for Collecting Input Parameters

```
<!DOCTYPE HTML PUBLIC "-//W3C//DTD HTML 4.0 Transitional//EN">

<HTML>
<HEAD>
    <TITLE>New Book</TITLE>
</HEAD>

<BODY>
<H2>Adding A New Book</H2>


  <CFFORM ACTION="ProcAddNewBookGo.cfm" METHOD="POST">

    <P>Category:<BR>
    <CFINPUT TYPE="Text"
       NAME="CategoryID"
       MESSAGE="Please enter a number for the Category."
       VALIDATE="integer"
       REQUIRED="Yes"
       SIZE="5">

    <P>ISBN:<BR>
    <CFINPUT TYPE="Text"
       NAME="ISBN"
       MESSAGE="Please don't leave the ISBN blank."
       REQUIRED="Yes"
       MAXLENGTH="13">

    <P>Title:<BR>
    <CFINPUT TYPE="Text"
       NAME="Title"
       MESSAGE="Please don't leave the Title blank."
       REQUIRED="Yes"
       SIZE="40"
       MAXLENGTH="50">

    <P>
    <INPUT TYPE="SUBMIT" NAME="AddBookNow" VALUE="Add New Book Now">

  </CFFORM>


</BODY>
</HTML>
```

FIGURE 20.5

The user supplies the values for the procedure's input parameters.

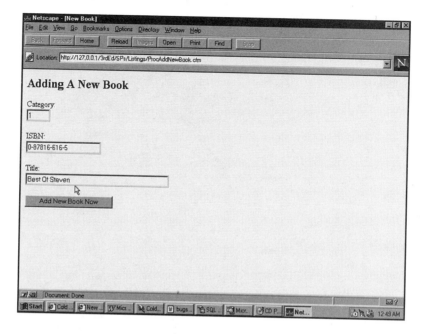

Listing 20.4 shows the `ProcAddNewBookGo.cfm` template that accepts the form input and executes the stored procedure. As you can see, when the form is submitted, three CFPROCPARAM tags are used to supply the values from the form as input parameters to the stored procedure. Each CFPROCPARAM tag in Listing 20.4 has four attributes:

- The TYPE attribute tells ColdFusion whether the stored procedure's parameter is an input parameter, an output parameter, or an input/output parameter. In this example, all the CFPROCPARAM tags use TYPE="IN" to indicate that these parameters are input parameters. You learn about output parameters shortly.

- The DBVARNAME attribute provides the name of the stored procedure's parameter, as defined by whomever wrote the stored procedure.

- The VALUE attribute provides the actual value to be supplied to the stored procedure. In this case, the appropriate form values are being used for each parameter's VALUE.

- The CFSQLTYPE attribute tells ColdFusion what the data type of the stored procedure's parameter is, as defined by whoever wrote the stored procedure. More detail about the possible data types to supply to CFSQLTYPE is provided in the next section.

Part

IV

Ch

20

TIP If you are using ColdFusion Studio 4 to edit your templates, you can use the Tag Inspector or the CFPROCPARAM Tag Editor to help you add the CFPROCPARAM tag to your code (see Figure 20.6).

FIGURE 20.6
Using ColdFusion Studio as your editor makes it easy to code CFPROCPARAM tags.

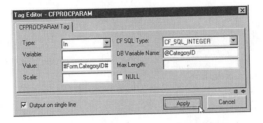

Listing 20.4   ProcAddNewBookGo.cfm—Providing Input Parameters to a Stored Procedure

```
<!DOCTYPE HTML PUBLIC "-//W3C//DTD HTML 4.0 Transitional//EN">

<HTML>
<HEAD>
    <TITLE>New Book</TITLE>
</HEAD>

<BODY>
<H2>Adding A New Book</H2>

    <!--- Go ahead and execute the stored procedure --->
    <CFSTOREDPROC
      PROCEDURE="AddNewBook"
      DATASOURCE="A2Z Server">

      <CFPROCPARAM TYPE="IN"
        DBVARNAME="@CategoryID"
        VALUE="#Form.CategoryID#"
        CFSQLTYPE="CF_SQL_INTEGER">

      <CFPROCPARAM TYPE="In"
        CFSQLTYPE="CF_SQL_VARCHAR"
        DBVARNAME="@ISBN"
        VALUE="#Form.ISBN#">

      <CFPROCPARAM TYPE="In"
        CFSQLTYPE="CF_SQL_VARCHAR"
        DBVARNAME="@Title"
        VALUE="#Form.Title#">

    </CFSTOREDPROC>

    <!--- Set #AddedOK# variable to value of return code --->
    <CFSET AddedOK = CFSTOREDPROC.STATUSCODE>

    <!--- Check the return code to see what actually happened --->
    <CFSWITCH EXPRESSION="#AddedOK#">

      <CFCASE VALUE="-1">
        Sorry, but that book already exists in the database.
```

```
  </CFCASE>

  <CFCASE VALUE="-2">
    Sorry, but the Category number you provided is invalid.
  </CFCASE>

  <CFCASE VALUE="1">
    Yay, the new book was added successfully!
  </CFCASE>

  <CFDEFAULTCASE>
    <!--- Display return code if we don't know how to handle it --->
    Error: The add-new-book routine returned an unknown status code:
    <CFOUTPUT>#AddedOK#</CFOUTPUT>
  </CFDEFAULTCASE>

</CFSWITCH>

</BODY>
</HTML>
```

After the procedure does its work, the CFSWITCH block examines the return code to make sure the new book was recorded successfully. Different messages are presented to the user to indicate what exactly happened. Figure 20.7 shows what the user will see, assuming that the stored procedure is able to insert the information and generates a return code of 1.

FIGURE 20.7
ColdFusion makes it easy to provide parameters to stored procedures.

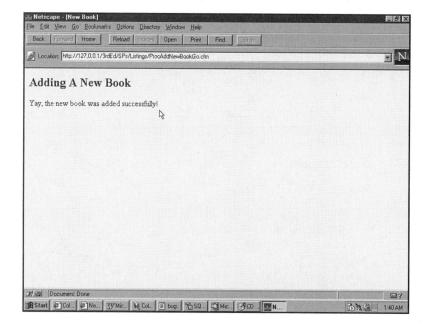

Part
IV

Ch
20

The template in Listing 20.4 uses ColdFusion 4's new CFSWITCH and CFCASE tags to analyze the return code from the stored procedure. Making decisions based on return codes is a perfect situation to use these new case-switching tags because there is a single expression (the return code) that will have one of several predetermined values. See Appendix A, "ColdFusion Tag Reference," for more information on CFSWITCH and related tags.

Parameter Data Types   As you saw in Listing 20.4, when you provide parameters to a stored procedure with the CFPROCPARAM tag, you must specify the data type of the parameter, as defined by whoever created the procedure. ColdFusion requires that you provide the data type for each parameter that you refer to in your templates, so that it does not have to determine the data type itself on-the-fly each time the template runs. That would require a number of extra steps for ColdFusion, which in turn would slow your application.

It's important to specify the correct data type for each parameter. If you use the wrong data type, you may run into problems. The data type you provide for CFSQLTYPE in a CFPROCPARAM tag must be one of ColdFusion's SQL data types, as listed in Table 20.1. These data types are based on the data types defined by the ODBC standard—one of them will map to each of the database-system–specific data types that was used when your stored procedure was created.

For instance, if you have a stored procedure sitting on a Microsoft SQL Server that takes a parameter of SQL Server data type int, you should specify the CF_SQL_INTEGER data type in the corresponding CFPROCPARAM tag.

Table 20.1 Which ColdFusion SQL Data Types to Use for What Native Data Type

ColdFusion SQL Data Type	SQL Server/Sybase	Oracle
CF_SQL_BIT	bit	
CF_SQL_BIGINT		
CF_SQL_CHAR	char, nchar*	char, nchar
CF_SQL_DATE	date	
CF_SQL_DECIMAL	decimal, numeric, double	
CF_SQL_DOUBLE		
CF_SQL_FLOAT	float	
CF_SQL_IDSTAMP		
CF_SQL_INTEGER	int	
CF_SQL_LONGVARCHAR	text	long
CF_SQL_MONEY	money	
CF_SQL_MONEY4	smallmoney	
CF_SQL_NUMERIC		number

ColdFusion SQL Data Type	SQL Server/Sybase	Oracle
CF_SQL_REAL	real	
CF_SQL_SMALLINT	smallint	
CF_SQL_TIME		
CF_SQL_TIMESTAMP	datetime, smalldatetime	
CF_SQL_TINYINT	tinyint	
CF_SQL_VARCHAR	varchar, nvarchar*	varchar2, nvarchar2

Supplying a NULL Value to an Input Parameter   If you need to supply the special value NULL to a input parameter, you can use the CFPROCPARAM tag's optional NULL attribute. The NULL attribute can be set to either YES or NO. When set to YES, a NULL value is sent to the database server. The tag's VALUE attribute is ignored.

> **N O T E**   If you don't know what null values are, see Chapter 19, "Advanced SQL," for a discussion
> about the general concept of nulls in database tables. ▪

If you need to send a null value when a form field is left blank, you have a couple of options. One way is to set a separate variable that's in charge of supplying a YES or NO to the NULL attribute. For instance, in Listing 20.4 you could place this snippet at the top of the template, before the CFSTOREDPROC tag:

```
<CFIF Form.Title is "">
  <CFSET IsTitleNull = "YES">
<CFELSE>
  <CFSET IsTitleNull = "NO">
</CFIF>
```

Then you would just add NULL=#IsTitleNull# to the third CFPROCPARAM tag. If the user leaves the title blank, the IsTitleNull variable is YES, which causes ColdFusion to send a null value to the database. Otherwise, IsTitleNull gets set to NO, which causes the CFPROCPARAM tag to behave normally.

Another, more concise approach is to forget the CFIF block, using ColdFusion's IIf function to get the same thing done in one step. For instance, you could replace the same CFPROCPARAM tag with the following:

```
<CFPROCPARAM TYPE="In"
  CFSQLTYPE="CF_SQL_VARCHAR"
  DBVARNAME="@Title"
  VALUE="#Form.Title#"
  NULL=#IIf(Form.Title is "", 1, 0)#>
```

> **N O T E**   See Appendix B, "ColdFusion Function Reference," for more information about the IIf
> function. While you're at it, check out the related DE function. ▪

Part

IV

Ch

20

Getting an Output Parameter from a Stored Procedure   You've seen that a stored procedure can accept input parameters that the procedure uses internally to carry out its work. Stored procedures can also accept *output parameters*, which a stored procedure makes available to the calling application (in this case, a ColdFusion template) after the procedure finishes executing.

For instance, considering the AddNewBook stored procedure as an example, it might be handy if your application could be aware of the primary key value (the new BookID) that was assigned to the new book as it was inserted into the Inventory table. One easy way to do this is to ask whoever wrote the stored procedure to add an output parameter called @NewBookID that your template can refer to after the procedure runs.

> **N O T E**   Parameters for stored procedures on Microsoft SQL Server and Sybase servers always begin with the @ symbol. With Oracle, however, the @ sign is illegal as a parameter name. If this were an Oracle stored procedure you were working with, the output parameter would just be called NewBookID, rather than @NewBookID. ▨

ColdFusion allows you to "capture" the value of an output parameter by specifying a name for a ColdFusion variable that you would like the output parameter's value put into as the procedure executes. For example, you could tell ColdFusion to put the value of the @NewBookID output parameter into a template variable called #MyNewBookID#, which you would then be able to use just like any other variable in the remainder of your template.

Listing 20.5 shows a slightly modified version of the ProcAddNewBookGo.cfm template from Listing 20.4. The only real change is an additional CFPROCPARAM tag to handle the procedure's output parameter. The new CFPROCPARAM tag is similar to those that were there before, except that TYPE="OUT" is used instead of TYPE="IN" (to indicate that @NewBookID is an output parameter rather than an input parameter), and a CFVARNAME attribute is supplied, which indicates the template variable that the output parameter's value should be stored in.

Listing 20.5   ProcAddNewBookGo2.cfm—Capturing an Output Parameter from a Stored Procedure

```
<!DOCTYPE HTML PUBLIC "-//W3C//DTD HTML 4.0 Transitional//EN">

<HTML>
<HEAD>
   <TITLE>New Book</TITLE>
</HEAD>

<BODY>
<H2>Adding A New Book</H2>


   <!--- Go ahead and execute the stored procedure --->
   <CFSTOREDPROC
     PROCEDURE="AddNewBook"
     DATASOURCE="A2Z Server"
     RETURNCODE="YES">
```

```
      <CFPROCPARAM TYPE="IN"
        DBVARNAME="@CategoryID"
        VALUE="#Form.CategoryID#"
        CFSQLTYPE="CF_SQL_INTEGER">

      <CFPROCPARAM TYPE="IN"
        DBVARNAME="@ISBN"
        VALUE="#Form.ISBN#"
        CFSQLTYPE="CF_SQL_VARCHAR"
        MAXLENGTH="2">

      <CFPROCPARAM TYPE="IN"
        DBVARNAME="@Title"
        VALUE="#Form.Title#"
        CFSQLTYPE="CF_SQL_VARCHAR">

      <!--- Get new BookID from the @NewBookID output parameter --->
      <CFPROCPARAM TYPE="OUT"
        DBVARNAME="@NewBookID"
        CFVARNAME="MyNewBookID"
        CFSQLTYPE="CF_SQL_INTEGER">

   </CFSTOREDPROC>


   <!--- Set #AddedOK# variable to value of return code --->
   <CFSET AddedOK = CFSTOREDPROC.STATUSCODE>

   <!--- Check the return code to see what actually happened --->
   <CFSWITCH EXPRESSION="#AddedOK#">

     <CFCASE VALUE="-1">
       Sorry, but that book already exists in the database.
     </CFCASE>

     <CFCASE VALUE="-2">
       Sorry, but the Category number you provided is invalid.
     </CFCASE>

     <CFCASE VALUE="1">
       Yay, the new book was added successfully!<BR>
       Its BookID in the Inventory table is: <CFOUTPUT>#MyNewBookID#</CFOUTPUT>
     </CFCASE>

     <CFDEFAULTCASE>
       <!--- Display return code if we don't know how to handle it --->
       Error: The add-new-book routine returned an unknown status code:
       <CFOUTPUT>#AddedOK#</CFOUTPUT>
     </CFDEFAULTCASE>

   </CFSWITCH>

</BODY>
</HTML>
```

Part
IV

Ch
20

NOTE You need to change the `ACTION` of the form in Listing 20.3 from `ProcAddNewBookGo.cfm` to `ProcAddNewBookGo2.cfm` in order to see Listing 20.5 in action.

The value of the `#MyNewBookID#` variable is displayed to the user at the bottom of Listing 20.5, to show that the template was able to get the value of the output parameter without a problem. Figure 20.8 shows the results.

FIGURE 20.8

The output parameter is captured from the stored procedure and displayed to the user.

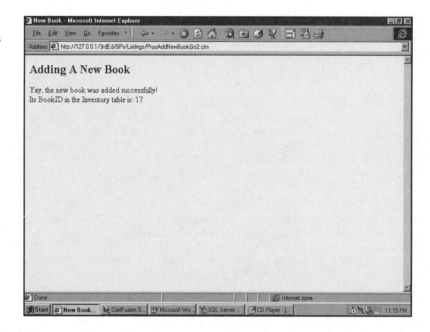

In an actual application, you would probably do more than just display the new `BookID`—you might provide some kind of Click Here link to a screen where the user could do further data entry about the book, for instance; you might also use the `CFMAIL` tag to alert some kind of inventory supervisor that a new book is now being carried by the bookstore. The point is that a stored procedure can give back whatever information its creator desires as output parameters, and you can use that information in just about any way you please.

Stored Procedures That Return Record Sets

You've seen that stored procedures can provide feedback and information to your ColdFusion templates by generating return codes and output parameters. Stored procedures can also send back record sets to your ColdFusion templates. *Record sets* are columns and rows of data—usually from one or more of the database's tables—which you can then use the way you'd use rows of data fetched by a `CFQUERY` tag.

For instance, consider a stored procedure called `GetCustomerInfo` that returns customer information for a given customer, straight from the Customers table in the A2Z database. Rather than using output parameters, this stored procedure sends back its information as a query result set, just as if you had done a simple SELECT * FROM Customers type of query with a CFQUERY tag.

Using the CFPROCRESULT Tag   The ProcGetCustomerInfo.cfm template in Listing 20.6 shows how to retrieve and use a record set returned from a stored procedure. As you can see, a CFSTOREDPROC tag is used to refer to the stored procedure itself (just like the other examples in this chapter); a CFPROCPARAM tag is used to supply the requested customer number to the procedure's @CustID input parameter.

N O T E   ColdFusion 4 dos not support the CFPROCRESULT tag with Oracle. You cannot use record sets returned by Oracle stored procedures. What is new here is the CFPROCRESULT tag, which is used to simply give a name to the result set by specifying the name in the tag's NAME parameter. It's been explained to you by whomever created the stored procedure that the record set will return one row and will contain four columns: FirstName, LastName, Company, and EMail. This template simply outputs these four pieces of information to create a little report for the user. Figure 20.9 shows the results. ■

FIGURE 20.9

The CFPROCRESULT tag gets a record set from a stored procedure.

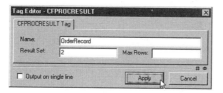

Listing 20.6   ProcGetCustomerInfo.cfm—Retrieving a Record Set from a Stored Procedure

```
<!DOCTYPE HTML PUBLIC "-//W3C//DTD HTML 4.0 Transitional//EN">

<HTML>
<HEAD>
    <TITLE>Quick Customer Report</TITLE>
</HEAD>

<BODY>
<H2>Quick Customer Report</H2>

<!--- Set default value of "" (blank) for the RequestedID variable --->
<CFPARAM NAME="RequestedID" DEFAULT="">

<!--- Quick form to collect/change RequestedID variable --->
<CFFORM ACTION="ProcGetCustomerInfo.cfm" METHOD="POST">

  Customer number:<BR>
  <CFINPUT TYPE="Text"
      NAME="RequestedID"
      VALUE="#RequestedID#"
```

Part
IV

Ch

20

continues

Listing 20.6 Continued

```
             MESSAGE="Please provide a Customer number."
             VALIDATE="integer"
             REQUIRED="Yes"
             SIZE="10">

  <INPUT TYPE="Submit" VALUE="Show">

</CFFORM>


<!--- Process the request --->
<CFIF RequestedID IS NOT "">

   <!--- Get the customer information via stored procedure --->
   <CFSTOREDPROC
     PROCEDURE="GetCustomerInfo"
     DATASOURCE="A2Z Server"
     RETURNCODE="YES">

     <!--- Supply the requested CustomerID number to procedure --->
     <CFPROCPARAM TYPE="IN"
       DBVARNAME="@CustomerID"
       VALUE="#RequestedID#"
       CFSQLTYPE="CF_SQL_VARCHAR">

     <!--- Receive the customer data recordset from procedure --->
     <CFPROCRESULT
       NAME="CustRecord">

   </CFSTOREDPROC>


   <CFOUTPUT QUERY="CustRecord">
   <TABLE>
     <TR> <TH BGCOLOR="SILVER">First Name:</TH> <TD>#FirstName#</TD> </TR>
     <TR> <TH BGCOLOR="SILVER">Last Name:</TH>  <TD>#LastName#</TD>  </TR>
     <TR> <TH BGCOLOR="SILVER">Company:</TH>    <TD>#Company#</TD>   </TR>
     <TR> <TH BGCOLOR="SILVER">E-Mail:</TH>     <TD>#Email#</TD>     </TR>
   </TABLE>
   </CFOUTPUT>


</CFIF>


</BODY>
</HTML>
```

TIP

If you are using ColdFusion Studio 4 to edit your templates, you can use the Tag Inspector or the CFPROCRESULT Tag Editor to help you add the CFPROCRESULT tag to your code (see Figure 20.10).

FIGURE 20.10

ColdFusion Studio can be used to add CFPROCRESULT tags to your code.

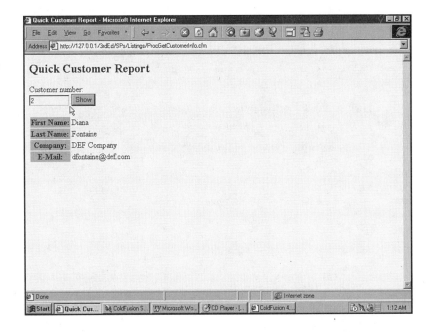

The key to being able to refer to the contents of the procedure's record set is the CFPROCRESULT tag's NAME parameter. In this case, NAME="CustRecord", so you are free to use the rows and columns returned by the procedure just as if CustRecord were a "normal" query result set. In other words, at this point the entire CFSTOREDPROC block shown in Listing 20.6 is functionally equivalent to the following CFQUERY:

```
<CFQUERY NAME="CustRecord" DATASOURCE="A2Z Server">
  SELECT FirstName, LastName, Company, EMail
  FROM Customers
  WHERE CustomerID = #RequestedID#
</CFQUERY>
```

TIP If you don't know the column names that the procedure outputs, you could run the procedure and output the value of the automatic #CustRecord.ColumnList# variable, just as you could do for any normal query result set.

Multiple Record Sets Are Fully Supported Some stored procedures return more than one record set. For instance, consider a stored procedure called GetMoreCustomerData. It returns the basic name/email information that the GetCustomerData procedure returns, but it also returns a second record set about orders placed, and a third record set about the customer's orders by category. (Whoever created the stored procedure has explained what each of the three record sets represents, the order in which the record sets are returned, and the names of the columns returned by each of the record sets.)

As you can see in Listing 20.7, the key to receiving more than one record set from a stored procedure is to specify a RESULTSET parameter for the CFPROCRESULT tag. For instance, the

Part

IV

Ch

20

second `CFPROCRESULT` tag assigns the name `OrderRecord` to the second `resultset` (that is, `resultset` number 2) returned by the stored procedure. The `RESULTSET` parameter defaults to 1 when not provided, which is why it's okay for the first `CFPROCRESULT` tag to not specify a `RESULTSET` parameter—it will still know to grab the first set of data output by the procedure.

Listing 20.7 `ProcGetMoreCustomerInfo.cfm`—**Dealing with Multiple Record Sets from a Single Stored Procedure**

```
<!DOCTYPE HTML PUBLIC "-//W3C//DTD HTML 4.0 Transitional//EN">

<HTML>
<HEAD>
    <TITLE>Quick Customer Report</TITLE>
</HEAD>

<BODY>
<H2>Quick Customer Report</H2>

<!--- Set default value of "" (blank) for the RequestedID variable --->
<CFPARAM NAME="RequestedID" DEFAULT="">

<!--- Quick form to collect/change RequestedID variable --->
<CFFORM ACTION="ProcGetMoreCustomerInfo.cfm" METHOD="POST">

  Customer number:<BR>
  <CFINPUT TYPE="Text"
      NAME="RequestedID"
      VALUE="#RequestedID#"
      MESSAGE="Please provide a Customer number."
      VALIDATE="integer"
      REQUIRED="Yes"
      SIZE="10">

  <INPUT TYPE="Submit" VALUE="Show">

</CFFORM>


<!--- Process the request --->
<CFIF RequestedID IS NOT "">

  <!--- Get the customer information via stored procedure --->
  <CFSTOREDPROC
    PROCEDURE="GetMoreCustomerInfo"
    DATASOURCE="A2Z Sybase"
    RETURNCODE="YES">

    <!--- Supply the requested CustomerID number to procedure --->
    <CFPROCPARAM TYPE="IN"
      DBVARNAME="@CustID"
      VALUE="#RequestedID#"
      CFSQLTYPE="CF_SQL_INTEGER">

    <!--- Receive the customer data recordset from procedure --->
    <CFPROCRESULT
```

```
              NAME="CustRecord">

        <!--- Receive the titles/dates ordered for customer --->
        <CFPROCRESULT
          NAME="OrderRecord"
          RESULTSET="2">

        <!--- Receive the category breakdown for customer --->
        <CFPROCRESULT
          NAME="CatSummary"
          RESULTSET="3">

    </CFSTOREDPROC>


    <!--- Output data from first result set --->
    <CFOUTPUT QUERY="CustRecord">
    <TABLE>
      <TR> <TH BGCOLOR="SILVER">First Name:</TH> <TD>#FirstName#</TD> </TR>
      <TR> <TH BGCOLOR="SILVER">Last Name:</TH>  <TD>#LastName#</TD>  </TR>
      <TR> <TH BGCOLOR="SILVER">Company:</TH>    <TD>#Company#</TD>   </TR>
      <TR> <TH BGCOLOR="SILVER">E-Mail:</TH>     <TD>#Email#</TD>     </TR>
    </TABLE>
    </CFOUTPUT>


    <!--- Output data from second result set --->
    <TABLE>
      <TR> <TH BGCOLOR="SILVER">Order Date</TH>
  <TH BGCOLOR="SILVER">Title</TH> </TR>
        <CFOUTPUT QUERY="OrderRecord">
          <TR> <TD>#DateFormat(OrderDate)#</TD> <TD>#Title#</TD> </TR>
        </CFOUTPUT>
    </TABLE>


    <!--- Output data from third result set --->
    <TABLE BORDER>
      <TR> <TH>Store Category</TH> <TH>Books Ordered</TH> </TR>
        <CFOUTPUT QUERY="CatSummary">
          <TR> <TD>#Category#</TD> <TH>#BookCount#</TH> </TR>
        </CFOUTPUT>
    </TABLE>


  </CFIF>


</BODY>
</HTML>
```

Part
IV

Ch
20

After the `CFSTOREDPROC` tag, the ColdFusion template is free to refer to the three record sets named in the `CFPROCRESULT` tags just as if they were the results of three separate `CFQUERY`-type queries. Since only one database transaction needed to happen, though, you can expect performance to be faster using the single stored procedure. Figure 20.11 shows what the user might see after submitting a customer number for which to retrieve information.

FIGURE 20.11

ColdFusion makes it easy to grab more than one record set from a procedure.

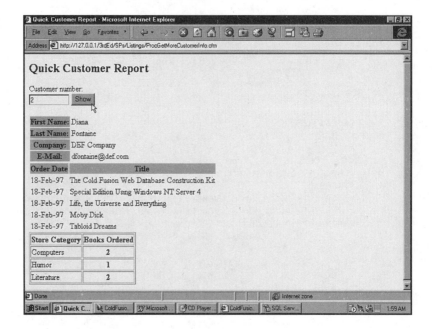

 TIP Your template doesn't have to handle or receive all of the record sets that a stored procedure spits out. For instance, if you weren't interested in the second record set from the `GetMoreCustomerInfo` procedure, you could simply leave out the second `CFPROCRESULT` tag. Neither ColdFusion nor your database server should mind.

Additional Parameters for the CFSTOREDPROC Tags

The `CFSTOREDPROC` tag can take a few optional parameters that aren't covered in specific examples in this chapter. These extra parameters do the same thing as the equivalent parameters of the `CFQUERY` tag do, so they won't be discussed here. The parameters listed in Table 20.2 deal with how ColdFusion connects to the database server. See `CFQUERY` in Appendix A for more information about working with these parameters.

Table 20.2 Additional CFSTOREDPROC Parameters

Parameter	Purpose
USERNAME	Provides a database username to the database server when ColdFusion connects to it. Overrides any username provided for the data source in the ColdFusion Administrator.

Parameter	Purpose
PASSWORD	Provides a database password (to go along with the USERNAME) to the database server. Overrides any password provided in the ColdFusion Administrator.
DBSERVER	The name of the database server that you need to connect to. Overrides the setting provided in the ColdFusion Administrator.
DBNAME	The name of the specific database on the database server that contains the stored procedure you want to use. Overrides the setting in the ColdFusion Administrator.
BLOCKFACTOR	Allows you to tweak how many data rows at a time are fetched from the server at once. Relevant only if you are using a CFPROCRESULT tag.
DEBUG	Displays debugging information.

Calling Procedures with CFQUERY Instead of CFSTOREDPROC

The CFSTOREDPROC and related tags are new for ColdFusion 4. Prior to this version of ColdFusion, the only way to call a stored procedure from a ColdFusion template was to use special procedure-calling syntax in a normal CFQUERY tag, where you would normally provide a SQL statement. ColdFusion then treats the response from the database server just like it would treat the response from an ordinary SELECT query. In fact, ColdFusion doesn't even realize that it's executing a stored procedure exactly; it's just passing on what it assumes to be a valid SQL statement and hopes to get some rows of table-style data in return.

The fact that ColdFusion is treating the stored procedure in the same way it treats a SELECT statement brings with it several important limitations, all of which are overcome with the new CFSTOREDPROC tag:

- ColdFusion cannot directly access the return code generated by the stored procedure.
- ColdFusion cannot directly access any output parameters generated by the stored procedure.
- If the stored procedure returns more than one record set, only one of the record sets will be captured by ColdFusion and available for your use in your templates. Details about this limitation may vary between types of database servers. With some database servers, only the first record set will be available for your use; with others, only the last. The point is that stored procedures that return multiple record sets are not fully supported when using CFQUERY.

Of course, now that ColdFusion includes tags specifically designed to deal with stored procedures, you shouldn't use CFQUERY to call stored procedures anymore. As you write new templates, use CFSTOREDPROC and related tags. If you have other templates already in use that call stored procedures with CFQUERY, you might want to consider going back and replacing the CFQUERY method with CFSTOREDPROC, so that you can get access to the return codes, output parameters, and so on.

Part
IV

Ch
20

Using ODBC's CALL Command The most common method of calling stored procedures in versions of ColdFusion prior to version 4 was to use the CALL command (as defined by the ODBC standard) inside a CFQUERY tag. Listing 20.8 demonstrates how the GetCustomerInfo stored procedure could be called using this method.

N O T E This method of calling stored procedures can be used only with ODBC and OLE-DB data sources. It cannot be used with ColdFusion's native driver support. ▪

Note that this template is almost exactly the same as the ProcGetCustomerInfo.cfm template shown in Listing 20.6. The only change is that CFQUERY is being used instead of CFSTOREDPROC. When this template is brought up in a browser, it should display its results exactly the same way (as shown in Figure 20.10).

Listing 20.8 `CallGetCustomerInfo.cfm`—**Calling a Stored Procedure Using CALL in a CFQUERY**

```
<!DOCTYPE HTML PUBLIC "-//W3C//DTD HTML 4.0 Transitional//EN">

<HTML>
<HEAD>
    <TITLE>Quick Customer Report</TITLE>
</HEAD>

<BODY>
<H2>Quick Customer Report</H2>

<!--- Set default value of "" (blank) for the RequestedID variable --->
<CFPARAM NAME="RequestedID" DEFAULT="">

<!--- Quick form to collect/change RequestedID variable --->
<CFFORM ACTION="ProcGetCustomerInfo.cfm" METHOD="POST">

  Customer number:<BR>
  <CFINPUT TYPE="Text"
      NAME="RequestedID"
      VALUE="#RequestedID#"
      MESSAGE="Please provide a Customer number."
      VALIDATE="integer"
      REQUIRED="Yes"
      SIZE="10">

  <INPUT TYPE="Submit" VALUE="Show">

</CFFORM>


<!--- Process the request --->
<CFIF RequestedID IS NOT "">

    <!--- Get the customer information via stored procedure --->
    <CFQUERY NAME="CustRecord" DATASOURCE="A2Z Server">
      { CALL GetCustomerInfo(#RequestedID#) }
```

```
</CFQUERY>

<CFOUTPUT QUERY="CustRecord">
<TABLE>
  <TR> <TH BGCOLOR="SILVER">First Name:</TH> <TD>#FirstName#</TD> </TR>
  <TR> <TH BGCOLOR="SILVER">Last Name:</TH>  <TD>#LastName#</TD>  </TR>
  <TR> <TH BGCOLOR="SILVER">Company:</TH>    <TD>#Company#</TD>   </TR>
  <TR> <TH BGCOLOR="SILVER">E-Mail:</TH>     <TD>#Email#</TD>     </TR>
</TABLE>
</CFOUTPUT>


</CFIF>


</BODY>
</HTML>
```

N O T E Remember that the CFQUERY method of calling stored procedures should be considered outdated. Don't use this kind of code as you write new templates—use CFSTOREDPROC instead. It's only being covered in this book so that you can understand what's happening in any legacy templates that may already exist in an application you're working on. ▥

As you can see in Listing 20.8, the syntax for using the CALL command is simply the word CALL and then the procedure name. The entire command is surrounded by a set of curly braces, which indicate that the command needs to be interpreted by ODBC before it gets sent on to the database server.

Input parameters are supplied in parentheses after the procedure name and are separated by commas. If there are no input parameters for the procedure, leave out the parentheses. Since you are not referring to them by name, input parameters must be supplied in the proper order (as defined by whoever wrote the stored procedure). If an input parameter is of a character type (like char, varchar, or text), enclose the parameter's value in single quotation marks. For instance, to call the AddNewBook stored procedure from Listing 20.4, you could replace the CFSTOREDPROC block in that template with this:

Part
IV

Ch
20

```
<CFQUERY DATASOURCE="A2Z Server">
  { CALL AddNewBook(#Form.CategoryID#, '#Form.ISBN#', '#Form.Title#') }
</CFQUERY>
```

Remember, however, that ColdFusion is not aware of the return code or output parameters returned by the procedure, so the code in the rest of the listing fails. You need to have the stored procedure rewritten so that the information provided by the return code or output parameters instead get returned as a record set. In a word, ick!

Using Your Database's "Native" Syntax In addition to using the CALL command, most database drivers also allow you to use whatever native syntax you would use normally with that database system. All the same limitations (regarding return codes, output parameters, and so on) listed at the beginning of this section apply.

The native syntax to use varies according to the database server you're using. You need to consult your database server documentation for the details. Just as an example, if you were using Microsoft SQL Server, you could replace the CFQUERY shown in Listing 20.8 with the following code; the results would be the same.

```
<CFQUERY NAME="CustRecord" DATASOURCE="A2Z Server">
   EXEC GetCustomerInfo #RequestedID#
</CFQUERY>
```

One advantage of using the native syntax over the CALL syntax is that you may be able to refer to the input parameters by name, which leads to cleaner and more readable code. Again, just as an example, if you were using Microsoft SQL Server, the AddNewBook procedure could be called with the following. Consult your database server documentation for details.

```
<CFQUERY DATASOURCE="A2Z Server">
  EXEC AddNewBook
    @CategoryID = #Form.CategoryID#,
    @ISBN = '#Form.ISBN#',
    @Title = '#Form.Title#'
</CFQUERY>
```

N O T E   Remember, the CFQUERY method of calling stored procedures should be considered outdated. Don't use this kind of code as you write new templates—use CFSTOREDPROC instead. It's only being covered in this book so that you can understand what's happening in any legacy templates that may already exist in an application. ■

Creating Stored Procedures

Now that you've seen how to use stored procedures in your ColdFusion templates, you are probably curious about how you can create some stored procedures of your own. While it's impossible to cover all of the advanced aspects of creating stored procedures in this book, you do learn how to create the simple stored procedures that were used in the example templates earlier in this chapter.

Before you begin, a short note: The examples you see in this section—and the procedure-creating code that you're likely to use as you write your own stored procedures—are not standard SQL. Stored procedures are implemented slightly differently by different database servers, and you will often want to use code within the stored procedures that take advantage of various extensions that are proprietary to the database system that you are using. In other words, when you get to the point of writing your own stored procedures, it's likely that you will be tying yourself to the database system you're using to some extent. The procedures will probably not be portable to other database systems (like ordinary SQL generally is) without reworking the procedures to some extent.

Creating Stored Procedures with Microsoft SQL Server

You use the SQL Server Enterprise Manager tool to create a stored procedure with Microsoft SQL Server, which helps you submit a CREATE PROCEDURE statement to the SQL Server machine. Once created, the procedure is available to whoever has appropriate permissions.

It is also possible to execute the CREATE PROCEDURE statements shown in this section with the Query Analyzer (called iSQL/w in SQL Server 6.5 and earlier) or the isql.exe command-line utility that ships with SQL Server. You could even execute these CREATE PROCEDURE statements in a CFQUERY tag within a ColdFusion template.

On the CD

N O T E To follow along with this chapter, you need to have a database on your SQL Server machine that has the same tables and columns as the A2Z example database. With SQL Server 7.0, choose Tools, Wizards from the Enterprise Manager's menu to start the DTS Import Wizard. In just a few steps, the wizard imports the a2z.mdb file from the CD-ROM onto your SQL Server, with all tables, columns, and data intact.

For SQL Server 6.5, you can use the Access upsizing tools for Microsoft Access 97, which provides a standalone wizard that does the same thing. The wizard is available from http://www.microsoft.com. ■

N O T E The figures shown in this section show screens using the SQL Server Enterprise Manager tool that ships with SQL Server 7.0, which ships as a snap-in for the new Microsoft Management Console on Windows NT. Earlier versions of SQL Server came with a standalone SQL Enterprise Manager tool that looked somewhat different. However, the overall designs of the tools and the steps you take to work with stored procedures are essentially the same. ■

Creating Your First Stored Procedure As a simple example, you can create the ImportCustomers stored procedure that was used in Listing 20.1. This procedure is a good one to start with because it's very simple and does not use any input or output parameters.

To create the stored procedure, follow these simple steps:

1. Start the SQL Server Enterprise Manager. Click your server, expand the databases tree, and click your database.

2. Click the Stored Procedures folder; right-click to choose New Stored Procedure from the pop-up menu, as shown in Figure 20.12. (With SQL Server 6.0 and 6.5, the Stored Procedures folder is inside the Objects folder, so you have one more mouse-click to make.)

3. Type the actual code for the procedure—provided in Listing 20.9—in the window that appears, as shown in Figure 20.13.

4. Click the OK button to create the stored procedure. (With SQL Server 6.0 and 6.5, you click the green arrow button instead of an OK button.)

Listing 20.9 shows the actual code for the ImportCustomers stored procedure. This is the code that you should enter after choosing New Procedure from the pop-up menu (see Figure 20.12). As you can see, it's fairly simple. First, a CREATE PROCEDURE statement is used to provide a name for the new stored procedure, followed by the AS keyword. Everything after AS is the code for the stored procedure itself—the actual SQL statements that you want to execute each time the procedure is called.

Part

IV

Ch

20

FIGURE 20.12

Use the Enterprise Manager to create a new stored procedure.

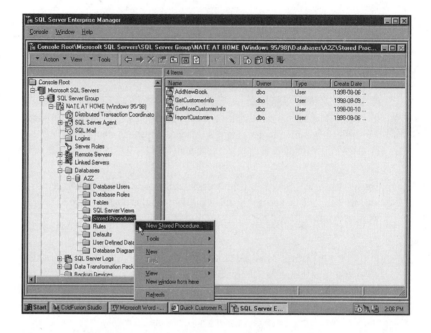

FIGURE 20.13

Simply enter the procedure's code in the New Stored Procedure window.

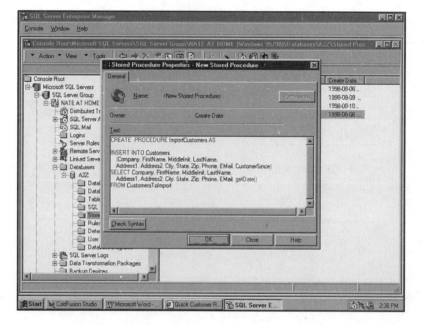

Listing 20.9 The `ImportCustomers` Stored Procedure

```
CREATE PROCEDURE ImportCustomers AS

INSERT INTO Customers
    (Company, FirstName, MiddleInit, LastName,
    Address1, Address2, City, State, Zip, Phone, EMail, CustomerSince)
SELECT Company, FirstName, MiddleInit, LastName,
    Address1, Address2, City, State, Zip, Phone, EMail, getDate()
FROM CustomersToImport
```

This procedure's actual body is also quite simple. It just uses a simple INSERT/SELECT state-ment to copy all of the names from the CustomersToImport table into the Customers table. Please refer to Listing 19.24 in Chapter 19, "Advanced SQL," for a complete explanation of using INSERT and SELECT together in this way.

Note that the only real difference between Listing 19.24 and Listing 20.9 is the fact that SQL Server's own getDate() function is used to insert the current date and time into the CustomerSince column, rather than ColdFusion's Now() function. It is always necessary to use your database server's native functions for this type of thing, since your database server cannot understand ColdFusion functions. Consult your SQL Server documentation for more informa-tion on the getDate() and other functions.

Returning Result Codes to ColdFusion   As it stands, the ImportCustomers procedure will always have a return code of 0, which, with SQL Server, is the default return code for any stored procedure that does not specify one on its own.

Recall that Listing 20.2 uses the return code from this procedure to display the number of customers actually imported. To cause the stored procedure to return this information as the return code, the RETURN keyword needs to be used within the procedure itself.

Listing 20.10 shows a revised version of the ImportCustomers procedure that returns the num-ber of rows inserted into the Customers table as the return code.

Listing 20.10   Generating a Return Code with the RETURN Keyword

```
CREATE PROCEDURE ImportCustomers AS

-- Insert data rows waiting in the CustomersToImport table
INSERT INTO Customers
    (Company, FirstName, MiddleInit, LastName,
    Address1, Address2, City, State, Zip, Phone, EMail, CustomerSince)
SELECT Company, FirstName, MiddleInit, LastName,
    Address1, Address2, City, State, Zip, Phone, EMail, getDate()
FROM CustomersToImport

-- Return the "rows affected" count to calling app as the Return Code
RETURN @@ROWCOUNT
```

The RETURN keyword basically tells SQL Server to end the procedure and return the integer value that follows it as the procedure's return code. Something like RETURN 1 causes the stored procedure to always generate a return code of 1. Here, SQL Server's built-in @@ROWCOUNT variable is used to supply the integer value. @@ROWCOUNT always contains the number of rows affected by the last SQL statement (the number of rows fetched by the last SELECT statement, the number of rows removed by the last DELETE statement, and so on). The result is that the procedure's return code will always be set to the number of rows actually inserted into the Customers table, even if that number is 0.

See your SQL Server documentation for more information about the @@ROWCOUNT variable.

Accepting Input Parameters from ColdFusion Templates As demonstrated in Listing 20.4, stored procedures can accept input parameters. *Input parameters* are like variables that are provided by the calling application (in this case, a ColdFusion template) and can then be used by the procedure internally.

With SQL Server, you define input parameters in the CREATE PROCEDURE part of the procedure code, between the procedure name and the AS keyword. Each input parameter is given a name, which must begin with the @ symbol and which cannot contain any spaces or other unusual characters. The SQL Server data type for each parameter is provided after the parameter's name. If there is more than one parameter, separate them with commas.

For instance, Listing 20.11 shows the code to create the AddNewBook stored procedure that was used in Listing 20.4. As you can see, each of the parameters provided in CFPROCPARAM tags in that template matches the corresponding parameters in the CREATE PROCEDURE statement here. Then, in the SQL statements that follow, the procedure is free to refer to the parameters by name—kind of how you refer to ColdFusion variables in your CFML templates. The values of the parameters are automatically plugged in with the appropriate values each time the procedure is actually used.

Listing 20.11 The AddNewBook Procedure Accepts Input Parameters

```
CREATE PROCEDURE AddNewBookx
  @CategoryID smallint,
  @ISBN varchar(13),
  @Title varchar(50)
AS

-- Make sure that this book is not already in the Inventory
IF EXISTS (SELECT * FROM Inventory WHERE ISBN = @ISBN)
  RETURN -1

-- Check that given @CategoryID exists in the Category table
IF NOT EXISTS (SELECT * FROM Category WHERE ID = @CategoryID)
  RETURN -2

-- Go ahead and insert new row into the Inventory table
INSERT INTO Inventory (CategoryID, ISBN, Title)
  VALUES (@CategoryID, @ISBN, @Title)

-- Return a value of 1 to indicate "success"
RETURN 1
```

Note that the AddNewBook procedure uses SQL Server's IF keyword to do some conditional processing as the template executes. Similar conceptually to the CFIF tag in CFML, the IF keyword as used here allows you to execute certain chunks of SQL code depending on conditions you define. You'll find IF extremely helpful when you need to write a stored procedure that needs to perform some kind of "sanity check" before committing changes to the database. For instance, the first IF line in Listing 20.11 halts processing and sends a return code of –1 to the calling application if the SELECT subquery inside the parentheses returns any rows.

Note that IF is not part of SQL as most people would define it, but is rather part of SQL Server's extensions to SQL, which Microsoft calls Transact-SQL.

 TIP Transact-SQL provides many other control-of-flow keywords that you might want to make yourself familiar with, such as BEGIN, END, ELSE, DECLARE, and WHILE. Sybase also supports the Transact-SQL extensions to standard SQL. Consult your database documentation about these keywords.

Adding Output Parameters   As you saw in Listing 20.5, stored procedures can return output parameters as well as input parameters. *Output parameters* have @-style names and data types just like input parameters do, but they are in charge of delivering a piece of information to the calling template (in this case, a ColdFusion template) rather than collecting a piece of information from it.

Listing 20.12 shows how to add the @NewBookID output parameter to the AddNewBook stored procedure, which is what the ProcAddNewBookGo2.cfm template in Listing 20.5 expects. As you can see, the main difference is in the CREATE PROCEDURE part of the code. The @NewBookID parameter is named and given a data type just like the other parameters, followed by two additional items.

- First, the parameter is given a default value using the = sign. Once a parameter has a default value, it becomes optional when the procedure is actually run. In other words, the default value keeps the calling application from having to provide some kind of dummy value for the @NewBookID parameter when calling the procedure. Here, the default value given to the parameter is the value NULL, which means that the parameter holds a blank or empty value until a real value is assigned to it within the procedure itself.

- Second, the OUTPUT keyword is used to identify the parameter as an output parameter. In other words, it's the word OUTPUT that tells SQL Server to pass the value of this parameter back to the CFPROCPARAM tag in your ColdFusion template as the procedure finishes executing.

Part
IV

Ch
20

Listing 20.12   Providing an Output Parameter to the Calling Template

```
CREATE PROCEDURE AddNewBook
  @CategoryID SmallInt,
  @ISBN varchar(13),
  @Title varchar(50),
  @NewBookID Int = NULL OUTPUT
AS
```

continues

Listing 20.12 Continued

```
-- Make sure that this book is not already in the Inventory
IF EXISTS (SELECT * FROM Inventory WHERE ISBN = @ISBN)
  RETURN -1

-- Check that given @CategoryID exists in the Category table
IF NOT EXISTS (SELECT * FROM Category WHERE ID = @CategoryID)
  RETURN -2

-- Go ahead and insert new row into the Inventory table
INSERT INTO Inventory (CategoryID, ISBN, Title)
  VALUES (@CategoryID, @ISBN, @Title)

-- Assign new Book_ID to the @NewBookID output parameter
SELECT @NewBookID = @@IDENTITY

-- Return a value of 1 to indicate "success"
RETURN 1
```

In this procedure, the SELECT statement near the end is what actually assigns a value to the @NewBookID parameter. This is a use of the SELECT statement that you haven't seen before, and is another feature of Microsoft's Transact-SQL extensions to SQL. Basically, if SELECT is followed by an @-style variable or parameter name and an = sign, SQL Server sets the parameter to whatever comes after the = sign. In other words, SELECT can behave a lot like CFSET does in ColdFusion templates. Of course, when not used with a parameter name, SELECT goes back to what SELECT statements do normally—fetch rows from database tables.

For instance, if the procedure contained something like SELECT @NewBookID = 10, the value of the @NewBookID output parameter would always be set to 10 whenever the procedure was used. Here, the parameter is set to the value of SQL Server's built-in @@IDENTITY variable, which always contains the newly generated identity value for the last INSERT to a table that contained an Identity-type column. (Identity columns are just like AutoNumber columns in Access tables.) Thus, the parameter gets set to the BookID that was just assigned to the row that was just inserted into the Inventory table.

N O T E You might be thinking that it's redundant to have to specify a default value even though the parameter is being identified as an output parameter. The reason for this is that stored procedure parameters can actually behave as input and output parameters at the same time. In other words, it's possible to create a stored procedure that actually changes the value of a parameter in place, kind of like a custom function. This really only makes sense when dealing with stored procedures that call other stored procedures, and so isn't directly related to what's being covered in this chapter. Still, you might want to take a look at your SQL Server documentation about using parameters in this way. ■

Returning Record Sets to ColdFusion   As you saw in Listing 20.6 and Listing 20.7 in this chapter, stored procedures can also return record sets. A *record set* is a set of rows and columns generated by a SELECT statement that outputs data from a database table.

To return record sets, simply use the appropriate SELECT statements as you would normally. Whatever would be returned by the SELECT statement outside a stored procedure is what will be returned to the calling application (in this case, your ColdFusion template) as a record set each time the procedure executes.

Your stored procedure can output as many record sets as it pleases. The calling ColdFusion template need only provide a CFPROCRESULT tag for each record set that it wants to be aware of after the procedure runs. The second SELECT statement in the procedure that outputs rows can be captured by using RECORDSET="2" in the CFPROCRESULT tag, and so on.

For instance, Listing 20.13 provides the code to create the GetMoreCustomerInfo procedure that is used by the GetMoreCustomerInfo.cfm template from Listing 20.7. As you can see, each CFPROCRESULT tag used in that template matches with a corresponding SELECT statement in the procedure code itself.

Listing 20.13   Returning Record Sets from a Stored Procedure

```
CREATE PROCEDURE GetMoreCustomerInfo
  @CustID Int
AS

-- Get basic information from Customers table
SELECT FirstName, LastName, Company, EMail
FROM Customers
WHERE CustomerID = @CustID

-- Get orders placed by this customer, by date
SELECT o.OrderDate, i.Title
FROM Orders o, OrderItems oi, Inventory i
WHERE o.OrderID = oi.OrderID
AND oi.BookID = i.BookID
AND o.CustomerID = @CustID
ORDER BY OrderDate

-- Get a cat/count rundown of customer's orders by category
SELECT c.Category, Count(i.Title) As BookCount
FROM Orders o, OrderItems oi, Inventory i, Category c
WHERE o.OrderID = oi.OrderID
AND oi.BookID = i.BookID
AND c.ID = i.CategoryID
AND o.CustomerID = @CustID
GROUP BY c.Category
ORDER BY c.Category
```

Part
IV

Ch
20

Creating Stored Procedures with Oracle

Stored procedures work somewhat differently with Oracle than they do with SQL Server and Sybase. The basic concepts are the same, and many of the stored procedure examples in this chapter can be implemented on an Oracle server quite easily.

N O T E This section assumes that you are using Oracle8 for Windows NT. If you're using an earlier version of Oracle, some of the figures shown in this chapter will look a little different from what you see on your screen. ■

Two important limitations affect what you can do with stored procedures when using Oracle with ColdFusion:

- ■ ColdFusion does not support record sets returned by Oracle stored procedures. In other words, you cannot use the CFPROCRESULT tag with Oracle.

- ■ With Oracle, procedures that send back a return value are actually called *stored functions*, rather than stored procedures. Stored functions are not supported by the CFSTOREDPROC tag. Therefore, you need to write your procedures so that they send back any status information as an output parameter instead of a return value.

N O T E To follow along with this chapter, you need to have the tables from the A2Z example database available on your Oracle server. You can do this very easily by using the Oracle Migration Assistant for Microsoft Access, which is a simple wizard that you can use to automatically migrate the a2z.mdb file from this book's CD to your Oracle server. The Migration Assistant installs with Oracle8 by default; if you don't have the Assistant available on your system, you can download it from http://www.oracle.com. ■

Creating the *ImportCustomers* Stored Procedure The easiest way to create a stored procedure is to use Oracle's Schema Manager, which is installed as part of the standard Oracle8 installation. For instance, follow these steps to create the ImportCustomers stored procedure:

1. Using the Windows Start menu, start the Oracle Schema Manager application and enter a valid username and password when prompted. If you used Oracle's Migration Assistant for Microsoft Access to import the A2Z.mdb database, you should be able to use A2Z as the username and ORACLE as the password.

2. Choose By Schema from the View menu.

3. Expand the tree for the A2Z Schema.

4. Right-click the Procedures folder, then choose Create from the pop-up menu as shown in Figure 20.14. The Create Procedure dialog box appears.

5. For the procedure's Name, type **IMPORTCUSTOMERS**.

6. Type the code shown in Listing 20.14 into the Source box, as shown in Figure 20.15. Do not include the first line of the listing (the Procedure IMPORTCUSTOMERS line). The dialog box includes this line for you.

7. Click the Create button. Your new procedure is created and the dialog box disappears. You can now expand the Procedures folder along the left side of the screen (see Figure 20.14) and click on the new procedure to confirm that it was created correctly.

T I P Instead of following the steps, you can just execute the code in Listing 20.14 directly into the Oracle SQL Worksheet utility. See your Oracle documentation for details.

FIGURE 20.14

Creating a stored procedure is simple with Oracle's Schema Manager.

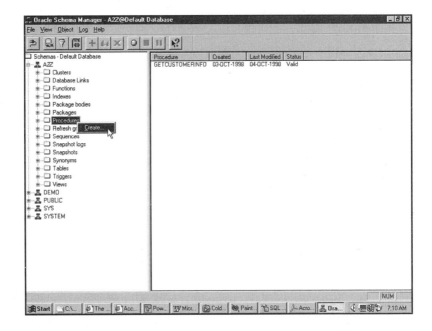

FIGURE 20.15

Enter the actual SQL code for the procedure into the Create Procedure dialog box.

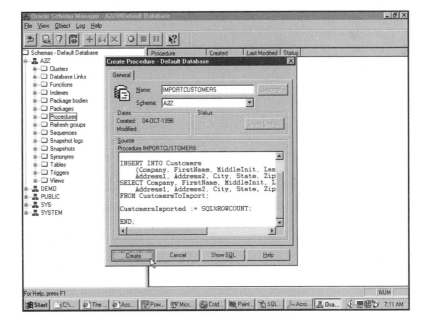

Part

IV

Ch

20

Listing 20.14   Creating the `ImportCustomers` Stored Procedure for Oracle

```
CREATE PROCEDURE IMPORTCUSTOMERS
(ImportCount OUT Number)
IS
BEGIN

INSERT INTO Customers
    (Company, FirstName, MiddleInit, LastName,
    Address1, Address2, City, State, Zip, Phone, EMail, CustomerSince)
SELECT Company, FirstName, MiddleInit, LastName,
    Address1, Address2, City, State, Zip, Phone, EMail, SYSDATE
FROM CustomersToImport;

ImportCount := SQL%ROWCOUNT;

END;
```

Note that the SQL syntax for creating the stored procedure is slightly different than it is for SQL Server, but the basic idea is the same. There's nothing here that's conceptually different from the SQL Server version of the procedure (see Listing 20.10).

The procedure name is provided first and follows the words CREATE PROCEDURE. Then the procedure's parameters, if any, are provided within a pair of parentheses. The parentheses are followed by the IS keyword and then the procedure's actual SQL code is provided between BEGIN and END keywords. Within the code, the actual value for the output parameter is set using Oracle's assignment operator, which is a colon followed by an equal sign (:=).

 TIP

Oracle requires that you place a semicolon after each statement in your SQL code. If you've done any work with C or C++ in the past, that semicolon is a familiar friend. See your Oracle documentation for details.

N O T E   Because the Oracle version of the `ImportCustomers` stored procedure sends the number of customers actually imported as an output parameter rather than as a return value, you would need to modify the `ImportCustomers2.cfm` template slightly before it can display the number to the user. The `ImportCustomers3.cfm` template on the CD shows the changed version of the template. Basically, a single CFPROCPARAM tag has been added to take the place of the CFSET from the original listing. ▪

Returning Output Parameters Instead of Record Sets   As noted earlier, ColdFusion cannot use the CFPROCRESULT tag to access record sets returned by Oracle stored procedures. While this is a real problem if you need multiple rows to come back from the stored procedure, there is a workaround if you just need a single row of information. Just use output parameters instead of returning a result set. For instance, the code shown in Listing 20.15 creates the `GetCustomerInfo` stored procedure for Oracle.

Listing 20.15 Creating the `GetCustomerInfo` Procedure for Oracle

```
CREATE PROCEDURE GETCUSTOMERINFO
(custid IN Number,
firstname OUT varchar2, lastname OUT varchar2, company OUT varchar2,
➥ email OUT varchar2)
IS
BEGIN

SELECT FIRSTNAME, LASTNAME, COMPANY, EMAIL
  INTO firstname, lastname, company, email
FROM Customers
WHERE CustomerID = custid;

END;
```

On the CD

To actually use the procedure in a ColdFusion template, just use `CFPROCPARAM` tags to capture each output variable from the procedure as it executes. For instance, the `ProcGetCustomerInfo2.cfm` template on the CD provides a version of the original `ProcGetCustomerInfo.cfm` template that will work with the Oracle version of the procedure.

Note that the `GetMoreCustomerInfo` stored procedure shown in Listing 20.13 could not be created in any reasonable manner for use in a ColdFusion application. That's because ColdFusion cannot retrieve record sets from Oracle stored procedures, and the nature of the procedure is such that record sets would be necessary. You would have to use traditional `SELECT`-style queries and `CFQUERY` tags to mimic the procedure's functionality.

Creating Stored Procedures with Sybase

Creating stored procedures with Sybase is extremely similar to creating them with Microsoft SQL Server. This has a lot to do with the fact that SQL Server was originally developed as a joint effort between Microsoft and Sybase. Both products supported almost the same functionality until relatively recently.

There are some differences between the products in the latest versions, but the structure of the SQL statements allowed and the way that stored procedures work remains nearly identical. For instance, both products use the @ sign to identify input and output parameters, and both products support the same kind of `CREATE PROCEDURE` statements.

> **N O T E** This section assumes that you're using a Sybase System 11–generation database server, such as Sybase Adaptive Server 11.5 for Windows NT. If you're using an earlier version of Sybase, some of the figures here may not match exactly what you see on your computer screen. The basic concepts and steps will be the same, however. ■

> **T I P** To follow along in this section, you need to have a database on your Sybase server that has the same tables and columns as the A2Z example database. You can use the PowerDesigner SQL Modeler's Reverse Engineering feature to migrate the Access version of the database to your Sybase server nearly automatically. PowerDesigner SQL Modeler comes with Sybase Adaptive Server for Windows NT. See your Sybase documentation for details.

Part
IV

Ch

20

Creating the ImportCustomers Procedure The easiest way to create a new stored procedure on a Sybase server is to use the Sybase Central application that is normally installed with Sybase Adaptive Server. Sybase Central is similar to Microsoft's SQL Server Enterprise Manager and Oracle's Schema Manager.

Follow these simple steps to create the ImportCustomers procedure on your Sybase server:

1. Start Sybase Central by using the Windows Start menu.

2. Using the Explorer-like interface on the left side of the screen, expand the tree for your Sybase server; expand the databases tree and then expand the tree for the database that you want to add the procedure to.

3. Click the database's Procedures folder. Double-click the Add Procedure icon that appears in the list on the right side of the screen.

4. The Create a New Procedure dialog box appears, as shown in Figure 20.16. Type ImportCustomers for the name of the procedure.

FIGURE 20.16

The Sybase Central application makes it easy to create stored procedures.

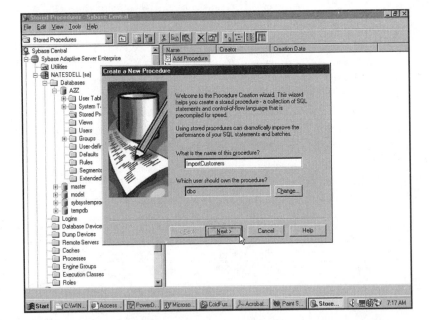

5. Just click the Next button through all the other steps, accepting the default options. When you get to the last step, click the Finish button.

6. A code-editor window appears with a basic code outline written for you. Replace the prewritten code with the code from Listing 20.10; this is shown in Figure 20.17.

7. Choose Execute Script from the File menu. The procedure is immediately created and ready for your use. You can now close the code-editor window and test the procedure with the ProcImportCustomers2.cfm template from earlier in this chapter (see Listing 20.2 and Figure 20.4).

FIGURE 20.17

You can use the same code for Sybase and SQL Server in most situations.

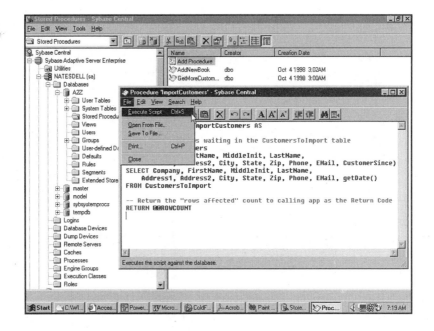

 TIP

Instead of following the steps listed here, you can execute the code from Listing 20.10 directly, using Sybase's SQL Advantage utility. See your Sybase documentation for details.

The other SQL Server procedures from this chapter can be created using the same basic steps. In general, no code changes are needed to make the SQL Server code legal for Sybase. ●

Advanced ColdFusion Templates

Reusing Code

I've talked a bit about code reuse before, and I'll mention it several more times before the end of this book. Code reuse, and writing code so that it is reusable, is a practice worth learning, understanding, and implementing.

To see why code reuse is so important, let's look at a simple example. Figure 21.1 shows a simple search screen. There is a navigation menu on the left of the screen and a search dialog in the main section. Once you have entered your search criteria, the results screen shown in Figure 21.2 displays the matching books.

FIGURE 21.1

The book search screen displays a navigation menu on the left and a search dialog in the main section of the screen.

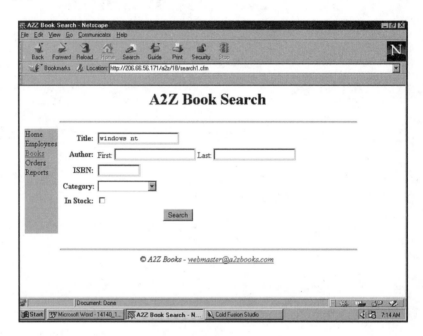

Notice that the results screen displays the same navigation bar as the search screen. In fact, the title, header, and copyright information are all identical as well.

The code for these two screens is shown in Listing 21.1 and Listing 21.2.

FIGURE 21.2

The search results screen displays the same navigation menu as the search screen, in addition to the search results.

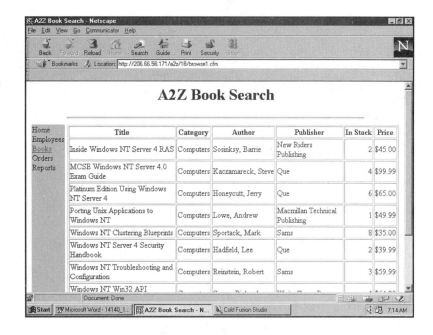

Listing 21.1 `C:\A2Z\SCRIPTS\21\SEARCH1.CFM`—**Source for**
`SEARCH1.CFM` **Template**

```
<CFQUERY DATASOURCE="A2Z" NAME="categories">
SELECT id, category
FROM category
ORDER BY category
</CFQUERY>

<HTML>

<HEAD>
 <TITLE>A2Z Book Search</TITLE>
</HEAD>

<BODY>

<CENTER>
 <H1>A2Z Book Search</H1>
 <HR WIDTH="80%">
</CENTER>

<TABLE>

<TR VALIGN="TOP">
 <TD NOWRAP BGCOLOR="C0C0C0">
```

Part
IV

Ch
21

continues

Listing 21.1 Continued

```
 Home<BR>
 Employees<BR>
 <A HREF="search1.cfm">Books</A><BR>
 Orders<BR>
 Reports<BR>
</TD>
<TD>

<CFFORM ACTION="browse1.cfm">

<TABLE>

<TR>
 <TH ALIGN="RIGHT">Title:</TH>
 <TD>
  <INPUT TYPE="text" NAME="Title" SIZE="20" MAXLENGTH="30">
 </TD>
</TR>

<TR>
 <TH ALIGN="RIGHT">Author:</TH>
 <TD>
  First: <INPUT TYPE="text" NAME="AuthorFirstName" SIZE="20" MAXLENGTH="20">
  Last: <INPUT TYPE="text" NAME="AuthorLastName" SIZE="20" MAXLENGTH="20">
 </TD>
</TR>

<TR>
 <TH ALIGN="RIGHT">ISBN:</TH>
 <TD>
  <INPUT TYPE="text" NAME="ISBN" SIZE="10" MAXLENGTH="10">
 </TD>
</TR>

<TR>
 <TH ALIGN="RIGHT">Category:</TH>
 <TD>
  <CFSELECT NAME="CategoryID" QUERY="categories" VALUE="id" DISPLAY="category"
  ➥SIZE="1">
  <OPTION VALUE="" SELECTED>
  </CFSELECT>
 </TD>
</TR>

<TR>
 <TH ALIGN="RIGHT">In Stock:</TH>
 <TD>
  <INPUT TYPE="checkbox" NAME="InStock" VALUE="Yes">
 </TD>
</TR>

<TR>
 <TH COLSPAN="2">
  <INPUT TYPE="submit" VALUE="Search">
```

```
    </TH>
  </TR>

  </TABLE>

  </CFFORM>

  </TD>

</TR>
</TABLE>

<CENTER>
 <P>
 <HR WIDTH="80%">
 <I>&copy; A2Z Books - <A HREF="mailto:webmaster@a2zbooks.com">
➥webmaster@a2zbooks.com</A></I>
</CENTER>

</BODY>
</HTML>
```

Listing 21.2 `C:\A2Z\SCRIPTS\21\BROWSE1.CFM`—**Source for
`BROWSE1.CFM` Template**

```
<CFPARAM NAME="Title" DEFAULT="">
<CFPARAM NAME="AuthorFirstName" DEFAULT="">
<CFPARAM NAME="AuthorLastName" DEFAULT="">
<CFPARAM NAME="isbn" DEFAULT="">
<CFPARAM NAME="CategoryID" DEFAULT="">
<CFPARAM NAME="InStock" DEFAULT="">

<CFQUERY DATASOURCE="A2Z" NAME="books">
SELECT Title, AuthorFirstName, AuthorLastName,
       NumberInStock, Category, Publisher, Price
FROM Inventory, Category
WHERE Inventory.CategoryID = Category.id

<CFIF Trim(Title) IS NOT "">
 AND Title LIKE '%#Trim(Title)#%'
</CFIF>

<CFIF Trim(AuthorFirstName) IS NOT "">
 AND AuthorFirstName LIKE '#Trim(AuthorFirstName)#%'
</CFIF>

<CFIF Trim(AuthorLastName) IS NOT "">
 AND AuthorLastName LIKE '#Trim(AuthorLastName)#%'
</CFIF>

<CFIF Trim(isbn) IS NOT "">
 AND isbn = '#Trim(isbn)#'
</CFIF>
```

Part
IV

Ch

21

continues

Listing 21.2 Continued

```
<CFIF Trim(CategoryID) IS NOT "">
 AND CategoryId = #Trim(CategoryID)#
</CFIF>

<CFIF Trim(InStock) IS NOT "">
 AND NumberInStock > 0
</CFIF>

ORDER BY title
</CFQUERY>

<HTML>

<HEAD>
 <TITLE>A2Z Book Search</TITLE>
</HEAD>

<BODY>

<CENTER>
 <H1>A2Z Book Search</H1>
 <HR WIDTH="80%">
</CENTER>

<TABLE>

<TR VALIGN="TOP">
 <TD NOWRAP BGCOLOR="C0C0C0">
  Home<BR>
  Employees<BR>
  <A HREF="search.cfm">Books</A><BR>
  Orders<BR>
  Reports<BR>
 </TD>
 <TD>

 <TABLE BORDER="1">

 <TR>
  <TH>Title</TH>
  <TH>Category</TH>
  <TH>Author</TH>
  <TH>Publisher</TH>
  <TH>In Stock</TH>
  <TH>Price</TH>
 </TR>

 <CFOUTPUT QUERY="books">
  <TR>
   <TD>#Trim(Title)#</TD>
   <TD>#Trim(Category)#</TD>
   <TD>#Trim(AuthorLastName)#, #Trim(AuthorFirstName)#</TD>
   <TD>#Trim(Publisher)#</TD>
   <TD ALIGN="RIGHT">#NumberFormat(NumberInStock)#</TD>
```

```
    <TD ALIGN="RIGHT">#DollarFormat(Price)#</TD>
    </TR>
  </CFOUTPUT>

  </TABLE>

  </TD>

 </TR>
 </TABLE>

 <CENTER>
 <P>
 <HR WIDTH="80%">
 <I>&copy; A2Z Books - <A HREF="mailto:webmaster@a2zbooks.com">
➥webmaster@a2zbooks.com</A></I>
 </CENTER>

 </BODY>
 </HTML>
```

Let's take a look at these two code listings. Everything contained within these templates is code you have seen before. <CFQUERY> retrieves a list of categories in Listing 21.1, and to perform the book search in Listing 21.2. <CFFORM> and <CFSELECT> display the category list in Listing 21.1, and <CFOUTPUT> is used to display the search results in Listing 21.2. For more information about using <CFQUERY> and <CFOUTPUT>, see Chapter 11, "ColdFusion Basics."

Now look at the HTML interface code, the code that creates the page's body, displays the title and copyright information, and shows the navigation bar on the left. The code is identical for both listings. (In fact, when creating this example, I just copied and pasted the code from one source file to the other!)

There is nothing wrong with copying chunks of code between files. That's exactly what Web page designers do within their HTML pages. HTML developers have no choice but to do this, as HTML itself has no mechanism with which to share common code.

What happens the first time you need to make changes to that common code? Perhaps it's something as simple as changing the color of the navigation bar background, or maybe your are fixing a typo or changing the order or color of some text? Whatever the change, no matter how simple and trivial, you must make sure you update every single occurrence of it manually. Of course, manually updating multiple files exposes you to the risk of introducing mistakes.

Obviously this is far from ideal, and definitely not scalable or manageable. What you really need is a way to share common code between files, and ColdFusion allows you to do this using a tag called <CFINCLUDE>.

Using <CFINCLUDE>

The <CFINCLUDE> tag is used to include the entire contents of one ColdFusion template into another. The syntax is as follows:

```
<CFINCLUDE TEMPLATE="FILE.CFM">
```

This includes the entire contents of FILE.CFM at the location where the <CFINCLUDE> tag appeared in your code.

To better understand this, let's modify the example we used earlier to use common header and footer code. To do this, we create two new templates, HEADER.CFM and FOOTER.CFM. HEADER.CFM, shown in Listing 21.3, contains all the header text to use on both the search page and the results page, including the title and the navigation bar. FOOTER.CFM, shown in Listing 21.4, contains the common footer code, including the copyright information and the end of the navigation bar table.

Listing 21.3   C:\A2Z\SCRIPTS\21\HEADER.CFM—**Source for HEADER.CFM Template**

```
<HTML>

<HEAD>
 <TITLE>A2Z Book Search</TITLE>
</HEAD>

<BODY>

<CENTER>
 <H1>A2Z Book Search</H1>
 <HR WIDTH="80%">
</CENTER>

<TABLE>

<TR VALIGN="TOP">
<TD NOWRAP BGCOLOR="C0C0C0">
Home<BR>
Employees<BR>
<A HREF="search.cfm">Books</A><BR>
Orders<BR>
Reports<BR>
</TD>
 <TD>
```

Listing 21.4   C:\A2Z\SCRIPTS\21\FOOTER.CFM—**Source for FOOTER.CFM Template**

```
</TD>
</TR>
</TABLE>

<CENTER>
 <P>
 <HR WIDTH="80%">
 <I>&copy; A2Z Books - <A HREF="mailto:webmaster@a2zbooks.com">
➥webmaster@a2zbooks.com</A></I>
</CENTER>
```

```
</BODY>
</HTML>
```

Now that we have the header and footer code broken into their own files, we can modify the search and results pages to include these files directly. Listings 21.5 and 21.6 contain the updated files. You'll see that all header and footer text has been pulled out and replaced with two <CFINCLUDE> calls, one for HEADER.CFM and the other for FOOTER.CFM.

Listing 21.5 C:\A2Z\SCRIPTS\21\SEARCH2.CFM—**Source for**
SEARCH2.CFM Template

```
<CFQUERY DATASOURCE="A2Z" NAME="categories">
SELECT id, category
FROM category
ORDER BY category
</CFQUERY>

<CFINCLUDE TEMPLATE="header.cfm">

<CFFORM ACTION="browse2.cfm">

<TABLE>

<TR>
 <TH ALIGN="RIGHT">Title:</TH>
 <TD>
  <INPUT TYPE="text" NAME="Title" SIZE="20" MAXLENGTH="30">
 </TD>
</TR>

<TR>
 <TH ALIGN="RIGHT">Author:</TH>
 <TD>
  First: <INPUT TYPE="text" NAME="AuthorFirstName" SIZE="20" MAXLENGTH="20">
  Last: <INPUT TYPE="text" NAME="AuthorLastName" SIZE="20" MAXLENGTH="20">
 </TD>
</TR>
<CFQUERY DATASOURCE="A2Z" NAME="catego

<TR>
 <TH ALIGN="RIGHT">ISBN:</TH>
 <TD>
  <INPUT TYPE="text" NAME="ISBN" SIZE="10" MAXLENGTH="10">
 </TD>
</TR>

<TR>
 <TH ALIGN="RIGHT">Category:</TH>
 <TD>
  <CFSELECT NAME="CategoryID" QUERY="categories" VALUE="id" DISPLAY="category"
  ➥SIZE="1">
  <OPTION VALUE="" SELECTED>
```

continues

Part
IV

Ch
21

Listing 21.5   Continued

```
   </CFSELECT>
  </TD>
 </TR>

 <TR>
  <TH ALIGN="RIGHT">In Stock:</TH>
  <TD>
   <INPUT TYPE="checkbox" NAME="InStock" VALUE="Yes">
  </TD>
 </TR>

 <TR>
  <TH COLSPAN="2">
   <INPUT TYPE="submit" VALUE="Search">
  </TH>
 </TR>

</TABLE>

</CFFORM>


<CFINCLUDE TEMPLATE="footer.cfm">
<CFQUERY DATASOURCE="A2Z" NAME="catego
```

**Listing 21.6   C:\A2Z\SCRIPTS\21\BROWSE2.CFM—Source for
BROWSE2.CFM Template**

```
<CFQUERY DATASOURCE="A2Z" NAME="catego
<CFPARAM NAME="Title" DEFAULT="">
<CFPARAM NAME="AuthorFirstName" DEFAULT="">
<CFPARAM NAME="AuthorLastName" DEFAULT="">
<CFPARAM NAME="isbn" DEFAULT="">
<CFPARAM NAME="CategoryID" DEFAULT="">
<CFPARAM NAME="InStock" DEFAULT="">

<CFQUERY DATASOURCE="A2Z" NAME="books">
SELECT Title, AuthorFirstName, AuthorLastName,
       NumberInStock, Category, Publisher, Price
FROM Inventory, Category
WHERE Inventory.CategoryID = Category.id

<CFIF Trim(Title) IS NOT "">
 AND Title LIKE '%#Trim(Title)#%'
</CFIF>

<CFIF Trim(AuthorFirstName) IS NOT "">
 AND AuthorFirstName LIKE '#Trim(AuthorFirstName)#%'
</CFIF>

<CFIF Trim(AuthorLastName) IS NOT "">
 AND AuthorLastName LIKE '#Trim(AuthorLastName)#%'
</CFIF>
```

```
<CFIF Trim(isbn) IS NOT "">
 AND isbn = '#Trim(isbn)#'
</CFIF>

<CFIF Trim(CategoryID) IS NOT "">
 AND CategoryId = #Trim(CategoryID)#
</CFIF>

<CFIF Trim(InStock) IS NOT "">
 AND NumberInStock > 0
</CFIF>

ORDER BY title
</CFQUERY>

<CFINCLUDE TEMPLATE="header.cfm">

<TABLE BORDER="1">

<TR>
 <TH>Title</TH>
 <TH>Category</TH>
 <TH>Author</TH>
 <TH>Publisher</TH>
 <TH>In Stock</TH>
 <TH>Price</TH>
</TR>

<CFOUTPUT QUERY="books">
 <TR>
  <TD>#Trim(Title)#</TD>
  <TD>#Trim(Category)#</TD>
  <TD>#Trim(AuthorLastName)#, #Trim(AuthorFirstName)#</TD>
  <TD>#Trim(Publisher)#</TD>
  <TD ALIGN="RIGHT">#NumberFormat(NumberInStock)#</TD>
  <TD ALIGN="RIGHT">#DollarFormat(Price)#</TD>
 </TR>
</CFOUTPUT>

</TABLE>

<CFINCLUDE TEMPLATE="footer.cfm">
```

Take a look at the new page in your browser; you'll see that the end result is exactly the same as when the header and footer code was entered directly into the files.

While the end result looks the same, things are very different under the hood. If you need to change a color or an option, fix a typo, or make any other change to the HEADER.CFM or FOOTER.CFM file, every file that includes these files is updated automatically. These changes are dynamic because ColdFusion includes the header and footer files every time the page is requested.

Writing Code with Reuse in Mind

Now that you've seen how to reuse code using <CFINCLUDE>, here are some guidelines to help you write reusable code:

- When writing code, isolate components that can be shared.
- Try to break out code that is slightly more generic than the main file itself. Code that is very template-specific is harder to reuse.
- Organize your code so that template-specific tasks and more generic tasks are separated from each other. (We look at this one later in this chapter.)
- Menus, toolbars, and headers and footers are prime candidates for breaking out into separate files.

TIP   Many Web page designers use CFM files for all their HTML pages, not just for pages that use ColdFusion code, so that they may use <CFINCLUDE> to share HTML code between files.

N O T E   One very important thing to remember when using <CFINCLUDE> is that the included file shares the scope of the calling file. This means that any variables, queries, form fields, or other data that is available in the caller file is also available to the included file. Similarly, any data created in the included file is visible to the caller file. This means that code in your included file must be careful not to overwrite variables or data in the caller file by mistake. ■

Organizing Your Code

Most of the code samples and applications that we have written so far have been small, and are therefore quite manageable. As you start writing bigger and more complex applications, you are going to find that your code becomes harder and harder to manage—particularly if you need to revisit code that you have not looked at in a while.

It is therefore very important to pay attention to the organization of your code from day one, taking the time to ensure that your code is clean and manageable.

Two of the most important components of code organization are the use of comments and the breaking up of templates into logical sections.

Using Comments and Headers

Programmers don't like writing comments. It's a sad fact, but that's just the way it is. Documenting and commenting code is not glamorous, nor is it as much fun as writing brand new code. Commenting code is also time consuming, and when time is running out, commenting and documentation are usually the first tasks to be sacrificed.

I have only one comment to make about commenting your code: Do it! View it as an investment, whatever time you put into commenting your code up front is time saved when you have to modify or debug the application at a later date. For more information about commenting your code and other development guidelines, see Chapter 17, "Debugging and Troubleshooting."

As an example, look at the code in Listing 21.7. The first thing you see is that the page has an entire header block that describes the page contents. This block contains the filename, description, author, date, and usage notes. You may add additional fields to this block if needed, but at least these five fields should be used.

In addition, you see comments like this through the code:

```
<!--- Retrieve category list for SELECT box --->
```

This makes the following code very clear. Anyone—yourself at a later date or another developer—will know right away what the query is and what it is used for.

Listing 21.7 `C:\A2Z\SCRIPTS\21\SEARCH3.CFM`—**Code for SEARCH3.CFM**

```
<!---
NAME: SEARCH3.CFM

DESCRIPTION: Search page for book inventory search. Sends
             search request to BROWSE3.CFM.

AUTHOR: Ben Forta

DATE: 7/26/98

NOTES: This file includes HEADER.CFM and FOOTER.CFM, both
       must be present in the current directory or an error
       will be displayed.
--->

<!--- Retrieve category list for SELECT box --->
<CFQUERY DATASOURCE="A2Z" NAME="categories">
SELECT id, category
FROM category
ORDER BY category
</CFQUERY>

<!--- Include header code --->
<CFINCLUDE TEMPLATE="header.cfm">

<!--- This is the search form --->
<CFFORM ACTION="browse3.cfm">

<TABLE>

<TR>
 <TH ALIGN="RIGHT">Title:</TH>
 <TD>
  <INPUT TYPE="text" NAME="Title" SIZE="20" MAXLENGTH="30">
 </TD>
```

continues

Listing 21.7 Continued

```
</TR>

<TR>
 <TH ALIGN="RIGHT">Author:</TH>
 <TD>
  First: <INPUT TYPE="text" NAME="AuthorFirstName" SIZE="20" MAXLENGTH="20">
  Last: <INPUT TYPE="text" NAME="AuthorLastName" SIZE="20" MAXLENGTH="20">
 </TD>
</TR>

<TR>
 <TH ALIGN="RIGHT">ISBN:</TH>
 <TD>
  <INPUT TYPE="text" NAME="ISBN" SIZE="10" MAXLENGTH="10">
 </TD>
</TR>

<TR>
 <TH ALIGN="RIGHT">Category:</TH>
 <TD>
  <CFSELECT NAME="CategoryID" QUERY="categories" VALUE="id" DISPLAY="category"
  ➥SIZE="1">
  <OPTION VALUE="" SELECTED>
  </CFSELECT>
 </TD>
</TR>

<TR>
 <TH ALIGN="RIGHT">In Stock:</TH>
 <TD>
  <INPUT TYPE="checkbox" NAME="InStock" VALUE="Yes">
 </TD>
</TR>

<TR>
 <TH COLSPAN="2">
  <INPUT TYPE="submit" VALUE="Search">
 </TH>
</TR>

</TABLE>

</CFFORM>

<!--- Include footer code --->
<CFINCLUDE TEMPLATE="footer.cfm">
```

Embedded comments obviously increase the size of the physical ColdFusion files, but the amount of data sent to the end user's browser is not increased at all. The screen shown in Figure 21.3 is the source code for the updated search screen (the one with the comments in it) as it appears on the browser. As you can see, ColdFusion stripped out all the comments before the page was sent. This saves download time and protects your comments from being viewed by your visitors.

FIGURE 21.3
ColdFusion strips embedded comments from your code before it is sent to the user's browser.

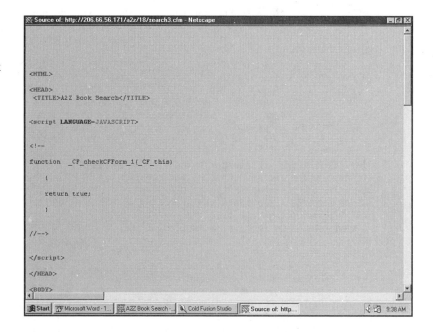

N O T E Make sure you use < ! - - - and - - - > for your comments (using three dashes, not two). If you use two dashes, your comment is an HTML comment—not a CFML comment. Unlike CFML comments, HTML comments are not stripped out by ColdFusion and are sent to the user's browser. ▨

 Studio users can use the Studio Tag Snippets feature to save an empty header block that can easily be inserted into your code.

Breaking Templates into Logical Sections

As mentioned earlier, an important part of code organization is breaking your code into logical sections. Take a look at an updated version of the results page; it is the same as the example earlier, except that this one has comments embedded in it. The code is shown in Listing 21.8.

Part
IV

Ch
21

Listing 21.8 C:\A2Z\SCRIPTS\21\BROWSE3.CFM—Source for
BROWSE3.CFM

```
<!---
NAME: BROWSE3.CFM
```

continues

Listing 21.8 Continued

```
DESCRIPTION: Perform search for books in the Inventory
             table. All search fields are optional.

AUTHOR: Ben Forta

DATE: 7/26/98

NOTES: This file includes HEADER.CFM and FOOTER.CFM, both
       must be present in the current directory or an error
       will be displayed.
--->

<!--- Initialize all fields if they do not exist --->
<CFPARAM NAME="Title" DEFAULT="">
<CFPARAM NAME="AuthorFirstName" DEFAULT="">
<CFPARAM NAME="AuthorLastName" DEFAULT="">
<CFPARAM NAME="isbn" DEFAULT="">
<CFPARAM NAME="CategoryID" DEFAULT="">
<CFPARAM NAME="InStock" DEFAULT="">

<!--- Perform actual search, search is on a
      JOIN between Inventory and Category so that
      the category names are retrieved --->
<CFQUERY DATASOURCE="A2Z" NAME="books">
SELECT Title, AuthorFirstName, AuthorLastName,
       NumberInStock, Category, Publisher, Price
FROM Inventory, Category
WHERE Inventory.CategoryID = Category.id

<!--- Filter by title if needed --->
<CFIF Trim(Title) IS NOT "">
 AND Title LIKE '%#Trim(Title)#%'
</CFIF>

<!--- Filter by author first name if needed --->
<CFIF Trim(AuthorFirstName) IS NOT "">
 AND AuthorFirstName LIKE '#Trim(AuthorFirstName)#%'
</CFIF>

<!--- Filter by author last name if needed --->
<CFIF Trim(AuthorLastName) IS NOT "">
 AND AuthorLastName LIKE '#Trim(AuthorLastName)#%'
</CFIF>

<!--- Filter by isbn if needed --->
<CFIF Trim(isbn) IS NOT "">
 AND isbn = '#Trim(isbn)#'
</CFIF>

<!--- Filter by category if needed --->
<CFIF Trim(CategoryID) IS NOT "">
 AND CategoryId = #Trim(CategoryID)#
</CFIF>
```

```
<!--- Filter by stock number if needed --->
<CFIF Trim(InStock) IS NOT "">
 AND NumberInStock > 0
</CFIF>

ORDER BY title
</CFQUERY>

<!--- Include header file --->
<CFINCLUDE TEMPLATE="header.cfm">

<!--- Create table for display --->
<TABLE BORDER="1">

<!--- Table headers --->
<TR>
 <TH>Title</TH>
 <TH>Category</TH>
 <TH>Author</TH>
 <TH>Publisher</TH>
 <TH>In Stock</TH>
 <TH>Price</TH>
</TR>

<!--- Write out the retrieved data --->
<CFOUTPUT QUERY="books">
 <TR>
  <TD>#Trim(Title)#</TD>
  <TD>#Trim(Category)#</TD>
  <TD>#Trim(AuthorLastName)#, #Trim(AuthorFirstName)#</TD>
  <TD>#Trim(Publisher)#</TD>
  <TD ALIGN="RIGHT">#NumberFormat(NumberInStock)#</TD>
  <TD ALIGN="RIGHT">#DollarFormat(Price)#</TD>
 </TR>
</CFOUTPUT>

</TABLE>

<!--- Include footer file --->
<CFINCLUDE TEMPLATE="footer.cfm">
```

The first item in the code is the header block.

Next comes variable initialization code using a series of `<CFPARAM>` tags. This code ensures that the fields that will be used later in the file exist. If they do not exist (either because the form changed, or because the field was not submitted), `<CFPARAM>` creates them right then and there. Either way, the variables will exist once that block of initialization code has been processed.

What's the advantage of doing this? These fields are used in the `<CFQUERY>` tag, the next item in the file. We could have enclosed every `<CFIF>` statement in another conditional statement to check that the field existed, but that would have made the code harder to read. The `<CFQUERY>` is cleaner when you break out the initialization code, and it does just what it is supposed to do: retrieve data.

Part
IV

Ch
21

The rest of the file follows the same pattern. <CFQUERY> (to retrieve the data) could have appeared in the middle of the HTML output, right before the <CFOUTPUT> tag. Why not do it that way? That would have made the code harder to read. More importantly, you might inadvertently reuse a query name as your files get bigger and more complex, not realizing that it was already used; either that or you might refer to a query before it was processed; you could commit other, similar errors. Keeping the queries isolated from the interface prevents this from happening.

This also makes managing your HTML code simpler because the HTML code does not have calls to ColdFusion tags embedded in it. This makes finding mismatched tags, broken tables, and other common HTML problems much easier to locate.

This kind of organization becomes even more important when you need to verify the contents of a field or abort processing if a field does not exist. You could put all that verification code above any actual processing, keeping your core processing cleaner and more manageable.

The basic rule of thumb here is to avoid embedding initialization and verification code in your core processing. Separate the code into logical blocks; it will be easier to maintain and manage.

While there is no hard and fast rule as to breaking up your code, the following layout is a good place to start:

- File description—Comments at the top of the page
- Variable initialization—Using <CFPARAM>
- Verification—Often using <CFIF>, <CFABORT>, and <CFLOCATION>
- All database retrieval—Using <CFQUERY>
- User interface—The HTML itself

N O T E   A nice side effect of breaking your code up this way is that this type of code lends itself very well to code reuse. For example, the header and footer text you saw earlier can be broken out into separate files because they are cleanly isolated. We couldn't have done that as easily if there were ColdFusion code embedded in the middle of the header or footer text. ∎

Browsing "Next n" Records

One of the most popular interface types used by Web-based applications is one that allows the user to browse the "next n" records; the n stands for any number of records you indicate. This kind of interface is used by the popular online search engines, as well as many sites that allow users to browse through catalogs.

Creating a Browse "Next n" Records Interface

Creating this kind of interface with ColdFusion is very simple, as long as you remember one basic rule. As explained in Chapter 2, "Introduction to ColdFusion," every request made by a Web browser must stand on its own. There is no relationship between a request made and any future request. This means that in order to continue a previous search (display the next five records, for example), you must pass back to the server all the information needed to reconstruct the original search.

Even though from the user's perspective they are continuing an existing search, from your perspective it is a brand new search. The only difference is from where to start displaying data. For the first page of results you'd display records 1 through 5 (assuming this was a "next 5" display), for the second page you'd display records 6 through 10, and so on.

Figure 21.4 shows an example of this. A search for Windows NT was performed, and the first five matching records are displayed. A Next 5 button at the bottom of the display allows the user to browse though five records at a time. To try this out yourself, run the SEARCH4.CFM file.

Listing 21.9 contains the updated results page. It is very similar to the browser page used earlier, but there are some important differences.

FIGURE 21.4
ColdFusion can be used to create "next n" records-style interfaces.

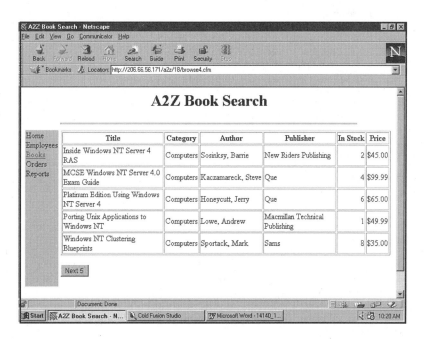

Listing 21.9 C:\A2Z\SCRIPTS\21\BROWSE4.CFM—**Code for BROWSE4.CFM File**

```
<!---
NAME: BROWSE4.CFM

DESCRIPTION: Perform search for books in the Inventory
             table. All search fields are optional. Results
             are shown 5 records at a time, and a "Next 5"
             button is shown to allow the user to browse
             through the results.
```

Part

IV

Ch

21

continues

Listing 21.9 Continued

```
AUTHOR: Ben Forta

DATE: 7/26/98

NOTES: This file includes HEADER.CFM and FOOTER.CFM, both
       must be present in the current directory or an error
       will be displayed.
--->

<!--- Initialize constants --->
<CFSET MaxRows = 5>

<!--- Initialize all fields if they do not exist --->
<CFPARAM NAME="start" DEFAULT="1">
<CFPARAM NAME="Title" DEFAULT="">
<CFPARAM NAME="AuthorFirstName" DEFAULT="">
<CFPARAM NAME="AuthorLastName" DEFAULT="">
<CFPARAM NAME="isbn" DEFAULT="">
<CFPARAM NAME="CategoryID" DEFAULT="">
<CFPARAM NAME="InStock" DEFAULT="">

<!--- Perform actual search, search is on a
       JOIN between Inventory and Category so that
       the category names are retrieved --->
<CFQUERY DATASOURCE="A2Z" NAME="books">
SELECT Title, AuthorFirstName, AuthorLastName,
       NumberInStock, Category, Publisher, Price
FROM Inventory, Category
WHERE Inventory.CategoryID = Category.id

<!--- Filter by title if needed --->
<CFIF Trim(Title) IS NOT "">
 AND Title LIKE '%#Trim(Title)#%'
</CFIF>

<!--- Filter by author first name if needed --->
<CFIF Trim(AuthorFirstName) IS NOT "">
 AND AuthorFirstName LIKE '#Trim(AuthorFirstName)#%'
</CFIF>

<!--- Filter by author last name if needed --->
<CFIF Trim(AuthorLastName) IS NOT "">
 AND AuthorLastName LIKE '#Trim(AuthorLastName)#%'
</CFIF>

<!--- Filter by isbn if needed --->
<CFIF Trim(isbn) IS NOT "">
 AND isbn = '#Trim(isbn)#'
</CFIF>

<!--- Filter by category if needed --->
<CFIF Trim(CategoryID) IS NOT "">
 AND CategoryId = #Trim(CategoryID)#
</CFIF>
```

```
<!--- Filter by stock number if needed --->
<CFIF Trim(InStock) IS NOT "">
 AND NumberInStock > 0
</CFIF>

ORDER BY title
</CFQUERY>

<!--- Include header file --->
<CFINCLUDE TEMPLATE="header.cfm">

<!--- Create table for display --->
<TABLE BORDER="1">

<!--- Table headers --->
<TR>
 <TH>Title</TH>
 <TH>Category</TH>
 <TH>Author</TH>
 <TH>Publisher</TH>
 <TH>In Stock</TH>
 <TH>Price</TH>
</TR>

<!--- Write out the retrieved data --->
<CFOUTPUT QUERY="books" STARTROW="#start#" MAXROWS="#MaxRows#">
 <TR>
  <TD>#Trim(Title)#</TD>
  <TD>#Trim(Category)#</TD>
  <TD>#Trim(AuthorLastName)#, #Trim(AuthorFirstName)#</TD>
  <TD>#Trim(Publisher)#</TD>
  <TD ALIGN="RIGHT">#NumberFormat(NumberInStock)#</TD>
  <TD ALIGN="RIGHT">#DollarFormat(Price)#</TD>
 </TR>
</CFOUTPUT>

</TABLE>

<!--- What is the next row to start at --->
<CFSET NextStart = Start + MaxRows>

<!--- Next button code --->
<CFOUTPUT>
<FORM ACTION="browse4.cfm" METHOD="POST">
<INPUT TYPE="hidden" NAME="start" VALUE="#NextStart#">
<INPUT TYPE="hidden" NAME="Title" VALUE="#Title#">
<INPUT TYPE="hidden" NAME="AuthorFirstName" VALUE="#AuthorFirstName#">
<INPUT TYPE="hidden" NAME="AuthorLastName" VALUE="#AuthorLastName#">
<INPUT TYPE="hidden" NAME="ISBN" VALUE="#isbn#">
<INPUT TYPE="hidden" NAME="CategoryID" VALUE="#CategoryID#">
<INPUT TYPE="hidden" NAME="InStock" VALUE="#InStock#">
<INPUT TYPE="submit" VALUE="Next #MaxRows#">
</FORM>
</CFOUTPUT>

<!--- Include footer file --->
<CFINCLUDE TEMPLATE="footer.cfm">
```

Part
IV

Ch
21

First of all we created a constant variable called MaxRows. This value is the maximum number of records to display at once. We used a value of 5 so that just 5 records are displayed at a time. To display 10 records at a time, just change this value to 10.

N O T E   Experienced programmers should note that ColdFusion has no real concept of constants, in that these values are not read-only and may be overwritten. The term *constant* is used here more as a descriptive notice than anything else. ▪

We added a new variable, start, to the initialization list. This variable contains the record number of the first record to display. If a start value was provided, then it is used later in this file. A value of 1 (the first record) is used if no start value is provided.

The <CFQUERY> tag did not change at all here. The process of displaying a subset of the retrieved data happens at the <CFOUTPUT> level, not at the <CFQUERY> level. <CFQUERY> retrieves all the data that matches your search, regardless of what you actually intend to display.

The filtering occurs in the <CFOUTPUT> tag, which was changed to look like this:

```
<CFOUTPUT QUERY="books" STARTROW="#start#" MAXROWS="#MaxRows#">
```

We added two attributes to this tag. The STARTROW attribute tells <CFOUTPUT> where to start displaying the data from. The variable passed to it is the variable we initialized earlier on. The MAXROWS attribute is the maximum number of rows to display. The value is the constant we set earlier, but we could have entered MAXROWS="5" as well.

Now that <CFOUTPUT> knows what data you want to display, it handles the filtering itself. If STARTROW is 1 (first page) and MAXROWS is 5, then <CFOUTPUT> displays just the first 5 records (or, if there were fewer than five, as many records as there are).

The last thing left to do now is to create the Next 5 button. As explained earlier, the next request must be self-contained, meaning that it must contain all the information needed to reconstruct the search. We added this code to the bottom of the file:

```
<!--- What is the next row to start at --->
<CFSET NextStart = Start + MaxRows>

<!--- Next button code --->
<CFOUTPUT>
<FORM ACTION="browse4.cfm" METHOD="POST">
<INPUT TYPE="hidden" NAME="start" VALUE="#NextStart#">
<INPUT TYPE="hidden" NAME="Title" VALUE="#Title#">
<INPUT TYPE="hidden" NAME="AuthorFirstName" VALUE="#AuthorFirstName#">
<INPUT TYPE="hidden" NAME="AuthorLastName" VALUE="#AuthorLastName#">
<INPUT TYPE="hidden" NAME="ISBN" VALUE="#isbn#">
<INPUT TYPE="hidden" NAME="CategoryID" VALUE="#CategoryID#">
<INPUT TYPE="hidden" NAME="InStock" VALUE="#InStock#">
<INPUT TYPE="submit" VALUE="Next #MaxRows#">
</FORM>
</CFOUTPUT>
```

First we created a new variable called NextStart, which is set to the sum of the current start value, plus the MaxRows value. This way NextStart will always be correct no matter what the start value is. You can also see now why we used a constant for the MaxRows value and didn't hard code it to 5. By using a constant, we could safely reuse that value. If you change MaxRows from 5 to 10, the calculation to determine the NextStart value would still be correct.

Next comes a form. The form has a Submit button and a whole set of hidden fields. The Submit button text uses the same MaxRows variable, again ensuring that the button text will change accordingly if you change the value. The hidden form fields embed all the original search fields into this new form. This way all the original form field values are submitted when the form is submitted, which allows you to recreate the search. We also embed NextStart as the value for the Start field. When this form is submitted, a start value that contains the correct start position is passed.

Using Previous and Next Buttons

The last task to complete our application is supporting a Previous 5 button. This allows a user to browse back and forth through the results, as shown in Figure 21.5.

FIGURE 21.5
Previous and Next buttons allow users to browse through search results.

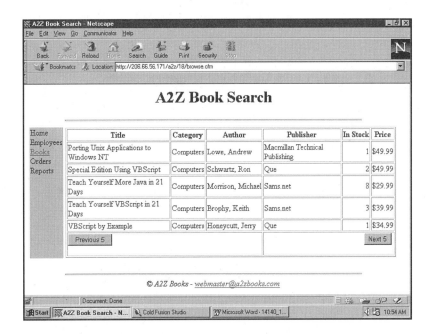

Creating a Previous 5 button is exactly the same as creating a Next 5 button, except that you need to subtract instead of add MaxRows to the current start position. The code for this updated file is shown in Listing 21.10.

Part
IV

Ch
21

Listing 21.10 `C:\A2Z\SCRIPTS\21\BROWSE5.CFM`—**Source for**
BROWSE5.CFM

```
<!---
NAME: BROWSE5.CFM

DESCRIPTION: Perform search for books in the Inventory
             table. All search fields are optional. Results
             are shown 5 records at a time, "Next 5" and
             "Previous 5" buttons are shown to allow the
             user to browse through the results.

AUTHOR: Ben Forta

DATE: 7/26/98

NOTES: This file includes HEADER.CFM and FOOTER.CFM, both
       must be present in the current directory or an error
       will be displayed.
--->

<!--- Initialize constants --->
<CFSET MaxRows = 5>

<!--- Initialize all fields if they do not exist --->
<CFPARAM NAME="start" DEFAULT="1">
<CFPARAM NAME="Title" DEFAULT="">
<CFPARAM NAME="AuthorFirstName" DEFAULT="">
<CFPARAM NAME="AuthorLastName" DEFAULT="">
<CFPARAM NAME="isbn" DEFAULT="">
<CFPARAM NAME="CategoryID" DEFAULT="">
<CFPARAM NAME="InStock" DEFAULT="">

<!--- Perform actual search, search is on a
      JOIN between Inventory and Category so that
      the category names are retrieved --->
<CFQUERY DATASOURCE="A2Z" NAME="books">
SELECT Title, AuthorFirstName, AuthorLastName,
       NumberInStock, Category, Publisher, Price
FROM Inventory, Category
WHERE Inventory.CategoryID = Category.id

<!--- Filter by title if needed --->
<CFIF Trim(Title) IS NOT "">
 AND Title LIKE '%#Trim(Title)#%'
</CFIF>

<!--- Filter by author first name if needed --->
<CFIF Trim(AuthorFirstName) IS NOT "">
 AND AuthorFirstName LIKE '#Trim(AuthorFirstName)#%'
</CFIF>

<!--- Filter by author last name if needed --->
<CFIF Trim(AuthorLastName) IS NOT "">
 AND AuthorLastName LIKE '#Trim(AuthorLastName)#%'
```

```
</CFIF>

<!--- Filter by isbn if needed --->
<CFIF Trim(isbn) IS NOT "">
 AND isbn = '#Trim(isbn)#'
</CFIF>

<!--- Filter by category if needed --->
<CFIF Trim(CategoryID) IS NOT "">
 AND CategoryId = #Trim(CategoryID)#
</CFIF>

<!--- Filter by stock number if needed --->
<CFIF Trim(InStock) IS NOT "">
 AND NumberInStock > 0
</CFIF>

ORDER BY title
</CFQUERY>

<!--- Include header file --->
<CFINCLUDE TEMPLATE="header.cfm">

<!--- Create table for display --->
<TABLE BORDER="1">

<!--- Table headers --->
<TR>
 <TH>Title</TH>
 <TH>Category</TH>
 <TH>Author</TH>
 <TH>Publisher</TH>
 <TH>In Stock</TH>
 <TH>Price</TH>
</TR>

<!--- Write out the retrieved data --->
<CFOUTPUT QUERY="books" STARTROW="#start#" MAXROWS="#MaxRows#">
 <TR>
  <TD>#Trim(Title)#</TD>
  <TD>#Trim(Category)#</TD>
  <TD>#Trim(AuthorLastName)#, #Trim(AuthorFirstName)#</TD>
  <TD>#Trim(Publisher)#</TD>
  <TD ALIGN="RIGHT">#NumberFormat(NumberInStock)#</TD>
  <TD ALIGN="RIGHT">#DollarFormat(Price)#</TD>
 </TR>
</CFOUTPUT>

<TR>

<!--- What are the previous and next row to start positions --->
<CFSET PrevStart = Start - MaxRows>
<CFSET NextStart = Start + MaxRows>

<!--- Previous button code --->
```

continues

Part
IV

Ch
21

Listing 21.10 Continued

```
<TD COLSPAN="3" ALIGN="LEFT">
<CFIF PrevStart GTE 1>
 <CFOUTPUT>
 <FORM ACTION="browse.cfm" METHOD="POST">
 <INPUT TYPE="hidden" NAME="start" VALUE="#PrevStart#">
 <INPUT TYPE="hidden" NAME="Title" VALUE="#Title#">
 <INPUT TYPE="hidden" NAME="AuthorFirstName" VALUE="#AuthorFirstName#">
 <INPUT TYPE="hidden" NAME="AuthorLastName" VALUE="#AuthorLastName#">
 <INPUT TYPE="hidden" NAME="ISBN" VALUE="#isbn#">
 <INPUT TYPE="hidden" NAME="CategoryID" VALUE="#CategoryID#">
 <INPUT TYPE="hidden" NAME="InStock" VALUE="#InStock#">
 <INPUT TYPE="submit" VALUE="Previous #MaxRows#">
 </FORM>
 </CFOUTPUT>
</CFIF>
</TD>

<TD COLSPAN="3" ALIGN="RIGHT">
<!--- Next button code --->
<CFIF NextStart LTE Books.RecordCount>
 <CFOUTPUT>
 <FORM ACTION="browse.cfm" METHOD="POST">
 <INPUT TYPE="hidden" NAME="start" VALUE="#NextStart#">
 <INPUT TYPE="hidden" NAME="Title" VALUE="#Title#">
 <INPUT TYPE="hidden" NAME="AuthorFirstName" VALUE="#AuthorFirstName#">
 <INPUT TYPE="hidden" NAME="AuthorLastName" VALUE="#AuthorLastName#">
 <INPUT TYPE="hidden" NAME="ISBN" VALUE="#isbn#">
 <INPUT TYPE="hidden" NAME="CategoryID" VALUE="#CategoryID#">
 <INPUT TYPE="hidden" NAME="InStock" VALUE="#InStock#">
 <INPUT TYPE="submit" VALUE="Next #MaxRows#">
 </FORM>
 </CFOUTPUT>
</CFIF>
</TD>

</TR>

</TABLE>

<!--- Include footer file --->
<CFINCLUDE TEMPLATE="footer.cfm">
```

This time we create variables for both the previous and next start positions:

```
<!--- What are the previous and next row to start positions --->
<CFSET PrevStart = Start - MaxRows>
<CFSET NextStart = Start + MaxRows>
```

Because both calculations use MaxRows instead of a hard coded value, you need change the MaxRows just once; the rest of your code changes automatically.

We embed two forms this time, one for the Previous 5 and one for the Next 5 button. Each one has the entire set of search fields embedded in it, as well as the appropriate start position. In addition, we also put a `<CFIF>` statement around each of the forms to prevent the buttons from displaying an invalid selection. The code `<CFIF PrevStart GTE 1>` ensures that the Previous 5 button is displayed only if the there if there are any previous records (thus, the Previous 5 button is never displayed on the first results page). The code `<CFIF NextStart LTE Books.RecordCount>` ensures that the next start position is not greater than the number of records retrieved (thus, the Next 5 button is never displayed on the last results page).

N O T E   We used forms here for the previous and next buttons. You could just as easily have used text or images and embedded the fields as URL parameters. If you do decide to use URL parameters, make sure you use the `URLEncodedFormat()` function to convert any passed text into URL safe text. ▨

Caching Query Results

The next *n* records interface is very popular within Web-based applications, particularly when there is the need to present large amounts of data within very limited screen real estate. Allowing users to browse through subsets of retrieved data, moving forward and backward as needed, is extremely convenient.

This convenience comes with a price. As you saw in Listing 21.10, the `<CFQUERY>` retrieves all the data that matches the search criteria. It is the `<CFOUTPUT>` block that restricts the display to the desired data subset. This means that if a user browses the Next 5 button 10 times, ColdFusion would have retrieved the entire result set 11 times, once for the initial results page and once for every time the Next 5 button was clicked.

As the amount of data in your application grows, and the number of concurrent users increases, the load placed on the server grows accordingly. Forcing ColdFusion to perform the same database search repeatedly can severely impact the performance of both ColdFusion and the database application. This, in turn, can bring your application's performance to a crawl.

Understanding Cached Queries

Caching your queries is the solution to this problem. *Caching* is a mechanism by which data is stored in memory when it is first read; all subsequent requests for that data use the cached data rather than the underlying database itself.

In our example, caching the results of the search allows ColdFusion to read the data only on the first results page (the one displayed by filling in the search form). All subsequent data reads (each time Next 5 or Previous 5 button is clicked) are read from the cache, not from the database.

N O T E   Cached data is stored in system memory, and the more data that is cached, the less memory there is for other applications and processes. ColdFusion administrators can control the number of queries that ColdFusion may cache, and can also disable caching altogether if required. Caching control is managed using the ColdFusion Administrator program. ▨

Cached data usually has a relatively short lifetime. At some point the data in the cache needs to be updated with newer data from the underlying database. Typically there are two ways that this can occur:

- ▪ *Timeout values* can be set when data is cached. The timeout specifies the maximum amount of time the data is to be cached; the first time the cache is used after the timeout period, the cache is flushed and the data is reread into it.

- ▪ *Manual flushing* of cached data is also allowed. This allows developers to programmatically force the cached data to be reread whenever needed.

Obviously not all queries are suited for caching. Cached data, by its very nature, can be inaccurate. The data being displayed is only as accurate as the last time data was read into the cache. The decision regarding whether to cache queries is entirely up to the developer. If data is mission critical and must always be 100% accurate, it should probably not be cached. On the other hand, data that changes less frequently might benefit substantially from being cached.

Using ColdFusion Query Caching

ColdFusion queries are cached by specifying one of two optional <CFQUERY> attributes:

- ▪ CACHEDAFTER takes an actual date/time value. Cached data will be used only if the query was retrieved after the date and time specified. This attribute takes date and time values in any of the formats supported by the ColdFusion date and time functions. Use this attribute to specify that cached is to be used only after a known date or time, or after a fixed time on each day.

- ▪ CACHEDWITH takes a time span value (created with the CreateTimeSpan() function). It specifies the maximum age of a query in days, hours, minutes, seconds, or any combination thereof. This attribute takes *relative time values*, meaning the amount of time that the query is to be considered up-to-date after it is cached. Use this attribute to specify that a cache be refreshed every 10 minutes or once an hour.

 T I P   Relative time values are generally preferred when caching data. Therefore, for most applications use caching with the CACHEDWITHIN attribute.

To improve the performance of a database query, all you need to do is include one of these two attributes. ColdFusion automatically caches the results as instructed, and subsequent references to the query results (in <CFOUTPUT>, <CFLOOP>, or any other tags or functions) will actually refer to the cached results. There is nothing you have to do to instruct ColdFusion to use the cache data rather than performing a database query; all that happens transparently and automatically.

Listing 21.11 is the final version of the browse code. Notice that the following attribute has been added to the <CFQUERY> tag:

```
CACHEDWITHIN="#CreateTimeSpan(0,0,10,0)#"
```

This CreateTimeSpan() functions returns a 10 minute time span, and the cache therefore is valid for 10 minutes from the time it was created. To change the cache interval, all you need to do is change that values passed to CreateTimeSpan(). For more information about the CreateTimeSpan() function, see Appendix B, "ColdFusion Function Reference."

Listing 21.11 C:\A2Z\SCRIPTS\21\BROWSE.CFM—**Source for BROWSE.CFM**

```
<!---
NAME: BROWSE.CFM

DESCRIPTION: Perform search for books in the Inventory
             table. All search fields are optional. Results
             are shown 5 records at a time, "Next 5" and
             "Previous 5" buttons are shown to allow the
             user to browse through the results.

AUTHOR: Ben Forta

DATE: 7/26/98

NOTES: This file includes HEADER.CFM and FOOTER.CFM, both
       must be present in the current directory or an error
       will be displayed.
--->

<!--- Initialize constants --->
<CFSET MaxRows = 5>

<!--- Initialize all fields if they do not exist --->
<CFPARAM NAME="start" DEFAULT="1">
<CFPARAM NAME="Title" DEFAULT="">
<CFPARAM NAME="AuthorFirstName" DEFAULT="">
<CFPARAM NAME="AuthorLastName" DEFAULT="">
<CFPARAM NAME="isbn" DEFAULT="">
<CFPARAM NAME="CategoryID" DEFAULT="">
<CFPARAM NAME="InStock" DEFAULT="">

<!--- Perform actual search, search is on a
      JOIN between Inventory and Category so that
      the category names are retrieved
      data is cached for 10 minutes --->
<CFQUERY DATASOURCE="A2Z" NAME="books" CACHEDWITHIN="#CreateTimeSpan(0,0,10,0)#">
SELECT Title, AuthorFirstName, AuthorLastName,
       NumberInStock, Category, Publisher, Price
FROM Inventory, Category
WHERE Inventory.CategoryID = Category.id

<!--- Filter by title if needed --->
<CFIF Trim(Title) IS NOT "">
 AND Title LIKE '%#Trim(Title)#%'
</CFIF>

<!--- Filter by author first name if needed --->
<CFIF Trim(AuthorFirstName) IS NOT "">
 AND AuthorFirstName LIKE '#Trim(AuthorFirstName)#%'
```

continues

Listing 21.11   Continued

```
</CFIF>

<!--- Filter by author last name if needed --->
<CFIF Trim(AuthorLastName) IS NOT "">
 AND AuthorLastName LIKE '#Trim(AuthorLastName)#%'
</CFIF>

<!--- Filter by isbn if needed --->
<CFIF Trim(isbn) IS NOT "">
 AND isbn = '#Trim(isbn)#'
</CFIF>

<!--- Filter by category if needed --->
<CFIF Trim(CategoryID) IS NOT "">
 AND CategoryId = #Trim(CategoryID)#
</CFIF>

<!--- Filter by stock number if needed --->
<CFIF Trim(InStock) IS NOT "">
 AND NumberInStock > 0
</CFIF>

ORDER BY title
</CFQUERY>

<!--- Include header file --->
<CFINCLUDE TEMPLATE="header.cfm">

<!--- Create table for display --->
<TABLE BORDER="1">

<!--- Table headers --->
<TR>
 <TH>Title</TH>
 <TH>Category</TH>
 <TH>Author</TH>
 <TH>Publisher</TH>
 <TH>In Stock</TH>
 <TH>Price</TH>
</TR>

<!--- Write out the retrieved data --->
<CFOUTPUT QUERY="books" STARTROW="#start#" MAXROWS="#MaxRows#">
 <TR>
  <TD>#Trim(Title)#</TD>
  <TD>#Trim(Category)#</TD>
  <TD>#Trim(AuthorLastName)#, #Trim(AuthorFirstName)#</TD>
  <TD>#Trim(Publisher)#</TD>
  <TD ALIGN="RIGHT">#NumberFormat(NumberInStock)#</TD>
  <TD ALIGN="RIGHT">#DollarFormat(Price)#</TD>
 </TR>
</CFOUTPUT>
```

```
<TR>

<!--- What are the previous and next row to start positions --->
<CFSET PrevStart = Start - MaxRows>
<CFSET NextStart = Start + MaxRows>

<!--- Previous button code --->
<TD COLSPAN="3" ALIGN="LEFT">
<CFIF PrevStart GTE 1>
 <CFOUTPUT>
 <FORM ACTION="browse.cfm" METHOD="POST">
 <INPUT TYPE="hidden" NAME="start" VALUE="#PrevStart#">
 <INPUT TYPE="hidden" NAME="Title" VALUE="#Title#">
 <INPUT TYPE="hidden" NAME="AuthorFirstName" VALUE="#AuthorFirstName#">
 <INPUT TYPE="hidden" NAME="AuthorLastName" VALUE="#AuthorLastName#">
 <INPUT TYPE="hidden" NAME="ISBN" VALUE="#isbn#">
 <INPUT TYPE="hidden" NAME="CategoryID" VALUE="#CategoryID#">
 <INPUT TYPE="hidden" NAME="InStock" VALUE="#InStock#">
 <INPUT TYPE="submit" VALUE="Previous #MaxRows#">
 </FORM>
 </CFOUTPUT>
</CFIF>
</TD>

<TD COLSPAN="3" ALIGN="RIGHT">
<!--- Next button code --->
<CFIF NextStart LTE Books.RecordCount>
 <CFOUTPUT>
 <FORM ACTION="browse.cfm" METHOD="POST">
 <INPUT TYPE="hidden" NAME="start" VALUE="#NextStart#">
 <INPUT TYPE="hidden" NAME="Title" VALUE="#Title#">
 <INPUT TYPE="hidden" NAME="AuthorFirstName" VALUE="#AuthorFirstName#">
 <INPUT TYPE="hidden" NAME="AuthorLastName" VALUE="#AuthorLastName#">
 <INPUT TYPE="hidden" NAME="ISBN" VALUE="#isbn#">
 <INPUT TYPE="hidden" NAME="CategoryID" VALUE="#CategoryID#">
 <INPUT TYPE="hidden" NAME="InStock" VALUE="#InStock#">
 <INPUT TYPE="submit" VALUE="Next #MaxRows#">
 </FORM>
 </CFOUTPUT>
</CFIF>
</TD>

</TR>

</TABLE>

<!--- Include footer file --->
<CFINCLUDE TEMPLATE="footer.cfm">
```

TIP To determine if a query is being returned from the cache or from an actual database read, turn on debugging output and look at the debug information at the bottom of the page. If the data were returned using an actual database read, the time value shown for each query will show the number of milliseconds a database request took. If the data were returned from the cache, the time value will contain the text Cached Query.

Part

IV

Ch

21

Correctly used, caching query results can dramatically improve the performance of applications that repeatedly perform the same database requests.

N O T E It is worth noting that the caching logic within ColdFusion is an example of true engineering genius. ColdFusion queries are dynamic—they can change based on passed variables, entire clauses can be changed based on embedded <CFIF> or <CFLOOP> statements, and different data may be returned if an overriding database login and password are used. The ColdFusion caching logic takes all of these into account, ensuring that caching is safe to use even within such a dynamic environment.

Lists, Arrays, and Structures

Using Advanced Data Types

The code introduced in this book's previous chapters uses ColdFusion variables extensively. *Variables*, you will recall, are named locations in memory used to store values. Variables are used to temporarily store values during processing.

Some variables are explicitly created; an example includes local variables, which are created using the <CFSET> or <CFPARAM> tags. Other variables are created automatically—FORM field and URL parameters, for example. Regardless of its type and how it was created, the variable can be used within your ColdFusion code. You simply refer to the variable by its name; ColdFusion processes the contents of that variable.

The important point here is that all of these variables are simple data types. All of these variables—whether they are local variables, cookies, FORM fields, URL parameters, or any other variable type—contain a single value. That value may be literal text, numeric data, dates, or any other data. ColdFusion variables may contain any data of any length or type.

In addition to these data types, ColdFusion supports three additional advanced data types:

- *Lists* are used to store lists of items separated by a common delimiter (for example, a comma).
- *Arrays* are used to store related information in one-, two-, or three-dimensional grids.
- *Structures* are used to manage key-value pairs or data grouped together as a set.

Don't worry if these don't make sense yet. Read on—the rest of this chapter is divided into three sections, one on each of these data types.

Working with ColdFusion Lists

ColdFusion lists are simply collections of data separated by a common delimiter or set of delimiters. Take a look at a few examples. This first is a comma-delimited list of seven states.

```
"CA,CO,FL,MA,MI,OH,PA"
```

This example is a list of words delimited by a space:

```
"ColdFusion web application language"
```

As you can see, lists can contain any data as long as there is a common delimiter.

A comma is the default list delimiter because both HTML form values and SQL lists are comma-delimited lists. Using the comma as the default delimiter makes it easier to work with these values.

To understand why you would want to use lists, look at an example. A2Z Books needs to charge tax in seven states. The following code is a ColdFusion if statement that determines whether tax is to be charged on an order:

```
<CFIF state IS "CA"
 OR state IS "CO"
 OR state IS "FL"
```

```
OR state IS "MA"
OR state IS "MI"
OR state IS "OH"
OR state IS "PA"
>
```

While the code is now readable, it is not exactly manageable. If A2Z Books were to open offices in additional states, that <CFIF> statement would have to be updated, as would every other occurrence of this logic.

This is a simpler <CFIF> statement:

```
<CFIF ListFindNoCase("CA,CO,FL,MA,MI,OH,PA", state)>
```

This example uses the ColdFusion ListFindNoCase() function, which searches for a value within a list of values. If the value is found, ListFindNoCase() returns the matching item's offset; a value of 5 is returned if state is MI. If there is no match, 0 is returned.

TIP Comparisons using simple <CFIF> operators like IS and CONTAINS are not case sensitive. List comparisons, however, can be case sensitive or not, depending on the list function used. For example, ListFind() performs a case-sensitive search; no match would have been found if state had been mi in the preceding example.

Obviously this code is simpler than the long <CFIF> statement with all of its OR conditions. The values, however, are still hard coded, so if the list of taxable states changes, you also have to change every <CFIF> statement that uses this logic.

A better solution is to use a variable that contains a list:

```
<CFIF ListFindNoCase(taxable_states, state)>
```

This way you could just use the variable taxable_states wherever needed—the list would be correct. The code is now cleaner, easier to read, and more manageable.

Creating Lists

Using the same <CFSET> or <CFPARAM> tags that you would use to create any variables is the simplest way to create a list. For example, you could use the following to create the list of states shown earlier:

```
<CFSET taxable_states="CA,CO,FL,MA,MI,OH,PA">
```

This code creates a variable named taxable_states, which is a comma-delimited list of states in which tax is to be charged.

Lists can also be created and managed programmatically using any of the list manipulation functions. The following code example creates the same list as the one just created, but it uses the ListAppend() function to append a value to an existing list. The first <CFSET> creates an empty list (a simple variable), and the subsequent <CFSET> statements append the states to the list.

```
<CFSET taxable_states="">
<CFSET taxable_states=ListAppend(taxable_states, "CA")>
```

```
<CFSET taxable_states=ListAppend(taxable_states, "CO")>
<CFSET taxable_states=ListAppend(taxable_states, "CA")>
<CFSET taxable_states=ListAppend(taxable_states, "FL")>
<CFSET taxable_states=ListAppend(taxable_states, "MA")>
<CFSET taxable_states=ListAppend(taxable_states, "MI")>
<CFSET taxable_states=ListAppend(taxable_states, "OH")>
<CFSET taxable_states=ListAppend(taxable_states, "PA")>
```

There is no right or wrong way to create lists; use whatever method works best for your application.

> **T I P** You can easily find the list manipulation functions in ColdFusion documentation or this book's
> Appendix B, "ColdFusion Function Reference." Almost all of these function start with List—
> `ListAppend()`, `ListFind()`, and `ListFindNoCase()`, for example.

Creating Data-Driven Lists

You will often find yourself working with lists that contain data retrieved from a database table. For example, the list of taxable states you used earlier would likely be stored in a database, not hard coded in your application.

You can create data-driven lists by looping through the query results and using the `ListAppend()` function to add the row to the list. The code would look something like this:

```
<!--- Get taxable states --->
<CFQUERY DATASOURCE="A2Z" NAME="taxed_states">
SELECT state_abbrev FROM taxable_states ORDER BY state_abbrev
</CFQUERY>

<!--- Create empty list --->
<CFSET taxable_states="">

<!--- Loop through results --->
<CFOUTPUT QUERY="taxed_states">
 <!--- Add this state to the list --->
 <CFSET ListAppend(taxable_states, state_abbrev)>
</CFOUTPUT>
```

While this code is neither overly complicated or difficult, ColdFusion always tries to make your coding even easier. As such, CFML included two functions for creating data-driven comma-delimited lists:

- ■ `QuotedValueList()` returns a data-driven list of values with each value enclosed within single quotation marks (which might be needed within SQL IN statements).
- ■ `ValueList()` returns a simple data-driven comma-delimited list of values.

The code preceding could be simplified by using the `ValueList()` function:

```
<!--- Get taxable states --->
<CFQUERY DATASOURCE="A2Z" NAME="taxed_states">
SELECT state_abbrev FROM taxable_states ORDER BY state_abbrev
</CFQUERY>
```

```
<!--- Create list --->
<CFSET taxable_states=ValueList(taxed_states.state_abbrev)>
```

As you can see, the code now is even cleaner than it was before.

 TIP Use the ValueList() and QuotedValueList() functions to pass the results of one <CFQUERY> to another. You might use this within an IN statement, for example.

Looping Through Lists with <CFLOOP>

In addition to using ColdFusion functions to manipulate lists, the CFML <CFLOOP> tag can be used to loop through lists one element at a time. To demonstrate this, you create a series of search forms that can be used to perform sophisticated searches against the A2Z Books inventory.

FIGURE 22.1

<TEXTAREA> boxes are useful for collecting large amounts of search data.

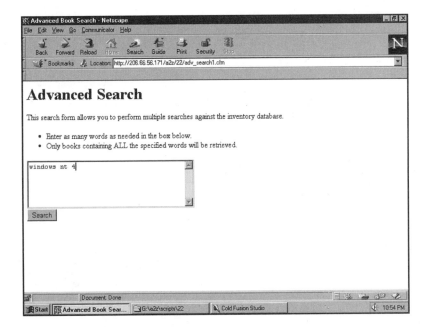

The search screen is shown in Figure 22.1. Listing 22.1 is the code that displays usage instructions and creates this simple HTML form.

Listing 22.1 ADV_SEARCH1.CFM—**Advanced Search Form**

```
<!---
NAME: ADV_SEARCH1.CFM

DESCRIPTION: Simple search form, allows specifying
             multiple search words, all of which must
```

continues

Listing 22.1 Continued

```
                match for records to be retrieved.

AUTHOR: Ben Forta

DATE: 8/16/98

--->

<HTML>

<HEAD>
<TITLE>Advanced Book Search</TITLE>
</HEAD>

<BODY>

<H1>Advanced Search</H1>
This search form allows you to perform multiple
searches against the inventory database.
<UL>
<LI>Enter as many words as needed in the box below.
<LI>Only books containing ALL the specified words will be retrieved.
</UL>
<FORM ACTION="adv_results1.cfm" METHOD="post">
<TEXTAREA NAME="search_for" COLS="40" ROWS="5" WRAP="PHYSICAL"></TEXTAREA>
<BR>
<INPUT TYPE="submit" VALUE="Search">
</FORM>

</BODY>

</HTML>
```

The results of this search are shown in Figure 22.2.

Now look at the result screenshot in Figure 22.2. Even though the search text was windows nt 4, books containing all those words were retrieved, even if the words were not in the exact order specified. In other words, the search looked for all the words individually, rather than treating the search text as a simple phrase.

To understand how this was accomplished, take a look at the actual search code shown in Listing 22.2.

Listing 22.2 ADV_RESULTS1.CFM—**Advanced Search Processing Page**

```
<!---
NAME: ADV_RESULTS1.CFM

DESCRIPTION: Perform search for books in the Inventory
             table. Allows multiple search words that are
             ANDd together.
```

```
AUTHOR: Ben Forta

DATE: 8/16/98

--->

<!--- Query --->
<CFQUERY DATASOURCE="a2z" NAME="books">
SELECT Title, AuthorFirstName, AuthorLastName,
        NumberInStock, Category, Publisher, Price
FROM Inventory, Category
WHERE Inventory.CategoryID = Category.id

<!--- Is there any search text? --->
<CFIF search_for IS NOT "">

<!--- Loop through the words  --->
<CFLOOP INDEX="word" LIST="#search_for#" DELIMITERS=" ">
 <!--- Add the AND clause --->
 AND Title LIKE '%#word#%'
</CFLOOP>

</CFIF>

ORDER BY Title
</CFQUERY>

<HTML>

<HEAD>
<TITLE>Advanced Book Search</TITLE>
</HEAD>

<BODY>

<!--- Create table for display --->
<TABLE BORDER="1">

<!--- Table headers --->
<TR>
 <TH>Title</TH>
 <TH>Category</TH>
 <TH>Author</TH>
 <TH>Publisher</TH>
 <TH>In Stock</TH>
 <TH>Price</TH>
</TR>

<!--- Write out the retrieved data --->
<CFOUTPUT QUERY="books">
 <TR>
```

continues

Listing 22.2 Continued

```
  <TD>#Trim(Title)#</TD>
  <TD>#Trim(Category)#</TD>
  <TD>#Trim(AuthorLastName)#, #Trim(AuthorFirstName)#</TD>
  <TD>#Trim(Publisher)#</TD>
  <TD ALIGN="RIGHT">#NumberFormat(NumberInStock)#</TD>
  <TD ALIGN="RIGHT">#DollarFormat(Price)#</TD>
 </TR>
</CFOUTPUT>

</TABLE>

</BODY>

</HTML>
```

FIGURE 22.2

Searches can be performed on individual words rather than complete phrases when using <CFLOOP> to loop through search text.

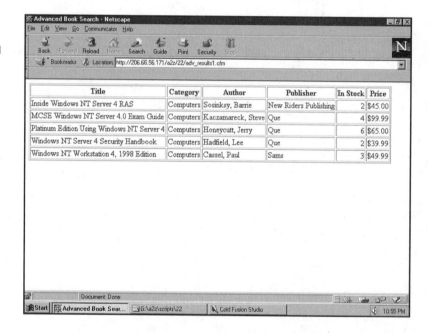

Title	Category	Author	Publisher	In Stock	Price
Inside Windows NT Server 4 RAS	Computers	Sosinksy, Barrie	New Riders Publishing	2	$45.00
MCSE Windows NT Server 4.0 Exam Guide	Computers	Kaczamareck, Steve	Que	4	$99.99
Platinum Edition Using Windows NT Server 4	Computers	Honeycutt, Jerry	Que	6	$65.00
Windows NT Server 4 Security Handbook	Computers	Hadfield, Lee	Que	2	$39.99
Windows NT Workstation 4, 1998 Edition	Computers	Cassel, Paul	Sams	3	$49.99

The code in Listing 22.2 starts with a standard <CFQUERY>. The SELECT statement creates a join on two tables, the Inventory and Category tables, and the WHERE clause creates the join. There is a <CFIF> following the WHERE clause; that tag determines whether search_for contains text for which to search. If it does, the following code is executed:

```
<CFLOOP INDEX="word" LIST="#search_for#" DELIMITERS=" ">
```

This code loops through the text in the search_for variable one word at a time. This is accomplished by specifying a space as the delimiter. This way <CFLOOP> returns each word in the word variable—one word at a time.

Each word is then added to the WHERE clause using the following code:

```
AND Title LIKE '%#word#%'
```

Processing your windows nt 4 search text generates a SQL statement that looks like this:

```
SELECT Title, AuthorFirstName, AuthorLastName,
       NumberInStock, Category, Publisher, Price
FROM Inventory, Category
WHERE Inventory.CategoryID = Category.id
AND Title LIKE '%windows%'
AND Title LIKE '%nt%'
AND Title LIKE '%4%'
ORDER BY Title
```

The rest of Listing 22.2 is standard query output code, generating the output shown in Figure 22.2.

Lists of Lists

So far you have seen lists of text and words delimited by commas and spaces. ColdFusion lists can contain any data, even other lists. To demonstrate this, enhance the advanced search screens you just created. Figure 22.3 shows the new search screen, complete with detailed usage instructions.

The code to create this form is shown in Listing 22.3.

FIGURE 22.3
Complex search screens should always contain usage instructions (and examples, if appropriate).

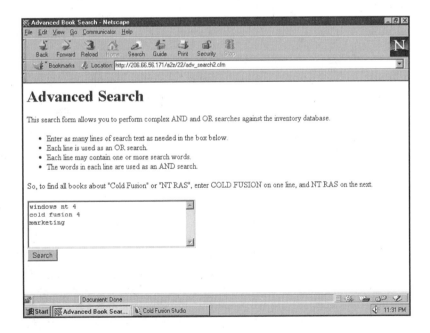

Listing 22.3 `ADV_SEARCH2.CFM`—**Advanced Search Form**

```
<!---
NAME: ADV_SEARCH2.CFM

DESCRIPTION: Advanced search form, allows specifying
             multiple search lines and words to create
             sophisticated AND and OR conditions.

AUTHOR: Ben Forta

DATE: 8/16/98

--->

<HTML>

<HEAD>
<TITLE>Advanced Book Search</TITLE>
</HEAD>

<BODY>

<H1>Advanced Search</H1>
This search form allows you to perform complex AND and OR
searches against the inventory database.
<UL>
<LI>Enter as many lines of search text as needed in the box below.
<LI>Each line is used as an OR search.
<LI>Each line may contain one or more search words.
<LI>The words in each line are used as an AND search.
</UL>
So, to find all books about &quot;ColdFusion&quot; or
&quot;NT RAS&quot;, enter COLD FUSION on one line, and
NT RAS on the next.
<FORM ACTION="adv_results2.cfm" METHOD="post">
<TEXTAREA NAME="search_for" COLS="40" ROWS="5" WRAP="PHYSICAL"></TEXTAREA>
<BR>
<INPUT TYPE="submit" VALUE="Search">
</FORM>

</BODY>

</HTML>
```

This new search screen allows the user to perform very sophisticated searches. Searches may be comprised of multiple searches, and each search may be comprised of multiple words. To find books containing one or more words, those words are typed on one line. Only books containing all the words in that line are retrieved. Additional searches may be specified too, one on each line.

The screen shot in Figure 22.3 is performing three different searches: any books containing the words windows, nt, and 4, any books containing the word coldfusion and 4, and any books containing the word marketing. The search results are shown in Figure 22.4.

FIGURE 22.4

<CFLOOP> tags can be nested to perform sophisticated list manipulation.

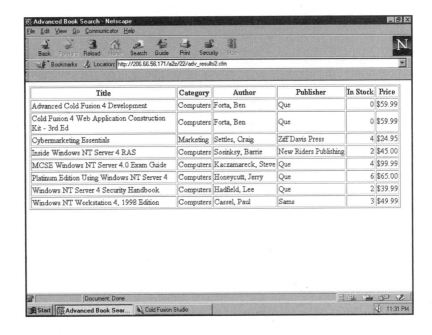

The code that performed the actual search is shown in Listing 22.4.

Listing 22.4 ADV_RESULTS2.CFM—Advanced Search Processing Page

```
<!---
NAME: ADV_RESULTS2.CFM

DESCRIPTION: Perform search for books in the Inventory
             table. Allows sophisticated AND and OR searching,
             each line in "search_for" is a OR clause, and each
             word in each line is a AND clause within that OR
             clause.

EXAMPLE: If the following text was specified:
         COLDFUSION
          NT RAS
         MARKETING
         then any books that contained COLDFUSION, or
         NT and RAS, or MARKETING, would be selected.

AUTHOR: Ben Forta

DATE: 8/16/98

--->

<!--- Initialize constants --->
<CFSET CRLF="#Chr(13)##Chr(10)#">
```

continues

Listing 22.4 Continued

```
<!--- Query --->
<CFQUERY DATASOURCE="a2z" NAME="books">
SELECT Title, AuthorFirstName, AuthorLastName,
        NumberInStock, Category, Publisher, Price
FROM Inventory, Category
WHERE Inventory.CategoryID = Category.id

<!--- Is there any search text? --->
<CFIF search_for IS NOT "">

<!--- Dummy clause for first of the ORd clauses --->
AND (0=1
<!--- Loop through each line --->
<CFLOOP INDEX="line" LIST="#search_for#" DELIMITERS="#CRLF#">
 <!--- For each line, OR another list of ANDd clauses --->
 OR (0=0
 <!--- Loop through the words in this line --->
 <CFLOOP INDEX="word" LIST="#line#" DELIMITERS=" ">
  <!--- Add the AND clause --->
  AND Title LIKE '%#word#%'
 </CFLOOP>
 )
</CFLOOP>
)

</CFIF>

ORDER BY Title
</CFQUERY>

<HTML>

<HEAD>
<TITLE>Advanced Book Search</TITLE>
</HEAD>

<BODY>

<!--- Create table for display --->
<TABLE BORDER="1">

<!--- Table headers --->
<TR>
 <TH>Title</TH>
 <TH>Category</TH>
 <TH>Author</TH>
 <TH>Publisher</TH>
 <TH>In Stock</TH>
 <TH>Price</TH>
</TR>

<!--- Write out the retrieved data --->
<CFOUTPUT QUERY="books">
```

```
<TR>
 <TD>#Trim(Title)#</TD>
 <TD>#Trim(Category)#</TD>
 <TD>#Trim(AuthorLastName)#, #Trim(AuthorFirstName)#</TD>
 <TD>#Trim(Publisher)#</TD>
 <TD ALIGN="RIGHT">#NumberFormat(NumberInStock)#</TD>
 <TD ALIGN="RIGHT">#DollarFormat(Price)#</TD>
 </TR>
</CFOUTPUT>

</TABLE>

</BODY>

</HTML>
```

Listing 22.4 is very similar to Listing 22.3, with one major difference: The dynamic WHERE clause is now constructed via nested <CFLOOP> tags. The outer <CFLOOP> loops through one line at a time, using carriage return and linefeed characters as delimiters. A variable containing these variables (which are not printable) simplify working with these characters:

```
<CFSET CRLF="#Chr(13)##Chr(10)#">
```

CRLF can be used as a delimiter this way.

The outer <CFLOOP> returns one line at a time in the variable line; the inner <CFLOOP> then loops through that line, extracting each word within it by specifying a space as a delimiter.

The search text specified in the screenshot shown in Figure 22.3 would thus generate the following SQL:

```
SELECT Title, AuthorFirstName, AuthorLastName,
       NumberInStock, Category, Publisher, Price
FROM Inventory, Category
WHERE Inventory.CategoryID = Category.id
AND (0=1
     OR
➡(0=0 AND TITLE LIKE '%windows%' AND Title LIKE '%nt%' AND Title LIKE '%4%')
     OR
➡(0=0 AND TITLE LIKE '%cold%' AND Title LIKE '%fusion%' AND Title LIKE '%4%')
     OR (0=0 AND TITLE LIKE '%marketing%')
     )
ORDER BY Title
```

There you have it: extremely powerful and flexible searching, with minimal changes to your code.

List Manipulation Functions

In addition to supporting looping through lists, ColdFusion provides a complete set of list manipulation functions, as listed in Table 22.1. Most of these functions take an optional last attribute, which specifies the list delimiter to be used. If this parameter is omitted, the default delimiter (a comma) is used.

Table 22.1   List Manipulation Functions

Function	Description
ArrayToList()	Converts an array to a list; returns a list
ListAppend()	Appends an element to a list; returns updated list
ListChangeDelims()	Changes a list's delimiters; returns new list using new delimiters
ListContains()	Case-sensitive substring search; returns index of matching element or 0 if not found
ListContainsNoCase()	Non–case-sensitive substring search; returns index of matching element or 0 if not found
ListDeleteAt()	Deletes an element from a list; returns updated list
ListFind()	Case-sensitive search for an element within a list; returns index of matching element or 0 if not found
ListFindNoCase()	Non–case-sensitive search for an element within a list; returns index of matching element or 0 if not found
ListFirst()	Returns the first element in a list
ListGetAt()	Returns a specific element in a list
ListInsertAt()	Inserts an element into a list at a specified position; returns updated list
ListLast()	Returns the last element in a list
ListLen()	Returns the number of elements in a list
ListPrepend()	Inserts an element at the front of a list; returns updated list
ListRest()	Returns all elements after the first element in a list
ListSetAt()	Updates a specific element in a list; returns updated list
ListToArray()	Converts a list to an array; returns an array
QuotedValueList()	Creates a data-driven list with each element enclosed within single quotation marks; returns the list
ValueList()	Creates a data-driven list; returns the list

Working with ColdFusion Arrays

Arrays are special variables that contain sets of data rather than individual bits of information. Whereas a variable contains one piece of information, an array is a list of variables that each contain information. Like lists, array elements are referenced by number. Unlike lists, arrays have no special delimiter, nor are they limited to a single dimension. In fact, ColdFusion has built in support for one-, two-, and three-dimensional arrays.

N O T E   ColdFusion arrays may contain any data, including text, numbers, lists, and even other arrays. ■

Understanding Arrays

To understand when you would want to use arrays, look at a sample scenario. A2Z Books has an online store that allows customers to browse books and add them to a shopping cart. As users browse the inventory and add items to the shopping cart, you need some place to store their selections. You would probably not want to store these selections in a database table because they are temporary selections and need only be maintained for the duration of the online session. In addition, users will often leave the site without completing the transaction; if the selections were stored in a database table, you'd have to perform maintenance and remove any incomplete transactions.

The solution is to store these values in variables in memory until a transaction is completed. You add or remove data within these variables as users add to or remove from the shopping cart. Only once a transaction is completed would you actually commit it to the database.

The information you need to track is the book identifier (ISBN) and the quantity ordered. How do you actually store the data?

One solution is to use standard variables. You could create a series of variables perhaps named ISBN_1, ISBN_2, ISBN_3 and QUANTITY_1, QUANTITY_2, QUANTITY_3 and so on—but how do you manipulate these? You can only support a fixed number of items, and if the second item in the shopping cart were removed you'd have to shift all the values between the various variables. That code could get rather complex and unmanageable.

A better solution is to store the data in a two-dimensional array. Imagine a two-dimensional array as a spreadsheet-style grid. You'd define an array two columns wide, one for the ISBN and one for the quantity. The code that creates the array looks like this:

```
<CFSET shopping_cart=ArrayNew(2)>
```

This creates a two-dimensional array named shopping_cart. The array is initially empty, and a call to the ArrayLen() function returns 0.

Elements are added to the array as items are added to the shopping cart. If the first item the user ordered was three copies of ISBN 078971809X, you could use the following <CFSET> statements to set the appropriate elements in the array:

```
<CFSET shopping_cart[1][1]="078971809X">
<CFSET shopping_cart[1][2]="3">
```

Array elements are set using the standard <CFSET> tags. The variables passed to <CFSET> specify the array element to be set. shopping_cart[1][1] refers to the first column in the fist row of array shopping_cart; shopping_cart[1][2] refers to the second column in the fist row of array shopping_cart. You keep adding rows to the array as items are added to the shopping cart. To add a second book, you need to add the items into the second row in the array:

```
<CFSET shopping_cart[2][1]="0789718103">
<CFSET shopping_cart[2][2]="2">
```

Of course, doing this requires that you manually keep track of the number of rows in the array. A better solution follows:

```
<CFSET shopping_cart[ArrayLen(shopping_cart)+1][1]="078971809X">
<CFSET shopping_cart[ArrayLen(shopping_cart)][2]="3">
```

Here you use the `ArrayLen()` function to return the size of the array. The following code lines are equivalent to one another:

```
<CFSET shopping_cart[ArrayLen(shopping_cart)+1][1]="078971809X">
```

```
<CFSET shopping_cart[2][1]="078971809X">
```

ColdFusion arrays are *dynamic*. This means that if you refer to a row that does not exist, it is automatically created. If an array has 5 rows and you try to set a value in row 10, rows 6 through 10 are automatically created and the value you specified is saved in row 10. Rows 6 through 9 would be empty, but they would exist. The following code returns the current length of the array plus 1:

```
ArrayLen(shopping_cart)+1
```

When you set a value in that row the array is automatically resized.

To delete or change items in the shopping cart, just remove or overwrite values in the array.

N O T E This is not a complete discussion of shopping carts and online commerce. For details on these topics see Chapter 25, "Online Commerce." ■

Array Manipulation Functions

ColdFusion provides a complete set of array manipulation functions; they're listed in Table 22.2.

Table 22.2   Array Manipulation Functions

Function	Description
ArrayApend()	Appends an element to an array; returns TRUE if successful, FALSE if not
ArrayAvg()	Returns the average value of values in an array
ArrayClear()	Deletes the data in an array (but not the array itself); returns TRUE if successful, FALSE if not
ArrayDeleteAt()	Deletes a specific element in an array, renumbering any elements after the deleted one; returns TRUE if successful, FALSE if not
ArrayInsertAt()	Inserts data into an array; returns TRUE if successful, FALSE if not
ArrayIsEmpty()	Determines whether an array is empty; returns TRUE if empty, FALSE if not
ArrayLen()	Returns the length of an array
ArrayMax()	Returns the largest value in an array

Function	Description
ArrayMin()	Returns the smallest value in an array
ArrayNew()	Creates a new array; returns the array itself
ArrayPrepend()	Inserts an element at the front of an array; returns TRUE if successful, FALSE if not
ArrayResize()	Resizes an array; returns TRUE if successful, FALSE if not
ArraySet()	Sets the elements in an array to a specific value; returns TRUE if successful, FALSE if not
ArraySort()	Sorts the contents of an array; returns the sorted array
ArraySum()	Returns the sum of the contents in an array
ArraySwap()	Swaps the values in two array elements; returns TRUE if successful, FALSE if not
ArrayToList()	Converts an array to a list; returns a list
IsArray()	Determines if a variable is an array; returns TRUE if yes, FALSE if not
ListToArray()	Converts a list to an array; returns an array

TIP Finding the array manipulation functions in ColdFusion documentation or in Appendix B is easy. Almost all of these functions start with Array—ArrayAppend(), ArrayNew(), and ArrayLen(), for example.

N O T E Database queries returned by the <CFQUERY> tag are actually two-dimensional arrays. As such, you can refer to specific query rows and columns using array syntax if needed. ▨

Working with ColdFusion Structures

Structures are similar to arrays, but elements are referred to by name rather than by index. Structures can be used to create custom data types, whereas a single variable contains multiple variables.

N O T E Unlike arrays, structures are not multidimensional. Structures store name value pairs only. ▨

Understanding Structures

These structure examples start simple. Suppose you have a block of code that manipulates employee information. The code that creates the variables might look like this:

```
<CFSET FirstName="Ben">
<CFSET LastName="Forta">
<CFSET HomePage="http://www.forta.com">
<CFSET EMail="ben@forta.com">
```

You would have to pass each variable separately in order to pass them between templates (perhaps as tag attributes). Similarly, if you need to reset the data so you can work with another employee's data, you need to clear and set each variable individually.

A better way to manage the data is to create a structure in which to store it. The code would look like this:

```
<CFSET Employee=StructNew()>
<CFSET Employee.FirstName="Ben">
<CFSET Employee.LastName="Forta">
<CFSET Employee.HomePage="http://www.forta.com">
<CFSET Employee.EMail="ben@forta.com">
```

The individual variables within a structure are called *keys*. A value is accessed by referring to its key. You can access these values via referring to them by their fully qualified key names. For example, the following code displays the first and last names:

```
<CFOUTPUT>
#Employee.FirstName# #Employee.LastName#
</CFOUTPUT>
```

To pass this data to another tag, all you need to pass is the structure, not the individual variables. Similarly, you could use a single function (StructClear()) to reinitialize the data; any keys are reinitialized automatically, without specifying individual names.

Structures can also be used as associative arrays. To understand this concept, imagine arrays where elements are referred to by name rather than by index. The following example adds two employees to a structure and assigns an email address for each:

```
<CFSET Employees=StructNew()>
<CFSET temp=StructInsert(Employees, "Ben", "ben@forta.com">
<CFSET temp=StructInsert(Employees, "John", "webmaster@a2z.com">
```

There are three ways to refer to Ben's email address. Depending on the code you are writing and the contents of the structure, one method may work better than another.

As an associative array:

```
#Employees[Ben]#
```

As a structured variable:

```
#Employees.Ben#
```

Using structure functions:

```
#StructFind(Employees, Ben)#
```

It is also possible to loop through arrays using the <CFLOOP> tag's COLLECTION attribute.

Structure Manipulation Functions

Many of the standard ColdFusion tags and functions can be used to manipulate structures. This includes `IsDefined()`, which determines whether a key exists, and `<CFSET>`, which sets a value. For more precise structure manipulation, ColdFusion provides a complete set of structure manipulation functions. These are listed in Table 22.3

Table 22.3   Structure Manipulation Functions

Function	Description
`IsStruct()`	Determines whether a specified variable is a valid ColdFusion structure
`StructClear()`	Removes all data from a structure, keeping the structure itself intact
`StructCopy()`	Makes a copy of a structure
`StructCount()`	Returns the number of keys in a structure
`StructDelete()`	Deletes a structure
`StructFind()`	Returns the value for a specified key
`StructInsert()`	Inserts a key value pair into a structure
`StructIsEmpty()`	Determines whether a structure is empty
`StructKeyExists()`	Checks to see if a key exists within a structure
`StructNew()`	Creates a new structure
`StructUpdate()`	Updates a key value pair within a structure

Enhancing Forms with CFFORM

Working with CFFORM

This chapter covers two concepts. The major concept, which encompasses the entire chapter, is that although forms are good, they can be better. ColdFusion goes beyond the standard HTML form capabilities by incorporating easy-to-use controls that allow data validation, enhanced population from queries, and totally new form types with Java. This brings us to the chapter's second concept.

If you are morally opposed to Java, prepare to have your views challenged. ColdFusion has incorporated several small, stable, and useful Java applets into its core system with easy-to-program controls for them. You should find these tags not only easy to use, but also a major enhancement to some ways of viewing data. All the standard Java fear should go out the window after you see these new tags in action. You don't have to worry about programming Java, learning applet syntax, or even looking at class files. This is Java without fear. On the other hand, those who feel that Java is a religion may be a bit disappointed. ColdFusion uses Java as a tool to enhance a Web page and allow better display of information. The Java here is used in a controlled way that allows non-Java programmers and even non-programmers to take advantage of its power.

Almost all the tags in this chapter use JavaScript for data validation and value control. This is JavaScript that's already written for you and that does not have to be touched at all. You'll probably never even look at it. You can actually go and see the JavaScript used by looking at a file named cfform.js in the C:\CFusion\Scripts\directory. (Some systems may vary on CFusion directory placement.)

Using CFFORM

Before you get into the CFFORM subtags, you have to discuss the tag that controls them all—CFFORM. To avoid confusion, I will refer to the various tags that go inside the CFFORM block as *subtags*. Every tag discussed in this chapter (with the exception of CFGRIDUPDATE) must be placed within a CFFORM block. CFFORM is a small replacement for the standard HTML form tag that allows you to include the CFFORM subtags onto a page. When a page is actually run, the CFFORM tag creates a standard HTML form element containing links to the JavaScript code mentioned earlier as well as to the Java tags mentioned later. On the whole, there's really very little difference between the CFFORM tag and the HTML form tag. First you read about the tag itself and then you go back to CFFORM in general. Table 23.1 shows the various attributes of the CFFORM tag.

On the CD

Table 23.1 CFFORM **Attributes**

Name	Status	Description
NAME	Optional	A name for the form you are creating.
ACTION	Required	The name of the ColdFusion page that is executed when the form is submitted for processing. This is the same thing as the

Name	Status	Description
		standard HTML form action. For more information, look at the HTML reference on the CD-ROM that accompanies this book.
ENABLECAB	Optional	Values are Yes or No with a default of No. This element provides downloadable Microsoft cabinet (*.cab) files containing the Java classes used for CFFORM that include Java. If ENABLECAB is Yes, the users are asked whether they want to download the *.cab file. Note that these files are digitally signed using VeriSign digital IDs to ensure file security. Downloading the Java class *.cab files dramatically reduces the time required to load pages with CFFORM controls that incorporate a Java applet. The ENABLECAB attribute is supported only for MS Internet Explorer clients that have Authenticode 2.0 installed. At the time of this writing, there is no Netscape version of this technology.
METHOD	Required	This is the standard HTML method attribute that specifies how the form is sent. The standard options are Get and Post, with Get being the usual default. For more information, look at the HTML reference on the CD-ROM accompanying this book.
TARGET	Optional	This is the standard HTML target syntax. This is used to specify what frame the form should be posted to. For more information, look at the HTML reference on the CD-ROM.
ENCTYPE	Optional	This is the standard HTML form encoding declaration. Currently, the options are application/x-www-form-urlencoded for standard forms and multipart/form-data for forms using file uploading. The default is application/x-www-form-urlencoded. For more information, look at the HTML reference on the CD-ROM.
ONSUBMIT	Optional	JavaScript function to execute after other input validation returns. Use this attribute to execute JavaScript for preprocessing data before the form is submitted.

As you can see, most of the CFFORM attributes are the same as the standard HTML form attributes. In truth, the CFFORM tag will even accept attributes not specified in Table 23.1. Any HTML form attribute that exists now or in the future can be added, and it will be passed directly to the page.

Because CFFORM itself does nothing other than hold ColdFusion and HTML form subtags, I'm not going to give any specific examples. On the other hand, every CFFORM tag example will have a CFFORM tag around it. This emphasizes the nature of the tag; it holds form elements.

Types of CFFORM Subtags

Now that you understand the basic framework of the CFFORM tag, you can examine the subtags. To do so, I'm going to divide the tags into classes.

The first class comprises CFSELECT and the various types of CFINPUT tags. These tags are processed on the server side and give an output of standard HTML. These server-side tags are basically there to enhance both the population and validation of what can be seen as standard tags.

The remainder tags are all processed on the client side using small, standardized Java applets. These client-side tags are further divided into classes based on functionality:

- The first class can be referred to as *simple tags*. They are called simple because they have a single tag do all their work. The tags of this class are currently limited to CFTEXTINPUT and CFSLIDER.

- The second class is referred to as the *container tags*. This class is currently made up of the CFTREE and the CFGRID tags as well as their subelements. These are called containers because they can contain subtags that allow greater control over their functionality.

- The third class is the *container class*. They have no function on their own and can only be used inside the appropriate container. These tags are CFGRIDROW, CFGRIDCOLUMN, and CFTREEITEM.

- The CFAPPLET tag is a special case that falls outside the standard definition of classes. This tag is used to include a foreign Java applet in ColdFusion. You learn more about this tag later. Just be aware that few of the standard CFFORM tag rules apply to CFAPPLET.

The only other exception is the CFGRIDUPDATE tag. This is actually not a CFFORM tag but only works in conjunction with the CFGRID tag. As such it will be discussed here, but none of the CFFORM rules apply to CFGRIDUPDATE.

Other CFFORM-Related Issues

Before discussing the individual tags, a few other CFFORM-related issues should be examined.

Speed and CFFORMs   The CFFORM tag by itself adds only a tiny amount of extra code to the HTML page and takes almost no time to process. The speed problem comes in when you start to use the Java elements. These can take a few moments to download and start running on a system. To combat this, ColdFusion uses a technique created by Microsoft for use with its browser. By setting the EnableCab attribute to Yes, any Java form element on a page can be installed on a Microsoft Web browser. This does require Authenticode security on the client side, but most Microsoft browsers already have it installed. The end result is that instead of downloading a new copy of the applet every time you want to use it on a page, the version installed on the client is called. Clients have the option to disregard this if they want, so there will be few complaints.

Images and CFFORM Tags   Many of the CFFORM tags allow the inclusion of images in various manners. Because the CFFORM tags are Java, these images must be in a special directory in relation to the Java class files. The standard location is in your Web server's \CFIDE\Classes\images\ directory. Any images that you may want to include in a CFFORM tag must be either in this directory or a subdirectory of this location. Both .gif and .jpg files can be used, and the size of the file is relatively unlimited. Remember that the graphic has to be downloaded with the Java applet for a CFFORM tag, so don't try to use a 5MB file. ColdFusion ships with a number of default images that are mainly used for CFTREE and CFGRID. Figure 23.1 shows these standard images by name.

FIGURE 23.1

Standard images shipped with ColdFusion.

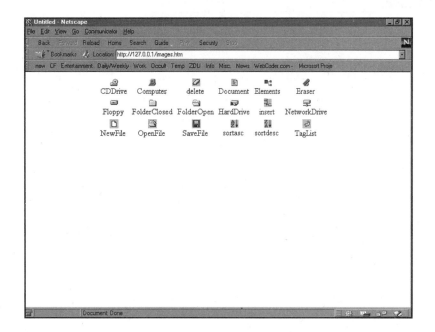

These images are all square .gif files with a byte size of less than 1KB and a graphic size of either 18×18 or 16×16. These graphics were included so that you can easily show disks, folders, drives, and so on. Because the main reason for the CFFORM tags is to enhance the data display, the inclusion of these graphics just makes it better. It should be noted that some tags use an alias for some of these images. The exact name of the alias is included in the attributes for the tags in question.

Colors and CFFORM Tags   Many CFFORM elements allow different colors to be used in many places. These colors can either be placed in a standard hexadecimal format or as predefined color names. If the hexadecimal format is used, the value must either use two pound (#) signs before it or none at all. If you are using the predefined colors, you are limited to black, magenta, cyan, orange, darkgrey, pink, gray, white, lightgray, and yellow. Note that these colors should be written as single words.

Common Attributes for Client-Side Tags   All client side tags have many of the same attributes in common. These attributes have been divided into tables that describe their general functions.

Table 23.2 contains the standard attributes supported by all the CFFORM Java tags. These range from the required NAME attribute through error validation calls on to formatting codes. These are supported by all the standard CFFORM tags. Of all these attributes, the ones that will seem most familiar are the formatting codes. Many of these attributes mirror the HTML of the same type.

Part

IV

Ch

23

Table 23.2 Common Attributes for CFFORM Java Tags

Name	Status	Description
NAME	Required	A name for the CFFORM element. This has the same effect as any name element in a standard form tag. Every CFFORM tag must have a name element associated with it. Two CFFORM tags with the same name will result in the later element being sent. The receiving template will see the result as Form.Name.
NoTSUPPORTED	Optional	The text you want to display if the page containing a Java applet-based CFFORM control is opened by a browser that does not support Java or has Java support disabled. This must be in standard HTML. For example: `NoTSUPPORTED="<B> Browser must support Java to view ColdFusion Java Applets</B>"` By default, the following message appears if no message is specified: `<B>Browser must support Java to  view ColdFusion Java Applets!</B>`
ONVALIDATE	Optional	The name of a valid JavaScript function used to validate user input. The form object, input object, and input object value are passed to the specified routine, which should return `true` if validation succeeds and `false` otherwise. The use of this element overrides the VALIDATE attribute when it exists.
ONERROR	Optional	The name of a valid JavaScript function you want to execute in the event of a failed validation. This only applies if ONVALIDATE is used.
ALIGN	Optional	Alignment value for the CFFORM element. Valid entries are `top`, `middle`, `left`, `right`, `bottom`, `baseline`, `texttop`, `absbottom`, and `absmiddle`. This is the same as standard HTML alignment format.
BOLD	Optional	Enter `Yes` for boldface text, `No` for regular text. This has the same effect as `<B></B>` in HTML. The default is `No`.
FONT	Optional	Font name for text. The available fonts are limited to those built in to the Java language and are listed on the CD-ROM that accompanies this book.
FONTSIZE	Optional	Font size for text.
HEIGHT	Optional	The control's height value in pixels. This is the same as standard HTML height formatting.
HSPACE	Optional	Horizontal spacing of the control. This is the same as standard HTML HSPACE formatting.
ITALIC	Optional	Enter `Yes` for italicized text, `No` for normal text. This has the same effect as `<I></I>` in HTML. Default is `No`.

Name	Status	Description
VSPACE	Optional	Vertical spacing of the control. This is the same as standard HTML VSPACE formatting.
WIDTH	Optional	The control's width value in pixels. This is the same as standard HTML width formatting.

CFFORMs and ColdFusion Studio   In general, ColdFusion Studio makes the creation of CFFORMs rather easy. You can just select the tag you want, fill in the attributes, and it's ready to roll. There are a few limitations though. The first can stop any CFFORM-containing page in its tracks. As mentioned earlier, hexadecimal colors have to be prefixed either with two pound (#) signs or with none. The CFFORM wizards always give you the hexadecimal color with a single pound sign. This means that you have to go over all the code to either add or remove a sign to avoid an error. The other killer problem is a little over-enthusiasm when the tag wizards were being written up. Tags were written for CFINPUT with the types submit, hidden, file, button, and image. Not only are these not part of the CFINPUT tag, but using any of these options will cause an error on the processing of the ColdFusion page. The only other limitation of the Studio tag wizards is that they do not give options for the NOTSUPPORTED, ONVALIDATE, and ONERROR attributes. If you want these attributes, you have to add them by hand or depend on the tag-completion helper. Because of the number of tags and other considerations, I won't show all the tag wizards in action.

Using CFSELECT

CFSELECT was created just to help out ColdFusion programmers. In the old days, when someone wanted to populate an HTML form select with a query, she had to write some rather long code. This was easy for those who used ColdFusion a lot, but for new people it was just something that had to be learned. CFSELECT took away the need for that chunk of code and wrapped it in a simple interface. Compare the two pieces of code that had to be used. Both use the this query:

```
<CFQUERY NAME="GetData" DATASOURCE="CF 3.0 Examples">
        SELECT Employee_ID, FirstName + ' ' + LastName AS FullName FROM Employees
</CFQUERY>
```

This was the old way:

```
<Form ACTION="Test.cfm"
     METHOD="POST">
<SELECT NAME="Employees"
              Size="1">
<CFOUTPUT QUERY="GetData">
    <OPTION VALUE="#Employee_ID#" <CFIF #Employee_ID# is "12">
➥TED</CFIF>>#FullName#
</CFOUTPUT>
</SELECT>
</form>
The new way, using the CFSELECT tag:
```

```
<CFFORM ACTION="Test.cfm"
        METHOD="POST">
<CFSELECT NAME="Employees"
        SIZE="1"
        QUERY="GetData"
        VALUE="Employee_ID"
        DISPLAY="FullName"
        SELECTED="12">
</CFSELECT>
</CFFORM>
```

Now the CFSELECT method is a bit tighter, probably faster to write, and a bit nicer to look at. The results are exactly the same, but you have a slight difference in power. The old method allows you much finer control over the outputted variables. What happens if you want to select more than one Employee_ID? CFSELECT doesn't allow that, but it's rather easy to add an OR statement to the old method. The entire point is that you should look at the job in question and use the method that best suits it.

The result of a CFSELECT method is the same as a standard HTML form element. Table 23.3 shows this tag's attributes.

```
Form.Select_name=select_value
```

Table 23.3 CFSELECT Attributes

Name	Status	Description
NAME	Required	A name for the form you are creating.
SIZE	Required	Size of the drop-down list box in number of entries.
REQUIRED	Optional	Yes or No. If Yes, a list element must be selected when the form is submitted. Default is No.
MESSAGE	Optional	Message that appears if REQUIRED="Yes" and no selection is made.
ONERROR	Optional	The name of a valid JavaScript function you want to execute in the event of a failed validation.
MULTIPLE	Optional	Yes or No. Yes permits selection of multiple elements in the drop-down list box. The default is No.
QUERY	Optional	Name of the query to be used to populate the drop-down list box.
SELECTED	Optional	Enter a value matching at least one entry in VALUE to preselect the entry in the drop-down list box.
VALUE	Optional	The query column value for the list element. Used with the QUERY attribute.
DISPLAY	Optional	The query column displayed. Defaults to the value of VALUE. Used with the QUERY attribute.

Using CFINPUT

As you've seen, the CFSELECT tag helped with the population of query results. The CFINPUT tag exists to help more with data validation than with straight population. As mentioned earlier, this data validation is done by JavaScript. In a moment, you look at this tag and compare it to both the standard HTML input tag and to the client-side Java CFTEXTINPUT tag. First look at the variables for the tag. Table 23.4 shows the attributes for CFINPUT.

Table 23.4 CFINPUT **Attributes**

Name	Status	Description
TYPE	Optional	Valid entries are:
		Text(default)—Creates a text entry box control.
		Radio—Creates a radio button control.
		Checkbox—Creates a check box control.
		Password—Creates a password entry control.
		All other CFINPUT types are invalid.
NAME	Required	A name for the form input element.
VALUE	Optional	An initial value for the form input element.
REQUIRED	Optional	Enter Yes or No. Default is No.
RANGE	Optional	Enter a minimum value; maximum value range separated by a comma. Valid only for numeric data.
VALIDATE	Optional	Valid entries are:
		date—Verifies U.S. date entry in the form mm/dd/yyyy.
		eurodate—Verifies valid European date entry in the form dd/mm/yyyy.
		time—Verifies a time entry in the form hh:mm:ss.
		float—Verifies a floating-point entry.
		integer—Verifies an integer entry.
		telephone—Verifies a telephone entry. Telephone data must be entered as ###-###-####. The hyphen separator (-) can be replaced with a blank. The area code and exchange must begin with a digit between 1 and 9.
		zipcode—(U.S. formats only) Number can be a five-digit or nine-digit zip in the form #####-####. The hyphen separator (-) can be replaced with a blank.

continues

Part
IV

Ch

23

Table 23.4   Continued

Name	Status	Description
		creditcard—Blanks and dashes are stripped, and the number is verified using the mod10 algorithm.
		social_security_number—Number must be entered as ###-##-####. The hyphen separator (-) can be replaced with a blank.
ONVALIDATE	Optional	The name of a valid JavaScript function used to validate user input. The form object, input object, and input object value are passed to the specified routine, which should return true if validation succeeds and false otherwise. When used, the VALIDATE attribute is ignored.
MESSAGE	Optional	Message text to appear if validation fails.
ONERROR	Optional	The name of a valid JavaScript function you want to execute in the event of a failed validation.
SIZE	Optional	The size of the input control. Ignored if TYPE is Radio or Checkbox.
MAXLENGTH	Optional	The maximum length of text entered when TYPE is Text.
CHECKED	Optional	Places checkmark when TYPE is Checkbox; preselects radio buttons when TYPE is Radio.

To get the best idea of the CFINPUT tag, I'm going to hold off the description until the next section, which is on CFTEXTINPUT. This is the Java version of the input tag and by comparing the methods, you can see which is best in what circumstances.

Using CFTEXTINPUT

The CFTEXTINPUT tag is a close relative to the HTML INPUT=text tag. To really show what the CFTEXTINPUT tag is, you should compare it to the other methods of inputting text.

Figure 23.2 shows the three different forms of text input supported by ColdFusion. You'll notice that they are almost exactly the same except that the Java version (third) is smaller and slightly nicer looking. This is discussed later.

The three displays are built on three different pieces of code that do the same basic thing. The first is the basic form input code. Notice that the actual code is two tags rather than one because the second is needed to specify that the value is required. The advantage to this is that no Java or JavaScript is involved, and you can specify the message returned when validation or required status fails. The disadvantage is that there is a very small range of data validation, and the validation does not take place until the form result page loads:

```
<INPUT TYPE="Text"
       NAME="Name"
```

```
        VALUE="Value"
        SIZE="10"
        MAXLENGTH="15">
<INPUT TYPE="Hidden"
        NAME="Name_Required"
        VALUE="You must enter a name/value">
```

FIGURE 23.2

The three text input methods.

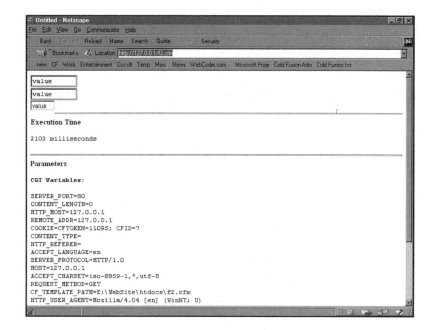

The second piece is a CFINPUT tag for the same thing. Although this is a ColdFusion tag, the results are in standard HTML. The advantages to this are a wide range of data validation and the data validation taking place before the form is sent. This is done with client-side JavaScript error checking. This, of course, is also one of the disadvantages. There is no data validation if someone either has JavaScript turned off or does not support it. In addition, this tag has to be within a CFFORM tag rather than a standard FORM tag. Although there is almost no speed difference between the two, it has to be noted.

```
<CFINPUT TYPE="Text"
        NAME="Name"
        VALUE="Value"
        ALIGN="Left"
        REQUIRED="Yes"
        SIZE="10"
        MAXLENGTH="15">
```

The third piece of code is CFTEXTINPUT. This tag has the power of the CFINPUT, but includes the capability to format both the text and the text box. As you've noticed earlier, the basic font and structure of the text box is different (some would say nicer). This is the primary advantage of this tag—being able to alter its display. This tag shares the disadvantages of the CFINPUT tag as well as any disadvantages relating to it being a Java applet. This means that people who have

Java turned off or do not support it are in a small amount of trouble. The fact that it takes more time to come down is also a factor. One advantage to this tag—to combat part of its Java disadvantages—is the capability (which is shared by all the Java tags) to specify a non-Java alternative.

```
<CFTEXTINPUT NAME="Name"
            VALUE="Value"
            ALIGN="Left"
            SIZE="10"
            MAXLENGTH="15"
            REQUIRED="Yes">
```

Now the question is, when would you use each of these tags? Is the CFINPUT any better than the standard tag, and is the Java version any better than the others? The answer is both yes and no. The major power of the CFFORM tags in this case is the data validation capabilities. If you just want to make sure that a value is present, the hidden/required version is good. The CFFORM tags on the other hand allow more forms of data validation. In addition, the Java version allows you to control the font, size, and colors of the text and box. The tag to use in a given situation really depends on what you need. Don't go crazy with the Java version just because it's there. As I've said, Java is a tool, not a way of life.

Now look at the attributes for the CFTEXTINPUT Java control. In addition to the standard tag elements mentioned in the previous sections, CFTEXTINPUT has a few that are specific to its use (see Table 23.5).

Table 23.5 CFTEXTINPUT **Attributes**

Name	Status	Description
VALUE	Optional	Default value for the tag. There is no limit on the size of this value, but the display is limited to the size element mentioned later.
REQUIRED	Optional	Yes or No. If Yes, the user must enter or change text.
RANGE	Optional	When using numeric data in the CFTEXTINPUT, this allows a minimum, maximum range to be set. Only useful for numeric data.
VALIDATE	Optional	Defines what sort of validation the data in the CFFORM element will be passed through. Valid entries are:
		Date—Verifies U.S. date entry in the form mm/dd/yy.
		Eurodate—Verifies valid European date entry in the form dd/mm/yyyy.
		Time—Verifies a time entry in the form hh:mm:ss.
		Float—Verifies a floating-point entry.
		Integer—Verifies an integer entry.

Name	Status	Description
		`Telephone`—Verifies a telephone entry. Telephone data must be entered as ###-###-####. The hyphen separator (-) can be replaced with a blank. The area code and exchange must begin with a digit between 1 and 9.
		`Zipcode`—(U.S. formats only) Number can be a five-digit or nine-digit zip in the form #####-####. The hyphen separator (-) can be replaced with a blank.
		`Creditcard`—Blanks and dashes are stripped, and the number is verified using the mod10 algorithm.
		`social_security_number`—Number must be entered as ###-##-####. The hyphen separator (-) can be replaced with a blank.
		This element is ignored if the `ONVALIDATE` element is used.
MESSAGE	Optional	Message text to appear if validation fails. This only applies if the `VALIDATE` element is used.
SIZE	Optional	Number of characters displayed before horizontal scrollbar appears. This does not seem to work because a tag is limited to a single line. Both this attribute and the `WIDTH` attribute seem to be able to control the actual size of the tag.
BGCOLOR	Optional	Background color of the control. Uses the standard color definitions for `CFFORM`.
TEXTCOLOR	Optional	Text colors for the control. Uses the standard color definitions for `CFFORM`.
MAXLENGTH	Optional	The maximum length of text entered.

Part IV

Ch 23

Listing 23.1 shows two different CFTEXTINPUT boxes. The first is the minimum script needed, whereas the second shows some of the features.

Listing 23.1   Two Different CFTEXTINPUT Boxes

```
<CFFORM ACTION="TEST.CFM"
        METHOD="POST"
        NAME="TEST">

<CFTEXTINPUT NAME="TEST1"
        VALUE="STANDARD, MINIMAL TAG">
<BR>
<CFTEXTINPUT NAME="TEST2"
        VALUE="TAG WITH A DIFFERENT BACKGROUND AND TEXT
        ➥COLOR WITH A NoN-SUPPORTED FONT IN ITALIC."
        WIDTH="750"
        FONT="ALEFBET"
        FONTSIZE="20"
```

continues

Listing 23.1 Continued

```
              BGCOLOR="##000000"
              TEXTCOLOR="##000FFF"
              ITALIC="Yes">
</CFFORM>
```

The form values returned from a page with a CFTEXTINPUT are straightforward. They take the same form as a standard form value. The preceding examples would result in the following:

```
TEST1= STANDARD, MINIMAL TAG
test2= Tag with a different background and text
➥color with a non-supported font in italic.
```

CFTEXTINPUT gets a rather raw deal when it comes to ColdFusion Studio. The button for this tag is not on the tag choicer, and there's no easy way to put it there. On the other hand, the tag is there and will pop up if you have the tag completion helper on or try to edit it after it's written.

Using CFSLIDER

The CFSLIDER tag is more fun than it is of any extreme value. It places a sliding bar control on a page that allows you to select a numeric value by moving a knob. The only analogy in HTML is a form select box with numbers in it. The slider control can be defined with a number of settings for range, default values, colors, formatting, and other features. Table 23.6 shows the attributes for this tag.

Table 23.6 CFSLIDER Attributes

Name	Status	Description
LABEL	Optional	A label that appears with the slider control. For example: LABEL="Volume %value%" You can use %value% to reference the slider value. If % is omitted, the slider value appears immediately following the label. Remember to set the REFRESHLABEL attribute to Yes when using %value%.
REFRESHLABEL	Optional	Yes or No. If Yes, the label is not refreshed when the slider is moved. Default is Yes.
IMG	Optional	Filename of the image to be used in the slider groove. This image must be in the standard CFFORM image directory or below it.
IMGSTYLE	Optional	Style of the image to appear in the slider groove. Valid entries are Centered, Tiled, and Scaled. Default is Scaled.

Name	Status	Description
RANGE	Optional	Determines the values of the left and right slider range. The slider value appears as the slider is moved. Separate values by a comma. For example: RANGE="1,100" Default is 0,100. Valid only for numeric data.
SCALE	Optional	An unsigned integer. SCALE defines the slider scale within the value of RANGE. For example, if RANGE=0,1000 and SCALE=100, the incremental values for the slider is 0, 100, 200, 300, and so on.
VALUE	Optional	Determines the default slider setting. Must be within the values specified in RANGE. Defaults to the minimum value specified in RANGE.
ONVALIDATE	Optional	The name of a valid JavaScript function used to validate user input, in this case, a change to the default slider value.
MESSAGE	Optional	Message text to appear if validation fails.
ONERROR	Optional	The name of a valid JavaScript function you want to execute in the event of a failed validation.
GROOVECOLOR	Optional	Color value of the slider groove. The *slider groove* is the area in which the slider box moves. Uses the standard color definitions for CFFORM.
BGCOLOR	Optional	Background color of slider label. Uses the standard color definitions for CFFORM.
TEXTCOLOR	Optional	Slider label text color. Uses the standard color definitions for CFFORM.

Part

IV

Ch

23

Listing 23.2 shows three different CFSLIDER tags (see Figure 23.3).

The first is the minimum code needed to make this tag work. As you can see, it's gray, dull, and tells us nothing. The second example has a bit more in terms of display and usability. Here, we have some nice colors and an updating label. The third example takes us another step by adding in size, fonts, and a picture in the groove. Notice that when a picture is specified for the groove, the color specified for the area is ignored.

Listing 23.2 Three Different CFSLIDER Tags

```
<CFFORM ACTION="TEST.CFM"
        METHOD="POST"
        NAME="TEST">
<CFSLIDER NAME="TEST1">
```

continues

Listing 23.2   Continued

```
<BR>
<CFSLIDER NAME="TEST2"
          LABEL="LABEL %VALUE%"
          BGCOLOR="##00FF00"
          TEXTCOLOR="##FF0000"
          GROOVECOLOR="##FFFF00"
          REFRESHLABEL="Yes">
<BR>
<CFSLIDER NAME="TEST3"
          VALUE="50"
          LABEL="TEST3 %VALUE%"
          RANGE="1,100"
          IMG="NETWORKDRIVE.GIF"
          IMGSTYLE="TILED"
          SCALE="10"
          HEIGHT="200"
          WIDTH="250"
          REFRESHLABEL="Yes">
</CFFORM>
```

FIGURE 23.3

Three CFSLIDER
examples.

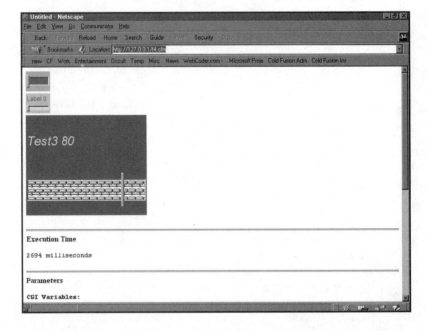

The values returned from a page with a CFSLIDER follow the same format as the standard
HTML form tags (and CFTEXTINPUT, for that matter). The preceding examples result in the
following:

```
test1= standard, minimal tag
test2= Tag with a different background and text
➥color with a non-supported font in italic.
```

Using CFTREE and CFTREEITEM

The CFTREE tag creates one of the most powerful and useful controls in ColdFusion—a branched tree control for the display of data. The CFTREE tag is actually composed of two tags (CFML): the CFTREE tag itself (which is like a container for the data) and the CFTREEITEM (which describes how the data will be formatted).

To truly describe the CFTREE tag, you have to build one and see it in action. Table 23.7 contains the attributes needed to build the CFTREE shell.

Part
IV
Ch
23

Table 23.7   Attributes to Build CFTREE Shell

Name	Status	Description
REQUIRED	Optional	Yes or No. User must select an item in the tree control. Default is No.
DELIMITER	Optional	The character used to separate elements in the form variable PATH. The default is \.
COMPLETEPATH	Optional	Yes passes the root level of the *treename.path* form variable when the CFTREE is submitted. If omitted or No, the root level of this form variable is not included.
APPENDKEY	Optional	Yes or No. When used with HREF. Yes passes the CFTREEITEMKEY variable along with the value of the selected tree item in the URL to the application page specified in the CFFORM ACTION attribute. The default is Yes.
HIGHLIGHTHREF	Optional	Yes highlights links associated with a CFTREEITEM with an URL attribute value. No disables highlight. Default is Yes.
BORDER	Optional	Places a border around the tree. Default is Yes.
HSCROLL	Optional	Permits horizontal scrolling. Default is Yes.
VSCROLL	Optional	Permits vertical scrolling. Default is Yes.
MESSAGE	Optional	Message text to appear if validation fails.

You have to put the data in after you build the CFTREE container. This is done using the CFTREEITEM tag.

All data inside a CFTREE must be contained within a CFTREEITEM tag. This can range from data retrieved from queries (DataBase, LDAP, POP, and so on) to data created by hand. After you've examined the attributes (see Table 23.8), you build a few examples so that you can get a better idea of what's going on.

Table 23.8 CFTREEITEM **Attributes**

Name	Status	Description
VALUE	Required	Value passed when the CFFORM is submitted. When populating a CFTREE with data from a CFQUERY, columns are specified in a comma-separated list: VALUE="dept_id,emp_id"
DISPLAY	Optional	Optional. The label for the tree item. Default is VALUE. When populating a CFTREE with data from a CFQUERY, display names are specified in a comma-separated list: DISPLAY="dept_name,emp_name"
PARENT	Optional	Value for tree item parent.
IMG	Optional	Image name or filename for the tree item. When populating a CFTREE with data from a CFQUERY, images or filenames for each level of the tree are specified in a comma-separated list. The default image name is Folder. A number of images are supplied and can be specified using only the image name (no file extension): folder floppy fixed cd document element Use commas to separate image names corresponding to tree level. For example: IMG="folder,document" IMG=",document To specify your own custom image, specify the path and file extension: IMG="../images/page1.gif"
IMGOPEN	Optional	Icon displayed with open tree item. You can specify the icon filename using a relative path. As with IMG, you can use an image supplied with ColdFusion.
HREF	Optional	URL to associate with the tree item or a query column for a tree that is populated from a query. If HREF is a query column, the HREF value is the value populated by the query. If HREF is not recognized as a query column, it is assumed that the HREF text is an actual HTML HREF. When populating a CFTREE with data from a CFQUERY, HREFs can be specified in a comma-separated list: HREF="http://dept_server,http://emp_server"

Name	Status	Description
TARGET	Optional	Target attribute for HREF URL. When populating a CFTREE with data from a CFQUERY, targets are specified in a comma-separated list: TARGET="FRAME_BODY,_blank"
QUERY	Optional	Query name used to generate data for the tree item.
QUERYASROOT	Optional	Yes or No. Defines specified query as the root level. As in Example 1, this option prevents having to create an additional parent CFTREEITEM.
EXPAND	Optional	Yes or No. Yes expands tree to show tree item children. No keeps tree item collapsed. Default is Yes.

Part
IV

Ch
23

Now build a minimal CFTREE (see Figure 23.4). The data from this tree will come from a query (see Listing 23.3).

FIGURE 23.4

A minimal CFTREE example.

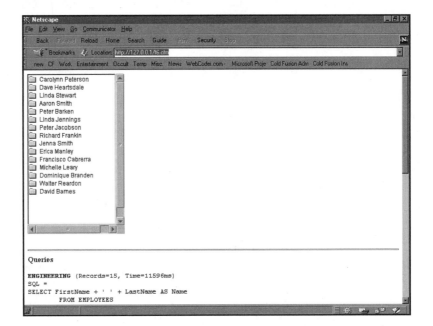

Listing 23.3   Building a Minimal CFTREE

```
<CFQUERY NAME="ENGINEERING" DATASOURCE="CF 3.0 EXAMPLES">
SELECT FIRSTNAME + ' ' + LASTNAME AS NAME
        FROM EMPLOYEES
</CFQUERY>
```

continues

Listing 23.3   Continued

```
<CFFORM ACTION="TEST.CFM"
        METHOD="POST"
        ENABLECAB="No"
        NAME="TEST">
<CFTREE NAME="TREE1">
<CFTREEITEM VALUE="NAME"
            IMG="FOLDER,DOCUMENT"
            QUERY="ENGINEERING">
</CFTREE>
```

As you can see both from the code and the figure, the results are not exactly useful or pretty. To really play with this, you should add in pieces such as images, altered sizes, and other attributes (see Figure 23.5 and Listing 23.4).

FIGURE 23.5

A sample multirow query.

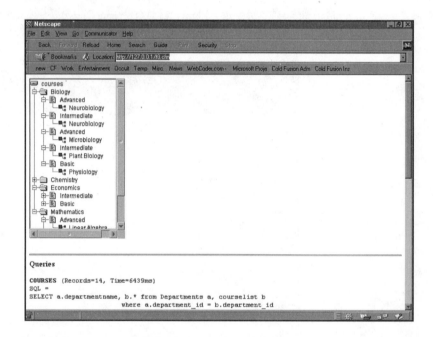

Listing 23.4   Multirow Query Example

```
<CFQUERY NAME="COURSES" DATASOURCE="CF 3.0 EXAMPLES">
        SELECT A.DEPARTMENTNAME, B.* FROM DEPARTMENTS A, COURSELIST B
            WHERE A.DEPARTMENT_ID = B.DEPARTMENT_ID
            ORDER BY B.DEPARTMENT_ID
</CFQUERY>
<CFFORM ACTION="TEST.CFM"
        METHOD="POST"
        ENABLECAB="No"
        NAME="TEST">
```

```
<CFTREE NAME="TREE1"
        BORDER="Yes"
        HSCROLL="Yes"
        VSCROLL="Yes"
        REQUIRED="Yes"
        APPENDKEY="Yes"
        HIGHLIGHTHREF="Yes">
<CFTREEITEM VALUE="DEPARTMENTNAME,COURSELEVEL, COURSENAME"
            IMG="FLOPPY, FOLDER, DOCUMENT, ELEMENT"
            QUERY="COURSES"
            QUERYASROOT="Yes"
            EXPAND="Yes">
</CFTREE>
```

As you can see, this example shows much of the CFTREE tag in action. You have a multirowed query being outputted in a nice, easy-to-view manner. This is exactly what CFTREE was designed for.

The final CFTREE example creates a tree from scratch with no query (see Listing 23.5 and Figure 23.6). This also shows hyperlinks embedded inside a CFTREEITEM.

FIGURE 23.6

An example of creating a tree from scratch.

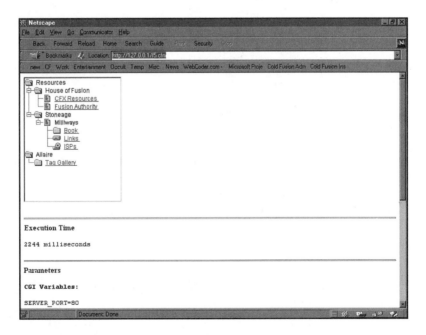

Listing 23.5   Creating a Tree from Scratch

```
<CFFORM ACTION="TEST.CFM"
        METHOD="POST"
        NAME="TEST">
<CFTREE NAME="TEST3"
```

continues

Listing 23.5 Continued

```
            HIGHLIGHTHREF="Yes"
            HEIGHT="250"
            WIDTH="200"
            HSCROLL="No"
            VSCROLL="No">
<CFTREEITEM VALUE="RESOURCES" EXPAND="Yes">
<CFTREEITEM VALUE="HOUSE OF FUSION"
                PARENT="RESOURCES"
                EXPAND="No">
<CFTREEITEM VALUE="CFX RESOURCES"
                PARENT="HOUSE OF FUSION"
                IMG="DOCUMENT"
                HREF="HTTP://WWW.HOUSEOFFUSION.COM">
<CFTREEITEM VALUE="FUSION AUTHORITY"
                PARENT="HOUSE OF FUSION"
                IMG="DOCUMENT"
            HREF="HTTP://WWW.HOUSEOFFUSION.COM/CF_COURSE/CF_INST_FRAME.HTML">
<CFTREEITEM VALUE="STONEAGE" PARENT="RESOURCES">
<CFTREEITEM VALUE="MILLIWAYS"
                PARENT="STONEAGE"
                IMG="DOCUMENT">
<CFTREEITEM VALUE="BOOK"
                PARENT="MILLIWAYS"
                IMG="FOLDER"
                HREF="HTTP://MILLIWAYS.STONEAGE.COM/CF/BOOK.HTML">
<CFTREEITEM VALUE="LINKS"
                PARENT="MILLIWAYS"
                IMG="FLOPPY"
                HREF="HTTP://MILLIWAYS.STONEAGE.COM/CF/LINKS.CFM">
<CFTREEITEM VALUE="ISPS"
                PARENT="MILLIWAYS"
                IMG="CD"
                HREF="HTTP://MILLIWAYS.STONEAGE.COM/CF/ISP/INDEX.CFM">
<CFTREEITEM VALUE="ALLAIRE">
<CFTREEITEM VALUE="TAG GALLERY"
                PARENT="ALLAIRE"
                EXPAND="Yes"
                HREF="HTTP://WWW.ALLAIRE.COM/TAGGALLERY">
</CFTREE>
</CFFORM>
```

Data is sent from a CFTREE tag in a slightly different form than you've seen before. Rather than one form value being sent, there are two. The first value is the element you chose. In the example illustrated in Listing 23.5, if you clicked MILLIWAYS, your first form result would be just that. The second result would actually be the path that you took to get there: Resources/Stoneage/Milliways. The values can be retrieved by using the following syntax:

```
form.test3.node = Milliways
form.test3.path = Resources/Stoneage/Milliways
```

As mentioned in the attributes section, the delimiter attribute allows you to change the delimiters in the path results. Although the default is a backslash (\), almost any character can be used. In addition, if the `completepath` attribute is set to `Yes`, the full root is appended to the beginning of the path.

Using CFGRID

Although `CFGRID` was originally a spreadsheet-style grid for outputting data, it has grown. The current version allows for the adding of new data rows, deleting of rows, sorting of columns, and instant updating of all data in the grid. This tag gives a nice, clean way of displaying spreadsheet type data on a Web page.

As with the other `CFFORM` tags, you really have to build some example applications to see what this tag looks like and what it does.

`CFGRID` has more than 30 attributes that you can use to customize its appearance and behavior. Any attributes set in the `CFGRID` tag affect the entire grid. You can also specify options for specific rows or columns by passing attributes to `CFGRIDCOLUMN` and `CFGRIDROW`. Options passed to `CFGRIDCOLUMN` and `CFGRIDROW` override any options set at the `CFGRID` level.

Table 23.9 shows the attributes supported by `CFGRID`.

Table 23.9 CFGRID **Attributes**

Name	Status	Description
APPENDKEY	Optional	Controls whether the URL `CFGRIDKEY` variable should be set containing the selected cell's value; default is `Yes`.
BGCOLOR	Optional	Background color of the control. Valid entries are `black`, `magenta`, `cyan`, `orange`, `darkgray`, `pink`, `gray`, `white`, `lightgray`, and `yellow`.

A hex value can also be entered in this form: `BGCOLOR="##xxxxxx"`, where *x* is 0–9 or A–F. Use either two pound signs or no pound signs. |
COLHEADERALIGN	Optional	Alignment of column header text, valid entries are `left`, `right`, and `center`. Default is `center`.
COLHEADERBOLD	Optional	`Yes` to use boldface text in column header; `No` for regular text. Default is `No`.
COLHEADERFONT	Optional	Column header font name.
COLHEADERFONTSIZE	Optional	Column header font size.
COLHEADERITALIC	Optional	`Yes` to use italic text in column header; `No` for regular text. Default is `No`.
COLHEADERS	Optional	`Yes` to display column headers, `No` to hide column headers. Default is `Yes`.

continues

Table 23.9   Continued

Name	Status	Description
GRIDDATAALIGN	Optional	Alignment of cell text; valid entries are left, right, and center. Default is left.
HIGHLIGHTHREF	Optional	Controls whether URLs in cells are highlighted and underlined. Default is Yes.
HREF	Optional	URL (or template) to go to upon cell selection.
MAXROWS	Optional	Maximum number of query rows to display, same as CFOUTPUT MAXROWS.
QUERY	Optional	The name of the query to be displayed in the grid.
ROWHEADER	Optional	Yes to display row headers; No to hide row headers. Default is Yes.
ROWHEADERALIGN	Optional	Alignment of row header text; valid entries are left, right, and center. Default is left.
ROWHEADERBOLD	Optional	Yes to use boldface text in row header; No for regular text. Default is No.
ROWHEADERFONT	Optional	Row header font name.
ROWHEADERFONTSIZE	Optional	Row header font size.
ROWHEADERITALIC	Optional	Yes to use italic text in row header; No for regular text. Default is No.
ROWHEADERWIDTH	Optional	The width, in pixels, of the row header. Defaults to whatever is the best fit.
SELECTCOLOR	Optional	Background color for selected cells. See BGCOLOR for valid options.
SELECTMODE	Optional	Controls selection mode. Valid entries are SINGLE (selection of a single cell); ROW (selection of an entire row when a cell is selected); COLUMN (selection of an entire column when a cell is selected); BROWSE (no selection, just browsing is permitted). Default is BROWSE.
TARGET	Optional	Target window for URL; same as HTML TARGET attribute.

To see how CFGRID could be used, see Figure 23.7 and Listing 23.6.

Listing 23.6   Minimal Grid Example

```
<CFQUERY NAME="GETDATA" DATASOURCE="A2Z">
     SELECT * FROM EMPLOYEES
```

```
</CFQUERY>
<CFFORM NAME="TEST1" ACTION="TEST.CFM" METHOD="POST">
<CFGRID NAME="TESTGRID1" QUERY="GETDATA">
</CFGRID>
</CFFORM>
```

FIGURE 23.7

An example of a minimal grid.

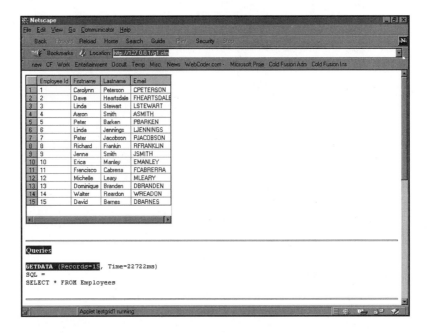

This example uses the minimum code necessary for a grid. No CFGRIDCOLUMN tag is needed because the database fields were used as the default column names. The disadvantage to this is that all the columns returned from the query must be used.

The next example (see Figure 23.8 and Listing 23.7) accomplishes the exact same thing, but this time the grid columns are explicitly provided.

Listing 23.7 Grid Columns Explicitly Provided

```
<CFQUERY NAME="GETDATA" DATASOURCE="A2Z">
        SELECT * FROM EMPLOYEES
</CFQUERY>
<CFFORM NAME="TEST1" ACTION="TEST.CFM" METHOD="POST">
<CFGRID NAME="TESTGRID1" QUERY="GETDATA">
<CFGRIDCOLUMN NAME="FIRSTNAME">
<CFGRIDCOLUMN NAME="LASTNAME">
</CFGRID>
</CFFORM>
```

As you can see, this has allowed you to limit the data displayed.

FIGURE 23.8

An example with grid columns explicitly provided.

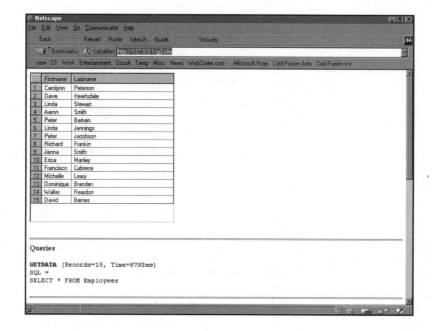

The control of colors, size, fonts, and other attributes can all be set using CFGRID attributes. The next code sample (see Listing 23.8 and Figure 23.9) is the same grid, but this time the font and color are specified.

FIGURE 23.9

An example of a grid enhanced with display features.

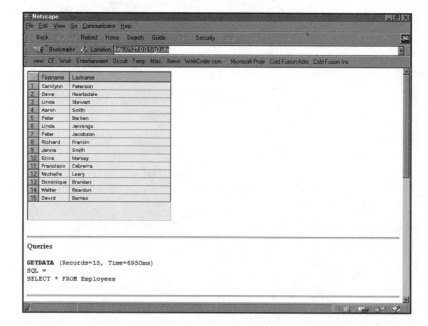

Listing 23.8 Grid Enhanced with Display Features

```
<CFQUERY NAME="getdata" DATASOURCE="CF 3.0 Examples">
        SELECT * FROM Employees
</CFQUERY>
<CFFORM NAME="test1" ACTION="test.cfm" METHOD="POST">
<CFGRID NAME="testgrid1" QUERY="getdata" FONT="Verdana" FONTSIZE="10"
➥ BGCOLOR="yellow" BOLD="Yes">
<CFGRIDCOLUMN NAME="Firstname">
<CFGRIDCOLUMN NAME="Lastname">
</CFGRID>
</CFFORM>
```

The cells in a CFGRID can be links to other URLs. To do this, you must allow selection to occur within the grid. The CFGRID SELECTMODE attribute instructs CFGRID to allow or disallow selection. The URL itself is passed to the CFGRID HREF attribute. The URL may be a fully qualified URL (starting with http) or just a ColdFusion template. When a user clicks a cell, the specified URL is called and the selected cell's value is passed as an URL parameter called CFGRIDKEY. The next example sets SELECTMODE to single (to allow the selection of a single cell) and provides the name of a ColdFusion template to be called when any state is selected:

```
<CFQUERY NAME="getdata" DATASOURCE="CF 3.0 Examples">
        SELECT * FROM Employees
</CFQUERY>
<CFFORM NAME="test1" ACTION="test.cfm" METHOD="POST">
<CFGRID NAME="testgrid1" QUERY="getdata" FONT="Verdana" FONTSIZE="10"
➥ BGCOLOR="yellow" BOLD="Yes" SELECTMODE="Single" HREF="process.cfm">
<CFGRIDCOLUMN NAME="Firstname">
<CFGRIDCOLUMN NAME="Lastname">
</CFGRID>
</CFFORM>
```

Using CFGRIDCOLUMN

As mentioned earlier, CFGRIDCOLUMN is used to specify the individual columns within a CFGRID. CFGRIDCOLUMN allows you to override grid-wide settings with the column-specific attributes listed in Table 23.10.

Table 23.10 CFGRIDCOLUMN Attributes

Name	Status	Description
DATAALIGN	Optional	Alignment of cell text; valid entries are left, right, and center. Default is left.
HEADER	Optional	Header text; NAME attribute text is used if this is omitted.
HEADERALIGN	Optional	Alignment of header text; valid entries are left, right, and center. Default is center.

continues

Table 23.10   Continued

Name	Status	Description
HEADERBOLD	Optional	Yes to use boldface text in header; No for regular text. Default is No.
HEADERFONT	Optional	Header font name.
HEADERFONTSIZE	Optional	Header font size.
HEADERITALIC	Optional	Yes to use italic text in header; No for regular text. Default is No.
HREF	Optional	URL (or template) to go to upon cell selection.
TARGET	Optional	Target window for URL; same as HTML TARGET attribute.

Using CFGRIDROW

Up to this point you've been dealing with grids built with a query. As with the CFTREE tag, you have the option to build a grid from scratch. This is where the CFGRIDROW tag comes in. A separate CFGRIDROW tag must be provided for each row of data to be added to the grid. CFGRIDROW takes a single attribute (see Table 23.11).

Table 23.11   CFGRIDROW Attribute

Name	Status	Description
DATA	Required	Comma-delimited list of values for each cell in this row; must have a value for each cell. If a value has a comma in it, that value must be escaped with two commas.

In the following example (see Listing 23.9 and Figure 23.10), you've created a grid with data written directly into the code.

Listing 23.9   A Grid Without a Query

```
<CFFORM NAME="GridForm" ACTION="catchme.cfm" >
        <CFGRID NAME="grid_one"
            HEIGHT=300
            WIDTH=400
            HSPACE=20
            VSPACE="6"
            SELECTCOLOR="magenta"
            SELECTMODE="row"
            ROWHEADERS="Yes"
            BOLD="no"
            COLHEADERITALIC="No"
            COLHEADERBOLD="Yes"
```

```
                    ROWHEADERITALIC="No"
                    ROWHEADERBOLD="Yes">
                    <CFGRIDCOLUMN NAME="full_name" HEADER="Full Name">
                    <CFGRIDCOLUMN NAME="email_address" HEADER="Email Address">
                    <CFGRIDROW DATA="Michael Dinowitz, mdinowit@i-2000.com">
                    <CFGRIDROW DATA="Ben Forta, ben@stoneage.com">
                    <CFGRIDROW DATA="Nancy Warner, warner@infinet-is.com">
                </CFGRID>
                <INPUT TYPE="Submit" VALUE=" Submit "> <BR>
            </CFFORM>
```

FIGURE 23.10

An example of a grid without a query.

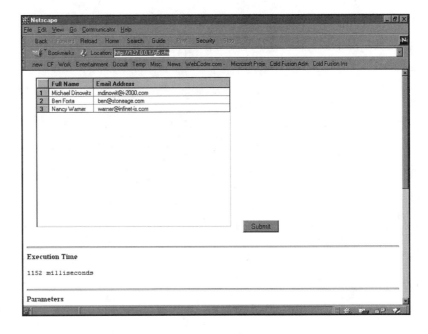

Like CFTREE, the CFGRID tag sends back more than one form element to a result page. Not only does the CFGRID send back multiple elements, these elements are one-dimensional arrays as well (see Table 23.12). These arrays are referenced like any other ColdFusion arrays. The primary use of this data is for record adding and updating using the CFGRIDUPDATE tag.

Table 23.12   CFGRID Results

Form Attribute	Description
gridname.colname [row_index]	Stores the new value of an edited grid cell
Gridname.Original.colname [row_index]	Stores the original value of the edited grid cell
Gridname.RowStatus.Action [row_index]	Stores the edit type made against the edited grid cell

Using CFGRIDUPDATE

One problem with using the CFGRID tag is that it is a pain to update. New data is added, rows are deleted, and things are changed all the time. To make it easier to add all this data to a database, the CFGRIDUPDATE tag was added. As mentioned previously, this is not really a CFFORM tag but is included here because it needs a CFGRID tag to operate. This tag takes the current values of the grid, compares them to the original values, and then goes to work. All the rows that have been deleted are removed, the new rows are inserted, and then the updating occurs. Table 23.13 shows the attributes for this tag.

Table 23.13   CFGRIDUPDATE Attributes

Name	Status	Description
GRID	Required	The name of the CFGRID form element that is the source for the update action.
DATASOURCE	Required	The name of the ODBC data source for the update action.
TABLENAME	Required	The name of the table you want to update.
USERNAME	Optional	If specified, USERNAME overrides the username value specified in the ODBC setup.
PASSWORD	Optional	If specified, PASSWORD overrides the password value specified in the ODBC setup.
TABLEOWNER	Optional	For data sources that support table ownership (such as SQL Server, Oracle, and Sybase SQL Anywhere), use this field to specify the owner of the table.
TABLEQUALIFIER	Optional	For data sources that support table qualifiers, use this field to specify the qualifier for the table. The purpose of table qualifiers varies across drivers. For SQL Server and Oracle, the qualifier refers to the name of the database that contains the table. For the Intersolv dBASE driver, the qualifier refers to the directory where the DBF files are located.
KEYONLY	Optional	Yes or No. Yes specifies that in the update action, the WHERE criteria is confined to the key values. No specifies that in addition to the key values, the original values of any changed fields are included in the WHERE criteria. Default is Yes.

Using the following example grid, you can do all the changes you want and then submit it to a page containing the CFGRIDUPDATE code for it to go directly into the database:

```
PAGE 1:
<CFQUERY NAME="GETDATA" DATASOURCE="A2Z">
        SELECT * FROM EMPLOYEES
```

```
</CFQUERY>
<CFFORM NAME="TEST1" ACTION="TEST.CFM" METHOD="POST">
<CFGRID NAME="TESTGRID1" QUERY="GETDATA">
</CFGRID>
</CFFORM>
PAGE 2:
<CFGRIDUPDATE GRID="TESTGRID1"
        DATASOURCE="A2Z"
        TABLENAME="EMPLOYEES"
        KEYONLY="No">
```

Using CFAPPLET

One of the least used or understood ColdFusion form features is the CFAPPLET tag. This tag allows you to extend the power of CFFORM by adding new Java elements that you can create. This goes beyond a simple Java applet in that you can have the results of the Java applet sent through like a form element. In addition, much of the code you would normally write for a Java applet is handled by ColdFusion using default values you set during registration.

Assume that you have a Java calculator applet that you want to add to a form. You want the end user to be able to do a calculation, select a few other things on the form, and send the whole thing to be processed. The first step is to write or acquire the applet.

N O T E You must know the METHOD used by the applet to return data to the screen. Currently CFAPPLET only supports a single return METHOD. ▮

You have to register your applet after you have it. Go to the ColdFusion Administrator and select the Applets button. It shows you a list of all registered applets and allows you to add new ones.

As you can see, the Calculator applet is already registered (see Figure 23.11). To register a new applet, type in the applet name and click the Register button (see Figure 23.12).

The first thing to do is set the codebase and code arguments for the applet, which are basically the location and name of the applet. This must appear exact as it will be used to point to the exact location of the applet. The method is the part of the Java code that returns a value to the screen. You have to specify which method is supplying the information you want to capture and pass. The alignment settings (HEIGHT, WIDTH, VSPACE, HSPACE, ALIGN) here are the defaults and can be changed later when the applet is used on a page. The Java-unsupported message allows you to set a message or perform an operation when the end user has a browser that doesn't support Java. The final pieces are the default parameters needed for the operation of the methods within the applet. These are default parameters and can be changed on actual usage.

Now that you've registered the applet, use it. The standard syntax for your calculator is as follows:

```
<CFFORM NAME="CalculatorForm" ACTION="CalculatorResult.cfm">
<CFApplet APPLETSOURCE="Calculator" NAME="Calculator">
</CFFORM>
```

This is the minimum needed to use a registered applet. CFAPPLETs do not share most of the standard tag elements with the other CFFORM tags. The only ones that are equivalent are NAME and the alignment codes (HEIGHT, WIDTH, VSPACE, HSPACE, ALIGN). All others are specific to CFAPPLET (see Table 23.14).

FIGURE 23.11

The applet registration, part 1.

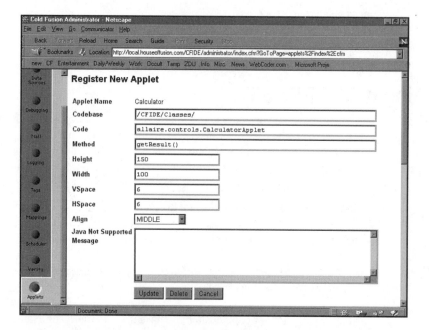

FIGURE 23.12

The applet registration, part 2.

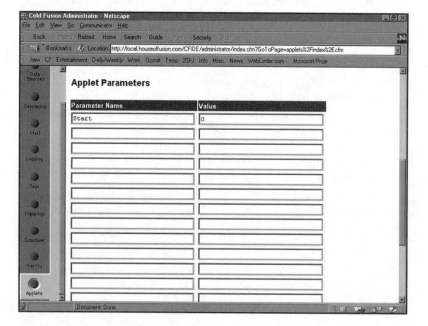

Table 23.14 CFAPPLET **Attributes**

Name	Status	Description
APPLETSOURCE	Required	The name of the registered applet.
PARAM	Optional	The valid name of a registered parameter for the applet. Specify a parameter only if you want to override parameter values already defined for the applet using the ColdFusion Administrator. You can set as many parameters as there are available to the applet.

The results of the CFAPPLET tag can be retrieved on the form action page in the same method as standard HTML forms. That means that the example used will have this result:

```
Calculator=value
```

Part

IV

Ch

23

Interacting with Email

What is the single Internet application that people use more often than any other? Email. Although the NCSA's Mosaic World Wide Web browser was probably the killer application that led to the Internet's current level of popularity, it is email that people use most often. The ability to send and receive potentially critical information almost instantaneously—to and from almost anywhere on the planet—is a compelling reason to use the Internet. Email has had a profound impact on virtually all aspects of how we do business and stay in touch with each other.

Although the Web is probably the most compelling reason people connect to the Internet, its usefulness is significantly enhanced by the integration of email. Of course, the usefulness of your Web Web applications: is enhanced by the incorporation of email. The following are some examples of how email can be used in conjunction with a Web application to enhance its usefulness.

- A simple order entry application sends an order confirmation by email.
- A complex database application sends an email to the developer when a user encounters a runtime error.
- A billing application sends invoices to customers through email.
- An office supply manufacturer uses email to send multimedia catalogs to a group of distributors throughout the world. Different versions of the catalog are sent to different distributors, based on information listed in the manufacturer's database.
- A Web-based mailing list archive gives new customers access to older technical support information.

There are lots of excellent examples of integrating email with Web Web applications:. In many of the other chapters you've seen how ColdFusion makes it easy to manage databases on the Web. As you'll see in this chapter, it is also quite simple to integrate email into your Web/database Web applications:.

Generating SMTP Mail

Simple Mail Transport Protocol (SMTP) is the standard method of sending and receiving email over the Internet. Post Office Protocol (POP) is the standard method of retrieving mail from an email server. SMTP involves the use of client and server software. When you want to get your mail, you use your client software to log into a POP server and download the mail. When you send mail, you post your message to your SMTP server, which sends it to the intended destination.

If you haven't configured ColdFusion to use a particular SMTP server, you can still send email by explicitly referring to the optional SERVER attribute in your CFMAIL tag (see Table 24.1). This approach is a bit cumbersome and may create a maintenance problem if used frequently. It's really much simpler to use the ColdFusion Administrator to set up your SMTP server (see Figure 24.1). If you don't take one of these approaches, your CFMAIL commands will fail.

FIGURE 24.1

Specify a valid SMTP mail server before using CFMAIL in your Web applications.

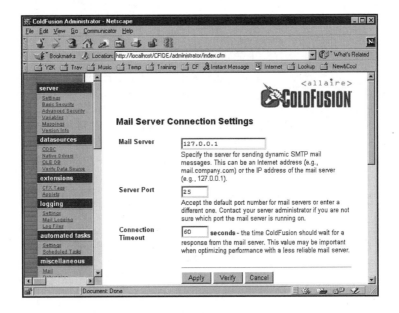

ColdFusion can be used to generate SMTP mail using the CFMAIL tag. In its most common application, the email's body resides in a template and is sent to an address specified in the CFMAIL tag. For example, Listing 24.1 contains code that a simple order entry application could use to send the customer an email order confirmation. The code that generates the email is in the same template as the HTML code used to generate a "thank you" page.

On the CD

Listing 24.1 LISTRESULTS.CFM—A ColdFusion Template with a Simple Email Message

```
<CFMAIL
FROM="orders@A2Z.com"
TO="#URL.Email#"
SUBJECT="Order Confirmation"
>
This letter confirms your recent order from our Web site. Your order
has been placed in our system and will be processed as quickly as
possible. Thanks again for your order.
</CFMAIL>

<HTML>
<HEAD>
<TITLE>Thank You for Your Order</TITLE>
</HEAD>
<BODY>
<H1>Thank You!</H1>
Thanks for your recent order. It will be processed as quickly as possible.
Feel free to continue reviewing our site. If there's anything we can
do to make our site more useful, please
<A HREF="mailto:Webmaster@a2zbooks.com">drop us a line</A>.
</BODY>
</HTML>
```

Part
IV

Ch
24

As you can see in LISTRESULTS.CFM, shown in Listing 24.1, the email address is defined at runtime from an URL parameter. Virtually every parameter in the CFMAIL tag can be specified with a variable. The complete list of CFMAIL attributes is shown in Table 24.1.

Note that the body of an email message is plain, unformatted text—not HTML. There are two implications: First, using HTML formatting tags won't work in this text; they appear in the email as text. Second, you must enter carriage returns where they are needed because the text won't wrap by itself. This functionality may be inadequate in some cases. When this is the case, you can set the TYPE attribute to HTML and use HTML to format the output. This is discussed later in this chapter in "Using HTML to Make Your Email Look Better."

Table 24.1 CFMAIL **Attributes**

Attribute	Required	Description
TO	Yes	The email address(es) to which messages are sent. Use commas to delimit addresses if more than one is used. Can be defined with a variable. Can also be defined as a field in a query result.
FROM	Yes	The sender's email address. Can be defined as a variable.
CC	No	Email addresses of people to be copied. Use commas to delimit more than one address. Can be defined with a variable or query output, such as TO.
SUBJECT	No	The subject of the message.
TYPE	No	Defines optional data type for the content of the message. The only currently valid value is HTML.
MIMEATTACH	No	Defines the path and name of the file to be attached to the email.
QUERY	No	Specifies the name of CFQUERY that is used in this message. The query can be used to create a list of people to send the message to or to create the content of the message.
MAXROWS	No	Used in conjunction with the QUERY attribute; this specifies the maximum number of people to whom you want to send the message.
GROUP	No	Used in conjunction with the QUERY attribute; this specifies the query result column to be used to group sets of related rows.
SERVER	No	Specifies the address of an alternative SMTP server. This is needed only if you want to specify the use of a server other than the server specified in the ColdFusion Administrator.
PORT	No	Specifies an alternative port number. By default, SMTP mail uses TCP/IP port 25; this is also what is used in the ColdFusion Administrator by default. Needed only if you want to specify the use of a port other than the port specified in the ColdFusion Administrator.

Attribute	Required	Description
TIMEOUT	No	If a connection cannot be made to the SMTP server specified in the ColdFusion Administrator, this value is the number of seconds that ColdFusion waits before timing out the connection. By default, this is specified in the ColdFusion Administrator as 180 seconds. Use this attribute only if you want to use a value other than the value defined in the ColdFusion Administrator.

The SERVER, PORT, and TIMEOUT attributes duplicate parameters that are defined using the ColdFusion Administrator. You need to use these parameters only if you want to override the values already specified in the ColdFusion Administrator.

Including Query Results in Email

Listing 24.1 demonstrates how simple it is to include automatically generated email in a ColdFusion application. It sent a simple confirmation to a customer who had just placed an order, but did not include any information about the order itself. The email message would probably be more helpful if it contained a bit more information about the order.

Suppose you want to actually send a list of the items in the order. Retrieve the line items in the order from the OrderItems table (using the A2Z.dbm database, which contains the sample data for this application); this requires the OrderId. When you have this information, you can specify the query in CFMAIL's QUERY attribute. Of course, the CFQUERY tag itself must be placed ahead of the CFMAIL tag in this template, as shown in Listing 24.2. To use SENDLIST.CFM, you must add URL parameters for OrderId and email, such as http://localhost/cfdocs/sendlist.cfm?email=ashley@aspx.com&OrderID=3.

On the CD

> **Listing 24.2** SENDLIST.CFM—**Including the Results of a Query in an Email Message**

```
<CFQUERY
DATASOURCE="A2Z"
NAME="GetOrder"
>
SELECT DISTINCTROW OrderItems.*
FROM OrderItems
WHERE OrderID = #URL.OrderId#
</CFQUERY>

<!-- Error processing code goes here -->

<CFIF GetOrder.RecordCount is 0>

    <HEAD>
    <TITLE>Error</TITLE>
    </HEAD>
```

continues

Listing 24.2 Continued

```
    <BODY>

    There were no matching orders.

    </BODY>

    <CFABORT>

</CFIF>

<CFMAIL
QUERY="GetOrder"
FROM="orders@A2Z.com"
TO="#URL.Email#"
SUBJECT="Order Confirmation"
>
This letter confirms your recent order for the items listed below.

## Book                  Qty  Unit Price Extd Price
- - - - - - - - - - - - - - - - - - - - - - - -
<CFOUTPUT>
#RJustify(OrderLine, 2)# #Ljustify(BookID,20)# #Rjustify(Quantity,2)
➥# #RJustify(NumberFormat(UnitPrice, '
➥$(_____.__)'),10)# #RJustify(NumberFormat
➥(SalePrice, '$(_____.__)'),10)#
</CFOUTPUT>
Please let us know if there are any changes that need to be made.
Thanks again for your order.
</CFMAIL>

<!-- HTML to build 'thank you' doc goes here -->
<HEAD>
<TITLE>Thank you!</TITLE>
</HEAD>
<BODY>
<H2>Thank you!</H2><P>
A confirmation has been sent to you via email.
<P>
</BODY>
</HTML>
```

You can see in Listing 24.2 that the query GetOrder was referred to in the CFMAIL tag. This allows you to include the query result in the email body's CFOUTPUT section.

Because the body of the message is just text, you can use ColdFusion 2.0 string and number formatting functions to get the query's output to line up with the "header" defined just above the CFOUTPUT section. You know exactly how wide each column is in the header, so the formatting functions (Rjustify() and Ljustify()) can be used to ensure that the output values are formatted to the same width. This works fine as long as the user who receives the email uses fixed pitch fonts (for example, Courier) to display the email. If she uses proportionally spaced fonts (such as Times Roman), this method of formatting won't work very well.

There may be situations in which you want to group the items that appear in the output. In the sample application, for example, it might be nice to group the books ordered by their categories. In other words, all computer books would be grouped together—all math books grouped, and so on.

This is easily accomplished, but requires a slightly more complex query, as shown in Listing 24.3. To use GROUPOUTPUT.CFM, you must add URL parameters for OrderID and email, such as http://localhost/cfdocs/groupoutput.cfm?email=ashley@aspx.com&OrderID=3.

On the CD

Listing 24.3 GROUPOUTPUT.CFM—Including the Results of a Query in an Email Message

```
<CFQUERY
DATASOURCE="A2Z"
NAME="GetOrder"
>
SELECT DISTINCTROW Category.Category, OrderItems.*
FROM Category INNER JOIN (Inventory INNER JOIN OrderItems ON
Inventory.BookID = OrderItems.BookID)
ON Category.ID = Inventory.CategoryID
WHERE OrderItems.OrderID=#URL.OrderID#
ORDER BY Category.Category
</CFQUERY>

<!-- Error processing code goes here -->
<CFMAIL
QUERY="GetOrder"
GROUP="Category"
FROM="orders@A2Z.com"
TO="#URL.Email#"
SUBJECT="Order Confirmation"
>
This letter confirms your recent order for the items listed below.

<CFOUTPUT GROUP="Category">
#Category#
<CFOUTPUT>
## Book                   Qty  Unit Price Extd Price
---------------------
#RJustify(OrderLine, 2)# #Ljustify(BookID,20)# #Rjustify(Quantity,2)
➥# #RJustify(NumberFormat(UnitPrice, '$
➥(_____.__)'),10)# #RJustify(NumberFormat
➥(SalePrice, '$(_____.__)'),10)#
</CFOUTPUT>
</CFOUTPUT>
Please let us know if there are any changes that need to be made.
Thanks again for your order.
</CFMAIL>

<!-- HTML to build 'thank you' doc goes here -->
```

Part
IV
Ch
24

The grouping requirement doesn't really make the ColdFusion coding much more complex. You merely add the GROUP attribute to the CFMAIL tag and add a pair of CFOUTPUT tags for the inner group (see Listing 24.3). The complexity comes from the nature of how data is stored in a relational database. The various categories into which books can be classified are stored in the Category table; they are identified by numbers. The category identification number, which is used to key rows in the Category table, is an attribute of the book—in the Inventory table—and is not found in the OrderItems table.

To get a book's category identification number, you must join the OrderItems records with the Inventory records in the BookID field. To get the actual name of the category—it's the category name that you're grouping on—you must join the Inventory records to the Category records by CagetoryID. Thus, there are two inner joins required.

◊ **See** "Joining Tables withINNER JOIN ON," **p. 399**.

Sending Email to a List of People

If you've been plugged into the Internet for at least one day, you've probably received at least 1,000 junk email letters. You know, these messages all say essentially the same thing, "How would you like to help us grow our account balance while simultaneously shrinking yours?" You weren't the only one who received this delightfully entertaining, unsolicited message. You can usually tell because the friendly, helpful person who sent it was nice enough to include all the other 3,000 recipients in the To list.

You'll be glad to know that it's easy to return the favor by using ColdFusion. Suppose that each time you receive one of these unsolicited emails, you decide to keep track of the person who sent you the message in a database. Now suppose you want to write them all a nice thank you letter. Now look at a more appropriate example of how to send email to a list of people that is stored in a table.

You may recall that A2Z Books' Marketing department is looking for a way to notify customers when books they may be interested in have arrived. The A2Z Books sample application includes a customer survey in which customers can identify book categories in which they are interested. Customers can request to be notified when new books in their favorite categories arrive. (You see, the folks at A2Z are sensitive to what happens when Internet-based marketing campaigns run out of control.)

Every so often, someone from the Marketing department uses a Web page to produce a listing of all new inventory arrivals. The user can select books that she wants to let customers know about from the new-arrivals list. If the user selects a book that is classified in the education category, for example, the process emails all customers who indicated that they want to be notified when such books arrive.

Listing 24.4 contains the form that the A2Z Marketing department uses to get the process started. It enables users to answer questions such as "Which books arrived within 14 days of September 16, 1996?" The defaults are set up so that it lists all the books that arrived within the last week. This form invokes the template SHOW_ARRIVALS.CFM (see Listing 24.5), which produces the list of books that recently arrived. Finally, Listing 24.6 contains the SEND_NOTIFICATIONS.CFM template—the code that actually sends the emails.

On the CD

Listing 24.4   SPECIFY_ARRIVALS.HTML—Producing a List of New Book Arrivals

```
<HTML>
<HEAD>
<TITLE>Specify Customer Notifications</TITLE>
</HEAD>
<BODY>
<H2>Specify Customer Notifications</H2>
This form allows you to identify books that we have received within the
specified number of days prior to the specified date. It will generate
a list of books.
<P>
<FORM ACTION="show_arrivals.cfm" METHOD="post">
<INPUT TYPE="hidden" NAME="FromDate_date"
➥VALUE="You must enter a valid 'from _date'">
<INPUT TYPE="hidden" NAME="FromDate_required" VALUE="You must enter a valid
➥ _'from date'">
<INPUT TYPE="hidden" NAME="Days_range" VALUE="MIN=0 MAX=99">
<INPUT TYPE="hidden" NAME="Days_required" VALUE="You must enter a valid 'from
➥ _date'">

<CFOUTPUT>
List all books that arrived up to <INPUT TYPE="text" NAME="Days" VALUE="7"
➥ SIZE="3" MAXLENGTH="3">
day(s) prior to <INPUT TYPE="text" NAME="FromDate"
_VALUE="#DateFormat(Now(),'mm-dd-yyyy')#" SIZE="12">.
</CFOUTPUT>
<BR>
<BR><INPUT TYPE="submit" VALUE="Produce recent arrivals list">
</FORM>
</BODY>
</HTML>
```

Note that the date validation performed in Listing 24.4 results in an ODBC date object being passed to SHOW_ARRIVALS.CFM in Listing 24.5. Data validation is described in detail in Chapter 15, "Form Data Validation." This example requires a bit of date math:

n days are subtracted from the user-specified date, where n is a user-specified number.

The first line of code easily does the trick. The DateAdd() function enables you to add n-time increments to a date. In this case, the increment is a day (specified by a d) and n is the negative value of the number entered by the user in the Form.Days variable. CFSET saves the result of the expression in the variable Date, which is then used in the SQL statement that follows.

N O T E   When you're doing SQL queries in which you're using parameterized date values, the dates must be in canonical form: { d 'YYYY-MM-DD' }, for example. ColdFusion 2.0 produces dates this way if you use a date validation on the INPUT object to create the date. If you don't do the date validation, the INPUT tag simply produces a string value, and this is not interpreted properly in your SQL. ▪

CAUTION

Note that in Listing 24.5 you must also use the `PreserveSingleQuotes()` function to use a parameterized date value. The problem is that ColdFusion automatically "escapes" the single quotation marks generated when the `INPUT` object casts a string into a canonical date.

On the CD

Listing 24.5 `SHOW_ARRIVALS.CFM`—Producing a List of New Books

```
<!-- Produce set of books that arrived within x days of specified date -->
<CFSET #Date# = #DateAdd("d",-Days,Form.FromDate)#>
<CFQUERY
NAME="GetArrivals"
DATASOURCE="A2Z"
>
SELECT DISTINCTROW Inventory.BookID, Inventory.ArrivalDate,
    _Category.Category, Inventory.Title
FROM Category INNER JOIN Inventory ON Category.ID = Inventory.CategoryID
WHERE Inventory.ArrivalDate>=#PreserveSingleQuotes(Date)#
ORDER BY Category.Category, Inventory.ArrivalDate
</CFQUERY>

<!-- Let user know none found and abort further processing -->
<CFIF GetArrivals.Recordcount is 0>
<HTML>
<HEAD>
<TITLE>No Arrivals</TITLE>
</HEAD>
<BODY>
<H1>No Arrivals</H1>
There were no arrivals in this date range. Go back and expand the range.
</BODY>
</HTML>
<CFABORT>
</CFIF>

<HTML>
<HEAD>
<TITLE>Recent Arrivals</TITLE>
</HEAD>

<BODY>
<H2>Recent Arrivals</H2>

<!-- Display output in tabular format -->
<TABLE BORDER=1 CELLPADDING=4>
<TR>
<TH ALIGN="left">Category</TH>
Arrival Date</TH>
Title</TH>
</TR>

<CFOUTPUT
QUERY="GetArrivals"
```

```
GROUP="Category"
>
<TR>
<TD>#Category#</TD>
<TD>#DateFormat(ArrivalDate)#</TD>
<TD>
<A HREF="/A2Z/send_notifications.cfm&BookID=#BookID#">#Title#</A>
</TD>
</TR>
</CFOUTPUT>
</TABLE>
</BODY>
</HTML>
```

This application is based on a separate A2Z.mdb that is included on the CD-ROM for Chapter 20, "Working with Stored Procedures." Please see the enclosed database.

Listing 24.6 SEND_NOTIFICATIONS.CFM—**Sending and Counting Notification Request Emails**

Part
IV

Ch
24

```
<!--
Identify book and all customers that requested notification upon
arrival of books in this book's category.
-->
<CFQUERY
NAME="MakeBookList"
DATASOURCE="A2Z"
>
SELECT DISTINCTROW Inventory.BookID, Inventory.ISBN, Inventory.Title,
Inventory.Publisher, Inventory.AuthorFirstName,
Inventory.AuthorLastName, Inventory.Description,
Category.Category, Customers.FirstName, Customers.EMail
          FROM CustomerSurvey INNER JOIN Customers ON CustomerSurvey.
➥CustomerID = _Customers.CustomerID,
Inventory INNER JOIN Category ON Inventory.CategoryID = Category.ID
WHERE ( (Inventory.BookID=#URL.BookID#) AND
(Inventory.CategoryID=CustomerSurvey.Category1 OR
Inventory.CategoryID=CustomerSurvey.Category2 OR
Inventory.CategoryID=CustomerSurvey.Category3 OR
Inventory.CategoryID=CustomerSurvey.Category4
)
)
ORDER BY Customers.LastName, Category.Category
</CFQUERY>

<!-- If no customer's requested notification, tell user and abort process -->
<CFIF MakeBookList.Recordcount is 0>
<HTML>
<HEAD>
<TITLE>No Notification Requests</TITLE>
</HEAD>
<BODY>
```

continues

Listing 24.6 Continued

```
<H1>No Notification Requests</H1>
There were no customers that requested notification upon arrival
of books in the same category as the selected book. Use the
Back button to return to the Recent Arrivals page.
</BODY>
</HTML>
<CFABORT>
</CFIF>

<!-- Send e-mails to all customers in list -->
<CFMAIL
QUERY="MakeBookList"
SUBJECT="Arrival of '#Title#'"
TO="#EMail#"
FROM="sales@A2ZBooks.com"
>
Dear #FirstName#:

Based on your request to be notified when certain categories of
books come in, we're writing to let you know about a book which
we recently received. You can purchase this book by visiting
our Web site or by dropping by our store.

Category: #Category#
Title: #Title#
Author: #AuthorFirstName# #AuthorLastName#
Description: #Description#

</CFMAIL>

<!-- Tell A2Z user how many e-mails were sent -->
<HTML>
<HEAD>
<TITLE>Notifications Sent</TITLE>
</HEAD>
<BODY>
<H2>E-mail sent</H2>
<CFOUTPUT QUERY="MakeBookList">
#MakeBookList.RecordCount# customers were notified about
➥the arrival of _#Title#.
</CFOUTPUT>
Use the Back button to return to the Recent Arrivals page.
</BODY>
</HTML>
```

Figure 24.2 shows the listing of books that recently arrived.

Figure 24.3 shows what the email message looks like when the user receives it in Netscape mail.

FIGURE 24.2

The
SHOW_ARRIVALS.CFM
template produces this
listing of all books that
have recently arrived.

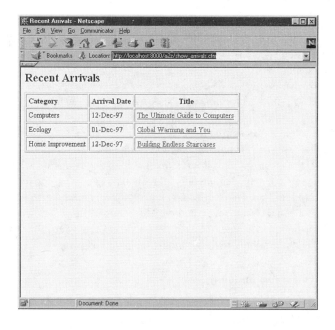

FIGURE 24.3

Here is the email
message that notifies
A2Z customers that
books they may be
interested in have
arrived.

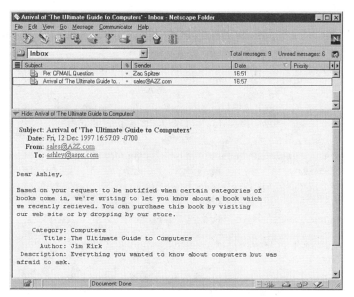

The SEND_NOTIFICATIONS.CFM template (see Listing 24.6) does most of the work you're interested in here. When you want to send mail to a list of people, you usually wind up using a similar approach: Use a query to identify the recipients and then refer to the query in the TO
attributes of the CFMAIL tag.

The query in the previous example generates a result set with one record for each customer. The resulting record also contains information needed in the body of the email (the book's title, category, and so forth).

Note that using this query-driven approach, an email message is sent to each recipient one at a time. Each recipient will not see the entire recipient list. ▨

It should be noted, however, that there is another technique for generating emails for multiple recipients. This approach is used when you do want each recipient to see all the other people who received the message. This is sometimes valuable information. This second technique involves building a comma-delimited list of recipients and assigning the value of the list to the CFMAIL tag's TO attribute. One way to accomplish this is to use a query to produce a list of email addresses in one of the result set columns. The values in this column can be easily converted into a comma-delimited list using ColdFusion's ValueList() function. You then set the value of the CFMAIL tag's TO attribute to the value list, as in the following:

```
<CFMAIL
TO="#ValueList(Query.ColumnName)#"
FROM="sales@A2Zbooks.com"
SUBJECT="Fan mail from some flounder"
>

-
</CFMAIL>
```

This is pretty cool, but there is still another way to skin this cat. Suppose, for example, that folks in the A2Z Marketing department want to scroll through a customer list, picking and choosing customers to whom they want to send an email message. The next set of listings shows how this is done.

The CREATE_CUSTOMER_LIST.CFM template is displayed in Listing 24.7. The resulting document is shown in the browser window in Figure 24.4. This template allows users to select an inventory category. It then calls GET_CUSTOMER_LIST.CFM (see Listing 24.8), which identifies any customers who specified an interest in this category of books in the customer survey. The GET_CUSTOMER_LIST.CFM template then generates a form that enables users to create an email message and select the customers to whom they want to send the message. This form is displayed in Figure 24.5. When the user selects the submit button in GET_CUSTOMER_LIST.CFM, EMAIL_CUSTOMERS.CFM (see Listing 24.9) is called to do the emailing.

This approach for building the list takes advantage of two interesting check box object behaviors. Note that check box objects in GET_CUSTOMER_LIST.CFM are created for each customer that winds up in the result set, and that each check box object is given the same name: CustList. Neat check box trick number one is that when a group of related check boxes are all given the same name, you can tell whether any of them was checked with ColdFusion's ParameterExists() function. If none of the check boxes are selected, ParameterExists(CheckBoxFieldName) returns No.

The page in Figure 24.4, produced by the CREATE_CUSTOMER_LIST.CFM template in Listing 24.7, enables the user to produce a list of customers that have expressed an interest in books in the selected category.

FIGURE 24.4

The resulting document is shown in the browser window.

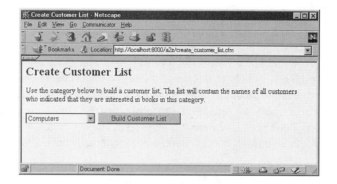

On the CD

Listing 24.7 CREATE_CUSTOMER_LIST.CFM—**Building a Customer List Based on a Specific Category**

```
<!-- Must first get names of all categories -->
<CFQUERY
NAME="GetCategories"
DATASOURCE="A2Z"
>
SELECT Category from Category
</CFQUERY>

<!--
Present form allowing user to select a category and build customer
list.
-->
<HTML>
<HEAD>
<TITLE>Create Customer List</TITLE>
</HEAD>
<BODY>

<H2>Create Customer List</H2>
Use the category below to build a customer list. The list will contain
the names of all customers who indicated that they are interested in
books in this category.
<P>

<FORM ACTION="/A2Z/get_customer_list.cfm" _METHOD="post">
<SELECT NAME="Category">
<CFOUTPUT QUERY="GetCategories">
<OPTION>#Category#
</CFOUTPUT>
</SELECT>
<INPUT TYPE="submit" VALUE="Build Customer List">
</FORM>
</BODY>
</HTML>
```

Look again at GET_CUSTOMER_LIST.CFM and at Figure 24.5. Although each check box is given the same name, each one has a different value; in this example it's the customer's email address. What is neat check box trick number two? A group of identically named check boxes that return one value. The value returned by the check box group is a comma-delimited list of the value of each selected check box. In your case, the object named CustList (which is the name of the check box group) returns a comma-delimited list of the email addresses of selected customers. This list is fed into the TO attribute of the CFMAIL tag in Listing 24.9. Note that in this case you don't need to use the ValueList() function because you're not trying to convert a query column into a comma-delimited list; you already have a comma-delimited list.

On the CD

Listing 24.8 GET_CUSTOMER_LIST.CFM—Template That Builds a Customer List

```
<!-- Must first get ID of category user selected from list -->
<CFQUERY
NAME="GetCategory"
DATASOURCE="A2Z"
MAXROWS=1
>
SELECT ID from Category
WHERE Category = '#Form.Category#'
</CFQUERY>

<!--
Get names, e-mail addr of all customers that expressed any interest
in the selected category (from the customer survey)
-->
<CFQUERY
NAME="GetCustomers"
DATASOURCE="A2Z"
>
SELECT DISTINCTROW Customers.FirstName, Customers.LastName, Customers.EMail
FROM Customers INNER JOIN CustomerSurvey ON
➥ Customers.CustomerID = CustomerSurvey.CustomerID
WHERE CustomerSurvey.Category1=#GetCategory.ID# OR
CustomerSurvey.Category2=#GetCategory.ID# OR
CustomerSurvey.Category3=#GetCategory.ID# OR
CustomerSurvey.Category4=#GetCategory.ID#
</CFQUERY>
<CFIF GetCustomers.Recordcount is 0>
<HTML>
<HEAD>
<TITLE>No Customers Found</TITLE>
</HEAD>
<BODY>
<H2>No Customers Found</H2>
There were no customers interested in <CFOUTPUT>#Form.Category#</CFOUTPUT>.
Use the Back button to go back and make a different selection.
</BODY>
</HTML>
<CFABORT>
</CFIF>
```

```
<HTML>
<HEAD>
<CFOUTPUT>
<TITLE>Customers Who Selected #Form.Category#</TITLE>
</CFOUTPUT>
</HEAD>
<BODY>

<CFOUTPUT>
<H2>Customers Interested in #Form.Category#</H2>

This form allows you to create a custom e-mail message to customers
that have indicated that they're interested in #Form.Category# books.
</CFOUTPUT>

<P>Use the following form to send selected customers a custom
e-mail message.

<FORM ACTION="email_customers.cfm" METHOD="post">
<INPUT TYPE="hidden" NAME="Subject_required" VALUE="You must enter a
➥message subject">
<INPUT TYPE="hidden" NAME="Message_required" VALUE="You must enter a message">
<TABLE>
<TR>
<TD ALIGN="right">Subject:</TD>
<TD><INPUT TYPE="text" NAME="Subject" SIZE="40" MAXLENGTH="100"></TD>
</TR>
<TR>
<TD ALIGN="right" VALIGN="top">Text:</TD>
<TD><TEXTAREA NAME="Message" ROWS="4" COLS="50"></TEXTAREA></TD>
</TR>
<TR>
<TD ALIGN="right">Attachment:</TD>
<TD><INPUT TYPE="text" NAME="Attachment" SIZE="40" MAXLENGTH="120"></TD>
</TR>
</TABLE>

<H2>Select Customers to Receive E-Mail</H2>
<TABLE>
<CFOUTPUT QUERY="GetCustomers">
<TR>
<TD><INPUT TYPE="checkbox" NAME="CustList" VALUE="#EMail#" CHECKED></TD>
<TD>#FirstName# #LastName#</TD>
</TR>
</CFOUTPUT>
</TABLE>
<INPUT TYPE="submit" VALUE="Send the E-Mail">
</FORM>
</BODY>
</HTML>
```

Part
IV

Ch
24

The page in Figure 24.5, produced by the GET_CUSTOMER_LIST.CFM template in Listing 24.8, is where the user creates an email message and selects individual users to whom the letter will be sent. In Listing 24.9, MIME attachments are sent using CFMAIL. You learn more about MIME attachments later in this chapter.

FIGURE 24.5

This is the form used to create an email list.

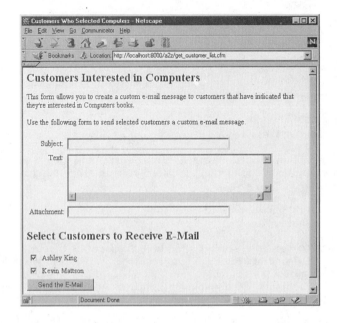

Listing 24.9 EMAIL_CUSTOMERS.CFM—Using CFMAIL **to Send MIME Attachments**

```
<!-- Make sure at least one customer was selected -->
<CFIF #ParameterExists(CustList)# is "No">
<HTML>
<HEAD>
<TITLE>No Names Selected</TITLE>
</HEAD>
<BODY>
<H2>No Names Selected</H2>
You must select at least one person to send this e-mail to.
</BODY>
</HTML>
<CFABORT>
</CFIF>

<!-- Make sure attached file exists -->
<CFIF #Form.Attachment# is not "">
<CFIF #FileExists(Form.Attachment)# is "No">
<HTML>
<HEAD>
<TITLE>Attachment Not Found</TITLE>
</HEAD>
<BODY>
<H2>Attachment Not Found</H2>
The file you specified as an attachment,
<CFOUTPUT>
<STRONG>#Form.Attachment#</STRONG>,
```

```
</CFOUTPUT>
could not be found.
<P>You can only attach valid files to your e-mail. Use the
Back button to go back and enter a valid file name or
erase the Attachment name.
</BODY>
</HTML>
<CFABORT>
</CFIF>

<!-- Send the e-mail, using the comma delimited list and attachment -->
<CFMAIL
TO=#CustList#
FROM="sales@A2ZBooks.com"
SUBJECT="#Form.Subject#"
MIMEATTACH="#Form.Attachment#"
>
#Form.Message#
</CFMAIL>
<CFELSE>
<!-- Send the e-mail, using the comma delimited list and NO attachment -->
<CFMAIL
TO=#CustList#
FROM="sales@A2ZBooks.com"
SUBJECT="#Form.Subject#"
>
#Form.Message#
</CFMAIL>
</CFIF>

<HTML>
<HEAD>
<TITLE>EMail Sent</TITLE>
</HEAD>
<BODY>

<H2>EMail Sent</H2>
<CFOUTPUT>
<CFIF #ListLen(CustList)# is 1>
<CFSET #Customer# = "customer">
<CFELSE>
<CFSET #Customer# = "customers">
</CFIF>
The e-mail message was sent to #ListLen(CustList)# #Customer#.

<p>#CustList#

</CFOUTPUT>

</BODY>
</HTML>
```

Part

IV

Ch

24

Using HTML to Make Your Email Look Better

If you have experimented with CFMAIL, you've probably recognized one of its shortcomings: The body of the message is unformatted text. In other words, it works sort of like an HTML PRE tag—what you see is what you get. When you're hard coding the content of the message, you have control over the formatting and can at least put in carriage returns where needed. When the body of the message includes text that you cannot explicitly control, however, things can get ugly.

Suppose, as in the previous example, you're providing users with a form in which they can create the body of the message themselves. If a user creates a long paragraph without any carriage returns, the message body extends off the right side of the screen.

The fact that CFMAIL messages are just plain text also creates other problems. In the A2Z Books online order system, the customer is sent an email message confirming his order. This confirmation contains all the line items that were ordered. Presenting these items in a format-ted, tabular structure is difficult using plain text. (An example was provided earlier, however, in "Including Query Results in Email.") In fact, unless the recipient has his email reader set up to display messages in a fixed pitch font, creating this tabular display is virtually impossible.

There is another solution: Set the CFMAIL TYPE attribute to "HTML". This allows you to use HTML formatting tags in your email message body. You can use HTML tables to format the order in your example.

Here's an example: A2Z Books is mailing a special notice to all customers who indicated in the customer survey that they are interested in science. A2Z Books needs to identify all these customers and send them a special notice.

N O T E It is important to note that the recipient's email client must be capable of displaying HTML. For example, the Netscape email client can display HTML documents. If the recipient is using an email client that doesn't know how to interpret and format HTML code, the message will appear as plain text—HTML codes and all. Be careful when you use this approach. ▪

Figure 24.6 and Listing 24.10 display the CFML code and the resulting HTML-formatted letter.

On the CD

Listing 24.10 HTML-EMAIL.CFM—Producing an HTML-Formatted Email Message

```
<!-- First get category ID of the 'Science' category -->
<CFQUERY
NAME="GetCategory"
DATASOURCE="A2Z"
>
SELECT DISTINCTROW Category.ID
FROM Category
WHERE Category = 'Science'
</CFQUERY>

<!-- error processing here -->
```

```
<!-- Now get customers who indicated they like science books in survey -->
<CFQUERY
NAME="GetScienceCustomers"
DATASOURCE="A2Z"
>
SELECT DISTINCTROW Customers.FirstName, Customers.LastName,
Customers.Email
FROM Customers INNER JOIN CustomerSurvey ON Customers.CustomerID
➥= CustomerSurvey.CustomerID
WHERE CustomerSurvey.Category1=#GetCategory.ID# OR
CustomerSurvey.Category2=#GetCategory.ID# OR
CustomerSurvey.Category3=#GetCategory.ID# OR
CustomerSurvey.Category4=#GetCategory.ID#
</CFQUERY>

<!-- error processing here -->
<CFIF GetScienceCustomers.RecordCount is 0>

<h2>An error has occurred</h2>
<p>
There were no matching records.

</CFIF>

<CFMAIL
QUERY="GetScienceCustomers"
SUBJECT="Steven Sagan To Appear at A2Z Books!"
TO="#EMail#"
FROM="sales@A2ZBooks.com"
TYPE="HTML"
>
<H2>Renowned Scientist Steven Sagan To Appear for Signing
at A2Z Books!</H2>
Howdy, #FirstName#. We're writing to let you know about
Steven Sagan's upcoming book signing at A2Z Books. Please
find the detail below.
<P>
<TABLE BORDER=1 CELLPADDING=5>
<TR>
<TD ALIGN="right"><STRONG><EM>Who:</EM></STRONG></TD>
<TD ALIGN="left">
All of our <EM>science</EM> club members are being sent
this special invitation.
</TD>
</TR>
<TR>
<TD ALIGN="right"><STRONG><EM>What:</EM></STRONG></TD>
<TD ALIGN="left">
The renowned science fiction writer, Steven Sagan,
will be appearing to sign copies of his latest book,
&quot;Was, Not Is&quot;.
</TD>
```

continues

Listing 24.10 Continued

```
</TR>
<TR>
<TD ALIGN="right"><STRONG><EM>Where:</EM></STRONG></TD>
<TD ALIGN="left">
A2Z Books<BR>
3456 Coolidge Road<BR>
Oak Park, MI 48027<BR>
(313) 55-55
</TD>
</TR>
<TR>
<TD ALIGN="right"><STRONG><EM>When:</EM></STRONG></TD>
<TD ALIGN="left">Saturday, February 30, 197, 10:30 AM EST</TD>
</TR>
</TABLE>
<P>Be there or be...cubed!
</CFMAIL>
```

FIGURE 24.6

This email was produced by using HTML formatting.

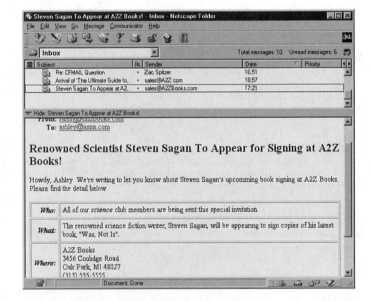

Sending Attachments with Your Email

With ColdFusion versions 2.0 and later, you have the ability to attach documents to your email messages. This powerful feature makes creating new types of Web applications: extremely simple. Here are some examples:

- A software developer uses email to send software patches to its registered users on an ongoing basis.

- A sales organization sends its geographically dispersed sales force updates to the customer database via email.

■ Our favorite bookstore notifies customers when books they may be interested in arrive from the publisher. A picture of the book cover is attached as a PCX file.

As you may recall from the example in the preceding section, the A2Z Bookstore's Marketing department has this nifty little function in its system that allows it to identify groups of customers and then send them custom email messages. You may have noticed in Listing 24.9 and Figure 24.5 that this function also enables the user to attach documents. Look for the field named Attachments in the listing.

Take a look at Listing 24.9, specifically the chunk of code that starts with this:

```
<!- Make sure attached file exists ->
<CFIF #Form.Attachment# is not "">
<CFIF #FileExists(Form.Attachment)# is "No">
```

This code chunk first tests to see whether the user entered a filename for the attachment. If she did, you need to make sure the file actually exists. If the file doesn't exist, ColdFusion won't tell you that it doesn't. When you're attaching a file to your email—unless you're absolutely certain that the file attachment exists—you'll probably want to use the `FileExists()` function to verify that the file does indeed exist before sending the email.

It's also worth noting that if you're allowing the user to specify the MIME attachment file and he doesn't specify one, you must use a CFMAIL tag that does not include the MIMEATTACH attribute. The following chunk of code, also from Listing 24.9, is used to create the CFMAIL tag without the MIMEATTACH attribute:

```
<CFELSE>
<!- Send the email, using the comma delimited list and NO attachment ->
<CFMAIL
TO=#CustList#
FROM="sales@A2ZBooks.com"
SUBJECT="#Form.Subject#"
>
```

Your ColdFusion Web applications: can also retrieve mail from a POP server and display the results like a simple mail client, or use the results in the form of a query. You can enhance many common Web Web applications: with CFPOP, as well as create new and useful tools:

■ A Web-based email client on a corporate intranet makes email retrieval easy for users and saves administrators money on software and support.

■ A software company creates a mailing list with an archive to make technical support questions and answers available both on the Web and by email.

■ An Internet service provider sends a customer satisfaction questionnaire to its customers using email and automatically tabulates the results received.

Using CFPOP

CFPOP encapsulates all the complexity of using the POP protocol into a simple ColdFusion tag. CFPOP takes an ACTION attribute to specify the operation to be performed. CFPOP supports three ACTION types:

Part
IV
Ch
24

1. GETHEADERONLY instructs CFPOP to retrieve all the header information for any messages in the mailbox. Header information includes the sender address, the date and time the mail was sent, and the message subject. In fact, the only information not in the header is the actual message itself.

2. GETALL is used to retrieve header information, as well as the message text. GETALL is used only when the message body is needed because retrieving the header information along with the message body can take quite a bit longer than retrieving just the header information.

3. DELETE can be used to delete one or more messages from a mailbox. Mail is not automatically deleted when it is read (with GETHEADERONLY or GETALL); to delete mail, a specific DELETE operation must be performed.

The following code snippet demonstrates how to retrieve POP mail headers:

```
<!--- Get mail headers --->
<CFPOP
 SERVER="mail.domain.com"
 USERNAME="bob"
 PASSWORD="gr8nHpnGy"
 ACTION="GETHEADERONLY"
 NAME="messages"
>
```

The messages retrieved are stored in a query result set, just like the results returned by CFQUERY. In this example, they are stored in a result set named "messages". CFOUTPUT can be used to process the retrieved list. The following code snippet outputs the sender and the subject of each message retrieved in the previous code example:

```
<!--- List retrieved messages --->
<UL>
<CFOUTPUT QUERY="messages">
 <LI>From: #from# - Subject: #subject#
</CFOUTPUT>
```

The query result set retrieved by CFPOP contains the following columns:

- DATE contains the date and time that the message was sent. (This is the contents of the SMTP message date header, and it might not be formatted suitably for use with the ColdFusion date functions.)

- FROM contains the name of the message sender.

- ATTACHMENTS contains a tab-delimited list of attachments, if there are any. This column is available only if the ACTION were GETALL and if the ATTACHMENTPATH attribute were specified.

- ATTACHMENTFILES contains a tab-delimited list of the temporary files created on the server. This column is available only if the ACTION were GETALL and if the ATTACHMENTPATH attribute were specified.

- TO contains the email address to which the message was sent.

- CC contains a comma-delimited list of names and email addresses to whom the message was carbon-copied.

- REPLYTO contains the email address to which any replies should be sent.
- SUBJECT contains the message subject.
- MESSAGENUMBER is a number that uniquely identifies a retrieved message, and it is used to drill down into or delete a specific message. The ID is a relative ID, not an actual ID. This means that IDs should be used immediately after being obtained, not stored for later use.
- BODY contains the actual message text. This column is available only if the ACTION were GETALL and not if the ACTION were GETHEADERONLY.

In addition to these basic attributes, CFPOP also supports additional attributes that you can use within your Web applications:. The complete list of additional attributes follows:

- ACTION specifies the operation to be performed. Valid values are GETHEADERONLY, GETALL, and DELETE. If this attribute is omitted, the default value GETHEADERONLY is used. It is a good idea to always specify the ACTION explicitly.
- ATTACHMENTPATH specifies the fully qualified name of the directory in which to save any email attachments. Attachments are retrieved only if the ACTION is GETALL.
- MAXROWS specifies the maximum number of messages to retrieve. All messages are retrieved if no value is provided.
- MESSAGENUMBER is an optional attribute that specifies one or more message numbers on which to perform an operation. It is required, however, if ACTION is DELETE. Multiple message numbers are specified as a ColdFusion list (a comma-delimited list).
- NAME contains the name of the query to be created if ACTION is GETALL or GETHEADERONLY, in which case it is a required attribute.
- PASSWORD must contain the POP password if the account has one.
- PORT specifies the POP server's port and defaults to 110 if not specified. Use this attribute only if your mail administrator tells you to.
- SERVER is the host name or IP address of the POP server. This attribute is required, and unlike the ColdFusion SMTP tag, there is no way to set a systemwide default value.
- STARTROW specifies the position of the first message to be retrieved. It defaults to 1 if no value is specified.
- TIMEOUT specifies the mail server timeout value (in seconds) and defaults to 60 seconds.
- USERNAME is the POP login name, and it should always be specified. An anonymous login is used if this is omitted.

Part
IV

Ch
24

Creating a Complete Mail Client

To better understand how CFPOP may be used, create a complete mail client using ColdFusion's mail tags. The supported functions follow:

- Allowing a user to log in to a mailbox on any POP mail server
- Displaying a list of waiting messages
- Allowing the user to drill down to view message details

■ The ability to delete unwanted mail

■ A reply function to reply to received mail (uses both CFOP and CFMAIL)

The email client is made up of seven templates:

■ LOGIN.CFM (Listing 24.11) is the user login screen.

■ MAIL.CFM (Listing 24.12) creates the frames for the mail interface.

■ HEADERS.CFM (Listing 24.13) displays the list of available mail messages.

■ MESSAGE.CFM (Listing 24.14) displays message details, including the body text.

■ DELETE.CFM (Listing 24.15) deletes a message.

■ REPLY.CFM (Listing 24.16) is the reply form.

■ SENDREPLY.CFM (Listing 24.17) sends the reply.

Creating LOGIN.CFM

This first template, LOGIN.CFM, prompts the user for a POP server name, login name, and password. The user may also specify an email address that is used when replying to mail. The POP server name and username are the only required fields in this form. The data collected in this form is submitted to MAIL.CFM for processing.

On the CD

Listing 24.11 LOGIN.CFM—**User Login Screen**

```
<HTML>

<HEAD>
<TITLE>E-Mail Login</TITLE>
</HEAD>

<BODY BGCOLOR="FFFFFF">

<CENTER>

<H1>CF Mail Client</H1>

<FORM ACTION="mail.cfm" METHOD="POST">

<INPUT TYPE="hidden" NAME="pop_server_required" VALUE="MAIL SERVER must be
➥specified!">
<INPUT TYPE="hidden" NAME="pop_username_required" VALUE="LOGIN must be
➥specified!">

<TABLE BGCOLOR="000000">
 <TR>
  <TH ALIGN="RIGHT" BGCOLOR="C0C0C0">Mail Server:</TH>
  <TD BGCOLOR="FFFFFF"><INPUT TYPE="text" NAME="pop_server"></TD>
 </TR>
 <TR>
  <TH ALIGN="RIGHT" BGCOLOR="C0C0C0">Login:</TH>
  <TD BGCOLOR="FFFFFF"><INPUT TYPE="text" NAME="pop_username"></TD>
```

```
    </TR>
    <TR>
     <TH ALIGN="RIGHT" BGCOLOR="C0C0C0">Password:</TH>
     <TD BGCOLOR="FFFFFF"><INPUT TYPE="password" NAME="pop_password"></TD>
    </TR>
    <TR>
     <TH ALIGN="RIGHT" BGCOLOR="C0C0C0">E-Mail Address:</TH>
     <TD BGCOLOR="FFFFFF"><INPUT TYPE="text" NAME="email_address"></TD>
    </TR>
    <TR>
     <TH BGCOLOR="C0C0C0" COLSPAN=2><INPUT TYPE="SUBMIT" VALUE="Login"></TR>
    </TR>
  </TABLE>
</FORM>

</CENTER>

</BODY>

</HTML>
```

Creating MAIL.CFM

This mail client uses a split screen window, which is created via two frames. The left frame contains the list of messages and the right frame displays a message when one is selected from the list. MAIL.CFM contains the HTML code to create the frames. The right window is populated with BLANK.CFM, an empty template. The left frame contains HEADERS.CFM, which retrieves the email messages. The POP login and server information must be passed down to the HEADERS.CFM template, and because the fields contain invalid URL characters, the values are all encoded using the URLEncodedFormat() function.

On the CD

Listing 24.12 MAIL.CFM—Creating Frames for the Mail Interface

```
<CFOUTPUT>

<HTML>

<HEAD>
<TITLE>E-Mail for #Trim(pop_username)#</TITLE>
</HEAD>

<FRAMESET COLS="50%,50%">
 <FRAME NAME="header" SRC="headers.cfm?pop_server=
➥#URLEncodedFormat(pop_server)#&pop_username=#URLEncodedFormat
➥(pop_username)#&pop_password=#URLEncodedFormat(pop_password)
➥#&email_address=#URLEncodedFormat(email_address)#" SCROLLING="AUTO">
 <FRAME NAME="message" SRC="blank.cfm" SCROLLING="AUTO">
</FRAMESET>

</HTML>

</CFOUTPUT>
```

Creating HEADERS.CFM

The HEADERS.CFM template retrieves the message headers and displays them in a table. Because the messages are returned in a standard ColdFusion query, the query variables RecordCount and CurrentRow are available for use. Listing 24.13 uses RecordCount to display the number of messages retrieved. The template starts with a CFPOP tag that has an ACTION of GETHEADERONLY. Because the message body is not needed in this template, time can be saved using GETHEADERONLY instead of GETALL. The template also contains two buttons at the top of the page. The REFRESH button calls the same HEADERS.CFM template again and is used to refresh the list of messages. The LOGOUT function returns the user to the login screen.

The list of messages itself is displayed in an HTML table; the message number field can be clicked in order to drill down to see the message details displayed in the right window.

On the CD

Listing 24.13 HEADERS.CFM—Displaying the List of Available Mail Messages

```
<!--- Get mail headers --->
<CFPOP
 SERVER="#pop_server#"
 USERNAME="#pop_username#"
 PASSWORD="#pop_password#"
 ACTION="GETHEADERONLY"
 NAME="messages"
>

<BODY BGCOLOR="FFFFFF">

<P ALIGN="RIGHT">

<!--- Table for REFRESH and LOGOUT buttons --->
<TABLE>
 <TR>
  <TD>
   <!--- REFRESH button --->
   <FORM ACTION="headers.cfm" METHOD="POST">
   <CFOUTPUT>
   <INPUT TYPE="hidden" NAME="pop_server" VALUE="#pop_server#">
   <INPUT TYPE="hidden" NAME="pop_username" VALUE="#pop_username#">
   <INPUT TYPE="hidden" NAME="pop_password" VALUE="#pop_password#">
   <INPUT TYPE="hidden" NAME="email_address" VALUE="#email_address#">
   </CFOUTPUT>
   <INPUT TYPE="submit" VALUE="Refresh">
   </FORM>
  </TD>
  <TD>
   <!--- LOGOUT button --->
   <FORM ACTION="login.cfm" METHOD="POST" TARGET="_parent">
   <INPUT TYPE="submit" VALUE="Logout">
   </FORM>
  </TD>
 </TR>
</TABLE>
```

```
</P>

<CENTER>

<!--- How many messages retrieved? --->
<CFOUTPUT>#messages.RecordCount# messages</CFOUTPUT>

<TABLE BGCOLOR="000000" WIDTH="100%">
 <TR>
  <TH></TH>
  <TH BGCOLOR="C0C0C0">Date</TH>
  <TH BGCOLOR="C0C0C0">From</TH>
  <TH BGCOLOR="C0C0C0">Subject</TH>
 </TR>

<!--- Display list of messages, first column links to drill down to message
itself --->
<CFOUTPUT QUERY="messages">
 <TR>
  <TD BGCOLOR="FFFFFF"><A HREF="message.cfm?pop_server=#URLEncodedFormat
➡(pop_server)#&pop_username=#URLEncodedFormat(pop_username)
➡#&pop_password=#URLEncodedFormat(pop_password)#&email_address=
➡#URLEncodedFormat(email_address)#&messagenumber=#messagenumber#"
TARGET="message">#messagenumber#</A></TD>
  <TD BGCOLOR="FFFFFF">#date#</TD>
  <TD BGCOLOR="FFFFFF">#from#</TD>
  <TD BGCOLOR="FFFFFF">#subject#</TD>
 </TR>
</CFOUTPUT>

</TABLE>

</CENTER>

</BODY>
</HTML>
```

Creating MESSAGE.CFM

The MESSAGE.CFM template displays the message details. The CFPOP tag has an ACTION of GETALL because the message body is needed. If you want a single message (the one the user selected), the message number is passed to the CFPOP MESSAGENUMBER attribute. The NAME attribute once again specifies the name of the query to be created; in this example, it is named "message". This template also has two buttons at the top of the page: The REPLY button allows the user to respond to a message and the DELETE button deletes the current message from the mail server. Each of these buttons is FORM submit buttons; the POP server, account information, and message number are passed as hidden fields. The message body itself is displayed using the ColdFusion ParagraphFormat() function so that paragraph breaks are honored.

Listing 24.14 MESSAGE.CFM—**Displaying Message Details**

```
<!--- Get message --->
<CFPOP
 SERVER="#pop_server#"
 USERNAME="#pop_username#"
 PASSWORD="#pop_password#"
 ACTION="GETALL"
 MESSAGENUMBER="#messagenumber#"
 NAME="message"
>

<BODY BGCOLOR="FFFFFF">

<P ALIGN="RIGHT">

<!--- Table for REPLY and DELETE button --->
<TABLE>
 <TR>
  <TD>
   <!--- REPLY button --->
   <FORM ACTION="reply.cfm" METHOD="POST">
   <CFOUTPUT>
   <INPUT TYPE="hidden" NAME="pop_server" VALUE="#pop_server#">
   <INPUT TYPE="hidden" NAME="pop_username" VALUE="#pop_username#">
   <INPUT TYPE="hidden" NAME="pop_password" VALUE="#pop_password#">
   <INPUT TYPE="hidden" NAME="email_address" VALUE="#email_address#">
   <INPUT TYPE="hidden" NAME="messagenumber" VALUE="#messagenumber#">
   </CFOUTPUT>
   <INPUT TYPE="submit" VALUE="Reply">
   </FORM>
  </TD>
  <TD>
   <!--- DELETE button --->
   <FORM ACTION="delete.cfm" METHOD="POST" TARGET="_parent">
   <CFOUTPUT>
   <INPUT TYPE="hidden" NAME="pop_server" VALUE="#pop_server#">
   <INPUT TYPE="hidden" NAME="pop_username" VALUE="#pop_username#">
   <INPUT TYPE="hidden" NAME="pop_password" VALUE="#pop_password#">
   <INPUT TYPE="hidden" NAME="email_address" VALUE="#email_address#">
   <INPUT TYPE="hidden" NAME="messagenumber" VALUE="#messagenumber#">
   </CFOUTPUT>
   <INPUT TYPE="submit" VALUE="Delete">
   </FORM>
  </TD>
 </TR>
</TABLE>

</P>

<CFOUTPUT QUERY="message">

<TABLE BGCOLOR="000000">

 <!--- Display message header info --->
 <TR>
```

```
     <TH BGCOLOR="C0C0C0" ALIGN="RIGHT">Date:</TH>
     <TD BGCOLOR="FFFFFF">#date#</TD>
    </TR>
    <TR>
     <TH BGCOLOR="C0C0C0" ALIGN="RIGHT">From:</TH>
     <TD BGCOLOR="FFFFFF">#from#</TD>
    </TR>
    <TR>
     <TH BGCOLOR="C0C0C0" ALIGN="RIGHT">Subject:</TH>
     <TD BGCOLOR="FFFFFF">#subject#</TD>
    </TR>
    <TR>
     <TH BGCOLOR="C0C0C0" ALIGN="RIGHT">To:</TH>
     <TD BGCOLOR="FFFFFF">#to#</TD>
    </TR>
    <TR>
     <TH BGCOLOR="C0C0C0" ALIGN="RIGHT">CC:</TH>
     <TD BGCOLOR="FFFFFF">#cc#</TD>
    </TR>

    <!--- Display message body --->
    <TR>
     <TD COLSPAN="2" BGCOLOR="FFFFFF">#ParagraphFormat(body)#</TD>
    </TR>

   </TABLE>

  </CFOUTPUT>

 </BODY>
</HTML>
```

Creating DELETE.CFM

DELETE.CFM deletes a message from the mail server. It calls CFPOP with an ACTION of DELETE and specifies the message number of the message to be deleted. The MAIL.CFM template (the template that defines the frames) is then called so that both the left and right windows get updated.

On the CD

Listing 24.15 LOGIN.CFM—Deleting a Message

```
<!--- Delete a message --->
<CFPOP
 SERVER="#pop_server#"
 USERNAME="#pop_username#"
 PASSWORD="#pop_password#"
 ACTION="DELETE"
 MESSAGENUMBER="#messagenumber#"
>

<!--- And redisplay entire frame so that headers is updated --->
<CFLOCATION
URL="mail.cfm?pop_server=#URLEncodedFormat(pop_server)#&pop_username=
➥#URLEncodedFormat(pop_username)#&pop_password=#URLEncodedFormat
➥(pop_password)#&email_address=#URLEncodedFormat(email_address)#">
```

Creating REPLY.CFM

REPLY.CFM displays a reply form that can be used to reply to email. First of all, the message is retrieved with a CFPOP call. A form is then displayed with the To name (the REPLYTO field) and the subject filled in, along with a TEXTAREA box in which to type a reply. The original message is also displayed so that it appears in the reply (beneath a dashed line). When the user clicks the Send button, the form is submitted to the SENDREPLY.CFM template.

On the CD

Listing 24.16   REPLY.CFM—The Reply Form

```
<!--- Get message to reply to --->
<CFPOP
 SERVER="#pop_server#"
 USERNAME="#pop_username#"
 PASSWORD="#pop_password#"
 ACTION="GETALL"
 MESSAGENUMBER="#messagenumber#"
 NAME="message"
>

<BODY BGCOLOR="FFFFFF">

<CFOUTPUT QUERY="message">

<!--- Reply form --->
<FORM ACTION="sendreply.cfm" METHOD="POST">

<INPUT TYPE="hidden" NAME="pop_server" VALUE="#pop_server#">
<INPUT TYPE="hidden" NAME="pop_username" VALUE="#pop_username#">
<INPUT TYPE="hidden" NAME="pop_password" VALUE="#pop_password#">
<INPUT TYPE="hidden" NAME="email_address" VALUE="#email_address#">
<INPUT TYPE="hidden" NAME="messagenumber" VALUE="#messagenumber#">
<INPUT TYPE="hidden" NAME="mail_from" VALUE="#email_address#">

<TABLE BGCOLOR="000000">
 <TR>
  <TH ALIGN="RIGHT" BGCOLOR="C0C0C0">To:</TH>
  <TD BGCOLOR="FFFFFF"><INPUT TYPE="text" NAME="mail_to" VALUE="#Trim
➥(replyto)#"></TD>
 </TR>
 <TR>
  <TH ALIGN="RIGHT" BGCOLOR="C0C0C0">Subject:</TH>
  <TD BGCOLOR="FFFFFF"><INPUT TYPE="text" NAME="mail_subject" VALUE=
➥"Re: #Trim(subject)#"></TD>
 </TR>
 <TR>
  <TD COLSPAN=2 BGCOLOR="FFFFFF">
  <TEXTAREA NAME="mail_body" WRAP="VIRTUAL">

#RepeatString("=", 40)#
#from# wrote:
#body#
  </TEXTAREA>
  </TD>
```

```
  </TR>
  <TR>
   <TH COLSPAN=2 BGCOLOR="C0C0C0"><INPUT TYPE="submit" VALUE="Send"></TH>
  </TABLE>

  </FORM>

  </CFOUTPUT>

  </BODY>
  </HTML>
```

Creating SENDREPLY.CFM

Listing 24.17, which displays SENDREPLY.CFM, sends the message using the ColdFusion CFMAIL tag (the SMTP interface) and then redisplays the message (see Figure 24.7).

Part
IV
Ch
24

On the CD

Listing 24.17   SENDREPLY.CFM—Sending the Reply

```
<!--- Send a reply using CFMAIL --->
<CFMAIL FROM="#mail_from#" TO="#mail_to#" SUBJECT="#mail_subject#">
#mail_body#
</CFMAIL>

<!--- And then redisplay message --->
<CFLOCATION URL="message.cfm?pop_server=#URLEncodedFormat(pop_server)
➡#&pop_username=#URLEncodedFormat(pop_username)#&pop_password=
➡#URLEncodedFormat(pop_password)#&email_address=#URLEncodedFormat
➡(email_address)#&messagenumber=#messagenumber#">
```

FIGURE 24.7
The Web-based email client.

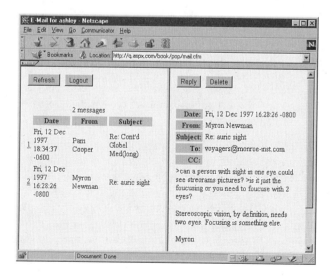

Enhancing the Mail Client

This is a very basic, albeit functional, email client and is a good base on which to write your own email client. Here are some suggested enhancements to this application:

- Allow the sending of new mail (not just replies) and sending attachments (using CFFILE ACTION="UPLOAD").
- Allow mail forwarding.
- Use cookies or client variables to store the POP server and account information so that the user does not have to enter it each time.
- Use cookies or client variables to store the date and time mail was last retrieved, so that on the next visit users can see only new mail.
- Allow mail filtering (by sender, subject, date) and searching (subject and body).
- Save attachments and allow the user to click and retrieve them.
- Use the ColdFusion CFLDAP tag to retrieve address book entries from a directory service.
- Replace all forms (login, reply, send mail) with CFFORM tags to create a more powerful and intuitive user interface.

Mail Daemons

CFPOP is well suited for use within mail daemons. A *daemon* is a program that sits waiting for some activity and then performs set processes when that activity occurs. A good example of this is a list server daemon. *List servers* are email-based discussion groups that users subscribe to or unsubscribe from.

To subscribe to a list, a user sends email to a specific email address with a subject such as SUBSCRIBE; the subject could be anything, but SUBSCRIBE has become the accepted keyword. When the daemon encounters a SUBSCRIBE message, it adds the user's email address to a database and sends a confirmation message to the user. From that point on, any mail sent to the list of users is also sent to the newly subscribed user, who is now part of that list.

To unsubscribe from a list, a user sends a mail message with a subject of UNSUBSCRIBE. When the daemon encounters this message, it removes the email address from the database and sends back a confirmation message.

The code example in Listing 24.18 is not a complete listserver interface, but it demonstrates the basic components required to create your own listserver. The template first retrieves a list of messages in the mailbox. Because the message body is not needed, the ACTION is set to GETHEADERONLY. A CFLOOP is used to loop through the query when the mail is retrieved. A good reason to use CFLOOP instead of CFOUTPUT is that CFOUTPUT does not allow some CF tags to be executed within it (such as CFMAIL or CFQUERY). CFLOOP does not have these limitations and can therefore be safely used as long as you place CFOUTPUT tags around your output sections within the loop. The CFLOOP itself contains a CFIF statement that checks the message subject and performs some code. Replace the ellipses (...) with your own code as appropriate.

Listing 24.18 Basic Elements of a Listserver

```
<!--- Get mail headers --->
<CFPOP
 SERVER="mail.domain.com"
 USERNAME="listserv"
 PASSWORD="g8g7ty"
 ACTION="GETHEADERONLY"
 NAME="messages"
>

<!--- Loop through messages --->
<CFLOOP QUERY="messages">

 <CFIF #subject# IS "SUBSCRIBE">

  <!--- User wants to subscribe --->

  ...

 <CFELSEIF #subject# IS "UNSUBSCRIBE">

  <!--- User wants to unsubscribe --->

  ...

 <CFELSE>

  <!--- Not sure what users wants, send HELP information --->

  ...

 </CFIF>

</CFLOOP>
```

Working with Attachments

Email is not used just to transmit text messages. Email has become a popular way to send and receive files of all types because of MIME.

You must do the following in order to retrieve attached files with CFPOP:

1. Retrieve messages with CFPOP using an ACTION value of GETALL and specifying the location (drive and directory) in which to store temporary copies of the attached files. This path is passed to the ATTACHMENTPATH attribute.

2. Examine the ATTACHMENTS field for a list of attachments. The list is tab delimited and can be used with the ColdFusion list function (and CFLOOP) if the tab character is specified as the delimiter (ASCII character with a value of 9).

3. The attached files are stored in the path specified in the ATTACHMENTPATH attribute. The files are not stored using their actual filenames because the file may have originated on

an operating system that had different file naming conventions. The physical filenames are stored in the ATTACHMENTFILES column, in a tab-delimited list. This list always has the same number of elements as the ATTACHMENTS list, and the first attachment listed in ATTACHMENTS is named with the value in the first element in the ATTACHMENTFILES list.

4. ColdFusion does not automatically delete the temporary files. It is your responsibility to do so; if you don't, they'll simply take up space. The files can be deleted with the CFFILE tag (via ACTION="DELETE").

If you are going to allow users to retrieve the attached files as Web pages (using an URL that points to the file directly), you must make sure that the path specified in the ATTACHMENTPATH attribute is within a Web server path (beneath the Web server root or in any other mapped drive). The Windows temporary directory (which is generally a good place to store temporary files) is therefore not a good choice for this. ●

CHAPTER 25

Online Commerce

Leveraging the Internet with ColdFusion

The vast growth of the Internet has been fueled by commerce. As you've heard in the commercials, businesses large and small have benefited from use of the Internet. Small companies and individuals now market products and services to new markets worldwide, and large companies are saving in sales and delivery costs by setting up shop on the Internet.

ColdFusion facilitates the construction of highly interactive, easily managed sites for commerce. Merchants have the choice of using many different payment systems, simplifying the purchasing process for customers. *Shopping cart systems* allow customers to easily browse a product selection, marking products for purchase and even retaining these selections between visits. Merchants can track purchases and use this data to recommend other items to customers, increasing the bottom line. In this chapter you construct a shopping cart system and show how this system can integrate with several different payment systems.

Understanding the Mechanics of Internet Commerce

The first element in Internet commerce is marketing. That specific subject is way beyond the scope of this book, but they'll only visit if they know it's there. When you create an Internet site, the goal is to make it easy and fun for potential customers to find what they want, and then make it as painless as possible for them to purchase it.

The purchase must be supported after the sale, and further offers and updates should be given to customers, which encourages them to return. This process can be broken down into five steps: navigating, selecting, purchasing, delivering, and supporting.

Navigating

If a customer is going to purchase something from your site, he first must be able to find it. Navigation includes several elements. First, the customer must know what is in the store in general terms. Second, the products on the site must be organized in a logical manner. Third, and very important, a means should be provided to search for products based on dynamic criteria. In the nonvirtual world, sales agents help customers find their way through a store and assist in the purchase. Your site must make it easy for customers to find what they need quickly and easily.

A good way to put this concept in context is to visualize the organization of your products in terms of a traditional store. As you walk in, there may be several special items on display, encouraging impulse purchases. As you venture into the store, departments are usually clearly defined and logically organized. If things are hard to find, they don't sell and customers go elsewhere.

Selecting

When you find the items you are looking for (and many that you weren't looking for but decide to buy anyway), you place the item in a basket so you can continue shopping. Allowing customers to queue items for purchase encourages greater sales. After all, stores wouldn't sell much if you could buy only what you could carry to the checkout. This is also an important feature for commerce sites on the Internet. If your site sells more than a few products, a shopping cart is a must.

Purchasing

Purchases require several elements. First, information about the customer must be obtained. Second, a payment method that is mutually feasible for both customer and merchant must be chosen. Third, the merchant must process the customer's payment information. Finally, the customers receive confirmation of their purchases. Gathering data from customers is a step that is different for almost every merchant, but usually name, address, and email are collected—at minimum. Check, credit card, or billing information for the chosen payment method is also collected from the customer for processing.

Of great concern to both developers and consumers is security and encryption of data between the customer and the merchant. This can be accomplished by using the SSL or SHTTP capabilities of your Web server to establish a secure connection between the customer and the merchant. ColdFusion uses these capabilities transparently, via your Web server's security features. For some Web servers, such as WebSite from O'Reilly and Associates, you can simply direct the user to an URL using port 443, such as `http://www.myserver.com:443/order.cfm`. Other servers use `https://` to precede a secure URL. The documentation for your Web server can provide more information on using encryption capabilities in your application.

Processing and confirmation steps depend entirely on the method of payment chosen. Later in the chapter you explore several popular methods of payment processing and how to use them in your application. Most payment processing systems provide automatic and immediate payment processing—a far cry from the early days of Internet commerce.

Part

IV

Ch

25

Delivering the Product

Delivering the product is different for almost every merchant. For paid access sites, delivery might simply include access to a protected area of the site. For software purchases, a file may be made available for a user to download. Other sites need to fulfill purchases by mail or other form of delivery. Each method of delivery can be supported using ColdFusion. For protected access sites, a customer could be given a username and password using CFMAIL or by displaying a secure Web page. Files can be made available using CFCONTENT or retrieved using CFFTP for software delivery.

Support After the Sale

Support after the sale not only keeps customers happy but also encourages future sales. Some items may not necessarily need support, but newsletters or customized offers can be sent to let the customer know about new specials or other items of interest. For items that need more complex support, a threaded conferencing area allows customers to post problems and receive quick responses from support staff and other users. Let's see how these elements come together in an example application: the QuickStore custom tag.

Building the QuickStore Application

This example brings together the elements necessary in a basic Internet store. Because many Webmasters would like to integrate a store into an existing Web site, you'll create a custom tag that can be placed into any page. The custom tag will use client and session management, so these must be enabled in the APPLICATION.CFM file for your application. See Chapter 27, "Session Variables and Cookies," for tips on enabling client and session management. The tag also uses a database to store products, categories, customer information, and sales data. This data can be used for delivery, support, and marketing. When viewing Listings 25.1 through 25.6, remember that each listing represents a separate custom tag. These tags must be placed in the same directory of the application you want to use them in, or the CUSTOMTAGS directory underneath your ColdFusion server's root directory. When the QuickStore.cfm template is called from another ColdFusion template, as shown in Listing 27.7, you will have a complete online shopping cart system. The following sections walk you through the application.

The Store.mdb Database Schema

The database used for QuickStore is small and simple and contains four tables. The Categories table contains the name and description for the product categories. The Products table is the most complex table. It contains the name, description, image paths, category ID, and text for a product, along with its price. The Customers table contains customer data, and the Sales table links Customer records to the products they purchased. The complete schema is shown in Table 25.1.

Table 25.1   Store.mdb **Schema**

Table	Fields	Data Type
Categories	CategoryID	Integer (Primary Key)
	Name	Text
	Description	Text or Memo
Customers	CustomerID	Integer (Primary Key)
	CFID	Integer
	FirstName	Text
	LastName	Text
	Address	Text
	City	Text
	State	Text
	Country	Text

Table	Fields	Data Type
	PostalCode	Text
	Email	Text
Products	ProductID	Integer (Primary Key)
	CategoryID	Integer
	DescriptionShort	Text or Memo
	DescriptionLong	Memo
	ProductName	Text
	Keywords	Text
	UnitPrice	Currency
	ImageSmall	Text
	ImageLarge	Text
Sales	CustomerID	Integer (Primary Key)
	ProductID	Integer
	Quantity	Integer
	SaleDate	Date/Time

Flow and Initialization in the QuickStore Application

The QuickStore tag, shown in Listing 25.1, sets up default values for the administration password, whether the URLToken will be appended to internal URLs, the data source to use, and what type of payment processing will be used. Because each payment processing system has its own parameters, no default values are specified. Client variables are used to identify customers, and session variables are used to store the contents of the shopping basket and the state of the application, or what it is to do next.

The QuickStore tag also controls the flow of the application. Depending on the values passed to it, the QuickStore tag will call other custom tags to execute functions such as displaying products, managing the application, and adding products to the basket. In addition, the ItemsLong query is cached in order to minimize the amount of queries per page. Navigation through the catalog does not require any other queries until a user views the detail of a product.

Listing 25.1 `QUICKSTORE.CFM`—**Initialization and Program Flow**

```
<!-- QuickStore custom tag

This tag is a complete online store with a shopping cart and Web based
➥ administration.

Usage:
<cf_quickStore
 dsn="data source name"
 password="administration password"
 addtoken="yes|no"
 cc="yes|no"
 processor="icverify|cybercash">

-->

<!-- Set defaults -->
<cfparam name="attributes.dsn" default="QuickStore">
<cfparam name="attributes.password" default="password">
<cfparam name="attributes.addToken" default="no">
<cfparam name="attributes.cc" default="yes">
<cfparam name="attributes.processor" default="ivcerify">
<cfparam name="form.productID" default="0">
<cfset cacheItemList = createTimeSpan(0,0,15,0)>

<cfset thispage = getfilefrompath(gettemplatepath())>

<!-- Create and cache the product list -->
<cfquery name="application.ItemsShort" data source="#attributes.dsn#"
➥ cachedWithin="#cacheItemList#">

    SELECT      Products.ProductID, Products.ProductName, Categories.Name,
➥ Categories.Description, Categories.CategoryID
    FROM        Products, Categories
    WHERE       Products.CategoryID = Categories.CategoryID
    ORDER BY  Categories.Name, Products.ProductName

</cfquery>

<!-- Create the shopping basket -->
<cfif not isDefined("session.basket")>

    <cfset session.basket = queryNew("ProductID, Quantity, saleDate")>

</cfif>

<cfif isdefined("url.do")>

    <cfset session.do = url.do>

<cfelse>

    <cfset session.do = "index">

</cfif>
```

```
<!-- Build query string -->
<cfif attributes.addtoken>

    <cfset variables.querystring = "?#client.URLToken#&">

<cfelse>

    <cfset variables.querystring = "?">

</cfif>

<!-- Do what we need to do -->

<cfif session.do is "action">

    <!-- Handle events -->

    <cfif action is "Add Category">

        <cf_quickStore_category
         action="add"
         dsn="#attributes.dsn#"
         name="#form.name#"
         description="#form.description#">

    <cfelseif action is "Delete Category">

        <cf_quickStore_category
         action="delete"
         dsn="#attributes.dsn#"
         categoryID="#form.categoryID#">

    <cfelseif action is "Add Product">

        <cf_quickStore_product
         dsn="#attributes.dsn#"
         action="add"
         productname="#form.Productname#"
         categoryID="#form.categoryID#"
         DescriptionShort="#form.descriptionShort#"
         DescriptionLong="#form.descriptionLong#"
         Keywords="#form.keywords#"
         UnitPrice="#form.unitPrice#"
         ImageSmall="#form.imageSmall#"
         ImageLarge="#form.imageLarge#">

    <cfelseif action is "Edit Product">

        <cf_quickStore_product
         productID="#form.productID#"
         dsn="#attributes.dsn#"
         action="edit">

    <cfelseif action is "Update Product">
```

Part

IV

Ch

25

continues

Listing 25.1 Continued

```
        <cfif form.editAction is "Update">

            <cfset this.action = "Update">

        <cfelse>

            <cfset this.action = "Delete">

        </cfif>

        <cf_quickStore_product
         dsn="#attributes.dsn#"
         action="#this.action#"
         productID="#form.productID#"
         productname="#form.Productname#"
         categoryID="#form.categoryID#"
         DescriptionShort="#form.descriptionShort#"
         DescriptionLong="#form.descriptionLong#"
         Keywords="#form.keywords#"
         UnitPrice="#form.unitPrice#"
         ImageSmall="#form.imageSmall#"
         ImageLarge="#form.imageLarge#">

    <cfelseif action is "Add to basket">

        <cf_quickStore_basket
         action="add"
         productID="#form.productID#"
         quantity="#form.quantity#">

        <cfset session.do = "basket">

    <cfelseif action is "Update basket">

        <cf_quickStore_basket
         action="update"
         productID="#form.productID#">

        <cfset session.do = "basket">

    <cfelseif action is "Purchase Products">

        <cf_quickStore_process
         action="purchase"
         dsn="#attributes.dsn#"
         cfid="#client.cfid#"
         name="#form.firstname# #form.lastname#"
         address="#form.address#"
         city="#form.city#"
         state="#form.state#"
         postalCode="#form.postalCode#"
         country="#form.country#"
         email="#form.country#">
```

```
            <cfset session.do = "process">

        </cfif>

</cfif>

<cfswitch expression="#session.do#">

    <cfcase value="admin">

        <!-- Administration page -->

        <cfparam name="session.edit" default="no">

        <cfif isdefined("form.pass")>

            <cfif form.pass is attributes.password>

                <cfset session.authenticated = "yes">

            </cfif>

        </cfif>

        <cfif not isdefined("session.authenticated")>

            <cf_quickStore_admin
             action="login"
             thispage="#thispage#"
             querystring="#querystring#"
             dsn="#attributes.dsn#">

        <cfelse>

            <cf_quickStore_admin
            action="admin"
             thispage="#thispage#"
             querystring="#querystring#"
             dsn="#attributes.dsn#">

        </cfif>

    </cfcase>

    <cfcase value="index">

        <!-- Main page -->
        <cf_quickStore_catalog
         action="index"
         thispage="#thispage#"
         querystring="#querystring#"
         dsn="#attributes.dsn#">

    </cfcase>
```

continues

Listing 25.1 Continued

```
<cfcase value="search">

    <!-- Search results -->
    <cf_quickStore_catalog
     action="search"
     thispage="#thispage#"
     querystring="#querystring#"
     dsn="#attributes.dsn#">

</cfcase>

<cfcase value="list">

    <!-- Product listing -->
    <cf_quickStore_catalog
     action="list"
     thispage="#thispage#"
     querystring="#querystring#"
     dsn="#attributes.dsn#">

</cfcase>

<cfcase value="detail">

    <!-- Product detail -->
    <cf_quickStore_catalog
     action="detail"
     thispage="#thispage#"
     querystring="#querystring#"
     dsn="#attributes.dsn#">

</cfcase>

<cfcase value="basket">

    <!-- The shopping basket -->
    <cf_quickStore_basket
     action="show"
     thispage="#thispage#"
     querystring="#querystring#"
     dsn="#attributes.dsn#">

</cfcase>

<cfcase value="form">

    <!-- Customer Information form -->
    <cf_quickStore_orderForm
     cc="#attributes.cc#"
     thispage="#thispage#"
     querystring="#querystring#">

</cfcase>
```

```
<cfcase value="process">

    <!-- Process the order -->
    <cf_quickStore_process
     method="#attributes.processor#"
     thispage="#thispage#"
     querystring="#querystring#"
     dsn="#attributes.dsn#"
     action="process"
     cfid="#client.cfid#"
     name="#form.firstname# #form.lastname#"
     address="#form.address#"
     city="#form.city#"
     state="#form.state#"
     postalCode="#form.postalCode#"
     country="#form.country#"
     email="#form.email#">


</cfcase>

</cfswitch>
```

Administering QuickStore

The administration area of the application, shown in Listing 25.2, is accessed by appending the URL parameter do=admin to the starting URL. When the admin page is accessed, the merchant is asked for the administration password. The administration forms are displayed when the correct password is entered. Merchants add, delete, and edit products. In the product entry dialog, images are entered using relative paths. For instance, if the store template is in the /store/ directory and the images are in the /store/images directory, the image pencil.gif is entered as images/pencil.gif. The administration page is shown in Figure 25.1.

On the CD

Listing 25.2 QUICKSTORE_ADMIN.CFM—**The Administration Interface**

```
<!-- QuickStore_admin custom tag

-->

<!-- Initialize -->
<cfparam name="attributes.thispage" default="">
<cfparam name="attributes.querystring" default="">
<cfparam name="attributes.dsn" default="">
<cfparam name="attributes.action" default="">
<cfparam name="attributes.thispage" default="#GetFileFromPath
➥(GetTemplatePath())#">
<cfparam name="attributes.querystring" default="?">
<cfparam name="attributes.productID" default="0">

<cfset thisPage = attributes.thisPage>
<cfset queryString = attributes.queryString>
```

continues

Listing 25.2   Continued

```
<cfswitch expression="#attributes.action#">

<cfcase value="login">

    <table cellspacing="0" cellpadding="2" border="1">
    <tr>
        <td><b>Administration</b>
        </td>
    </tr>
    <tr>
        <td>
            <table border=0>
            <tr><td colspan=2>
            <b>Enter your password:</b><p>
            </td></tr>

            <cfform method="post" action="#thisPage##queryString#do=admin">

            <tr><td>
            <input type="hidden" name="pass_required"
➡ value="You must enter a password">
            <input type="Password" name="Pass">
            </td>
            <td>
            <input type="Submit" value="Enter">
            </td></tr>
            </cfform>
            </table>
        </td>
    </tr>
    </table>

</cfcase>

<cfcase value="admin">

    <cfquery name="categories" data source="#attributes.dsn#">

        SELECT * FROM Categories
        ORDER BY Name ASC

    </cfquery>

    <table cellspacing="0" cellpadding="2" border="1">
    <tr>
        <td>
            <b>Administration</b>
        </td>
    </tr>

    <cfif categories.recordcount is not 0>

        <!-- Delete category dialog -->
```

```
      <tr>
          <td>
              <table border=0>
              <tr>
                  <td colspan=2>
                  <b>Delete a category:</b><p>
                  </td>
              </tr>
              <cfform action="#thisPage##queryString#do=action">
              <tr>
                  <td>
                  <b>Category:</b>
                  <cfselect name="CategoryID" size="1"
➥ query="Categories" value="categoryID" display="Name">
                  </cfselect>
                  </td>
                  <td>
                  <input type="Submit" name="action" value="Delete Category">
                  </td>
              </tr>
              </cfform>
              </table>
          </td>
      </tr>

  </cfif>

  <!-- Add category dialog -->

  <tr>
      <td>
          <table border=0>
          <tr>
              <td colspan=2>
              <b>Add a category:</b><p>
              </td>
          </tr>
          <cfform method="post" action="#thisPage##queryString#do=action">
          <tr>
              <td>
              <input type="hidden" name="name_required"
➥ value="You must enter    a category">
              <b>Category:</b> <input type="text" name="name">
              </td>
              <td>
              <input type="hidden"
               name="description_required"
               value="You must enter a description">
              <b>Description:</b>
              <cfinput type="text"
               name="Description"
               required="yes"
               message="You must enter a description">
              </td>
          </tr>
```

continues

Part

IV

Ch

25

Listing 25.2   Continued

```
            <tr>
                <td colspan=2>
                <input type="Submit" name="action" value="Add Category">
                </td>
            </tr>
            </cfform>
            </table>
        </td>
</tr>


<cfquery name="products" data source="#attributes.dsn#">

    SELECT * FROM Products
    ORDER BY ProductName ASC

</cfquery>


<cfif categories.recordcount is not 0
 and products.recordcount is not 0>

    <!-- Edit product dialog -->

    <tr>
        <td>
            <table border=0>
            <tr><td colspan=2>
            <b>Edit a product:</b><p>
            </td></tr>
            <cfform
             action="#thisPage##queryString#do=action">
            <tr><td>
            <b>Product:</b>
            <cfselect name="ProductID"
             size="1"
             query="Products"
             value="ProductID"
             display="ProductName">
            </cfselect>
            </td>
            <td>
            <input type="Submit" name="action" value="Edit Product">
            </td></tr>
            </cfform>
            </table>
        </td>
    </tr>
                    <table border=0>
                    <tr>
                    <td colspan=2>
                    <b>Edit product:</b><p>
                    </td>
```

```
              </tr>

              <cfform
               action="#thisPage##queryString#do=action">

               type="Text"
               name="DescriptionShort"
               value="#ItemsLong.DescriptionShort#"
               required="yes"
               message="You must enter a short description">
              </td>
              </tr>
              <tr>
              <td>
              <input
               type="hidden"
               name="UnitPrice_required"
               value="You must enter a unit price">
              <b>Unit price:</b>
              <cfinput
               type="Text"
               name="UnitPrice"
               value="#DecimalFormat(ItemsLong.UnitPrice)#"
               required="Yes"
               message="You must enter a unit price">
              </td>
              <td>
              <input
              type="hidden"
              name="keywords_required"
              value="You must enter keywords">
              <b>Keywords:</b>
              <cfinput
               type="Text"
               name="Keywords"
               value="#ItemsLong.Keywords#"
               required="yes"
               message="You must enter keywords">
              </td>
              </tr>
              <tr>
              <td colspan=2>
              <input
               type="hidden"
               name="descriptionLong_required"
               value="You must enter a long description">
              <b>Long Description:</b><br>
              <textarea
               name="DescriptionLong"
               cols="60"
               rows="6"
               wrap="VIRTUAL"><cfoutput>#ItemsLong.DescriptionLong#
➥</cfoutput></textarea>
              </td>
              </tr>
```

continues

Listing 25.2   Continued

```
                      <tr>
                      <td>
                      <input
                       type="hidden"
                       name="ImageSmall_required"
                       value="You must enter a path to your image      (small)">
                      <b>Image Thumbnail path:</b><br>
                      <cfinput
                      type="Text"
                      name="ImageSmall"
                      value="#ItemsLong.ImageSmall#"
                      required="yes"
                      message="You must enter a path to your image      (small)">
                      </td>
                      <td>
                      <input
                       type="hidden"
                       name="ImageLarge_required"
                       value="You must enter a path to your image      (large)">
                      <b>Image Path:</b><br>
                      <cfinput
                       type="Text"
                       name="ImageLarge"
                       value="#ItemsLong.ImageLarge#"
                       required="yes"
                       message="You must enter a path to your image      (large)">
                      </td>
                      </tr>
                      <tr>
                      <td colspan="2">
                      <cfif session.edit>
                      <select name="EditAction">
                          <option>Update
                              <option>Delete
                      </select>
                      </cfif>
                      <input type="Submit" name="action"      value="<cfoutput>#iif
➥(session.edit, de("Update Product"), de("Add Product"))#</cfoutput>"">
                      </td>
                      </tr>
                      </cfform>
                      </table>
                  </td>
              </tr>


      </cfif>

      </table>

  </cfcase>

  </cfswitch>
```

FIGURE 25.1

The administration page.

Products and categories are managed in the database using the `QuickStore_Product` and `QuickStore_Category` tags, respectively. Categories can be created or deleted as shown in Listing 25.3, and products can be added, deleted, or edited as shown in Listing 25.4. The HTML forms for these functions are separated so that changes and updates in the interface won't affect the application's underlying functionality. After any update to categories or products, the `ItemsShort` query is run again so that cached version in Listing 25.1 will reflect the changes made in the database.

Listing 25.3 QUICKSTORE_CATEGORY—Category Management in the QuickStore Application

```
<!-- cf_quickStore_category

Creates and deletes categories.

<cf_quickStore_category
 dsn="data source name"
 action="add|delete">

-->


<!-- Set default for attributes -->
<cfparam name="attributes.action" default="">
<cfparam name="attributes.dsn" default="">
<cfparam name="attributes.categoryID" default="">
<cfparam name="attributes.name" default="">
<cfparam name="attributes.description" default="">
```

continues

Listing 25.3   Continued

```
<!-- Show error if no data source is specified -->
<cfif trim(attributes.dsn) is "">

    <cfthrow message="ERROR IN QUICKSTORE:
➥ No data source specified in cf_quickStore_category.">

</cfif>

<!-- Add a new category to database -->
<cfswitch expression="#attributes.action#">

    <cfcase value="add">

        <cfquery data source="#attributes.dsn#">

            INSERT INTO Categories ('Name', 'Description')
            VALUES('#attributes.name#', '#attributes.description#')

        </cfquery>

    </cfcase>

    <!-- Remove a category from the database -->
    <cfcase value="delete">

        <cfquery data source="#attributes.dsn#">

            DELETE * FROM Categories
            WHERE CategoryID = #attributes.CategoryID#

        </cfquery>

    </cfcase>

</cfswitch>


<!-- Set admin mode -->
<cfset session.do = "admin">

<!-- Refresh product list -->
<cfquery name="application.ItemsShort" data source="#attributes.dsn#">

    SELECT     Products.ProductID, Products.ProductName, Categories.Name,
    Categories.Description, Categories.CategoryID
    FROM       Products, Categories
    WHERE      Products.CategoryID = Categories.CategoryID
    ORDER BY   Categories.Name, Products.ProductName

</cfquery>

<!-- End -->
```

Listing 25.4 QUICKSTORE_CATEGORY—**Category Management in the QuickStore Application**

```
<!-- cf_quickStore_product

Creates, edits and deletes products.

<cf_quickStore_product
 dsn="data source name"
 action="add¦delete¦edit¦update"
 productname="product name"
 categoryID="Category ID"
 DescriptionShort="Short description of product"
 DescriptionLong="Long description of product"
 Keywords="Keywords"
 UnitPrice="Price"
 ImageSmall="URL to thumbnail image"
 ImageLarge="URL to large image">

-->


<!-- Set default for attributes -->
<cfparam name="attributes.action" default="">
<cfparam name="attributes.dsn" default="">
<cfparam name="attributes.productname" default="">
<cfparam name="attributes.categoryID" default="">
<cfparam name="attributes.DescriptionShort" default="">
<cfparam name="attributes.DescriptionLong" default="">
<cfparam name="attributes.Keywords" default="">
<cfparam name="attributes.UnitPrice" default="">
<cfparam name="attributes.ImageSmall" default="">
<cfparam name="attributes.ImageLarge" default="">

<!-- Show error if no data source is specified -->
<cfif trim(attributes.dsn) is "">

    <cfthrow message="ERROR IN QUICKSTORE:
➥ No data source specified in cf_quickStore_category.">

</cfif>

<cfswitch expression= "#attributes.action#">

    <!-- Add a new product to database -->
    <cfcase value="add">

        <cfquery data source="#attributes.dsn#">

            INSERT INTO Products ('ProductName', 'CategoryID',
➥    'DescriptionShort', 'DescriptionLong', 'Keywords',
➥ 'UnitPrice',      'ImageSmall', 'ImageLarge')
            VALUES('#form.Productname#', #form.categoryID#,
➥    '#form.descriptionShort#', '#form.descriptionLong#',
```

continues

Part

IV

Ch

25

Listing 25.4   Continued

```
➥     '#form.keywords#', #form.unitPrice#, '#form.imageSmall#',
➥     '#form.imageLarge#')

       </cfquery>

   </cfcase>

   <!-- Edit product -->
   <cfcase value="edit">

       <!-- Set edit flag -->
       <cfset session.edit = "yes">

   </cfcase>

   <!-- Update a product -->
   <cfcase value="update">

       <cfquery data source="#attributes.dsn#">

           UPDATE Products
           SET ProductName = '#form.Productname#',
           CategoryID = #form.categoryID#,
           DescriptionShort = '#form.descriptionShort#',
           DescriptionLong = '#form.descriptionLong#',
           Keywords = '#form.keywords#',
           UnitPrice = #form.unitPrice#,
           ImageSmall = '#form.imageSmall#',
           ImageLarge = '#form.imageLarge#'
           WHERE ProductID = #form.productID#

       </cfquery>

   </cfcase>

   <!-- Delete a product -->
   <cfcase value="delete">

       <cfquery data source="#attributes.dsn#">

           DELETE * FROM Products
           WHERE ProductID = #form.productID#

       </cfquery>

       <cfset session.edit = "no">

   </cfcase>

</cfswitch>

<!-- Set admin flag -->
<cfset session.do = "admin">
```

```
<!-- Refresh product query -->
<cfquery name="application.ItemsShort" data source="#attributes.dsn#">

    SELECT      Products.ProductID, Products.ProductName, Categories.Name,
➥Categories.Description, Categories.CategoryID
    FROM        Products, Categories
    WHERE       Products.CategoryID = Categories.CategoryID
    ORDER BY  Categories.Name, Products.ProductName

</cfquery>

<!-- End -->
```

Navigating QuickStore

The navigation interface, shown in Listing 25.5, allows either drill-down navigation by category or a keyword search of products. On the second level, shown in Figure 25.2, products are listed alphabetically with thumbnail images and short descriptions of each. On the third level, the customer sees product detail, including a full description, the unit price, a large image, and a purchase dialog. Customers move up from this level by clicking the category link or return to the top level by clicking the Home link. This is accomplished by using simple database queries to retrieve the categories and items. Again, the main category query is cached to cut down on database accesses.

On the CD

Listing 25.5 QUICKSTORE_CATALOG.CFM—**The Navigation and Catalog Section**

```
<!-- QuickStore_catalog custom tag

-->

<!-- Initialize -->
<cfparam name="attributes.action" default="">
<cfparam name="attributes.dsn" default="">
<cfparam name="attributes.thispage" default="#GetFileFromPath
➥(GetTemplatePath())#">
<cfparam name="attributes.querystring" default="?">

<cfset thisPage = attributes.thisPage>
<cfset queryString = attributes.queryString>

<cfif attributes.action is "index">

    <!-- Main page -->

    <table cellspacing="0" cellpadding="2" border="1">
    <tr>

        <cfform action="#thisPage##queryString#do=search">

        <td><b>Search</b><cfinput type="Text" name="SearchTerms">
```

continues

Part

IV

Ch

25

Listing 25.5   Continued

```
        <input type="Submit" value="Search">
        </td>
        </cfform>
    </tr>
    <tr>
        <td>
            <table border=0>
            <tr><td colspan=2>
            <b>Categories</b><p>
            </td></tr>
            <cfoutput query="application.ItemsShort" group="Name">
            <tr>
            <td><b><a
href="#thisPage##queryString#CategoryID=#CategoryID#&do=list">
➥#Name#</a></b></td>
            <td>#Description#</td>
            </tr>
            </cfoutput>
            </table>
        </td>
    </tr>
    <tr>
        <td>
        <cfoutput>
        <b><a href="#thisPage##queryString#do=admin">Administration</a></b>
        </cfoutput>
        </td>
    </tr>
    </table>


<cfelseif attributes.action is "search">

    <!-- Search results -->


    <cfquery name="ItemsLong" data source="#attributes.dsn#">

        SELECT      ProductID, ProductName, DescriptionShort, ImageSmall
        FROM        Products
        WHERE       (ProductName like '%#form.searchTerms#%'
                    OR Keywords like '%#form.searchTerms#%'
                    OR DescriptionShort like '%#form.searchTerms#%')
        ORDER BY    ProductName

    </cfquery>

    <table cellspacing="0" cellpadding="2" border="1" width=80%>
    <tr>
        <td><b>Search Results</b>
        </td>
    </tr>
    <tr>
        <td>
```

```
            <table border=0>
            <tr><td colspan=2>
            <b>Products</b><p>
            </td></tr>
            <cfoutput query="ItemsLong">
            <tr>
            <td valign="top"><b>
➡<ahref="#thisPage##queryString#ProductID=#ProductID#&do=detail">
➡#ProductName#</a></b></td>
            <td valign="top"><img src="#ImageSmall#" border=0 align="right">
➡#DescriptionShort#</td>
            </tr>
            </cfoutput>
            </table>
        </td>
    </tr>
    <tr>
        <td><cfoutput query="ItemsLong" maxrows=1><b>[<a
href="#thisPage##queryString#">Home</a>]</b></cfoutput>
        </td>
    </tr>
    </table>

<cfelseif attributes.action is "list">

    <!- Product listing -->

    <cfquery name="ItemsLong" data source="#attributes.dsn#">

        SELECT      Products.ProductID, Products.ProductName,
➡   Products.DescriptionShort,      Products.ImageSmall,
➡ Categories.CategoryID, Categories.Name
        FROM        Products, Categories
        WHERE       Products.CategoryID = Categories.CategoryID AND
                        (Categories.CategoryID = #URL.categoryID#)
        ORDER BY  Products.ProductName

    </cfquery>

    <table cellspacing="0" cellpadding="2" border="1" width=80%>
    <tr>
        <td><cfoutput query="ItemsLong" maxrows=1><b>#name#</b></cfoutput>
        </td>
    </tr>
    <tr>
        <td>
            <table border=0>
            <tr><td colspan=2>
            <b>Products</b><p>
            </td></tr>
            <cfoutput query="ItemsLong">
            <tr>
            <td valign="top"><b>
➡<ahref="#thisPage##queryString#ProductID=#ProductID#&do=detail">
➡#ProductName#</a></b></td>
```

continues

Part

IV

Ch

25

Listing 25.5 Continued

```
            <td valign="top"><img src="#ImageSmall#" border=0 align="right">
➥#DescriptionShort#</td>
            </tr>
            </cfoutput>
            </table>
        </td>
    </tr>
    <tr>
        <td><cfoutput query="ItemsLong" maxrows=1><b>
➥[<a href="#thisPage##queryString#">Home</a>]
➥[<a href="#thisPage##queryString#do=basket">View basket</a>]</b></cfoutput>
        </td>
    </tr>
    </table>

<cfelseif attributes.action is "detail">

    <!-- Product detail -->

    <cfquery name="ItemsLong" data source="#attributes.dsn#">

        SELECT        Products.ProductID, Products.ProductName,
➥    Products.DescriptionLong, Products.CategoryID, Products.UnitPrice,
➥ Products.ImageLarge, Categories.Name, Categories.CategoryID
        FROM          Products, Categories
        WHERE         Products.CategoryID = Categories.CategoryID
                      AND (Products.ProductID = #URL.ProductID#)

    </cfquery>

    <table cellspacing="0" cellpadding="2" border="1" width=80%>
    <tr>
        <td><cfoutput query="ItemsLong" maxrows=1><b>#ProductName#</b></
cfoutput>
        </td>
    </tr>
    <tr>
        <td>
            <table border=0>
            <tr><td colspan=2 width=100%>
            <b>Detail</b><p>
            </td></tr>
            <cfoutput query="ItemsLong">
            <tr>
            <td valign="top" width=20%><b>#DollarFormat(UnitPrice)#</b></td>
            <td valign="top" width=80%>
➥<img src="#ImageLarge#" border=0 align="left">#DescriptionLong#</td>
            </tr>
            <cfform action="#thisPage##queryString#do=action">
            <tr><td colspan=2>
            <input type="Hidden" name="Quantity_integerinteger"
➥ value="You must enter a quantity as a numeric value.">
            <b>Quantity</b>
```

```
                <cfinput type="Text" name="Quantity" value="1"
➡ validate="integer" required="No" size="2" maxlength="3">
                <input type="Hidden" name="ProductID" value="#ProductID#">
                <input type="Submit" name="action" value="Add to basket">
                </td></tr>
                </cfform>
                </cfoutput>
                </table>
            </td>
        </tr>
        <tr>
            <td><cfoutput query="ItemsLong" maxrows=1><b>
➡ [<ahref="#thisPage##queryString#do=list&CategoryID=#CategoryID#">#Name#</a>]
➡ [<a href="#thisPage##queryString#">Home</a>]
➡ [<a href="#thisPage##queryString#do=basket">View basket</a>]</b></cfoutput>
            </td>
        </tr>
        </table>

    </cfif>
```

FIGURE 25.2

The category menu.

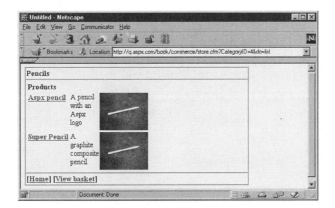

Part

IV

Ch

25

Selecting a QuickStore Item

From the product detail page shown in Listing 25.6, customers select items by entering a quantity and clicking the Add to Basket button, which is shown in Figure 25.3. This returns a listing of the current products in the customer's shopping bag and a current total, as shown in Figure 25.4. The customer then continues to shop or moves on to the purchase step from this page. The customer can return to this page by clicking the View Basket link. Items can also be deleted from the shopping cart by selecting the check box next to the product and clicking Delete. If the customer purchases the same product twice, the application simply updates the quantity of the first selected product.

The shopping cart is stored in session variables and will time out after a customer leaves your site. To keep the shopping cart persistent, the items can be stored in a database table that references the customer's cfid, as available in the client.cfid variable. See Chapter 27 for more information on client variables.

Listing 25.6 QUICKSTORE_BASKET.CFM—The Selection Section

```
<!-- QuickStore_basket custom tag

-->

<!-- Initialize -->
<cfparam name="attributes.productID" default="">
<cfparam name="attributes.quantity" default="">
<cfparam name="attributes.thispage"
default="#GetFileFromPath(GetTemplatePath())#">
<cfparam name="attributes.querystring" default="?">

<cfset thisPage = attributes.thisPage>
<cfset queryString = attributes.queryString>

<cfif attributes.action is "show">

    <!-- The shopping basket -->

    <table cellspacing="0" cellpadding="2" border="1">
    <tr>
        <td><cfoutput><b>Shopping Basket</b></cfoutput>
        </td>
    </tr>
    <tr>
        <td>
            <table border=0>
            <tr><td colspan=2>
            <b>Items</b>
            </td></tr>
            <tr>
            <td>
            <b><font size="-1">Name</font></b>
            </td>
            <td>
            <b><font size="-1">Qty.</font></b>
            </td>
            <td>
            <b><font size="-1">Price</font></b>
            </td>
            <td>
            <b><font size="-1">Total</font></b>
            </td>
            <td>
            <b><font size="-1">Remove</font></b>
            </td>
            </tr>
            <cfset session.total = 0>
```

```
                    <cfform action="#thisPage##queryString#do=action">
                    <cfloop query="session.basket">

                    <!-- Get product information -->
                    <cfquery name="Item" data source="#attributes.dsn#">

                        SELECT * FROM Products
                        WHERE ProductID = #session.basket.productID#

                    </cfquery>

                    <tr>
                    <cfoutput>
                    <td valign="top"><b>
➥<ahref="#thisPage##queryString#ProductID=#item.ProductID#&do=detail">
➥#item.ProductName#</a></b></td>
                    <td valign="top">#session.basket.quantity#
                    </td>
                    <td valign="top">#DollarFormat(item.UnitPrice)#</td>
                    <td valign="top">#DollarFormat
➥(item.UnitPrice * session.basket.quantity)#</td>
                    <td valign="top">
                    <input type="checkbox" name="productID" value="#item.productID#">
                    </td>
                    </cfoutput>
                    </tr>

                    <cfset session.total =
➥ evaluate(session.total + (item.UnitPrice * session.basket.quantity))>
                    </cfloop>
                    <tr>
                    <cfoutput>
                    <td colspan="2"> </td>
                    <td valign="top"><b>Total:</b></td>
                    <td valign="top">#DollarFormat(session.total)#</td>
                    <td valign="top">
                    <input type="submit" value="Delete">
                    </td>
                    </cfoutput>
                    </tr>
                    </table>

                    <input type="hidden" name="action" value="Update basket">
                    </cfform>

            </td>
        </tr>
        <tr>
            <td><cfoutput><b>[<a href="#thisPage##queryString#">Home</a>]
➥[<a href="#thisPage##queryString#do=form">Check out</a>]</b></cfoutput>
            </td>
        </tr>
        </table>

<!-- Update shopping cart -->
```

Listing 25.6 Continued

```
<cfelseif attributes.action is "update">

    <!-- Loop through basket and remove selected items -->
    <cfset newBasket = queryNew("ProductID, Quantity, saleDate")>

    <cfloop query="session.basket">

        <!-- Add anything that isn't in the delete list -->
        <cfif not listFind(attributes.productID, productID)>

            <cfset tempValue = queryAddRow(newBasket)>
            <cfset tempValue = querySetCell(newBasket, "saleDate", saleDate)>
            <cfset tempValue = querySetCell(newBasket, "ProductID", ProductID)>
            <cfset tempValue = querySetCell(newBasket, "Quantity", quantity)>

        </cfif>

    </cfloop>

    <!-- set the basket to the new values -->
    <cfset session.basket = newBasket>

<!-- Add product to query -->
<cfelseif attributes.action is "add">

    <!-- check to see if the product is in the baset already -->
    <cfset productRow = listFind(valueList(session.basket.productID),
➥ attributes.productID)>

    <!-- Product is in basket, update quantity -->
    <cfif productRow neq 0>

        <!-- determine the new quantity and the correct row -->
        <cfset oldQuantity = listGetAt
➥(valueList(session.basket.quantity), productRow)>
        <cfset newQuantity = attributes.quantity + oldQuantity>
        <cfset tempValue = querySetCell
➥(session.basket, "Quantity", newQuantity, productRow)>

    <!-- Product is not in basket, add it -->
    <cfelse>

        <cfset tempValue = queryAddRow(session.basket)>
        <cfset tempValue = querySetCell(session.basket, "saleDate", "#Now()#")>
        <cfset tempValue = querySetCell
➥(session.basket, "ProductID", attributes.ProductID)>
        <cfset tempValue = querySetCell
➥(session.basket, "Quantity", attributes.quantity)>

    </cfif>

</cfif>
```

FIGURE 25.3

The product detail.

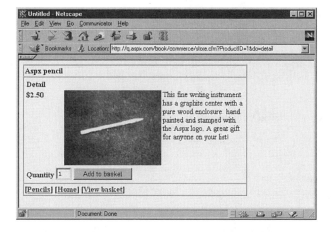

FIGURE 25.4

The shopping basket.

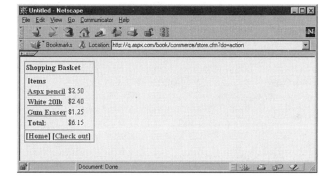

Purchasing a QuickStore Item

The purchase form, shown in Listing 25.7, requires the customer to enter basic personal and payment information. Figure 25.5 shows this form's layout. Upon submission, the application inserts this information into the database along with the contents of the customer's shopping basket. Other information can be added to this form, including additional shipping information and survey information.

On the CD

Listing 25.7 QUICKSTORE_ORDERFORM.CFM—The Purchase Form

```
<!-- QuickStore_orderForm custom tag

-->

<!-- Initialize -->
<cfparam name="attributes.cc" default="No">
<cfparam name="attributes.thispage" default="#GetFileFromPath
➡(GetTemplatePath())#">
```

continues

Listing 25.7   Continued

```
<cfparam name="attributes.querystring" default="?">

<cfset thisPage = attributes.thisPage>
<cfset queryString = attributes.queryString>


<!-- Customer Information form -->

<table cellspacing="0" cellpadding="2" border="1">

<tr>
    <td colspan=2>
    <b>Please enter your personal information:</b><p>
    </td>
</tr>
<cfform action="#thisPage##queryString#do=action" method="POST">
<tr>
    <td>
    <input type="hidden" name="FirstName_required" value="You must enter a
name">
    <b>First Name:</b>
    </td>
    <td>
    <cfinput type="Text" name="FirstName" message=
➥"Please enter your first name" required="Yes">
    </td>
</tr>
<tr>
    <td>
    <input type="hidden" name="LastName_required" value="You must enter a name">
    <b>Last Name:</b>
    </td>
    <td>
    <cfinput type="Text" name="LastName" message=
➥"Please enter your last name" required="Yes">
    </td>
</tr>
<tr>
    <td>
    <input type="hidden" name="Address_required" value="You must enter an
address">
    <b>Address:</b>
    </td>
    <td>
    <cfinput type="Text" name="Address" message=
➥"Please enter your address" required="Yes">
    </td>
</tr>
<tr>
    <td>
    <input type="hidden" name="City_required" value="You must enter a city">
    <b>City:</b>
    </td>
    <td>
```

```
        <cfinput type="Text" name="City" message=
➥"Please enter your city" required="Yes">
        </td>
</tr>
<tr>
        <td>
        <input type="hidden" name="State_required" value=
➥"You must enter a state or province">
        <b>State:</b><br>
        </td>
        <td>
        <cfinput type="Text" name="State" message=
➥"Please enter your state" required="Yes">
        </td>
</tr>
<tr>
        <td>
        <input type="hidden" name="PostalCode_required" value=
➥"You must enter a postal code">
        <b>Postal code:</b>
        </td>
        <td>
        <cfinput type="Text" name="PostalCode" message=
➥"Please enter your zip code" validate="zipcode" required="Yes">
        </td>
</tr>
<tr>
        <td>
        <input type="hidden" name="Country_required" value="You must enter a coun-
try">
        <b>Country:</b><br>
        </td>
        <td>
        <cfinput type="Text" name="Country" message=
➥"Please enter your country" required="Yes">
        </td>
</tr>

<cfif attributes.cc>

    <tr>
        <td>
        <b>Credit card number:</b>
        </td>
        <td>
        <cfinput type="Text" name="CCNum" message=
➥"Please enter a valid credit card number" validate="creditcard" required="No">
        </td>
    </tr>
    <tr>
        <td>
        <b>Expires:</b><br>
        </td>
        <td>
```

Listing 25.7   Continued

```
        <cfinput type="Text" name="ExpDate" value="xx/xx" message=
➥"Please enter a valid date" required="No">
        </td>
    </tr>

</cfif>

<tr>
    <td>
    <input type="hidden" name="Email_required" value=
➥"You must enter an email address">
    <b>Email:</b>
    </td>
    <td>
    <cfinput type="Text" name="Email" message=
➥"Please enter your email address" required="Yes">
    </td>
</tr>
<tr>
    <td colspan=2>
    <input type="Submit" name="action" value="Purchase Products">
    </td>
</tr>
</cfform>
</table>
```

FIGURE 25.5

The customer information form.

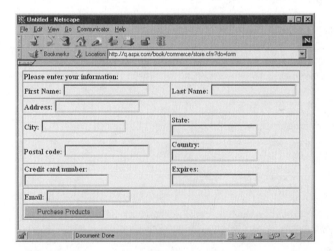

Processing Payments

The payment processing section of QuickStore is shown in Listing 25.8. This is where the application hands off to the selected processing system. The application includes Cybercash and ICVerify, which you look at later. Each requires separate attributes to be passed to the template. When processing is complete, each tag sets variables so that the success of the transaction can be determined and recorded.

Security can be enhanced at this point by redirecting the user to an SSL or SHTTP version of this page. Data is then encrypted between the user and your Web site.

On the CD

Listing 25.8 `QUICKSTORE_PROCESS.CFM`—**The Order Processing Template**

```
<!-- QuickStore_process custom tag

-->



<cfif attributes.action is "purchase">

    <cftransaction>

    <cfquery data source="#attributes.dsn#">

        INSERT INTO Customers ('CFID', 'FirstName', 'LastName', 'Address',
➥ 'City', 'State', 'PostalCode', 'Country', 'Email')
        VALUES(#client.cfid#, '#form.FirstName#', '#form.LastName#',
➥ '#form.Address#', '#form.city#', '#form.state#', '#form.PostalCode#',
'#form.Country#','#form.email#')

    </cfquery>

    <cfquery name="getLastID" data source="#attributes.dsn#">

        SELECT Max(CustomerID) AS LastCustomer
        FROM Customers

    </cfquery>

    </cftransaction>


    <cfloop query="session.basket">

        <cfquery data source="#attributes.dsn#">

            INSERT INTO Sales ('CustomerID', 'ProductID', 'Quantity',
'SaleDate')
            VALUES(#client.cfid#, '#session.basket.ProductID#',
➥ '#session.basket.Quantity#', #session.basket.saleDate#)

        </cfquery>

    </cfloop>

<cfelseif attributes.action is "process">
```

Part
IV

Ch

25

continues

Listing 25.8   Continued

```
<cfif attributes.method is "icverify">

    <CFX_ICV NAME="process_card"
        IC_SHAREDIR="#attributes.ic_sharedir#"
        TRANS_TYPE="C1"
        ACCOUNT="#form.ccnum#"
        EXPIRES_MO="#left(form.expdate, 2)#"
        EXPIRES_YR="#right(form.expdate, 2)#"
        AMOUNT="#session.total#" >

    <CFOUTPUT QUERY="VALIDATE_CC">
    <CFIF #VALIDATED# is "Y">
        #VALIDATED# - Credit card was authorized.
        #AUTH_NO#
    <CFELSE>
        <CFIF #VALIDATED# is not "IC_TIMEOUT">
            #AUTH_NO# - Credit card was NOT authorized.
        <CFELSE>
            #AUTH_NO#
            A Timeout occurred waiting to process this order.
            Credit card was NOT authorized.
        </CFIF>
    </CFIF>
    </CFOUTPUT>



<cfelseif attributes.method is "cybercash">

    <CFX_CYBERCASH
            SERVER="#attributes.server#"
            MERCHANTPASSWORD="#attributes.merchantpassword#"
            TRANSTYPE="mauthonly"
            ORDERID="#client.cftoken#"
            AMOUNT="#session.total#"
            CCNUMBER="#form.ccnum#"
            CCEXP="#form.expdate#"
            CCNAME="#form.firstname# #form.lastname#"
            CCADDRESS="#form.address#"
            CCCITY="#form.city#"
            CCSTATE="#form.state#"
            CCZIP="#form.postalcode#"
            CCCOUNTRY="#form.country#"
        >

    <!-- Add post processing here such as mailing receipts,    etc.
    Cold Fusion variables MStatus,
    MAuthNumber, and MErrMsg are now available for
    processing -->
```

```
</cfif>

<!-- Add post processing here such as mailing receipts,    etc. -->

<b>Thank you!</b><p>
Your order has been processed.

</cfif>
```

Now that the QuickStore application is complete, you can add it to any existing ColdFusion template. Listing 25.9 shows how to call QuickStore from an existing template. Because QuickStore uses the URL of the page calling it, it can be used without modification to your existing application structure.

On the CD

Listing 25.9 `index.CFM`**—Calling QuickStore from an Existing Application**

```
<!DOCTYPE HTML PUBLIC "-//W3C//DTD HTML 3.2 Final//EN">
<HTML>
<HEAD>
    <TITLE>A Basic Store</TITLE>
</HEAD>
<BODY>
<CF_QUICKSTORE>
</BODY>
</HTML>
```

Part

IV

Ch

25

Using Payment Processing Systems

Payment processing systems provide the critical link between Web applications and the financial world. There are many commercial payment processing systems available for use with your commerce site, and most allow customers to use credit cards as a payment method. Security is of utmost concern to the majority of potential customers. You can help the customer feel safe purchasing on your site by incorporating encrypted pages into your application (using SSL or SHTTP) and by providing customers with means to contact you if they have concerns.

For you, ease-of-use and reliability are also requirements in a payment processing system. Take a look at a few established payment processing systems that are in widespread use on the Internet today: Cybercash, ICVerify, Redi-Check, and Open Market. Table 25.2 shows a comparison of these payment processing systems.

Table 25.2   Payment Processing Systems

Vendor and Product	Accepted Types	Comments
Cybercash	Credit cards, micro payments, checks	Requires the Cash Register software to be installed on your server. Payments are processed over the Internet securely. For more information, visit http://www.cybercash.com.
ICVerify	Credit cards	Requires ICVerify software to be installed on your server. Payments are processed via modem connection to a processing network. Information on ICVerify software is available at http://www.icverify.com. The CFX tag for integration with ColdFusion is available at http://www.programmersWeb.com.
Redi-Check	Credit cards, checks	Payments are processed via secure HTTP connection. No software is required on your server. For more information, visit http://www.redicheck.com.
Open Market	Credit cards, debit cards, SET, purchase orders	Requires Transact server. Distributed architecture enables centralization of processing enterprisewide. For more information on the Open Market commerce system, visit http://www/openmarket.com. The Open Market Fuel Pack is available at http://www.allaire.com.

Using Cybercash

Cybercash offers credit card processing, check processing, and micropayment processing. *Micropayments* involve smaller payments, ranging from around $.25 to $10.00 (U.S.). Cybercash also allows customers using Cybercash wallets to pay without entering a credit card number on your site. Cybercash requires that the Cash Register software be installed on your server. The Cybercash CFX tag communicates with Cash Register, which processes the transaction using a secure connection to the Cybercash network. Cash Register returns success codes for your application to evaluate. An example of the use of the CFX Cybercash tag is included in the QuickStore application in Listing 25.8. The CFX Cybercash tag is part of a ColdFusion Fuel Pack available from Allaire.

Using ICVerify

ICVerify gives you the most control over payment processing. The entire system resides on your server, which means you are also responsible for monitoring and maintaining the payment system, in addition to your Web servers and other concerns. The advantage of this is lower processing fees per transaction, depending on your merchant account. When the ICVerify server receives a processing request, it dials the appropriate processing network, using your modem, and completes the transaction in real time. Settlements, chargebacks, and other transactions can also be performed, and all records are stored on your server. ICVerify can reuse connections for heavy-use sites, connecting to the processing network once for several transactions at a time. The CFX_ICV custom tag is a third-party tool developed to integrate the functions of ICVerify into the ColdFusion language. An example of the use of this tag is included in the QuickStore application in Listing 25.8.

Using Redi-Check

Redi-Check processes both credit cards and checks using secure HTTP connections, making it very simple to integrate in any Web commerce site. When a transaction is initiated, the customer is redirected to the Redi-Check secure server for processing, then returned to the URL of your choice for confirmation. Payments can be mailed to you or deposited directly in your account. Redi-Check requires no additional software and can be set up very quickly. An example of a Redi-Check–enabled site is shown in Listing 25.10.

On the CD

Listing 25.10 `REDI_CHECK.CFM`—**Payment Processing Using Redi-Check**

```
        <FORM METHOD="POST" ACTION="https://secure.redi-check.com/cgi-bin/
➥rc3/ord.cgi">
        <INPUT TYPE="hidden" NAME="vendor_id" VALUE="XXXXXX">
        <INPUT TYPE="hidden" NAME="home_page" VALUE="http://www.aspx.com">
        <INPUT TYPE="hidden" NAME="ret_addr" VALUE=
➥"http://www.aspx.com/store/thanks.cfm">
        <INPUT TYPE="hidden" NAME="email_text" VALUE="Thank you for
purchasing MrPost! Your key and instructions will follow by email.">
        <CFOUTPUT>
        <INPUT TYPE="hidden" NAME="passback" VALUE="Identifier">
        <INPUT TYPE="hidden" NAME="Identifier" VALUE="#variables.
➥identifier#">
        <INPUT TYPE="hidden" NAME="passback" VALUE="Total">
        <INPUT TYPE="hidden" NAME="Total" VALUE="#DollarFormat(form.Total)#">
        <INPUT TYPE="hidden" NAME="first_name" VALUE="#form.first_name#">
        <INPUT TYPE="hidden" NAME="last_name" VALUE="#form.Last_name#">
        <INPUT TYPE="hidden" NAME="address" VALUE="#form.address#">
```

continues

Listing 25.10   Continued

```
        <INPUT TYPE="hidden" NAME="city" VALUE="#form.city#">
        <INPUT TYPE="hidden" NAME="state" VALUE="#form.state#">
        <INPUT TYPE="hidden" NAME="zip" VALUE="#Form.zip#">
        <INPUT TYPE="hidden" NAME="country" VALUE="#form.country#">
        <INPUT TYPE="hidden" NAME="phone" VALUE="#Form.Phone#">
        <INPUT TYPE="hidden" NAME="email" VALUE="#form.email#">
        <INPUT TYPE="hidden" NAME="1-desc" VALUE="Aspx Products" SIZE=8>
        <INPUT TYPE="hidden" NAME="1-cost" SIZE=8 VALUE=
➥"#DecimalFormat(form.thisTotal)#"></CFOUTPUT>
        <INPUT TYPE="hidden" NAME="1-qty" VALUE="1">
        <TABLE BORDER=1 CELLSPACING=0 CELLPADDING=0>
        <TR>
    <TD VALIGN=TOP COLSPAN=2  BGCOLOR=MAROON><A HREF=
➥"http://www.redi-check.com"><B>Redi-Check Payment</B></A>
    </TD>
    </TR>
        <TR>
    <TD COLSPAN=2 BGCOLOR=PURPLE><FONT SIZE="-1">For your convenience, we use
➥ Redi-Check's real-time secure transaction gateway. <IMG SRC="http://
➥www.redi-check.com/images/securekey.gif" BORDER=0> <A HREF="https://
➥secure.redi-check.com/support/security.html">Security information
➥</A></FONT><P>
        </TD>
        </TR>
        <TR>
    <TD VALIGN=TOP COLSPAN=2  BGCOLOR=MAROON><B>Checking Account
➥Information</B>
    </TD>
    </TR>
        <TR>
    <TD COLSPAN=2 BGCOLOR=PURPLE>
<I><FONT SIZE="-1">At the bottom of your check is a series of numbers,
➥separated by symbols.  It is not necessary to enter symbols or spaces
➥in the fields provided below.</FONT><BR>
    </TD>
    </TR>
    <TR>
    <TD VALIGN=TOP BGCOLOR=PURPLE>
    <B> Enter the series of <I>nine</I> numbers <I>between</I>
➥this symbol </B>
    </TD>
    <TD VALIGN=TOP BGCOLOR=PURPLE>
    <IMG SRC="http://www.redi-check.com/images/1.gif">
➥<INPUT NAME="aba" SIZE=9 MAXLENGTH=9>
➥<IMG SRC="http://www.redi-check.com/images/1.gif"><BR>
    </TD>
    </TR>
    <TR>
    <TD VALIGN=TOP BGCOLOR=PURPLE>
    <B>Enter the series of numbers  found <I>before</I> this symbol </B>
    </TD>
    <TD VALIGN=TOP BGCOLOR=PURPLE>
    <IMG SRC="http://www.redi-check.com/images/2.gif"><INPUT NAME="account"
➥SIZE=20 MAXLENGTH=25><IMG SRC="http://www.redi-check.com/images/2.gif">
```

```
        </TD>
        </TR>
        <TR>
        <TD COLSPAN=2 BGCOLOR=PURPLE><FONT SIZE=-1>Note: Some banks use a
➥non-standard format in this series of numbers.  If your account number
➥includes this symbol <IMG SRC="http://www.redi-check
➥.com/images/3.gif">,
➥simply disregard the symbols and enter this section of numbers.
        </FONT></TD>
        </TR>
            </TABLE>
        </FORM>
```

Using Open Market

Open Market is a commerce platform with many options and components, the most important of which are Transact and SecureLink. The Open Market system creates *digital offers* (DOs) that customers can add to a shopping cart. When the customer is ready to purchase, the transaction is handled by the Transact server. Digital offers can be created and modified using the set of CFX tools in the Open Market Fuel Pack, available from Allaire. The Open Market platform is aware of all elements of the merchant site, from digital offers to fulfillment, providing a highly integrated commerce solution.

Using the Open Market Fuel Pack

The Open Market Fuel Pack consists of six CFX tags. These tags make the creation and manipulation of *predigital offers* (PDOs) much simpler and integrate conversion into digital offers. The tag names are CFX_CREATEPDO, CFX_GETPDO, CFX_SETPDO, CFX_READPDO, CFX_WRITEPDO, and CFX_PDO2DO. For a more detailed discussion of the mechanics of the Open Market platform, specifications of the Transact and SecureLink systems are available at the Open Market Web site at http://www.openmarket.com. This discussion assumes familiarity with the Open Market components.

Using CFX_CREATEPDO The CFX_CREATEPDO tag creates a PDO. This is the starting point for creating a digital offer. The attributes for this tag are listed in Table 25.3.

Table 25.3 CFX_CREATEPDO

Attribute	Description
OfferName	The variable that will hold the PDO. This is required.
Attribute	Any of the available attributes for a PDO. All required attributes of a PDO must be included to create a PDO: Name, Type, UniqueID, OfferURL, and Price.

Using CFX_GETPDO The CFX_GETPDO tag queries any of a PDO's attributes created using CFX_CREATEPDO. These attributes can then be changed using CFX_SETPDO. The attributes for this tag are listed in Table 25.4.

Table 25.4 CFX_GETPDO

Attribute	Description
OfferValue	The variable that contains the PDO. This is required.
Attribute	Any of the available attributes for a PDO. This is also required.
Variable	The variable that will contain the value of the above attribute. This is required.

Using CFX_SETPDO   The CFX_SETPDO tag dynamically sets any attribute in a PDO. The current value of an attribute can be queried by CFX_GETPDO and then set using dynamic data from a database or other source. The attributes for this tag are listed in Table 25.5.

Table 25.5 CFX_SETPDO

Attribute	Description
OfferName	The variable that contains the PDO. This is required.
OfferValue	A variable that contains a PDO. If this does not match the value in OfferName, a copy of the PDO will be made. This is required.
Attribute	Any of the available attributes for a PDO. This is required.
Variable	The value the attribute will be set to.
Validate	Determines whether the offer will be validated. Optional; defaults to YES.

Using CFX_READPDO   PDOs contained in files are read using CFX_READPDO. The files are created using CFX_WRITEPDO and are derived from existing PDOs. The attributes for this tag are listed in Table 25.6.

Table 25.6 CFX_READPDO

Attribute	Description
OfferName	The name of the variable that contains the PDO. This is required.
File	The filename to read the PDO from. This is required.
Validate	Determines whether the offer will be validated. Optional; defaults to YES.

Using CFX_WRITEPDO   CFX_WRITEPDO saves an existing PDO to a file. The file can then be read using CFX_READPDO. The attributes for this tag are listed in Table 25.7.

Table 25.7 `CFX_WRITEPDO`

Attribute	Description
OfferValue	The variable that contains the PDO. This is required.
File	The name of the file that the PDO will be saved to. This is required.

Using `CFX_PDO2DO`   `CFX_PDO2DO` converts an existing PDO into a digital offer URL. The attributes for this tag are listed in Table 25.8.

Table 25.8 `CFX_PDO2DO`

Attribute	Description
OfferValue	The variable that contains the PDO. This is required.
URLVariable	The variable in which the DO will be stored. This is required.
ContentURL	The URL of the content server. This is required.
TransactionURL	The URL of the transaction server. This is required.
FulfillmentURL	The URL of the fulfillment server. This is required.
SubscriptionURL	The URL of the subscription server. This is required.
StoreID	The store identification. This is required.
KeyFile	The filename for the store encryption file.
Encoding	Can be none, z, or radix. Defaults to z.

Part

IV

Ch

25

Web Application Framework

Introducing the Web Application Framework

The ColdFusion Web Application Framework is a collection of essential tools that can both ease your development effort, as well as help you create a more reliable and robust application. Although these tools are not dependent on one another, they are designed to work together and complement each other.

The Web Application Framework is made up of several functions:

- The APPLICATION.CFM application template is a special ColdFusion application-level template that is processed every time any other template is requested.

- Persistent client variables, session variables, and application variables enable you to save variables associated with a specific client's connections, even between sessions.

- Setting application scope by uniquely naming parts of an application so that variables can be kept within the scope of the appropriate application.

- Custom error handling is a mechanism by which you can override the standard ColdFusion error messages, allowing you to create more polished and complete applications. Custom error handling is not covered in this book, but it is covered extensively in *Advanced ColdFusion 4.0 Application Development* (Que, 1999).

Using the Application Template

Every time ColdFusion processes a template, it looks for a special template file called APPLICATION.CFM. If ColdFusion finds this template, known as the *application template*, it processes it before the requested template is processed.

The application template can contain any ColdFusion tags or functions; it can perform database queries, set variables, or perform any other processing required. You may even include a conditional call to <CFABORT> to halt processing of the requested template under specific conditions.

Listing 26.1 contains a sample application template. This template does just two things: It sets the application name and enables the use of client and session variables and also sets constant values that may be used throughout the application. The variable ODBC_DataSource, for example, contains the name of a data source to be used throughout the application. This variable could be used in place of hard-coded, data-source names in <CFQUERY> tags. See Appendix A, "ColdFusion Tag Reference," for more information about the <CFAPPLICATION> or <CFSET> tag.

Listing 26.1   Sample Application Template

```
<!--- Name application --->
<CFAPPLICATION NAME="A2Z_Internal" CLIENTMANAGEMENT="ON">

<!--- Set application constants --->
<CFSET ODBC_DataSource = "A2Z">
<CFSET BG_Color = "FFFFFF">
<CFSET Font_Face = "Arial">
```

◊ **See** "The CFQUERY Tag," for more information about <CFQUERY> and how it is used, **p. 201**.

 TIP

The application template is the perfect place for establishing applicationwide settings—installing custom error messages, implementing application-level security, setting applicationwide defaults, and setting variable defaults.

Locating the Application Template

Whenever a template is requested, ColdFusion looks for an application template in the current directory—the directory that the requested template itself is in. If no application template is found, ColdFusion looks in the requested template's parent directory and then gradually up the directory tree, one directory at a time. As soon as the first file named APPLICATION.CFM is found, it is used as the application template file.

To understand how application templates are located, look at a sample directory tree. Figure 26.1 shows a Web server directory tree. The root directory (\A2Z\SCRIPTS) contains a file— APPLICATION.CFM—so that when requests are made for any of the templates in that directory, or in any directory beneath it, \A2Z\SCRIPTS\APPLICATION.CFM is processed as well.

FIGURE 26.1

An application template file in the document root directory is used as the default application template for all directories.

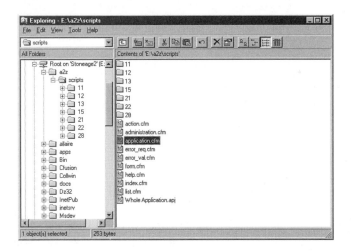

Part

IV

Ch

26

Directory \A2Z\SCRIPTS\13 does not contain any application template files, as seen in Figure 26.2. If a template in that directory is requested, ColdFusion tries to locate an application template in the parent directory, \A2Z\SCRIPTS. When the parent directory contains an application template file, that file will be processed.

Directory \A2Z\SCRIPTS\15 contains its own application template file, as seen in Figure 26.3. Therefore, if a template in that directory were requested, that local application template file would be processed—the one in the parent directory would not be processed.

FIGURE 26.2

If there is no application template in a directory, a template in a parent directory is used instead.

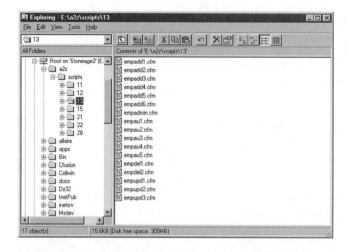

FIGURE 26.3

To override the default application template in a specific directory (and any directories beneath it), provide a different APPLICATION.CFM file in that directory.

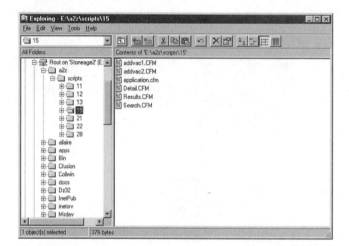

> **N O T E**   Only one application template file is ever processed. Assume your document root contains an application template file and that you create another application template file in a subdirectory. That second application template file is processed instead of the first one when a template is requested from that subdirectory. If you need to process both templates, you need to include the first one from within the second. ■

Application Template-Based Security

ColdFusion application templates are an ideal place to implement application-level security. Because the application template is processed prior to any other templates, any security checking implemented in it applies to all templates.

One form of security commonly implemented in intranets is domain-based security. Because intranets are usually internal corporate networks, and the IP addresses of hosts on most networks are within one or more known domains, you can restrict access based on the IP address of the requesting host within one of those known domains.

The application template in Listing 26.2 determines whether the first three sets of numbers in the remote address (the client IP address) are not the first part of a known domain address. An error message is displayed if the test returns TRUE, meaning the client is not within the known domain; processing is halted with a <CFABORT> tag.

Listing 26.2 Sample Security Application Template

```
<!--- Check that host IP address is in allowed domain --->
<CFIF Left(CGI.REMOTE_ADDR, 11) IS NOT "208.193.16.">

  <!--- Unknown host, display "unauthorized" screen --->
  <HTML>
  <HEAD>
  <TITLE>Unauthorized host detected!</TITLE>
  </HEAD>
  <BODY>
  <H1>Unauthorized host detected!</H1>
  </BODY>
  </HTML>

  <!--- And abort processing --->
  <CFABORT>

</CFIF>
```

The application template can also be used to allow users to log in to applications. The template can perform the following steps:

1. Check to see if this client has logged in yet.
2. If user logged in, allow processing of requested template.
3. If user is not logged in, but a login form has been submitted, attempt the login.
4. If not logged in, and login form fields are not present, display the login form.

This kind of security mechanism usually involves creating ODBC tables that list the valid user accounts and passwords. Once you have verified that a user-supplied name and password matches a table row, you have to set a flag or variable indicating the successful login. You can do this using fields in your database table, or you can use *persistent client variables* or *session variables*, which are discussed next.

N O T E ColdFusion only processes one application template file per request. If your template includes other templates that are in other directories (using the <CFINCLUDE> tag), application templates in those other directories are not processed.

Addressing the Web's Statelessness

As explained in Chapter 2, "Introduction to ColdFusion," Web clients do not maintain open connections with Web servers while interacting with Web-based applications. Rather, every client request stands on its own, with no knowledge of any prior interaction. It is the Web's lack of persistence between sessions that is referred to as its *statelessness*. This limitation means that variables or flags set during one processed request are not available during the next processed request.

To get around this problem, Web application developers use a variety of techniques to maintain variables and values between sessions:

■ URL parameters can be used to pass values back and forth between the server and the client with each request. This technique is used by Internet search engines, for example, which embed a field indicating what results have been displayed so that Next and Previous buttons can work correctly.

■ Form fields can be used to embed values in hidden fields—in multipart forms, for example.

■ HTTP cookies are variables that are stored on the client browser, and these are submitted along with future requests so that prior set values are known to the server.

See Chapter 21, "Advanced ColdFusion Templates," for more information on creating previous- and next-style interfaces.

All of these techniques have their own advantages and drawbacks. The biggest drawback with all of them is that they are time consuming to implement and require lots of manual manipulation.

ColdFusion provides application developers several types of variables that address this problem. While each variable type is different and has its own purpose, the common goal is providing a mechanism that stores information which persists across requests or sessions. The basic variable types are the following:

■ Client variables are variables associated with a particular client. By default, they are stored on the server in the system registry. They allow you to maintain state as a user moves from page to page in an application.

■ Server variables are associated with the current Web server and are available until the ColdFusion server is shut down. This server scope allows you to define variables that all your ColdFusion application pages can reference.

■ Session variables are tied to an individual client and persist for as long as that client ID maintains a session. Session variables, such as current client variables, require a client name to work; they are only available to that client ID.

■ Application variables are tied to an individual application as defined in the CFAPPLICATION NAME attribute, typically used in the APPLICATION.CFM file. Application variables only work if an application name has been defined.

Session and application variables are enabled or disabled in the ColdFusion Administrator's Server tab. Client variables must be enabled within your templates via the `<CFAPPLICATION>` tag. If you decide to use client variables, the `APPLICATION.CFM` file is the ideal place to enable this feature.

See Chapter 27, "Session Variables and Cookies," for information about HTTP cookies and session and application variables, as well as how to use them within your ColdFusion applications. ●

Session Variables and Cookies

Using Client-State Management Techniques

The Web is a stateless environment. Cookies were developed to keep track of visitors. ColdFusion has taken this concept a step further with client and session management. In conjunction with application and server variables, an efficient means of keeping track of users and their information is achieved.

There are four basic ways to keep track of a client browser using ColdFusion, as shown in Table 27.1. The most obvious is by keeping track of a user's IP address. The drawbacks of this are that many Internet users browse the Web via a proxy server. A *proxy server* actually receives the files from your server and re-sends this information to the client browser. This means that a virtually unlimited number of users can share a few or even one IP address. In addition, many Internet users have dial-up accounts that change IP addresses each time they log on to their ISP. All in all, IP tracking isn't an effective client management scheme.

As a rule, avoid using IP addresses for session tracking. Many service providers, America Online for example, reassign and reuse IP addresses dynamically. This causes session information to be confused and lost.

Another way to keep track of a user is to send a cookie to the user's browser. A *cookie* is a variable stored on the user's hard drive by the client browser and generally can only be viewed or manipulated by the server that sent it. Cookies also have drawbacks. First of all, not all browsers are compatible with cookies, and even if they are, many users turn them off because of security concerns. In addition, more than one cookie may be required in order to store a useful set of data on a client browser. You must also build cookie management in your application.

A third way to keep track of users is to append data in an URL or pass it with a form. This method's drawbacks include lengthy URLs for complex data sets and users sharing URLs, thus mixing users sessions. To make client-state management easier, ColdFusion features built-in client and session management that works with or without cookies.

Table 27.1   Client Management Techniques

Scheme	Components	Pros/Cons
IP tracking	`CGI.REMOTE_ADDR`	Can track client browsers by IP address. Ineffective with clients using proxy servers or dynamic IPs.
Cookies	`<CFCOOKIE>`, cookie variable scope	Data is stored on client browser and can easily be retrieved for use by applications. Some browsers do not support cookies, and many users disable them. Cookies can also be lost.
URL data	URL variable scope, `URLEncodedFormat()`	Does not require cookies; user data can be stored in bookmarks. Not secure. Users can share data by sharing links. Cannot be used to distinguish sessions.

Scheme	Components	Pros/Cons
ColdFusion client	`<CFAPPLICATION>`, scope client management scope, session	Can be used with or without cookies; large capacity for data storage, sessions are distinguished, secure. CFID must be stored in database to match user records to client data.

Using ColdFusion Client and Session Management

ColdFusion client and session management keeps track of client browser activity transparently and is compatible with virtually any browser. In addition to tracking client and session state, ColdFusion allows you to store information in the context of a particular client or session. Information can also be stored in context with an application, making it available to all an application's users.

Using Client and Session Management

Client and session management enable Web applications to maintain a virtual state for each client. This is essential for commerce applications such as shopping carts, document publishing, application security, collaboration applications, and virtually all other highly interactive applications. They are also useful in optimizing Web applications by allowing a database to be queried once with the results stored in RAM for application or client use. Data can also be passed from client to client using the application scope, allowing efficient user interaction.

Client and session management also enables you to develop applications without creating a separate management scheme for browsers that do not accept cookies. Data that would normally be passed using URL parameters or stored on the client browser using cookies can be hidden from users and eavesdroppers by storing it securely on the ColdFusion server. Cookies and other management schemes can be used in conjunction with ColdFusion client and session management, allowing the greatest freedom in application development.

Using Variable Scopes and `application.cfm`

Several variable scopes are available to ColdFusion developers. The ones you should be concerned with here are application, client, session, and cookie. These help you develop applications that track users and make data available to both the user and the application. The `application.cfm` file in an application defines the status of an application, client and session scope variables, and how long they are active. To demonstrate how these scopes interact, you construct a virtual pet application that uses only application, session, and client variables to pass data between users. This chapter requires an understanding of how variables work and how to create applications in ColdFusion. The main and most important tag in the `application.cfm` file is `<CFAPPLICTION>`. This tag defines the name of the application, whether ColdFusion client and session management are active, and how long application and session data will be active on the ColdFusion server. See Table 27.2 for examples of the usage of `<CFAPPLICATION>`. These values are restricted by global settings in the ColdFusion Administrator, where maximum and default values can be set serverwide.

Part
IV

Ch
27

Table 27.2 `<CFAPPLICATION>` **Parameters**

Parameter	Required/Optional	Description
NAME	Required	Enables application scope variables. The name of the application.
CLIENTMANAGEMENT	Optional	Enables ColdFusion client management.
SESSIONMANAGEMENT	Optional	Enables ColdFusion session variables.
APPLICATIONTIMEOUT	Optional	The time span for the persistence of application scope variables. Default is specified in the ColdFusion administrator. Uses `CreateTimeSpan()`.
SESSIONTIMEOUT	Optional	The time span for the persistence of session scope variables. Uses `CreateTimeSpan()`.

For the example application, the `application.cfm` in Listing 27.1 must enable client and session management, set some default values, and test to see if the client browser accepts cookies. If the client browser does not accept cookies, `CFID` and `CFTOKEN` are appended to all links in the application using the reserved client variable `client.URLToken`.

Listing 27.1 `application.cfm`—**Application Initialization**

```
<!--- My CF_Pet - A ColdFusion virtual pet --->
<!--- Define the application parameters --->
<CFAPPLICATION NAME="MyPet"
              CLIENTMANAGEMENT="Yes"
              SESSIONMANAGEMENT="Yes"
              SESSIONTIMEOUT=" #CreateTimeSpan(0,0,30,0)#"
              APPLICATIONTIMEOUT=" #CreateTimeSpan(1,0,0,0)#">
<!--- Initialize application variables --->
<CFPARAM NAME="application.lastMessage" DEFAULT="Hello!">
<CFPARAM NAME="application.lastUser" DEFAULT="Nobody">
<!--- Check to see if this is the first time the application has been
accessed by a particular client. If so, set values. --->
<CFIF NOT ISDEFINED("session.rollCount")>
   <CFSET SESSION.ROLLCOUNT = 1>
   <CFSET APPLICATION.LASTUSER = IIF(ISDEFINED("application.currentUser")
➥, "application.currentUser", DE("Nobody"))>
   <CFSET APPLICATION.CURRENTUSER = IIF(ISDEFINED("client.clientName"),
➥ "client.clientName", DE("guest from #CGI.REMOTE_ADDR#"))>
   <!--- Try to set a cookie for testing later --->>--->
   <CFCOOKIE NAME="isOn" VALUE="testing">
   <CFSET APPLICATION.ADDTOKEN = "cfid=#client.cfid#&cftoken=#client.
➥cftoken#">
<CFELSE>
   <!--- Check to see if cookies are on. If no, make a query string
variable with the CFID and CFTOKEN. --->
```

```
    <CFSET APPLICATION.ADDTOKEN = IIF(NOT ISDEFINED("cookie.isOn"),
DE("cfid=#client.cfid#&cftoken=#client.cftoken#"), DE("")))>

</CFIF>
```

Using Application Scope   Now that the application is defined, application scope variables can be used. All variable types can be used in the application scope including arrays and queries. In `application.cfm`, application scope variables are used to show users who visited before them, and also to pass the session key to all links in the application if the client browser does not accept cookies. These values are both used in `index.cfm`, shown in Listing 27.2. These values can also be read from any template in the application. Notice that `index.cfm` automatically appends the session key to its links. This is because a cookie may not be set and retrieved from within the same template. The cookie test will not be complete by the time the links in `index.cfm` are constructed. The completed welcome page is shown in Figure 27.1.

Listing 27.2   `index.cfm`—The Welcome Page

```
<!--- The welcome page --->
<HTML>
<HEAD>
<TITLE>My CF_Pet </TITLE>
</HEAD>
<BODY BGCOLOR="white" TEXT="black" LINK="blue" VLINK="green" ALINK="yellow">
<TABLE ALIGN="center" BGCOLOR="#0000cc" WIDTH="100%" CELLSPACING="0"
➥ CELLPADDING="0" BORDER="1">
<TR>
    <TD WIDTH="100%" VALIGN="top">
    <FONT SIZE="+3" COLOR="Yellow"><B><I>My CF_Pet</I></B></FONT>
    </TD>
</TR>
</TABLE>
<P>
<TABLE ALIGN="center" BGCOLOR="#ffffcc" WIDTH="100%" CELLSPACING="0"
➥ CELLPADDING="0" BORDER="1">
<TR>
    <TD WIDTH="100%" VALIGN="top">
<CFOUTPUT>
<B>Welcome to the home of the CF_Pet, a web-based virtual pet!  You can
raise your pet from infancy and test your virtual parenting skills!  The
last user to visit, #application.lastUser#, says "#application.lastMessage#".
</B>
</CFOUTPUT>
<P>
<!--- Show separate messages for users and guests --->
<CFIF ISDEFINED("client.status")>
    <CFOUTPUT>
    Welcome back, #client.clientName#! You last visited on #dateFormat(client.
➥lastVisit, "ddd, mmmm dd, yyyy")# at #timeFormat(client.lastVisit,
➥ "h:mm tt")#.  Your pet, #client.petName# is ready for your visit.

    <P>
```

continues

Listing 27.2 Continued

```
    <B>[<A HREF="main.cfm?#application.addToken#">Visit #client.petName#
➡</A>]</B>
    <B>[<A HREF="register.cfm?#application.addToken#">Edit your Preferences
➡</A>]</B>
    <B>[<A HREF="action.cfm?endLife=yes&#application.addToken#">
➡Euthanize your pet</A>]</B>
    </CFOUTPUT>
<CFELSE>
    <CFOUTPUT>
    To login and create your pet, <B><A HREF="register.cfm?#application.
➡addToken#">start here!</A></B>
    </CFOUTPUT>
</CFIF>
    </TD>
</TR>
</TABLE>
</BODY>
</HTML>
```

FIGURE 27.1

The user is greeted with a welcome page.

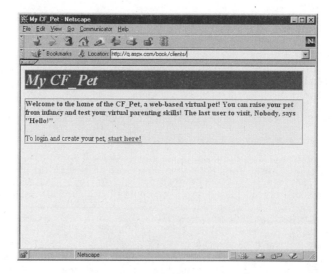

Using Client Scope   Users must be able to register and create a pet. When a client accesses any page in your application with client management enabled, CFID and CFTOKEN are automatically generated. If the client browser accepts cookies, these values are stored as cookies on the client browser. If these cookies are not accepted, it is up to your application to pass these values between templates to maintain client state. Only the CFID and CFTOKEN must be passed. ColdFusion makes all other client and session scope variables available to your application automatically based on these two values. In the CF_Pet application, more information than just a session key is needed to make the application useable. Listing 27.3 shows register.cfm, where user attributes such as name and email address are collected, as well as the pet's attributes. When this form is submitted, `action.cfm` (shown in Listing 27.4) adds this data to the client data already stored by ColdFusion.

On the CD

Listing 27.3 `register.cfm`—**The Form for the Creation and Modification of the Pet**

```
<!--- Form for creating or modifying a pet --->
<HTML>
<HEAD>
<TITLE>My CF_Pet - Registration </TITLE>
</HEAD>
<BODY BGCOLOR="white" TEXT="black" LINK="blue" VLINK="green" ALINK="yellow">
<TABLE ALIGN="center" BGCOLOR="#0000cc" WIDTH="100%" CELLSPACING="0"
➥ CELLPADDING="0" BORDER="1">
<TR>
    <TD WIDTH="100%" VALIGN="top">
    <FONT SIZE="+3" COLOR="Yellow"><B><I>My CF_Pet</I></B></FONT>
    </TD>
</TR>
</TABLE>
<P>
<TABLE BGCOLOR="#ffffcc" WIDTH="100%" CELLSPACING="0" CELLPADDING="0"
➥ BORDER="1">
<TR>
    <TD WIDTH="100%" VALIGN="top">
<CFIF ISDEFINED("client.status")>
    <B>To modify your preferences, fill out the form below!</B>
<CFELSE>
    <B>To create a new CF_Pet, fill out the form below!</B>
</CFIF>
<P>
<CFOUTPUT>
<FORM METHOD="post" ACTION="action.cfm?#application.addToken#">
<INPUT TYPE="hidden" NAME="clientName_required" VALUE="Please enter
➥ your name.">
<INPUT TYPE="hidden" NAME="petName_required" VALUE="Please enter a name for
➥ your pet.">
<INPUT TYPE="hidden" NAME="email_required" VALUE="Please enter your email
➥ address.">
<TABLE CELLSPACING="2" CELLPADDING="2">
<TR>
    <TD><B>Your Name:</B></TD>
    <TD><INPUT TYPE="Text" NAME="clientName" SIZE="20" <CFIF
ISDEFINED("client.status")>value="#client.clientName#"</CFIF>></TD>
</TR>
<TR>
    <TD><B>Your Pet's Name:</B></TD>
    <TD><INPUT TYPE="Text" NAME="petName" SIZE="20" <CFIF
ISDEFINED("client.status")>value="#client.petName#"</CFIF>></TD>
</TR>
<TR>
    <TD><B>Your Email Address:</B></TD>
    <TD><INPUT TYPE="Text" NAME="email" SIZE="20"  <CFIF
```

Part

IV

Ch

27

continues

Listing 27.3   Continued

```
ISDEFINED("client.status")>value="#client.email#"</CFIF>></TD>
</TR>
<TR>
    <TD><B>Your Pet's Color</B></TD>
    <TD><SELECT NAME="petColor">
    <CFIF ISDEFINED("client.status")><OPTION SELECTED>#client.petColor#</CFIF>
    <OPTION>Yellow
    <OPTION>Brown
    <OPTION>Blue
    </SELECT></TD>
</TR>
<TR>
    <TD><B>Put My Pet In:</B></TD>
    <TD><SELECT NAME="windows">
    <CFIF ISDEFINED("client.status")><OPTION SELECTED>#client.windows#</CFIF>
    <OPTION VALUE="window">A separate window
    <OPTION VALUE="page">The same page
    </SELECT></TD>
</TR>
</TABLE>
<INPUT TYPE="Submit" VALUE="Make My Pet!">
</FORM>
</CFOUTPUT>
    </TD>
</TR>
</TABLE>
</BODY>
</HTML>
```

Client variables are a good place to store user preferences, since they persist between client visits. Because client variables are stored in the registry by default, you should be careful not to store too much data in client variables, especially in high-traffic applications. If you need to store large amounts of information, you should configure client variables for database storage. This is done in the ColdFusion Administrator (as explained in Chapter 4, "Administering ColdFusion").

If your servers are configured in a server cluster, you should definitely use client variables and configure them for database storage. This allows you to share session state information between multiple servers.

Shared session state management in a clustered environment is covered in more detail in *Advanced ColdFusion 4.0 Application Development* (ISBN 0-7897-1810-3, Que).

The register.cfm template, shown in Figure 27.2, is also used for modifying preferences, so you check for the existence of the client variable client.status, which is not created until the form is submitted. Once a user has created a pet, this form is used for modification only.

FIGURE 27.2

The registration page.

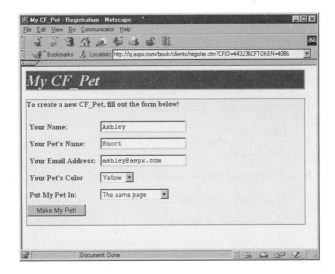

On the CD

Listing 27.4 `action.cfm`—Template for Handling Form Submissions

```
<!--- action.cfm - Let the owner take care of the pet. --->
<CFIF ISDEFINED("form.feed")>
   <CFSET CLIENT.PETFED = INCREMENTVALUE(CLIENT.PETFED)>

<CFELSEIF ISDEFINED("form.clean")>
   <CFSET CLIENT.PETCLEANED = INCREMENTVALUE(CLIENT.PETCLEANED)>

<CFELSEIF ISDEFINED("url.endLife")>
   <CFLOOP INDEX="listElement" LIST="#getClientVariablesList()#">
      <CFSET ISSUCCESS = DELETECLIENTVARIABLE("#listElement#")>
   </CFLOOP>

   <CFLOCATION URL="index.cfm" ADDTOKEN="yes">
<CFELSE>
   <!--- Create a new pet. --->
   <!--- Grab all of the values from the form and add them to the
client varibles     scope --->
   <CFLOOP INDEX="listElement" LIST="#form.fieldnames#">
      <CFSET "client.#listElement#" = EVALUATE("form.#listElement#")>
   </CFLOOP>
   <!--- If this is an update, skip the preliminaries --->
   <CFIF NOT ISDEFINED("client.status")>
      <CFSET CLIENT.STATUS="active">
      <CFSET CLIENT.PETBORN = "#Now()#">
      <CFSET CLIENT.PETFED = "1">
      <CFSET CLIENT.PETCLEANED = "1">
      <CFSET SESSION.EMOTION_VALUE = 100>
      <CFSET SESSION.HEALTH_VALUE = 100>
   </CFIF>
   <!--- Go to the main page --->
   <CFLOCATION URL="main.cfm" ADDTOKEN="yes">
</CFIF>
<CFLOCATION URL="#cgi.http_referer#" ADDTOKEN="yes">
```

Part

IV

Ch

27

Now all client variables necessary for maintaining the pet have been created. Remember that client scope variables cannot be used to store complex data types such as queries and arrays. Table 27.3 shows the additional reserved variables automatically created and maintained by ColdFusion in the client scope.

Table 27.3   Reserved Client Variables

Name	Description
CFID	The unique client ID. Part of the session key.
CFTOKEN	A unique ID that forms part of the session key.
LastVisit	Records the date and time of the last visit for a client.
URLToken	The CFID and CFTOKEN together, used to append to an URL.
HitCount	The number of times a client has visited the site.
TimeCreated	The date and time of the creation of the CFID.

When adding variables in this scope, remember that client variables are stored in the registry. Again, this is not a good place to store large amounts of data for each client. In the pet application, store simple values that are manipulated and used elsewhere in the application. These variables are used in main.cfm, shown in Listing 27.5, to determine how the pet is to be displayed in the custom tag checkUp.cfm. Determining how to compute the current state of the pet is shown in Listing 27.6.

On the CD

Listing 27.5   main.cfm—The Virtual Pet Management Area

```
<!--- The main window. --->
<HTML>
<HEAD>
<TITLE>My CF_Pet - <CFOUTPUT>#client.petName#</CFOUTPUT>'s kennel</TITLE>
<!--- window open script --->
<SCRIPT LANGUAGE="JavaScript">
<!--
    function openWin( windowURL, windowName, windowFeatures ) {
        return window.open( windowURL, windowName, windowFeatures ) ;
    }
// -->
</SCRIPT>
</HEAD>
<BODY BGCOLOR="white" TEXT="black" LINK="blue" VLINK="green" ALINK="yellow">
<TABLE ALIGN="center" BGCOLOR="#0000cc" WIDTH="100%"
➥CELLSPACING="0" CELLPADDING="0" BORDER="1">
<TR>
    <TD WIDTH="100%" VALIGN="top">
    <FONT SIZE="+3" COLOR="Yellow"><B><I>My CF_Pet</I></B>  </FONT>
    <FONT SIZE="+2" COLOR="White"><CFOUTPUT>
➥#client.petName#</CFOUTPUT>'s kennel</FONT>
    </TD>
```

```
</TR>
</TABLE>
<P>
<TABLE ALIGN="center" BGCOLOR="#ffffcc" WIDTH="100%"
➡CELLSPACING="0" CELLPADDING="0" BORDER="1">
<TR>
    <TD WIDTH="100%" VALIGN="top">
<CFOUTPUT>
<B>Welcome to CF_Kennels, #client.clientName#!  We do our best to take care
of the needs of your pet, but your pet needs your attention and care.
You must feed your pet at least 3 times a day, and clean up after your
pet as necessary.  And the more you visit your pet, the happier it gets. </B>
<P>
    <B>[<A HREF="register.cfm?#application.addToken#">
➡Edit your Preferences</A>]</B>
    <B>[<A HREF="action.cfm?endLife=yes&#application.addToken#">
➡Euthanize your pet</A>]</B>
</CFOUTPUT>
<!--- Check preferences and display contents accordingly --->
<CFIF CLIENT.WINDOWS IS "window">
    <CFOUTPUT>
    <B>[<A HREF="JavaScript: newWindow = openWin( 'kennel.cfm?show=
➡pet&#application.addToken#', 'kennel', 'width=250,height=300,
➡toolbar=0,location=0,directories=0,status=
➡0,menuBar=0,scrollBars=1,resizable=1' ); newWindow.focus()">
Open your kennel</A>]</B>
    </CFOUTPUT>
<CFELSE>

    <CFINCLUDE TEMPLATE="pet.cfm">
</CFIF>
    </TD>
</TR>
</TABLE>
</BODY>
</HTML>
```

In `action.cfm`, the application provides for the complete deletion of the pet and associated client variables. The function `GetClientVariablesList()` returns a comma-delimited list of all non–read-only client variables. You can use this in conjunction with `DeleteClientVariable()` and `<CFLOOP>` to delete all the variables created in the application. If the variable does not exist, `DeleteClientVariable()`returns `NO`; it returns `YES` when successful.

Part

IV

Ch

27

Notice also in Listing 27.6 that you're using JavaScript in a new way. Instead of using it for validation, you're using it here to open a new browser window, one that is sized to fit your virtual kennel. This JavaScript was generated by the ColdFusion Studio Open Window Wizard. For more information on using the ColdFusion Studio wizards, see Chapter 10.

Using Session Scope   Now that the user has created a pet and is ready to care for it, the basic values stored in the client scope need to be converted into useable statistics and displayed in an appropriate manner. To do this, create session scope variables for the data you need to use for this session only. Session scope variables can only be defined in the context of a session key, so it is important to make sure any session variables are defined and used only within the same application and only with both client and session management enabled in `application.cfm`.

In the `CF_Pet` application, you've encapsulated the conversions in a custom tag, `checkUp.cfm`. This custom tag, shown in Listing 27.6, reads the current values in the client scope, runs calculations for the pet's health and happiness, and stores these temporary values in the session scope. This is an efficient way to pass data between templates and custom tags because no database queries, form fields, or URL parameters are needed. All of the data is stored in RAM for quick retrieval.

Listing 27.6 `checkUp.cfm`—Template That Calculates How Well the Pet Is

```
<!--- checkUp custom tag.  This template calculates the well-being of the
pet. --->
<!--- First, figure out if the pet has been visited. Figure it should take
about 20 hits per visit to constitute "quality time". --->
<CFSET SESSION.VISITVALUE = EVALUATE("#iif(dateDiff("D", client.petBorn,
➥ now()) GT 0, DE("((#CLIENT.HITCOUNT# / 20) / #DATEDIFF("d", CLIENT.
➥PETBORN, NOW())#)"), DE("((#CLIENT.HITCOUNT# / 20) / 1)"))# * 100")>
<CFSET SESSION.VISITVALUE = IIF(SESSION.VISITVALUE LTE 100, DE("#session.
➥visitValue#"), DE("100"))>
<!--- Next, figure out if the pet has received three square meals a day. --->
<CFIF CLIENT.PETFED GT EVALUATE("(#dateDiff("D", client.petBorn, now())
➥# * 3)")>
   <CFSET CLIENT.PETFED = IIF(DATEDIFF("d", CLIENT.PETBORN, NOW()) GT 0,
➥DE("#evaluate("((#DATEDIFF("d", CLIENT.PETBORN,
➥ NOW())# * 3) + 1)")#"), DE("4"))>
</CFIF>
<CFSET SESSION.HUNGER = EVALUATE("#iif(dateDiff("D", client.petBorn, now())
➥ GT 0, DE("(#CLIENT.PETFED# / (#DATEDIFF("d", CLIENT.PETBORN, NOW
➥())# * 3))"), DE("(#CLIENT.PETFED# / 3)"))# * 100")>
<CFSET SESSION.HUNGER = IIF(SESSION.HUNGER LTE 100, DE("#session.hunger#"),
➥ DE("100"))>
<!--- Now, figure out how many times the pooper - scooper has been used.
And remember, not all pets make the same amount of mess. The more it is fed,
the more the mess. --->
<CFSET SESSION.CLEANED = EVALUATE("#iif(dateDiff("D", client.petBorn,
➥ now()) GT 0, DE("(#CLIENT.PETCLEANED# / (#DATEDIFF("d", CLIENT.
➥PETBORN, NOW())# * ((#RANDOMIZE(DAY(NOW()))# * 2) +
➥(#CLIENT.PETFED# / (#DATEDIFF("d", CLIENT.PETBORN, NOW())# * 3)))))"),
➥DE("(#CLIENT.PETCLEANED# / ((#RANDOMIZE(DAY(NOW()))# * 2) +
➥(#CLIENT.PETFED# / 3)))"))# * 100")>
<CFSET SESSION.CLEANED = IIF(SESSION.CLEANED LTE 100,
➥ DE("#session.cleaned#"), DE("100"))>
<!--- Use the above to figure out how healthy and happy it is. Combine
these for an overall value.  There's no substitute for time well spent.--->
<CFSET SESSION.EMOTION_VALUE = EVALUATE("(((#session.visitValue# * 2) +
➥ #session.hunger# + #session.cleaned#) / 4)")>
<CFSET SESSION.HEALTH_VALUE = EVALUATE("((#session.hunger# + #session.
➥cleaned#) / 2)")>
<CFSET VARIABLES.EMOTIONALSTATE = EVALUATE("((((#session.Health_value# * 2)
➥ + #session.Emotion_value#) / 3)")>
```

```
<!--- Give the emotion a name --->
<CFIF VARIABLES.EMOTIONALSTATE GT 66
 AND VARIABLES.EMOTIONALSTATE LTE 100>

    <CFSET SESSION.EMOTION = "Happy">
<CFELSEIF VARIABLES.EMOTIONALSTATE GT 33
 AND VARIABLES.EMOTIONALSTATE LTE 66>

   <CFSET SESSION.EMOTION = "Sad">

 <CFELSE>

    <CFSET SESSION.EMOTION = "Dead">
</CFIF>
```

Notice how the variable scopes interact in Listing 27.6. You pass data from more persistent scopes, such as client and application, to less persistent scopes, such as the session scope. You use the variables scope to store temporary values that are not used elsewhere in the application. When using the scopes in an application, it is important to qualify your variables by adding the scope to their name, such as `application.myVar` instead of `myVar`. Not only does this speed your template's execution, it also keeps confusion to a minimum.

Server, application, client, and session scope variables are available to multiple templates, so you must make sure that your variable names do not clash. Errors of this type can be hard to debug. Keep track of your variables, and all will turn out well.

Now that the pet has been evaluated by its health professional, this data can be displayed in a graphical manner. One way to do this is to create a *Sprite* a la the old Commodore 64 graphics engine. A *sprite* in this context is simply an 8×8 grid (in pixels) used to represent an image. ColdFusion arrays can be stored in application, server, and session scopes, so you'll use the session scope to create and store a graphic array as shown in Listing 27.7.

On the CD

Listing 27.7 makeSprite.cfm—Template to Generate a Sprite and Store It as an Array

Part
IV

Ch
27

```
<!--- makeSprite.cfm CF_MyPet.MakeSprite custom tag
      Constructs a sprite (like the old time Commodore 64 sprites)
using an array.

--->
<!--- How is the pet feeling?  If it has no feelings, give it some. --->
<CFPARAM NAME="Session.Emotion" DEFAULT="happy">
<!--- Give the pet data on how to make faces --->
<CFSET HAPPY = "66,102,126,219,255,189,66,60">
<CFSET SAD = "66,102,126,219,255,231,90,60">
<CFSET DEAD = "66,102,126,153,255,255,66,60">
<!--- Set array based on emotion --->
<CFSET SESSION.SPRITE = ARRAYNEW(2)>
<CFLOOP INDEX="currentValue" LIST="#evaluate(""variables.#Session.
➥Emotion#"")#">
```

continues

Listing 27.7   Continued

```
<CFPARAM NAME="loopStep" DEFAULT="1">
<!--- Convert value to binary --->
<CFSET CURRENTBYTE = FORMATBASEN(CURRENTVALUE, 2)>
<CFLOOP INDEX="currentBit" FROM="8" TO="1" STEP="-1">

    <CFIF CURRENTBIT GT LEN(CURRENTBYTE)>
        <CFSET SESSION.SPRITE[LOOPSTEP][CURRENTBIT] = "0">

    <CFELSE>

        <CFSET SESSION.SPRITE[LOOPSTEP][CURRENTBIT] = MID(REVERSE
➥(CURRENTBYTE), CURRENTBIT, 1)>

    </CFIF>
</CFLOOP>

<CFSET LOOPSTEP = INCREMENTVALUE(LOOPSTEP)>

</CFLOOP>
```

Now you can use HTML tables to display this sprite on the client browser. Using session scope variables to pass the sprite from custom tag to custom tag allows the tags to be called from separate templates. As long as the current client session does not time out, this sprite is available to any template in the application. The drawSprite.cfm custom tag (shown in Listing 27.8) takes the information stored in the session array variable and converts it to a table display.

On the CD

Listing 27.8   drawSprite.cfm—Retrieving the Sprite and Drawing on the Client Browser

```
<!--- drawSprite.cfm CF_MyPet.drawSprite
   Draws the face of the pet
--->
<!--- Check to see if makeSprite ran.  If not, kill process --->
<CFIF NOT ISDEFINED("session.sprite")>
   CF_MyPet.makeSprite has not run!
   <CFEXIT>
</CFIF>
<!--- Build table --->
<TABLE BORDER="0" CELLSPACING="0" CELLPADDING="0" ALIGN="CENTER"
➥VALIGN="TOP" BGCOLOR="white">
<!--- Read data from the array --->
<CFLOOP INDEX="currentByte" FROM="1" TO="8">
   <!--- Read bits and make table --->
   <TR>
   <CFLOOP INDEX="currentBit" FROM="1" TO="8">
      <!--- Check to see if bit is on --->
      <CFIF #SESSION.SPRITE[CURRENTBYTE][CURRENTBIT]# IS "1">
         <CFOUTPUT>
         <TD ALIGN="CENTER" VALIGN="TOP" BGCOLOR="#client.petColor#">
➥<FONT SIZE="1"> </FONT></TD>
```

```
        <TD ALIGN="CENTER" VALIGN="TOP" BGCOLOR="#client.petColor#">
➥<FONT SIZE="1"> </FONT></TD>
        <TD ALIGN="CENTER" VALIGN="TOP" BGCOLOR="#client.petColor#">
➥<FONT SIZE="1"> </FONT></TD>
        </CFOUTPUT>
      <CFELSE>
        <TD ALIGN="CENTER" VALIGN="TOP" BGCOLOR="black">
➥<FONT SIZE="1"> </FONT></TD>
        <TD ALIGN="CENTER" VALIGN="TOP" BGCOLOR="black">
➥<FONT SIZE="1"> </FONT></TD>
        <TD ALIGN="CENTER" VALIGN="TOP" BGCOLOR="black">
➥<FONT SIZE="1"> </FONT></TD>
        </CFIF>
    </CFLOOP>
    </TR>
</CFLOOP>
</TABLE>
```

The custom tags that check the pet's health and draw the sprite are called from the pet.cfm template, shown in Listing 27.9. A table is constructed to contain the pet display and allow it to be portable to any section of the application.

On the CD

Listing 27.9 pet.cfm—Displaying the Pet

```
<!--- Show the pet --->
  <CF_CHECKUP>
  <CF_MAKESPRITE>
  <TABLE ALIGN="center" CELLSPACING="0" CELLPADDING="0" BORDER=1>
  <TR>
      <TD WIDTH="100%" BGCOLOR="navy"><B><CFOUTPUT><FONT SIZE="+1"
COLOR="White">#client.petName#</FONT></CFOUTPUT></B></TD>
  </TR>
  <TR>
      <TD WIDTH="100%" ALIGN="center" BGCOLOR="#ffffcc">
      <CF_DRAWSPRITE>
      </TD>
  </TR>
  <TR>
      <TD WIDTH="100%">
      <B>Happiness:</B><CFOUTPUT>#round(session.Emotion_value)#</CFOUTPUT><BR>
      <CF_MAKEBAR BARVALUE="#session.Emotion_value#" BARSIZE="1" BARCOLOR=
➥"##9966cc" SCALE="2">

      </TD>
  </TR>
  <TR>
      <TD WIDTH="100%">
      <B>Health:</B><CFOUTPUT>#round(session.Health_value)#</CFOUTPUT><BR>
      <CF_MAKEBAR BARVALUE="#session.Health_value#" BARSIZE="1" BARCOLOR=
➥"##9966cc" SCALE="2">
      </TD>
  </TR>
```

Part

IV

Ch

27

continues

Listing 27.9   Continued

```
<TR>
    <TD WIDTH="100%">
    <TABLE BORDER=0 ALIGN="center">
    <CFOUTPUT>
    <FORM ACTION="action.cfm?#application.addToken#" METHOD="POST">
    </CFOUTPUT>
    <TR><TD>
    <INPUT TYPE="Submit" NAME="Feed" VALUE="Feed">
    </TD><TD>
    <INPUT TYPE="Submit" NAME="Clean" VALUE="Clean">
    </TD>
    </FORM>
    <CFIF CLIENT.WINDOWS IS "window">

        <FORM>
        <TD>
            <INPUT TYPE="button" ONCLICK="self.close()" VALUE="Close">
        </TD>
        </FORM>
    </CFIF>
    </TR>
    </TABLE>
    </TD>
</TR>
<TR>
    <TD WIDTH="100%">
    <TABLE BORDER=0 ALIGN="center">
    <TR>
    <CFIF SESSION.HUNGER LT 100>
    <TD>
        <CFOUTPUT><FONT SIZE="-1">I'm hungry!</FONT></CFOUTPUT>
    </TD>
    </CFIF>
    <CFIF SESSION.CLEANED LT 100>
    <TD>
        <CFOUTPUT><FONT SIZE="-1">I'm dirty!</FONT></CFOUTPUT>
    </TD>
    </CFIF>
    </TR>
    </TABLE>
    </TD>
</TR>
</TABLE>
```

In Listing 27.9 additional data is displayed to help the user take care of the pet. Two bar graphs are displayed, along with notices if the pet is hungry or needs to be cleaned. The bar graph is displayed using a simple custom tag that uses tables.

Finally, CF_Pet allows users to keep their pet in a separate window. The template `kennel.cfm`, shown in Listing 27.11, creates the pet display in the window and includes the `pet.cfm` template. Figure 27.3 shows the pet in its virtual habitat.

On the CD

Listing 27.10 `makeBar.cfm`—**Generating Bar Graphs Without the Use of Images**

```
<!--- makeBar.cfm --->
<!--- Draw a bar graph.  Parameters:
    scale: Display scale of the bar.  Value is x in 1:x
    color: A hex value including hash
    size:  The size of the bar.  Values 1 - 3   --->
<TABLE BORDER="0" CELLSPACING="0" CELLPADDING="0">
<TR>
    <CFLOOP INDEX="loopCount" FROM="1" TO="#evaluate(""100 / #attributes.
➡scale#"")#">
        <CFOUTPUT>
        <CFIF LOOPCOUNT LTE #EVALUATE("#attributes.barValue# / #attributes.
➡scale#")#>
            <TD BGCOLOR="#attributes.barColor#"><FONT
➡SIZE="#attributes.barSize#"> </FONT></TD>
        <CFELSE>
            <TD BGCOLOR="black"><FONT SIZE="#attributes.barSize#"> 
➡</FONT></TD>
        </CFIF>
        </CFOUTPUT>
    </CFLOOP>
</TR>
</TABLE>
```

On the CD

Listing 27.11 `kennel.cfm`—**The Pet Kennel Window Template**

```
<!--- For separate window users.  Show the kennel or the chat window --->
<!DOCTYPE HTML PUBLIC "-//W3C//DTD HTML 3.2 Final//EN">
<HTML>
<HEAD>
</HEAD>
<CFPARAM NAME="show" DEFAULT="pet">
<BODY BGCOLOR="White" TEXT="Black" LINK="Blue" VLINK="Green" ALINK="Yellow">
<CFIF SHOW IS "pet">
    <CFHTMLHEAD TEXT="<TITLE>#Client.petName#'s Kennel</TITLE>">
    <CFINCLUDE TEMPLATE="pet.cfm">
</CFIF>
</BODY>
</HTML>
```

Part
IV

Ch

27

Using Cookies

Cookies can be created, read, and manipulated on the client browser independently of ColdFusion client and session management. The <CFCOOKIE> tag creates and deletes cookies on the client browser. Values set using <CFCOOKIE> can be read and set using the cookie variable scope. Table 27.4 describes the parameters available for the <CFCOOKIE> tag.

FIGURE 27.3

The pet in its virtual environment.

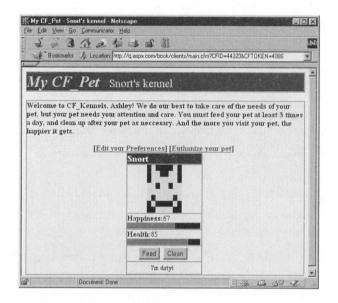

Table 27.4 `<CFCOOKIE>` **Parameters**

Name	Value	Description
NAME	String	Required. The name of the variable.
VALUE	Any	Required. The value of the variable.
EXPIRES	Date, number of days	Optional. Describes when the cookie is NOW or NEVER scheduled to expire.
SECURE	None	Optional. Requires the cookie to be sent securely using SSL. Cookie is not sent if client browser does not support SSL.
DOMAIN	Domain name	Required only if PATH is used. The domain for which the cookies are valid. Separate multiple domains with a ; character.
PATH	Web path	Optional. Subset of the URL to which the cookie applies. Separate multiple paths with a ; character.

Setting a Cookie

Cookies are set using the `<CFCOOKIE>` tag by specifying a name, value, and expiration date for the cookie. The expiration date can be absolute, such as 12/6/2006, or it can be relative, such as 1. Relative values are represented in days, so if your cookie is set as EXPIRES="7", it will expire in one week. You can also specify that the cookie never expire by adding EXPIRES="NEVER". This will, in effect, cause your cookie to reside permanently on the client browser.

Reading a Cookie

When reading a cookie, it is a good idea to check for the existence of the cookie first using IsDefined(). To read the value of the cookie, simply reference the fully qualified variable. If the name of your cookie is ITEMS and you would like to see if it is 0, use the same syntax as for any other variable. Look at Listing 27.12.

On the CD

Listing 27.12 cookie.cfm—Determining Whether a Browser Accepts Cookies

```
<!--- Check for the existence of the cookie -*
<cfif IsDefined("cookie.items")>
   <cfif cookie.items is 0>
      There are no items in your basket.
   </cfif>
</cfif>
```

Deleting Cookies

Removing cookies is similar to setting a cookie, but instead of specifying an expiration date in the future, add EXPIRES="NOW". This immediately deletes the cookie from the client browser. ●

Part

IV

Ch

27

Working with Files and Directories

Manipulating Files and Directories

File and directory manipulation in ColdFusion is provided through the `<CFFILE>` and `<CFDIRECTORY>` tags. These tags take advantage of features introduced in Web browsers that support file upload using the HTTP protocol. The method by which files are uploaded to the server using HTTP is documented in the Internet Request for Comment (RFC) 1867, which can be found at `http://www.cis.ohio-state.edu/htbin/rfc/rfc1867.html`. These features are browser specific; you therefore use them carefully to provide the maximum capability to your users, while also providing the maximum level of flexibility.

In addition to the ability to upload files, `<CFFILE>` also permits local file access through CFML templates. Files can be moved, copied, or deleted by using different action attributes for the `<CFFILE>` tag. Additionally, `<CFFILE>` provides mechanisms for reading and writing ASCII files with ColdFusion. Taking advantage of the `<CFFILE>` tag provides you with the ability to produce complex applications with file manipulation using a single interface, without having to deal with the additional complexities of protocols such as FTP or NFS. The templates, in which the `<CFFILE>` tag are used, can be protected using native server security when the templates are stored in directories below the document root defined for the HTTP server.

N O T E RFC 1867 is the formal documentation of the HTTP file upload process. It specifies the concepts relating to file uploads using MIME file extensions. ■

CAUTION

The file upload mechanism is browser specific. Netscape Navigator 2.0 and later support this feature. Microsoft Internet Explorer 4.0 supports this feature natively, while Internet Explorer 3.02 provides file upload support through the addition of an ActiveX control. Other browsers, such as Lynx and Mosaic, may not support this feature. Use of the file upload mechanism should be implemented with this in mind.

On the CD

The file upload plug-in for Microsoft Internet Explorer 3.02 on Windows 95/NT is on the CD-ROM in the file `RFC1867.EXE`.

For more information about HTTP file uploads and Microsoft Internet Explorer, check out Microsoft's Web page at `http://www.microsoft.com/ie/`.

Understanding the `<CFFILE>` Tag and Its Attributes

The `<CFFILE>` tag utilizes standard HTTP protocols to permit file uploads using a POST operation. The files are transmitted from the client to the server using a multipart form field definition. The general syntax for the `<CFFILE>` tag is in Listing 28.1, with specific values for the ACTION parameter and the other attributes shown in Table 28.1.

Listing 28.1 `<CFFILE>` **Tag Syntax**

```
<CFFILE ACTION=action ATTRIBUTE=attribute
ÂATTRIBUTE=attribute ATTRIBUTE=attribute>
```

The CFFILE tag's attributes can be set to multiple values, which permits the behavior of the tag to be modified to fit your needs. Each of the attributes can be set dynamically using variables created via the CFSET tag, or the values of query or form fields. When using form fields, extreme care should be taken to ensure that security restrictions are in place to prevent malicious action as a result of dynamic file action. Table 28.1 indicates the attributes and the valid values permitted. Table 28.2 shows the possible values for the NAMECONFLICT attribute, and the corresponding ColdFusion actions that will occur based on those values.

Table 28.1   **<CFFILE> Tag ACTION Attributes**

Action	Attributes	Comments
APPEND	OUTPUT FILE	Writes the contents of the string specified in OUTPUT to the end of the file specified in FILE.
COPY	SOURCE DESTINATION	Copies file from location specified in SOURCE to location specified in DESTINATION.
DELETE	FILE	Deletes file specified in FILE attribute.
MOVE	SOURCE DESTINATION	Moves file from location specified in SOURCE to location specified in DESTINATION.
READ	FILE VARIABLE	Reads the contents of the file specified in FILE into the variable specified in VARIABLE. The VARIABLE is created if it does not exist.
RENAME	SOURCE DESTINATION	Renames file specified in SOURCE to the filename specified in DESTINATION.
UPLOAD	ACCEPT DESTINATION FILEFIELD NAMECONFLICT	Used to upload files to the server using the filename found in FILEFIELD from the form and resolves filename conflicts using the value of the NAMECONFLICT attribute.
WRITE	OUTPUT FILE	Writes the contents of the string specified as OUTPUT to the file specified in FILE. The file is overwritten if it exists.

Table 28.2   **Explanation of NAMECONFLICT Attribute**

Value	Meaning
ERROR	Generates an error if the file specified already exists.
SKIP	Allows the problem file to be skipped. The file cannot be saved.
OVERWRITE	The file is overwritten with a new file.
MAKEUNIQUE	Automatically generates a unique filename for the uploaded file.

Once a file is uploaded (or any other file manipulation operation is completed), information about the file is available in reference attributes of the file object. Similar to the URL, FORM, and CGI objects, the FILE object maintains status information about the most recent file operation completed or attempted. Attributes in the FILE object are referenced in the same manner as other variables (for example, #FILE.ContentType#). Table 28.3 identifies the attributes maintained and their meanings.

Table 28.3   File Object Attributes

Attribute	Explanation
AttemptedServerFile	Did ColdFusion attempt to save the file? (Yes/No)
ClientDirectory	Client-side directory where the file was located.
ClientFile	Client-side filename (with extension).
ClientFileExt	Client-side filename extension without the period.
ClientFileName	Client-side filename (without extension).
ContentSubType	MIME content subtype of file.
ContentType	MIME content type of file.
DateLastAccessed	Returns the date and time the uploaded file was last accessed.
FileExisted	Did a file with same name exist in the specified destination prior to upload, copy, or move? (Yes/No)
FileSize	Size of the uploaded file.
FileWasAppended	Was the file appended to an existing file by ColdFusion? (Yes/No)
FileWasOverwritten	Was an existing file overwritten by ColdFusion? (Yes/No)
FileWasRenamed	Was the uploaded file renamed to avoid a conflict? (Yes/No)
FileWasSaved	Was the file saved by ColdFusion? (Yes/No)
OldFileSize	Size of the file that was overwritten during an upload operation. ServerDirectoryDirectory on server where file was saved.
ServerFile	Filename of the saved file.
ServerFileExt	Extension of the uploaded file without the period.
ServerFileName	Filename without extension of the uploaded file.
TimeCreated	Returns the time the uploaded file was created.
TimeLastModified	Returns the date and time of the last modification to the uploaded file.

Uploading Files Using the <CFFILE> Tag

The syntax of the <CFFILE> tag can be used with selected attributes in order to facilitate the uploading of files to the server. You must carefully examine a number of issues prior to writing the HTML/CFML necessary to process a file upload. First and foremost is security. The directory where the files will be uploaded must be secure from outside view, and the templates used to perform the file operations must be protected from unauthorized access. Because the threat of computer viruses is increasing, you must take precautions to protect your system from malicious users. The second issue to examine is the reason you are providing file operations to the users. Is it necessary? Can it be accomplished using other means?

You can move on to the next step once you decide on <CFFILE>—preparing the user interface. This requires the development of an HTML form, either through writing static HTML or by creating an HTML form using dynamic code generated via CFML. In either case, the form's structure is basically the same. Listing 28.2 shows the HTML code necessary to create a form that prompts the user for a file to be uploaded to the server. The result of Listing 28.2 is shown in Figure 28.1. Listing 28.3 shows the form after a file has been selected for uploading.

Listing 28.2 UPLOADFORM.HTML—**HTML Form for File Upload Using the** <CFFILE> **Tag**

```
<!-- This document was created with ColdFusion Studio -->
<!DOCTYPE HTML PUBLIC "-//W3C//DTD HTML 3.2 Final//EN">

<HTML>
<HEAD>
<TITLE>CF CFFILE Upload Demonstration - Example 1</TITLE>
</HEAD>
<BODY BGCOLOR=="#000000">
<CENTER>CF CFFILE Upload Demonstration - Example 1</CENTER>
<HR>
<FORM ACTION="uploadfile.cfm" ENCTYPE="multipart/form-data" METHOD=POST>
File to upload: <INPUT NAME="FileName" SIZE=50 TYPE=FILE><BR>
<INPUT TYPE=SUBMIT VALUE="Upload the File">
</FORM>
</BODY>
</HTML>
```

The primary difference between this form and a "standard" HTML form is the specification of the ENCTYPE value—multipart/form-data—which is necessary to process the uploaded file. A second difference is the addition of a new INPUT type called FILE, which tells the browser to process file selection using the standard user-interface functionality of the underlying operating system. The FORM tag's ACTION attribute identifies which ColdFusion template will be used to process the file. The METHOD attribute is set to POST, which is required by ColdFusion. Figure 28.2 shows the operating system File Selection dialog box.

Part
IV

Ch
28

FIGURE 28.1

Example HTML form for file upload.

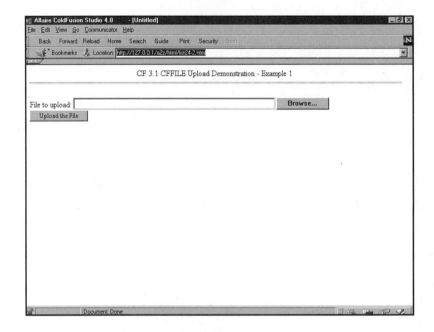

FIGURE 28.2

Example File Selection dialog box.

The dialog box shown in Figure 28.2 is specific to the operating system that a browser is running on and changes from one operating system to another. Figure 28.3 shows the HTML form with the text box filled with the selected filename.

When this form is submitted, the FORM tag's ACTION attribute causes the selected file to be uploaded. Listing 28.3 shows the CFML code required to process the uploaded file.

On the CD

Listing 28.3 UPLOADFILE.CFM—**CFML Code Required to Process an Uploaded File**

```
<!--- This document was created with ColdFusion Studio --->
<HTML>
<HEAD>
<TITLE>CF CFFILE Tag File Upload Demonstration
➥Results - Example 1</TITLE>
</HEAD>
```

```
<BODY BGCOLOR="#FFFFFF"="white">
<CFFILE
DESTINATION="H:\website\uploads\"
ACTION="UPLOAD"
NAMECONFLICT="OVERWRITE"
FILEFIELD="FileName">
<CFOUTPUT>
<CENTER>
CF CFFILE Tag File Upload Demonstration Results - Example 1<P>
File Upload was Successful! Information about the file is detailed below
</CENTER>
<HR>
<TABLE>
<CAPTION><B>File Information</B></CAPTION>
<TR>
<TH VALIGN=top ALIGN=LEFT>File Name:</TH>
➡<TD>#File.ServerDirectory#\#FILE.ServerFile#</TD>
<TH VALIGN=top ALIGN=LEFT>Content Type:</TH><TD>#File.ContentType#</TD>
</TR>
<TR>
<TH VALIGN=top ALIGN=LEFT>Content SubType:</TH>
➡<TD>#File.ContentSubType#</TD>
<TH VALIGN=top ALIGN=LEFT>Client Path:</TH>
➡<TD>#File.ClientDirectory#</TD>
</TR>
<TR>
<TH VALIGN=top ALIGN=LEFT>Client File:</TH><TD>#File.ClientFile#</TD>
<TH VALIGN=top ALIGN=LEFT>Client FileName:</TH>
➡<TD>#File.ClientFileName#</TD>
</TR>
<TR>
<TH VALIGN=top ALIGN=LEFT>Client FileExt:</TH>
➡<TD>#File.ClientFileExt#</TD>
<TH VALIGN=top ALIGN=LEFT>Server Path:</TH><TD>#File.ServerDirectory#</TD>
</TR>
<TR>
<TH VALIGN=top ALIGN=LEFT>Server File:</TH><TD>#File.ServerFile#</TD>
<TH VALIGN=top ALIGN=LEFT>Server FileName:</TH>
➡<TD>#File.ServerFileName#</TD>
</TR>
<TR>
<TH VALIGN=top ALIGN=LEFT>Server FileExt:</TH>
➡<TD>#File.ServerFileExt#</TD>
<TH VALIGN=top ALIGN=LEFT>Attempted ServerFile:</TH>
➡<TD>#File.AttemptedServerFile#</TD>
</TR>
<TR>
<TH VALIGN=top ALIGN=LEFT>File Existed?</TH><TD>#File.FileExisted#</TD>
<TH VALIGN=top ALIGN=LEFT>File Was Saved?</TH><TD>#File.FileWasSaved#</TD>
</TR>
<TR>
<TH VALIGN=top ALIGN=LEFT>File Was Overwritten?</TH>
➡<TD>#File.FileWasOverWritten#</TD>
<TH VALIGN=top ALIGN=LEFT>File Was Appended?</TH>
➡<TD>#File.FileWasAppended#</TD>
```

continues

Listing 28.3   Continued

```
</TR>
<TR>
<TH VALIGN=top ALIGN=LEFT>File Was Renamed?</TH>
➥<TD>#File.FileWasRenamed#</TD>
<TH VALIGN=top ALIGN=LEFT>File Size:</TH><TD>#File.Filesize#</TD></TH>
</TR>
<TR>
<TH VALIGN=top ALIGN=LEFT>Old File Size:</TH><TD>#File.OldFileSize#</TD>
<TH VALIGN=top align=LEFT>Date Last Accessed:</TH>
➥<TD>#DateFormat(File.DateLastAccessed,'DD MMM YY')#</TD>
</TR>
<TR>
<TH VALIGN=top align=LEFT>Date/Time Created:</TH>
➥<TD>#DateFormat(File.TimeCreated,'DD MMM YY')# #Timeformat(File.
➥TimeCreated,'HH:MM:SS')#</TD>
<TH VALIGN=top align=LEFT>Date/Time Modified:</TH>
➥<TD>#DateFormat(File.TimeLastModified,'DD MMM YY')
➥# #Timeformat(File.TimeLastModified,'HH:MM:SS')#</TD>
</TR>
</TABLE>
</CFOUTPUT>
</BODY>
</HTML>
```

FIGURE 28.3

Example HTML form for file upload with selected filename.

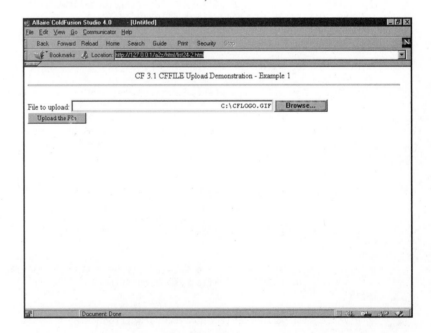

The CFML template shown in Listing 28.3 processes the uploaded file, stores it in the directory indicated in the <CFFILE> tag's DESTINATION attribute, and then prints out the contents of the attributes in the FILE object. Some of the FILE object attributes may not have values, depending on the attributes passed to the <CFFILE> tag. Figure 28.4 shows the output resulting from the file upload.

FIGURE 28.4

Example CFML output of uploaded file information.

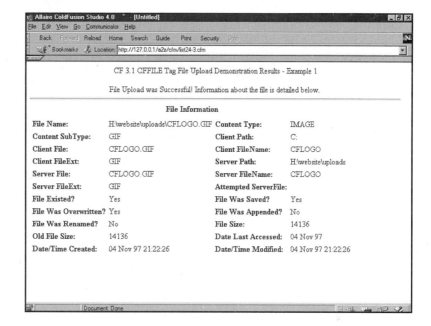

Now take a look at the use of the <CFFILE> tag in Listing 28.3. Four of the attributes for the <CFFILE> tag were used:

```
<CFFILE
ACTION="UPLOAD"
DESTINATION="H:\website\uploads\"
NAMECONFLICT="OVERWRITE"
FILEFIELD="FileName">
```

The ACTION attribute is set to "UPLOAD". The DESTINATION attribute was set to the value "H:\website\uploads\", which is a directory created on a server specifically for storing uploaded files. The directory you choose may be anywhere on the server, provided the appropriate file access privileges (read, write, delete, and so on) are set. The NAMECONFLICT attribute is set to "OVERWRITE", indicating that ColdFusion should overwrite the file if it finds a file with the same name in the destination directory. The last attribute set is the FILEFIELD attribute. Its value is "FileName", indicating the name of the field on the form from which the multipart/form-data containing the file data will be passed. The remaining code in the example uses attributes from the FORM object to show details about the selected file.

Part
IV

Ch
28

CAUTION

The trailing slash (\) in the destination directory name is required.

Listing 28.4 shows an example that builds on the HTML/CFML code you just wrote; it demonstrates the utilization of variables to set the various attributes of the <CFFILE> tag. The HTML form is modified by adding a radio button group that sets the NAMECONFLICT attribute in the <CFFILE> tag.

On the CD

Listing 28.4   UPLOADFORM2.HTML—Modification of HTML to Demonstrate Data-Driven Attribute Setting

```
<!-- This document created by ColdFusion Studio -->
<HTML>
<HEAD>
<TITLE>CF CFFILE Upload Demonstration - Example 2</TITLE>
</HEAD>
<BODY BGCOLOR="#FFFFFF"="">
<CENTER>CF CFFILE Upload Demonstration - Example 2</CENTER>
<HR>
<FORM ACTION="uploadfile2.cfm" ENCTYPE="multipart/form-data" METHOD=POST>
File to upload: <INPUT NAME="FileName" SIZE=50 TYPE=FILE><BR>
Action if File Exists:
<INPUT TYPE=RADIO NAME="FileAction" VALUE="OVERWRITE" CHECKED>Overwrite
<INPUT TYPE=RADIO NAME="FileAction" VALUE="MAKEUNIQUE">Make Unique
<INPUT TYPE=RADIO NAME="FileAction" VALUE="SKIP">Skip
<INPUT TYPE=SUBMIT VALUE="Upload the File">
</FORM>
</BODY>
</HTML>
```

The radio group was added with the name of FileAction, which is used in the template to identify the appropriate action to take if a duplicate file is detected. Figure 28.5 shows what the modified form looks like in the browser.

The CFML from Listing 28.3 has to be modified to specify the action to take when data is being passed to the template and a duplicate file exists. Listing 28.5 shows the modifications required.

On the CD

Listing 28.5   UPLOADFILE2.CFM—Modified CFML Code with Data-Driven Attribute Setting

```
<!--- This document was created with ColdFusion Studio -->
<HTML>
<HEAD>
<TITLE>CF CFFILE Tag File Upload Demonstration
➥Resul-s - Example 2</TITLE>
</HEAD>
<BODY BGCOL"R="#FFF"FF">
<CFFILE
DESTINATI"N="H:\website\uploa"s\"
ACTI"N="UPL"AD"
NAMECONFLI"T="#FORM.FILEACTI"N#"
FILEFIE"D="FileN"me">
```

```
<CFOUTPUT>
<CENTER>
CF CFFILE Tag File Upload Demonstration Resul-s - Example 2<P>
File Upload was Successful! Information about the file is detailed below.
</CENTER>
<HR>
<TABLE>
<CAPTION><B>File Information</B></CAPTION>
<TR>
<TH VALIGN=top ALIGN=LEFT>File
Name:</TH><TD>#File.ServerDirectory#\#FILE.ServerFile#</TD>
<TH VALIGN=top ALIGN=LEFT>Content Type:</TH><TD>#File.ContentType#</TD>
</TR>
<TR>
<TH VALIGN=top ALIGN=LEFT>Content SubType:</TH>
<TD>#File.ContentSubType#</TD>
<TH VALIGN=top ALIGN=LEFT>Client Path:</TH>
<TD>#File.ClientDirectory#</TD>
</TR>
<TR>
<TH VALIGN=top ALIGN=LEFT>Client File:</TH><TD>#File.ClientFile#</TD>
<TH VALIGN=top ALIGN=LEFT>Client
FileName:</TH><TD>#File.ClientFileName#</TD>
</TR>
<TR>
<TH VALIGN=top ALIGN=LEFT>Client
FileExt:</TH><TD>#File.ClientFileExt#</TD>
<TH VALIGN=top ALIGN=LEFT>Server Path:</TH><TD>#File.ServerDirectory#</TD>
</TR>
<TR>
<TH VALIGN=top ALIGN=LEFT>Server File:</TH><TD>#File.ServerFile#</TD>
<TH VALIGN=top ALIGN=LEFT>Server
FileName:</TH><TD>#File.ServerFileName#</TD>
</TR>
<TR>
<TH VALIGN=top ALIGN=LEFT>Server
FileExt:</TH><TD>#File.ServerFileExt#</TD>
<TH VALIGN=top ALIGN=LEFT>Attempted
ServerFile:</TH><TD>#File.AttemptedServerFile#</TD>
</TR>
<TR>
<TH VALIGN=top ALIGN=LEFT>File Existed?</TH><TD>#File.FileExisted#</TD>
<TH VALIGN=top ALIGN=LEFT>File Was Saved?</TH><TD>#File.FileWasSaved#</TD>
</TR>
<TR>
<TH VALIGN=top ALIGN=LEFT>File Was
Overwritten?</TH><TD>#File.FileWasOverWritten#</TD>
<TH VALIGN=top ALIGN=LEFT>File Was
Appended?</TH><TD>#File.FileWasAppended#</TD>
</TR>
<TR>
<TH VALIGN=top ALIGN=LEFT>File Was
Renamed?</TH><TD>#File.FileWasRenamed#</TD>
<TH VALIGN=top ALIGN=LEFT>File Size:</TH><TD>#File.Filesize#</TD></TH>
```

Part

IV

Ch

28

continues

Listing 28.5   Continued

```
</TR>
<TR>
<TH VALIGN=top ALIGN=LEFT>Old File Size:</TH><TD>#File.OldFileSize#</TD>
<TH VALIGN=top align=LEFT>Date Last
Accessed:</TH><TD>#DateFormat(File.DateLastAccess'd,'DD MMM'YY')#</TD>
</TR>
<TR>
<TH VALIGN=top align=LEFT>Date/Time
Created:</TH><TD>#DateFormat(File.TimeCreat'd,'DD MMM'YY')#
#Timeformat(File.TimeCreat'd,'HH:MM'SS')#</TD>
<TH VALIGN=top align=LEFT>Date/Time
Modified:</TH><TD>#DateFormat(File.TimeLastModifi'd,'DD MMM'YY')#
#Timeformat(File.TimeLastModifi'd,'HH:MM'SS')#</TD>
</TR>
</TABLE>
</CFOUTPUT>
</BODY>
</HTML>
```

FIGURE 28.5

Modified file upload form with radio buttons.

Note that in the example in Figure 28.5, the radio button marked Make Unique was checked. This caused the CFML to dynamically change its behavior. Because in the first example you uploaded cflogo.gif to the server, the result of submitting the same file (with the make unique parameter) is that the server is forced to create a unique name for the file when it is uploaded the second time. Figure 28.6 shows the results, with the new filename ACF16.GIF and the fact that the FILE.FileWasRenamed variable was set to Yes.

FIGURE 28.6

Example output with user-specified NAMECONFLICT attribute.

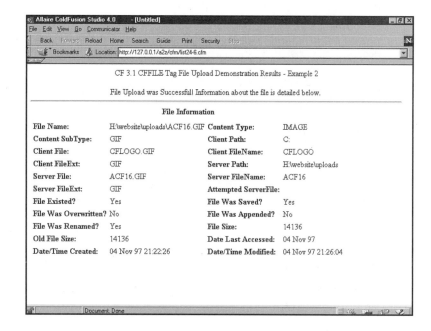

The <CFFILE> tag in this example uses data passed from the form in the FileAction field to set the value of the NAMECONFLICT attribute. The field was referenced in the <CFFILE> tag as follows:

```
NAMECONFLICT="#FORM.FILEACTION#"
```

Any of the other attributes can also be set using CFSET variables, FORM attributes, or URL attributes. Note, however, that setting the SOURCE or DESTINATION attributes based on user input can have far-reaching consequences. For security reasons, users should not be permitted to specify SOURCE or DESTINATION attributes using TEXT input fields. The SOURCE and DESTINATION attributes should only be set using template-based code, which is conditionally executed, to provide maximum security.

Accessing the Local File System with <CFFILE>

The <CFFILE> tag provides the ability to perform local file operations such as COPY, MOVE, and DELETE. *Local* in this example means local to the HTTP server, not local to the client. These actions have the potential for causing severe damage to the file system. Security considerations should therefore be evaluated carefully before developing ColdFusion templates that provide the ability to copy, move, or delete files.

N O T E Security measures can vary by operating system and from one Web server to another. Consult documentation specific to the configuration of your Web server for detailed information about security issues. ▪

Part
IV

Ch
28

To provide local file access, the <CFFILE> tag is used with the ACTION attribute set to COPY, MOVE, or DELETE. The DESTINATION attribute is not required in the case of the DELETE action value; it is required in all other cases.

Listing 28.6 shows ColdFusion's capability to copy files on the local file system. The ACTION attribute is set to COPY; the SOURCE attribute is set to the name of the file that is to be copied. The DESTINATION attribute is set to the directory into which the file will be copied. The DESTINATION attribute may also specify a filename in addition to the directory name, which allows you to copy one file to another while changing the name in the process.

Listing 28.6   <CFFILE> Tag with ACTION Attribute Set to COPY

```
<CFFILE ACTION="COPY" SOURCE="H:\WEBSITE\UPLOADS\FILE1.TXT"
➡ DESTINATION="H:\WEBSITE\PROCESS\">
```

Listing 28.7 shows ColdFusion's ability to move files on the local file system. The ACTION attribute is set to MOVE; the SOURCE attribute is set to the name of the file that is to be moved. The DESTINATION attribute is set to the directory into which the file will be moved. The next listing shows the use of the DELETE value of the ACTION attribute.

Listing 28.7   <CFFILE> Tag with ACTION attribute Set to MOVE

```
<CFFILE ACTION="MOVE" SOURCE="H:\WEBSITE\UPLOADS\FILE2.TXT"
➡DESTINATION="H:\WEBSITE\PROCESS\">
```

The ACTION attribute in Listing 28.8 is set to DELETE. The FILE attribute is set to the name of the file you are going to delete. The DESTINATION attribute is not used when the ACTION attribute is set to DELETE.

Listing 28.8   <CFFILE> Tag with ACTION Attribute Set to DELETE

```
<CFFILE ACTION="DELETE" FILE="H:\WEBSITE\UPLOADS\FILE3.TXT">
```

CAUTION

Use the DELETE action carefully. Access to templates that delete files should be carefully restricted.

Now that you have seen the <CFFILE> tag used in simple examples, you can modify the example application to add file upload capabilities. You accomplish this by creating three CFML templates for the purposes of uploading an employee photo to the server and updating the employee record to reflect the location of the photo. The first template provides a list of employees from which to pick. The second template prompts you for the name of the file containing the photo. The third template actually accepts the file and updates the employee record. You start by creating the template to provide the employee list, which is shown in Listing 28.9.

Listing 28.9 EMPLOYEE_PHOTO1.CFM—Employee Listing Template

```
<CFQUERY DATASOURCE="A2Z" NAME="Employees">
SELECT FirstName, LastName, EmployeeId FROM Employees
     ORDER BY LastName, FirstName
</CFQUERY>

<HTML>

<HEAD>
<TITLE>Maintain Employee Photos</TITLE>
</HEAD>

<BODY BGCOLOR="#FFFFFF">

<H1>Maintain Employee Photos</H1>
<HR>
<H3>Click on Employee Name to Add Employee Photo</H3>
<TABLE BORDER>
<TR>
<TH>Name</TH>
<TH>ID</TH>
</TR>
<CFOUTPUT QUERY="Employees">
<TR>
<TD><A HREF="employee_photo2.cfm?EmployeeId=#EmployeeId#">
➥#LastName#, #FirstName#</A></TD>
<TD>#NumberFormat(EmployeeId,'0000')#</TD>
</TR>
</CFOUTPUT>
</TABLE>
</BODY>
</HTML>
```

Figure 28.7 shows what the screen looks like using the template created in Listing 28.9. This template selects a list of employees from the Employees table and presents a table to select an employee for photo processing.

A link is created for each employee in the Employees table; the link takes you to another template, where the photo information can be added or updated. Listing 28.10 shows the CFML code used to create the form necessary to upload the file to the server.

Listing 28.10 EMPLOYEE_PHOTO2.CFM—Employee Photo Maintenance Form

```
<CFQUERY NAME="Employee" DATASOURCE="A2Z">
SELECT LastName,FirstName,EmployeeId from Employees where
EmployeeId=#URL.EmployeeId#
</CFQUERY>

<HTML>
<TITLE>Employee Photo Maintenance Form</TITLE>
<BODY BGCOLOR="#FFFFFF">
```

Part
IV

Ch
28

continues

FIGURE 28.7

Employee photo
maintenance list.

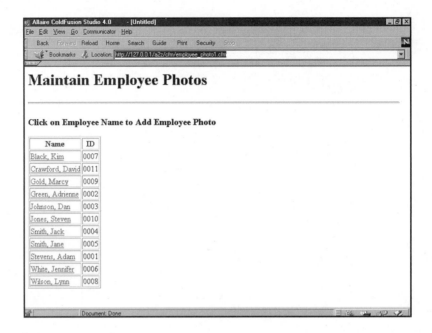

Listing 28.10   Continued

```
<CENTER>Employee Photo Maintenance Form</CENTER>
<HR>
<FORM ACTION="employee_photo3.cfm"
ENCTYPE="multipart/form-data"
METHOD=POST>
<CFOUTPUT>
<INPUT TYPE="hidden" NAME="EmployeeId" VALUE=#Employee.EmployeeId#>
<B>
Employee ID: #NumberFormat(Employee.EmployeeId,'0000')#<BR>
Name: #Employee.LastName#, #Employee.FirstName#<BR>
</B>
</CFOUTPUT>
<BR>
Photo File to upload: <INPUT NAME="PhotoFile" SIZE=50 TYPE=FILE><BR>
<INPUT TYPE=SUBMIT VALUE="Upload the Photo">
</FORM>
</BODY>
</HTML>
```

This template is a simple modification of the first file upload template that you wrote. Figure 28.8 shows what this template would look like. The value of the employee number is retrieved from the URL.EmployeeId variable and used to retrieve the employee's name from the Employees table.

The employee name and employee number is displayed with leading 0s using the NumberFormat function. A file selection box is also displayed. The button labeled Upload the

Photo causes the browser to upload the file to the server, where it will be processed by the template in Listing 28.11.

FIGURE 28.8

Employee photo upload form.

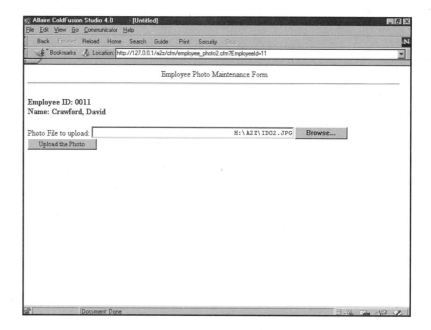

Listing 28.11 `\A2Z\CFM\EMPLOYEE_PHOTO3.CFM`—**Employee Photo Upload Process Template**

```
<CFQUERY NAME="Employee" DATASOURCE="A2Z">
SELECT LastName,FirstName,EmployeeId from Employees
➥ where EmployeeId=#Form.EmployeeId#
</CFQUERY>

<HTML>
<TITLE>A2Z Employee Photo Upload Results</TITLE>
<BODY BGCOLOR="#FFFFFF">
<CFFILE
DESTINATION="H:\a2z\employee\photos\"
ACTION="UPLOAD"
NAMECONFLICT="OVERWRITE"
FILEFIELD="PhotoFile"
ACCEPT="image/gif,image/jpeg">
<CFQUERY NAME="UPDATE_EMP" DATASOURCE="A2Z">
UPDATE Employees
SET Photo = '#FILE.ServerDirectory#\#FILE.ServerFile#'
WHERE EmployeeId=#FORM.EmployeeId#
</CFQUERY>
<CFOUTPUT>
Employee Photo File Upload was Successful!
Information about the file is detailed below.
```

Part
IV

Ch
28

continues

Listing 28.11   Continued

```
<HR>
<TABLE>
<CAPTION><B>Photo Information</B></CAPTION>
<TR>
<TH VALIGN=top ALIGN=LEFT>Employee
Id:</TH><TD>#NumberFormat(Employee.EmployeeId,'0000')#</TD>
<TH VALIGN=top ALIGN=LEFT>Employee Name:</TH>
<TD>#Employee.LastName#, #Employee.FirstName#</TD>
</TR>
<TR>
<TH VALIGN=top ALIGN=LEFT>Photo File Name:</TH>
<TD>#File.ServerDirectory#\#FILE.ServerFile#</TD>
<TH VALIGN=top ALIGN=LEFT>Content Type:</TH><TD>#File.ContentType#</TD>
</TR>
<TR>
<TH VALIGN=top ALIGN=LEFT>Content SubType:</TH>
<TD>#File.ContentSubType#</TD>
<TH VALIGN=top ALIGN=LEFT>Client Path:</TH>
<TD>#File.ClientDirectory#</TD>
</TR>
<TR>
<TH VALIGN=top ALIGN=LEFT>Client File:</TH><TD>#File.ClientFile#</TD>
<TH VALIGN=top ALIGN=LEFT>Client FileName:</TH>
<TD>#File.ClientFileName#</TD>
</TR>
<TR>
<TH VALIGN=top ALIGN=LEFT>Client FileExt:</TH>
<TD>#File.ClientFileExt#</TD>
<TH VALIGN=top ALIGN=LEFT>Server Path:</TH><TD>#File.ServerDirectory#</TD>
</TR>
<TR>
<TH VALIGN=top ALIGN=LEFT>Server File:</TH><TD>#File.ServerFile#</TD>
<TH VALIGN=top ALIGN=LEFT>Server FileName:</TH>
<TD>#File.ServerFileName#</TD>
</TR>
<TR>
<TH VALIGN=top ALIGN=LEFT>Server FileExt:</TH>
<TD>#File.ServerFileExt#</TD>
<TH VALIGN=top ALIGN=LEFT>Attempted ServerFile:</TH>
<TD>#File.AttemptedServerFile#</TD>
</TR>
<TR>
<TH VALIGN=top ALIGN=LEFT>File Existed?</TH><TD>#File.FileExisted#</TD>
<TH VALIGN=top ALIGN=LEFT>File Was Saved?</TH><TD>#File.FileWasSaved#</TD>
</TR>
<TR>
<TH VALIGN=top ALIGN=LEFT>File Was Overwritten?</TH>
<TD>#File.FileWasOverWritten#</TD>
<TH VALIGN=top ALIGN=LEFT>File Was Appended?</TH>
<TD>#File.FileWasAppended#</TD>
</TR>
<TR>
<TH VALIGN=top ALIGN=LEFT>File Was Renamed?</TH>
<TD>#File.FileWasRenamed#</TD>
```

```
<TH VALIGN=top ALIGN=LEFT>File Size:</TH><TD>#File.Filesize#</TD></TH>
</TR>
<TR>
<TH VALIGN=top ALIGN=LEFT>Old File Size:</TH><TD>#File.OldFileSize#</TD>
<TH VALIGN=top align=LEFT>Date Last Accessed:</TH>
<TD>#DateFormat(File.DateLastAccessed,'DD MMM YY')#</TD>
</TR>
<TR>
<TH VALIGN=top align=LEFT>Date/Time Created:</TH>
<TD>#DateFormat(File.TimeCreated,'DD MMM YY')#
#Timeformat(File.TimeCreated,'HH:MM:SS')#</TD>
<TH VALIGN=top align=LEFT>Date/Time Modified:</TH>
<TD>#DateFormat(File.TimeLastModified,'DD MMM YY')#
#Timeformat(File.TimeLastModified,'HH:MM:SS')#</TD>
</TR>
</TABLE>
</CFOUTPUT>
</BODY>
</HTML>
```

Figure 28.9 shows the screen results. The template you just completed processes the uploaded file and stores it in the specified directory. It also updates the employee record to indicate that an employee photo is on file. The <CFFILE> tag's ACCEPT attribute is set to only allow GIF and JPEG images to be uploaded to the server.

Make sure that your Employee table has a field called Photo, which is a character string at least 65 characters long.

FIGURE 28.9

Employee photo upload results.

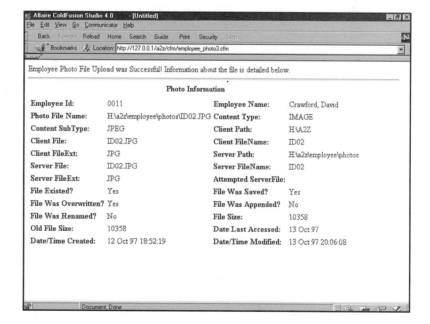

Part
IV

Ch
28

Reading and Writing Files with <CFFILE>

You have demonstrated the capabilities of <CFFILE> to upload a file to the server, as well as to manipulate files on the local file system by moving, copying, deleting, or renaming them. The last piece of the puzzle is to demonstrate its capability to read and write ASCII files using the <CFFILE> tag. This capability, combined with other constructs available in ColdFusion—looping over the results of a query and evaluating expressions—provides a powerful tool to developers. The next simple example highlights the capability to read and write files.

In order to demonstrate the capability, you write a template that queries the Employees table and writes out an ASCII file containing the following items:

- The name of the employee
- The employee ID
- If present, the name of the file where the employee's photo is maintained

The template then reads the file into a variable and displays it in the browser window. Listing 28.12 shows the code necessary to accomplish these tasks.

On the CD

> **Listing 28.12   READWRITE.CFM—Read and Write an ASCII File Using <CFFILE>**

```
<!-- This document was created with ColdFusion Studio -->
<!DOCTYPE HTML PUBLIC "-//W3C//DTD HTML 3.2 Final//EN">
<CFQUERY NAME="EMPLOYEE" DATASOURCE="A2Z">
select LastName,FirstName,EmployeeId,photo from Employees
</CFQUERY>
<!--- Setup variables to be used in writing the file --->
<!--- Variable to hold output string --->
<CFSET TXTOUTPUT = "">
<!--- File Name to write string into --->
<CFSET OUTFILE = "h:\a2z\employee\photolist.txt">

<CFIF #FileExists(OUTFILE)# is "Yes">
    <CFFILE ACTION="DELETE" FILE="#OUTFILE#">
</CFIF>
<CFLOOP QUERY="EMPLOYEE">
    <CFSET TXTOUTPUT = '"#LASTNAME#","#FIRSTNAME#","
➥#NumberFormat(EMPLOYEEID,'0000')#","#PHOTO#"'>
    <CFIF #FileExists(OUTFILE)# is "No">
        <CFFILE ACTION="WRITE" FILE="#OUTFILE#" OUTPUT="#TXTOUTPUT#">
    <CFELSE>
        <CFFILE ACTION="APPEND" FILE="#OUTFILE#" OUTPUT="#TXTOUTPUT#">
    </CFIF>
</CFLOOP>
<CFFILE ACTION="READ" FILE="#OUTFILE#" VARIABLE="TXTINPUT">

<HTML>
<HEAD>
    <TITLE>CF CFFILE Read/Write Demonstration</TITLE>
</HEAD>
```

```
<BODY BGCOLOR="#FFFFFF">
<CFOUTPUT>
The contents of the query where written into
➥ the file located at #OUTFILE#.<P>
The contents of the file are shown below:
<HR>
<PRE>
#TXTINPUT#
</PRE>
</CFOUTPUT>
</BODY>
</HTML>
```

Figure 28.10 shows the output from the template you just created. The code in the template created a comma-delimited ASCII file containing the LastName, FirstName, EmployeeID, and Photo fields from the Employees table.

FIGURE 28.10

Output from the read/write demonstration template.

Take a closer look at this template to see what makes it tick. The first part of the template runs a simple query, which selects a number of fields from the Employees table. The following lines are responsible for the query:

```
<CFQUERY NAME="EMPLOYEE" DATASOURCE="A2Z">
select LastName,FirstName,EmployeeId,photo from Employees
</CFQUERY>
```

The next few lines of code set up a number of variables that is used to pass values to the `<CFFILE>` tag. The comments in the following code indicate what the variables are to be used for:

```
<!--- Setup variables to be used in writing the file --->
<!--- Variable to hold output string --->
<CFSET TXTOUTPUT = "">
<!--- File Name to write string into --->
<CFSET OUTFILE = "h:\a2z\employee\photolist.txt">
```

After setting up the variables, you use the `FileExists` function to determine if the output file you want to create is on the disk. If it does exist there, you use the `<CFFILE>` tag with the `DELETE` action to remove it before proceeding:

```
<CFIF #FileExists(OUTFILE)# is "Yes">
    <CFFILE ACTION="DELETE" FILE="#OUTFILE#">
</CFIF>
```

The next few lines of code perform the meat of the work in this template. The `CFLOOP` tag processes each record in the result set from your query; a text variable is set with the values of the fields, separated by commas and enclosed in quotation marks. The following code results in a comma-delimited file when you are done:

```
<CFLOOP QUERY="EMPLOYEE">
    <CFSET TXTOUTPUT = '"#LASTNAME#","#FIRSTNAME#","
➡#NumberFormat(EMPLOYEEID,'0000')#","#PHOTO#"'>
    <CFIF #FileExists(OUTFILE)# is "No">
        <CFFILE ACTION="WRITE" FILE="#OUTFILE#" OUTPUT="#TXTOUTPUT#">
    <CFELSE>
        <CFFILE ACTION="APPEND" FILE="#OUTFILE#" OUTPUT="#TXTOUTPUT#">
    </CFIF>
</CFLOOP>
```

The `<CFFILE>` tag is executed within the loop and its behavior is changed depending on the existence of the output file specified in the variable `#OUTFILE#`. If it does not exist (which is true for the first iteration of the loop), the `<CFFILE>` tag's `ACTION` attribute is set to `"WRITE"`, which creates the file and writes the contents of the `#TXTOUTPUT#` variable into the file. Because the file exists, the `ACTION` attribute is set to `"APPEND"` on the remaining iterations through the loop; this results in the value of the `#TXTOUTPUT#` variable being written to the end of the file.

The last few lines of the template are used to read the contents of the file you created into a variable and then display the contents in the browser window. This is accomplished by setting the `<CFFILE>` tag's `ACTION` attribute to `"READ"` and specifying the name of the variable where the file contents will be stored:

```
<CFFILE ACTION="READ" FILE="#OUTFILE#" VARIABLE="TXTINPUT">

<HTML>
<HEAD>
    <TITLE>CF CFFILE Read/Write Demonstration</TITLE>
</HEAD>

<BODY BGCOLOR="#FFFFFF">
<CFOUTPUT>
The contents of the query where written
into the file located at #OUTFILE#.<P>
The contents of the file are shown below:
<HR>
```

```
<PRE>
#TXTINPUT#
</PRE>
</CFOUTPUT>
</BODY>
</HTML>
```

Directory Manipulation with <CFDIRECTORY>

Just as <CFFILE> can be used to read, write, and manipulate local files, <CFDIRECTORY> can be used to manage directories. Like <CFFILE>, <CFDIRECTORY> takes an ACTION attribute, which specifies the action to be performed. The supported actions are listed in Table 28.4.

Table 28.4 <CFDIRECTORY> **ACTION**

Action	Description
CREATE	Creates the directory specified in the DIRECTORY attribute.
DELETE	Deletes the directory specified in the DIRECTORY attribute.
LIST	Returns the contents of the directory specified in the DIRECTORY attribute into a query named in the NAME attribute. An optional FILTER can be specified as well, as can a SORT order.
RENAME	Renames the directory specified in the DIRECTORY attribute to the name specified in the NEWDIRECTORY attribute.

Part
IV

Ch
28

Full-Text Searching with Verity

Getting to Know Verity

By now you're convinced that ColdFusion is the greatest package on the planet for publishing database data to the Web—but you haven't really uncovered how to put together that most popular of Web-based applications: the search engine. The success of Yahoo!, Excite, and the like have made the concept of a Web-based search tool nearly as ubiquitous on the Internet as the word *ubiquitous* itself. An intelligent search tool is a must-have for an increasing number of sites. This chapter shows how to integrate the Verity search engine into your ColdFusion applications.

Verity's search technology—which is included and can be integrated with ColdFusion—is a high-performance search engine that is built specifically for searching text. It excels at finding words in large chunks of unstructured text, such as the documents that human beings tend to write. As a developer, you tell it what to search—and what to search for—and it faithfully tries to find it.

Verity can search a variety of files in a variety of languages, and it does all the fancy stuff you'd expect from a sophisticated search engine, like handling ANDs, ORs, wildcards, and so on. If you've ever used the search interface provided by LEXIS/NEXIS, you can expect the same kind of functionality from your own applications that use Verity.

Conceptually, the Verity layer you learn about in this chapter is a lot like the ODBC/SQL layer that you've learned so much about elsewhere in this book. The main difference is that where ODBC and SQL excel at accessing neat rows and columns of information in structured database tables, Verity excels at accessing messy chunks of text, strewn about in various folders on your hard drives.

Most of the inner workings of the Verity engine are thoughtfully hidden from ColdFusion developers. All you need to be concerned with is creating collections of documents with the ColdFusion Administrator and including the CFINDEX and CFSEARCH tags in your ColdFusion templates.

N O T E The word *Verity* in this chapter really refers to ColdFusion's integration with search technology from a company called Verity. Just as people tend to say Netscape when they are really referring to the program called Navigator (which is made by Netscape Communications), ColdFusion developers tend to just say Verity when they are talking about putting together full-text search applications. ■

You may not have realized it yet, but you probably already have a Verity-based application running on your server. Unless you chose not to install the documentation files when you installed ColdFusion, full online documentation was installed for you in the CFDOCS folder, directly off your Web server's root directory. As you can see in Figure 29.1, the documentation has a handy search tool. The search tool uses the same Verity functionality that you'll learn about in this chapter.

T I P Check out your ColdFusion documentation's search tool anytime by opening this URL in your browser and then clicking Search: http://localhost/CFDOCS/index.htm. (localhost is your computer's name or IP address.)

FIGURE 29.1

The search tool for the ColdFusion online documentation uses Verity to carry out its searches.

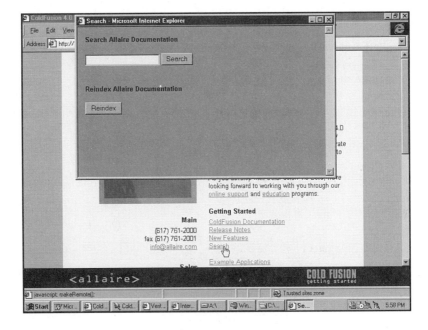

Searching for Different Types of Files with Verity

ColdFusion's Verity functionality supports a wide variety of file types, including native files, such as documents produced with many of the Microsoft Office applications. This provides great flexibility when it comes to making files searchable via a Web browser.

For instance, in an intranet situation, employees can continue to use the word-processing and spreadsheet applications they use every day. All they have to do is save the documents in a folder tree that is indexed by a Verity collection. With literally a few lines of code, you can turn those documents into a fully searchable company library. Table 29.1 shows the different types of files that Verity can index and search.

N O T E Support for searching binary file formats (word processor, spreadsheet, and other native types of files) was introduced in ColdFusion 3.1; version 3.0 supported only plain-text files (which included HTML files). ■

N O T E The term *document files* is used in reference to files that are being indexed with Verity. As you can see, Verity can handle 1-2-3 spreadsheets, PowerPoint presentations, and so on. Document files means any word processor, spreadsheet, or other file type listed in Table 29.1. ■

TIP Different file types can be freely mixed and matched in a Verity collection. Don't worry about keeping the HTML and Word files in separate folders or collections. Store them wherever you want.

Table 29.1 File Types That Verity Can Index and Search

Category	File Type	Limited to Versions
Word Processing	Lotus AMI Pro	2.x, 3.0, 3.1
	WordPerfect	DOS: 5.0, 5.1, 6.0x, 6.1, 7.0
		Windows: 5.1, 5.2, 6.0x, 6.1, 7.0
		Macintosh: 2.0, 2.1, 3.0-3.5
	Microsoft Word	Windows: 2.0, 6.0, 95 (7.0), '97 (8.0)
		DOS: 4.x, 5.x, 6.x
		Macintosh: 4.0, 5.0, 6.0
WordPad		Write for Windows
Spreadsheets	1-2-3	DOS, Windows: 2.0, 3.0, 4.0, 5.0
		OS/2: Release 2
	Microsoft Excel	Windows: 3.0, 4.0, 5.0, '95 (7.0), 97 (8.0)
		Macintosh: 3.0, 4.0
Text-Based Files	HTML	
	Plain Text	
	Rich Text Format (RTF)	1.x, 2.0
	ASCII and ANSI Text	
	Acrobat PDF files	
Other	Microsoft PowerPoint	Windows: 95 (7.0), 97 (8.0)

Integrating ColdFusion with Other Search Engines

Including Verity functionality is a terrific way to add search capability to your application, making it behave somewhat like a mini-Yahoo! or mini-AltaVista. However, it has nothing to do with actually integrating with Yahoo!, AltaVista, or any other commercial search engines. If you want to integrate with one of these search engines, you certainly can include standard HREF links from your application to a commercial search engine—but doing so really has nothing to do with the Verity functionality explained in this chapter.

You could also place a search form on one of your pages that has an appropriate URL (within the commercial search engine's domain) as the form's ACTION parameter. Many of the commercial search engines have instructions about how to set this up—like what to name the form <INPUT> tags, for instance. See their sites for details.

Finally, you could use the <CFHTTP> tag to place a search request to a commercial search engine and display the results on your page with the #CFHTTP.FileContent# variable. See Appendix A, "ColdFusion Tag Reference," for information about this extremely flexible tag.

Creating a Search Tool for Your Documents

Say that A2Z's Human Resources department wants to make the company's personnel policies available online so that employees can see what they are allowed to do (and not do) at any time.

The documents are saved as various Word, plain text, and Excel files. Collect all the documents into one folder on your Web server's local drive; explore what is necessary to make these documents searchable and retrievable from a Web browser using ColdFusion's Verity functionality as the back end. It's really pretty simple.

N O T E   If you want to follow along with the examples in this section exactly, make a copy of the folder named HR from this chapter's directory on the CD-ROM. You can either place the folder directly off your Web server's document root, or use any random folder of your own documents that you like. Just make sure that the folder is accessible to your Web server. ▓

Creating a New Collection for the Documents

Verity's search functionality centers around a concept of a collection. A Verity *collection* is a mass of documents you want Verity to keep track of and make searchable.

Once Verity has been told which documents belong to a collection, it can index the documents and compile *meta-data* about them for its own use. This allows it to answer questions about your documents quickly, without actually parsing through them line-by-line at runtime. Conceptually, the key to Verity's strength is its capability to invest a certain amount of time up front to indexing and compiling information about your documents. You get the payoff on that investment when your users run their searches; Verity has already studied the documents and can therefore return information about them very quickly.

Again, you may find it useful to think of Verity collections as being the full-text search equivalent of ODBC data sources. Just as you need to set up an ODBC data source before you can use CFQUERY to retrieve data with SQL, you need to set up a collection before you can get started with Verity. Just as with setting up a new ODBC data source, you go to the ColdFusion Administrator to set up a new collection.

Creating a New Verity Collection

To set up a new collection, go to the ColdFusion Administrator and click the Verity tab, as shown in Figure 29.2.

You'll probably notice right away that a document collection named CFDocumentation is already created and visible. This collection represents the ColdFusion documentation, which uses the Verity engine for its search interface.

Now you create the Verity collection that your Human Resources documents will belong to. Under the Create a New Collection heading, type HRDocs as the Name of the new collection.

You can change Path if you want the collection to be stored in a different location than the default, but you might as well use the default unless you have a specific reason not to (such as drive space or file-permissions issues).

FIGURE 29.2

All collections on your server are shown on the Verity page of the ColdFusion Administrator.

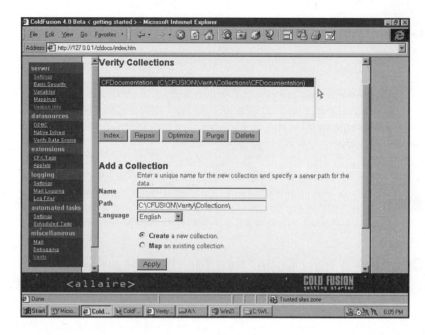

When you're done filling in the blanks, click the Apply button (see Figure 29.3). After a moment, your new collection will appear in the list at the top of the page, right along with the predefined CFDocumentation collection.

FIGURE 29.3

Simply type the name for the new collection and then click Create.

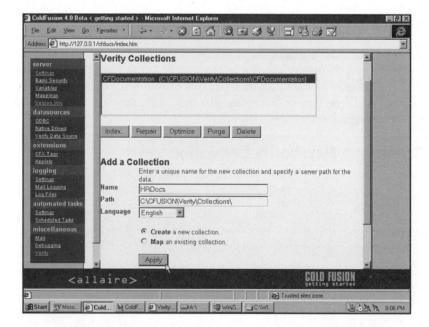

N O T E The path you fill in when creating a new collection is simply where the Verity's internal data about your documents will be kept. You don't have to point to the path to where the actual documents are at this point. ■

N O T E If you already had created this collection on another ColdFusion server on your local network, you could check the Map an Existing Collection radio button and enter a complete UNC path to the collection's folder on the other server.

This feature is new to ColdFusion 4.0 and can be used in situations where you have several ColdFusion servers—perhaps operating in a cluster—that all need to be able to search the same information. By creating this mapped collection, the Verity engine will use the index files maintained by the other ColdFusion server. When the collection is re-indexed on the other server, all collections that are mapped to it reflect the new data in search results. This keeps you from having to maintain separate collections on each ColdFusion server. ■

Specifying a Language

If you have the optional ColdFusion International Search Pack, you can specify a language other than English when creating a new collection. The language should match the language that the documents were written in. Verity can pull off a few neat tricks when it knows what language the documents are written in, such as understanding the role of accented characters. It also uses knowledge of the language to pull off variations on the same word *stem*, or *root*.

You must choose the language when you are creating the collection. Simply select the language from the drop-down list in the Administrator before you click the Create button (see Figure 29.2). The International Search Pack supports the following languages: English, German, French, Danish, Dutch, Finnish, Italian, Norwegian, Portuguese, Spanish, and Swedish. Support for the language pack was added to ColdFusion in version 3.1.

N O T E You must have purchased the ColdFusion International Search Pack from Allaire to use languages other than English. If you attempt to do so without the Search Pack installed, you get an error message when you click Create. ■

Try not to mix documents written in different languages in the same collection. If you have documents in several different languages, make separate collections for them.

Creating a Working Search Interface

Now that you've created the HRDocs collection, you can start putting together the ColdFusion templates to make your documents searchable. You'll see that the code you use to do this is similar in concept and structure to the employee search application you worked through in Chapter 12, "ColdFusion Forms."

A terrific way to get started is to use the Verity Wizard included in ColdFusion Studio. The wizard helps you create a search tool page, search results page, and a detail page. After letting the wizard create these basic templates for you, you can examine each of the templates to see how they work and what you can add to them.

N O T E If you're not using ColdFusion Studio, don't worry. All the code that the wizard generates is included here as you work through the steps, and is on the CD-ROM that comes with this book for your convenience. The wizard makes it quick and easy to set up basic Verity templates, but it is by no means required.

In ColdFusion Studio, follow these steps to bring the Verity Wizard up on your screen:

1. Choose New from the File menu. The New Document window appears.
2. Click the CFML tab in the New Document window.
3. Double-click the Verity Wizard from the list of wizards.

 You can also start the Verity Wizard—or any other wizard—by right-clicking anywhere in the editor and choosing File, New from the pop-up menu.

As you can see in Figure 29.4, the first step of the Verity Wizard wants you to choose a title for the application and where the ColdFusion templates should be stored. To complete the first step, do the following:

1. Type `Personnel Policy Documents` for Title. The wizard puts this title at the top of each of the ColdFusion (.cfm) templates that it generates.
2. Select the directory that the ColdFusion (.cfm) templates should be generated in. The folder must already exist, and should be located somewhere within your Web server's document root (so people will be able to access the .cfm files with their Web browsers). My Web server's document root is `c:\WEBSHARE\WWWROOT`, so I've created a folder named `c:\WEBSHARE\WWWROOT\HRSearch` and selected the path on the server to that folder.

FIGURE 29.4

The first step of the Verity Wizard wants an application title and location for the generated .cfm files.

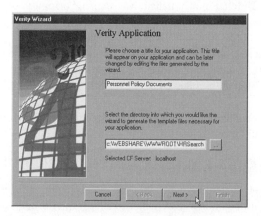

When you're done with the first step, click the Next button to get to step 2. As you can see in Figure 29.5, this second step asks you about the Verity collection that the generated ColdFusion templates should refer to. Do the following to complete this second step:

1. For the collection name, enter `HRDocs`, which is the name of the collection that you created in the ColdFusion Administrator.

2. Leave the language selection at English, unless you chose a different language when creating the HRDocs collection. The language you choose here should always match the language that you created the collection with in the ColdFusion Administrator.

FIGURE 29.5

The second step of the wizard asks you about the Verity collection to be used by the generated .cfm files.

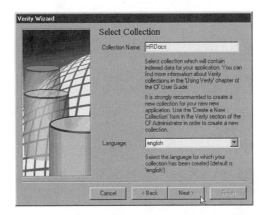

When you're done with the second step, click the Next button to get to the third step. As you can see in Figure 29.6, you're asked about the document files you actually want Verity to index and make searchable. Do the following to complete this third step:

1. For Directory Path, select the folder that contains the actual documents you want to make searchable. The documents on my server are in a folder called Docs, which is in a folder called HR, directly off my Web server's root directory. I've entered c:\WEBSHARE\WWWROOT\HR\Docs\ here.

2. The Recursively Index Subdirectories check box indicates whether Verity is to look inside any subdirectories of the directory path you just entered. My c:\WEBSHARE\WWWROOT\HR\Docs folder includes a Days Off subfolder that has documents in it that I want searched, so I've left this check box selected.

3. For File Extensions, type a list of file extensions that Verity should index. Separate the extensions with commas. I want Verity to make all of the HTML, Word, Excel, and plain text files available for searching, so I've entered .htm, .html, .txt, .doc, .xls in this field. I do not, however, want any files with the .cfm extension to be indexed, so I've excluded .cfm from the list.

4. For Return URL, type the URL version of the document path that you entered earlier. In other words, what would a user need to type before a filename in order to pull a file from the folder up in his Web browser? I have entered http://127.0.0.1/HR/Docs here because that is what I would need to enter to get to my Web server's c:\WEBSHARE\WWWROOT\HR\Docs\ folder with my browser.

Click the Finish button when you are done with the third step. The wizard generates and saves four files to the c:\WEBSHARE\WWWROOT\HRSearch folder (or whatever directory you specified in the first step of the wizard). As you can see in Figure 29.7, the wizard then displays the four files that it generated in the Wizard Output Summary.

FIGURE 29.6

The third step of the Verity Wizard asks about the actual document files.

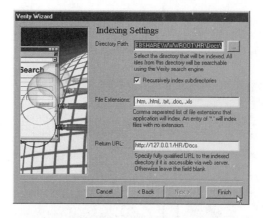

FIGURE 29.7

The Verity Wizard generates four .cfm files in all.

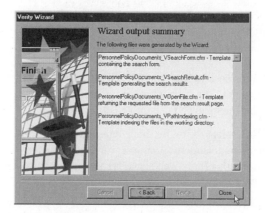

Finally, click the Close button to exit the wizard. ColdFusion Studio automatically brings up the four files in the editor for your convenience.

Take a look at the search interface the Verity Wizard put together. Bring up the search form in your Web browser. The URL depends on what you entered in step 1 of the wizard—on my system, it's called PERSONNELPOLICYDOCUMENTS_VSEARCHFORM.CFM. (The PERSONNELPOLICYDOCUMENTS part came from the application title I supplied in step 1 of the wizard). Make sure to bring it up in your browser with a HTTP URL (starting with http://), rather than as a local file (starting with c:/ or some other drive letter). Figure 29.8 shows what the search form looks like.

It looks the way you'd expect a search tool to look—there's a text INPUT field to type keywords into and a Submit button to start the search.

However, no documents would be found if you were to try to run a search right now, regardless of what you were searching for. That's because the Verity collection you created in the ColdFusion Administrator has not been indexed yet. In other words, the collection has been set up, but it's still empty.

FIGURE 29.8

The search form includes a link that indexes the actual documents.

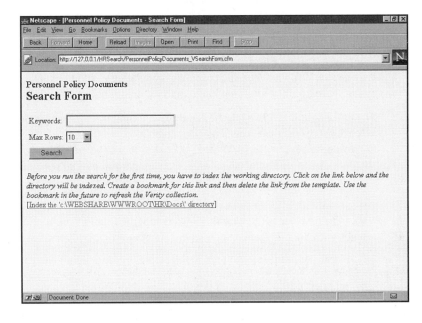

At the bottom of the search page (shown in Figure 29.8), the Verity Wizard has provided a link that indexes the collection. Go ahead and click that link now. Your server's hard drive will whir around for a bit as Verity examines the actual documents and saves its internal data about the documents to disk. When the indexing is complete, an Indexing Finished message appears, as shown in Figure 29.9.

FIGURE 29.9

The PERSONNELPOLICY DOCUMENTS_ VPATHINDEXING.CFM file indexes the collection, populating it with your actual documents.

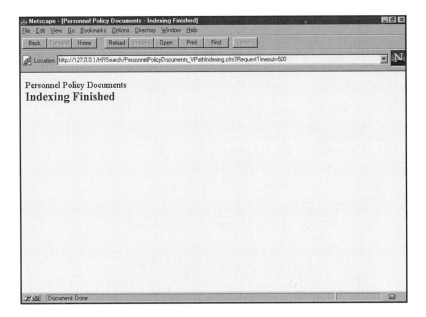

If you run a search with the search form shown in Figure 29.8, it should work. The documents have successfully been indexed by Verity and are searchable.

Indexing Your Files with the CFINDEX Tag   You've seen that clicking that link on the search page causes Verity to index the collection, populating it with the contents of your actual documents. Take a look at what that link is actually doing.

The link is bringing up a separate ColdFusion template which was generated by the Verity Wizard. On my machine, this template is named PERSONNELPOLICYDOCUMENTS_VPATHINDEXING.CFM. It's shown in Listing 29.1 and is actually a simple template, with only one ColdFusion tag that you haven't seen before: <CFINDEX>.

The <CFINDEX> tag is what cues Verity to wake up and index (or re-index) the files in the folder you specify. This is the second step in the overall process of making a Verity application come alive. (The first step is creating the collection in the ColdFusion Administrator, and the third is actually searching the collection with the <CFSEARCH> tag, which is covered shortly.)

TIP

Remember, there's nothing special about the code that the Verity Wizard generates. You can use this code—or any code that uses CFINDEX in a similar way—to get the job done, whether you use ColdFusion Studio and its Verity Wizard or not.

On the CD

Listing 29.1   PERSONNELPOLICYDOCUMENTS_VPATHINDEXING.CFM—
Indexing a Collection

```
<CFSET IndexCollection = "HRDocs">
<CFSET IndexDirectory = "C:\WEBSHARE\WWWROOT\HR\Docs">
<CFSET IndexRecurse = "YES">
<CFSET IndexExtensions = ".htm, .html, .txt, *.">
<CFSET IndexLanguage = "english">

<CFINDEX
  collection="#IndexCollection#"
  action="REFRESH"
  type="PATH"
  key="#IndexDirectory#\"
  extensions="#IndexExtensions#"
  recurse="#IndexRecurse#"
  language="#IndexLanguage#"
  urlPath="http://127.0.0.1/HR/Docs"
>

<HTML><HEAD>
    <TITLE>Personnel Policy Documents - Indexing Finished</TITLE>
</HEAD><BODY bgcolor="ffffff">

<FONT size="+1">Personnel Policy Documents</FONT> <BR>
<FONT size="+2"><B>Indexing Finished</B></FONT>
```

This template simply sets a few constants at the top of the template with some CFSET tags. It then plugs the values of those constants into the CFINDEX tag. The Verity Wizard has used the CFSET tags at the top—rather than hard coding the values in the parameters of the CFINDEX tag itself—so it is easy for you to change the values later on.

Since the CFINDEX tag is what tells Verity to index your actual documents, the CFINDEX tag's various parameters simply give Verity the particulars about what you want it to do. Take a look at each of the parameters:

- ▇ COLLECTION simply tells Verity which collection to use. In Listing 29.11, the value passed to the COLLECTION parameter is HRDocs, which is the value I supplied to the wizard.

- ▇ ACTION tells Verity that you're interested in refreshing any data currently in the collection with new information. There are other possible values for ACTION other than REFRESH, which are discussed in "Maintaining Collections" at the end of this chapter.

- ▇ TYPE tells Verity that you're interested in adding documents from a directory path on your Web server. You learn about another possible value for TYPE later, when using Verity to index database data rather than document files is covered.

- ▇ KEY tells Verity from which directory path to add documents. This must evaluate to a complete physical file system path to the actual documents you want to index.

- ▇ EXTENSIONS tells Verity which documents in the specified folder should be indexed. This is useful if you only want certain types of documents to become searchable.

- ▇ RECURSE tells Verity whether you want it to index files that are sitting in subfolders of the folder you specified with the KEY parameter. Possible values are YES and NO—usually you specify YES for this parameter.

- ▇ LANGUAGE tells Verity what language the documents are written in. For the possible values, see "Specifying a Language" earlier in this chapter.

- ▇ URLPATH tells Verity to maintain URLs for each document, as it does its indexing, by appending the filename to the value you supply with this parameter. If RECURSE="YES" and the file is in a subfolder, the folder name is appended as well. In other words, as long as the value you supply here is the URL version of the value you supplied for KEY, Verity automatically records the correct URL for each file as it does its indexing. You see this in action later, when you use the #URL# column returned by the CFSEARCH tag.

That's about all there is to indexing document files. Now all you have to do is make sure that the code in Listing 29.1 runs whenever somebody saves new documents to the c:\WEBSHARE\WWWROOT\HR\Docs folder.

You can now delete the link to the PERSONNELPOLICYDOCUMENTS_VSEARCHFORM.CFM template as the message at the bottom of the search page suggests (see Figure 29.8 and Listing 29.2), or you can leave it there so that your users can re-index the documents on their own whenever they want.

The Search Form Page Take a look at the search form that the Verity Wizard created for you. The name of the file depends on what application title you supplied in the first step of the wizard; on my machine, the file is called `PERSONNELPOLICYDOCUMENTS_VSEARCHFORM.CFM` (see Listing 29.2).

This search form is very similar to the search forms you worked through in Chapter 12. Refer to that chapter if you need to refresh your memory about the `INPUT` and `SELECT` tags that appear in Listing 29.2.

On the CD

Listing 29.2 `PERSONNELPOLICYDOCUMENTS_VSEARCHFORM.CFM`—**The Search Form Page That the Wizard Created**

```
<!--- template settings --->
<CFSET SearchDirectory = "C:\WEBSHARE\WWWROOT\HR\Docs">

<HTML><HEAD>
    <TITLE>Personnel Policy Documents - Search Form</TITLE>
</HEAD><BODY bgcolor="ffffff">

<FONT size="+1">Personnel Policy Documents</FONT> <BR>
<FONT size="+2"><B>Search Form</B></FONT>


<!--- search form definition --->
<FORM action="PersonnelPolicyDocuments_VSearchResult.cfm" method="post">
  <INPUT type="hidden" name="StartRow" value="1">

  <TABLE>

    <TR>
      <TD>Keywords:</TD>
      <TD><INPUT type="text" name="Criteria" size="30"></TD>
    </TR>

    <TR>
      <TD>Max Rows:</TD>
      <TD>
➥<SELECT name="MaxRows"> <OPTION> 10 <OPTION> 25 <OPTION> 100 </SELECT></TD>
    </TR>

    <TR>
      <TD colspan=2><INPUT type="submit" value="   Search   "></TD>
    </TR>

  </TABLE>

</FORM>

<P>
<I>
```

Before you run the search for the first time, you have to index the working directory. The directory is indexed when you click the link. Create a bookmark for it and then delete the link from the template. Use the bookmark in the future to refresh the Verity collection.

```
</I>
<BR>
[<A href="PersonnelPolicyDocuments_VPathIndexing.cfm?RequestTimeout=500">
➥Index the 'C:\WEBSHARE\WWWROOT\HR\Docs' directory</A>]

</BODY></HTML>
```

As you can see in Figure 29.8, your search form template contains a form that collects two pieces of information from the user. Most importantly, it collects the keywords that the user wants to search for (the INPUT named Criteria). It also collects the maximum number of hits to display per-page of search results (the SELECT named MaxRows).

The Search Results Page   The Verity Wizard's search form submits these two pieces of information to the PERSONNELPOLICYDOCUMENTS_VSEARCHRESULT.CFM template, which contains the code that actually runs the Verity search and displays the results of the search to the user.

Take a look at that template now. As you can see in Listing 29.3, it contains only one ColdFusion tag that you're not familiar with yet—the <CFSEARCH> tag.

On the CD

Listing 29.3   PERSONNELPOLICYDOCUMENTS_VSEARCHRESULT.CFM—The
Search Results Page That the Wizard Created

```
<!--- template settings --->
<CFSET SearchDirectory = "C:\WEBSHARE\WWWROOT\HR\Docs">
<CFSET SearchCollection = "HRDocs">
<CFSET UseURLPath = "YES">


<!--- retrieve requested files --->
<CFSEARCH
  name = "GetResults"
  collection = "#SearchCollection#"
  criteria = "#Form.Criteria#"
  maxRows = "#Evaluate(Form.MaxRows + 1)#"
  startRow = "#Form.StartRow#"
>


<HTML><HEAD>
    <TITLE>Personnel Policy Documents - Search Results</TITLE>
</HEAD><BODY bgcolor="ffffff">

<FONT size="+1">Personnel Policy Documents</FONT> <BR>
<FONT size="+2"><B>Search Results</B></FONT>

<P>

<!--- no files found for specified criteria? --->
<CFIF GetResults.RecordCount is 0>
  <B>No files found for specified criteria</B>
```

continues

Listing 29.3 Continued

```
<!--- ... else at least one file found --->
<CFELSE>

  <TABLE cellspacing=0 cellpadding=2>

  <!--- table header --->
  <TR bgcolor="cccccc">
    <TD><B>No</B></TD>
    <TD><B>Score</B></TD>
    <TD><B>File</B></TD>
    <TD><B>Title</B></TD>
  </TR>

  <CFOUTPUT query="GetResults" maxRows="#Form.MaxRows#">
  <TR bgcolor="#IIf(CurrentRow Mod 2, DE('ffffff'), DE('ffffcf'))#">

    <!--- current row information --->
    <TD>#Evaluate(Form.StartRow + CurrentRow - 1)#</TD>

    <!--- score --->
    <TD>#Score# </TD>

    <!--- file name with the link returning the file --->
    <TD>
      <CFIF UseURLPath>
  <!--- URL parameter from cfsearch contains URL path info --->
        <CFSET href = Replace(URL, " ", "%20", "ALL")>
      <CFELSE>        <!--- ... else use OpenFile to return the file --->
        <CFSET href =
  "MyApplication_VOpenFile.cfm?serverFilePath=#URLEncodedFormat(Key)#">
      </CFIF>
      <A href="#href#">#GetFileFromPath(Key)#</A>
    </TD>

    <!--- title for HTML files --->
    <TD>#Title# </TD>

  </TR>
  </CFOUTPUT>

  </TABLE>


  <!--- CFSEARCH tried to retrieve one more file than the number specified in
the
    Form.MaxRows parameter. If number of retrieved files is greater than MaxRows
    we know that there is at least one file left. The following form contains
only
    one button which reloads this template with the new StartRow parameter. --->

  <CFIF GetResults.RecordCount gt Form.MaxRows>
    <FORM action="PersonnelPolicyDocuments_VSearchResult.cfm" method="post">
    <CFOUTPUT>
```

```
        <INPUT type=
➥"hidden" name="Criteria" value="#Replace(Form.Criteria, """", "'", "ALL")#">
        <INPUT type="hidden" name="MaxRows" value="#Form.MaxRows#">
        <INPUT type="hidden" name="StartRow" value="#Evaluate
➥(Form.StartRow + Form.MaxRows)#">
        <INPUT type="submit" value="    More ...    ">
    </CFOUTPUT>
    </FORM>
  </CFIF>

</CFIF>

</BODY></HTML>
```

Clearly, the focus of this template is the CFSEARCH tag near the top. The CFSEARCH tag tells Verity to actually run a search—take the search criteria that the user supplies and try to find documents that match.

Do you remember that Verity searches are a lot like ODBC/SQL queries? With that similarity in mind, it's worth noting that the CFSEARCH tag acts a lot like the CFQUERY tag when you're dealing with database tables.

Take a look at the specific parameters you're supplying to the CFSEARCH tag in Listing 29.3. As you do so, keep in mind that most of these parameters look a lot like the kind of parameters that you'd supply to a CFQUERY tag.

N O T E   The MAXROWS and STARTROW parameters listed here are used in the templates the wizard generated to create a Next 10 Records feature—where the user can move through pages of search results—just like you see on commercial search engines. The Next 10 Records functionality isn't explained in this chapter because it's not directly related to Verity. Refer to Chapter 21, "Advanced ColdFusion Templates," for an explanation of how to use MAXROWS and STARTROW to put together Next 10 Records types of solutions.

The following are the parameters for CFSEARCH, as used in Listing 29.3:

- NAME gives the search a name. Whatever results are found by Verity are available, for your use as a developer, as a query that has the name you supply here. You can use the search results in CFOUTPUT tags and in any of the other ways you normally use query results.

- COLLECTION tells Verity in which collection to search for documents. In this case, I'm directing it to the HRDocs collection that I created and indexed in this chapter.

- CRITERIA is probably the most important parameter here. This is what you're actually asking Verity to look for. Here, you're simply passing whatever the user types in the search form to this parameter.

- MAXROWS tells Verity to return only a certain number of rows. This is just like using the MAXROWS parameter with the CFQUERY tag. Here, you're taking whatever the user indicated in the MaxRows SELECT on the search form and adding one to it.

■ STARTROW tells Verity to return only the search results from a certain row in the search results on down. Here, you're taking the value specified by the hidden field named StartRow on the search form, so this value is always 1 for now. In other words, you're telling Verity to start returning the search results starting with the very first row.

> **N O T E**   CFSEARCH also takes another parameter, TYPE. You can use TYPE="SIMPLE" or TYPE="EXPLICIT" in your search templates. TYPE="SIMPLE" places the STEM and MANY operators into effect automatically (see Appendix C, "Verity Search Language Reference," for information on the STEM and MANY operators). Unless you specify EXPLICIT, SIMPLE is used by default. I recommend that you do not use EXPLICIT unless you have a specific reason to do so. ■

After the CFSEARCH is executed, the rest of Listing 29.3 displays the results to the user; it's fairly straightforward. The main thing to keep in mind is that now that the CFSEARCH has found its results, you're going to treat it just as if it were a CFQUERY named GetResults.

First, there is a CFIF tag that does the now-familiar check to make sure that the built-in RecordCount variable is not 0 (which would mean that Verity didn't find any results). See Chapter 12 for more information on the RecordCount variable.

Provided there are results to display, your code moves into the large CFELSE block that encompasses the remainder of the template. TABLE, TR, and TD tags are used to establish an HTML table in which to display the results, with headers. Look back at Chapter 11, "ColdFusion Basics," for more examples of building tables row-by-row with query results.

Most of the important stuff happens in the large CFOUTPUT block that follows. The QUERY="GetResults" parameter in the CFOUTPUT tag causes this code to be executed once for each row in the search results, where each row represents a document found. Unlike a result set returned by a CFQUERY—where you've specified what columns your result set will contain by including them in the SELECT part of your SQL statement—result sets returned by Verity searches always contain the same, predefined column names, which are shown in Table 29.2.

Table 29.2   Columns Returned by Verity Searches

Column	Contains
Key	The document's filename.
Title	The title of the document, if Verity is able to determine what the title is. For example, if the file is an HTML document, Verity obtains the title from the TITLE tags in the document's HEAD section. Verity may not provide a title for other types of documents.
Score	The *relevancy score* for the document, which indicates how closely the document matched the search criteria. The score is always a value between 0 and 1, where a score of 1 indicates a perfect match.
URL	The URL that can be used to obtain the file from your Web server. This is based on the information you supplied to the CFINDEX tag with its URLPATH parameter. If you did not specify an URLPATH parameter when indexing the collection, this column is blank.

Column	Contains
CurrentRow	This works just like the CurrentRow column that is returned by a CFQUERY. In a CFOUTPUT block that uses the search results in its QUERY parameter, CurrentRow is 1 for the first document returned by the CFSEARCH, 2 for the second document, and so on. See Chapter 23 for more discussion on CurrentRow.

As you can see, the code in Listing 29.3 uses these columns to display the score, title, and filename for each document. It also uses the URL column in an HTML anchor tag's HREF attribute to provide a link to the document.

In addition, two predefined variables are available to you after a search runs. Table 29.3 explains these variables.

Table 29.3 Properties Available After a CFSEARCH Tag Executes

Property	Indicates
RecordCount	Just as with CFQUERY, the number of matches Verity found. In this example, you access this variable using #GetResults.RecordCount# in your code.
RecordsSearched	The number of records Verity searched. In other words, the number of records in the collection(s).

You saw RecordCount in action in Listing 29.3. RecordsSearched can be used in much the same way, if you want to let the user know how many documents were searched to find their hits. For example, a code similar to the following would display something like 10 out of 4363 documents found:

```
<CFOUTPUT>
#GetResults.RecordCount#
out of
#GetResults.RecordsSearched#
documents found.
</CFOUTPUT>
```

Running a Search   Your search tool should already be operational. Pull the search form up in your browser and type **employee** in the blank. When you click Search, you should get a list of relevant documents from your Human Resources department, as shown in Figure 29.10.

> **N O T E**   If you look at Listing 29.3, you'll see there's a reference to a file called
> PERSONNELPOLICYDOCUMENTS_VOPENFILE.CFM. That code is in the template to
> provide access to documents that do not reside in the Web server's document root, and only goes into
> effect if the URL path is left blank when the collection is indexed. This OPENFILE template uses the
> CFCONTENT tag to get its job done. See Appendix A and the Coffee Valley Document Library example
> application that installs with ColdFusion for more information on using the CFCONTENT tag. ▪

FIGURE 29.10

Your search results page shows a relevancy score, filename, and title (when available) for each document found.

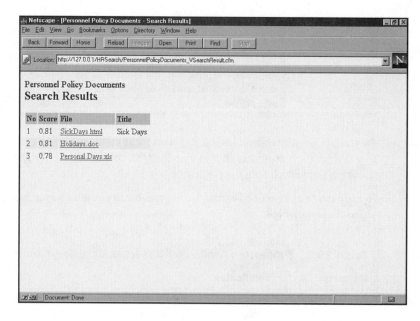

Refining Your Search   Often, just typing a few keywords isn't enough to find the documents you want. Verity provides a wealth of search operators to help you get the job done. By including special words like AND, OR, and NOT in your search criteria, or by using various wildcards, your users can tweak their searches so they find exactly what they're looking for.

As you're reading through this section, note how Verity search criteria end up looking a lot like SQL statements. It's nice that there's some common ground between the two, but it's also important to keep in mind that Verity's search language is not the same thing as SQL.

Using AND, OR, *and* NOT   If you want to refine your search a little, you can use special search operators in your search criteria to get more specific. Only the most common search operators are discussed at this point. There are many others available for your use. Refer to Appendix C for all the details on each of the search operators in Verity's search language.

Table 29.4 briefly describes the effect of using AND, OR, and NOT in your search criteria. These operators are very much like the AND, OR, and NOT Boolean operators discussed in Chapter 8, "Introduction to SQL."

Table 29.4   Basic Search Operators

Operator	Effect	Example
AND	Searches for documents that have both words in it.	Verity AND Allaire
OR	Searches for documents that has either word in it.	Verity OR Allaire
NOT	Eliminates documents where the word is found.	Verity NOT Allaire

T I P A comma can be used instead of OR in search criteria. A search for Verity, Allaire is therefore
the same as a search for Verity OR Allaire.

Using Parentheses and Quotation Marks Search criteria can look ambiguous once there are
more than two search words present. For instance, if you typed in Verity AND Allaire OR
ColdFusion, what would that mean exactly? Documents that definitely contained Verity but that
only needed to contain Verity or ColdFusion? Documents that contained ColdFusion in addition
to documents that contained both Verity and Allaire?

Use parentheses and quotation marks to indicate this type of criteria, where the order of evaluation needs to be specified. They make your intentions clear to Verity and are fairly easy to
explain to users. Table 29.5 summarizes the use of parentheses and quotation marks.

Table 29.5 Examples: Quotation Marks and Parentheses

Character	Purpose	Examples
(Parentheses)	Determines how ANDs and ORs are treated. Words within parentheses are considered a unit, and are considered first.	"Allaire OR (Cold AND Fusion)" "Fusion AND (Cold NOT Hot)"
"Quotation Marks"	Quoted words or phrases are searched for literally. Useful when you want to search for the actual words *and* or *or*.	"Simple AND Explicit" Allaire AND "not installed"

Using Wildcards Verity provides a few wildcards that you can use in your searches, so you
can find documents based on incomplete search words or phrases. The wildcards should look
pretty familiar to you if you've used the LIKE operator with SQL queries, as discussed in
Chapter 8. Table 29.6 summarizes the use of wildcard operators.

Table 29.6 The Two Most Common Wildcards

Wildcard	Purpose
*	Like the % wildcard in SQL, * stands in for any number of characters (including 0). A search for Fu* would find Fusion, Fugazi, and Fuchsia.
?	Just as in SQL, ? stands in for any single character. More precise—and thus generally less helpful—than the * wildcard. A search for ?ar?et would find both carpet and target, but not Learjet.

◊ These aren't the only wildcards available for your use. **See** the WILDCARD operator in "Understanding Evidence Operators," **p. 937.**

Taking Case Sensitivity into Account By default, a Verity search automatically becomes case
sensitive whenever the characters provided as the CRITERIA parameter are of mixed case. A
search for employee—or for EMPLOYEE—finds employee, Employee, or EMPLOYEE, but a search

for `Employee` only finds `Employee`, not `employee` or `EMPLOYEE`. You may want to make this fact clear to your users by providing a message on your search forms such as "Type in all upper-case or all lowercase unless you want the search to be case sensitive."

To have your application always ignore case regardless of what the user types, use ColdFusion's `LCase` function to convert the user's search words to lowercase when you supply them to `CFSEARCH`. For instance, by replacing the `CFSEARCH` in Listing 29.3 with the code in Listing 29.4, you guarantee that the search criteria passed to Verity is not of mixed case—you know the search will not be case sensitive.

Listing 29.4   Using `LCase` to Defeat Case-Sensitivity Even if User's Keywords Are of Mixed Case

```
<!--- retrieve requested files --->
<CFSEARCH
    name = "GetResults"
    collection = "#SearchCollection#"
    criteria = "#LCase(Form.Criteria)#"
    maxRows = "#Evaluate(Form.MaxRows + 1)#"
    startRow = "#Form.StartRow#"
>
```

Indexing Your Files Interactively

You've explored how to use the `CFINDEX` tag to index your collections. ColdFusion provides two different ways to index a Verity collection:

- Programmatically, with the `CFINDEX` tag (see Listing 29.11)
- Interactively, with the ColdFusion Administrator

The *programmatic* method that you've explored is best suited for the following situations:

- When the documents are always changing
- When it's critical that new documents become searchable right away
- When it's important that your application is as self-tuning as possible; if you are working as an outside consultant, for instance
- More complicated applications

However, you also have the option of indexing your documents interactively, using the Index button in the ColdFusion Administrator. This method is handy for the following situations:

- When the documents change infrequently, or not on a fixed or predictable schedule
- When the documents live outside your ColdFusion application, such as a folder full of Word files that employees may save and edit without your application knowing about it
- Testing and development
- Less complicated, in-house applications

Take a look at the interactive approach. To do this, go to the ColdFusion Administrator's Verity page, highlight your collection, and click the Index button. As you can see, all you have to do is fill in a few form fields and click the Update button (see Figure 29.11). After a few seconds—or minutes, depending on the number of files you're indexing—you see a message in the Administrator that the operation is complete.

FIGURE 29.11

Indexing your files interactively is as simple as filling in a few blanks.

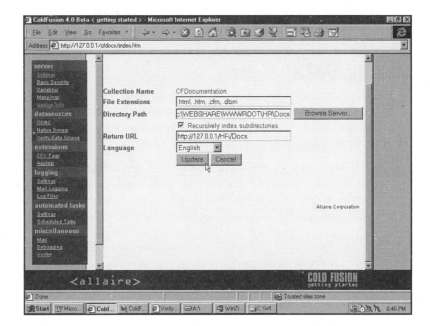

To index files, you must supply four pieces of information:

- File extensions
- Directory path
- Recursively index subdirectories
- Return URL

The File Extensions field corresponds to the CFINDEX tag's EXTENSIONS parameter. Just provide a simple list of file extensions—including the periods—that indicate which documents you want to index.

The Directory Path field corresponds to the KEY parameter of the CFINDEX tag. Just indicate which directory on your Web server—or local network—that Verity should index. This value must be given as an absolute file system path, not an URL, which means that it cannot start with http://.

The Recursively Index Subdirectories check box corresponds to the RECURSE parameter of the CFINDEX tag. Check this box if you want Verity to search all folders within the directory you specify.

The Return URL field corresponds to the URLPATH parameter of the CFINDEX tag. Enter the URL equivalent of the directory path you entered. In other words, what would you put before the filename if you wanted to open a file in this directory in a Web browser? This value should start with http:// or https://.

A collection indexed using this method will work the same way as a collection indexed using the CFINDEX tag in a ColdFusion template. It's really just a matter of whether you want to create a template that uses the CFINDEX tag.

Indexing Data

You've seen how easy it is to use ColdFusion's Verity functionality to index all sorts of files on your system. What if you want to index and search information in your database files? ColdFusion makes it possible to make a Verity index your database data just as if it were a bunch of document files.

In this section you see how Verity allows you to very neatly get around the limitations that make SQL less-than-perfect for true text-based searching. By the time you're through, you'll have a good understanding of when it makes sense to unleash Verity's rich search capabilities on your database data, and when you're best off leaving things to SQL instead.

N O T E   The examples in this section use the populated A2Z.mdb file located in this chapter's folder on the CD-ROM. The tables are populated with some actual book and order data with which to work. ▢

Doing It Without Verity

You don't need to use Verity to make your database searchable, but it can make it much easier for you to implement a search interface, and easier for your users to find what they want. Take a look at what you'd need to do to search your data using the tools you already know: CFQUERY and SQL.

Say you want to set up a little search tool to allow your users to search the A2Z database's Inventory table. You just want the user to be able to type a word or two into a form field and click Search to get the matching books.

The code in Listing 29.5 a simple search form. This will remind you a lot of the search forms that are explained in Chapter 12. The form is displayed in a browser, as shown in Figure 29.12.

On the CD

Listing 29.5   INVSRCH1.CFM—A Simple Inventory Search Form

```
<HTML>

<HEAD>
<TITLE>Inventory Search</TITLE>
</HEAD>

<BODY>
```

```
<H2>Please enter keywords to search for.</H2>

<FORM ACTION="invsrch2.cfm" METHOD="POST">

Keywords: <INPUT TYPE="text" NAME="Criteria"><BR>
<P>
<INPUT TYPE="submit" VALUE="Search">

</FORM>

</BODY>

</HTML>
```

Part

IV

Ch

29

FIGURE 29.12

The Inventory Search tool collects one or more keywords from the user.

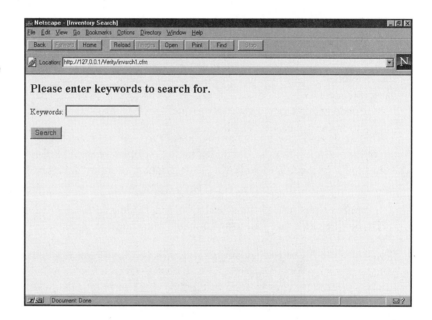

Again borrowing heavily from Chapter 12, you come up with the code in Listing 29.6 for searching and displaying the results from the Inventory table. Note that the LIKE keyword is used along with the % wildcard to search any part of the description. Refer to Chapter 12 if you need to jog your memory on the use of the LIKE keyword.

On the CD

Listing 29.6 INVSRCH2.CFM—**Code for Searching the Inventory Table**

```
<CFQUERY NAME="GetResults" DATASOURCE="A2Z">
  SELECT BookID, Title
  FROM Inventory
  WHERE (Description LIKE '%#Form.Criteria#%')
</CFQUERY>
```

continues

Listing 29.6 Continued

```
<HTML>

<HEAD>
<TITLE>Search Results</TITLE>
</HEAD>

<BODY>

<H2><CFOUTPUT>
➥#GetResults.RecordCount# books found for "#Form.Criteria#".</CFOUTPUT></H2>

<UL>
<CFOUTPUT QUERY="GetResults">
  <LI>#Title#
</CFOUTPUT>
</UL>

</BODY>

</HTML>
```

This would work fine, as long as your application only required simple searching. If the user entered *guide* for the search criteria, SQL's LIKE operator would faithfully find all the books that had the word *guide* somewhere in the description, as shown in Figure 29.13.

What if the user entered something like *Hitchhiker Guide*? No records would be found because there are no records with those exact words in it (only *Hitchhiker's Guide*, with an apostrophe). That's a limitation that your users probably won't find acceptable.

FIGURE 29.13

Your Verity-free code works fine for simple, one-word searches.

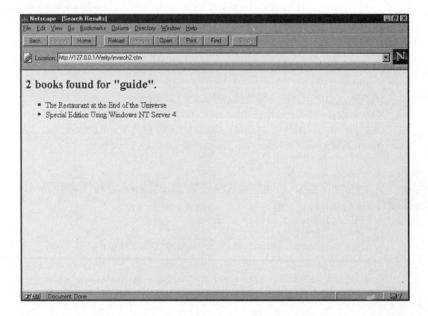

Maybe you need to modify your CFQUERY a little, to account for multiple-word searches. Listing 29.8 contains a revised query that should take multiple words into account. Each word is treated separately because the CFLOOP adds an additional AND condition to the query for each word in the user's input. Only books that contain all of the words entered in the blank will be found. See Chapter 21, "Advanced ColdFusion Templates," for a detailed discussion of the CFLOOP tag.

On the CD

Listing 29.7 INVSRCH2A.CFM—**Getting SQL to Account for Multiple Words**

```
<CFQUERY NAME="GetResults" DATASOURCE="A2Z">
  SELECT BookID, Title
  FROM Inventory
  WHERE (0=0
  <CFLOOP LIST="#Form.Criteria#" INDEX="ThisWord" DELIMITERS=" ">
    AND (Description LIKE '%#ThisWord#%')
  </CFLOOP>)
</CFQUERY>


<HTML>

<HEAD>
<TITLE>Search Results</TITLE>
</HEAD>

<BODY>

<H2><CFOUTPUT>
➥#GetResults.RecordCount# books found for "#Form.Criteria#".</CFOUTPUT></H2>

<UL>
<CFOUTPUT QUERY="GetResults">
  <LI>#Title#
</CFOUTPUT>
</UL>

</BODY>

</HTML>
```

Now the appropriate books will be found if the user enters *Hitchhiker Guide*. What if your user wants to search for all books with *Guide*, but without *Hitchhiker*? What about all books with either *Hitchhiker* or *Guide*, rather than *Hitchhiker* and *Guide*? What if the user doesn't know quite the right words, so types in *Hitchhikers Guide* or *Hitchhiker's Guides*? What about *Guide, Hitchhiker's*?

This is the kind of intelligence users have come to expect from a search engine. It is theoretically possible to come up with various CFLOOPs and CFIFs that build SQL code to cover all of those scenarios, but that many WHEREs, LIKEs, ANDs, and ORs would be a real pain to code, debug, and maintain. In addition, performance degrades as the number of books grows. Indexing the text columns won't improve performance because the LIKE operator cannot take advantage of indexes when a wildcard operator precedes the search string. There has to be a better way.

Indexing Your Table Data: Verity to the Rescue

ColdFusion's Verity functionality provides a well-performing, easy-to-implement solution that addresses all of these concerns. You create a *custom* Verity collection filled with documents that aren't really documents at all. Each "document" is actually just a record from your database tables.

It works like this: You write a CFQUERY that retrieves the data you want to make searchable. You pass this data to a CFINDEX tag, which indexes the data as if it were documents. Additionally, you tell Verity which column from the query should be considered a document "filename," which column should be considered a document "title," and which column(s) should be considered a document's "body." Figure 29.14 illustrates the idea.

FIGURE 29.14

Database data becomes searchable, just like regular documents.

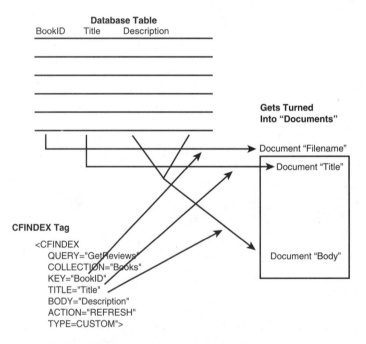

Assume you've just used the ColdFusion Administrator to create a new Verity collection called Books, as discussed earlier in this chapter. You'll populate this new collection with data from the Inventory database table.

Take a look at the code in Listing 29.8. Notice that the CFINDEX tag looks a lot like Listing 29.1, where you indexed your document files. The central differences here are the fact that you're setting TYPE to CUSTOM instead of PATH, and that you're referring to column names from a CFQUERY.

On the CD

Listing 29.8 `INDEXDATA.CFM`—**Code to Index a Collection with Database Data**

```
<CFQUERY NAME="GetResults" DATASOURCE="A2Z">
  SELECT BookID, Title, Description
  FROM Inventory
</CFQUERY>

<CFINDEX ACTION="REFRESH"
         COLLECTION="Books"
         KEY="BookID"
         TYPE="CUSTOM"
         TITLE="Title"
         QUERY="GetResults"
         BODY="Description">


<HTML>

<HEAD>
<TITLE>Indexing Complete</TITLE>
</HEAD>

<BODY>

<H2>Indexing Complete</H2>

</BODY>

</HTML>
```

The CFQUERY part is very simple—just get the basic information about the books. (Obviously, if you only want certain books to be indexed, a WHERE clause could be added to the CFQUERY's SQL statement.) Next comes a CFINDEX tag, which looks a lot like the CFINDEX tag you used earlier to index your normal document files.

This time around, though, you specify a few new parameters that are necessary when indexing a database table instead of normal documents.

`ACTION="REFRESH"`	As before, tells Verity that you're supplying new data.
`TYPE="CUSTOM"`	Says that you're dealing with table data, rather than document files.
`QUERY="GetResults"`	Specifies from which CFQUERY to get the data.
`KEY, TITLE, BODY`	Specifies which query columns should be treated like which parts of a document.

That's really about all there is to it! Once the INDEXDATA.CFM template is executed, you should be able to search the Books collection in much the same way as you searched the HRDocs collection back in Listing 29.3.

The code in Listing 29.9 searches through the newly indexed Books collection, based on whatever criteria the user types in the search form. Except for the introduction of the CFSEARCH tag, this code is virtually unchanged from Listing 29.6; the results will be displayed to the user as shown in Figure 29.13.

N O T E You're still using Listing 29.5's Inventory Search form—just be make sure to change the ACTION parameter of the FORM tag to "InvSrch3.cfm". ■

Listing 29.9 Searching and Displaying Records That Came from a Database

```
<CFSEARCH COLLECTION="Books"
          NAME="GetResults"
          CRITERIA="#Form.Criteria#">

<HTML>

<HEAD>
<TITLE>Search Results</TITLE>
</HEAD>

<BODY>

<H2><CFOUTPUT>#GetResults.RecordCount# books found for
➥"#Form.Criteria#".</CFOUTPUT></H2>

<UL>
<CFOUTPUT QUERY="GetResults">
  <LI>#Title#
</CFOUTPUT>
</UL>

</BODY>

</HTML>
```

As you can see, it was pretty easy to expose your database data to Verity. You really didn't have to do much work at all. Of course, the user will notice a tremendous difference: All of Verity's AND, OR, NOT, wildcarding, and other searching niceties are all of a sudden very much available to her.

Displaying a Summary for Each Record   In addition to the score and title, Verity also provides a Summary for each record in the search results. The summary will be the first 3 sentences—or the first 500 characters—of the information you specified for the BODY back when you indexed the collection with the CFINDEX tag. The summary is helpful for the user to "eyeball" which documents she is interested in.

To display the Summary to the user, simply refer to it in your ColdFusion templates in the same way you refer to the KEY, SCORE, or TITLE. Listing 29.10 adds the summary to your Search Results page. Figure 29.15 shows what the search results will look like to the user.

Listing 29.10 `INVSRCH4.CFM`—**Code to Include a Summary for Each Document**

```
<CFSEARCH COLLECTION="Books"
          NAME="GetResults"
          CRITERIA="#Form.Criteria#">

<HTML>

<HEAD>
<TITLE>Search Results</TITLE>
</HEAD>

<BODY>

<H2><CFOUTPUT>#GetResults.RecordCount# books found for
➡"#Form.Criteria#".</CFOUTPUT></H2>

<DL>
<CFOUTPUT QUERY="GetResults">
  <DT><I>#NumberFormat(Round(Score * 100))#%</I>
       <B>#Title#</B>
  <DD><FONT SIZE="-1">#Summary#</FONT>
</CFOUTPUT>
</DL>

</BODY>

</HTML>
```

FIGURE 29.15

Displaying the
document summary is
a slick, professional-
looking touch.

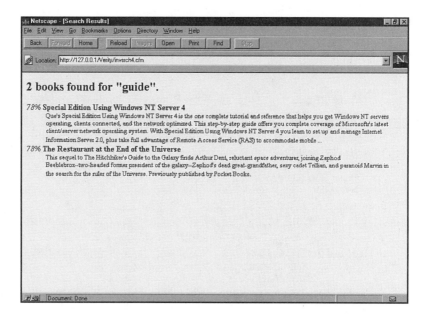

Don't expect Verity summaries to always show the parts of the document that contain the search keywords; that's not how Verity summarization works. Verity selects each record's summary at the time the collection is indexed, and is always the same for any given record, regardless of whatever the search criteria were that found it. The summary does not necessarily contain the keywords that were used as the search criteria.

Indexing Multiple Query Columns as the BODY   In Listing 29.8 you indexed the Books collection with the results from a query. In that listing, you declared that the Description column from the Inventory table should be considered the body of each book record (by setting the BODY parameter of the CFINDEX tag to "Description").

By default, when your application runs a Verity search, only the BODY part of each record is actually searched for matching words. The information in the TITLE part of the record is not searched.

There are two ways to make the title searchable. One is to specify the title in the CRITERIA parameter, using relational operators and the SUBSTRING operator.

An easier way is to go back to your CFINDEX tag and simply supply the information that you're giving to the TITLE parameter to the BODY parameter as well. The BODY parameter can take a comma-separated list of column names ("Description, Title"), rather than only one column name ("Description"). The searchable part of each record in your database is comprised of the Description of the book, followed by the Title of the book.

There's no need to stop there. You can put a bunch of column names in the BODY parameter, as shown in Listing 29.11. For each row returned by the query, ColdFusion concatenates the Description, Publisher, AuthorFirstName, AuthorLastName, and Title columns and presents it to Verity as the BODY of each document. The result is that all textual information about the title, publisher, author, and so on is now part of your collection and instantly searchable. You don't have to change a thing about the code in any of your search templates.

On the CD

Listing 29.11   INDEXDATA2.CFM—Supplying More Than One Column to the BODY Parameter

```
<CFQUERY NAME="GetResults" DATASOURCE="A2Z">
  SELECT BookID, Title, Description,
         Publisher, AuthorFirstName, AuthorLastName
  FROM Inventory
</CFQUERY>

<CFINDEX ACTION="UPDATE"
         COLLECTION="Books"
         KEY="BookID"
         TYPE="CUSTOM"
         TITLE="Title"
         QUERY="GetResults"
         BODY="Description, Publisher, AuthorFirstName, AuthorLastName">

<HTML>
```

```
<HEAD>
<TITLE>Indexing Complete</TITLE>
</HEAD>

<BODY>

<H2>Indexing Complete</H2>

</BODY>

</HTML>
```

It's important to note that when you supply several columns to the BODY like this, Verity is not maintaining the information in separate columns, fields, or anything else. The underlying table's structure is not preserved. All the information is pressed together into one big, searchable mass. Don't expect to be able to refer to a #Publisher# variable, for instance, in the same way that you can refer to the #Title# and #Score# variables after a CFSEARCH is executed.

That may or may not feel like a limitation, depending on the nature of the applications that you're building. In a way, it's just the flip side of Verity's concentrating on text in a natural-language kind of way, rather than being obsessed with columns the way that SQL is.

However, ColdFusion and Verity do allow you to store a limited amount of information in a more database-type of way, using something called *custom fields*.

Indexing Additional Columns with Custom Fields   ColdFusion allows you to index up to two additional Verity fields when you're indexing database data. The fields—CUSTOM1 and CUSTOM2—and are treated very much like the Title field you've already worked with. These custom fields come in handy when you have precise, code-style data you want to keep associated with each record.

In Listing 29.12, you adjust the code from Listing 29.8 to fill the CUSTOM1 field with your ISBN column, and the CUSTOM2 field with your CategoryID column. Conceptually, it's as if Verity is making two little notes on each document that it makes from the rows of your query. The CUSTOM1 note is the ISBN number, and the CUSTOM2 note is the CategoryID.

On the CD

Listing 29.12   INDEXDATA3.CFM—**Adding Custom Fields to a Collection**

```
<CFQUERY NAME="GetResults" DATASOURCE="A2Z">
  SELECT BookID, Title, Description, ISBN, CategoryID
  FROM Inventory
</CFQUERY>

<CFINDEX ACTION="UPDATE"
         COLLECTION="Books"
         KEY="BookID"
         TYPE="CUSTOM"
         TITLE="Title"
         QUERY="GetResults"
         BODY="Description"
```

continues

Listing 29.12   Continued

```
            CUSTOM1="ISBN"
            CUSTOM2="CategoryID">

<HTML>

<HEAD>
<TITLE>Indexing Complete</TITLE>
</HEAD>

<BODY>

<H2>Indexing Complete</H2>

</BODY>

</HTML>
```

Now that Verity knows the CategoryID and ISBN for each record in the collection, it's easy to create a more sophisticated search tool that allows the user to choose Categories or ISBN numbers along with their search words, like Listing 29.13. Figure 29.16 shows what the search form looks like.

On the CD

Listing 29.13   INVSRCH1A—Search Form with User Interface for Custom Search Criteria

```
<HTML>

<HEAD>
<TITLE>Inventory Search</TITLE>
</HEAD>

<BODY>

<H2>Please enter keywords to search for.</H2>

<FORM ACTION="invsrch5.cfm" METHOD="POST">

Keywords: <INPUT TYPE="text" NAME="Criteria"><BR>

Category: <INPUT TYPE="Radio" NAME="CategoryID" VALUE="1">Literature
          <INPUT TYPE="Radio" NAME="CategoryID" VALUE="2">Humor
          <INPUT TYPE="Radio" NAME="CategoryID" VALUE="3">Computers
<P>
Or ISBN:  <INPUT TYPE="text" NAME="ISBN"><BR>

<INPUT TYPE="submit" VALUE="Search">

</FORM>

</BODY>

</HTML>
```

FIGURE 29.16

Custom fields provide a simple way to handle search forms like this one.

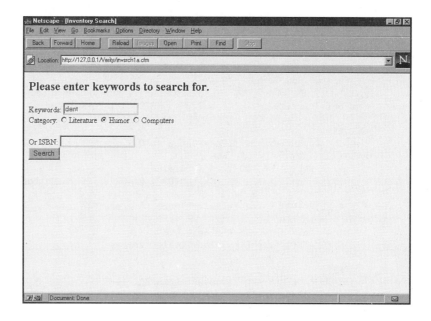

Now you just need to teach the receiving template how to deal with the user's entries for the CategoryID and ISBN form fields. To specify the additional criteria, you make use of Verity's MATCHES operator, which you use here for the first time.

The MATCHES operator searches specific document fields—rather than the body—and finds only exact matches. Document fields that you can use MATCHES with include CF_CUSTOM1, CF_CUSTOM2, CF_TITLE, and CF_KEY, all of which correspond to the values you supply to the CFINDEX tag when you indexed the data.

N O T E Depending on the situation, you could use the Verity operators CONTAINS, STARTS, ENDS, or SUBSTRING in the place of MATCHES in the this code. You could also use numeric operators such as =, <, and > with the CF_CUSTOM2 field. See "Relational Operators" in Appendix C for more information. █

Listing 29.14 demonstrates the use of the MATCHES search operator. At the top of the template, you use some CFIF, CFELSE, and CFELSEIF tags to decide what you're going to ask Verity to look for.

If the user specifies an ISBN number, you're not concerned with anything else; you ignore the other form fields if the ISBN is not blank. If the ISBN is blank, however, there are still two possibilities: the category could be specified, keywords could be specified, or both.

Depending on which fields the user may have left blank, the TheCriteria variable will have slightly different values. The TheCriteria variable is then supplied to the CFSEARCH tag in its CRITERIA parameter.

Listing 29.14 INVSRCH5.CFM—**Using the** MATCHES **Operator to Search Custom Fields**

```
<!--- DECIDE WHAT CRITERIA WE'LL PASS TO VERITY --->
<CFIF Form.ISBN is not "">
  <!--- IF AN ISBN NUMBER IS GIVEN, USE IT AND IGNORE OTHER INPUT --->
  <CFSET TheCriteria = "CF_CUSTOM1 <MATCHES> #Form.ISBN#">

<CFELSE>
  <CFIF (ParameterExists(Form.CategoryID))
➥AND (Form.Criteria is "")>
    <!--- ONLY A CATEGORY IS SPECIFIED --->
    <CFSET TheCriteria = "(CF_CUSTOM2 <MATCHES> #Form.CategoryID#) ">

  <CFELSEIF (NOT ParameterExists(Form.CategoryID))
➥AND (Form.Criteria is not "")>
    <!--- ONLY KEYWORDS ARE SPECIFIED --->
    <CFSET TheCriteria = "#Form.Criteria#">

  <CFELSE>
    <!--- CATEGORY AND KEYWORDS ARE SPECIFIED --->
    <CFSET TheCriteria = "(CF_CUSTOM2 <MATCHES> #Form.CategoryID#)
➥AND (#Form.Criteria#)">

  </CFIF>
</CFIF>

<CFSEARCH COLLECTION="Books"
          NAME="GetResults"
          CRITERIA="#TheCriteria#">

<HTML>

<HEAD>
<TITLE>Search Results</TITLE>
</HEAD>

<BODY>

<H2><CFOUTPUT>#GetResults.RecordCount# books found.</CFOUTPUT></H2>

<P ALIGN="RIGHT"><CFOUTPUT>Actual Criteria Used:
➥#HTMLEditFormat(TheCriteria)#</CFOUTPUT></P>

<DL>
<CFOUTPUT QUERY="GetResults">
  <DT><I>#NumberFormat(Round(Score * 100))#%</I>
      <B>#Title#</B>
  <DD><FONT SIZE="-1"><I>ISBN #Custom1#.</I> #Summary#</FONT>
</CFOUTPUT>
</DL>

</BODY>

</HTML>
```

As you can see in Figure 29.17, this code presents the ISBN number to the user by using the #Custom1# variable in the CFOUTPUT block, along with the Summary, Score, and other information. Also note that this code displays the criteria that is actually being passed to Verity at the top of the page, so you can fool around with the template a bit if you want and see the effect your CFIF logic is having.

FIGURE 29.17

Custom fields let you display related information about each record found.

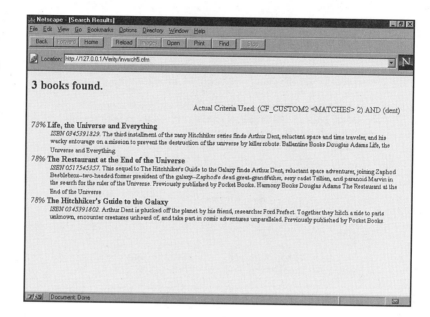

Combining Verity Searches with SQL Queries On-The-Fly

The custom fields you just learned about give you a lot of flexibility. In most cases, you'll be able to search and display records straight from your Verity collection(s), without bothering the underlying database tables.

You may encounter situations where you want to get information from Verity and from your database tables, presenting the information together to the user. This kind of thing is quite easy to pull off: use ColdFusion's ValueList function along with SQL's IN operator.

Say you want to run a Verity search on the Books collection, but you want to be able to show the number of copies in stock for each book. You consider the idea of feeding the NumberInStock column to CUSTOM1 or CUSTOM2, but you decide that the number of copies in stock is such a volatile, ever-changing piece of information that you always want to display the live value directly from the database table.

You run a CFSEARCH just as you already have, but you won't display anything from it. Instead, you just use Verity's results as criteria for a normal SQL query. Verity supplies you with the key value for each document that it finds, which you know happens to be the BookID from your Inventory table. You'll supply those BookIDs to a normal CFQUERY.

Listing 29.15 shows how to use CFSEARCH results to drive a CFQUERY in this manner. Figure 29.18 shows the results.

Listing 29.15   INVSRCH6.CFM—Using Verity Results as Criteria for a Normal SQL Query

```
<!--- RUN THE VERITY SEARCH --->
<CFSEARCH COLLECTION="Books"
          NAME="VeritySearch"
          CRITERIA="#Form.Criteria#">

<!--- GET THE RECORDS THAT VERITY FOUND --->
<CFQUERY NAME="GetResults" DATASOURCE="A2Z">
  SELECT BookID, Title, NumberInStock FROM Inventory
  WHERE BookID IN (#ValueList(VeritySearch.KEY)#)
  ORDER BY Title
</CFQUERY>

<HTML>

<HEAD>
<TITLE>Search Results</TITLE>
</HEAD>

<BODY>

<H2><CFOUTPUT>#GetResults.RecordCount# books found for
➥"#Form.Criteria#".</CFOUTPUT></H2>

<CFTABLE QUERY="GetResults" COLHEADERS HTMLTABLE BORDER>
  <CFCOL HEADER="BookID" TEXT="#BookID#">
  <CFCOL HEADER="Title" TEXT="#Title#">
  <CFCOL HEADER="In stock" TEXT="#NumberInStock#">
</CFTABLE>

</BODY>

</HTML>
```

TIP

When you use this strategy, the search results will no longer be sorted by relevance. Instead, they are sorted according to the ORDER BY part of your SQL statement. This can be a good or a bad thing, depending on your situation. Keep it in mind.

Understanding Verity and Your Table's Key Values

When you're indexing table data, it's important to understand that Verity doesn't think of the concept of a key in the same way that your database tables do. Specifically, Verity does not assume or enforce any rules about uniqueness of values that you feed to it with the CFINDEX's KEY parameter. This means that Verity can and will index two separate documents that have the same key value. This can lead to problems, especially if the data you're indexing is derived from two tables that have a master-detail relationship to one another.

FIGURE 29.18

CFSEARCH and
CFQUERY can work well
together, through SQL's
IN keyword and
ColdFusion's
ValueList function.

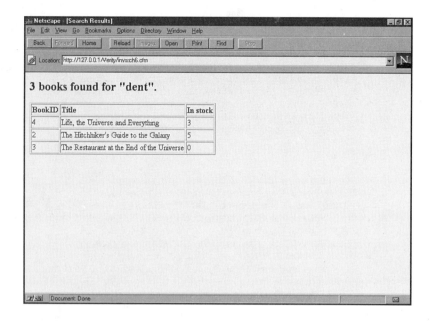

For instance, say you want to include the names of the people who placed orders for each of the books into the Verity collection. As you learned in Chapter 19, "Advanced SQL," it's fairly simple to create a join query that retrieves this information from your database tables.

The problem is that there can be any number of orders placed for each book. This means that if a book has been ordered by seven different customers, there will be seven rows for that book in the result set. This poses a problem. Verity will dutifully index each of these rows as a separate document, without understanding that the seven rows all represent the same book. This means that a search that matches with the text of the book finds all seven records and displays them to the user. This can make your application look buggy.

ColdFusion provides no built-in way out of this. CFINDEX doesn't have a GROUP parameter like CFOUTPUT does; you can't use GROUP when you're displaying the records because the seven rows aren't guaranteed to be in consecutive rows when Verity finds them. You either need to avoid this kind of situation altogether or figure out some way of processing the data between the CFQUERY and the CFINDEX.

Here's one approach. The code in Listing 29.16 takes the query results and manually creates a second query, line-by-line. The new query has the same structure as the original, except that it is guaranteed to have only one row for each book. If the original query had more than one row for a particular BookID (because of multiple orders), the customer names from all the rows are turned into a comma-separated list when they are put into the new query. The result is a query that can be used to index a Verity collection without problems.

Listing 29.16   `INDEXDATA4.CFM`—**Solving the Problem by Creating a New, Uniqued Query**

```
<CFQUERY NAME="GetResults" DATASOURCE="A2Z">
  SELECT i.BookID, i.Title, i.Description, c.Company
  FROM Inventory i, OrderItems oi, Orders o, Customers c
  WHERE i.BookID = oi.BookID
      AND oi.OrderID = o.OrderID
      AND o.CustomerID = c.CustomerID
  ORDER BY i.BookID
</CFQUERY>

<!--- Create new query with same column names --->
<CFSET MyQuery = QueryNew(GetResults.ColumnList)>
<CFOUTPUT QUERY="GetResults" GROUP="BookID">
  <!--- Make a comma-separated list of all papers for this BookID --->
  <CFSET CompanyList = "">
  <CFOUTPUT><CFSET CompanyList = ListAppend(CompanyList, GetResults.
➥Company)></CFOUTPUT>
  <!--- Make new row in MyQuery, with other data just copied from
➥GetResults --->
  <CFSET Temp = QueryAddRow(MyQuery)>
  <CFSET Temp = QuerySetCell(MyQuery,"BookID",GetResults.BookID)>
  <CFSET Temp = QuerySetCell(MyQuery,"Title",GetResults.Title)>
  <CFSET Temp = QuerySetCell(MyQuery,"Description",GetResults.Description)>
  <CFSET Temp = QuerySetCell(MyQuery,"Company",CompanyList)>
</CFOUTPUT>

<CFINDEX ACTION="UPDATE"
        COLLECTION="Books"
        KEY="BookID"
        TYPE="CUSTOM"
        TITLE="Title"
        QUERY="MyQuery"
        BODY="Description, Company">

<HTML>

<HEAD>
<TITLE>Indexing Complete</TITLE>
</HEAD>

<BODY>

<H2>Indexing Complete</H2>

</BODY>

</HTML>
```

Once this code is run, if the user typed a company name in a search form, the CFSEARCH would find books that the specified company has actually ordered.

Searching on More Than One Collection

To specify more than one Verity collection in a CFSEARCH tag, just specify all of the collection names for the COLLECTION parameter and separate them with commas. All of the collections are searched for matching documents.

N O T E If you have Allaire Forums 2.02 installed on your system, this is how the Search Message Titles and Search Titles and Text options work on the search page. The titles and text are separate collections. ■

If you want to allow your users to choose from several collections, you could add the code from Listing 29.17 to your search form.

On the CD

Listing 29.17 INVSRCH1B.CFM—Adding Check Boxes for Multiple Collections

```
<HTML>

<HEAD>
<TITLE>Inventory Search</TITLE>
</HEAD>

<BODY>

<H2>Please enter keywords to search for.</H2>

<FORM ACTION="invsrch3a.cfm" METHOD="POST">
<INPUT TYPE="Hidden" NAME="Collections_required"
➥ VALUE="You must chose at least one collection.">

Keywords: <INPUT TYPE="text" NAME="Criteria"><BR>

<INPUT TYPE="Checkbox" NAME="Collections" VALUE="Books">Book Inventory
<INPUT TYPE="Checkbox" NAME="Collections" VALUE="HRDocs">Personnel Policies

<P>
<INPUT TYPE="submit" VALUE="Search">

</FORM>

</BODY>

</HTML>
```

Because of the convenient way check boxes are handled by ColdFusion, the value of the Form.Collections variable is set to "Books,HRDocs" if the user checks both boxes. You would pass the variable directly to the COLLECTION parameter of the receiving template's CFSEARCH tag.

T I P   Note that you can freely mix normal document collections with database-table collections within a single CFSEARCH operation.

Displaying Records in a Different Order   The search results returned by a CFSEARCH tag are ranked in *order of relevance*. The closest matches—the ones with the highest score—are first, and the weakest matches are last.

Verity provides a few ways to tweak the way the score is computed (see "Score Operators" in Appendix C), which gives you a little bit of control over how the documents are ordered. What if you wanted to display the search results in, say, alphabetical order by title?

There is no built-in function to handle this in ColdFusion. At the time of this writing, there is no CFX_QuerySort or similar tag available either. In lieu of these options, Listing 29.18 provides a CFML custom tag that you can use to order your Verity results. Actually, you can use it to sort the output of any ColdFusion tag that presents its data as a query, such as CFPOP, CFLDAP, and the like.

On the CD

Listing 29.18   QUERYSORT.CFM—A Custom Tag That Sorts Query (and Verity) Results

```
<!--- Example of use

<CF_QuerySort
  QUERY="MyQuery"
  SORTCOLUMN="MyColumn"
  SORTORDER="Desc"                 <- optional, defaults to Asc
  SORTTYPE="Numeric"               <- optional, defaults to Textnocase
  SORTEDQUERY="MySortedQuery">     <- optional, defaults to "Sorted"

 --->

<!--- SUSPEND OUTPUT --->
<CFSETTING CFOUTPUTONLY="YES">

<!--- REQUIRED PARAMETERS --->
<CFPARAM NAME="Attributes.QUERY">
<CFPARAM NAME="Attributes.SortColumn">
<!--- OPTIONAL PARAMETERS --->
<CFPARAM NAME="Attributes.SortType" DEFAULT="Textnocase">
<CFPARAM NAME="Attributes.SortOrder" DEFAULT="Asc">
<CFPARAM NAME="Attributes.SortedQuery" DEFAULT="Sorted">

<!--- ESTABLISH LOCAL VERSIONS OF QUERIES --->
<CFSET MyArray = ArrayNew(1)>
<CFSET MyQuery = Evaluate("Caller.#Attributes.Query#")>
<CFSET NewQuery = QueryNew(MyQuery.ColumnList)>
<CFIF MyQuery.RecordCount greater than 999999><CFABORT SHOWERROR="Only
➥Queries with less than one million rows can be sorted.
➥Your Query has #MyQuery.RecordCount# rows."></CFIF>

<!--- ADD ROWNUMBER TO END OF EACH ROW'S VALUE --->
<CFOUTPUT QUERY="MyQuery">
  <CFSET MyArray[CurrentRow] = Evaluate("MyQuery.#Attributes.SortColumn#")
➥& NumberFormat(CurrentRow, "000009")>
  <CFSET Temp = QueryAddRow(NewQuery)>
```

```
</CFOUTPUT>

<!--- SORT ARRAY --->
<CFSET Temp = ArraySort(MyArray, Attributes.SortType, Attributes.SortOrder)>

<!--- POPULATE NEW QUERY, ROW BY ROW, WITH APPROPRIATE ROW OF OLD QUERY --->
<CFLOOP FROM=1 TO=#MyQuery.RecordCount# INDEX="This">
  <CFSET Row = Val(Right(MyArray[This], 6))>
  <CFLOOP LIST="#MyQuery.ColumnList#" INDEX="Col">
    <CFSET Temp = QuerySetCell(NewQuery, Col, Evaluate("MyQuery.#Col#
➥[Row]"), This)>
  </CFLOOP>
</CFLOOP>

<!--- PASS SORTED QUERY BACK TO CALLING TEMPLATE --->
<CFSET "Caller.#Attributes.SortedQuery#" = NewQuery>

<!--- RESTORE OUTPUT --->
<CFSETTING CFOUTPUTONLY="NO">
```

If you save the QUERYSORT.CFM file to your server's CustomTags directory, it should be quite easy to use it to sort your Verity results, as shown in Listing 29.19.

On the CD

Listing 29.19   SORTED.CFM—Sorting Verity Results by Title

```
<CFSEARCH COLLECTION="Books"
          NAME="GetResults"
          CRITERIA="#Form.Criteria#">

<CF_QUERYSORT QUERY="GetResults"
              SORTEDQUERY="GetResults"
              SORTCOLUMN="Title">

<HTML>

<HEAD>
<TITLE>Search Results</TITLE>
</HEAD>

<BODY>

<H2><CFOUTPUT>#GetResults.RecordCount# books found for
➥"#Form.Criteria#".</CFOUTPUT></H2>

<UL>
<CFOUTPUT QUERY="GetResults">
  <LI>#Title#
</CFOUTPUT>
</UL>

</BODY>

</HTML>
```

Maintaining Collections

In some situations, you may be able to simply create a Verity collection, index it, and forget about it. If the documents or data that make up the collection never change, you're in luck—you get to skip this whole section of the chapter.

It's likely that you'll have to refresh that data at some point. Even when you don't have to refresh it, you may want to get it to run faster.

Repopulating Your Verity Collection

Whenever the original documents change from what they were when you indexed them, your collection will be a little bit out of sync with reality. The search results will be based on Verity's knowledge of the documents back when you did your indexing. If a document or database record has since been edited so that it no longer has certain words in it, it may be found in error if someone types in a search for those words. If the document is deleted altogether, Verity will still find it in its own records, which means that your application might show a bad link that leads nowhere.

In a perfect world, Verity would dynamically watch your document folders and data tables and immediately reflect any changes, additions, or deletions in your collections. Unfortunately, the world isn't totally perfect, and this stuff doesn't happen automatically for you. The good news is that it's no major chore.

If You Index Your Collections Interactively If you recall, there are two ways of indexing a Verity collection: *interactively* with the ColdFusion Administrator or *programmatically* with the CFINDEX tag. If you did it interactively, there's not much I need to tell you; just go back to the Verity page in the Administrator and hit the Purge button for your collection. Select the Index button and do the same thing you did the first time. This should bring your collection up-to-date.

TIP   You'd do the same basic thing if the location of the documents had changed.

If You Index Your Collections Programmatically If you indexed the collection using CFINDEX—and you used ACTION="REFRESH" in the CFINDEX tag, as shown in Listing 29.1 and Listing 29.8—you should be able to bring your collection up-to-date simply by running it again.

TIP   You might want to consider scheduling this refresh template to be executed automatically at the end of each week, during off-peak hours. For more information on ColdFusion's built-in template scheduler, see Chapter 32, "Event Scheduling."

Instead of ACTION="REFRESH", you can use ACTION="UPDATE" in your CFINDEX tag. This updates information on documents already indexed, but without deleting information on documents that no longer exist. You can also use ACTION="PURGE" to completely remove all data from the collection. The ACTION="REFRESH" previously recommended is really the same thing as a PURGE followed by an UPDATE.

Deleting/Repopulating Specific Records   If your application is aware of the moment that a document or table record is deleted or edited, you may want to update the Verity collection right then, so your collection stays in sync with the actual information. Clearly it's not necessary to repopulate the entire collection just because one record has changed. ColdFusion and Verity address this by allowing you to delete items from a collection via the key value.

For instance, after an edit has been made to the Inventory database table, you could use the code shown in Listing 29.20 to remove the record from the Books collection and put the new data in its place. This should run much faster than a complete repopulation. This listing assumes that a form that passes the BookID as a hidden field has just been submitted, and contains some other fields that are meant to allow them to update certain columns in the Inventory table (the description, perhaps) for a particular book.

On the CD

Listing 29.20   DELADD.CFM—Deleting and Re-Adding a Specific Record to a Collection

```
<!--- Perform the update to the database table --->
<CFUPDATE DATASOURCE="A2Z" TABLENAME="Inventory">

<!--- Retrieve updated data back from the database --->
<CFQUERY NAME="GetBook" DATASOURCE="A2Z">
  SELECT BookID, Title, Description
  FROM Inventory
  WHERE BookID = #Form.BookID#
</CFQUERY>

<!--- Delete the old record from the Verity collection --->
<CFINDEX ACTION="DELETE"
  COLLECTION="Books"
  KEY="#Form.BookID#">

<!--- Get updated version back into the Verity collection --->
<CFINDEX ACTION="UPDATE"
  COLLECTION="Books"
  TYPE="CUSTOM"
  QUERY="GetBook"
  KEY="BookID"
  TITLE="Title"
  BODY="Description">

<HTML>

<HEAD>
<TITLE>Update Complete</TITLE>
</HEAD>

<BODY>

<H2>Update Complete</H2>

</BODY>

</HTML>
```

Administrating Collections with CFCOLLECTION

ColdFusion 4.0 includes a new tag called CFCOLLECTION, which allows you to administer collections programmatically in your own templates, as an alternative to using the ColdFusion Administrator. If you want your application to be able to create, delete, and maintain a collection on its own, the CFCOLLECTION tag is here to help.

This section may be especially interesting if you are developing pre-built applications that other people will deploy on their servers without your help, or if you are presented with a project where you want to completely remove any need for anyone to interact with the ColdFusion Administrator interface. For example, you could use CFCOLLECTION in a template that acted as a kind of setup script, creating the various files, registry entries, database tables, and Verity collections that your application need to operate.

Optimizing a Verity Collection

After a Verity collection gets hit many times, performance may start to degrade. Depending on your application, this may never become a problem. If you notice your Verity searches becoming slower over time, you may want to try optimizing your collection. Optimizing your collection is similar conceptually to running Disk Defragmenter on a Windows 95 machine.

There are two ways to optimize a collection: You can use the ColdFusion Administrator or create a ColdFusion template that uses the CFCOLLECTION tag to optimize the collection programmatically.

To optimize a collection with the ColdFusion Administrator, highlight the collection in the ColdFusion Administrator and click Optimize (see Figure 29.2). Verity whirs around for a minute or two as the collection is optimized. Because optimization can take some time—especially with large collections—it's best to optimize a collection during off-peak hours if possible.

To optimize a collection with the CFCOLLECTION tag, just include the tag in a simple ColdFusion template. The tag must include a ACTION="OPTIMIZE" parameter, and the collection name must be provided in the COLLECTION parameter. For instance, the code in Listing 29.21 can be used to optimize the HRDocs collection that was created earlier in this chapter.

 TIP You may find that you want to optimize your collections on a regular basis. You could schedule the template shown in Listing 29.21 to be automatically run once a week, for example, by using the ColdFusion scheduler (see Chapter 32).

Listing 29.21 OPTIMIZE.CFM—Optimizing a Collection with the CFCOLLECTION Tag

```
<!--- Optimize the Verity collection --->
<CFCOLLECTION
  ACTION="OPTIMIZE"
  COLLECTION="HRDocs">
```

```
<HTML>

<HEAD>
<TITLE>Optimizing Verity Collection</TITLE>
</HEAD>

<BODY>

<H2>Optimizing Complete</H2>
The HRDocs collection has been optimized successfully.

</BODY>

</HTML>
```

N O T E In previous versions of ColdFusion, the way to optimize a collection programmatically was to use ACTION="OPTIMIZE" in a CFINDEX tag. This use of CFINDEX is now deprecated. Instead, use ACTION="OPTIMIZE" in a CFCOLLECTION tag when coding for ColdFusion 4 and later. ▪

Repairing or Deleting a Collection

If for some reason Verity's internal index files for a collection become damaged, ColdFusion provides repairing functionality that makes it possible to get the collection back up and running quickly in most cases. It's quite likely that you will never need to repair a Verity collection. If you need to, use the CFCOLLECTION tag with ACTION="REPAIR". For instance, you could use the code shown in Listing 29.21—just change the ACTION parameter to REPAIR.

T I P You can also use the Repair button on the Verity page of the ColdFusion Administrator (see Figure 29.2) to repair a collection.

N O T E While a collection is being repaired, searches against the collection will not be able to take place. ▪

To delete a collection altogether, use the CFCOLLECTION tag with ACTION="DELETE". Again, you could use the basic code shown in Listing 29.21 by simply changing the ACTION to DELETE. Once the collection has been deleted, ColdFusion displays an error message if a CFSEARCH tag that uses that collection name is encountered. The collection name will no longer appear in the ColdFusion Administrator and Verity's index files will be removed from your server's hard drive. Note that only Verity's internal index files will be deleted, not the actual documents that had been made searchable by the collection.

T I P Alternatively, you could use the Delete button on the Verity page of the ColdFusion Administrator (see Figure 29.2) to delete the collection.

Creating a Collection Programmatically

The CFCOLLECTION tag can also be used to create a collection from scratch. Basically, you supply the same information to the tag as you would normally supply to the ColdFusion Administrator when creating a new collection there. Provide a name for the new collection in the tag's NAME parameter and provide the path for the new collection's internal index files with the PATH parameter.

Under most circumstances, you would supply the same path that appears by default in the ColdFusion Administrator, which would typically be c:\CFUSION\Verity\Collections\ on Windows platforms, as shown in Figure 29.3. Verity will create a new subfolder within the directory that you specify as the PATH.

Listing 29.22 demonstrates how to use CFCOLLECTION to create a new collection called MoreHRDocs.

N O T E If you have the ColdFusion International Search Pack installed on your ColdFusion server, you can also provide a LANGUAGE attribute to specify a language other than English. The languages that you can supply with the LANGUAGE attribute include German, French, Danish, Dutch, Italian, Norwegian, Portuguese, Spanish, and Swedish. ▪

Listing 29.22 CREATE.CFM—Creating a Collection with the CFCOLLECTION Tag

```
<!--- Create the Verity collection --->
<CFCOLLECTION
  ACTION="CREATE"
  COLLECTION="MoreHRDocs"
  PATH="c:\CFUSION\Verity\Collections\">

<HTML>

<HEAD>
<TITLE>Creating Verity Collection</TITLE>
</HEAD>

<BODY>

<H2>Collection Created</H2>
The MoreHRDocs collection has been created successfully.

</BODY>

</HTML>
```

N O T E Remember that the newly created collection cannot be searched yet, since no information has been indexed. You still need to use the CFINDEX tag—after the CFCOLLECTION tag—to index documents or data from your database tables, as discussed earlier in this chapter. ▪

If the collection already exists on another server in your local network, you can create a mapping to the existing collection, rather than creating a new one. This is useful when you are using several ColdFusion servers in a cluster, since only one copy of Verity's internal index files will need to be maintained.

To create the mapping, change the ACTION parameter in Listing 29.22 to MAP and provide a complete UNC-style path to the collection's folder on the other ColdFusion server. For instance, Listing 29.23 shows the code that you might use to create a mapping to the collection named HRDocs, which is on another machine named MAINSERVER (it's assumed that the Collections folder on the other server is available as a share called Collections). Note that you cannot use an URL in the PATH parameter—PATH cannot start with http:// to point to another server over the Internet.

TIP You can also create a mapping with the ColdFusion Administrator by using the Map an Existing Collection option when filling out the onscreen form for a new collection (see Figure 29.3).

Once the mapping has been created, you can use the HRDocs collection name normally in CFINDEX and CFSEARCH tags. The Verity engine installed on the local ColdFusion server does the indexing and searching work, but it accesses the index files that are located on the other ColdFusion server.

Listing 29.23 MAP.CFM—**Creating a Mapping to an Existing Collection on Another Server**

```
<!--- Create the Verity collection --->
<CFCOLLECTION
  ACTION="MAP"
  COLLECTION="HRDocs"
  PATH="\\MAINSERVER\Collections\HRDocs">

<HTML>

<HEAD>
<TITLE>Creating Verity Collection</TITLE>
</HEAD>

<BODY>

<H2>Collection Created</H2>
The HRDocs collection has been mapped successfully.

</BODY>

</HTML>
```

TIP Depending on how your local network is configured, you may have permissions issues to deal with before ColdFusion can access the files on the other server. On Windows NT, you may need to go to the Services applet in the Control Panel; there you adjust the Windows NT username that the Allaire ColdFusion service logs in as.

N O T E If you delete a collection that was created with ACTION="MAP", Verity's internal index files on the other ColdFusion server do not get deleted—only the mapping itself does. The same goes for collections that are created using the Map an Existing Collection option in the ColdFusion Administrator, as shown in Figure 29.3. ∎

Understanding Verity's Search Syntax

You've explored a number of ways to index information and make it searchable on the Web. You've also discovered using AND, OR, and wildcards, which make your search criteria work easier for you.

It doesn't stop at AND and OR. Verity practically provides a fairly rich set of operators that you can use in your search criteria. In general, don't expect that your users will be using these operators along with their keywords when they are running a search. Most people aren't going to go beyond ANDs and ORs. You may, in certain circumstances, want to use some of these operators behind the scenes. Table 29.7 lists all of the operators available by category. Refer to Appendix C for explanations of each of the operators listed in Table 29.7.

Table 29.7 Verity Operator Quick Reference

Category	Operator	Purpose	Description
Concept Operators	AND	To find *documents*:	all words/conditions are found
	OR		any one word/condition is found
Evidence Operators	STEM	To find *words* that:	are derived from the search words
	WORD		match the search words
	WILDCARD		match search words with *, ?, and so on.
Proximity Operators	NEAR	To find *words* that are:	close together
	NEAR/N		within N words of each other
	PARAGRAPH		in same paragraph
	PHRASE		in same phrase
	SENTENCE		in same sentence
Relational Operators	CONTAINS	To find *words* that are:	within a specific field
	MATCHES		the text of an entire field
	STARTS		at the start of a specific field
	ENDS		at the end of a specific field
	SUBSTRING		within a specific field as fragments
	=, <, >, <=, >=		(for numeric and date values only)

Category	Operator	Purpose	Description
Search Modifiers	CASE	To change Verity's behavior so that:	the search is case-sensitive
	MANY		documents are ranked by relevance
	NOT		matching documents should not be found
	ORDER		words must appear in documents in order
Score Operators	YESNO	To *rank* documents found:	equally (no ranking)
	COMPLEMENT		in reverse order
	PRODUCT		by pushing multiple hits up faster
	SUM		by pushing multiple hits up much faster

Directory Services

Understanding Directory Services

Directories are lists of objects, usually lists of users. Anyone who has ever logged in to a network or accessed email has used a directory service. The *directory service* is the directory of users, login names, passwords, and other information used to validate user account and logins.

In the past, network operating systems and applications maintained their own directories. Network administrators have grown accustomed to having to add new users to multiple databases, perhaps one for the network, another for an email account, another for remote access, and yet others for specific applications. Obviously, managing these directories is both difficult and time consuming. Administrators must make sure to make changes to all directories, just as users changing passwords must make the change in multiple locations to ensure that the passwords are kept in synch.

But this is all changing. Network administrators are now establishing corporate directories. These directories can store all sorts of information:

- User names and login information
- Passwords
- Locations and addresses
- Phone numbers and extensions
- Group affiliation
- Security and access information
- Binary data, such as pictures of employees
- Encryption keys

These new directories are accessible by multiple applications and, in an ideal environment, by all applications on a network. The centralized directory helps ensure that data is always accurate, current, and easily managed.

The directories themselves, and the tools used to manage them, are referred to as *directory services*. Examples of directory services include the following:

- Banyan StreetTalk
- Microsoft Active Directory (part of NT5)
- Microsoft Exchange (MAPI)
- Novell NDS (Novell Directory Services)
- X.500-compliant directories

These directories are more than simple address books, although they can be that too. Directory services are complete databases of users, objects, resources, security equivalencies, rights, and the tools with which to manage this information. Directory services are usually extremely security conscious and have built-in access controls and restrictions enabling the administrator to specify who has access to what information, and what they can do to it.

Understanding LDAP

A directory service is only useful if applications can take advantage of it, and while every one of the directory service products previously listed is a powerful and useable solution, interfacing with them has never been a trivial task.

For application developers to support these directory services, they'd have to write code specifically for each product, using each product's API. Supporting multiple APIs is time consuming and usually requires that the developer have a very good understanding of the directory service, so he can write code at as low a level as is required.

To solve this problem—and to facilitate simple and consistent directory service interaction—the Lightweight Directory Access Protocol (LDAP) was developed by the University of Michigan at Ann Arbor. LDAP is a slimmed-down version of DAP, the Directory Access Protocol of the international X.500 standard for directories.

LDAP has broad industry support. The list of vendors that have committed themselves to LDAP includes AT&T, Banyan, Hewlett Packard, IBM, Lotus, Microsoft, Netscape, and Novell. In addition, many of the public Internet directories, such as BigFoot, Four11, Switchboard, and WhoWhere?, have created LDAP interfaces for public use.

LDAP is a client/server directory access protocol that enables LDAP-compliant clients to communicate with LDAP-compliant servers. All of the directory service products previously listed are LDAP-compliant (or have add-ons or gateways that provide LDAP support). Users can simply point their address books to any directory, whether it's on a local machine, their corporate address book, or a public Internet directory.

LDAP hides the differences between directory services from the client application. All the client needs to know is the address (DNS name or IP address) of the LDAP server so that LDAP requests can be submitted to it. The same LDAP client software can talk to any LDAP-compliant server, and no special drivers are needed on the client side. The LDAP software of the server itself handles the translation between the native databases and LDAP.

To help understand this concept, think of LDAP as being to directory services as ODBC is to databases. LDAP allows clients to talk to a single interface, and thereby access many different directory service products. The big difference between LDAP and ODBC, however, is that ODBC requires that the client install different database drivers and know the type of database being accessed. LDAP places this requirement on the server; the client needs no knowledge of the underlying directory service.

▶ **See** Chapter 2, "Introduction to ColdFusion," for more information about DNS and IP address, **p. 17**.

▶ **See** Chapter 8, "Introduction to SQL," for more information about ODBC, **p. 129**.

LDAP is most frequently used to search directory services, but the LDAP protocol also provides the means to manage directories. Using LDAP, a single client application could be used to search, add to, update, and delete from a directory.

Many new applications are being turned into LDAP clients. Netscape Communicator 4, Microsoft Exchange 5, and Microsoft Internet Mail are examples of applications that can talk to

LDAP servers to access directory service information. Figure 30.1 shows the LDAP-driven user search feature in the Netscape Navigator 4 Address Book.

FIGURE 30.1

The Netscape Messenger Address Book uses LDAP to allow users to search public user directories.

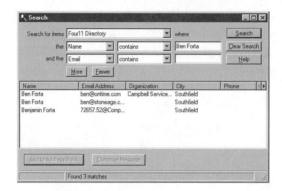

Keep in mind, however, that LDAP is a relatively new standard, and one that is still evolving. Not all LDAP servers and clients are created equally, and the ultimate goal of complete directory service independence has yet to be attained. In the short term, you probably need to familiarize yourself with the exact level of support provided by a specific LDAP server, paying close attention to the supported attributes (columns).

N O T E   Version 3 of LDAP is on the horizon. That version provides some of the key missing components that have prevented LDAP client from being totally server-independent. ColdFusion will support LDAP version 3 in the future. ■

Understanding <CFLDAP>

As mentioned earlier, directory services ideally need to be accessible by all network applications, and ColdFusion applications are no exception. ColdFusion developers often find themselves having to implement security systems, check passwords, determine email addresses, and more. All this information already exists if a directory service is already in place. All the ColdFusion developer needs is a mechanism with which to access this data.

This is where <CFLDAP> fits in. <CFLDAP> is the ColdFusion LDAP client tag. Yes, you read that right. <CFDLAP> encapsulates the entire LDAP client protocol and supporting code in a single, simple-to-use ColdFusion tag.

<CFLDAP> allows several different operations, specified using the ACTION attribute:

- ■ QUERY is used to browse or search a directory.
- ■ ADD is used to add records to a directory.
- ■ MODIFY and MODIFYDN are both used to update entries.
- ■ DELETE is used to remove data from a directory.

When used to retrieve data, <CFLDAP> returns data in the standard ColdFusion query format—into a query named as specified in the NAME attribute. This allows you to use standard query manipulation—including CFOUTPUT, CFTABLE, CFLOOP, CFMAIL, CFSELECT, CFGRID, and CFTREE—to display or process the data.

▶ **See** Chapter 11, "ColdFusion Basics," for more information about ColdFusion queries, **p. 191**.

▶ **See** Chapter 23, "Enhancing Forms with CCFORM," for more information about CFGRID and CFTREE, **p. 525**.

Retrieving Data with <CFLDAP>

The best way to learn how to use <CFLDAP> is to see examples. The first example uses <CFLDAP> to retrieve a list of employees whose last names are Smith (or begin with Smith).

The NAME attribute specifies the name of the query result set to be created, just like the NAME attribute in CFQUERY. The SERVER attribute specifies the DNS name of the LDAP server where the request is to be sent. As this is a query operation, the ACTION attribute is set to type QUERY. (Because ACTION="QUERY" is the default operation, this attribute could actually have been omitted). The ATTRIBUTES attribute specifies which LDAP attributes are to be returned. An LDAP attribute is kind of like a column in a database table. You must specify which columns, or attributes, you want returned to you whenever you query an LDAP server. This example requests the cn (common name or full name) attribute, and the email (URL) attribute. The attributes are specified as a comma-delimited list, and a column is created in the query for each attribute in the list. The SORT attribute specifies the sort order, and this example specifies that the data be sorted by common name (cn) in ascending (ASC) order. The final attribute is the required START, which specifies the actual search text.

The query results returned by <CFLDAP> are used to populate an unordered HTML list that displays the list of names and allows the user to click a name to send email to that employee.

```
<!--- Retrieve all employees named Smith --->
<CFLDAP
 NAME="Employees"
 SERVER="ldap.company.com"
 ACTION="QUERY"
 ATTRIBUTES="cn,email"
 SORT="cn ASC"
 START="cn=Smith"
>
<!--- Display list and create URL for mailto --->
<UL>
<CFOUTPUT QUERY= "">
<LI><A HREF=mailto:#email#>#cn#</A>
</CFOUTPUT>
</UL>
```

As this example demonstrates, ColdFusion makes interacting with a LDAP server simple and convenient.

Part

IV

Ch

30

Using <CFLDAP>

Now that you have seen what <CFLDAP> can do, take a look at the complete set of tag attributes shown in Table 30.1.

Table 30.1 <CFLDAP> **Attributes Description**

Name	Status	Description
ACTION	Required	Must be either ADD, DELETE, MODIFY, MODIFYDN, or QUERY.
ATTRIBUTES	Required	(Required if ACTION="QUERY", ACTION="ADD", or ACTION="MODIFY") Comma-delimited list of columns to be returned or updated. If ACTION="QUERY", the query result set contains a column for each entry in this list.
DN	Required	(Required if ACTION="ADD", ACTION="DELETE", ACTION="MODIFY", or ACTION="MODIFYDN") "distinguished name" of the entry to be changed. The "distinguished name" is the LDAP equivalent of a database table's primary key. A "distinguished name" uniquely identifies an entry in a directory.
FILTER	Optional	Filter to be used when querying data. May contain one or more conditions in a comma-delimited list in the format of attribute=filter, attribute=filter. If no FILTER is specified, all entries are returned.
MAXROWS	Optional	Maximum number of rows to be returned by CFLDAP. Note that many LDAP servers impose their own maximum that cannot be overridden. Similar to the <CFQUERY> MAXROWS attribute.
NAME	Required	(Required only if ACTION="QUERY") Name of the query result set to be created by CFLDAP. The query will contain the columns specified in the ATTRIBUTES attribute.
PASSWORD	Optional	Password to be used if a USERNAME is provided.
PORT	Optional	Port number that the LDAP server responds to. Defaults to 389 if not specified. (This attribute is rarely needed.)
SCOPE	Optional	Search scope used when "ACTION=QUERY". There are three possible values: ONELEVEL searches all entries one level beneath the entry specified in the Start attribute (the default value); BASE searches only the entry specified in the Start attribute; SUBTREE searches the entry specified in the Start attribute, as well all entries at all levels beneath it.
SERVER	Required	DNS name or IP address of the LDAP server to which the request is to be sent.

Name	Status	Description
SORT	Optional	Attribute to sort query results by. If specified, the attribute must be one of those listed in the ATTRIBUTES attribute. The column may be followed by the keyword ASC to sort ascending, or DESC to sort descending. If neither ASC nor DESC are specified, the column will be sorted in ascending order.
START	Required	(Required only if ACTION="QUERY") Search conditions. May contain one or more attributes in a comma-delimited list in the format of attribute=value, attribute=value.
TIMEOUT	Optional	Operation timeout value. Will default to 60 seconds if not specified. (60 seconds is more than enough time for most operations on most LDAP servers.)
USERNAME	Optional	Username to be used to log on to the LDAP server. If no name is specified, an anonymous login is used. LDAP servers are often configured to allow different levels of access (for both requesting data and changing data) based on login. Note that some LDAP servers deny anonymous login attempts; ask your network administrator for login details. All public Internet LDAP servers allow basic data retrieval via anonymous login.

Accessing Public LDAP Servers

As mentioned earlier, many of the public Internet directories have LDAP interfaces that you may freely access. Table 30.2 lists some of the more popular directories that support LDAP, their home pages, and their LDAP server names.

Table 30.2   Public LDAP Servers

Service	Homepage	LDAP Server
BigFoot	http://www.bigfoot.com	ldap.bigfoot.com
Four11	http://www.four11.com	ldap.four11.com
InfoSpace	http://www.infospace.com	ldap.infospace.com
Switchboard	http://www.switchboard.com	ldap.switchboard.com
WhoWhere?	http://www.whowhere.com	ldap.whowhere.com

To access any of these directories via <CFLDAP>, all you need is the name of that LDAP server. All of these services allow querying via anonymous login, so no login name and password are required.

Creating an LDAP Client

To demonstrate working with LDAP, take a look at a sample application. The A2Z Contact Lookup is designed to be used by customer service or support personnel, allowing them to try to locate names on any of five public user directories.

Figure 30.2 shows the search screen. The interface allows you to enter a name (or part thereof) and select a server from the list of available LDAP servers. Figure 30.3 shows the formatted returned results.

FIGURE 30.2

Many of the major online user directories support public LDAP lookups.

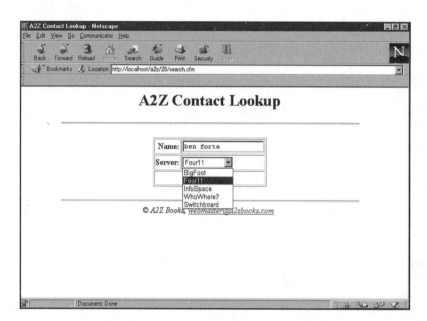

The application is made up of five files:

> HEADER.CFM is the header file shared by both the search and results screens.
>
> FOOTER.CFM is the footer file shared by both the search and results screens.
>
> SERVERS.CFM contains the list of available servers.
>
> SEARCH.CFM is the search screen, with a drop-down list of servers dynamically driven by the server list in SERVERS.CFM.
>
> RESULTS.CFM performs the actual LDAP lookup and displays the results.

See Chapter 21, "Advanced ColdFusion Templates," for more information about sharing common code using <CFINCLUDE>.

Creating the Services List

The list of servers is stored in SERVERS.CFM, shown in Listing 30.1.

FIGURE 30.3

The attributes (information) returned by each LDAP server may differ from one server to the next.

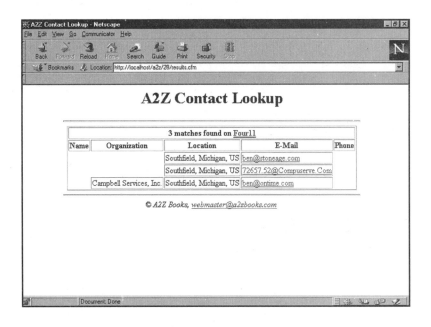

On the CD

Listing 30.1 `C:\A2Z\SCRIPTS\28\SERVERS.CFM`—**Source for SERVERS.CFM File**

```
<!--- Array columns --->
<CFSET LDAPService = 1>
<CFSET LDAPServer = 2>
<CFSET LDAPHome = 3>

<!--- Two dimensional array to hold servers --->
<CFSET Servers = ArrayNew(2)>

<!--- Number of services available --->
<CFSET ServiceCount = 0>

<!--- Add BigFoot to array --->
<CFSET ServiceCount = ServiceCount + 1>
<CFSET Servers[ServiceCount][LDAPService] = "BigFoot">
<CFSET Servers[ServiceCount][LDAPServer] = "ldap.bigfoot.com">
<CFSET Servers[ServiceCount][LDAPHome] = "http://www.bigfoot.com">

<!--- Add Four11 to array --->
<CFSET ServiceCount = ServiceCount + 1>
<CFSET Servers[ServiceCount][LDAPService] = "Four11">
<CFSET Servers[ServiceCount][LDAPServer] = "ldap.four11.com">
<CFSET Servers[ServiceCount][LDAPHome] = "http://www.four11.com">

<!--- Add InfoSpace to array --->
<CFSET ServiceCount = ServiceCount + 1>
<CFSET Servers[ServiceCount][LDAPService] = "InfoSpace">
```

continues

Listing 30.1   Continued

```
<CFSET Servers[ServiceCount][LDAPServer] = "ldap.infospace.com">
<CFSET Servers[ServiceCount][LDAPHome] = "http://www.infospace.com">

<!--- Add WhoWhere? to array --->
<CFSET ServiceCount = ServiceCount + 1>
<CFSET Servers[ServiceCount][LDAPService] = "WhoWhere?">
<CFSET Servers[ServiceCount][LDAPServer] = "ldap.whowhere.com">
<CFSET Servers[ServiceCount][LDAPHome] = "http://www.whowhere.com">

<!--- Add Switchboard to array --->
<CFSET ServiceCount = ServiceCount + 1>
<CFSET Servers[ServiceCount][LDAPService] = "Switchboard">
<CFSET Servers[ServiceCount][LDAPServer] = "ldap.switchboard.com">
<CFSET Servers[ServiceCount][LDAPHome] = "http://www.switchboard.com">
```

As you can see, the servers are stored in an *array*, a special type of variable that allows you to store sets of grouped data. The array being used here is two dimensional, kind of like a two-dimensional grid, created with this code:

```
<CFSET Servers = ArrayNew(2)>
```

This creates an array called `Servers` with two dimensions. (You can think of a two-dimensional array as having rows and columns, making up the two dimensions.)

As servers are added to the array, rows are automatically added. The following code sets the first column (LDAPServer is set to 1) of the first row to `Four 11`. (ServiceCount equals 1 for the first row.)

```
<CFSET Servers[ServiceCount][LDAPService] = "Four11">
```

While this might seem overly complex, you are in fact creating something that looks like a ColdFusion query, but is more flexible and dynamic. Once the SERVERS.CFM has been processed, a fully populated array will exist ready for use in both the search and results templates.

▶ **See** "Array Manipulation Functions" for more information about arrays, **p. 910**.

Creating the Search Screen

The code for the search screen itself, shown in Listing 30.2, is much like any of the forms you have created until now. `<CFINCLUDE>` tags are used to include the common headers and footers, and the SERVERS.CFM file.

On the CD

Listing 30.2   C:\A2Z\SCRIPTS\28\SEARCH.CFM—**Code for** SEARCH.CFM
File

```
<!--- Include LDAP server list --->
<CFINCLUDE TEMPLATE="servers.cfm">

<!--- Include page header --->
<CFINCLUDE TEMPLATE="header.cfm">
```

```
<CENTER>

<!--- Search form --->
<FORM ACTION="results.cfm" METHOD="POST">

<TABLE BORDER>

<TR>
 <!--- Name to search for --->
 <TH ALIGN="RIGHT">Name:</TH>
 <TD><INPUT TYPE="text" NAME="name"></TD>
</TR>
<TR>
 <!--- Server to search --->
 <TH ALIGN="RIGHT">Server:</TH>
 <TD>
  <!--- Dynamically build server list from server array --->
  <SELECT NAME="server">
   <CFLOOP INDEX="service" FROM="1" TO="#ArrayLen(Servers)#">
    <CFOUTPUT><OPTION VALUE="#service#">#Servers[service][LDAPService]
    ➥#</CFOUTPUT>
   </CFLOOP>
  </SELECT>
 </TD>
</TR>
<TR>
 <TH COLSPAN=2><INPUT TYPE="submit" VALUE="Search"></TH>
</TR>

</TABLE>

</FORM>

</CENTER>

<!--- Include page footer --->
<CFINCLUDE TEMPLATE="footer.cfm">
```

The SELECT box for the server selection is populated via a <CFLOOP>, using this code:

```
<CFLOOP INDEX="service" FROM="1" TO="#ArrayLen(Servers)#">
```

This creates a loop that loops through from 1 to the length of the array; in this case it is 5. Each time the loop repeats, a variable called "service" contains the current service number. It is 1 the first time, then 2, and so on.

The SELECT box OPTION tags are populated using this code:

```
<OPTION VALUE="#service#">#Servers[service][LDAPService]#
```

The #service# variable is replaced by the current service number (the loop counter). The displayed text is the service name. For the first item in the list, the code #Servers[service][LDAPService]# becomes #Servers[1][1]#, referring to first column of the first row, which as the value "BigFoot".

The end result is the screen shown in Figure 30.2.

Creating the Results Screen

Now look at the results screen, the code for which is in Listing 30.3.

On the CD

Listing 30.3   C:\A2Z\SCRIPTS\28\RESULTS.CFM—Code for RESULTS.CFM File

```
<!--- Include LDAP server list --->
<CFINCLUDE TEMPLATE="servers.cfm">

<!--- Perform LDAP lookup using passed server info --->
<CFLDAP
 SERVER="#Servers[server][LDAPServer]#"
 ACTION="QUERY"
 NAME="results"
 START="cn=#name#,c=US"
 FILTER="(cn=#name#)"
 ATTRIBUTES="cn,o,l,st,c,mail,telephonenumber"
 SORT="cn ASC"
>

<!--- Include page header --->
<CFINCLUDE TEMPLATE="header.cfm">

<!--- Display results --->
<CENTER>

<TABLE BORDER>
 <TR>
  <TH COLSPAN=5><CFOUTPUT>#results.RecordCount# matches found on <A
HREF="#Servers[server][LDAPHome]#">#Servers[server][LDAPService]#</A>
➥</CFOUTPUT></TH>
 </TR>
 <TR>
  <TH>Name</TH>
  <TH>Organization</TH>
  <TH>Location</TH>
  <TH>E-Mail</TH>
  <TH>Phone</TH>
 </TR>
<CFOUTPUT QUERY="results">
 <TR>
  <TD>#Trim(cn)#</TD>
  <TD>#Trim(o)#</TD>
  <TD>#Trim(l)#, #Trim(st)#, #Trim#</TD>
  <TD><A HREF="mailto:#Trim(mail)#">#Trim(mail)#</A></TD>
  <TD>#Trim(telephonenumber)#</TD>
 </TR>
</CFOUTPUT>
</TABLE>

</CENTER>

<!--- Include page footer --->
<CFINCLUDE TEMPLATE="footer.cfm">
```

Once again, this file uses <CFINCLUDE> to include the header, footer, and services files.

Then comes the LDAP call itself:

```
<!--- Perform LDAP lookup using passed server info --->
<CFLDAP
 SERVER="#Servers[server][LDAPServer]#"
 ACTION="QUERY"
 NAME="results"
 START="cn=#name#,c=US"
 FILTER="(cn=#name#)"
 ATTRIBUTES="cn,o,l,st,c,mail,telephonenumber"
 SORT="cn ASC"
>
```

The SERVER attribute is passed the name of the LDAP server as extracted from the servers array. The variable "server" contains the "row number" of the server that was selected in the SEARCH.CFM file.

As you want to perform a search, the ACTION is set to "QUERY" and the NAME attribute is used to provide the name of the query to be created.

The START and FILTER attributes specify the search to perform, using the "name" field submitted from the SEARCH.CFM screen.

ATTRIBUTES lists the columns that you want returned. The query that will be created by <CFLDAP> (the query named in the QUERY attribute) will have a column for each attribute listed here. Not all columns will have data—many will be empty.

The SORT attribute specifies the sort order for the data. The value "cn ASC" specifies that the data should be sorted by common name (full name) in ascending order.

The rest of the code should be very familiar by now. A <CFOUTPUT> block is used to display the results, and the output screen will look something like the one shown in Figure 30.3.

Adding, Modifying, and Deleting LDAP Entries

While LDAP is mostly used to retrieve data from directory services, it also provides the mechanisms to perform entry administration. Adding, modifying, and deleting entries is fully supported by <CFLDAP>.

Directory service entry manipulation is almost never allowed via an anonymous login. You need a login name and password to perform these functions. In addition, many directories are set up so that different levels of access are granted to different login names. Your network administrator should be able to provide you with login information if it is required.

When directly manipulating directory service entries, that entry's unique ID must be known. In LDAP terms this is known as the dn attribute, or the *distinguished name*. This is usually a comma-delimited list of attributes (containing, at minimum, the country, organization, and name) that together uniquely identity a specific entry. It is good practice to use LDAP to retrieve the dn attribute of the entry to be changed or deleted so that that same value may be passed for the MODIFY or DELETE operation.

When adding or modifying entries, the ATTRIBUTES attribute must be used to specify the list of attributes be set or altered, in addition to their values.

N O T E   University of Michigan at Ann Arbor is the birthplace of LDAP and is home to some of the most comprehensive information about the protocol can be found at http://www.umich.edu/~dirsvcs/ldap. ▨

Version Control

Using Revisions Control

Developing a ColdFusion application requires many different file versions to be integrated into the completed project. In development, a file may need to be changed several times, and keeping track of what was changed and by whom can become complicated. Version control systems provide a solution to this common problem by tracking changes made to any files and organizing projects in a single place.

You may develop your own version control system as you develop applications. Many developers save copies of a project into several different folders, while others rename older files in case they need to fall back to a previous version of code. Version 2.0 source control software is included with the ColdFusion Studio development environment and makes keeping track of your project intuitive and easy.

You may have tried experimental code in some of your files when developing an application or Web site, only to find yourself reverting to a previous version. Even worse, you may have spent hours on a file only to find it has been corrupted by some malevolent system gremlin. Version control keeps previous versions of your files in a safe place along with critical information about what has been changed, when it was changed, and by whom it was changed. Without a version control system, it may be difficult to figure out which file is the correct file to use, especially in a large project or a project that involves multiple developers.

Version control systems also help organize a project, keeping all related files in one place. Images, templates, notes, and specifications can be kept together, along with previous versions of all files in a project and a record of all changes. Security is also enhanced by version control systems, as all files can be protected by a password and all accesses can be recorded.

Version control systems also allow developers in disparate locations work together in a coordinated manner. Tasks in the development of an application can be assigned, and developers can only access files pertinent to their tasks. Project managers can more easily track the progress of development and better manage resources and time.

Understanding Version Control

An understanding of version control terminology will help you more quickly grasp how version control systems work. Definitions for frequently used terms are listed in Table 31.1.

Table 31.1   Version Control Terms

Term	Definition
Administrator	The project manager. By default, the creator of the project. Manages all settings, team members, and milestones.
Audit log	Contains audit entries detailing every action taken during the development of a project. These entries form the audit trail, which is used to track project modifications.

Term	Definition
Build	The act of gathering, linking, and assembling all necessary files to create an application. Also designating the completion of a step in the development of a project. When a build is specified, a set of non-permanent files is created and labeled with the name of the build.
Check out	The modification process begins with a team member checking out a file. This action creates a working copy of the file and logs an entry in the audit log. A lock is also placed on the file (*see* Lock).
Check in	Similar to saving a file, checking in occurs when a team member relinquishes control of a file. When a file is checked in, the new version of the file is stored in the vault, along with information about the file in the database. The lock is removed.
Database	The database in which information about the project, subprojects, team members, project files, and version information is stored.
Label	When a milestone or build is designated, a title or description is assigned to all files in the current version.
Lock	A file that is checked out cannot be modified by another team member and is considered locked until an administrator breaks the lock or the user who checked out the file checks it back in. Locks can be designated read only so that other team members can view the file as necessary.
Milestone	An event in project development that represents a major step toward completion. Designation of a milestone creates a set of permanent versions of files with the label of the milestone. Milestones can be alpha, beta, or final releases of products or any other significant step in progress.
Non-permanent version	A version of a file that is not part of a set of permanent version files and can be automatically deleted when the maximum number of non-permanent versions is reached or when the file is purged.
Permanent version	When a project file version is designated a permanent version. This file cannot be purged or removed automatically when the maximum number of non-permanent versions is reached. The project file must be locked to be deleted or designated non-permanent.
Project	A set of related files that compose an application and its documentation, images, and other files. Also includes all subprojects linked to it.
Project file	A file that is part of a project or subproject and is referenced in the database.
Purge	The deletion of non–permanent file versions. The last checked-in version and any permanent versions cannot be purged. A file must be locked to be purged.
Subproject	A subset of files within a project that are related.

Part

IV

Ch

31

continues

Table 31.1 Continued

Term	Definition
Team	All developers involved in the creation of an application.
Vault	Directory where all versions of all project files are stored. The vault can be compressed for efficient use of disk space and increased performance.
Working directory	Directory in which current versions of all checked-out files are stored. Can be determined by the team member or mandated by the administrator.

Your application or Web site is organized into a project, and usually subprojects. The overall application is the *project*, while *subprojects* contain components of the larger project. Images, documentation, and project subdirectories are all good candidates for subprojects. The developers working on a project and its subprojects are called the *team* and a project *administrator* manages the team.

The project administrator decides how a project is structured and how it progresses; he or she also manages access to project files, designates milestones, and oversees and audits the project. Information about project files, version history, team members, and milestones is stored in the project database. The vault is stored with the project database and contains all files that are a part of the project.

When a team member requires access to a project file, it is noted in the audit log. The audit log tracks all actions taken by team members. Once noted, the file is checked out and a copy is stored in a working directory. Checking a file out places a lock on it so no other members can modify the file until it is checked in or the lock is broken. Only an administrator or the team member who created the lock can break a lock placed on a file by another team member. When the modifications are completed, the project file is checked in and any working copies can be deleted. The system stores the latest version of the file, along with auditing data, including who modified the file and when it was modified. Difference data describing changes from the last saved version is also usually stored in the system at this time.

When a project milestone is reached, the administrator can designate this milestone and label the file versions with relevant information. A *build* or *permanent* version can also be designated, and non-permanent versions can be retained or purged.

Now that you have an understanding of version control, see these concepts in action as you create a project using Versions 2.0.

Using Versions 2.0

The version-control interface in ColdFusion Studio makes working with version control software fast and painless. Using this interface eliminates many of the steps required to create a project and makes checking files in and out virtually transparent to team members. To fully understand how the ColdFusion Studio version-control interface works and to better manage your projects, it is good to know some of the basics of using the Versions 2.0 software.

Planning Your Project

The first step in version control is deciding what your needs are. To properly create a project, you must first answer a few basic questions:

- Is this a single project or does this project require the use of subprojects?

  Most ColdFusion applications and Web sites use subdirectories that accomplish certain functions, such as an images or administration directory. Documentation, notes, and project specifications are also involved with most. These are all perfect candidates for subprojects. If you are developing a small project with no images, notes, or other related material, subprojects may not be useful to you.

- How many people are in my team, and how is my team structured?

  If more than one person is working on a project, each person's tasks should be analyzed. Decide what portions of the project each person requires access to.

- Where will the files be stored?

  A network-accessible directory must be chosen to store both the project database and the project vault. Choose a directory where the working copies of the project and subprojects will reside, or if each team member will choose a directory on his own machine. Decide if compression is to be used with your project.

- Are security and auditing required?

  It is a good idea to use security and auditing by default. Enabling security requires all team members to enter a password before gaining access to a project. This also limits the actions non-administrators can perform. Only a project administrator can create a subproject, delete files, modify project properties, change version information for a file, open locks, and designate permanent versions, milestones, builds, and non-permanent versions. Restricting these actions can save much frustration in the long run.

  Auditing records all actions taken by any team member on any file, project, or subproject. This is useful in tracking completed work and who is working on what items. It can also help you track bugs and changes. Auditing is a must in developing any project.

Creating a Project in Versions 2.0

To create a new project in Versions 2.0, complete the following steps:

1. Create a working directory. Create a directory on your C: drive named `Projects`.
2. Create a subdirectory in `C:\Projects` called `myproject`.
3. Copy some ColdFusion templates into this directory, such as the example application from Chapter 28, "Working with Files and Directories." This set of files becomes the new project.
4. From the Start menu, choose Programs, Versions 2.0. Click the Versions icon to start the Versions 2.0 software.

Part
IV

Ch
31

5. In Versions, create a new project from the Project menu by selecting New.

6. The New Project dialog box appears, as shown in Figure 31.1. Fill in the options in the dialog box.

You are prompted for a name for your new project. Project names must not contain forward slashes (/), backslashes (\), or exclamation marks (!) and can be up to 228 characters long. Enter My New Project.

FIGURE 31.1

Creating a new project in Versions 2.0.

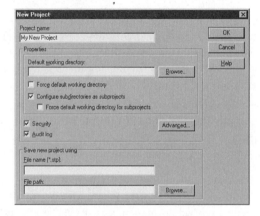

Choose a default working directory either by typing in the path you chose for your working directory, or by selecting a path using the Browse button.

If you want to require all team members to use this directory as their default, check the Force Default Working Directory box. This option applies to the team members' individual workstations. For instance, if you choose C:\Projects\myproject as the working directory, each team member will use C:\Projects\myproject on his or her workstation as the working directory, not on the machine where the project is created. Leaving this box unchecked allows team members to choose their own working directory. For this project, allow team members to choose their own working directory.

Your test project may contain subprojects in the future, so check the Configure Subdirectories as Subprojects box to cause Versions to create new subprojects for any of your working directory's subdirectories.

The Force Default Working Directory for Subprojects box, when checked, forces team members to use subproject directories within the default working directory. This box is only active if Configure Subdirectories as Subprojects is checked. Check this box to keep a consistent directory structure for your project for all team members.

The Security check box, when checked, forces all team members to use a password when accessing the project. Checking this box also limits the actions team members can perform and delegates these actions to the authority of the administrator. Check this box to make your project secure. Checking the Audit Log box causes Versions to log all actions taken on a project by team members. Check both boxes (Security and Audit Log) to create an audit trail for your project.

The Save New Project Using section defines the filename (myproject.stp) and file path for your new project's database. All Versions 2.0 project database files must have the filename extension .stp. Choose the path under which the database and project vault will be stored. The database can't reside in the same directory as the project itself, so choose C:\Projects. The project database must be in a location that is network accessible to all team members for this project.

Clicking the Advanced Project Settings button allows you to configure additional project options. The Advanced Project Settings dialog box appears, as shown in Figure 31.2. This dialog box is organized into four tabs: Defaults, Commands, Exclude, and Description.

FIGURE 31.2
Advanced project
options in Versions 2.0.

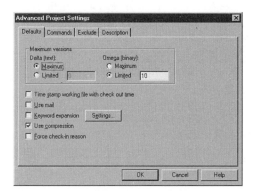

The Defaults tab sets project defaults for files. Maximum versions allows you to set the maximum number of previous versions that are retained for Delta (text, HTML, non-encrypted ColdFusion templates) and Omega (encrypted ColdFusion templates, executables, and other binary files) files. Setting the limit to Maximum retains up to 32,767 previous versions of any file, depending on disk space. For this project, click the Time Stamp Working File with Check Out Time to create an easy way to tell the last time of modification. Click OK in this dialog box, and click OK in the New Project dialog box.

Versions will now ask you for a user profile. Enter a username, your full name, and a password; click OK. Your project has been created!

Using ColdFusion Studio Source Control Integration

Now that you know the specifics of creating a project in Versions 2.0, use ColdFusion Studio's source control integration to create and manage a project. ColdFusion Studio's source control integration simplifies project management by giving you one set of controls that can be used with any software that's compliant with source-code control (SCC). SCC-compliant software packages include Versions 2.0, Microsoft Visual SourceSafe, and Intersolv PVCS.

ColdFusion Studio source control commands allow you to perform the following tasks with any SCC-compliant software:

- Create a new project.
- Add new files.
- Remove files.
- Check in files.
- Check out files.
- Get the latest version of a file and copy it, leaving the file checked in.
- Open the source control software.

With these basic commands, most day-to-day tasks can be completed without exiting the ColdFusion Studio environment; that way you can spend more time in development and less time in project management.

Creating a Project in ColdFusion Studio

Source control in ColdFusion Studio is project-based, so source control can only be used while working with an existing project. For more information using ColdFusion Studio, see Chapter 10, "Introduction to ColdFusion Studio."

First you need to create a ColdFusion Studio project. Complete the following steps:

1. In ColdFusion Studio, click the Projects tab in the Resource dialog box.
2. Click the new project icon (the wand with stars); the Project Wizard dialog box appears.
3. Create a project from an existing directory structure by entering My New Project in the Project Name field. Choose a directory that has an existing application as shown in Figure 31.3. Check Include Sub-Folders to recurse the application's full directory structure.
4. Click Next, Finish. Your project is now created in ColdFusion Studio.

FIGURE 31.3

Creating a project in ColdFusion Studio.

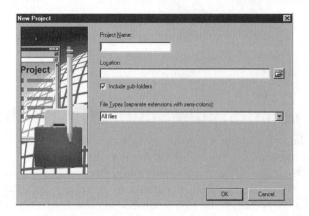

Now that you have a project, add this project to source control:

1. Select My New Project from the projects list; then right-click My New Project in the Projects pane.

2. Choose Add Project to Source Control from the Context menu. ColdFusion Studio asks you to specify a project for source code control. It is important to remember that source control projects are actually managed by your source control software, and are not the same as ColdFusion Studio projects. Either you can use an existing source control project or a new source control project can be created now. For now, use the project you created earlier in the chapter.

3. Click Open and the Select a Versions Project File For dialog box appears, as shown in Figure 31.4. Navigate to the C:\Projects directory and select myproject.stp.

4. Click Open to reveal the Log On dialog box. Enter the password you chose earlier in the chapter and click OK. The ColdFusion Studio project is added to your source control project.

FIGURE 31.4

Adding a project to an existing source control project.

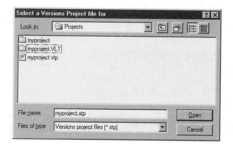

ColdFusion Studio's source control integration can also create a new source control project, saving you the step of creating it beforehand. First create a new ColdFusion Studio project as you did before. Once the project has been created, right-click the name of the project and select Add Project to Source Control. When you are asked to specify the project for source code control, click New. Does the dialog box in Figure 31.5 look familiar? You now see the New Project dialog box from Versions 2.0 (or your SCC-compliant application). Now you can create a new project using the techniques you learned earlier in the chapter. You didn't even have to open your source control application.

Adding Files to Source Control

Now that you've created projects in both ColdFusion Studio and your source control application, files in the project can be added to source control. To add files to source control, complete the following steps:

1. Select the file or files in your project that you want to add.

2. Right-click your selection, choose Source Control, Add to Source Control.

FIGURE 31.5

Adding a project to a new source control project.

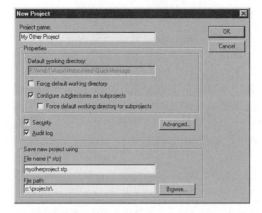

3. The Add Files dialog box appears with a list of all the files selected (see Figure 31.6). Make sure the box to the left of each file is checked. If you would like to use the files immediately, select Check Out Immediately.

4. Click OK; the files are now added to source control.

FIGURE 31.6

The selected files.

Managing Files in Source Control

The files in your project are now under source control management, and your source control application is now tracking your project's files in the background. This means you no longer can immediately open a file to edit—all files under source control must either be checked out or copied first. You can easily tell which files in your project are checked out by noting whether there is a small green check next to the filename, as shown in Figure 31.7. If it is present, the file is checked out by you and is available for editing. Double-clicking this file immediately opens it.

If a file is not checked out, there are two ways to check a file out from the file list:

FIGURE 31.7

Determining whether a file is checked out.

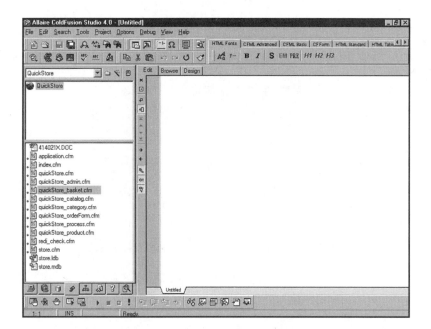

- The first method is to double-click the filename as you would when opening it. You are prompted to choose how you would like to open the file, as shown in Figure 31.8. Choosing Open It As Read-Only opens a read-only copy of the version of the selected file as stored in your working directory. If other team members are involved in this project, this version may not be the most current version. Selecting Get the Latest Copy From Source Control and Open It as Read-Only makes a copy of the most recent version of the file. Neither of these selections allows you to modify the file, so the best choice is Check It Out of Source Control (see Figure 31.8). This gives you exclusive access to the file.

  Another method of checking out a file is to right-click the file you want to check out, select Source Control from the Context menu, and then choose Check Out. If another user has not checked the file out, it is checked out immediately.

FIGURE 31.8

Checking a file out of source control.

It is a very good idea to check the file back in once it has been modified. This updates the version history for the file, adds entries to the audit log, and makes the file available to other team members. To check in a file, first save any changes you have made as you normally would. Right-click the file you want to check in, select Source Control from the Context menu, and choose Check In. You'll see the Check In Files dialog box pictured in Figure 31.9. Make sure the box next to the file you are checking in is selected and then click OK.

FIGURE 31.9

Checking a file in to source control.

You can also get additional information about your files—such as what changes have been made to them and to whom they are checked out—by right-clicking a file and choosing History. This dialog box lists what happened each time a file was checked in. To use source control features such as milestones, you need to open Versions itself. To do this easily, right-click a file and choose Source Control, Launch Source Control Application. This launches Versions with the current project open, allowing you to mark milestones and access other source control functions. ●

Event Scheduling

Scheduling Template Execution

One of the most awaited ColdFusion features is the capability to schedule template execution. Ever since the product's first release, people have been finding ways to set a template to run at specific times. With the release of ColdFusion 3.1, this feature was not only given to programmers, but several features were added, making it exceptionally well received. The capability to use the Administrator for clean control of scheduled tasks, the capability to program tasks from a template as well as from the Administrator, and the capability to have static pages generated from any task made this feature the pride of the 3.1 release. While ColdFusion 4 has done little to enhance the basic nature of this tag, some of the underlying functionality has been altered.

N O T E In ColdFusion 3.1, scheduling was only supported in the server version of the product. With the release of 4, all levels of ColdFusion support scheduling. ■

Understanding Scheduled Tasks

The CFSCHEDULE tag allows a programmer to execute a page to take place anytime from now to a specific point in the future. You can set a template to be run once at a specific time, continually with a set interval, with a specific time limit, or with any combination of these features.

Events are currently limited to calls to a Web page by CFHTTP. While this may seem like a limitation, there's almost no limit to what can actually be done with this. Despite how it looks, this does not mean that you are limited to pages on your own site. One of this tag's best features is that it allows you to call any Web page from anywhere and even save it to a physical file on your server. Combine this with using any of ColdFusion's capabilities in the called template and the sky's the limit.

Creating a Scheduled Task

As mentioned, there are two ways to create, run, and delete scheduled tasks. The first is to use the programmed interface provided by the ColdFusion Administrator. The major advantage to this is that it also gives you a list of all scheduled tasks. The disadvantage is that anyone who wants to set a scheduled task must have access to the Administrator. Luckily, you have an additional way to create scheduled tasks—code a task directly into a page that must be saved and executed in order to be recognized by the CFSCHEDULE service. This allows for a more customized interface and access for all, but does not include the list of tasks that already exist. Any task set this way need only be set once to be recognized by the scheduler. Additional executions of a task scheduling tag simply replace the previous tasks.

There is actually a third way of setting a scheduled event, but it's not a suggested method; go into the system registry and add, alter, or delete tasks directly. While I don't suggest doing this for tasks, there is a reason for going into the registry.

When a scheduled event is set, it is not recognized by the system until a certain interval is passed. This interval, shown in Figure 32.1, determines how often the scheduling service checks the scheduled task list for a new entry. When the service refreshes, the new (or modified) task is added to the list of tasks to do and are checked every minute for execution.

FIGURE 32.1

The Administrator page shows the schedule refresh interval.

The registry entry for this value is slightly different. This interval is set in the key called CheckInterval in the HKEY_LOCAL_MACHINE\SOFTWARE\Allaire\ColdFusion\CurrentVersion\ Schedule path. This entry has a default value of 3600, which is the number of seconds in an hour. Even though ColdFusion deals with intervals in a minute format, the entry in the registry is in a second format. You can alter this interval to any number, but it's suggested you not change it as a normal practice. One trick is to set your scheduled event, set the refresh interval to 1 minute, wait the time for it to be read, and then reset it to 60 minutes. This causes all of the new events to be read from the registry into the ColdFusion scheduling engine immediately. While the overhead of reading the scheduled events into the engine is miniscule, it is a good idea to keep the refresh rate high and to lower it only when new events are added. Stopping and restarting the ColdFusion service also resets the refresh counter, but is a bit more drastic than is necessary.

Using the Administrator to Create Tasks

The Administrator's scheduler section starts with a rundown of all the scheduled tasks that exist, what operation they are performing (currently limited to HTTP requests), when they will start and end, and the interval between each execution (see Figure 32.2). This information allows you to keep a good handle on your timed tasks and edit them when necessary.

To create a task, all you have to do is enter a name for it, select an operation, and press the Add New Task button (see Figure 32.3).

Part

IV

Ch

32

FIGURE 32.2

This is an Administrator list of all scheduled tasks.

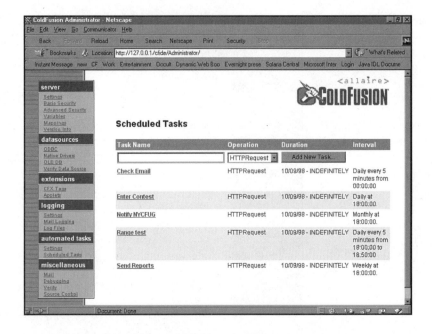

FIGURE 32.3

The Administrator screen shows a specific task.

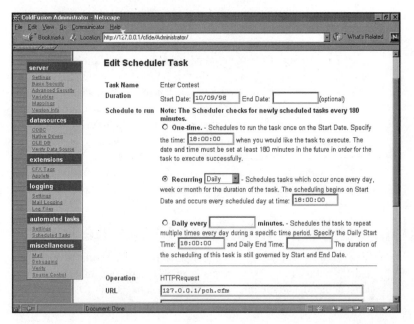

The resulting page is where you do all of your work when creating a new scheduled task. The start date and time defaults to the current date and time and usually isn't changed unless you want an action that starts on a future date. The end date is used to set a limit on how long your operation will run. Operations can be set for either a single use at a specific time, a recurring time every day, week, or month, or a recurring time in a single day.

An operation set for a one-time run is executed once and never again. The execution does not erase this operation's record, but it cannot be used again unless the time is reset. Actually, if no end date is set, it results in an operation that runs once a year. Operations set to daily, weekly, or monthly simply run once in the desired time period until the end date is reached, or forever if none is set. Daily events are a bit different than the other events. If an event is set with no end time, it simply runs every x number of minutes until the end date, or forever if none is set. This is useful for continuously changing data such as stock indexes, but should have some boundaries. Stock indexes, for example, are only updated between the hours of 9:00 a.m. and 5:00 p.m. (or so) and doing a call for them outside those times is wasteful. In this case, you can set a start and end time for this operation equal to the times in question. This causes the template to be called every day starting at 9:00 a.m. and stopping at 5:00 p.m.

 TIP Remember that every executed scheduled event is the same as any other user's HTTP request. The more that happens, the more a hit it is on your site. Try to set your scheduled executions to use the least amount of time and resources. Tight code is essential for big sites.

Now that you've set the time, you have to deal with the operation that will be performed (see Figure 32.4). The only required piece here is the URL; every timed event has to have an URL that will be executed. All of the other fields are just extras to enhance the HTTP process or control the creation of static pages. Remember that the URL can reside almost anywhere and is not limited to local files.

Part
IV

Ch
32

FIGURE 32.4
Additional schedule information.

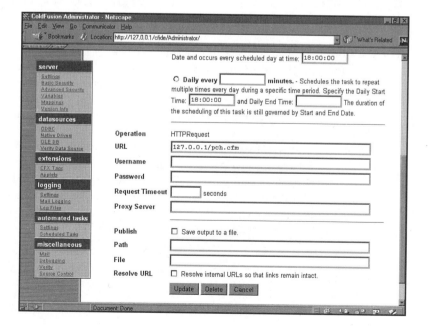

The Username and Password fields are used when the requested page is behind Web server-based security. These values are sent along, allowing the page to be executed in a secure environment. The Request Timeout field allows you to set the length (in seconds) that the HTTP request will run before returning an error. This is the same as the RequestTimeOut URL variable.

The Publish check box toggles the creation of static pages, which are created from the results of the HTTP request. If Publish is checked, the Path and File boxes must also be filled in. These boxes allow you to set the resultant static page's directory path and filename. The result of any page executed by the scheduler is then written to a file using these values. Included is the capability to resolve any URLs that are being saved. This is important when saving information from other sites because it keeps the links pointing to their proper locations.

Using the Administrator to Edit Tasks

The Administrator also allows you to edit a task by simply selecting it from the first screen and changing any values you want. This makes the one-time executions using the Now option more sensible. Once a task is selected, any value associated with it can be altered. Once the changes are done, selecting Update loads the task into the registry. You should note that this has the same effect as a new task in all ways; the old one is gone and the new one has to be recognized by the scheduling service. Deletion of tasks is handled the same way, but with a single button for removal.

Programming Control Tasks with the CFSCHEDULE Tag

The Administrator control is simply a form-based interface for using the CFSCHEDULE tag. The only difference between the Administrator and using the CFSCHEDULE tag is that the Administrator can access a record of all scheduled events and has error checking to make sure you write in the proper values for the tag attributes. The only advantage of the CFSCHEDULE tag over the Administrator is that your security is maintained. You don't have to allow someone Administrator access to create a scheduled event. This does not mean anything for most people, but this security is essential for ISPs who want to offer ColdFusion services. Copy the form template from the Administrator and use that as a front end when dealing with users who want to add tasks. This is helpful to them, maintains the security of your Administration pages, and ensures that the CFSCHEDULE tag is always formatted properly. This means you have to write a page to test the data before running the CFSCHEDULE tag, but that shouldn't be too hard. Chapter 15, "Form Data Validation," has information on data validation.

Table 32.1 shows all of the CFSCHEDULE tag's attributes, as well as provide a brief description of each. Status items with an asterisk (*) are optional in some cases and required in others. The specific cases in which the attribute is required is always noted.

Table 32.1 CFSCHEDULE Tag Attributes

Name	Status	Description
ACTION	Required	Valid entries are DELETE, UPDATE, or RUN. UPDATE creates a new task if one does not exist. If a task already exists, UPDATE overwrites the current task of the same name. RUN executes a task now. DELETE removes the task from the list of current tasks.
TASK	Required	The name of the task to delete, update, or run.
OPERATION	Required*	Required when creating tasks with ACTION="UPDATE". The type of operation the scheduler should perform when executing this task. ColdFusion currently only supports OPERATION="HTTPRequest" used for calling remote and local pages for execution.
STARTDATE	Required*	Required when creating tasks with ACTION="UPDATE". The date when scheduling of the task should start.
STARTTIME	Required*	Required when creating tasks with ACTION="UPDATE". The time when scheduling of the task should start. This should be a complete time value either in military standard (13:00:00=1:00:00pm) or with the a.m./p.m. appended to it.
URL	Required*	Required when creating tasks with ACTION="UPDATE". This is the URL to be executed by the scheduler.
INTERVAL	Required*	Required when creating tasks with ACTION="UPDATE". Interval at which task should be scheduled. Can be set in minutes or as DAILY, WEEKLY, MONTHLY, and EXECUTE. The default interval is one hour and the minimum interval is one minute. The EXECUTE interval seems to set to DAILY, while an interval of NOW sets the operation to execute immediately.
PUBLISH	Optional	YES or NO. Specifies whether the result should be saved to a file.
FILE	Optional*	Required with PUBLISH="YES". A valid filename for the published file.
PATH	Optional*	Required with PUBLISH="YES". The path location for the published file.
ENDDATE	Optional	The date when the scheduled task should end.
ENDTIME	Optional	The time when the scheduled task should end. This value should be in a valid time format.

continues

Part

IV

Ch

32

Table 32.1 Continued

Name	Status	Description
REQUESTTIMEOUT	Optional	Customizes the REQUESTTIMEOUT for the task operation. Can be used to extend the standard timeout for time-intensive operations.
USERNAME	Optional	Username if URL is protected.
PASSWORD	Optional	Password if URL is protected.
PROXYSERVER	Optional	Host name or IP address of a proxy server.
RESOLVEURL	Optional	YES or NO. If you are retrieving data from a remote server or an external server instance, this guarantees that links to other pages and graphics still work by changing relative links to fully qualified URLs.

Setting CFSCHEDULE Attributes

The first things you have to define in a CFSCHEDULE tag are the TASK name of the scheduled event and the ACTION you want to perform. At present there are three actions to choose from:

- UPDATE—Used to create a scheduled event. This writes an event to the registry that will be run either by the timer or by the RUN action.
- RUN—Used to execute a previously scheduled event now (useful for static page creation).
- DELETE—Used to remove a scheduled event.

You set the OPERATION and URL at this point. The problem is that the only operation you can do now is HTTP request. This is far from a limitation. With some creative code in the template being called, almost anything can be done. I expect that either this will be removed and HTTP request will be the only action allowed or others will be added and HTTP request will be made default. Neither case really affects anything you'll be doing. When creating or updating a task, an URL must be supplied as an attribute. If it's not, the tag fails to run and has to be fixed. There seems to be no difference whether you type an http:// before the URL, but it doesn't hurt for clean and descriptive code.

Now the only thing needed for a working CFSCHEDULE is some time code. This is basically the same as what was described in the Administration page, but you get to write it all down rather than setting it in a form.

At this point, you have a fully working schedule. Everything else is either an extra that enhances the scheduled task or static page generation code.

One fast and easy way to write up the CFSCHEDULE code is to use the CFSCHEDULE button (see Figure 32.5), which is located in the advanced ColdFusion toolbar in ColdFusion Studio.

FIGURE 32.5

The CFSCHEDULE button.

Selecting this button gives you a full editor for the tag with access to all of its attributes. In many ways it is like the Administration page, minus the layout or data verification. This tag generator (see Figure 32.6) does almost everything needed to write the tag. Note that there is a bug in the tag generator that adds an attribute called `limittime` to the `requesttimeout` setting. This is not used by the tag, but does not stop it from operating.

FIGURE 32.6

The CFSCHEDULE tag generator.

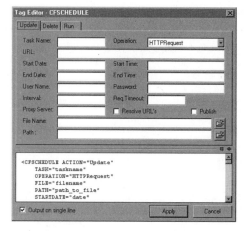

The interval setting is a pitfall to watch out for. This can either be a word or a number, as mentioned in the Administration section. The major problem is that the number is not in minutes but in seconds. This means that any number you want to set here should be multiplied by 60 in order to be near what you want. This is all due to the evolution of the scheduling engine and what values it can support. This will likely be addressed in a future release.

Dynamically Creating Static Pages

One of the great uses of CFSCHEDULE is combining it with server or application scope variables. This allows you to take some of the information that you may be calling or generating on every page and call it only once at a specific interval.

For example, I have a site that has a live stock feed for every page. Every time someone calls a page, a CFHTTP is called to get the live information from another server. This is nice, but a lot of overhead, especially if a lot of people are on at once. The solution is to call the same information from a scheduled page every minute, store the results as APPLICATION variables, and give the users the stored information. The reduction in overhead, network traffic, and pages being called makes the site just a little faster. Something to think about.

> **N O T E** The timers for the `GetIndex.cfm` template, UPDATE_GETINDEX.CFM, are the schedules
> and templates for a small stock index application. ■

Listing 32.1 is the schedule for the `GetIndex1.cfm` template. It's set to run every day between
the hours of 9:00 a.m. and 5:00 p.m., once a minute.

Listing 32.1 Schedule for `GetIndex1.cfm`

```
<cfschedule
    action="UPDATE"
    task="GetIndex1"
    operation="HTTPRequest"
    url="http://127.0.0.1/stocks/GetIndex1.cfm"
    startdate="01/01/97"
    starttime="9:00:00"
    endtime="17:00:00"
    interval="60"
    limittime="120">
```

Listing 32.2 is a template that gets the current stock index and saves the results to application
variables. This is used to provide the most up-to-date values to multiple people without having
each run the template.

On the CD

**Listing 32.2 `GETINDEX1.CFM`—A Scheduled Template for Getting Stock
Indexes**

```
<!--- Try to get the stock index from the first site. --->
<CF_RPC_StockIndex Server="PCQuote">
<!--- If it fails, try the next one. If this fails, the default values
➥ will be used --->
<CFIF live is "NO">
    <CF_RPC_StockIndex Server="Bloomberg">
</CFIF>
<!--- Set application values to the stock indexes returned --->
<CFSET application.djia=Dow>
<CFSET application.djia2=dow2>
<CFSET application.sp=spx>
<CFSET application.sp2=spx2>
<CFSET application.nq=comp>
<CFSET application.nq2=comp2>
```

While the `GetIndex1.cfm` template simply loads the indexes into application variables, you
want this to be a tight setup. That means that the `GetIndex1.cfm` will stop executing at
5:00 p.m. You now need a way for the last values to be preserved until 9:00 the next day. That's
where the publishing comes in. You call `GetIndex2.cfm`, which writes the values to a file in a
format you can use. `GetIndex3.cfm` is a static file containing some `CFSET` commands to load the
stock index data (defaulted to 0.00 for display) into the application variables. You then add
some code to `application.cfm` to see if the attributes have timed out. If they have, the

`GetIndex3.cfm` runs, loading them back into memory. Setups like this are needed in case the machine goes down, the application values time out, or something else happens. The key to a good dynamic site is making sure that you always have some data being returned. Nothing looks as bad as a missing data error.

Listing 32.3 is the scheduled event for the `GetIndex2.cfm` template. This runs once a day at 5:00 p.m. and writes the results to a file with the name and location listed in the tag.

Listing 32.3   Schedule for `GetIndex2.cfm`

```
<cfschedule action="UPDATE"
            task="GetIndex2"
            operation="HTTPRequest"
            url="http://127.0.0.1/stocks/GetIndex2.cfm"
            startdate="01/01/97"
            starttime="17:00:00"
            interval="Daily"
            limittime="240"
publish="Yes"
            file="GetIndex3.cfm"
            path="E:\WebSite\htdocs\stock">
```

Listing 32.4 is the `GetIndex2.cfm` template, which is called by the previous schedule and writes a static page to the Web server. This static page is called `GetIndex3.cfm` and contains the last stock index values for the day.

On the CD

Listing 32.4   `GETINDEX2.CFM`—A Scheduled Template for Writing the Stock Indexes to a File

```
<!--- Try to get the stock index from the first site. -->
<CF_RPC_StockIndex Server="PCQuote">
<!--- If it fails, try the next one.
➥If this fails, the default values will be used -->
<CFIF live is "NO">
    <CF_RPC_StockIndex Server="Bloomberg">
</CFIF>
<!--- Set application values to the stock indexes returned -->
<CFOUTPUT>
&lt;CFSET ##application.djia##="#Dow#"&gt;
&lt;CFSET ##application.djia2##="#dow2#"&gt;
&lt;CFSET ##application.sp##="#spx#"&gt;
&lt;CFSET ##application.sp2##="#spx2#"&gt;
&lt;CFSET ##application.nq##="#comp#"&gt;
&lt;CFSET ##application.nq2##="#comp2#"&gt;
</CFOUTPUT>
```

Listing 32.5 is a static page that simply contains the last stock indexes for the day, and when it is called it writes these values to application variables.

Listing 32.5 `GETINDEX3.CFM`—**Static Page Generated from** `GetIndex2.cfm`

```
<CFSET application.djia="0.00">
<CFSET application.djia2="0.00">
<CFSET application.sp="0.00">
<CFSET application.sp2="0.00">
<CFSET application.nq="0.00">
<CFSET application.nq2="0.00">
```

Logging Scheduled Events

The execution of all scheduled files is recorded in the `schedule.log` file, which is located in the `\cfusion\log\` directory. The log is a comma-delimited list of information, each surrounded by quotation marks (see Listing 32.6).

Listing 32.6 `SCHEDULE.LOG`—**Sample Line from Schedule Log**

```
"Information","TID=237","10/05/97","17:53:24","Scheduled action
➥Enter Contest, template http://127.0.0.1/testbed/pch.cfm
➥completed successfully."
```

The first simply gives information. This may hold more in the future, but for now seems to just be a placeholder. The second value is simply the process' thread ID, which has value only to Allaire personnel for debugging. The third and fourth values are for the date and time of the event's execution. The fifth value contains the name of the event run, the URL that was called, and the operation's success status. The schedule log simply records the fact that a template was run by a scheduled event. The event is also recorded in other log files as appropriate to the event. ●

Appendixes

ColdFusion Tag Reference

ColdFusion tags are the CFML extensions to HTML. These tags are the instructions to ColdFusion to perform database queries, process results, perform transaction processing, send email, and much more.

The tags are presented here in alphabetical order, and are cross referenced to any related tags wherever appropriate.

<CFABORT>

Description: The <CFABORT> tag is used to immediately halt processing of a ColdFusion template. <CFABORT> attributes are listed in Table A.1.

Syntax:

```
<CFABORT SHOWERROR="Error text">
```

Table A.1   **<CFABORT> Attributes**

Attribute	Description	Notes
SHOWERROR	Error message	This attribute is optional.

Example: The following example aborts template processing if the user is not in a specific range of valid IP addresses:

```
<CFIF Left(CGI.REMOTE_ADDR, 11) NEQ "208.193.16.">
 <H1>Unauthorized host detected! Access denied!</H1>
 <CFABORT SHOWERROR="You are not authorized to use this function!">
</CFIF>
```

TIP   <CFABORT> can be used to safely terminate the processing of a template if an error condition occurs. For example, if your template were expecting an URL parameter to be passed, you could use the ParameterExists or IsDefined functions to verify its existence and terminate the template with an appropriate error message if it did not exist.

See also: <CFEXIT>

<CFAPPLET>

Description: <CFAPPLET> is used to embed user-supplied Java applets into CFFORM forms. Table A.2 is the complete list of attributes supported by <CFAPPLET>. In addition, you may pass your own attributes as long as they have been registered along with the applet itself.

Before you can use an applet with <CFAPPLET>, it must be registered with the ColdFusion Administrator.

<CFAPPLET> must be used within <CFORM> and </CFORM> tags.

Syntax:

```
<CFAPPLET ALIGN="Alignment" APPLETSOURCE="Regsitered Name" HEIGHT="Height"
HSPACE="Horizontal Spacing" NAME="Field Name"
 NOTSUPPORTED="Text for non Java browsers" VSPACE="Vertical Spacing"
WIDTH="Width">
```

Table A.2 **<CFAPPLET> Attributes**

Attribute	Description	Notes
ALIGN	Applet alignment	Valid values are: left, right, bottom, top, texttop, middle, absmiddle, baseline, and absbottom. This attribute is optional.
APPLETSOURCE	Name of the registered applet.	This attribute is required.
HEIGHT	Height in pixels.	This attribute is optional.
HSPACE	Horizontal spacing in pixels.	This attribute is optional.
NAME	Form field name.	This attribute is required.
NOTSUPPORTED	Text to display on browsers that do not support Java.	This attribute is optional.
VSPACE	Vertical spacing optional in pixels.	This attribute is optional.
WIDTH	Width in pixels.	This attribute is optional.

Example: The following example embeds a Java spin control applet into a <CFFORM> form, passing the required attributes and two applet-specific attributes:

```
<CFFORM ACTION="process.cfm">
<CFAPPLET APPLETSOURCE="spin" NAME="quantity" MIN="1" MAX="10">
</CFFORM>
```

For more information about the ColdFusion Administrator and registering applets, see Chapter 4, "Administering ColdFusion." For more information about using <CFFORM> and <CFAPPLET>, see Chapter 23, "Enhancing Forms with CFFORM."

N O T E Controls embedded with <CFAPPLET> are accessible only by users with Java-enabled browsers. ▓

See also: <CFFORM>, <CFGRID>, <CFSLIDER>, <CFTEXTINPUT>, <CFTREE>

<CFAPPLICATION>

Description: <CFAPPLICATION> is used to name an application, or part thereof, to restrict the scope of any client, session, and application variables. By default, these variables are visible to all templates. <CFAPPLICATION> allows you to name part of an application so that variables created in other templates are not visible to it, and variables created within it are not visible to other parts of the application. <CFAPPLICATION> attributes are shown in Table A.3.

Syntax:

```
<CFAPPLICATION APPLICATIONTIMEOUT ="Timeout" CLIENTMANAGEMENT ="Yes or No"
 CLIENTSTOREAGE="Storage Type" NAME="Application Name"
 SESSIONMANAGEMENT ="Yes or No" SESSIONTIMEOUT ="Timeout"
 SETCLIENTCOOKIES="Yes or No">
```

Table A.3 <CFAPPLICATION> **Attributes**

Attribute	Description	Notes
APPLICATIONTIMEOUT	Timeout interval for application variables	Application variable timeout; default to value in ColdFusion Administrator.
CLIENTMANAGEMENT	Enable or disable client variables	This optional attribute defaults to No.
CLIENTSTORAGE	Mechanism for storage of client information	This optional attribute defaults to Registry; other values are Cookie and any ODBC data source name.
NAME	Name of application	This attribute is required if you are using application variables; may be up to 64 characters long.
SESSIONMANAGEMENT	Enable or disable session variables	This optional attribute defaults to No.
SESSIONTIMEOUT	Timeout interval for session variables	Session variable timeout; default to value in ColdFusion Administrator.
SETCLIENTCOOKIES	Enable or disable client cookies	This optional attribute defaults to Yes.

Example: The following example names part of an application Administration and enables session variables:

```
<CFAPPLICATION NAME="Administration" SESSIONMANAGEMENT="Yes">
```

 TIP The <CFAPPLICATION> tag is best used in the APPLICATION.CFM template, as explained in Chapter 26, "Web Application Framework."

For more information about enabling or disabling application and session variables, as well as setting default timeout values, see Chapter 4. For more information about client, session, and application variables, see Chapter 27, "Session Variables and Cookies."

See also: <CFCOOKIE>, <CFSET>

<CFASSOCIATE>

Description: The <CFASSOCIATE> tag is used to associate subtags with base tags. This tag may only be used within custom tags. <CFASSOCIATE> attributes are shown in Table A.4.

Syntax:

```
<CFASSOCIATE BASETAG="tag" DATACOLLECTION="collection">
```

Table A.4 <CFASSOCIATE> **Attributes**

Attribute	Description	Notes
BASETAG	Name of base tag associated with this subtag.	This attribute is required.
DELETEFILE	Name of the structure in the base tag to store attributes.	This attribute is optional; if not specified, the default structure of AssocAttribs is used.

Example: The following example associates a subtag with a base tag:

```
<CFASSOCIATE BASETAG="CF_MENU">
```

See also: <CFMODULE>

<CFAUTHENTICATE>

Description: The <CFAUTHENTICATE> tag authenticates a user, setting a security context for the application. The complete list of supported attributes is explained in Table A.5.

Syntax:

```
<CFAUTHENTICATE PASSWORD="password" SECURITYCONTEXT="context" USERNAME="user">
```

Table A.5   <CFAUTHENTICATE> **Attributes**

Attribute	Description	Notes
PASSWORD	User password.	Optional user password.
SECURITYCONTEXT	Context to authenticate against.	This is a required attribute; context must have been defined in the ColdFusion Administrator.
USERNAME	Username.	Required username.

Example: The following example authenticates a user-supplied username and password within an administrator context:

```
<CFAUTHENTICATE SECURITYCONTEXT="administrator" USERNAME="#username#"
 PASSWORD="#password#">
```

<CFCOLLECTION>

Description: The <CFCOLLECTION> tag can be used to programmatically create and administer Verity collections. The complete list of <CFCOLLECTION> attributes is explained in Table A.6.

Syntax:

```
<CFCOLLECTION ACTION="action" COLLECTION="collection" LANGUAGE="language"
 PATH="path">
```

Table A.6   <CFCOLLECTION> **Attributes**

Attribute	Description	Notes
ACTION	Action.	Required attribute; see Table A.7.
COLLECTION	Collection name.	Required; name of the collection to be indexed. If using external collections, this must be a fully qualified path to the collection

Attribute	Description	Notes
LANGUAGE	Collection language.	Optional language; default to English.
PATH	Collection path.	Required if ACTION is CREATE.

Table A.7 <CFCOLLECTION> **Actions**

Action	Description
CREATE	Create a new collection.
DELETE	Delete a collection.
OPTIMIZE	Purge and reorganize a collection.
REPAIR	Fixed a corrupt collection.

Example: The following example fixes a collection named `"all"`:

```
<CFCOLLECTION ACTION="REPAIR" COLLECTION="all">
```

N O T E   <CFCOLLECTION> works at the collection level only. To add content to a collection, use <CFINDEX>. ▨

For more information about using <CFCOLLECTION> and Verity collections, see Chapter 29, "Full-Text Searching with Verity."

For the complete list of search expressions and instructions, see Appendix C, "Verity Search Language Reference."

See also: <CFINDEX>, <CFSEARCH>

<CFCONTENT>

Description: The <CFCONTENT> tags allows you to send non-HTML documents to a client's browser. <CFCONTENT> lets you specify the MIME type of the file and an optional filename to transmit. The complete list of supported attributes is in Table A.8.

Syntax:

```
<CFCONTENT TYPE="MIME Type" FILE="File Name" DELETEFILE>
```

Table A.8   <CFCONTENT> **Attributes**

Attribute	Description	Notes
TYPE	Content MIME Type	This attribute is required.
FILE	Name of file to send to user	This is an optional attribute that specifies the fully qualified path of a file to be transmitted to the user's browser.
DELETEFILE	Deletes the file once sent	Useful if servingdynamically created graphics. This attribute is optional.

Example: The following example sends data-driven VRML to the user:

```
<CFCONTENT TYPE="x-world/x-vrml">
<CFOUTPUT QUERY="world">
#world#
</CFOUTPUT>
```

This next example sends a Microsoft Word document:

```
<CFCONTENT TYPE="application/msword" FILE="C:\MyDocs\Proposal.DOC">
```

This final example sends a dynamically created map to the user and then deletes it upon completion of the transmission:

```
<CFCONTENT TYPE="image/gif" FILE="C:\Images\Maps\Temp123.gif" DELETEFILE>
```

<CFCOOKIE>

Description: <CFCOOKIE> allows you to set *cookies*, persistent client-side variables, on the client browser. Cookies allow you to set variables on a client's browser, which are then returned every time a page is requested by a browser. Cookies may be sent securely if required.

To access a returned cookie, specify its name and precede it with the COOKIE designator, as in #COOKIE.USER_ID#.

As not all browsers support cookies. You must never make assumptions about the existence of the cookie. Always use the IsDefined function to check for the existence of the cookie before referencing it.

Syntax:

```
<CFCOOKIE NAME="Cookie Name" VALUE="Value" EXPIRES="Expiration" SECURE>
```

Table A.9   `<CFCOOKIE>` **Attributes**

Attribute	Description	Notes
DOMAIN	The domain for which the cookies are valid	Required only if PATH is used. Separate multiple domains with a ; character.
EXPIRES	Cookie expiration date	The cookie expiration date may be specified as a definite date (as in '10/1/97'), relative days (as in '100'), NOW, or NEVER. This attribute is optional.
NAME	Name of cookie	This attribute is required.
PATH	Subset of the URL to which the cookie applies	This attribute is optional. Separate multiple paths with a ; character.
SECURE	Specify that cookie must be sent securely	This attribute is optional. If it is specified and the browser does not support SSL, the cookie is not sent.
VALUE	Cookie value	This attribute is required.

Example: The following example sends a cookie containing a user ID and sets the expiration date to 60 days from now:

```
<CFCOOKIE NAME="USER_ID" VALUE="100">
```

This next example sets a secure cookie that never expires (until manually deleted):

```
<CFCOOKIR NAME="access" VALUE="admin" SECURE>
```

N O T E   If you use the SECURE attribute to specify that the cookie must be sent securely, it is only sent if the browser supports SSL. If the cookie cannot be sent securely, it is not sent at all. ▓

N O T E   Cookies are domain-specific, meaning they can be set so just the server that set them can retrieve them. ▓

 T I P   Setting a cookie expiration date of NOW effectively deletes the cookie from the client's browser.

For more information about using HTTP cookies, see Chapter 27.

See also: `<CFAPPLICATION>`

<CFDIRECTORY>

Description: <CFDIRECTORY> is used for all directory manipulation, including obtaining directory lists and creating or deleting directories.

<CFDIRECTORY> is a flexible and powerful tag, and has many attributes, some of which are mutually exclusive. The values passed to the ACTION attribute dictates what other attributes can be used. The possible ACTION values for <CFDIRECTORY> are listed in Table A.11. LIST is assumed if no ACTION is specified. Table A.12 contains the list of columns returns if ACTION="LIST".

Syntax:

```
<CFDIRECTORY ACTION="Action Type" DIRECTORY="Directory Name"
 FILTER="Search Filter" MODE="Unix Permissions Mode" NAME="Query Name"
 NEWDIRECTORY="New Directory Name" SORT="Sort Order">
```

Table A.10 <CFDIRECTORY> **Attributes**

Attribute	Description	Notes
ACTION	Tag action	This attribute is optional, and will default to LIST if omitted.
DIRECTORY	Directory name	This attribute is required.
FILTER	Filter spec	This attribute is optional and is only valid if ACTION="LIST". Filter may contain wildcard characters.
MODE	Permissions mode	This optional attribute is only valid if ACTION="CREATE". It is used only by the Solaris version of ColdFusion, and is ignored by the Windows versions.
NAME	Query name	Required if ACTION="LIST". Query to hold retrieved directory listing.
NEWDIRECTORY	New directory rename	Required if ACTION="RENAME", ignored by all other actions.

Attribute	Description	Notes
SORT	Sort order	Optional comma -delimited list of columns to sort by; each may use ASC for ascending or DESC for descending. Default is ascending.

Table A.11 <CFDIRECTORY> **Actions**

Action	Description
CREATE	Creates a new directory.
DELETE	Deletes a directory.
LIST	Obtains a list of directory contents.
RENAME	Renames a directory.

Table A.12 <CFDIRECTORY> LIST **Columns**

Action	Description
ATTRIBUTES	File attributes
DATELASTMODIFIED	Last modified date
MODE	Permissions mode (Solaris only)
NAME	File or directory name
SIZE	Size in bytes
TYPE	Type F for file or D for directory

Example: This first creates a new directory:

```
<CFDIRECTORY ACTION="CREATE"DIRECTORY="C:\STUFF">
```

This next example retrieves a directory list, sorted by filename:

```
<CFDIRECTORY ACTION="LIST"DIRECTORY="C:\STUFF" NAME="Stuff" SORT="Name">
```

For more information about ColdFusion's file and directory manipulation capabilities, see Chapter 28, "Working with Files and Directories."

See also: <CFFILE>

<CFERROR>

Description: `<CFERROR>` allows you to override the standard ColdFusion error messages and replace them with templates that you specify. `<CFERROR>` requires that you specify the type of error message to be overridden and the template containing the error message to be displayed.

There are two different types of error messages in ColdFusion. `REQUEST` errors occur while processing a template, and `VALIDATION` errors occur when `FORM` field validation errors occur. In each scenario, a special set of ColdFusion fields are available for inclusion in your error message template.

Syntax:

```
<CFERROR Type="Error Type" TEMPLATE="Error Message Template
MAILTO="Administrator's email Address">
```

Table A.13 `<CFERROR>` Attributes

Attribute	Description	Notes
MAILTO	The administrator's email address	The email address of the administrator to be notified of any error messages; this value is available with the error message template as #ERROR.MailTo#.
TEMPLATE	Error message template	Name of the template containing the error message to display. This attribute is required.
TYPE	Type of error message	Possible values are "REQUEST" or "VALIDATION". If this attribute is omitted, the default value of "REQUEST" is used.

Table A.14 ColdFusion Error Message Variables

Type	Field	Description
REQUEST	#ERROR.RemoteAddress#	Client's IP address.
REQUEST	#ERROR.Browser#	The browser the client was running, with version and platform information if provided by the browser.

Type	Field	Description
REQUEST	#ERROR.DateTime#	The date and time that the error occurred; can be passed to any of the date/time manipulation functions as needed.
REQUEST	#ERROR.Diagnostics#	Detailed diagnostic error message returned by ColdFusion.
REQUEST	#ERROR.HTTPReferer#	URL of the page from which the template was accessed.
REQUEST	#ERROR.MailTo#	Administrator's email address; can be used to send notification of the error.
REQUEST	#ERROR.QueryString#	The URL's query string.
REQUEST	#ERROR.Template#	Template being processed when the error occurred.
VALIDATION	#ERROR.InvalidFields#	List of the invalid form fields.
VALIDATION	#ERROR.ValidationFooter#	Text for footer of error message.
VALIDATION	#ERROR.ValidationHeader#	Text for header of error message.

Example: The following example establishes an error message template for REQUEST errors:

```
<CFERROR TYPE="REQUEST" NAME="ERROR_REQUEST.CFM" MAILTO="admin@a2zbooks.com">
```

Listing A.1 Sample Request Error Template

```
<HTML>

<HEAD>
<TITLE>Application Error!</TITLE>
</HEAD>

<BODY>
<H1>Application Error!</H1>
A critical error has occurred, please try your request later.

</BODY>

</HTML>
```

T I P The <CFERROR> tag is best used in the APPLICATION.CFM template, as explained in Chapter 26, "Web Application Framework."

<CFEXIT>

Description: <CFEXIT> aborts the processing of a custom tag without aborting processing of the calling template. <CFEXIT> can only be used within custom tags. Unlike <CFABORT>, which terminates caller template processing, <CFEXIT> stops processing the custom tag and returns control to the caller.

Syntax: <CFEXIT>

Example: This example checks to see if any form fields exist and stops processing if there are none:

```
<CFIF IsDefined("FORM.formfields") IS "No">
 <CFEXIT>
</CFIF>
```

See also: <CFABORT>

<CFFILE>

Description: <CFFILE> is used to perform various types of file management, including uploading files from a browser, moving, renaming, copying, and deleting files, and reading and writing of text files.

<CFFILE> is a flexible and powerful tag; it has many attributes, many of which are mutually exclusive. The values passed to the ACTION attribute dictate what other attributes may be used.

<CFFILE> creates a FILE object after every <CFFILE> operation. You can use the variables in this object as you would any other ColdFusion variables, allowing you to check the results of an operation. However, only one FILE object exists, and as soon as you execute a new <CFFILE> tag, the prior FILE object is overwritten with the new one.

Syntax:

```
<CFFILE ACCEPT="Filter" ACTION="Action Type"
 DESTINATION="Destination Directory or File Name" FILE="File Name"
 FILEFIELD="Field Containing File Name" NAMECONFLICT="Conflict Option"
 OUTPUT="Text To Output" SOURCE="Source File Name" VARIABLE="Variable Name">
```

Table A.15 <CFFILE> **Attributes**

Attribute	Description	Notes
ACCEPT	File type filter	This optional attribute restricts the types of files that may be uploaded, and may only be used if ACTION is UPLOAD. The filter is specified as a MIME type ("image/*", which allows all image types, but nothing else); multiple MIME types may be specified separated by commas.
ACTION	Desired action	This attribute is required.
DESTINATION	Destination file location	This attribute may only be used if ACTION is one the following: APPEND, COPY, MOVE, RENAME, UPLOAD. Destination may be a filename or a fully qualified file path.
FILE	Name of local file to access	This attribute may only be used if ACTION is DELETE, READ, or WRITE, in which case it is required.
FILEFIELD	Name of the form field containing the file	This attribute may only be used if ACTION is UPLOAD, in which case it is required.
NAMECONFLICT	What to do in case of name conflicts	This optional attribute may be used if ACTION is UPLOAD. It specifies the action to be performed if a name conflict arises. If this attribute is omitted, the default value of "ERROR" is used.
OUTPUT	Text to output to file	This attribute may only be used if ACTION is WRITE.
SOURCE	Source filename	Name of the source file to be written to, copied, or moved. May be used only if ACTION is APPEND, COPY, MOVE, or RENAME.
VARIABLE	Variable to store contents of read file	This attribute may only be used if ACTION is READ, in which case it is required.

App
A

Table A.16 `<CFFILE>` **Actions**

Action	Description
APPEND	Appends one text file to the end of another
COPY	Copies a file
DELETE	Deletes a specified file
MOVE	Moves a specified file from one directory to another, or from one filename to another
READ	Reads the contents of a text file
RENAME	Does the same thing as MOVE; see MOVE
UPLOAD	Receives an uploaded file
WRITE	Writes specified text to the end of a text file

Table A.17 **File Upload Name Conflict Options**

Option	Description
ERROR	The file will not be saved, and ColdFusion will immediately terminate template processing.
SKIP	Neither saves the file nor generates an error message.
OVERWRITE	Overwrites the existing file.
MAKEUNIQUE	Generates a unique filename and saves the file with that new name. To find out what the new name is, inspect the #FILE.ServerFile# field.

Table A.18 `<CFFILE>` `FILE` **Object Fields**

Field	Description
#FILE.AttemptedServerFile#	The original attempted filename; will be the same as #FILE.ServerFile# unless the name had to be changed to make it unique.
#FILE.ClientDirectory#	The client directory from where the file was up-loaded, as reported by the client browser.
#FILE.ClientFile#	The original filename as reported by the client browser.
#FILE.ClientFileExt#	The original file extension, as reported by the client browser.

Field	Description
#FILE.ClientFileName#	The original filename as reported by the client browser, but without the file extension.
#FILE.ContentSubType#	The MIME subtype of an uploaded file.
#FILE.ContentType#	The primary MIME type of an uploaded file.
#FILE.FileExisted#	Yes if file already existed, No if not.
#FILE.FileWasOverwritten#	Yes if file were overwritten, No if not.
#FILE.FileWasRenamed#	Yes if file were renamed, No if not.
#FILE.FileWasSaved#	Yes is file were saved, No if not.
#FILE.ServerDirectory#	The server directory in which the uploaded file was saved.
#FILE.ServerFile#	The name of the file as saved on the server. (Takes into account updated filename if it were modified to make it unique.)

Example: This first example receives any uploaded files and generates an error message if the specified filename already exists:

```
<CFFILE ACTION="Upload" FORMFIELD="UploadFile" DESTINATION="C:\UPLOADS\FILE.TXT">
```

This next example restricts the upload to Microsoft Word documents and changes the filename to something unique if it already exists:

```
<CFFILE
 ACTION="Upload"
 FORMFIELD="UploadFile"
 DESTINATION="C:\UPLOADS\FILE.TXT"
 ACCEPT="application/msword"
 NAMECONFLICT="MAKEUNIQUE"
>
```

This example appends a log entry to a text file:

```
<CFFILE
 ACTION="WRITE"
 FILE="C:\LOGS\DAILY.LOG"
 OUTPUT="#CGI.REMOTE_ADDR#, #Now()#"
>
```

The following example reads a file called C:\LOGS\DAILY\LOG into a variable called LOG and then displays the results:

```
<CFFILE
 ACTION="READ"
 FILE="C:\LOGS\DAILY.LOG"
 VARIABLE="LOG"
>
```

```
<CFOUTPUT>
<B>Log file:</B><P>#LOG#
</CFOUTPUT>
```

This next example deletes the C:\LOGS\DAILY.LOG file:

```
<CFFILE
 ACTION="DELETE"
 FILE="C:\LOGS\DAILY.LOG"
>
```

For more information about ColdFusion's file manipulation capabilities, see Chapter 28, "Working with Files and Directories."

See also: <CFDIRECTORY>

<CFFORM>, </CFFORM>

Description: <CFFORM> and </CFFORM> are replacements for the standard HTML <FORM> and </FORM> tags. <CFFORM> itself adds no real value to your forms, but <CFFORM> allows you to embed other tags (<CFGRID>, <CFINPUT>, <CFSELECT>, <CFTEXTINPUT>, <CFTREE>, or any Java applets of your own using <CFAPPLET>). The code generated by <CFFORM> is standard FORM HTML code.

Syntax:

```
<CFFORM ACTION="Action Page" …>
```

Table A.19 <CFFORM> **Attributes**

Attribute	Description	Notes
ACTION	Form action page	This attribute is required.
ENABLECAB	Header value	This optional attribute allows the downloading Java classes in Microsoft cabinet files. If Yes, users are asked upon opening the page if they want to download the CAB file.
NAME	Form name	This attribute is optional. If used, you must ensure that the form name is unique.
ONSUBMIT	JavaScript OnSubmit function	Optional name of function. JavaScript to be executed prior to form submission.
TARGET	Target window	Optional target window.

Example: A simple <CFFORM>:

```
<CFFORM ACTION="process.cfm">
…
</CFFORM>
```

N O T E   <CFFORM> automatically embeds METHOD="POST" into your form. ▪

See also: <CFAPPLET>, <CFGIRD>, <CFINPUT>, <CFSELECT>, <CFSLIDER>, <CFTEXTINPUT>, <CFTREE>

<CFFTP>

Description: <CFFTP> is the ColdFusion interface to the file transfer protocol. You may interact with remote file systems, retrieve directory lists, and GET and OUT files via <CFFTP>. It is a very powerful and complex tag; Table A.20 lists its attributes. When calls to <CFFTP> are completed, a series of variables is set so you can determine the success or failure of the operation. These variables are listed in Table A.22. An error code is set if an error occurs. Table A.24 lists the complete set of error codes and what they mean. <CFFTP> can be used to retrieve remote directory lists. Lists are returned in ColdFusion query format and Table A.23 lists the query columns.

<CFFTP> is designed to be used two ways: either for single operations or to batch operations together. To use the batch mode (called *cached mode*), you must specify a unique name in the CONNECTION attribute that you can use in future <CFFTP> calls.

Syntax:

```
<CFFTP ACTION="Action" AGENTNAME="Name" ASCIIEXTENSIONLIST="List"
 ATTRIBUTES="Attributes" CONNECTION="Connection Name" DIRECTORY="Directory"
 EXISTING="Name" FAILIFEXISTS="Yes¦No" ITEM="Name" LOCALFILE="Name"
 NAME="Query Name" NEW="Name" PASSWORD="Password" PORT="Port" REMOTEFILE="Name"
 RETRYCOUNT="Count" SERVER="Server Address" STOPONERROR="Yes¦No"
 TIMEOUT="Seconds" TRANSFERMODE="Mode" USERNAME="User Name">
```

Table A.20   <CFFTP> **Attributes**

Attribute	Description	Notes
ACTION	Action	Required attribute.
AGENTNAME	Agent name	Optional attribute; application name.
ASCIIEXTENSIONLIST	ASCII extensions	Optional attribute, semicolon-delimited list of extensions to be treated as ASCII extensions if using TRASNFERMODE of "AutoDetect"; default is "txt;htm;html;cfm;cfml;shtm;shtml;css;asp;asa".
ATTRIBUTES	Attributes list	Comma-delimited list of attributes; specifies the file attributes for the local file; possible values are

continues

Table A.20   Continued

Attribute	Description	Notes
		READONLY, HIDDEN, SYSTEM, ARCHIVE, DIRECTORY, COMPRESSED, TEMPORARY, and NORMAL.
CONNECTION	Connection name	Optional attribute; used to cache connections to perform batches of operations.
DIRECTORY	Directory name	Required if ACTION is CHANGEDIR, CREATEDIR, LISTDIR, or EXISTSDIR; specifies the directory on which to perform the operation.
EXISTING	Existing item name	Required if ACTION is RENAME.
FAILIFEXISTS	Fail if exists	Optional attribute; if Yes, will fail. If the file already exists, default is Yes.
ITEM	Item name	Required if ACTION is EXISTS or REMOVE.
LOCALFILE	Local filename	Required if ACTION is GETFILE or PUTFILE, local filename.
NAME	Query name	Required if ACTION is GETLIST; see Table A.23 for column list.
NEW	New item name	Required if ACTION is RENAME.
PASSWORD	Login password	Required attribute.
PORT	Server port	Optional attribute; defaults to 21.
REMOTEFILE	Remote filename	Required if ACTION is EXISTSFILE, GETFILE, or PUTFILE; local filename.
RETRYCOUNT	Retries	Optional retry count; defaults to 1.
SERVER	Server name	Required attribute; DNS or IP address of FTP server.
STOPONERROR	Error handling	Optional attribute; defaults to Yes.
TIMEOUT	Timeout value	Optional attribute; timeout value in seconds.
TRANSFERMODE	Transfer mode	Optional attribute; values can be ASCII, binary, or AutoDetect; default is AutoDetect.
USERNAME	Login username	Required attribute.

Table A.21 <CFFTP> **Actions**

Action	Description
CHANGEDIR	Changes directory
CLOSE	Closes a cached connection
CREATEDIR	Creates a directory
EXISTS	Checks to see if an object exists
EXISTSDIR	Checks for a directory's existence
EXISTSFILE	Checks for a file's existence
GETCURRENTDIR	Gets current directory
GETCURRENTURL	Gets current URL
GETFILE	Retrieves a file
LISTDIR	Retrieves directory list
OPEN	Opens a cached connection
PUTFILE	Sends a file
REMOVE	Deletes a file
RENAME	Renames a file

Table A.22 <CFFTP> **Status Variables**

Variable	Description
#CFFTP.ErrorCode#	Error codes
#CFFTP.ErrorText#	Error text
#CFFTP.Succeeded#	Success; Yes or No

Table A.23 <CFFTP> **Query Columns**

Column	Description
ATTRIBUTES	Comma-delimited list of attributes
ISDIRECTORY	Yes if directory, No if file
LASTMODIFIED	Date and time last modified
LENGTH	File length

continues

Table A.23   Continued

Column	Description
NAME	Object name
PATH	Full path to object
URL	Full URL to object

Table A.24   \<CFFTP\> Error Codes

Code	Description
0	Operation succeeded.
1	System error (OS or FTP protocol error).
2	An Internet session could not be established.
3	FTP session could not be opened.
4	File transfer mode not recognized.
5	Search connection could not be established.
6	Invoked operation valid only during a search.
7	Invalid timeout value.
8	Invalid port number.
9	Not enough memory to allocate system resources.
10	Cannot read contents of local file.
11	Cannot write to local file.
12	Cannot open remote file for reading.
13	Cannot read remote file.
14	Cannot open local file for writing.
15	Cannot write to remote file.
16	Unknown error.
18	File already exists.
21	Invalid retry count specified.

Examples:

The following example opens a connection and reads a directory list into a query named `dir`:

```
<CFFTP CONNECTION="FTP" USERNAME="#username#" PASSWORD="#password#"
 SERVER="ftp.a2zbooks.com" ACTION="Open">
<CFFTP CONNECTION="FTP" ACTION="LISTDIR" DIRECTORY="/*." NAME="dir">
<CFFTP CONNECTION="FTP" ACTION="CLOSE">
```

See also: <CFHTTP>

<CFGRID>, <CFGRIDCOLUMN>, <CFGRIDROW>, </CFGRID>

Description: <CFGRID> embeds a Java grid control into your HTML forms. Grids are similar to spreadsheet-style interfaces, and <CFGRID> grids can be used to browse, select, and even edit data. Grids can be populated either by a query or by specifying each row using the <CFGRIDROW> tag. <CFGRIDCOLUMN> can be used to configure the individual columns with a grid.

<CFGRID> must be used between <CFFORM> and </CFFORM> tags.

Syntax:

```
<CFGRID ALIGN="Alignment" APPENDKEY="Yes¦No" BGCOLOR="Color" BOLD="Yes¦No"
 COLHEADERALIGN="Alignment" COLHEADERBOLD="Yes¦No" COLHEADERFONT="Font Face"
 COLHEADERFONTSIZE="Font Size" COLHEADERS="Yes¦No" DELETE="Yes¦No"
 DELETEBUTTON="Button Text" FONT="Font Face" FONTSIZE="Font Size"
 GRIDDATAALIGN="Alignment" GRIDLINES="Yes¦No" HEIGHT="Control Height"
 HIGHLIGHTHREF="Yes¦No" HREF="URL" HREFKEY="Key" HSPACE="Horizontal Spacing"
 INSERT="Yes¦No" INSERTBUTTON="Button Text" ITALIC="Yes¦No" NAME="Field Name"
 NOTSUPPORTED="Non Java Browser Code" ONERROR="Error Function"
 ONVALIDATE="Validation Function" PICTUREBAR="Yes¦No" QUERY="Query"
 ROWHEADER="Yes¦No" Name" ROWHEADERALIGN="Alignment" ROWHEADERBOLD="Yes¦No"
 ROWHEADERFONT="Font Face" ROWHEADERFONTSIZE="Font Size" ROWHEADERWIDTH="Width"
 SELECTCOLOR="Color" SELECTMODE="Mode" SORT="Yes¦No"
 SORTASCENDINGBUTTON="Button Text" SORTDESCENDINGBUTTON="Button Text"
 TARGET="Target Window" VSPACE="Vertical Spacing" WIDTH="Control Width">

<CFGRIDCOLUMN BOLD="Yes¦No" DATAALIGN="Alignment" DISPLAY="Yes¦No"
 FONT="Font Face" FONTSIZE="Font Size" HEADER="Header Text"
 HEADERALIGN="Alignment" HEADERBOLD="Yes¦No" HEADERFONT="Font Face"
 HEADERFONTSIZE="Font Size" HEADERITALIC="Yes¦No" HREF="URL" HREFKEY="Key"
 ITALIC="Yes¦No" NAME="Column Name" NUMBERFORMAT="Format Mask" SELECT="Yes¦No"
 TARGET="Target Window" TYPE="Type" WIDTH="Column Width">
<CFGRIDROW DATA="Data">
```

Table A.25   `<CFGRID>` **Attributes**

Attribute	Description	Notes
ALIGN	Control alignment	Optional attribute; possible values are top, left, bottom, baseline, texttop, absbottom, middle, absmiddle, right.
APPENDKEY	Append item key to URL	Optional attribute; if Yes, a variable named GRIDKEY is appended to the URL containing the item selected; defaults to Yes.
BGCOLOR	Background color	Optional attribute; possible values are black, cyan, darkgray, gray, lightgray, magenta, orange, pink, white, yellow, or any color specified in RGB form.
BOLD	Bold face text	Optional attribute; must be Yes or No if specified; defaults to No.
COLHEADERALIGN	Column header alignment	Optional attribute; may be left, center, or right; default is left.
COLHEADERBOLD	Column header in bold	Optional; if Yes, column header is displayed in a bold font; default is No.
COLHEADERFONT	Column header font	Optional font to use for column header.
COLHEADERFONTSIZE	Column header font size	Optional font size to use for column header.
COLHEADERITALIC	Column header in italics	Optional; if Yes, row column is displayed in an italic font; default is No.
COLHEADERS	Display column headers	Optional attribute; column headers are displayed if Yes; default is Yes.
DELETE	Allow delete	Optional; if Yes, allows records to be deleted from the grid. Default is No.
DELETEBUTTON	Delete button text	Optional text to use for the Delete button; default is Delete.
FONT	Font face	Optional font face to use.
FONTSIZE	Font Size	Optional font size.
GRIDDATAALIGN	Data alignment	Data alignment; may be left, right, or center; may be overridden at the column level.
GRIDLINES	Display grid lines	Optional grid lines displayed if Yes; default is Yes.

Attribute	Description	Notes
HEIGHT	Control height	Optional height in pixels.
HIGHLIGHTHREF	Highlight links	Optional attribute; if Yes, links are highlighted and underlined; defaults to Yes.
HREF	URL	Optional URL to go to upon item selection; if populated by a query, this may be a query column.
HREFKEY	Primary key column	Optional name of column to be used as the primary key.
HSPACE	Control horizontal spacing	Optional horizontal spacing in pixels.
INSERT	Allow insert	Optional; if Yes, allows records to be added to the grid; default is No.
INSERTBUTTON	Insert button text	Optional text to use for the Insert button; default is Insert.
ITALIC	Italic face text	Optional attribute; must be Yes or No if specified; defaults to No.
NAME	Unique control name	This attribute is required.
NOTSUPPORTED	Text to be used for non Java browsers	Optional text (or HTML code) to be displayed on non–Java-capable browsers.
ONERROR	JavaScript error function	Optional override to your own JavaScript error message function.
ONVALIDATE	JavaScript validation function	Optional override to your own JavaScript validation function.
PICTUREBAR	Display picture bar with icons	Optional attribute; if Yes a button bar with icons is displayed for insert, delete, and sort; default is No.
QUERY	Query to populate grid	Optional name of query to be used to populate the grid.
ROWHEADER	Display row header	Optional attribute displays header if Yes; default is Yes.
ROWHEADERALIGN	Row header alignment	Optional attribute may be left, center, or right; default is left.

App
A

continues

Table A.25   Continued

Attribute	Description	Notes
ROWHEADERBOLD	Row header in bold	Optional; if Yes, row header is displayed in a bold font; default is No.
ROWHEADERFONT	Row header font	Optional font to use for row header.
ROWHEADERFONTSIZE	Row header font size	Optional font size to use for row header.
ROWHEADERITALIC	Row header in italics	Optional; if Yes, row header is displayed in an italic font; default is No.
ROWHEADERWIDTH	Row header width	Optional row header width in pixels.
ROWHEIGHT	Row height	Optional height of row in pixels.
SELECTCOLOR	Selection color	Optional attribute; possible values are black, cyan, darkgray, gray, lightgray, magenta, orange, pink, white, yellow, or any color specified in RGB form.
SELECTMODE	Selection mode	Optional attribute, may be EDIT SINGLE ROW COLUMN or BROWSE; default is BROWSE.
SORT	Allow sorting	Optional; if Yes, allows grid data to be sorted; default is No.
SORTASCENDINGBUTTON	Sort ascending button text	Optional text to use for the sort ascending button; default is A -> Z.
SORTDESCENDINGBUTTON	Sort descending button text	Optional text to use for the sort descending button; default is Z -> A.
TARGET	Link target window	Optional name of target window for HREF URL.
VSPACE	Control vertical spacing	Optional vertical spacing in pixels.
WIDTH	Control width	Optional width in pixels.

Table A.26   \<CFGRIDCOLUMN\> Attributes

Attribute	Description	Notes
BOLD	Bold face text	Optional attribute, must be Yes or No if specified; defaults to No.

Attribute	Description	Notes
DATAALIGN	Data alignment	Optional attribute may be `left`, `center`, or `right`; default is `left`.
DISPLAY	Display column	Optional attribute; if `No`, column is hidden; default is `Yes`.
FONT	Font face	Optional font face to use.
FONTSIZE	Font Size	Optional font size.
HEADER	Header text	Optional header text; defaults to column name.
HEADERALIGN	Header alignment	Optional attribute; may be `left`, `center`, or `right`; default is `left`.
HEADERBOLD	Header in bold	Optional; if `Yes`, header is displayed in a bold font; default is `No`.
HEADERFONT	Header font	Optional font to use for header.
HEADERFONTSIZE	Header font size	Optional font size to use for header.
HEADERITALIC	Header in italics	Optional; if `Yes`, header is displayed in an italic font; default is `No`.
HREF	URL	URL for selection in this column; may be absolute or relative.
HREFKEY	Primary key	Optional primary key to use for this column.
ITALIC	Italic face text	Optional attribute; must be `Yes` or `No` if specified; defaults to `No`.
NAME	Column name	Required attribute; if using a query to populate the grid, this must be a valid column name.
NUMBERFORMAT	Number formatting	Optional attribute, uses `NumberFormat()` function masks; see that function for mask details.
SELECT	Allow selection	Optional attribute; if `No`, selection or editing is not allowed in this column.
TARGET	Target window	Optional target window for `HREF`.
TYPE	Data type	Optional attribute; may be image or numeric. If image, an appropriate graphic is displayed for the cell value.
WIDTH	Column width	Optional column width in pixels.

Table A.27 `<CFGRIDROW>` **Attributes**

Attribute	Description	Notes
DATA	Row data	Comma-delimited list of data to be displayed; one item for each row in the grid.

Examples: This first example displays the results of a query in a simple browse-only grid:

```
<CFFRORM ACTION="process.cfm">
<CFGRID NAME="Users" QUERY="Users">
</CFGRID>
</CFFORM>
```

This next example specifies the columns to be displayed and allows editing, but prevents the primary key from being edited:

```
<CFFRORM ACTION="process.cfm">
<CFGRID NAME="Users" QUERY="Users" MODE="EDIT">
<CFGRIDITEM NAME="ID" DISPLAY="No">
<CFGRIDITEM NAME="LastName">
<CFGRIDITEM NAME="FirstName">
</CFGRID>
</CFFORM>
```

For more information about using `<CFGRID>`, see Chapter 23.

N O T E The `<CFGRID>` control is only accessible by users with Java-enabled browsers. ■

See also: `<CFFORM>`, `<CFGRIDUPDATE>`, `<CFINPUT>`, `<CFSELECT>`, `<CFSLIDER>`, `<CFTEXTINPUT>`, `<CFTREE>`

`<CFGRIDUPDATE>`

Description: `<CFGRIDUPDATE>` provides the action back end to support `<CFGRID>` in edit mode. `<CFGRIDUPDATE>` performs all inserts, deletes, and updates in one simple operation. `<CFGRIDUPDATE>` may only be used in an action page to which a form containing a `<CFGRID>` control was submitted. `<CFGRIDUPDATE>` attributes are listed in Table A.28.

Syntax:

```
<CFGRIDUPDATE DATASOURCE="ODBC Data Source Name" DBNAME="database name"
 DBPOOL="pool" DBTYPE="type" DBSERVER="dbms" GRID="Grid Name" KEYONLY="Yes¦No"
 PASSWORD="Password" PROVIDER="provider" PROVIDERDSN="data source"
 TABLENAME="Table Name" TABLEOWNER="Table Owner Name"
 TABLEQUALIFIER="Table Qualifier" USERNAME="User Name">
```

Table A.28 <CFGRIDUPDATE> **Attributes**

Attribute	Description	Notes
DATASOURCE	ODBD data source	This attribute is required.
DBNAME	Sybase database name	Optional attribute; only used if using native Sybase drivers.
DBPOOL	Database connection pool name	Optional database pool name.
DBSERVER	Database server	Optional database server, only used if using native database drives.
DBTYPE	Database type	Optional type; defaults to ODBC; other values are Oracle73, Oracle80, and Sybase11.
GRID	Grid name	This attribute is required; the name of the grid in the submitted form with which to update the table.
KEYONLY	WHERE clause construction	If Yes, the WHERE clause generated by <CFGRID> contains just the primary; default is Yes.
PASSWORD	ODBC login password	Optional ODBC login password.
PROVIDER	OLE-DB COM provider	Optional attribute; only used if using OLE-DB.
PROVIDERDSN	Data source OLE-DB COM provider	Optional attribute; only used if using OLE-DB.
TABLENAME	Table name	This attribute is required.
TABLEOWNER	Table owner	Optional ODBC table owner.
TABLEQUALIFIER	Table qualifier	Optional ODBC table qualifier.
USERNAME	ODBC username	Optional ODBC username.

Examples: The following example updates a table with the data in a editable grid:

```
<CFGRIDUPDATE DATASOURCE="A2Z" TABLE="Employees" GRID="Emp">
```

For more information about using <CFGRIDUPDATE>, see Chapter 23.

See also: <CFFORM>, <CFGRID>

<CFHEADER>

Description: <CFHEADER> allows you to control the contents of specific HTTP headers.

Syntax:

```
<CFHEADER NAME="Header Name" VALUE="Value">
```

Table A.29 <CFHEADER> **Attributes**

Attribute	Description	Notes
NAME	HTTP header to be set	This attribute is required.
VALUE	Header value	This attribute is required.

Example: The following example sets an expiration header to Now() in order to prevent it from being cached:

```
<CFHEADER NAME="Expires" VALUE="#Now()#">
```

N O T E There is usually little need to use <CFHEADER> because ColdFusion sets the HTTP headers automatically to optimum values. ■

<CFHTMLHEAD>

Description: <CFHTMLHEAD> writes text into the header section of your Web page.

Syntax:

```
<CFHTMLHEAD TEXT="Text">
```

Table A.30 <CFHTMLHEAD> **Attributes**

Attribute	Description	Notes
TEXT	Header text	This attribute is required.

Example: This example write a <TITLE> tag into the head section:

```
<CFHTMLHEAD TEXT="<TITLE>A2Z Home Page</TITLE>">
```

<CFHTTP>, <CFHTTPPARAM>, </CFHTTP>

Description: <CFHTTP> allows you to process HTTP GET and POST requests within your ColdFusion code. If using the POST method, parameters may be passed using the <CFHTTPPARAM> tag. <CFHTTPPARAM> can only be used between <CFHTTP> and </CFHTTP> tags.

<CFHTTP> attributes are listed in Table A.31, <CFHTTPPARAM> attributes are listed in Table A.32. <CFHTTP> sets special variables upon completion that you can inspect; they are listed in Table A.33.

Syntax:

```
<CFHTTP COLUMNS="Column Names" DELIMITER="Delimiter Character" FILE="File Name"
 METHOD="Get¦Post" NAME="Query Name" PASSWORD="Password" PATH="Directory"
 PROXYSERVER="Host Name" RESOLVEURL="Yes¦No" TEXTQUALIFIER="Text Qualifier"
 URL="Host Name" USERNAME="User Name">

<CFHTTPPARAM FILE="File Name" NAME="Field Name" TYPE="Type" VALUE="Value">
```

Table A.31   **<CFHTTP> Attributes**

Attribute	Description	Notes
COLUMNS	Query columns	Optional attribute; query columns for retrieved data.
DELIMITER	Column delimiter	Required if NAME is used; default delimiter is a comma.
FILE	Filename	Required only if PATH is used; file to save.
METHOD	Submission method	This attribute is required; must be either GET or POST; use POST to use <CFHTTPPARAM>.
NAME	Query name	Optional attribute; name of query to be constructed with HTTP results.
PASSWORD	User password	Optional attribute; user password if required by server.
PATH	File path	Optional attribute, path to save file if method is POST.
PROXYSERVER	Server name	Optional name of proxy server to use.
RESOLVEURL	Resolve URL	Optional attribute; defaults to No; if Yes, fully resolves embedded URLs.
TEXTQUALIFIER	Text qualifier	Required if NAME is used; delimiter indicating start and end of column.
URL	Host URL	This attribute is required; must be DNS name or IP address of a valid host.
USERNAME	Username	Optional attribute; username if required by server.

Table A.32 `<CFHTTPPARAM>` **Attributes**

Attribute	Description	Notes
FILE	Filename	Required if TYPE is File.
NAME	Field name	This attribute is required.
TYPE	Field type	This attribute is required; must be URL, FORMFIELD, COOKIE, CGI, or FILE.
VALUE	Field value	This attribute is optional unless TYPE is File.

Table A.33 `<CFHTTP>` **Returned Variables**

Field	Description
#FILE.FileContent#	Content returned by HTTP request
#FILE.MimeType#	MIME type of returned data

Examples: This example retrieves the A2Z home page:

```
<CFHTTP URL="www.a2zbooks.com/" METHOD="GET">
```

See also: `<CFFTP>`

`<CFIF>, <CFELSEIF>, <CFELSE>, </CFIF>`

Description: The `<CFIF>` set of tags are what allow you to create conditional CFML code. `<CFIF>` and its supporting tags (`<CFELSEIF>`, `<CFELSE>`, and `</CFIF>`) will likely be the tags your use most in your applications.

Every `<CFIF>` tag must have a matching `</CFIF>` tag. The `<CFELSEIF>` and `<CFELSE>` tags are entirely optional. You may use as many `<CFELSEIF>` tags as needed in a `<CFIF>` statement, but only one `<CFELSE>`. `<CFELSE>` must always be the last compare performed if it is used.

`<CFIF>` uses operators to compare values. Conditions can also be combined to perform more complex comparisons.

You may compare any values, including static text and numbers, ColdFusion fields, database column values, and function results.

Syntax:

```
<CFIF Condition><CFELSEIF Condition><CFELSE></CFIF>
```

Table A.34 ColdFusion Conditional Operators

Operator	Alternate	Description
IS	EQUAL, EQ	Check that the right value is equal to the left value.
IS NOT	NOT EQUAL, NEQ	Check that the right value is not equal to the left value.
CONTAINS		Check that the right value is contained within the left value.
DOES NOT CONTAIN		Check that the right value is not contained within the left value.
GREATER THAN	GT	Check that the left value is greater than the right value.
LESS THAN	LT	Check that the left value is less than the right value.
GREATER THAN OR EQUAL	GTE	Check that the left value is greater than or equal to the right value.
LESS THAN OR EQUAL	LTE	Check that the left value is less than or equal to the right value.

Table A.35 ColdFusion Boolean Operators

Operator	Description
AND	Conjunction; returns TRUE only if both expressions are true.
OR	Disjunction; returns TRUE if either expression is true.
NOT	Negation.

This first example checks to see if a field named LastName exists:

```
<CFIF ParameterExists(LastName)>
```

The following example checks to see if both the FirstName and LastName fields exist:

```
<CFIF (ParameterExists(FirstName)) AND (ParameterExists(LastName))>
```

You could use the following to check for either a first name or a last name:

```
<CFIF (ParameterExists(FirstName)) OR (ParameterExists(LastName))>
```

Often you will want to verify that a field is not empty and that it does not contain blank spaces. The following example demonstrates how this can be accomplished:

```
<CFIF Trim(LastName) IS NOT "">
```

You can use the CONTAINS operator to check if a values is within a range of values. Take a look at both these examples:

```
<CFIF "KY,MI,MN,OH,WI" CONTAINS State>
```

```
<CFIF TaxableStates CONTAINS State>
```

More complex expressions can be created by combining conditions within parentheses. For example, the following condition checks to see whether payment is by check or credit card; if payment is by credit card, it checks to ensure that there is an approval code:

```
<CFIF (PaymentType IS "Check") OR ((PaymentType IS "Credit")
AND (ApprovalCode IS NOT ""))>
```

The following example is a complete conditional statement that uses <CFELSEIF> to perform additional comparisons, and uses <CFELSE> to specify a default for values that pass none of the compares:

```
<CFIF State IS "MI">
 Code for Michigan only goes here
<CFELSEIF State IS "IN">
 Code for Indiana only goes here
<CFELSEIF (State IS "OH") OR (State IS "KY")>
 Code for Ohio or Kentucky goes here
<CFELSE>
 Code for all other states goes here
</CFIF>
```

◊ For more information about the<CFIF>tags, **see** "Using CFIFto Create Conditional Code," **p. 291**.

See also: <CFSWITCH>

<CFINCLUDE>

Description: <CFINCLUDE> includes the contents of another template into the one being processed.

Syntax:

```
<CFINCLUDE TEMPLATE="Template File Name">
```

Table A.36 <CFINCLUDE> **Attributes**

Attribute	Description	Notes
TEMPLATE	Name of template to include	This attribute is required. Only relative paths are supported.

Example: The following example includes the footer file in the current directory if it exists, a default footer if not:

```
<CFIF FileExists("FOOTER.CFM")>
`<CFINCLUDE TEMPLATE="FOOTER.CFM">
```

```
<CFELSE>
 <CFINCLUDE TEMPLATE="/DEFAULT/FOOTER.CFM">
</CFIF>
```

 TIP <CFINCLUDE> can help you reuse templates. You can use <CFINCLUDE> to break out common components (such as page headers and footers), which enables you to share them among multiple templates.

For more information about the <CFINCLUDE> tag, see Chapter 21, "Advanced ColdFusion Templates."

See also: <CFLOCATION>

<CFINDEX>

Description: <CFINDEX> is used to populate Verity collections with index data. A collection must be created with the ColdFusion Administrator before it can be populated. <CFINDEX> can be used to index physical files—in which case the filename is returned in searches—or query results—in which case the primary key is returned in searches.

<CFINDEX> attributes are listed in Table A.37.

Syntax:

```
<CFINDEX ACTION="Action" BODY="Text" COLLECTION="Collection Name" CUSTOM1="Data"
 CUSTOM2="Data" EXTENSIONS="File Extensions" EXTERNAL="Yes¦No" KEY="Key"
 QUERY="Query Name" RECURSE="Yes¦No" TITLE="Text" TYPE="Type" URLPATH="Path">
```

Table A.37 <CFINDEX> **Attributes**

Attribute	Description	Notes
ACTION	Action	Required attribute.
BODY	Body to index	Required if TYPE is Custom; if indexing files, this must be the path to the file to be indexed; if indexing a query, this must be the column to be indexed.
COLLECTION	Collection name	Required; name of the collection to be indexed; if using external collections, this must be a fully qualified path to the collection.
CUSTOM1	Custom data	Optional attribute for storing data during indexing.
CUSTOM2	Custom data	Optional attribute for storing data during indexing.

continues

Table A.37 Continued

Attribute	Description	Notes
EXTENSIONS	File extensions	Optional list of extensions of files to be indexed; list must be comma delimited; only used if TYPE is PATH.
EXTERNAL	External collection	Optional attribute; must be Yes if indexing an external collection.
KEY	Unique key	Optional attribute; used to indicate what makes each record unique, if TYPE is File, this should be the document filename; if TYPE is Path, this should be a full path to the document; if TYPE is Custom, this should be any unique identifier.
QUERY	Query name	Optional attribute.
RECURSE	Recurse directories	Optional attribute; if Yes then all subdirectories are indexed too TITLE Document title Required if TYPE is Custom.
TYPE	Index type	Optional attribute, must be FILE, PATH, or CUSTOM.
URLPATH	URL path	Optional attribute, specifies the URL path for files when TYPE = File or TYPE = Path.

Table A.38 <CFINDEX> Actions

Action	Description
DELETE	Deletes a key from a collection
OPTIMIZE	Optimizes a collection
PURGE	Clears all data from a collection
REFRESH	Clears all data from a collection and repopulates it
UPDATE	Updates a collection and adds a key if it does not exist

Examples: This examples indexes all HTM and HTML files in all directories beneath the Web server document root:

```
<CFINDEX COLLECTION="Docs" TYPE="Path" KEY="c:\inetpub\wwwroot"
URLPATH="http://127.0.0.1/" EXTENSIONS=".htm, .html" RECURSE="Yes">
```

For more information about using <CFINDEX> and Verity collections, see Chapter 29.

See also: <CFCOLLECTION>, <CFSEARCH>

<CFINPUT>

Description: <CFINPUT> is an enhancement to the standard HTML <INPUT> tag. <CFINPUT> allows you to automatically embed JavaScript client-side validation code in your HTML forms. <CFINPUT> must be used between <CFFORM> and </CFORM> tags; it is not a Java control.

Syntax:

```
<CFINPUT CHECKED MAXLENGTH="Length" MESSAGE="Message Text" NAME="Field Name"
 ONERROR="JavaScipt Error Function" ONVALIDATE="JavaScript Validation Function"
 RANGE="Range Values" REQUIRED="Yes|No" SIZE="Field Size" TYPE="Type"
 VALIDATE="Validation Type" VALUE="Initial Value">
```

Table A.39   <CFINPUT> **Attributes**

Attribute	Description	Notes
CHECKED	Checked state	Optional; only valid if type is RADIO or CHECKBOX and if present radio button or check box is pre-checked.
MAXLENGTH	Maximum number of characters	Optional attribute.
MESSAGE	Validation failure message	Optional message to display upon validation failure.
NAME	Unique control name	This attribute is required.
ONERROR	JavaScript error	Optional override to function your own JavaScript error message function.
ONVALIDATE	JavaScript validation function	Optional override to your own JavaScript validation function.
RANGE	Range minimum and maximum	Optional range for numeric values only; must be specified as two numbers separated by a comma.
REQUIRED	Field is required	Optional required flag; must be Yes or No if specified; defaults to No.
SIZE	Field size	Optional number of characters to display before needing horizontal scrolling.
TYPE	Input type	Must be TEXT, RADIO, CHECKBOX, or PASSWORD.
VALIDATE	Field validation	Optional field validation.
VALUE	Initial value	Optional initial field value.

Table A.40 `<CFINPUT>` **Validation Types**

Type	Description
Creditcard	Correctly formatted credit card number verified using `mod10`.
Date	Date in mm/dd/yy format.
Eurodate	European date in dd/mm/yy format.
Float	Number with decimal point.
Integer	Number with no decimal point.
Social_Security_Number	Social security number formatted as 999-99-9999 (using hyphens or spaces as separators).
Telephone	Phone number in 999-999-9999 format (using hyphens or spaces as separators); area code and exchange must not begin with 0 or 1.
Time	Time in hh:mm or hh:mm:ss format.
Zipcode	U.S. zipcode, either 99999 or 99999-9999 format.

Examples: This example creates a simple text field that is flagged as required:

```
<CFFORM ACTION="process.cfm">
<CFINPUT TYPE="text" NAME="name" REQUIRED="Yes" MESSAGE="NAME is required!">
</CFFORM>
```

This next example creates a field that accepts only a valid telephone number:

```
<CFFORM ACTION="process.cfm">
<CFINPUT TYPE="text" NAME="phone" VALIDATE="telephone"
 MESSAGE="You entered an invalid phone number!">
</CFFORM>
```

NOTE   `<CFINPUT>` does not support input fields of type HIDDEN. ■

For more information about `<CFINPUT>`, see Chapter 15.

See also: `<CFFORM>`, `<CFGIRD>`, `<CFSELECT>`, `<CFSLIDER>`, `<CFTEXTINPUT>`, `<CFTREE>`

`<CFINSERT>`

Description: `<CFINSERT>` adds a single row to a database table. `<CFINSERT>` requires that the database and table names be provided. All other attributes are optional.

Syntax:

```
<CFINSERT DATASOURCE="ODBC Data Source" DBNAME="database name" DBPOOL="pool"
 DBTYPE="type" DBSERVER="dbms" FORMFIELDS="List of File to Insert"
```

```
PASSWORD="Password" PROVIDER="provider" PROVIDERDSN="data source"
TABLENAME="Table Name" TABLEOWNER="owner" TABLEQUALIFIER="qualifier"
USERNAME="User Name">
```

Table A.41   <CFINSERT> **Attributes**

Attribute	Description	Notes
DATASOURCE	Name of ODBC data source	The specified data source must already exist. This attribute is required.
DBNAME	Sybase database name	Optional attribute; only used if using native Sybase drivers.
DBPOOL	Database connection pool name	Optional database pool name.
DBSERVER	Database server	Optional database server; only used if using native database drives.
DBTYPE	Database type	Optional type; defaults to ODBC; other values are Oracle73, Oracle80, and Sybase11.
FORMFIELDS	List of fields to insert	This optional attribute specifies which fields are to be inserted if they are present. Any fields present that are not in the list will not be inserted.
PASSWORD	ODBC data source password	This optional attribute is used to override the ODBC login password specified in the ColdFusion Administrator.
PROVIDER	OLE-DB COM provider	Optional attribute; only used if using OLE-DB.
PROVIDERDSN	Data source OLE-DB COM provider	Optional attribute; only used if using OLE-DB.
TABLENAME	Name of table to insert data into	Some ODBC data source require fully qualified table names. This attribute is required.
TABLEOWNER	Table owner name	Optional attribute used by databases that support table ownership.
TABLEQUALIFIER	Table qualifier	Optional attribute used by databases that support full qualifiers.
USERNAME	ODBC data source login name	The optional attribute is used to override the ODBC login name specified in the ColdFusion Administrator.

N O T E Your form field names must match the column names in the destination table for `<CFINSERT>` to work correctly. ■

 T I P If your form contains fields that are not part of the table into which you are inserting data, use the `FORMFIELDS` attribute to instruct ColdFusion to ignore those fields.

T I P For more control over the insertion of rows into a database table, you may use the `<CFQUERY>` tag specifying INSERT as the SQL statement.

Example: The following example inserts a new row into the Employees table in the A2Z data source:

```
<CFINSERT DATASOURCE="A2Z" TABLENAME="Employees">
```

The next example inserts a new row into the same table, but only inserts values into the three specified fields if they exist:

```
<CFINSERT DATASOURCE="A2Z" TABLENAME="Employees"
 FORMFIELD="LastName,FirstName,PhoneExtension">
```

For more information about the `<CFINSERT>` tag, see Chapter 13, "Using Forms to Add or Change Data."

See also: `<CFQUERY>`, `<CFUPDATE>`

`<CFLDAP>`

Description: `<CFLDAP>` is used to for all interaction with LDAP servers. It can be used to search an LDAP server, as well as to add, change, or delete data. Table A.42 lists the attributes for `<CFLDAP>`.

Syntax:

```
<CFLDAP ACTION="Action" ATTRIBUTES="Attributes List" DN="Name" FILTER="Filter"
 MAXROWS="Number" NAME="Query Name" PASSWORD="Password" PORT="Port Number"
 SCOPE="Scope" SERVER="Server Address" SORT="Sort Order" START="Start Position"
 STARTROW="Number" TIMEOUT="Timeout" USERNAME="Name">
```

Table A.42 `<CFLDAP>` **Attributes**

Attribute	Description	Notes
ACTION	Action	Required attribute.
ATTRIBUTES	Desired attributes	Required if ACTION is QUERY; comma-delimited list of desired attributes, query specified in NAME attribute will contain these columns.

Attribute	Description	Notes
DN	Distinguished name	Required if ACTION is ADD MODIFY MODIFYDN or delete.
FILTER	Search filter	Optional search filter used if ACTION is QUERY.
MAXROWS	Maximum rows to retrieve	Optional attribute.
NAME	Query name	Name of query for returned data; required if ACTION is QUERY.
PASSWORD	User password	Optional user password; might be required for update operations.
PORT	Port number	Optional port number; defaults to 389 if not specified.
SCOPE	Search scope	Optional search scope if ACTION is QUERY; valid values are ONELEVEL, BASE and SUBTREE; default is ONELEVEL.
SERVER	Server name	Required DNS name or IP address of LDAP server.
SORT	Sort order	Optional attribute used if ACTION is QUERY; specifies the sort order as a comma-delimited list; may use ASC for ascending and DESC for descending; default is ASC.
START	Start name	Required if ACTION is QUERY; distinguished name to start search at.
STARTROW	Start row	Optional start row; defaults to 1.
TIMEOUT	Timeout value	Optional timeout value.
USERNAME	User login name	Optional user login name; might be required for update operations.

Table A.43   <CFLDAP> Actions

Action	Description
ADD	Adds an entry to an LDAP server
DELETE	Deletes an entry from an LDAP server
MODIFY	Updates an entry on an LDAP server
MODIFYDN	Updates the distinguished name of an entry on an LDAP server
QUERY	Performs a query against an LDAP server

Example: The following example retrieves a list of names from a public directory:

```
<CFLDAP Name="seach" SERVER="ldap.four11.com" ACTION="Query" ATTRIBUTES="cn"
 SCOPE="Subtree" SORT="cn Asc" FILTER="(sn=*)" START="#search#, c=US">
```

For more information about <CFLDAP> and directory services, see Chapter 30, "Directory Services."

<CFLOCATION>

Description: <CFLOCATION> is used to redirect a browser to a different URL.

Syntax:

```
<CFLOCATION ADDTOKEN="Yes or No" URL="URL">
```

Table A.44 <CFLOCATION> **Attributes**

Attribute	Description	Notes
ADDTOKEN	Adds session tokens	Optional attribute; default is Yes.
URL	URL (or relative URL) to redirect to	This attribute is required.

Example: The following example redirects the user to a login page:

```
<CFLOCATION URL="login.cfm">
```

N O T E Unlike <CFINCLUDE>, any text or CFML after the <CFLOCATION> tag is ignored by ColdFusion. ■

See also: <CFINCLUDE>

<CFLOCK>, </CFLOCK>

Description: <CFLOCK> is used to restrict blocks of code to single threaded access. Once inside a locked block of code, all other threads are queued until the thread with the exclusive lock relinquishes control. Table A.45 lists all the <CFLOCK> attributes.

Syntax:

```
<CFLOCK TIMEOUT="timeout" THROWONTIMEOUT="Yes or No"> … </CFLOCK>
```

Table A.45 **<CFLOCK> Attributes**

Attribute	Description	Notes
TIMEOUT	Timeout interval	This attribute is required.
THROWONTIMEOUT	Timeout handling	This optional attribute specifies how timeouts should be handled; an exception is thrown if Yes, processing continues if No; defaults to Yes.

App

A

Example: The following code locks a call to a custom tag:

```
<CFLOCK TIMEOUT="60">
 <CF_MyTag>
</CFLOCK>
```

N O T E   <CFLOCK> is primarily designed for use with custom tags that are not multithreaded. ■

CAUTION

Avoid unnecessary use of <CFLOCK>. Forcing code to single threaded use only can seriously impact system performance.

See also: <CFCATCH>, <CFTRY>

<CFLOOP>, <CFBREAK>, </CFLOOP>

Description: <CFLOOP> allows you to create loops within your code. *Loops* are blocks of code that are executed repeatedly until a specific condition is met. <CFBREAK> allows you to unconditionally terminate a loop. ColdFusion supports five kinds of loops:

- For loops repeat a specific number of times.
- While loops repeat until a set condition returns FALSE.
- Query loops go through the results of a <CFQUERY> once for each row returned.
- List loops go through the elements of a specified list.
- Collection loops are used to loop over collections.

Syntax:

For loop:

```
<CFLOOP INDEX="Index" FROM="Loop Start" TO="Loop End" STEP="Step Value">
```

While loop:

```
<CFLOOP CONDITION="Expression">
```

Query loop:

`<CFLOOP QUERY="Query Name" STARTROW="Start Row Value" ENDROW="End Row Value">`

List loop:

`<CFLOOP INDEX="Index" LIST="List" DELIMITERS="Delimiters">`

Collection loop:

`<CFLOOP COLLECTION="Collection" ITEM="Item">`

N O T E The syntax and use of <CFLOOP> varies based on the type of loop being executed. ■

Table A.46 `<CFLOOP>` Attributes

Attribute	Description	Notes
COLLECTION	Collection to loop through	This attribute is required for Collection loops.
CONDITION	While loop condition	This attribute is required for While loops and must be a valid condition.
DELIMITERS	List loop delimiters	This is an optional List loop attribute; if it is omitted, the default delimiter of a comma is used.
ENDROW	Query loop end position	This is an optional Query loop attribute; if it is omitted, all rows are processed.
FROM	For loop start position	This attribute is required for For loops and must be a numeric value.
INDEX	Current element	This attribute is required for For loops and List loops and holds the name of the variable that will contain the current element.
ITEM	Current item	This attribute is required for Collection loops.
LIST	List loop list	This attribute is required for List loops and can be a ColdFusion list field or a static string.
QUERY	Query loop query	This attribute is required for Query loops and must be the name of a previously executed <CFQUERY>.
STARTROW	Query loop start position	Thus is an optional Query loop attribute; if it is omitted, the loop will start at the first row.

Attribute	Description	Notes
STEP	For loop step value	This is an optional For loop attribute; if it is omitted, the default value of 1 is used.
TO	For loop end position	This attribute is required for For loops and must be a numeric value.

Example: The following is a For loop used in a FORM to populate a select field with the years 1901 to 2000. The alternative would have been to enter 100 OPTION values manually:

```
<SELECT NAME="year">
 <CFLOOP INDEX="YearValue" FROM="1901" TO="2000">
 <OPTION><CFOUTPUT>#YearValue#</CFOUTPUT>
</SELECT>
```

The next example does the exact same thing, but presents the list in reverse order. This is done by specifying a STEP value of -1:

```
<SELECT NAME="year">
 <CFLOOP INDEX="YearValue" FROM="2000" TO="1901" STEP="-1">
  <OPTION><CFOUTPUT>#YearValue#</CFOUTPUT>
 </CFLOOP>
</SELECT>
```

This example loops until any random number between 1 and 10, excluding 5, is generated:

```
<CFSET RandomNumber = 0>
<CFLOOP CONDITION= "(#RandomNumber# GT 0) AND (#RandomNumber# NEQ 5)">
 <CFSET RandoNumber = RandRange(1, 10)>
</CFLOOP>
```

This example creates a Query loop that processes an existing <CFQUERY> named Orders, but only processes rows 100 through 150:

```
<CFLOOP QUERY="Orders" STARTROW="100" ENDROW="150">
 <CFOUTPUT>
  #OrderNum# - #DateFormat(OrderDate)# - #DollarFormat(Total)#<BR>
 </CFOUTPUT>
</CFLOOP>
```

This example loops through a user-supplied list of titles, displaying them one at a time:

```
<CFLOOP INDEX="Title" LIST="#FORM.Titles#">
 <CFOUTPUT>
  Title: #Title#<BR>
 </CFOUTPUT>
</CFLOOP>
```

This example uses <CFBREAK> to terminate a loop when a specific row is reached—in this case, an order number greater than 10000:

```
<CFLOOP QUERY="Orders" >
 <CFIF OrderNum GT 10000>
  <CFBREAK>
 </CFIF>
```

```
<CFOUTPUT>
 #OrderNum# - #DateFormat(OrderDate)# - #DollarFormat(Total)#<BR>
</CFOUTPUT>
</CFLOOP>
```

TIP Using <CFLOOP> to process queries is substantially slower than using <CFOUTPUT>. Whenever possible, use <CFOUTPUT> to loop through query results.

N O T E The <CFLOOP> tag may be nested, and there is no limit placed on the number of nested loops allowed. ▬

`<CFMAIL>`, `</CFMAIL>`

Description: `<CFMAIL>` generates SMTP mail from within ColdFusion templates. `<CFMAIL>` can be used to output query results, just like `<CFOUTPUT>`, or on its own. The `<CFMAIL>` tag itself is used to set up the mail message, all text between the `<CFMAIL>` and `</CFMAIL>` tags is sent as the message body. `<CFMAIL>` requires that you specify a sender address, recipient address, and subject. All other attributes are optional.

Syntax:

```
<CFLOCATION CC="Carbon Copy Addresses" FROM="Sender Address" GROUP="Group Name"
 MAXROWS="Maximum Mail Messages" PORT="SMTP TCP/IP Port" QUERY="Query Name"
 SERVER="SMTP Server Address" SUBJECT="Subject" TIMEOUT="SMTP Connection Timeout"
 TO="Recipient Address" TYPE="Message Type" MAILERID="id">
Message
</CFMAIL>
```

Table A.47 `<CFMAIL>` **Attributes**

Attribute	Description	Notes
CC	Carbon copy addresses	Optional one or more carbon copy addresses separated by commas.
FROM	Sender's address	Required sender's email address.
GROUP	Query column to group on	Optional attribute that specifies column to group on. See `<CFOUTPUT>` for more information on grouping data.
MAXROWS	Maximum message to send	Optional attribute specifying the maximum number of email messages to generate.
MAILERID	Mailer ID	Optional mailer ID; default is `Allaire ColdFusion Application Server`.
PORT	TCP/IP SMTP port	Optional TCP/IP SMTP port; overrides the default value of 25 if specified.

Attribute	Description	Notes
QUERY	`<CFQUERY>` to draw data from	Email can be generated based on the results of a `<CFQUERY>`; to do this specify the name of the `<CFQUERY>` here. This is an optional attribute.
SERVER	SMTP mail server	Optional SMTP mail server name; overrides the default setting if specified.
SUBJECT	Message subject	Required message subject.
TIMEOUT	Connection timeout interval	Optional SMTP connection timeout interval; overrides the default setting if specified.
TO	Recipient's address	Required recipient's email address.
TYPE	Message type	Optional message type; currently the only supported type is HTML, indicating that there is HTML code embedded in the message.

Example: The following is a simple email message based on a form submission. It uses form fields in both the attributes and the message body itself:

```
<CFMAIL
 FROM="#FORM.EMail#"
 TO="sales@a2zbooks.com"
 SUBJECT="Customer inquiry"
>
The following customer inquiry was posted to our web site:
Name: #FORM.name#
email: #FORM.EMail#

Message:
#FORM.Message#

</CFMAIL>
```

This next example sends an email message based on `<CFQUERY>` results. The message is sent once for each row retrieved:

```
<CFMAIL
 QUERY="MailingList"
 FROM="sales@a2zbooks.com"
 TO="#EMailAddress#"
 SUBJECT="Monthly Online Newsletter"
>
Dear #FirstName#,

This email message is to remind you that our new monthly online newsletter
is now on our web site.
```

You can access it at http://www.a2zbooks.com/newsletter

Thanks for you continued interest in our product line.

A2Z Books Sales

</CFMAIL>

TIP Unlike Web browsers, email programs do not ignore whitespace. Carriage returns are displayed in the email message if you embed carriage returns between the <CFMAIL> and </CFMAIL> tags.

N O T E To use <CFMAIL>, the ColdFusion SMTP interface must be set up and working. If email is not being sent correctly, use the ColdFusion Administrator to verify that ColdFusion can connect to your SMTP mail server. ■

N O T E The PORT, SERVER, and TIMEOUT attributes will never be used in normal operation. These are primarily used for debugging and troubleshooting email problems. ■

N O T E Email errors are logged to the \CFUSION\MAIL\LOG directory. Messages that cannot be delivered are stored in the \CFUSION\MAIL\UNDELIVR directory. ■

For more information about the <CFMAIL> tag, see Chapter 24, "Interacting with Email."

See also: <CFPOP>

<CFMODULE>

Description: <CFMODULE> is used to call a custom tag explicitly stating its full or relative path. Table A.48 lists the <CFMODULE> attributes. Your own tag attributes may also be added to this list.

Syntax:

```
<CFMODULE NAME="Path" TEMPLATE="Path" …>
```

Table A.48 <CFMODULE> **Attributes**

Attribute	Description	Notes
NAME	Fixed path to tag file	Either TEMPLATE or NAME must be used, but not both at once; use a period for directory delimiters.
TEMPLATE	Relative path to tag file	Either TEMPLATE or NAME must be used, but not both at once.

Examples: This example calls a custom tag named ShowMenu in the parent directory:

```
<CFMODULE TEMPLATE="../showmenu.cfm">
```

See also: <CFASSOCIATE>

<CFOBJECT>

Description: <CFOBJECT> allows you to use COM, DCOM, and CORBA objects within your ColdFusion applications. You need to know an object's ID or filename in order to use it, as well as its methods and properties. <CFOBJECT> attributes are listed in Table A.49.

To use an object with <CFOBJECT>, that object must be already installed on the server.

Syntax:

```
<CFOBJECT ACTION="Action" CLASS="Class ID" CONTEXT="Context" NAME="Name"
SERVER="Server Name" TYPE="COM or CORBA">
```

Table A.49 <CFMODULE> **Attributes**

Attribute	Description	Notes
ACTION	Action	Required attribute; must be either CREATE to instantiate an object or CONNECT to connect to a running object; only used when TYPE is COM.
CLASS	Component ProgID	This attribute is required.
CONTEXT	Operation context	Optional attribute, must be InProc, Local, or Remote. Uses registry setting is not specified.
NAME	Object name	This attribute is required.
SERVER	Valid server name	Server name as UNC, DNS, or IP address; required only if CONTEXT = "remote"; only used if TYPE is COM.
TYPE	Object type	Optional; defaults to COM; valid values are COM and CORBA.

Example: The following example instantiates a COM object named NT.Exec and invokes a method:

```
<CFOBJECT TYPE="COM" CLASS="NT.Exec" ACTION="CREATE" NAME="Exec">
<CFSET Exec.Command = "DIR C:\">
<CFSET temp = Exec.Run()>
```

◊ For more information about<CFOBJECT> and COM, see Chapter 12, "Interfacing with COM and DCOM Objects," of*Advanced ColdFusion 4.0 Application Development* (Que, 1999).

N O T E Use of <CFOBJECT> can be disabled in the ColdFusion Administrator program. ▪

\<CFOUTPUT>, \</CFOUTPUT>

Description: \<CFOUTPUT> is used to output the results of a \<CFQUERY>, or any time text includes variables that are to be expanded. If \<CFQUERY> is used to process the results of a \<CFQUERY> tag, any code between \<CFOUTPUT> and \</CFOUTPUT> is repeated once for every row. \<CFOUTPUT> can be used with the GROUP attribute to specify a data group. Data that is grouped together is displayed so that only the first occurrence of each value is output.

Syntax:

```
<CFOUTPUT QUERY="Query Name" MAXROWS="Maximum Rows" STARTROW="Start Row"
 GROUP="Group Column">

Code

</CFOUTPUT>
```

Table A.50 \<CFOUTPUT> **Attributes**

Attribute	Description	Notes
GROUP	Column to group on	This optional attribute allows you to define output groups.
MAXROWS	Maximum rows to display	This optional attribute specifies the maximum number of rows to display. If omitted, all rows are displayed.
QUERY	Query name	This optional query name refers to the query results within \<CFOUTPUT> text.
STARTROW	First row to display	The optional attribute specifies the output start row.

Table A.51 \<CFOUTPUT> **Fields Available When Using the** QUERY **Attribute**

Field	Description
#ColumnList#	Comma-delimited list of columns with a query
#CurrentRow#	The number of the current row, starting at 1, and incremented each time a row is displayed
#RecordCount#	The total number of records to be output

Example: Any time you use variables or fields within your template, you must enclose them within \<CFOUTPUT> tags as shown in this example. Otherwise the field name is sent as is and not expanded:

```
<CFOUTPUT>
 Hi #name#, thanks for dropping by again.<P>
```

```
You have now visited us #NumberFormat(visits)#
since your first visit on #DateFormat(first_visit)#.
</CFOUTPUT>
```

This example uses <CFOUTPUT> to display the results of a query in an unordered list:

```
<UL>
<CFOUTPUT QUERY="Employees">
 <LI>#LastName#, #FirstName# - Ext: #PhoneExtension#
</CFOUTPUT>
</UL>
```

You can use the GROUP attribute to group output results. This example lists employees within departments:

```
<UL>
 <CFOUTPUT QUERY="Employees" GROUP="Department">
  <LI><B>#Department#</B>
   <UL>
    <CFOUTPUT>
     <LI>#LastName#, #FirstName# - Ext: #PhoneExtension#
    </CFOUTPUT>
   </UL>
 </CFOUTPUT>
</UL>
```

N O T E There is no limit to the number of nested groups that you may use in a <CFOUTPUT>. However, every column used in a GROUP must be part of the SQL statement ORDER BY clause.

 T I P The STARTROW and MAXROWS attribute can be used to implement a "display next n of n" type display. You should note however, that even though only a subset of the retrieved data is displayed, it has *all* been retrieved by the <CFQUERY> statement. So, while the page might be transmitted to the browser quicker, because it contains less text, the SQL operation itself takes no less time.

For more information about <CFOUTPUT>, see Chapter 11, "ColdFusion Basics."

See also: <CFLOOP>, <CFMAIL>, <CFQUERY>, <CFTABLE>

<CFPARAM>

Description: <CFPARAM> lets you specify default values for parameters and specify parameters that are required. <CFPARAM> requires that a variable name be passed to it. If a VALUE is passed as well, that value will be used as the default value if the variable is not specified. If VALUE is not specified, <CFPARAM> requires that the named variable be passed; it will generate an error message if it is not.

Syntax:

```
<CFPARAM NAME="Parameter Name" DEFAULT="Default">
```

Table A.52   <CFPARAM> **Attributes**

Attribute	Description	Notes
NAME	Name of variable	Name should be fully qualified with variable type. This attribute is required.
DEFAULT	Default variable value	This attribute is optional. If specified, the value is used as the default value whenever this variable is used.

Example: The following specifies a default value for a field that is to be used in a <CFQUERY> tag, making it unnecessary to write conditional code to build a dynamic SQL statement:

```
<CFPARAM NAME="Minimum" DEFAULT="10">
<CFQUERY NAME="OverDue" DATASOURCE= "A2Z">
 SELECT * FROM Inventory WHERE NumberInStock < #Minimum#
</CFQUERY>
```

This example makes the Minimum field required; an error is generated if you request the template and the Minimum field is not specified:

```
<CFPARAM NAME="Minimum" >
<CFQUERY NAME="OverDue" DATASOURCE= "A2Z">
 SELECT * FROM Inventory WHERE NumberInStock < #Minimum#
</CFQUERY>
```

See also: <CFSET>

<CFPOP>

Description: <CFPOP> retrieves and manipulates mail in a POP3 mailbox. You must know three things in order to access a POP mailbox: the POP server name, the POP login name, and the account password. <CFPOP> has three modes of operation: It can be used to retrieve just mail headers, entire message bodies, and to delete messages. POP messages are not automatically deleted when they are read, and must be deleted explicitly with a DELETE operation. Table A.53 lists the <CFPOP> attributes; Table A.55 lists the columns returned when retrieving mail or mail headers.

Syntax:

```
<CFPOP ACTION="Action" ATTACHMENTSPATH="Path" MAXROWS="Number"
 MESSAGENUMBER="Messages" NAME="Query Name" PASSWORD="Password" PORT="Port
Number"
 SERVER="Mail Server" STARTROW="Number" TIMEOUT="Timeout" USERNAME="User Name">
```

Table A.53 <CFPOP> **Attributes**

Attribute	Description	Notes
ACTION	Action	Optional.
ATTACHMENTSPATH	Attachment path	Optional path to store mail attachments.
MAXROWS	Maximum messages to retrieve	Optional attribute; ignored ID MESSAGENUMBER is used.
MESSAGENUMBER	Message number	Optional message number (or comma-delimited list of message numbers); required if ACTION is DELETE; specifies the messages to be deleted or retrieved.
NAME	Query name	Required if ACTION is GETALL or GETHEADERONLY; name of query to be returned; query columns are listed in Table A.55.
PASSWORD	Password	Optional POP account password; most POP servers require this.
PORT	Mail server port	Optional attribute; defaults to port 110.
SERVER	Mail server	Required; DNS name or IP address of the POP mail server.
STARTROW	Start row	Optional start row; defaults to 1; ignored if MESSAGENUMBER is used.
TIMEOUT	Timeout value	Optional timeout value.
USERNAME	Login name	Optional POP login name; most POP servers require this.

Table A.54 <CFPOP> **Actions**

Action	Description
DELETE	Delete messages from a POP mailbox
GETALL	Gets message headers and body
GETHEADERONLY	Gets just message headers

Table A.55 <CFPOP> Query Columns

Column	Description
ATTACHMENTFILES	List of saved attachments; only present if ACTION is GETALL and an ATTACHMENT path was specified.
ATTACHMENTS	List of original attachment names; only present if ACTION is GETALL and an ATTACHMENT path was specified.
CC	List of any carbon copy recipients.
DATE	Message date.
FROM	Sender name.
HEADER	Mail header.
MESSAGENUMBER	Message number for use in calls with future calls.
REPLYTO	Email address to reply to.
SUBJECT	Message subject.
TO	Recipient list.

Examples: This example retrieves a list of waiting mail in a POP mailbox and then displays the message list in an HTML list:

```
<CFPOP SERVER="mail.a2zbooks.com" USERNAME=#username# PASSWORD=#pwd#
 ACTION="GETHEADERONLY" NAME="msg">
<UL>
<CFOUTPUT QUERY="msg">
<LI>From: #from# - Subject: #subject#
</CFOUTPUT>
</UL>
```

N O T E <CFPOP> is used to retrieve mail only. Use the <CFMAIL> tag to send mail. ■

For more information about the <CFPOP> tag, see Chapter 24.

See also: <CFMAIL>

<CFQUERY>, </CFQUERY>

Description: <CFQUERY> submits SQL statements to an ODBC driver. SQL statements are not limited to SELECT statements, but can also be INSERT, UPDATE, and DELETE statements, as well as calls to stored procedures. <CFQUERY> returns results in a named set if you specify a query name in the NAME attribute. The <CFQUERY> attributes set up the query, and any text between the <CFQUERY> and </CFQUERY> tags becomes the SQL statement that is sent to the ODBC driver. ColdFusion conditional code may be used between the <CFQUERY> and </CFQUERY> tags, allowing you to create dynamic SQL statements.

Syntax:

```
<CFQUERY NAME="Parameter Name" DATASOURCE="ODBC Data Source"
 DBNAME="database name" DBPOOL="pool" DBTYPE="type" DBSERVER="dbms"
 USERNAME="User Name" PASSWORD="Password" PROVIDER="provider"
 PROVIDERDSN="data source" BLOCKFACTOR="factor" TIMEOUT="timeout value"
 CACHEDAFTER="date" CACHEDWITHIN="time span" DEBUG="Yes or No">
SQL statement
</CFQUERY>
```

Table A.56   **<CFQUERY> Attributes**

Attribute	Description	Notes
BLOCKFACTOR	Number of rows to retrieve at once	This optional attribute is available if using ODBC or Oracle drivers; valid values are 1 to 100, default value is 1.
CACHEDAFTER	Cache date	Optional attribute; specifies that query is to be cached and cached copy is to be used after specified date.
CACHEDWITHIN	Cache time span	Optional attribute; specifies that query is to be cached and cached copy is to be used within a relative time span.
DATASOURCE	ODBC data source	This optional attribute is used to override the ODBC data source specified when the report was created.
DBNAME	Sybase database name	Optional attribute; only used if using native Sybase drivers.
DBPOOL	Database connection pool name	Optional database pool name.
DBSERVER	Database server	Optional database server; only used if using native database drives.
DBTYPE	Database type	Optional type; defaults to ODBC; other values are Oracle73, Oracle80, and Sybase11.
DEBUG	Enable query debugging	Optional attribute; turns on query debugging output.

continues

Table A.56 Continued

Attribute	Description	Notes
NAME	Query name	This optional query name is used to refer to the query results in <CFOUTPUT>, <CFMAIL>, or <CFTABLE> tags.
PASSWORD	ODBC data source	This optional attribute password is used to override the ODBC login password specified in the ColdFusion Administrator.
PROVIDER	OLE-DB COM provider	Optional attribute; only used if using OLE-DB.
PROVIDERDSN	Data source OLE-DB COM provider	Optional attribute; only used if using OLE-DB.
TIMEOUT	Timeout value	Optional timeout value in milliseconds.
USERNAME	ODBC data source login name	The optional attribute is used to override the ODBC login name specified in the ColdFusion Administrator.

The following example is a simple data retrieval query:

```
<CFQUERY
 DATASOURCE="A2Z"
 NAME="Employees"
>
 SELECT FirstName, LastName, PhoneExtension FROM Employees
</CFQUERY>
```

This example demonstrates how dynamic SQL statements can be constructed using the ColdFusion conditional tags:

```
<
 CFQUERY
 DATASOURCE="A2Z"
 NAME="Employees"
>
 SELECT FirstName, LastName, PhoneExtension, EmployeeID
     FROM Employees
     WHERE EmployeeID = EmployeeID

<CFIF #FirstName# IS NOT "">
 AND FirstName LIKE '#FirstName#%'
</CFIF>

<CFIF #LastName# IS NOT "">
```

```
 AND LastName LIKE '#LastName#%'
</CFIF>

<CFIF #PhoneExtension# IS NOT "">
 AND PhoneExtension LIKE '#PhoneExtension#%'
</CFIF>

ORDER BY LastName, FirstName

</CFQUERY>
```

<CFOUTPUT> can be used to execute any SQL statement, and the following example demonstrates how <CFOUTPUT> can be used to delete rows from a table:

```
<CFQUERY
 DATASOURCE="A2Z"
>
DELETE FROM Employees WHERE EmployeeID = #EmployeeID#"
</CFQUERY>
```

For more information about the <CFQUERY> tag, see Chapter 11. For more information about creating dynamic SQL statements, see Chapter 12, "ColdFusion Forms." For more information about using <CFQUERY> for INSERT, UPDATE, and DELETE operations, see Chapter 13, "Using Forms to Add or Change Data."

See also: <CFOUTPUT>, <CFMAIL>, <CFSTOREDPROC>

<CFREGISTRY>

Description: <CFREGISTRY> can be used to directly manipulate the system registry. The <CFREGISTRY> ACTION attribute specifies the action to be performed, and depending on the action, other attributes may or may not be needed.

<CFREGISTRY> attributes are listed in Table A.57.

Syntax:

```
<CFREGISTRY ACTION="action" BRANCH="branch" ENTRY="entry" NAME="query"
 SORT="sort order" TYPE="type" VALUE="value" VARIABLE="variable">
```

Table A.57   <CFREGISTRY> **Attributes**

Attribute	Description	Notes
ACTION	Action	Required attribute.
BRANCH	Registry branch	Required for all actions.
ENTRY	Branch entry	Required for all actions except GETALL.
NAME	Query name	Required if ACTION is GETALL.
SORT	Sort order	Optional; may be used if ACTION is GETALL.

continues

Table A.57   Continued

Attribute	Description	Notes
TYPE	Value type	Optional; and may be used for all actions except DELETE; valid types are STRING, DWORD, and KEY; default is STRING.
VALUE	Value to set	Required if ACTION is SET.
VARIABLE	Variable to save value in	Required if ACTION is GET.

Table A.58   <CFREGISTRY> Actions

Action	Description
DELETE	Deletes a registry key
GET	Gets a registry value
GETALL	Gets all registry keys in a branch
SET	Sets a registry value

Example: This example retrieves all the keys beneath the Allaire branch:

```
<CFREGISTRY ACTION="GETALL" NAME="reg"
 BRANCH= "HKEY_LOCAL_MACHINE\SOFTWARE\Allaire">
```

<CFREPORT>, </CFREPORT>

Description: <CFREPORT> is the ColdFusion interface to reports created with the Crystal Reports Professional report writer. <CFREPORT> only requires a single attribute: the name of the report to be processed. The full list of supported attributes is in Table A.59.

Syntax:

```
<CFREPORT REPORT="Report File" ORDERBY="Sort Order" DATASOURCE="ODBC Data Source"
 USERNAME="User Name" PASSWORD="Password" @FORMULANAME="Formula">
Optional filter conditions
</CFREPORT>
```

Table A.59   <CFREPORT> Attributes

Attribute	Description	Notes
DATASOURCE	ODBC data source	This optional attribute is used to override the ODBC data source specified when the report was created.

Attribute	Description	Notes
ORDERBY	Report sort order	This optional attribute overrides the default sort order specified when the report was created.
PASSWORD	ODBC data source password	This optional attribute is used to override the ODBC login password specified in the ColdFusion Administrator.
REPORT	Name of RPT file to process	This attribute is required.
USERNAME	ODBC data source login name	The optional attribute is used to override the ODBC login name specified in the ColdFusion Administrator.
@FORMULANAME	Crystal Reports formula override	This optional parameter allows you to override Crystal Reports formulas with passed formula text. Formula names must begin with an @ character.

Example: The following example processes a report created with Crystal Reports Professional and passes it an optional filter condition:

```
<CFREPORT REPORT="\a2z\scripts\emplist.rpt">
 {Departments.Department} = "Sales"
</CFREPORT>
```

This example processes a report and specifies parameters to override the ODBC data source, user login name and password, and a formula named `title` derived from an HTML form:

```
<CFREPORT REPORT="\a2z\scripts\emplist.rpt" DATASOURCE="A2ZInternal"
 USERNAME="HR" PASSWORD="anarchy" @Title="#FORM.title#">
 {Departments.Department} = "Sales"
</CFREPORT>
```

For more information about Crystal Reports Professional and how to embed reports into ColdFusion templates, see Chapter 16, "The Report Writer."

<CFSCHEDULE>

Description: <CFSCHEDULE> allows you to run a specified page at scheduled intervals with the option to write out static HTML pages. This allows you to offer users access to pages that publish data (such as reports) without forcing them to wait while a database transaction that populates the data on the page is performed. ColdFusion scheduled events must be registered using the ColdFusion Administrator before they can be executed. Information supplied by the user includes the scheduled ColdFusion page to execute, the time and frequency for executing the page, and whether the output from the task should be published. A path and file are specified if the output is to be published.

<CFSCHEDULE> attributes are listed in Table A.60.

Syntax:

```
<CFSCHEDULE ACTION="Action" ENDDATE="Date" ENDTIME="Time" FILE="File Name"
  INTERVAL="Interval" LIMITIME="Seconds" OPERATION="HTTPRequest"
  PASSWORD="Password" PATH="Path" PROXYSERVER="Server Name" PUBLISH="Yes¦No"
  RESOLVEURL="Yes¦No" STARTDATE="Date" STARTTIME="Time" TASK="Task Name"
  URL="URL" USERNAME="User Name">
```

Table A.60   <CFSCHEDULE> **Attributes**

Attribute	Description	Notes
ACTION	Action (see Table A.61)	Required attribute.
ENDDATE	Event end date	Optional attribute; date the scheduled task should end.
ENDTIME	Event end time	Optional attribute; time the scheduled task should end; enter value in seconds.
FILE	File to create	Required if PUBLISH is Yes.
INTERVAL	Execution interval	Required if ACTION is UPATE; may be specified as number of seconds, as daily, weekly, monthly, or as execute.
LIMITTIME	Maximum execution time	Optional attribute; maximum number of seconds allowed for execution.
OPERATION	Operation	Required if ACTION is UPDATE; currently only HTTPRequest is supported.
PASSWORD	Password	Optional password for protected URLs.
PATH	Path to save published files	Required if PUBLISH is Yes.
PROXYSERVER	Proxy server name	Optional name of proxy server.
PUBLISH	Publish static files	Optional attribute; Yes if the scheduled task should publish files; default is No.
RESOLVEURL	Resolve URLs	Optional attribute; resolve URLs to fully qualified URLs if Yes; default is No.
STARTDATE	Event start date	Optional attribute; date the scheduled task should start.

Attribute	Description	Notes
STARTTIME	Event start time	Optional attribute; time the scheduled task should start; enter value in seconds.
TASK	Task name	Required attribute; the registered task name.
URL	URL	Required if ACTION is UPDATE; the URL to be executed.
USERNAME	Username	Optional username for protected URLs.

Table A.61   <CFSCHEDULE> **Actions**

Action	Description
DELETE	Deletes a task
UPDATE	Updates a task
RUN	Executes a task

Example: This example executes a task and allows it to run for 30 minutes:

```
<CFSCHEDULE TASK="SalesReports" ACTION="RUN" LIMITTIME="1800">
```

For more information about <CFSCHEDULE> and scheduled events, see Chapter 32.

N O T E   Execution of <CFSCHEDULE> can be disabled in the ColdFusion Administrator. ▓

<CFSCRIPT>, </CFSCRIPT>

Description: <CFSCRIPT> and </CFSCRIPT> are used to mark blocks of ColdFusion script.

Syntax:

```
<CFSCRIPT> script </CFSCRIPT>
```

<CFSEARCH>

Description: <CFSEARCH> performs searches against Verity collections (in much the same way <CFQUERY> performs searches against ODBC data sources). To use <CFSEARCH> you must specify the collection to be searched and the name of the query to be returned. You may search more than one collection at once, and you may also perform searches against Verity collections created with applications other than ColdFusion. Table A.62 lists the `<CFSEARCH>` attributes.

Syntax:

```
<CFSEARCH COLLECTION="Collection Name" CRITERIA="Search Criteria" CUSTOM1="Data"
  CUSTOM2="Data" EXTERNAL="Yes¦No" MAXROWS="Number" NAME="Name"
  STARTROW="Number" TYPE="Type">
```

Table A.62 `<CFSEARCH>` **Attributes**

Attribute	Description	Notes
COLLECTION	Collection name	Required attribute; the name of the collection or collections to be searched. Multiple collections must be separated by commas; for external collections specify the full path to the collection.
CRITERIA	Search criteria	Optional attribute; search criteria as shown in Appendix C.
CUSTOM1	Custom data storage	Optional attribute; used to store custom data during an indexing operation.
CUSTOM2	Custom data storage	Optional attribute; used to store custom data during an indexing operation.
EXTERNAL	External collection	Optional attribute; must be Yes if using an external collection; default is No.
MAXROWS	Maximum rows to retrieve	Optional attribute; defaults to all.
NAME	Value column	Optional attribute; column to be used for OPTION VALUE attribute.
STARTROW	Start row	Optional attribute; default is first row.
TYPE	Search type	Optional attribute; may be SIMPLE or EXPLICIT.

Examples: This example performs a search with a user-supplied search criteria:

```
<CFSEARCH NAME="search" COLLECTION="site" TYPE="SIMPLE" CRITERIA="#search#">
```

For more information about using `<CFINDEX>` and Verity collections, see Chapter 29. For the complete list of search expressions and instructions, see Appendix C, "Verity Search Language Reference."

See also: `<CFCOLLECTION>`, `<CFINDEX>`

<CFSELECT>, </CFSELECT>

Description: <CFSELECT> is used to simplify the process of creating data driven SELECT controls. <CFSELECT> is not a Java control. <CFSELECT> requires that you pass it the name of a query for use populating the drop-down list box. <CFSELECT> attributes are listed in Table A.63.

You may add your own options to the SELECT list by adding <OPTION> tags between the <CFSELECT> and </CFSELECT> tags.

Syntax:

```
<CFSELECT DISPLAY="Column Name" MESSAGE="Message Text" MULTIPLE="Yes¦No"
 NAME="Field Name" ONERROR="JavaScript Error Function" QUERY="Query Name"
 REQUIRED="Yes¦No" SELECTED="Value" SIZE="Size" VALUE="Column Name"></CFSELECT>
```

Table A.63 <CFSELECT> **Attributes**

Attribute	Description	Notes
DISPLAY	Column to display	Optional query column to use as the displayed text.
MESSAGE	Validation failure message	Optional message to display upon validation failure.
MULTIPLE	Allow multiple selection	Optional attribute; defaults to No.
NAME	Unique field name	This attribute is required.
ONERROR	JavaScript error function	Optional override to your own JavaScript error message function.
QUERY	Query name	Required attribute; query to be used to populate the SELECT box.
REQUIRED	Field is required	Optional required flag; must be Yes or No if specified; defaults to No.
SELECTED	Selected value	Value of the OPTION to be pre-selected.
SIZE	List size	Required attribute; number of options to display without scrolling.
VALUE	Value column	Optional attribute; column to be used for OPTION VALUE attribute.

Example: This example creates a simple data-driven SELECT control:

```
<CFFORM ACTION="process.cfm">
<CFSELECT QUERY="Users" VALUE="id" DISPLAY="Name" SIZE="1">
</CFSELECT>
</CFFORM>
```

See also: <CFFORM>, <CFGIRD>, <CFINPUT>, <CFSLIDER>, <CFTEXTINPUT>, <CFTREE>

<CFSET>

Description: <CFSET> assigns values to variables. <CFSET> can be used for both client variables (type CLIENT) and standard variables (type VARIABLES). Unlike most other ColdFusion tags, <CFSET> takes no attributes—just the name of the variable being assigned and its value.

Syntax:

```
<CFSET "Variable" = "Value">
```

Example: The following example creates a local variable containing a constant value:

```
<CFSET MaxDisplay = 25>
```

The following example creates a client variable called #BGColor#, which contains a user-specified value and explicitly states the variable type:

```
<CFSET CLIENT.BGColor = FORM.Color>
```

This example stores tomorrow's date in a variable called Tomorrow:

```
<CFSET Tomorrow = Now() + 1>
```

<CFSET> can also be used to concatenate fields:

```
<CFSET VARIABLES.FullName = FORM.FirstName FORM.LastName>
```

Values of different data types also can be concatenated:

```
<CFSET Sentence = FORM.FirstName FORM.LastName & "is" & FORM.age & "years old">
```

 If you ever find yourself performing a calculation or combining strings more than once in a specific template, you're better off doing it once and assigning the results to a variable with <CFSET>; you can then use that variable instead.

See also: <CFAPPLICATION>, <CFCOOKIE>, <CFPARAM>

<CFSETTING>

Description: <CFSETTING> is used to control various aspects of page processing, such as controlling the output of HTML code in your pages or enabling and disabling debug output. One benefit is managing whitespace that can occur in output pages that are served by ColdFusion. <CFSETTING> attributes are listed in Table A.64.

When using <CFSETTING> to disable an option, make sure you have a matching enable option later in the file.

Syntax:

```
<CFSETTING ENABLECFOUTPUTONLY="Yes|No" SHOWDEBUGOUTPUT="Yes|No">
```

Table A.64 <CFSETTING> **Attributes**

Attribute	Description	Notes
ENABLECFOUTPUTONLY	Only output text within <CFOUTPUT>	This attribute is optional, and must be blocked. Yes or No is specified.
SHOWDEBUGOUTPUT	Display debug information at bottom of page	This optional attribute overrides the settings in the ColdFusion Administrator.

Examples:

The following demonstrates how <CFSETTING> can be used to control generated whitespace:

```
This text will be displayed
<CFSETTING ENABLECFOUTPUTONLY="Yes">
This text will not be displayed as it is not in a <CFOUTOUT> block
<CFOUTPUT>This will be displayed</CFOUTOUT>
<CFSETTING ENABLECFOUTPUTONLY="No">
This text will be displayed even though it is not in a <CFOUTPUT> block
```

<CFSLIDER>

Description: <CFSLIDER> embeds a Java slider control into your HTML forms. Slider controls are typically used to select one of a range of numbers. <CFSLIDER> must be used in between <CFFORM> and </CFFORM> tags. Table A.65 lists the entire set of <CFSLIDER> attributes.

Syntax:

```
<CFSLIDER ALIGN="Alignment" BGCOLOR="Background Color" BOLD="Yes|No"
 FONT="Font Face" FONTSIZE="Font Size" GROOVECOLOR="Groove Color"
 HEIGHT="Control Height" HSPACE="Horizontal Spacing" IMG="Groove Image"
 IMGSTYLE="Groove Image Style" ITALIC="Yes|No" LABEL="Slider Label"
 MESSAGE="Error Message" NAME="Field Name" NOTSUPPORTED="Non Java Browser Code"
 ONERROR="Error Function" ONVALIDATE="Validation Function" RANGE="Numeric Range"
 REFRESHLABEL="Yes|No" SCALE="Increment Value" TEXTCOLOR="Text Color"
 VALUE="Initial Value" VSPACE="Vertical Spacing" WIDTH="Control Width">
```

Table A.65 <CSLIDER> **Attributes**

Attribute	Description	Notes
ALIGN	Control alignment	Optional attribute; possible values are top, left, bottom, baseline, texttop, absbottom, middle, absmiddle, and right.

continues

Table A.65   Continued

Attribute	Description	Notes
BGCOLOR	Background color	Optional attribute; possible values are black, cyan, darkgray, gray, lightgray, magenta, orange, pink, white, yellow, or any color specified in RGB form.
BOLD	Bold face text	Optional attribute; must be Yes or No if specified; defaults to No.
FONT	Font face	Optional font face to use.
FONTSIZE	Font Size	Optional font size.
GROOVECOLOR	Groove color	Optional attribute; possible values are black, cyan, darkgray, gray, lightgray, magenta, orange, pink, white, yellow, or any color specified in RGB form.
HEIGHT	Control height	Optional height in pixels.
HSPACE	Control horizontal spacing	Optional horizontal spacing in pixels.
IMG	Groove image	Optional filename of image to be used for the slider groove.
IMGSTYLE	Grove image style	Optional attribute; may be Centered, Tiled, Scaled, default is Scaled.
ITALIC	Italic face text	Optional attribute; must be Yes or No is specified; defaults to No.
LABEL	Slider label	Optional attribute; may contain the variable %value%, in which case the current value is displayed as the slider is moved.
MESSAGE	Validation failure message	Optional message to display upon validation failure.
NAME	Unique control name	This attribute is required.
NOTSUPPORTED	Text to be used for non Java browsers	Optional text (or HTML code) to be displayed on non–Java-capable browsers.
ONERROR	JavaScript error function	Optional override to your own JavaScript error message function.
ONVALIDATE	JavaScript validation function	Optional override to your own JavaScript validation function.

Attribute	Description	Notes
RANGE	Range minimum and maximum	Optional range for numeric values only; must be specified as two numbers separated by a comma; defaults to `"0,100"`.
REFRESHLABEL	Refresh label as slider is moved	Optional attribute; default is `Yes`; if you are not using a variable label, this attributeshould be set to `No` to prevent unnecessary refreshing.
SCALE	Increment scale	Optional increment; defaults to 1.
TEXTCOLOR	Text color	Optional attribute; possible values are `black`, `cyan`, `darkgray`, `gray`, `lightgray`, `magenta`, `orange`, `pink`, `white`, `yellow`, or any color specified in RGB form.
VALUE	Initial value	Optional initial field value; this value must be within the specified range if range is used.
VSPACE	Control vertical spacing	Optional vertical spacing in pixels.
WIDTH	Control width	Optional width in pixels.

Example: The following example displays a Java slider control that specifies the height, width, font, color, and label:

```
<CFFORM ACTION="process.cfm">
<CFSLIDER NAME="volume" HEIGHT="100" WIDTH="200" FONT="Verdana"
 BGCOLOR="Black" TEXTCOLOR="White" GROOVECOLOR="White" LABEL="Volume %value%">
</CFFORM>
```

For more information about using <CFSLIDER>, see Chapter 23.

N O T E The <CFSLIDER> control is only accessible by users with Java-enabled browsers.

See also: <CFFORM>, <CFGIRD>, <CFINPUT>, <CFSELECT>, <CFTEXTINPUT>, <CFTREE>

<CFSTOREDPROC>, <CFPROCPARAM>, <CFPROCRESULT>, </CFSTOREDPROC>

Description: <CFSTOREDPROC> provides sophisticated support for database stored procedures. Unlike <CFQUERY> (which can also call stored procedures), <CFSTOREDPROC> and its supporting tags can pass and retrieve parameters and access multiple result sets. <CFSTOREDPROC> attributes are listed in Table A.66; <CFPROCPARAM> attributes are listed in Table A.67; <CFPROCRESULT> attributes are listed in Table A.68.

App

A

Syntax:

```
<CFSTOREDPROC DATASOURCE="ODBC Data Source" DBNAME="database name" DBPOOL="pool"
 DBTYPE="type" DBSERVER="dbms" USERNAME="User Name" PASSWORD="Password"
 PROCEDURE="Procedure" PROVIDER="provider" PROVIDERDSN="data source"
 BLOCKFACTOR="factor" DEBUG="Yes¦No" RETURNCODE="Yes¦No">
<CFPROCPARAM TYPE="In¦Out¦Inout" VARIABLE="variable" DBVARIABLE="variable"
 VALUE="value" CFSQLTYPE="type" MAXLENGTH="length" SCALE="decimal places">
<CFPROCRESULT NAME="name" RESULTSET="set" MAXROWS="rows">
</CFSTOREDPROC>
```

Table A.66   `<CFSTOREDPROC>` **Attributes**

Attribute	Description	Notes
BLOCKFACTOR	Number of rows to retrieve at once	This optional attribute is available if using ODBC or Oracle drivers; valid values are 1 to 100, default value is 1.
DATASOURCE	ODBC data source	This optional attribute is used to override the ODBC data source specified when the report was created.
DBNAME	Sybase database name	Optional attribute; only used if using native Sybase drivers.
DBPOOL	Database connection pool name	Optional database pool name.
DBSERVER	Database server	Optional database server; only used if using native database drives.
DBTYPE	Database type	Optional type; defaults to ODBC; other values are Oracle73, Oracle80, and Sybase11.
DEBUG	Enable query debugging	Optional attribute; turns on query debugging output.
PASSWORD	ODBC data source password	This optional attribute is used to override the ODBC login password specified in the Cold Fusion Administrator.
PROCEDURE	Stored procedure name	Name of stored procedure to execute.
PROVIDER	OLE-DB COM provider	Optional attribute; only used if using OLE-DB.
PROVIDERDSN	Data source OLE-DB COM provider	Optional attribute; only used if using OLE-DB.

Attribute	Description	Notes
USERNAME	ODBC data source login name	The optional attribute is used to override the ODBC login name specified in the ColdFusion Administrator.

Table A.67   <CFPROCPARAM> **Attributes**

Attribute	Description	Notes
CFSQLTYPE	Variable type	Required; see Table A.69 for list of supported types.
DBVARIABLE	Database variable name	Required if name notation is desired.
MAXLENGTH	Maximum parameter length	Optional attribute.
SCALE	Decimal places	Optional attribute.
TYPE	Parameter type	Optional parameter type; valid values are IN, OUT, or INOUT; defaults to IN.
VALUE	Parameter value	Required for IN and INOUT parameters.
VARIABLE	ColdFusion variable name	Required for OUT or INOUT parameters

Table A.68   <CFPROCRESULT> **Attributes**

Attribute	Description	Notes
MAXROWS	Maximum number of rows	Optional
NAME	Query name	Required
RESULTSET	Result set number	Optional attribute; specifies the desired result set; defaults to 1

Table A.69   CFSQLTYPE **Types**

Type
CF_SQL_BIGINT
CF_SQL_CHAR

continues

Table A.69 Continued
CF_SQL_DATE
CF_SQL_DECIMAL
CF_SQL_DOUBLE
CF_SQL_FLOAT
CF_SQL_IDSTAMP
CF_SQL_INTEGER
CF_SQL_LONGVARCHAR
CF_SQL_MONEY
CF_SQL_MONEY4
CF_SQL_NUMERIC
CF_SQL_REAL
CF_SQL_SMALLINT
CF_SQL_TIME
CF_SQL_TIMESTAMP
CF_SQL_TINYINT
CF_SQL_VARCHAR

For more information about using Stored Procedures, see Chapter 20, "Working with Stored Procedures."

See also: <CFQUERY>

<CFSWITCH>, <CFCASE>, </CFCASE>, <CFDEFAULTCASE>, </CFDEFAULTCASE>, </CFSWITCH>

Description: <CFSWITCH> is used to create case statements in ColdFusion. Every <CFSWITCH> must be terminated with a </CFSWITCH>. The individual case statements are specified using the <CFCASE> tag; a default case may be specified using the <CFDEFAULTCASE> tag. <CFSWITCH> attributes are listed in Table A.70; <CFCASE> attributes are listed in Table A.71.

Syntax:

```
<CFSWITCH EXPRESSION="expression"><CFCASE VALUE="value"></CFCASE><CFDEFAULTCASE>
</CFDEFAULTCASE></CFSWITCH>
```

Table A.70   **<CFSWITCH> Attributes**

Attribute	Description	Notes
EXPRESSION	Case expression	This attribute is required.

Table A.71   **<CFCASE> Attributes**

Attribute	Description	Notes
VALUE	Case value	This attribute is required.

Example: The following example checks to see if a state is a known state and displays an appropriate message:

```
<CFSWITCH EXPRESSION="#Ucase(state)#">
 <CFCASE VALUE="CA">California</CFCASE>
 <CFCASE VALUE="FL">Florida</CFCASE>
 <CFCASE VALUE="MI">Michigan</CFCASE>
 <CFCASEDEFAULT>One of the other 47 States</CFCASEDEFAULT>
</CFSWITCH>
```

See also: <CFIF>

<CFTABLE>, <CFCOL>, </CFTABLE>

Description: <CFTABLE> allows you to easily create tables in which to display data. <CFTABLE> can create HTML tables (using the <TABLE> tag) or preformatted text tables that display on all browsers. Using <CFTABLE> involves two tags: <CFTABLE> defines the table itself and one or more <CFCOL> tags define the table columns. The <CFTABLE> attributes are listed in Table A.72; the <CFCOL> attributes are listed in Table A.73.

Syntax:

```
<CFTABLE QUERY="Query Name" MAXROWS="Maximum Rows" COLSPACING="Column Spacing"
 COLHEADERS HEADERLINES ="Header Lines" HTMLTABLE>
<CFCOL HEADER="Header Text" WIDTH ="Width" ALIGN ="Alignment" TEXT="Body Text">
</CFTABLE>
```

Table A.72   **<CFTABLE> Attributes**

Attribute	Description	Notes
COLHEADERS	Display column headers	Column headers are displayed if this optional attribute is present.
COLSPACING	Spaces between columns	This optional attribute overrides the default column spacing of 2 if present.

continues

Table A.72 Continued

Attribute	Description	Notes
HEADERLINES	Number of header lines	The default number of header lines is 2, one for the header and a blank row between the header and the body. You may increase this number if needed.
HTMLTABLE	Create an HTML table	An HTML table is created if this attribute is present. If not, a preformatted text table is created.
MAXROWS	Maximum number of table rows	The optional attribute specifies the maximum number of rows to be displayed in the table.
QUERY	<CFQUERY> name	The name of the query from which to derive the table body text.

Table A.73 <CFCOL> Attributes

Attribute	Description	Notes
ALIGN	Column alignment	Valid values are LEFT, CENTER, or RIGHT.
HEADER	Column header text	
TEXT	Column text	The text attribute is the body of what is displayed in each column. Hypertext jumps can be included, as can any table fields. Expressions cannot be included in the TEXT attribute.
WIDTH	Column width	Optional column width; defaults to 20 if not specified. Any text that fits into the cell is truncated.

Example: The following example creates an HTML table with two columns, Name and Extension.

```
<CFTABLE QUERY="Employees" COLHEADERS HTMLTABLE>
 <CFCOL HEADER="Name" ALIGN=LEFT TEXT ="#LastName#, #FirstName#">
<CFCOL HEADER="Extension" ALIGN=LEFT TEXT ="#PhoneExtension#">
</CFTABLE>
```

 TIP The <CFTABLE> tag is an easy and efficient way to create tables for displaying query results. you should create HTML tables manually for greater control over table output, including cell spanning, text and background colors, borders, background images, and nested tables.

▶ **See** "Displaying Results in Tables" for more information on using table to display data, **p. 210**.

See also: <CFOUTPUT>, <CFQUERY>

<CFTEXTINPUT>

Description: <CFTEXTINPUT> embeds a highly configurable Java text input control into your HTML forms. <CFTEXTINPUT> must be used between <CFFORM> and </CFFORM> tags. Unlike the standard HTML INPUT, <CFTEXTINPUT> lets you configure the exact height and width of the edit control, as well as color, font, size, and spacing. <CFTEXTINPUT> can also automatically generate field JavaScript validation code. Table A.74 lists the entire set of <CFTEXTINPUT> attributes.

Syntax:

```
<CFTEXTINPUT ALIGN="Alignment" BGCOLOR="Background Color" BOLD="Yes¦No"
FONT="Font Face" FONTSIZE="Font Size" HEIGHT="Control Height"
HSPACE="Horizontal Spacing" ITALIC="Yes¦No" MAXLENGTH="Maximum Length"
MESSAGE="Error Message" NAME="Field Name" NOTSUPPORTED="Non Java Browser Code"
ONERROR="Error Function" ONVALIDATE="Validation Function" RANGE="Numeric Range"
REQUIRED="Yes¦No" SIZE="Field Size" TEXTCOLOR="Text Color"
VALIDATE="Validation Type" VALUE="Initial Value" VSPACE="Vertical Spacing"
WIDTH="Control Width">
```

Table A.74 <CFTEXTINPUT> **Attributes**

Attribute	Description	Notes
ALIGN	Control alignment	Optional attribute; possible values are top, left, bottom, baseline, texttop, absbottom, middle, absmiddle, right.
BGCOLOR	Background color	Optional attribute; possible values are black, cyan, darkgray, gray, lightgray, magenta, orange, pink, white, yellow, or any color specified in RGB form.
BOLD	Bold face text	Optional attribute; must be Yes or No if specified; defaults to No.
FONT	Font face	Optional font face to use.
FONTSIZE	Font size	Optional font size.
HEIGHT	Control height	Optional height in pixels.
HSPACE	Control horizontal spacing	Optional horizontal spacing in pixels.
ITALIC	Italic face text	Optional attribute; must be Yes or No if specified; defaults to No.

continues

Table A.74 Continued

Attribute	Description	Notes
MAXLENGTH	Maximum number of characters	Optional attribute.
MESSAGE	Validation failure message	Optional message to display upon validation failure.
NAME	Unique control name	This attribute is required.
NOTSUPPORTED	Text to be used for non Java browsers	Optional text (or HTML code) to be displayed on non–Java-capable browsers.
ONERROR	JavaScript error function	Optional override to your own JavaScript error message function.
ONVALIDATE	JavaScript validation	Optional override to your function own JavaScript validation function.
RANGE	Range minimum and maximum	Optional range for numeric values only; must be specified as two numbers separated by a comma.
REQUIRED	Field is required	Optional required flag; must be Yes or No if specified; defaults to No.
SIZE	Field size	Optional number of characters to display before needing horizontal scrolling.
TEXTCOLOR	Text color	Optional attribute; possible values are black, cyan, darkgray, gray, lightgray, magenta, orange, pink, white, yellow, or any color specified in RGB form.
VALIDATE	Field validation	Optional field validation. If specified, must be any of the validation types listed in Table A.75.
VALUE	Initial value	Optional initial field value.
VSPACE	Control vertical spacing	Optional vertical spacing in pixels.
WIDTH	Control width	Optional width in pixels.

Table A.75 `<CFTEXTINPUT>` **Validation Types**

Type	Description
Creditcard	Correctly formatted credit card number verified using mod10
Date	Date in mm/dd/yy format
Eurodate	European date in dd/mm/yy format
Float	Number with decimal point
Integer	Number with no decimal point
Social_Security_Number	Social security number formatted as 999-99-9999 (using hyphens or spaces as separators)
Telephone	Phone number in 999-999-9999 format (using hyphens or spaces as separators), area code and exchange must not begin with 0 or 1
Time	Time in hh:mm or hh:mm:ss format
Zipcode	U.S. zipcode; either 99999 or 99999-9999 format

Example: The following example displays a simple Java text edit control, specifying the height, width, font, and color:

```
<CFFORM ACTION="process.cfm">
<CFTEXTINPUT NAME="name" HEIGHT="100" WIDTH="200" FONT="Verdana" BGCOLOR="Black"
 TEXTCOLOR="White">
</CFFORM>
```

For more information about using `<CFTEXTINPUT>`, see Chapter 23.

N O T E The `<CFTEXTINPUT>` control is only accessible by users with Java-enabled browsers.

See also: `<CFFORM>`, `<CFGIRD>`, `<CFINPUT>`, `<CFSELECT>`, `<CFSLIDER>`, `<CFTREE>`

`<CFTHROW>`

Description: `<CFTHROW>` throws an exception. Program control is then handed to the catch code specified in a prior `<CFTRY>` and `<CFCATCH>` set. `<CFTHROW>` can be used to force an error condition, throwing an exception to an `application` or any catch block. `<CFTHROW>` attributes are listed in Table A.76.

Syntax:

```
<CFTHROW MESSAGE="message">
```

Table A.76 `<CFTHROW>` **Attributes**

Attribute	Description	Notes
MESSAGE	Error message	This attribute is optional.

Example: This example throws an exception because an invalid password was specified:

```
<CFTHROW MESSAGE="Invalid password specified">
```

See also: `<CFTRY>`

`<CFTRANSACTION>, </CFTRANSACTION>`

Description: `<CFTRANSACTION>` implements transaction and rollback processing. Any `<CFQUERY>` tags placed between `<CFTRANSACTION>` and `</CFTRANSACTION>` tags are automatically rolled back if an error occurs. The `<CFTRANSACTION>` attributes are list in Table A.77.

Syntax:

```
<CFTRANSACTION ISOLATION="Lock Type">
Queries
</CFTRANSACTION>
```

Table A.77 `<CFTRANSACTION>` **Attributes**

Attribute	Description	Notes
ISOLATION	Type of ODBC lock	Optional lock type; possible values are READ_UNCOMMITTED, READ_COMMITTED, REPEATABLE_READ, SERIALIZABLE, and VERSIONING.

Example: The following example shows how `<CFTRANSACTION>` ensures that an operation dependent on two queries does not leave the databases in an inconstant state if one operation fails:

```
<CFTRANSACTION>
 <CFQUERY
  DATASOURCE="Accounts"
 >
  UPDATE Accounts SET Total = Total - #Withdrawal# WHERE AccountNum =
#AccountNum#
 </CFQUERY>
 <CFQUERY
  DATASOURCE="Accounts"
 >
 UPDATE Accounts SET Total = Total + #Withdrawal# WHERE AccountNum = #AccountNum#
 </CFQUERY>
</CFTRANSACTION>
```

> **N O T E**   Not all lock types are supported by all ODBC drivers. Consult your database documentation
> before using the ISOLATION attribute. ▨

<CFTREE>, <CFTREEITEM>, </CFTREE>

Description: <CFTREE> embeds a Java tree control into your HTML forms. The tree control is similar to the Explorer window in Windows 95 and Windows NT. The tree is made up of root entries and branches that can be expanded or closed. Branches can be nested. Each branch has a graphic that is displayed next to it; you can select from any of the supplied graphics or use any of your own.

<CFTREE> trees are constructed using two tags. <CFTREE> creates the tree control and <CFTREEITEM> adds the entries into the tree. Trees may be populated one branch at a time or using query results. <CFTREEITEM> must be used between <CFTREE> and </CFTREE> tags. <CFTREE> attributes are listed in Table A.78; <CFTREEITEM> attributes are listed in Table A.79.

Syntax:
```
<CFTTREE ALIGN="Alignment" APPENDKEY="Yes¦No" BOLD="Yes¦No" BORDER="Yes¦No¦
 COMPLETEPATH="Yes¦No" DELIMITER="Delimiter Character" FONT="Font Face"
 FONTSIZE="Font Size" HEIGHT="Control Height" HIGHLIGHTHREF="Yes¦No"
 HSPACE="Horizontal Spacing" HSCROLL="Yes¦No" ITALIC="Yes¦No"
 MESSAGE="Error Message" NAME="Field Name" NOTSUPPORTED="Non Java Browser Code"
 ONERROR="Error Function" ONVALIDATE="Validation Function" REQUIRED="Yes¦No"
 VSPACE="Vertical Spacing" WIDTH="Control Width">

<CFTREEITEM DISPLAY="Display Text EXPAND="Yes¦No" HREF="URL" IMG="Images"
 IMGOPEN="Images" QUERY="Query Name" QUERYASROOT="Yes¦No" TARGET="Target Name"
 PARENT="Parent Branch" VALUE="Values">
```

Table A.78   <CFTREE> Attributes

Attribute	Description	Notes
ALIGN	Control alignment	Optional attribute; possible values are top, left, bottom, baseline, texttop, absbottom, middle, absmiddle, right.
APPENDKEY	Append item key to URL	Optional attribute; if Yes, variable named CFTREEITEMKEY is appended to the URL containing the item selected; defaults to Yes.
BOLD	Bold text	Optional attribute; must be Yes or No if specified; defaults to No.
BORDER	Display border around control	Optional attribute; defaults to Yes.

continues

Table A.78 Continued

Attribute	Description	Notes
COMPLETEPATH	Pass complete path	Optional attribute; to selected item the full tree path to the selected item is returned if Yes; defaults to No.
DELIMITER	Path delimiter	Optional attribute; defaults to \.
FONT	Font face	Optional font face to use.
FONTSIZE	Font size	Optional font size.
HEIGHT	Control height	Optional height in pixels.
HIGHLIGHTHREF	Highlight links	Optional attribute; links arehighlighted and underlined if Yes; defaults to Yes.
HSPACE	Control horizontal spacing	Optional horizontal in pixels.
HSCROLL	Display horizontal	Optional attribute; scrollbar default is Yes.
ITALIC	Italic face text	Optional attribute; must be Yes or No if specified, defaults to No.
MESSAGE	Validation failure	Optional message to message display upon validation failure.
NAME	Unique control name	This attribute is required.
NOTSUPPORTED	Text to be used for non-Java browsers	Optional text (or HTML code) to be displayed on non-Java–capable browsers.
ONERROR	JavaScript error function	Optional override to your own JavaScript error message function.
ONVALIDATE	JavaScript validation function	Optional override to your own JavaScript validation function.
REQUIRED	Selection is required	Optional attribute; must be Yes or No; defaults to No.
VSPACE	Control vertical spacing	Optional vertical spacing in pixels.
VSCROLL	Display vertical scrollbar	Optional attribute; default is Yes.
WIDTH	Control width	Optional width in pixels.

Table A.79 <CFTREEITEM> Attributes

Attribute	Description	Notes
DISPLAY	Display text	Optional attribute, defaults to value is not specified, if populating with a query result set this value should be a comma delimited list of values, one for each tree item.
EXPAND	Open expanded	Optional attribute; branch is initially expanded if Yes; defaults to No.
HREF	Item URL	Optional attribute; URL to go to when an item is selected; if populating with a query result set, this value can be a comma-delimited list of URLs (one for each tree item), or it can be a column name. In that case it is populated dynamically.
IMG	Image	Optional attribute; image to be displayed; if populating with a query result set, this value should be a comma-delimited list of images, one for each tree level; images may be folder, floppy, fixed, CD, document, element, or any image file of your own.
IMGOPEN	Open image	Optional attribute; image to be displayed when branch is open; if populating with a query result set, this value should be a comma-delimited list of images, one for each tree level; images may be folder, floppy, fixed, CD, document, element, or any image file of your own. If omitted, the IMG image is used; if populating with a query result set, this value should be a comma-delimited list of images, one for each tree item.
QUERY	Query name	Optional query name to be used to populate the list.
QUERYASROOT	Use query name as root	Optional attribute; if Yes, query name itself is the tree root branch; defaults to No.
TARGET	Link target window	Optional attribute; the page to open the link in; this value can be a comma-delimited list of targets if populating with a query result set, one for each tree item.
PARENT	Branch parent	Optional attribute; name of parent to attach this branch to.

continues

Table A.79   Continued

Attribute	Description	Notes
VALUE	Value to be returned	Required attribute; this value should be a comma-delimited list of values, one for each tree item, if populating with a query result set.

Examples: This example creates a simple Java tree control with three branches:

```
<CFFORM ACTION="process.cfm">
<CFTREE NAME="states">
<CFTREEITEM VALUE="US">
<CFTREEITEM VALUE="CA" DISPLAY="California" PARENT="US">
<CFTREEITEM VALUE="MI" DISPLAY="Michigan" PARENT="US">
<CFTREEITEM VALUE="NY" DISPLAY="New York" PARENT="US">
</CFTREE>
</CFFORM>
```

This next example populates a tree with a query called Users:

```
<CFFORM ACTION="process.cfm">
<CFTREE NAME="peopletree" HSPACE="20" HSCROLL="no" VSCROLL="Yes" DELIMITER="?"
BORDER="Yes">
<CFTREEITEM VALUE="cn" QUERYASROOT="Yes" QUERY="Users" IMG="folder,document">
</CFTREE>
</CFFORM>
```

For more information about using <CFTREE>, see Chapter 23.

N O T E   The <CFTREE> control is only accessible by users with Java-enabled browsers. ■

N O T E   For examples of using <CFTREE> with browser directories, take a look at the ColdFusion Administrator. ■

See also: <CFFORM>, <CFGIRD>, <CFINPUT>, <CFSELECT>, <CFSLIDER>, <CFTEXTINPUT>

<CFTRY>, <CFCATCH>, </CFCATCH>, </CFTRY>

Description: <CFTRY> is used to catch exceptions thrown by ColdFusion or explicitly with <CFTHROW>. All code between <CFTRY> and </CFTRY> can throw exceptions. Exceptions are caught by <CFCATCH> blocks. Explicit <CFCATCH> blocks may be created for different error types, or one block can catch all errors. <CFCATCH> attributes are listed in Table A.80.

Syntax:

```
<CFTRY> <CFCATCH TYPE="type"> </CFCATCH> </CFTRY>
```

Table A.80   **<CFCATCH> Attributes**

Attribute	Description	Notes
TYPE	Exception type	This attribute is optional.

Table A.81   **<CFCATCH> TYPE values**

Type
Any
Application
Database
MissingInclude
Object
Security
Synchronization
Template

Example: This example throws an exception because an invalid password was specified:

```
<CFTRY>
<CFCATCH TYPE= "Any">some error handling goes here</CFCATCH>
</CFTRY>
```

See also: <CFTHROW>

<CFUPDATE>

Description: <CFUPDATE> updates a single row to a database table; it requires that the database and table names be provided. All other attributes are optional. The full list of <CFUPDATE> attributes is explained in Table A.82.

Syntax:

```
<CFUPDATE DATASOURCE="ODBC Data Source" DBNAME="database name" DBPOOL="pool"
 DBTYPE="type" DBSERVER="dbms" FORMFIELDS="List of File to Update"
 PASSWORD="Password" PROVIDER="provider" PROVIDERDSN="data source"
 TABLENAME="Table Name" TABLEOWNER="owner" TABLEQUALIFIER="qualifier"
 USERNAME="User Name">
```

Table A.82   `<CFUPDATE>` **Attributes**

Attribute	Description	Notes
DATASOURCE	Name of ODBC data source	The specified data source must already exist. This attribute is required.
DBNAME	Sybase database name	Optional attribute, only used if using native Sybase drivers.
DBPOOL	Database connection pool name	Optional database pool name.
DBSERVER	Database server	Optional database server; only used if using native database drives.
DBTYPE	Database type	Optional type, defaults to ODBC, other values are Oracle73, Oracle80, and Sybase11.
FORMFIELDS	List of fields to insert	This optional attribute specifies which fields are to insert if they are present. Any fields present that are not in the list are not inserted.
PASSWORD	ODBC data source password	This optional attribute is used to override the ODBC login password specified in the ColdFusion Administrator.
PROVIDER	OLE-DB COM provider	Optional attribute; only used if using OLE-DB.
PROVIDERDSN	Data source OLE-DB COM provider	Optional attribute; only used if using OLE-DB.
TABLENAME	Name of table to insert	Some ODBC data source data into.require fully qualified table names. This attribute is required.
TABLEOWNER	Table owner name	Optional attribute used by databases that support table ownership.
TABLEQUALIFIER	Table qualifier	Optional attribute used by databases that support full qualifiers.
USERNAME	ODBC data source login name	The optional attribute is used to override the ODBClogin name specified inthe ColdFusion Administrator.

N O T E For <CFUPDATE> to work correctly, your form field names must match the column names in the destination table, and the primary key value of the row to be updated must be specified. ▓

T I P If your form contains fields that are not part of the table you are updating, use the FORMFIELDS attribute to instruct ColdFusion to ignore those fields.

T I P For more control over updating rows into a database table, you may use the <CFQUERY> tag specifying UPDATE as the SQL statement.

Example: The following example updates a row in the Employees table in the A2Z data source:

```
<
CFUPDATE
DATASOURCE="A2Z"
TABLENAME="Employees"
>
```

The next example updates a row in the same table, but will only update values into the three specified fields if they exist:

```
<
CFUPDATE
DATASOURCE="A2Z"
TABLENAME="Employees"
FORMFIELD="LastName,FirstName,PhoneExtension"
>
```

For more information about the <CFUPDATE> tag, see Chapter 13.

See also: <CFINSERT>, <CFQUERY>

<CFWDDX>

Description: <CFWDDX> is used to serialize and deserialize ColdFusion data structures to the XML based WDDX format. The ACTION attribute specifies the action to be performed.

Syntax:

```
<CFWDDX ACTION="action" INPUT="input" OUTPUT="output" TOPLEVELVARIABLE="name">
```

Table A.83   <CFWDDX> **Attributes**

Attribute	Description	Notes
ACTION	Action	This attribute is required. Actions are listed in Table A.84.
INPUT	Input value	This attribute is required.

continues

Table A.83   Continued

Attribute	Description	Notes
OUTPUT	Output variable	Required if ACTION is WDDX2CFML.
TOPLEVELVARIABLE	JavaScript top-level variable	Required if ACTION is WDDX2JS or CFML2JS.

Table A.84   `<CFWDDX>` Actions

Action	Description
CFML2JS	Serializes CFML to JavaScript format
CFML2WDDX	Serializes CFML to WDDX format
WDDX2CFML	Deserializes WDDX to CFML
WDDX2JS	Deserializes WDDX to JavaScript

ColdFusion Function Reference

Using ColdFusion Functions

ColdFusion provides a complete set of data manipulation and formatting functions. Here are some things to remember when using functions:

- Function names are not case sensitive, so NOW() is the same as now(), which is the same as Now().
- When functions are used in body text rather than within a ColdFusion tag, they must be enclosed within <CFOUTPUT> tags.
- Functions can be nested.

To make this function reference easier to use, the functions have been grouped into logical sets. As there are some functions that overlap these groupings, each function has a "see also" list of related functions.

- **String manipulation functions** are a complete set of text parsing, comparison, and conversion functions.
- **Date and time functions** can be used to create, parse, compare, and manipulate date and time values.
- **Data formatting functions** allow you to display data in a variety of formats.
- **Mathematical functions** can be used to perform calculations, conversions, and generate random numbers.
- **International functions** provide localization support for dates, times, and other data types.
- **List manipulation functions** are used to control lists of values.
- **Array manipulation functions** are used to create and manage two- and three-dimensional arrays.
- **Structure manipulation functions** are used to create and manage ColdFusion structures.
- **Query manipulation functions** are used to create and manage ColdFusion queries.
- **Security functions** give you access to security information returned by a <CFAUTHENTICATE> call.
- **System functions** give you access to system directories, temporary files, and path manipulation functions.
- **Client variable manipulation functions** allow you to control client variables.
- **Expression evaluation functions** enable you to create and evaluate expressions on-the-fly.
- **Bit and set manipulation functions** can be used to perform bit-level operations.
- **Miscellaneous functions** are an assortment of functions that you can use to check for the existence of parameters, format URLs, and manipulate lists to be passed to SQL statements.

String Manipulation Functions

The ColdFusion string manipulation functions can be used to perform operations on character data. Strings may be hard-coded constants, table column values, or ColdFusion fields. As with all ColdFusion functions, these string manipulation functions can be nested.

Asc

Description: Asc returns the ASCII value of the leftmost character of a string.

Syntax: Asc(character)

Example: The following example returns 72, the ASCII value of the character H:

#Asc("Hello")#

 TIP The Asc function only processes the leftmost character in a string. To return the ASCII characters of an entire string, you have to loop through the string at process each character individually.

See also: Chr, Val

Chr

Description: Chr converts an ASCII value into a printable character.

Syntax: Chr(number)

Example: The following example returns the letter H, whose ASCII value is 72:

#Chr(72)#

See also: Asc, Val

CJustify

Description: CJustify centers a string within a field of a specified length. It does this by padding spaces before and after the specified text. CJustify takes two parameters, the string to process, and the desired string length.

Syntax: CJustify(string, length)

Example: The following example justifies the word Hello so that it is centered within a 20-character–wide field:

#CJustify("Hello", 20)#

See also: LJustify, LTrim, RJustify, RTrim, Trim

Compare, CompareNoCase

Description: The Compare and CompareNoCase functions compare two string values. Compare performs a case-sensitive comparison; CompareNoCase performs a non–case-sensitive function.

App
B

Both of these functions return a negative number if the first string is less than the second string, a positive number if the first string is greater than the second string, and 0 if the strings are the same.

Syntax:

```
Compare(String1, String2)

CompareNoCase(String1, String2)
```

Example: This example returns a negative value because the first string is less than the second string:

```
#Compare("Ben", "Bill")#
```

This next example uses the non–case-sensitive comparison function and returns 0 because, aside from case, the strings are the same:

```
#CompareNoCase("Michigan", "MICHIGAN")#
```

N O T E The two comparison functions treat whitespace as characters to be compared. Therefore, if you compare two strings that are identical except for extra spaces at the end of one of them, the compare will not return 0. ■

Find, FindNoCase, REFind, REFindNoCase

Description: ColdFusion provides three functions to search for a specific text within another string. Find performs a case-sensitive search, FindNoCase performs a non–case-sensitive search, REFind performs a case-sensitive search using regular expressions, and REFindNoCase performs a non–case-sensitive search using regular expressions. The parameters for all these functions are the same. The first parameter is the string (or regular expression) to search for, the second parameter is the target string, or string to be searched. An optional third parameter may be provided to specify the position in the target string from which to start the search. All of these functions return the starting position of the first occurrence of the search string within the specified target string. If the search string is not found, 0 is returned.

◊ For more information about regular expressions and how they are used**see** the "Regular Expressions" chapter on the accompanying CD-ROM.

Syntax:

```
Find(SearchString, TargetString [, StartPosition])

FindNoCase(SearchString, TargetString [, StartPosition])

REFind(RegularExpression, TargetString [, StartPosition])

REFindNoCase(RegularExpression, TargetString [, StartPosition])
```

Example: This first example returns 18, the start position of the word America:

```
#Find("America", "United States of America")#
```

The next example returns 0 because Find performs a case-sensitive search:

```
#Find("AMERICA", "United States of America")#
```

The FindNoCase function performs a non–case-sensitive search, as this example shows:

```
#FindNoCase("AMERICA", "United States of America")#
```

The next example searched for the word of in the string The Flag of the United States of America, and specifies that the search should start from position 15. This example returns 31, the position of the second of. Had the optional start position parameter been omitted, the return value would have been 10, the position of the first of:

```
#Find("of", "The Flag of the United States of America", 15)#
```

See also: Find0neOf, GetToken, Left, Mid, Right

FindOneOf

Description: FindOneOf returns the position of the first target string character that matches any of the characters in a specified set. FindOneOf takes three parameters. The first parameter is a string containing the set of characters to search for, the second parameter is the *target string* (the string to be searched), the third parameter is an optional starting position from which to start the search. These functions return the starting position of the first occurrence of any characters in the search set within the specified target string. If no matching characters are found, 0 is returned.

Syntax:

```
FindOneOf(SearchSet, TargetString, [, StartPosition])
```

Example: The following example returns the position of the first vowel with a ColdFusion field called LastName:

```
The first vowel in your last name is at position #FindOneOf("aeiou", LastName)#
```

 The FindOneOf function is case sensitive, and there is no non–case-sensitive equivalent function. To perform a non–case-sensitive FindOneOf search, you must first convert both the search and target strings to either upper- or lowercase (using the UCase or LCase functions).

See also: Find, FindNoCase

GetToken

Description: *Tokens* are delimited sets of data within a string. The GetToken function allows you to extract a specific token from a string by specifying the *token number* or index. GetToken takes three parameters. The first is the string to search; the second is the index of the token to extract, so 3 will extract the third token and 5 will extract the fifth. The third parameter is an optional set of delimiters that GetToken uses to determine where each token starts and finishes. If the delimiter's parameter is not provided, the default of spaces, tabs, and new line characters is used. The default delimiters effectively allow this function to be used to extract specific words for a string. GetToken returns the token in the specified position, or any empty string if Index is greater than the number of token present.

Syntax:

GetToken(String, Index [, Delimiters])

Example: The following example uses a hyphen as a delimiter to extract just the area code from a phone number:

#GetToken("800-555-1212", 1, "-")#

 Use the ColdFusion list functions instead of GetToken when working with strings that contain lists of data.

InputBaseN

Description: InputBaseN converts a string into a number using the base specified by radix. Valid radix values are 2 through 36.

Syntax:

InputBaseN(String, Radix)

Example: The following example converts the string containing the binary number 10100010 into its base-10 equivalent of 162:

#InputBaseN("10100010", 2)#

 The code InputBaseN(String, 10) is functionally equivalent to the code Val(String). If you are converting a number that is base 10, the Val function is simpler to use.

See also: FormatBaseN, Val

Insert

Description: Insert is used to insert text into a string and takes three parameters. The first parameter, SourceString, is the string you want to insert. The second parameter, TargetString, is the string into which you are going to insert SourceString. The third parameter, Position, is a numeric value that specifies the location in the TargetString at which to insert the SourceString. Insert returns the modified string.

Syntax:

Insert(SourceString, TargetString, Position)

Example: The following example inserts a field called area code in front of a phone number:

#Insert(area_code, phone, 0)#

 To insert a string at the very beginning of another, use the Insert function specifying a Position of 0.

See also: RemoveChars, SpanExcluding, SpanIncluding

LCase

Description: LCase converts a string to lowercase. LCase takes a single parameter, the string to be converted, and returns the converted string.

Syntax:

```
LCase(String)
```

Example: The following example converts a user-supplied string to lowercase:

```
#LCase(string_field)#
```

See also: UCase

Left

Description: Left returns the specified leftmost characters from the beginning of a string. Left takes two parameters, the string from which to extract the characters and the number of characters to extract.

Syntax:

```
Left(String, Count)
```

Example: The following example returns the first three characters of a phone number column:

```
#Left(phone_number, 3)#
```

See also: Find, Mid, RemoveChars, Right

Len

Description: Len returns the length of a specified string. Len takes a single parameter, the string whose length you want to determine.

Syntax:

```
Len(String)
```

Example: The following example returns the length of a user-supplied address field after it has been trimmed:

```
#Len(Trim(address))#
```

LJustify

Description: LJustify left-aligns a string within a field of a specified length. It does this by padding spaces after the specified text. LJustify takes two parameters, the string to process and the desired string length.

Syntax:

```
LJustify(String, Length)
```

Example: The following example left-justifies the string `"First Name:"` so that it is left-aligned within a 25-character–wide field:

```
#LJustify("First Name:", 25)#
```

See also: CJustify, LTrim, RJustify, RTrim, Trim

LTrim

Description: LTrim trims whitespace (spaces, tabs, and new line characters) from the beginning of a string.

LTrim takes a single parameter, the string to be trimmed.

Syntax:

```
LTrim(String)
```

Example: The following example trims spaces from the beginning of a table note field:

```
#LTrim(notes)#
```

See also: CJustify, LJustify, RJustify, RTrim, Trim, StripCR

Mid

Description: Mid returns a string of characters from any location in a string. Mid takes three parameters, the first is the string from which to extract the characters, the second is the desired characters' starting position, and the third is the number of characters required.

Syntax:

```
Mid(String, StartPosition, Count)
```

Example: The following example extract eight characters from the middle of a table column, starting at position 3:

```
#Mid(order_number, 3, 8)#
```

See also: Find, Left, RemoveChars, Right

RemoveChars

Description: RemoveChars returns a string with specified characters removed from it. This function is the exact opposite of the Mid function. RemoveChars takes three parameters, the first is the string from which to remove the characters, the second is the starting position of the characters to be removed, and the third is the number of characters to be removed.

Syntax:

```
RemoveChars(String, StartPosition, Length)
```

Example: The following example returns a field with characters 10 through 15 removed:

```
#RemoveChars(product_code, 10, 5)#
```

See also: Left, Mid, Right

RepeatString

Description: RepeatString returns a string that is made up of a specified string multiple times. RepeatString takes two parameters, the first is the string to repeat and the second is the number of occurrences.

Syntax:

```
RepeatString(String, Count)
```

Example: The following example creates a horizontal line made up of equal signs:

```
#RepeatString("=", 80)#
```

Replace, REReplace, REReplaceNoCase

Description: Replace, REReplace, and REReplaceNoCase allow you to replace text within strings with alternative text. Replace does a simple text comparison to locate the text to be replaced; REReplace and REReplaceCase perform the same operation but use regular expressions.

All three functions take four parameters. The first parameter is the string to be processed, the second is the text to be replaced, and the third is the text to replace it with. The fourth parameter is optional and specifies the scope of the replacements. Possible scope values are "ONE" to replace the first occurrence only, "ALL" to replace all occurrences, and "RECURSIVE" to replace all occurrences recursively.

Syntax:

```
Replace(String, WhatString, WithString [, Scope])
REReplace(String, WhatString, WithString [, Scope])
REReplaceNoCase(String, WhatString, WithString [, Scope])
```

Example: The following example replaces all occurrences of the text "US" in an address field with the text "USA":

```
#Replace(address, "US", "USA", "ALL")#
```

This next example replaces the area code "(313)" with the area code "(810)", and because no scope is specified, only the first occurrence of "(313)" is replaced:

```
#Replace(phone, "(313)", "(810)")#
```

 The Replace function is case sensitive, and there is no non-case-sensitive equivalent function. In order to perform a non-case-sensitive replacement you must first convert both the search and target strings to either upper- or lowercase (using the UCase or LCase functions).

See also: ReplaceList

ReplaceList

Description: ReplaceList replaces all occurrences of elements in one string with corresponding elements in another. Both sets of elements must be specified as comma-delimited values, and there must be an equal number of values in each set. ReplaceList takes three parameters. The first is the string to be processed, the second is the set of values to be replaced, and the third is the set of values to replace them with.

Syntax:

```
ReplaceList(String, FindWhatList, ReplaceWithList)
```

Example: The following example replaces all occurrences of state names with their appropriate abbreviations:

```
#ReplaceList(address, "CA, IN, MI", "California, Indiana, Michigan")#
```

 TIP The ReplaceList function is case sensitive, and there is no non–case-sensitive equivalent function. To perform a non-case-sensitive replacements you must first convert both the search and target strings to either upper- or lowercase (using the UCase or LCase functions).

N O T E Unlike other replacement functions, the ReplaceList function takes no scope parameter. ReplaceList replaces all occurrences of matching elements. ▆

See also: Replace

Reverse

Description: Reverse reverses the characters in a string. Reverse takes a single parameter, the string to be reversed.

Syntax:

```
Reverse(String)
```

Example: The following example reverses the contents of a user-supplied field:

```
#Reverse(sequence_id)#
```

Right

Description: Right returns the specified rightmost characters from the end of a string. Right takes two parameters, the string from which to extract the characters and the number of characters to extract.

Syntax:

```
Right(String, Count)
```

Example: The following example returns the last seven characters of a phone number column:

```
#Right(phone_number, 7)#
```

T I P Right does not trim trailing spaces before extracting the specific characters. To ignore whitespace when using Right, you should nest the RTrim within Right, as in #Right(RTrim(String), Count)#.

See also: Find, Left, Mid, RemoveChars

RJustify

Description: RJustify right-aligns a string within a field of a specified length. It does this by padding spaces before the specified text. RJustify takes two parameters, the string to process, and the desired string length. The syntax of the RJustify function is:

Syntax: RJustify(string, length)

Example: The following example right-justifies the contents of a field named Zip so that it is right aligned within a 10-character–wide field:

#RJustify(Zip, 10)#

See also: CJustify, LJustify, LTrim, RTrim, Trim

RTrim

Description: RTrim trims whitespace (spaces, tabs, and new line characters) from the end of a string. RTrim takes a single parameter, the string to be trimmed.

Syntax:

RTrim(String)

Example: The following example trims spaces from the end of a user-supplied field:

#RTrim(first_name)#

See also: CJustify, LJustify, LTrim, RJustify, Trim, StripCR

SpanExcluding

Description: SpanExcluding extracts characters from the beginning of a string until a character that is part of a specified set is reached. SpanExcluding takes two parameters, the string to process and a comma-delimited set of values to compare against.

Syntax:

SpanExcluding(String, Set)

Example: The following example extracts the first word of a sentence by specifying a space as the character to compare against:

#SpanExcluding(sentence, " ")#

App
B

The SpanExcluding function is case sensitive, and there is no non–case-sensitive equivalent function. To perform a non–case-sensitive extraction you must first convert both the search and target strings to either upper- or lowercase (using the UCase or LCase functions).

See also: SpanIncluding

SpanIncluding

Description: SpanIncluding extracts characters from the beginning of a string only as long as they match characters in a specified set. SpanIncluding takes two parameters, the string to process and a comma-delimited set of values to compare against.

Syntax:

SpanIncluding(String, Set)

Example: The following example extracts the house number from a street address by specifying a set of values that are digits only:

#SpanIncluding(address, "1,2,3,4,5,6,7,8,9,0")#

 The SpanIncluding function is case sensitive, and there is no non–case-sensitive equivalent function. To perform a non–case-sensitive extraction you must first convert both the search and target strings to either upper- or lowercase (using the UCase or LCase functions).

See also: SpanExcluding

StripCR

Description: StripCR removes all carriage return characters from a string. StripCR takes a single parameter, the string to process.

Syntax:

StripCR(String)

Example: The following example removes carriage returns for a field to be displayed in a preformatted text block:

<PRE>#StripCR(comments)#</PRE>

 The StripCR function is particularly useful when displaying a string within HTML preformatted text tags (<PRE> and </PRE>) where carriage returns are not ignored.

See also: CJustify, LJustify, LTrim, RJustify, RTrim, Trim

Trim

Description: Trim trims whitespace (spaces, tabs, and new line characters) from both the beginning and the end of a string. Trim takes a single parameter, the string to be trimmed.

Syntax:

```
Trim(String)
```

Example: The following example trims spaces from both the beginning and the end of a user-supplied field:

```
#Trim(notes)#
```

See also: CJustify, LJustify, LTrim, RJustify, RTrim, StripCR

UCase

Description: UCase converts a string to uppercase. UCase takes a single parameter, the string to be converted, and returns the converted string.

Syntax:

```
UCase(String)
```

Example: The following example converts the contents of a table column called States to uppercase:

```
#UCase(State)#
```

See also: LCase

Val

Description: Val converts the beginning of a string to a number. Val takes a single parameter, the string to process. Conversion is only possible if the string begins with numeric characters. If conversion is impossible, 0 is returned.

Syntax:

```
Val(String)
```

Example: The following example extracts the hour portion from a time field:

```
Hour: #Val(time)#
```

TIP Val converts characters to numbers using a base of 10 only. To convert the string to numbers with a base other than 10, use the InputBaseN function.

See also: Asc, Chr, InputBaseN, IsNumeric

Date and Time Functions

The ColdFusion Date and Time functions allow you to perform date and time manipulation on table columns and user-supplied fields.

Many of these functions work with date/time objects. A *date/time object* is a ColdFusion internal representation of a complete date and time with accuracy to the second. These objects are designed to facilitate the passing of date/time information between different ColdFusion functions and are not designed to be displayed as is. If you need to display a date/time object, you need to use one of the date/time formatting functions.

N O T E   ColdFusion date/time objects are not the same as ODBC date/time fields. Use the CreateODBCDateTime function to convert ColdFusion date/time objects to the ODBC format. ■

Many ColdFusion date and time functions take date and time values as parameters. These parameters must be valid and within a set range; otherwise a ColdFusion syntax error is generated. The range of values allowed for each date and time field is listed in Table B.1.

Table B.1   Valid ColdFusion Date and Time Values

Field	Min	Max
Year	0	9999
Month	1	12
Day	1	31
Hour	0	23
Minute	0	59
Second	0	59

N O T E   Year values of less than 100 are treated as twentieth century values, and 1900 is added automatically to them. ■

Several of the ColdFusion date and time functions allow you to work with parts of the complete date/time object; to add days or weeks to a date, or to find out how many weeks apart two dates are, for example. These functions require that you pass a date/time part specifier that is passed as a string. (They must have quotation marks around them.) The complete list of specifiers is explained in Table B.2.

Table B.2   ColdFusion Date/Time Specifiers

Specifier	Description
D	Day
H	Hour
M	Month
N	Minute
Q	Quarter
S	Second
W	Weekday (day of week)
WW	Week
Y	Day of year
YYYY	Year

CreateDate

Description: The CreateDate function returns a ColdFusion date/time object that can be used with other date manipulation or formatting functions. CreateDate takes three parameters: the date's year, month, and day.

Syntax:

```
CreateDate(Year, Month, Day)
```

Example: The following example creates a date/time object based on three user-supplied fields:

```
#CreateDate(birth_year, birth_month, birth_day)#
```

N O T E Because the CreateDate function takes no time values as parameters, the time portion of the created date/time object is set to all 0s. ▪

See also: CreateDateTime, CreateODBCDate, CreateTime

CreateDateTime

Description: The CreateDateTime function returns a ColdFusion date/time object that can be used with other date- and time-manipulation or formatting functions. CreateDateTime takes six parameters: the date's year, month, and day, and the time's hour, minute, and second.

Syntax:

```
CreateDateTime(Year, Month, Day, Hour, Minute, Second)
```

App
B

Example: The following example creates a date/time object for midnight on New Year's Day, 1997:

```
#CreateDateTime(1997, 1, 1, 0, 0, 0)#
```

See also: CreateDate, CreateODBCDateTime, CreateTime, ParseDateTime

CreateODBCDate

Description: The CreateODBCDate function returns an ODBC date/time field that can safely be used in SQL statements. CreateODBCDate takes a single parameter, a ColdFusion date/time object.

Syntax:

```
CreateODBCDate(Date)
```

Example: The following example creates an ODBC date/time field for the current day (retrieved with the Now() function):

```
#CreateODBCDate(Now())#
```

 N O T E   CreateODBCDate always creates an ODBC date/time field that has the time values set to 0s, even if the passed date/time object had valid time values. ■

 T I P   CreateODBCDate takes a date/time object as a parameter. If you want to pass individual date values as parameters, use the CreateDate as the function parameter and pass it the values.

See also: CreateDate, CreateODBCDateTime, CreateODBCTime

CreateODBCDateTime

Description: The CreateODBCDateTime function returns an ODBC date/time field that can safely be used in SQL statements. CreateODBCDateTime takes a single parameter, a ColdFusion date/time object.

Syntax:

```
CreateODBCDate(Date)
```

Example: The following example creates an ODBC date/time field for the current day (retrieved with the Now() function):

```
#CreateODBCDateTime(Now())#
```

T I P   CreateODBCDateTime takes a date/time object as a parameter. If you want to pass individual date and time values as parameters, use the CreateDateTime as the function parameter and pass it the values.

See also: CreateDate, CreateODBCDate, CreateODBCTime

CreateODBCTime

Description: The CreateODBCTime function returns an ODBC date/time field that can safely be used in SQL statements. CreateODBCTime takes a single parameter, a ColdFusion date/time object.

Syntax:

```
CreateODBCTime(Date)
```

Example: The following example creates an ODBC date/time field for the current day (retrieved with the Now function):

```
#CreateODBCTime(Now())#
```

> **NOTE** CreateODBCTime always creates an ODBC date/time field that has the date values set to 0s, even if the passed date/time object had valid date values. ■

> **TIP** CreateODBCTime takes a date/time object as a parameter. If you want to pass individual time values as parameters, use the CreateTime as the function parameter and pass it the values.

See also: CreateODBCDate, CreateODBCDateTime, CreateTime

CreateTime

Description: The CreateTime function returns a ColdFusion date/time object that can be used with other time-manipulation or formatting functions. CreateTime takes three parameters: the time's hour, minute, and second.

Syntax:

```
CreateTime(Hour, Minute, Second)
```

Example: The following example creates a date/time object based on three ColdFusion fields:

```
#CreateTime(act_hr, act_mn, act_se)#
```

> **NOTE** Because the CreateTime function takes no date values as parameters, the date portion of the created date/time object is set to all 0s. ■

See also: CreateDate, CreateDateTime, CreateODBCTime

CreateTimeSpan

Description: CreateTimeSpan creates a date/time object that can be used to rapidly perform date- and time-based calculations. CreateTimeSpan takes four parameters: days, hours, minutes, and seconds. Any of these values can be set to 0 if not needed.

Syntax:

```
CreateTimeSpan(Days, Hours, Minutes, Seconds)
```

Example: The following example creates a date/time object with a time exactly six hours from now:

```
<CFSET #detonation# = #Now()# + #CreateTimeSpan(0, 6, 0, 0)#>
```

 The `CreateTimeSpan` function is designed to speed the process of performing date- and time-based calculations. Creating a date/time object with 30 days—and using standard addition operators to add this to an existing date/time object—is quicker than using the `DateAdd` function.

See also: DateAdd

DateAdd

Description: `DateAdd` is used to add or subtract values to a date/time object; to add a week or subtract a year, for example. `DateAdd` takes three parameters, the first is the date specifier (see Table B.2), the second is the number of units to add or subtract, and the third is the date/time object to be processed. `DateAdd` returns a modified date/time object.

Syntax:

```
DateAdd( Specifier, Units, Date)
```

Example: The following example returns tomorrow's date (it adds one day to today's date):

```
#DateAdd('D', 1, Now())#
```

The next example returns a date exactly 10 years earlier than the date in a table column:

```
#DateAdd('WW', -10, Now())#
```

 To subtract values from a date/time object, use the `DateAdd` function and pass a negative number of units. For example, -5 subtracts five units of whatever specifier was passed.

DateCompare

Description: `DateCompare` allows you to compare two dates to see if they are the same or if one is greater than the other. `DateCompare` takes two parameters, the dates to compare, which may be specified as date/time objects or string representations of dates. `DateCompare` returns -1 if the first date is less than the second date, 0 if they are the same, and 1 if the first date is greater than the second date.

Syntax:

```
DateCompare(Date1, Date2)
```

Example: The following example verifies that a user-supplied order ship date is valid (not already passed):

```
<CFIF DateCompare(ship_date, Now()) IS -1>
 We can't ship orders yesterday!
</CFIF>
```

See also: DateDiff, DatePart

DateDiff

Description: DateDiff returns the number of units of a passed specifier by which one date is greater than a second date. Unlike DateCompare, which returns the greater date, DateDiff tells you how many days, weeks, or months it is greater by. DateDiff takes three parameters, the first is the date specifier (see Table B.2), and the second and third are the dates to compare.

Syntax:

```
DateDiff(Specifier, Date1, Date2)
```

Example: The following example returns how many weeks are left in this century, by specifying today's date (using the Now() function) and the first date of the next century (using the CreateDate function) as the two dates to compare:

```
There are #DateDiff("WW", Now(), CreateDate(2000, 1, 1))
➥# weeks left in this century!
```

> **NOTE** If the first date passed to DateDiff is greater than the second date, a negative value is returned. Otherwise, a positive value is returned. ▪

See also: DateCompare, DatePart

DatePart

Description: DatePart returns the specified part of a passed date. DatePart takes two parameters, the first is the date specifier (see Table B.2) and the second is the date/time object to process.

Syntax:

```
DatePart(Specifier, Date)
```

Example: The following example returns the day of week that a user was born on (and converts it to a string date using the DayOfWeekAsString function):

```
You were born on a #DayOfWeekAsString(DatePart('W', dob))#
```

See also: DateCompare, DateDiff, Day, DayOfWeek, DayOfYear, Hour, Minute, Month, Quarter, Second, Week, Year

Day

Description: Day returns a date/time object's day of month as a numeric value with possible values of 1–31. Day takes a single parameter, the date/time object to be processed.

Syntax:

```
Day(Date)
```

Example: The following example returns today's day of month:

```
Today is day #Day(Now())# of this month
```

See also: DayOfWeek, DayOfYear, Hour, Minute, Month, Quarter, Second, Week, Year

App

B

DayOfWeek

Description: DayOfWeek returns a date/time object's day of week as a numeric value with possible values of 1–7. DayOfWeek takes a single parameter, the date/time object to be processed.

Syntax:

DayOfWeek(Date)

Example: The following example returns today's day of week:

Today is day #DayOfWeek(Now())# of this week

See also: Day, DayOfYear, Hour, Minute, Month, Quarter, Second, Week, Year

DayOfWeekAsString

Description: DayOfWeekAsString returns the English weekday name for a passed day of week number. DayOfWeekAsString takes a single parameter, the day of week to process, with a value of 1–7.

Syntax:

DayOfWeekAsString(DayNumber)

Example: The following example returns today's day of week:

Today is day #DayOfWeekAsString(DayOfWeek(Now()))# of this week

See also: DayOfWeek, MonthAsString

DayOfYear

Description: DayOfYear returns a date/time object's day of year as a numeric value taking into account leap years. DayOfYear takes a single parameter, the date/time object to be processed.

Syntax:

DayOfYear(Date)

Example: The following example returns the today's day of year:

Today is day #DayOfYear(Now())# of year #Year(Now())#

See also: Day, DayOfWeek, Hour, Minute, Month, Quarter, Second, Week, Year

DaysInMonth

Description: DaysInMonth returns the number of days in a specified month, taking into account leap years. DaysInMonth takes a single parameter, the date/time object to evaluate.

Syntax:

DaysInMonth(Date)

Example: The following example returns the number of days in the current month:

```
This month has #DaysInMonth(Now())# days
```

 TIP DaysInMonth takes a date/time object as a parameter, and there is no equivalent function that takes a year and month as its parameters. Fortunately, this can easily be accomplished by combining the DaysInMonth and CreateDate functions. For example, to determine how many days are in February 2000, you can create a statement that looks like this: #DaysInMonth(CreateDate(2000, 2, 1))#.

See also: DaysInYear, FirstDayOfMonth

App
B

DaysInYear

Description: DaysInYear returns the number of days in a specified year, taking into account leap years. DaysInYear takes a single parameter, the date/time object to evaluate.

Syntax:

```
DaysInYear(Date)
```

Example: The following example returns the number of days in the current year:

```
This year, #Year(Now())#, has #DaysInYear(Now())# days
```

 TIP DaysInYear takes a date/time object as a parameter, and there is no equivalent function that takes just a year as its parameter. Fortunately, this can easily be accomplished by combining the DaysInYear and CreateDate functions. For example, you can create a statement that looks like this to determine how many days are in the year 2000: #DaysInYear(CreateDate(2000, 1, 1))#.

See also: DaysInMonth, FirstDayOfMonth

FirstDayOfMonth

Description: FirstDayOfMonth returns the day of the year on which the specified month starts. FirstDayOfMonth takes a single parameter, the date/time object to evaluate.

Syntax:

```
FirstDayOfMonth(Date)
```

Example: The following example returns the day of the year that the current month starts on:

```
#FirstDayOfMonth(Now())#
```

TIP   FirstDayOfMonth takes a date/time object as a parameter, and there is no equivalent function that takes just a month and year as its parameters. Fortunately, this can easily be accomplished by combining the FirstDayOfMonth and CreateDate functions. For example, to determine the day of year that March 1999 starts on, you can create a statement that looks like this: #FirstDayOfMonth(CreateDate(1999, 3, 1))#.

See also: DaysInMonth, DaysInYear

Hour

Description: Hour returns a date/time object's hour as a numeric value with possible values of 0–23. Hour takes a single parameter, the date/time object to be processed.

Syntax:

Hour(Date)

Example: The following example returns the current hour of day:

This is hour #Hour(Now())# of the day

See also: Day, DayOfWeek, DayOfYear, Minute, Month, Quarter, Second, Week, Year

IsDate

Description: IsDate checks to see if a string contains a valid date; returns TRUE if it does, FALSE if it does not. IsDate takes a single parameter, the string to be evaluated.

Syntax:

IsDate(String)

Example: The following example checks to see if a user-supplied date string contains a valid date:

```
<CFIF IsDate(ship_date) IS "No">
 You entered an invalid date!
</CFIF>
```

NOTE   IsDate checks U.S.-style dates only. Use the LSIsDate function for international date support. ▪

See also: IsLeapYear, LSIsDate, ParseDateTime

IsLeapYear

Description: IsLeapYear checks to see if a specified year is a leap year. IsLeapYear takes a single parameter, the year to check, and returns TRUE if it is a leap year, FALSE if not.

Syntax:

IsLeapYear(Year)

Example: The following example checks to see if this year is a leap year:

```
<CFIF IsLeapYear(Year(Now()))>
 #Year(Now())# is a leap year
<CFELSE>
#Year(Now())# is a not leap year
</CFIF>
```

 T I P   IsLeapYear takes a year as a parameter, not a date/time object. To check if a date stored in a date/
time object is a leap year, use the Year function to extract the year and pass that as the parameter to
IsLeapYear.

App

B

See also: IsDate

IsNumericDate

Description: IsNumericDate checks to see that a value passed as a date in the ColdFusion
internal date format is in fact a legitimate date. IsNumericDate takes a single parameter, the
date to be checked. This date is a floating point value with precision until the year 9999.
IsNumericDate returns TRUE if the passed date value is valid, FALSE if it is not.

Syntax:

IsNumericDate(Real)

Example: The following example checks to see if a local variable contains a valid date:

```
<CFIF IsNumericDate(var.target_date) IS "Yes">
```

See also: IsDate

Minute

Description: Minute returns a date/time object's hour as a numeric value with possible values
of 0–59. Minute takes a single parameter, the date/time object to be processed.

Syntax:

Minute(Date)

Example: The following example returns the current time's minutes:

```
#Minute(Now())# minutes have elapsed since #Hour(Now())# o'clock
```

See also: Day, DayOfWeek, DayOfYear, Hour, Month, Quarter, Second, Week, Year

Month

Description: Month returns a date/time object's month as a numeric value with possible values
of 1–12. Month takes a single parameter, the date/time object to be processed.

Syntax:

Month(Date)

Example: The following example returns the current month:

```
It is month #Month(Now())# of year #Year(Now())#
```

See also: Day, DayOfWeek, DayOfYear, Hour, Minute, Quarter, Second, Week, Year

MonthAsString

Description: MonthAsString returns the English month name for a passed month number. MonthAsString takes a single parameter, the number of the month to process, with a value of 1–12.

Syntax:

```
MonthAsString(MonthNumber)
```

Example: The following example returns the English name of the current month:

```
It is #MonthAsString(Now())#
```

See also: DayOfWeek, Month

Now

Description: Now returns a date/time object containing the current date and time precise to the second. Now takes no parameters.

Syntax:

```
Now()
```

Example: The following example returns the current date and time formatted for correct display:

```
It is now #DateFormat(Now())# #TimeFormat(Now())#
```

N O T E   The Now function returns the system date and time of the computer running the ColdFusion service, not of the system running the Web browser. ■

ParseDateTime

Description: ParseDateTime converts a date in string form into a ColdFusion date/time object. ParseDateTime takes a single parameter, the string to be converted.

Syntax:

```
ParseDateTime(String)
```

Example: The following example converts a user-supplied string containing a date into a ColdFusion date/time object:

```
<CFSET ship_date = ParseDateTime(FORM.ship_date)>
```

NOTE ParseDateTime supports U.S.-style dates and times only. Use the LSParseDateTime function for international date and time support. ▨

See also: CreateDateTime, LSParseDateTime

Quarter

Description: Quarter returns a date/time object's quarter as a numeric value with possible values of 1–4. Quarter takes a single parameter, the date/time object to be processed.

Syntax:

Quarter(Date)

Example: The following example returns the current quarter:

We are in quarter #Quarter(Now())# of year #Year(Now())#

See also: Day, DayOfWeek, DayOfYear, Hour, Minute, Month, Second, Week, Year

Second

Description: Second returns a date/time object's hour as a numeric value with possible values of 0–59. Second takes a single parameter, the date/time object to be processed.

Syntax:

Second(Date)

Example: The following example returns the current minute's seconds:

We are now #Second(Now())# seconds into the current minute

See also: Day, DayOfWeek, DayOfYear, Hour, Minute, Month, Quarter, Week, Year

Week

Description: Week returns a date/time object's week in year as a numeric value with possible values of 1–52. Week takes a single parameter, the date/time object to be processed.

Syntax:

Week(Date)

Example: The following example returns the current week in year:

This is week #Week(Now())# of year #Year(Now())#

See also: Day, DayOfWeek, DayOfYear, Hour, Minute, Month, Quarter, Second, Year

Year

Description: Year returns a date/time object's year as a numeric value with possible values of 100–9999. Year takes a single parameter, the date/time object to be processed.

Syntax:

```
Year(Date)
```

Example: The following example returns the current year value:

```
It is year #Year(Now())#
```

See also: Day, DayOfWeek, DayOfYear, Hour, Minute, Month, Quarter, Second, Week

Data Formatting Functions

Powerful data manipulation functions and database interaction capabilities are pretty useless unless there are ways to display data in a clean, readable format. ColdFusion data addresses this need by providing an array of highly capable formatting functions.

Many of these functions take optional format masks as parameters, thereby giving you an even greater level of control over the final output.

DateFormat

Description: DateFormat displays the date portion of a date/time object in a readable format. DateFormat takes two parameters, the first is the date/time object to be displayed and the second is an optional mask value allowing you to control exactly how the data is formatted. If no mask is specified, the default mask of DD-MMM-YY is used. The complete set of date masks is listed in Table B.3.

Syntax:

```
DateFormat(Date [, mask ])
```

Table B.3 DateFormat Mask Characters

Mask	Description
D	Day of month in numeric form with no leading 0 for single-digit days.
DD	Day of month in numeric form with a leading 0 for single-digit days.
DDD	Day of week as a three-letter abbreviation (Sun for Sunday is an example).
DDDD	Day of week as its full English name.
M	Month in numeric form with no leading 0 for single-digit months.
MM	Month in numeric form with a leading 0 for single-digit months.
MMM	Month as a three-letter abbreviation (Jan for January is an example).
MMMM	Month as its full English name.
Y	Year as last two digits of year with no leading 0 for years less than 10.

Mask	Description
YY	Year as last two digits of year with a leading 0 for years less than 10.
YYYY	Year as full four digits.

Example: The following example displays today's date with the default formatting options:

```
Today is: #DateFormat(Now())#
```

The next example displays the same date but uses the full names of both the day of week and the month:

```
It is #DateFormat(Now(), "DDDD, MMMM DD, YYYY")#
```

The final example displays today's date in the European format (day/month/year):

```
It is #DateFormat(Now(), "DD/MM/YY")#
```

N O T E Unlike the TimeFormat function mask specifiers, the DateFormat function mask specifiers are non-case-sensitive. ■

N O T E DateFormat supports U.S.-style dates only. Use the LSDateFormat function for international date support. ■

See also: LSDateFormat, TimeFormat

DecimalFormat

Description: DecimalFormat is a simplified number formatting function that outputs numbers with two decimal places, commas to separate the thousands, and a minus sign for negative values. DecimalFormat takes a single parameter, the number to display.

Syntax:

```
DecimalFormat(Number)
```

Example: The following example displays a table column in the decimal format:

```
Quantity: #DecimalFormat(quantity)#
```

 T I P For more precise numeric display, use the NumberFormat function instead.

See also: NumberFormat

DollarFormat

Description: DollarFormat is a simplified U.S. currency formatting function that outputs numbers with a dollar sign at the front, two decimal places, commas to separate the thousands, and a minus sign for negative values. DollarFormat takes a single parameter, the number to display.

Syntax:

DollarFormat(Number)

Example: The following example displays the results of an equation (quantity multiplied by item cost) in the dollar format:

Total cost: #DollarFormat(quantity*item_cost)#

 TIP For more precise currency display, use the NumberFormat function instead.

N O T E DollarFormat supports U.S. dollars only. Use the LSCurrencyFormat function for international currency support. ■

See also: LSCurrencyFormat, NumberFormat

FormatBaseN

Description: FormatBaseN converts a number to a string using the base specified. Valid radix values are 2–36.

Syntax:

FormatBaseN(Number, Radix)

Example: The following example converts a user-supplied number into hexadecimal notation:

#FormatBaseN(Number, 16)#

To convert a number to its binary format, you can do the following:

#FormatBaseN(Number, 2)#

See also: InputBaseN

HTMLCodeFormat

Description: HTMLCodeFormat displays text with HTML codes with a preformatted HTML block (using the <PRE> and </PRE> tags). HTMLCodeFormat takes a single parameter, the text to be processed.

Syntax:

HTMLCodeFormat(Text)

Example: The following example uses preformatted text to display the code used to generate a dynamic Web page:

#HTMLEditFormat(page)#

 TIP HTMLCodeFormat is very useful for displaying data into FORM TEXTAREA fields.

See also: HTMLCodeFormat, ParagraphFormat

HTMLEditFormat

Description: HTMLEditFormat converts supplied text into a *safe* format, with any HTML control characters converted to their appropriate entity codes. HTMLEditFormat takes a single parameter, the text to convert.

Syntax:

```
HTMLEditFormat(Text)
```

Example: The following example displays the HTML code that is used to render a dynamic Web page inside a bordered box:

```
<TABLE BORDER>
 <TR>
  <TD>#HTMLEditFormat(page)#</TD>
 </TR>
</TABLE>
```

 TIP Use HTMLEditFormat to display HTML code and tags within your page.

See also: HTMLCodeFormat, ParagraphFormat

NumberFormat

Description: NumberFormat allows you to display numeric values in a readable format. NumberFormat takes two parameters, the number to be displayed and an optional mask value. If the mask is not specified, the default mask of "‚99999999999999" is used. The complete set of number masks is listed in Table B.4.

Syntax:

```
NumberFormat(Number [, mask ])
```

Table B.4 NumberFormat **Mask Characters**

Mask	Description
_	Optional digit placeholder.
9	Optional digit placeholder (same as _ but shows decimal place more clearly).
.	Location of decimal point.
0	Force padding with 0s.
()	Display parentheses around the number if it is less than 0.
+	Display a plus sign in front of positive numbers, a minus sign in front of negative numbers.

continues

Table B.4 Continued

Mask	Description
-	Display a minus sign in front of negative numbers, leave a space in front of positive numbers.
,	Separates thousands with commas.
C	Center number within mask width.
L	Left-justify number within mask width.
$	Place a dollar sign in front of the number.
^	Specify the exact location for separating left and right formatting.

Example: To demonstrate how the number masks can be used, Table B.5 lists examples of different masks being used to format the numbers 1453.876 and −1453.876:

Table B.5 Number Formatting Examples

Mask	Result	Notes
`NumberFormat(1453.876, "9999")`	1454	No decimal point was specified in the mask, so the number is rounded to the nearest integer value.
`NumberFormat(-1453.876, "9999")`	−1454	
`NumberFormat(1453.876, "9999.99")`	1453.88	Even though a decimal point is provided, the number of decimal places specified is less than needed; the decimal portion must be rounded to the nearest integer value.
`NumberFormat(1453.876, "(9999.99)")`	1453.88	The number is a positive number, so the parentheses are ignored.
`NumberFormat(-1453.876, "(9999.99)")`	(1453.88)	The number is a negative number, so parentheses are displayed around the number.
`NumberFormat(1453.876, "-9999.99")`	1453.88	The number is a positive number, so the minus is ignored.
`NumberFormat(-1453.876, "-9999.99")`	−1453.88	The number is a negative number, so the minus is displayed.
`NumberFormat(1453.876, "+9999.99")`	+1453.88	The number is a positive number, so a plus sign is displayed.

Mask	Result	Notes
NumberFormat(-1453.876, "+9999.99")	–1453.88	The number is a negative number, so a minus is displayed.
NumberFormat(1453.876, "$9999.99")	$1453.88	
NumberFormat(1453.876, "C99999^9999")	1453.876	Position six of the mask is a carat character, so the decimal point is positioned there even though there are less than six digits before the decimal point. This allows you to align columns of numbers at the decimal point.

N O T E Use the LSNumberFormat function for international number support. ▪

See also: DecimalFormat, DollarFormat, LSNumberFormat

TimeFormat

Description: TimeFormat displays the time portion of a date/time object in a readable format. TimeFormat takes two parameters, the first is the date/time object to be displayed and the second is an optional mask value allowing you to control exactly how the data is formatted. If no mask is specified, the default mask of hh:mm:tt is used. The complete set of date masks is listed in Table B.6.

Syntax:

```
TimeFormat(Date [, mask ])
```

Table B.6 TimeFormat **Mask Characters**

Mask	Description
h	Hours in 12-hour clock format with no leading 0 for single-digit hours.
hh	Hours in 12-hour clock format with a leading 0 for single-digit hours.
H	Hours in 24-hour clock format with no leading 0 for single-digit hours.
HH	Hours in 24-hour clock format with a leading 0 for single-digit hours.
m	Minutes with no leading 0 for single-digit minutes.
mm	Minutes with a leading 0 for single-digit minutes.
s	Seconds with no leading 0 for single-digit seconds.
ss	Seconds with a leading 0 for single-digit seconds.

continues

Table B.6   Continued

Mask	Description
t	Single character meridian specifier, either A or P.
tt	Two character meridian specifier, either AM or PM.

Example: The following example displays the current time with the default formatting options:

```
The time is: #TimeFormat(Now())#
```

The next example displays the current time with seconds in 24-hour clock:

```
The time is: #TimeFormat(Now(), "HH:mm:ss")#
```

NOTE   Unlike the DateFormat function mask specifiers, the TimeFormat function mask specifiers are case sensitive.

NOTE   TimeFormat supports U.S.-style times only. Use the LSTimeFormat function for international time support.

See also: DateFormat, LSTimeFormat

ParagraphFormat

Description: ParagraphFormat converts text with embedded carriage returns for correct HTML display. HTML ignores carriage returns in text, so they must be converted to HTML paragraph markers (the <P> tag) in order to be displayed correctly. ParagraphFormat takes a single parameter, the text to be processed.

Syntax:

```
ParagraphFormat(Text)
```

Example: The following example displays a converted text files inside a FORM TEXTAREA field:

```
<TEXTAREA NAME="comments">#ParagraphFormat(comments)#</TEXTAREA>
```

 TIP   ParagraphFormat is very useful for displaying data into FORM TEXTAREA fields.

See also: HTMLCodeFormat, HTMLEditFormat

YesNoFormat

Description: YesNoFormat converts TRUE and FALSE values to Yes and No. YesNoFormat takes a single parameter, the number, string, or expression to evaluate. When evaluating numbers, YesNoFormat treats 0 as FALSE, and any non-zero value as TRUE.

Syntax:

YesNoFormat(Value)

Example: The following example converts a table Boolean value to a Yes or No string:

Member: #YesNoFormat(member)#

See also: IsBoolean

Mathematical Functions

To assist you in performing calculations, ColdFusion comes with a complete suite of mathematical and random number generation functions, and arithmetic expressions. As with all ColdFusion functions, these mathematical functions can be nested.

Some of the mathematical functions take one or more numeric values as parameters. You may pass real values, integer values, and ColdFusion fields to these functions.

Table B.7 lists the complete set of ColdFusion mathematical functions. Table B.8 lists the supported arithmetic expressions.

Table B.7   ColdFusion Mathematical Functions

Function	Parameters	Returns
Abs	(number)	Absolute value of passed number.
Atn	(number)	Arc tangent of passed number.
Ceiling	(number)	The closest integer greater than passed number.
Cos	(number)	Cosine of passed number.
DecrementValue	(number)	Number decremented by 1.
Exp	(number)	E to the power of passed number.
Fix	(number)	If passed number is greater than or equal to 0, returns closest integer smaller than the passed number. If not, returns closest integer greater than passed number.
IncrementValue	(number)	Number incremented by 1.
Int	(number)	The closest integer smaller than passed number.
Log	(number)	Natural logarithm of passed number.
Log10	(number)	Base 10 log of passed number.

continues

Table B.7   Continued

Function	Parameters	Returns
Max	(number1, number2)	The greater of the two passed numbers.
Min	(number1, number2)	The smaller of the two passed numbers.
Pi		Value of pi as 3.14159265359.
Rand		A random number between 0 and 1.
Randomize	(number)	Seed the random number generator with the passed number.
RandRange	(number1, number2)	A random integer value between the two passed numbers.
Round	(number)	The integer closest (either greater or smaller) to the passed number.
Sgn	(number)	Sign—either –1, 0, or 1, depending on whether passed number is negative, 0, or positive.
Sin	(number)	Sine of passed number.
Sqr	(number)	Square root of passed number.
Tan	(number)	Tangent of passed number.

Table B.8   ColdFusion Arithmetic Expressions

Expression	Description
+	Addition
–	Subtraction
*	Multiplication
/	Division
MOD	Modular (finds remainder)
\	Integer division (both values must be integers)
^	Power

Example: This first example returns the natural logarithm of the number 10.

```
#Log(10)#
```

This next example returns the value of pi rounded to the nearest integer value, 3.

```
#Round(Pi())#
```

The following example uses the `Min()` and `Max()` functions to determine the greater and smaller of two ColdFusion fields:

```
Of the two numbers #Num1# and #Num2#, Max(#Num1#, #Num2#) is the greater,
➥ and Min(#Num1#, #Num2#) is the smaller
```

To generate random numbers, you can use the `Rand` and `RandRange` functions. The following example generates a random number between 1 and 1,000:

```
#RandRange(1, 1000)#
```

This next example creates a variable that contains a total cost of several items:

```
<CFSET total# = quantity * item_price>
```

> **N O T E** If the Rand() or RandRange() functions are used prior to issuing a Randomize()
> statement, the random number generator is seeded with a random value. ■

International Functions

ColdFusion fully supports the display, formatting, and manipulation of international dates, times, numbers, and currencies. In order to use ColdFusion's international support, you must specify the locale. A *locale* is an encapsulation of the set of attributes that govern the display and formatting of international date, time, number, and currency values. The complete list of supported locales is shown in Table B.9.

Table B.9   ColdFusion Locales

Locale
Dutch (Belgian)
Dutch (Standard)
English (Australian)
English (Canadian)
English (New Zealand)
English (U.K.)
English (U.S.)
French (Belgian)
French (Canadian)
French (Standard)

continues

Table B.9   Continued

Locale

French (Swiss)

German (Austrian)

German (Standard)

German (Swiss)

Italian (Standard)

Italian (Swiss)

Norwegian (Bokmal)

Norwegian (Nynorsk)

Portuguese (Brazilian)

Portuguese (Standard)

Spanish (Mexican)

Spanish (Modern)

Spanish (Standard)

Swedish

You must use the SetLocale function to set the locale. You can retrieve the name of the locale currently in use using the GetLocale function.

To utilize ColdFusion's international support, you must use the LS functions listed (later in this chapter). These functions behave much like the standard date, time, and formatting functions, but they honor the current locale setting.

N O T E   The ColdFusion server variable Server.ColdFusion.SupportedLocales contains a comma-delimited list of the supported locales. ■

GetLocale

Description: GetLocale returns the name of the locale currently in use.

Syntax:

```
GetLocale()
```

Example: The following example saves the current locale to a local variable:

```
<CFSET current_locale = GetLocale()>
```

See also: SetLocale

LSCurrencyFormat

Description: LSCurrencyFormat displays currency information formatted for the current locale. LSCurrencyFormat takes two parameters, the number to display and an optional format type. If type is specified, its value must be none, local, international. Type defaults to none.

Syntax:

```
LSCurrencyFormat(Number [, Type])
```

Example: The following example displays the results of an equation (quantity multiplied by item cost) in formatting appropriate for the French locale:

```
<CFSET previous_locale = SetLocale("French (Standard)")>
Total cost: #LSCurrencyFormat(quantity*item_cost)#
```

 T I P For more precise currency display, use the NumberFormat function instead.

N O T E You can use the simpler DollarFormat function for U.S. currency formatting.

See also: DollarFormat, NumberFormat

LSDateFormat

Description: LSDateFormat displays the date portion of a date/time object in a readable format. LSDateFormat is the locale specific version of the DateFormat function. Like DateFormat, LSDateFormat takes two parameters; the first is the date/time object to be displayed and the second is an optional mask value allowing you to control exactly how the data is formatted. If no mask is specified, a format suitable for the current locale is used. The complete set of date masks is listed in Table B.3 in the description of the DateFormat function.

Syntax:

```
LSDateFormat(Date [, mask ])
```

Example: The following example displays today's date with the default formatting options for the current locale:

```
Today is: #LSDateFormat(Now())#
```

The next example displays the same date but uses the current locale's full names of both the day of week and the month:

```
It is #LSDateFormat(Now(), "DDDD, MMMM DD, YYYY")#
```

N O T E You can use the simpler DateFormat function for U.S. dates.

See also: DateFormat, LSNumberFormat, LSTimeFormat

LSIsCurrency

Description: LSIsCurrency checks to see if a string contains a valid currency for the current locale; returns TRUE if it does, FALSE if it does not. LSIsCurrency takes a single parameter, the string to be evaluated.

Syntax:

LSIsCurrency(String)

Example: The following example checks to see if a user-supplied date string contains a valid German currency value:

```
<CFSET previous_locale = SetLocale("German (Standard)")>
<CFIF LSIsCurrency(total) IS "No">
 You entered an invalid currency amount!
</CFIF>
```

See also: IsNumber, LSIsNumeric

LSIsDate

Description: LSIsDate checks to see if a string contains a valid date for the current locale; returns TRUE if it does, FALSE if it does not. LSIsDate takes a single parameter, the string to be evaluated.

Syntax:

LSIsDate(String)

Example: The following example checks to see if a user-supplied date string contains a valid German date:

```
<CFSET previous_locale = SetLocale("German (Standard)")>
<CFIF LSIsDate(ship_date) IS "No">
 You entered an invalid date!
</CFIF>
```

N O T E To check U.S. dates, you can use the IsDate function.

See also: IsDate, IsLeapYear, LSParseDateTime, ParseDateTime

LSIsNumeric

Description: LSIsNumeric checks to see if a specified value is numeric. LSIsNumeric is the locale-specific version of the IsNumeric function. LSIsNumeric takes a single parameter, the value to be evaluated.

Syntax:

LSIsNumeric(Value)

Example: The following example checks to ensure that a user entered a valid locale-specific age (numeric characters only):

```
<CFIF LSIsNumeric(age) IS "No">
 You entered an invalid age!
</CFIF>
```

NOTE You can use the simpler IsNumeric function for U.S. number support. ▪

See also: InputBaseN, IsNumeric, Val

LSNumberFormat

Description: LSNumberFormat allows you to display numeric values in a locale-specific readable format. LSNumberFormat is the locale-specific version of the NumberFormat function. LSNumberFormat takes two parameters, the number to be displayed and an optional mask value. If the mask is not specified, the default mask of ,99999999999999 is used. The complete set of number masks is listed in Table B.4 in the description of the NumberFormat function.

Syntax:

LSNumberFormat(Number [, mask])

NOTE To display numbers in the any of the U.S. formats, you can use the NumberFormat function. ▪

Example: The following displays a submitted form field in the default format for the current locale:

#LSNumberFormat(FORM.quantity)#

See also: DecimalFormat, DollarFormat, LSCurrencyFormat, LSParseNumber, NumberFormat

LSParseCurrency

Description: LSParseCurrency converts a locale-specific number in string form into a valid number. LSParseCurrency takes two parameters, the string to be converted and an optional type. If type is specified, its value must be none, local, or international. Type defaults to all types if not provided.

Syntax:

LSParseCurrency(String [, Type])

Example: The following example converts a user-supplied currency string into a number:

<CFSET sale_price = LSParseCurrency(FORM.sale_price)>

See also: LSCurrencyFormat, LSParseNumber

LSParseDateTime

Description: LSParseDateTime converts a locale-specific date in string form into a ColdFusion date/time object. LSParseDateTime is the locale-specific version of the ParseDateTime function. LSParseDateTime takes a single parameter, the string to be converted.

Syntax:

LSParseDateTime(String)

Example: The following example converts a user-supplied string containing a date into a ColdFusion date/time object:

<CFSET ship_date = LSParseDateTime(FORM.ship_date)>

N O T E   For U.S. date and times you can use the simpler ParseDateTime function. ▪

> **CAUTION**
>
> Unlike the ParseDateTime function, the LSParseDateTime function does not support POP date/time fields. Passing a POP date/time field to LSParseDateTime generates an error.

See also: CreateDateTime, ParseDateTime

LSParseNumber

Description: LSParseNumber converts a locale-specific number in string form into a valid number. LSParseNumber takes a single parameter, the string to be converted.

Syntax:

LSParseNumber(String)

Example: The following example converts a user-supplied numeric string into a number:

<CFSET quantity = LSParseNumber(FORM.quantity)>

See also: LSCurrencyFormat, LSParseCurrency, Val

LSTimeFormat

Description: LSTimeFormat displays the time portion of a date/time object in a locale-specific readable format. LSTimeFormat is the locale-specific version of the TimeFormat function. LSTimeFormat takes two parameters, the first is the date/time object to be displayed and the second is an optional mask value that allows you to control exactly how the data is formatted. If no mask is specified, a mask appropriate for the current locale is used. The complete set of date masks is listed in Table B.6 in the description of the TimeFormat function.

Syntax:

LSTimeFormat(Date [, mask])

Example: The following example displays the current time with the default formatting options for the current locale:

The time is: #LSTimeFormat(Now())#

N O T E   You can use the simpler TimeFormat function for U.S. times.

See also: LSDateFormat, LSNumberFormat, TimeFormat

SetLocale

Description: SetLocale sets the name of the locale to be used by any subsequent calls to the LS functions. SetLocale also returns the name of the currently active locale so that it may be saved if needed.

Syntax:

SetLocale(locale)

Example: The following example sets the locale to British English and saves the current locale to a local variable:

<CFSET previous_locale = SetLocale("English (UK)")>

See also: GetLocale

List Manipulation Functions

ColdFusion lists are an efficient way to manage groups of information. Lists are made up of elements, values separated by delimiting characters. The default delimiter is a comma, but you can change it to any character or string if required. Lists are actually simple two-dimensional arrays. For more complex or multidimensional lists, you should use arrays instead.

This list format is very well suited for ColdFusion applications; it is both the format that HTML forms use to submit fields with multiple values and the format used by SQL to specify lists in SQL statements.

When using the list manipulation functions, remember the following:

- List manipulation functions that add to, delete from, or change a list do not alter the original list passed to them. Rather, they return an altered list to you for manipulation. If you do need to update the passed list itself, you must use <CFSET> to replace the list with the newly modified list.

- All list functions accept as an optional last parameter a string with delimiters to be used in the processing of the list. If this parameter is omitted, the default comma delimiter is used.

N O T E   All of the ColdFusion list manipulation functions have names that begin with the word *list*, making them easy to spot in your code.

T I P   Lists may be used in conjunction with the <CFLOOP> tag for processing.

ListAppend

Description: ListAppend adds an element to a list and returns the new list with the appended element. ListAppend takes two parameters; the first is the current list and the second is the element to be appended.

Syntax:

```
ListAppend(List, Element)
```

Example: The following example appends John to an existing list of users and replaces the old list with the new one:

```
<CFSET Users = ListAppend(Users, "John")>
```

See also: ListInsertAt, ListPrepend, ListSetAt

ListChangeDelims

Description: ListChangeDelims returns a passed list reformatted to use a different delimiter. ListChangeDelims takes two parameters; the first is the list to be reformatted and the second if the new delimiter character.

Syntax:

```
ListChangeDelims(List, Delimiter)
```

Example: The following example creates a new list containing the same elements as the original list, but separated by plus signs:

```
<CFSET URLUsers = ListChangeDelims(Users, "+")>
```

 The default list delimiter, a comma, is the delimiter used by SQL lists. If you are going to pass ColdFusion lists to SQL statements, you should use the default delimiter.

ListContains, ListContainsNoCase

Description: The ListContains and ListContainsNoCase functions search through a list to find the first element that contains the specified search text. If the search text is found, the position of the element containing the text is returned. If no match is found, 0 is returned. ListContains performs a case-sensitive search; ListContainsNoCase performs a non–case-sensitive search. Both functions take two parameters—the first parameter is the list to be searched and the second parameter is the value to search for.

Syntax:

```
ListContains(List, Value)
ListContainsNoCase(List, Value)
```

Example: The following example returns the position of the first element to contain the text cash (regardless of case):

```
Element #ListContainsNoCase(Payments, "cash")# contains the word "cash"
```

App
B

N O T E ListContains and ListContainsNoCase find substrings within elements that match
the specified search text. To perform a search for a matching element, use the ListFind
and ListFindNoCase functions instead. ▪

See also: ListFind, ListFindNoCase

ListDeleteAt

Description: ListDeleteAt deletes a specified element from a list. ListDeleteAt takes two
parameters; the first is the list to be processed and the second is the position of the element to
be deleted. ListDeleteAt returns a modified list with the specified element deleted. The specified element position must exist; an error message is generated if you specify an element that
is beyond the range of the list.

Syntax:

```
ListDeleteAt(List, Position)
```

Example: The following example deletes the second element in a list, but first verifies that it
exists:

```
<CFIF ListLen(Users) GTE 2>
 <CFSET Users = ListDeleteAt(Users, 2)>
</CFIF>
```

See also: ListRest

ListFind, ListFindNoCase

Description: The ListFind and ListFindNoCase functions search through a list to find the
first element that matches the specified search text. If a matching element is found, the position of that element is returned; if no match is found, 0 is returned. ListFind performs a case-
sensitive search; ListFindNoCase performs a non–case-sensitive search. Both functions take
two parameters—the first parameter is the list to be searched and the second parameter is the
element text to search for.

Syntax:

```
ListFind(List, Value)
```

```
ListFindNoCase(List, Value)
```

Example: The following example returns the position of the first element whose value is MI:

```
MI is element #ListFind(States, "MI")#
```

N O T E ListFind and ListFindNoCase only find elements that exactly match the specified
search text. To perform a search for substrings within elements, use the ListContains
and ListContainsNoCase functions. ▪

See also: ListContains, ListContainsNoCase

ListFirst

Description: ListFirst returns the first element in a list. ListFirst takes a single parameter, the list to be processed.

Syntax:

```
ListFirst(List)
```

Example: The following example returns the first selection from a field of book titles submitted by a user:

```
The first title you selected is #ListFirst(titles)#
```

See also: ListGetAt, ListLast, ListRest

ListGetAt

Description: ListGetAt returns the list element at a specified position. ListGetAt takes two parameters: the first is the list to process and the second is the position of the desired element. The value passed as the position parameter must not be greater than the length of the list; otherwise a ColdFusion error message is generated.

Syntax:

```
ListGetAt(List, Position)
```

Example: The following example returns the name of the fourth selection from a field of book titles submitted by a user:

```
The fourth title you selected is #ListGetAt(titles, 4)#
```

See also: ListFirst, ListLast, ListRest

ListInsertAt

Description: ListInsertAt inserts a specified element into a list, shifting all elements after it one position to the right. ListInsertAt takes three parameters; the first is the list to be processed, the second is the desired position for the new element, and the third is the value of the new element. The position parameter must be no greater than the number of elements in the list; a ColdFusion error message is generated if a greater value is provided.

Syntax:

```
ListInsertAt(List, Position, Value)
```

Example: The following example inserts John into the third position of an existing list of users and replaces the old list with the new one:

```
<CFSET Users = ListInsertAt(Users, 3, "John")>
```

See also: ListAppend, ListPrepend, ListSetAt

ListLast

Description: ListLast returns the first element in a list. ListLast takes a single parameter, the list to be processed.

Syntax:

```
ListLast(List)
```

Example: The following example returns the last selection from a field of book titles submitted by a user:

```
The last title you selected is #ListLast(titles)#
```

See also: ListFirst, ListGetAt, ListRest

ListLen

Description: ListLen returns the number of elements present in a list. ListLen takes a single parameter: the list to be processed.

Syntax:

```
ListLen(List)
```

Example: The following example returns the number of books selected by a user:

```
You selected #ListLen(titles)# titles
```

ListPrepend

Description: ListPrepend inserts an element at the beginning of a list, pushing any other elements to the right. ListPrepend returns the new list with the prepended element. ListPrepend takes two parameters: the first is the current list and the second is the element to be prepended.

Syntax:

```
ListPrepend(List, Element)
```

Example: The following example prepends John to an existing list of users and replaces the old list with the new one:

```
<CFSET Users = ListPrepend(Users, "John")>
```

See also: ListAppend, ListInsertAt, ListSetAt

ListRest

Description: ListRest returns a list containing all the elements after the first element. If the list contains only one element, an empty list (an empty string) is returned. ListRest takes a single parameter: the list to be processed.

Syntax: ListRest(List)

App

B

Example: The following example replaces a list with the list minus the first element:

```
<CFSET Users = ListRest(Users)>
```

See also: ListDeleteAt

ListSetAt

Description: ListSetAt replaces the value of a specific element in a list with a new value. ListSetAt takes three parameters: the first is the list to be processed, the second is the position of the element to be replaced, and the third is the new value. The value passed to the position parameter must be no greater than the number of elements in the list; otherwise a ColdFusion error message is generated.

Syntax: ListSetAt(List, Position, Value)

Example: The following searches for an element with the value of "Ben" and replaces it with the value "Benjamin":

```
<CFIF ListFindNoCase(Users, "Ben") GT 0>
 <CFSET Users = ListSetAt(Users, ListFindNoCase(Users, "Ben"), "Benjamin")>
</CFIF>
```

See also: ListAppend, ListInsertAt, ListPrepend

Array Manipulation Functions

Arrays are special variables made up of collections of data. Array elements are accessed via their index into the array; to access the third element of a simple array you would refer to array[3], for example.

ColdFusion supports arrays with one to three dimensions. A one-dimensional array is very similar to a list. A two-dimensional array is kind of like a grid. (In fact, under the hood, ColdFusion queries are essentially two-dimensional arrays.) Three-dimensional arrays are more like cubes.

Arrays are created using the ArrayNew function. To create an array you must specify the number of dimensions needed, between one and three. You do need to specify how many elements will be stored in the array, ColdFusion automatically expands the array as needed.

N O T E Array elements may be added in any order. If you add an element 10 to an array that has only 5 elements, ColdFusion will automatically create elements 6 to 9 for you. ■

ArrayAppend

Description: ArrayAppend adds an element to the end of an array. ArrayAppend takes two parameters: the array to append the element to and the data to be stored in that element. ArrayAppend returns TRUE if the operation was successful.

Syntax:

```
ArrayAppend(Array, Value)
```

Example: The following example appends an element containing the word January to an array:

```
#ArrayAppend(Month, "January")#
```

This next example appends an element to a three-dimensional array, setting the value of element [10][1]:

```
#ArrayAppend(Users[10][1], "January")#
```

N O T E You can set the values of explicit array elements using the <CFSET> tag. ■

See also: ArrayInsertAt, ArrayPrepend

ArrayAvg

Description: ArrayAvg returns the average numeric value in an array. ArrayAvg takes a single parameter: the array to be checked.

Syntax:

```
ArrayAvg(Array)
```

Example: The following example reports the average cost of items in an array:

```
The average cost of each item in the list is #DollarFormat(ArrayAvg(items))#
```

N O T E ArrayAvg only works with arrays containing numeric data. Do not use this function with arrays that contain text data. ■

See also: ArrayMin, ArrayMax, ArraySum

ArrayClear

Description: ArrayClear deletes all data from an array. ArrayClear takes a single parameter: the array to be deleted. ArrayClear returns TRUE if the operation was successful.

Syntax:

```
ArrayClear(Array)
```

Example: The following example empties an existing array:

```
<CFSET result = ArrayClear(Items)>
```

N O T E ArrayClear does not delete the actual array. Rather, it removes all the contents from it. The array itself remains and may be reused. ■

See also: ArrayDeleteAt, ArrayIsEmpty

App
B

ArrayDeleteAt

Description: `ArrayDeleteAt` deletes an element from an array at a specified position, pulling all remaining elements back one place. `ArrayDeleteAt` takes two parameters: the array to delete the element from and the position of the element to delete. `ArrayDeleteAt` returns TRUE if the operation was successful.

Syntax:

```
ArrayDeleteAt(Array, Position)
```

Example: The following example deletes the ninth element from an array:

```
#ArrayDeleteAt(Items, 9)#
```

See also: `ArrayClear`, `ArrayInsertAt`

ArrayInsertAt

Description: `ArrayInsertAt` inserts an element into an array at a specified position, pushing all existing elements over one place. `ArrayInsertAt` takes three parameters: the array to insert the element into, the position to insert the element at, and the data to be stored in that element. `ArrayInsertAt` returns TRUE if the operation was successful.

Syntax:

```
ArrayInsertAt(Array, Position, Value)
```

Example: The following example inserts an element containing the word `Alaska` into the second position of an existing two-dimensional array; it then sets the abbreviation `AK` into the matching second dimension:

```
<CFSET result = ArrayInsertAt(States[1], 2, "Alaska")>
<CFSET States[2][2] = "AK">
```

See also: `ArrayAppend`, `ArrayDeleteAt`, `ArrayPrepend`

ArrayIsEmpty

Description: `ArrayIsEmpty` checks to see if an array has data. `ArrayIsEmpty` takes a single parameter: the array to be checked. `ArrayIsEmpty` returns TRUE if the array is empty, FALSE if not.

Syntax:

```
ArrayIsEmpty(Array)
```

Example: The following example reports whether an array is empty:

```
<CFOUTPUT>Array empty: #YesNoFormat(ArrayIsEmpty(Users))#</CFOUTPUT>
```

See also: `ArrayClear`, `ArrayLen`, `IsArray`

ArrayLen

Description: `ArrayLen` returns the length of a specified array. `ArrayLen` takes a single parameter: the array to be checked.

Syntax: `ArrayLen(Array)`

Example: The following example reports the size of an array:

```
The items array has #ArrayLen(items)# elements
```

See also: `ArrayIsEmpty`, `ArrayResize`

App
B

ArrayMax

Description: `ArrayMax` returns the largest numeric value in an array. `ArrayMax` takes a single parameter, the array to be checked.

Syntax:

```
ArrayMax(Array)
```

Example: The following example reports the cost of the most expensive item in an array:

```
The most expensive item in the list costs #DollarFormat(ArrayMax(items))#
```

N O T E ArrayMax only works with arrays containing numeric data. Do not use this function with arrays that contain text data.

See also: `ArrayAvg`, `ArrayMin`, `ArraySum`

ArrayMin

Description: `ArrayMin` returns the smallest numeric value in an array. `ArrayMin` takes a single parameter: the array to be checked.

Syntax:

```
ArrayMin(Array)
```

Example: The following example reports the cost of the least expensive item in an array:

```
The least expensive item in the list costs #DollarFormat(ArrayMin(items))#
```

N O T E ArrayMin only works with arrays containing numeric data. Do not use this function with arrays that contain text data.

See also: `ArrayAvg`, `ArrayMax`, `ArraySum`

ArrayNew

Description: `ArrayNew` is used to create an array. `ArrayNew` takes a single parameter: the number of dimensions needed. Valid dimensions are one through three. `ArrayNew` returns the array itself.

Syntax:

```
ArrayNew(Dimensions)
```

Example: The following example creates a one-dimensional array:

```
<CFSET Users = ArrayNew(1)>
```

N O T E Once an array is created, ColdFusion automatically expands it as needed. Use the ArrayResize function to manually resize an array. ▪

See also: IsArray, ListToArray

ArrayPrepend

Description: ArrayPrepend adds an element to the beginning of an array. ArrayPrepend takes two parameters: the array to insert the element into and the data to be stored in that element. ArrayPrepend returns TRUE if the operation was successful.

Syntax:

```
ArrayPrepend(Array, Value)
```

Example: The following example inserts an element containing the word Alabama into the beginning of an array:

```
#ArrayPrepend(States, "Alabama")#
```

N O T E You can set the values of explicit array elements using the <CFSET> tag. ▪

See also: ArrayAppend, ArrayInsertAt

ArrayResize

Description: ArrayResize changes the size of an array, padding it with empty elements if needed. ArrayResize takes two parameters: the array to be resized and the size at which to resize it. ArrayResize returns TRUE if the operation is successful.

Syntax:

```
ArrayResize(Array, Size)
```

Example: The following example creates an array and immediately resizes it to hold 100 elements:

```
<CFSET Users = ArrayNew(1)>
<CFSET result = ArrayResize(Users, 100)>
```

 Dynamically expanding arrays is a slow operation. You can dramatically optimize ColdFusion's array processing by resizing the array to the anticipated size immediately after creating it with ArrayNew.

See also: ArrayLen, ArraySet

ArraySet

Description: ArraySet initializes one or more elements in an array with a specified value. ArraySet takes four parameters, the array itself, the element starting and ending positions, and the value to use. ArraySet returns TRUE if the operation is successful.

Syntax:

```
ArraySet(Array, Start, End, Value)
```

Example: The following example sets elements 1 through 100 with the value 0:

```
#ArraySet(OrderItems, 1, 100, 0)#
```

See also: ArrayResize, ArraySort, ArraySwap

App

B

ArraySort

Description: ArraySort sorts the data in an array. ArraySort takes three parameters: the array to be sorted, the sort type, and an optional sort order. If the sort order is omitted, the default order of ascending is used. ArraySort supports three sort types, as listed in Table B.10.

Table B.10   ArraySort Sort Types

Type	Description
Numeric	Sorts numerically.
Text	Sorts text alphabetically, uppercase before lowercase
TextNoCase	Sorts text alphabetically; case is ignored

Syntax:

```
ArraySort(Array, Type [, Order])
```

Example: The following example sorts an array alphabetically using a non–case-sensitive sort (also known as a *dictionary sort*):

```
#ArraySort(Users, "textnocase")#
```

N O T E ArraySort sorts the actual passed array, not a copy of it. ▪

See also: ArraySet, ArraySwap

ArraySum

Description: ArraySum returns the sum of all values in an array. ArraySum takes a single parameter: the array to be checked.

Syntax:

```
ArraySum(Array)
```

Example: The following example reports the total cost of all items in an array:

```
The total cost of all item in the list is #DollarFormat(ArraySum(items))#
```

N O T E ArraySum only works with arrays containing numeric data. Do not use this function with arrays that contain text data. ■

See also: ArrayAvg, ArrayMin, ArrayMax

ArraySwap

Description: ArraySwap is used to swap the values in two array elements. ArraySwap takes three parameters: the array itself and the positions of the two elements to be swapped. ArraySwap returns TRUE if the operation is successful.

Syntax:

```
ArraySwap(Array, Position1, Position2)
```

Example: The following example swaps elements 10 and 11 in an array:

```
#ArraySwap(Users, 10, 11)#
```

See also: ArraySet, ArraySort

ArrayToList

Description: ArrayToList converts a one-dimensional ColdFusion array into a list. ArrayToList takes two parameters: the array to be converted and an optional list delimiter. If no delimiter is specified, the default (comma) delimiter is used. ArrayToList creates a new list.

Syntax:

```
ArrayToList (Array [, Delimiter])
```

Example: The following example converts an array of users into a list:

```
<CFSET UserList = ArrayToList(UserArray)>
```

See also: ListToArray

IsArray

Description: IsArray checks to see if a variable is a valid ColdFusion array; it also determines that an array has a specific number of dimensions. IsArray takes two parameters: the variable to be checked and an optional number of dimensions to check for. IsArray returns TRUE if the variable is an array, FALSE if not.

Syntax:

```
IsArray (Array [, Dimension])
```

Example: The following example checks to see if a variable named Users is an array:

```
#IsArray(Users)#
```

This example checks to see if Users is a three-dimensional array:

```
#IsArray(Users, 3)#
```

See also: ArrayIsEmpty

ListToArray

Description: ListToArray converts a ColdFusion list to a one-dimensional array. ListToArray takes two parameters: the list to be converted and an optional list delimiter. If no delimiter is specified, the default (comma) delimiter is used. ListToArray creates a new array.

Syntax:

```
ListToArray(List [, Delimiter])
```

Example: The following example converts a list of users into an array:

```
<CFSET UserArray = ListToArray(UserList)>
```

See also: ArrayToList

Structure Manipulation Functions

ColdFusion *structures* are special data types that contain one or more other variables. Structures are a way to group related variables together.

StructClear

Description: StructClear deletes all data from a structure. StructClear takes a single parameter: the structure to be cleared. StructClear returns TRUE if the operation is successful.

Syntax:

```
StructClear(Structure)
```

Example: The following example empties an existing structure:

```
<CFSET result = StructClear(Items)>
```

> **N O T E** StructClear does not delete the actual structure. Rather, it removes all the contents from it. The structure itself remains and may be reused. ▪

See also: StructDelete, StructIsEmpty

StructCount

Description: StructCount returns the number of items in a specified structure. StructCount takes a single parameter: the structure to be checked.

Syntax:

```
StructCount(Structure)
```

Example: The following example reports the number of elements in a structure:

```
The items structure has #StructCount(items)# elements
```

See also: StructIsEmpty

StructDelete

Description: StructDelete deletes an item from a structure. StructDelete takes three parameters: the structure, the name of the key to be deleted, and an optional flag that specifies how to handle requests to delete a key that does not exist. StructDelete returns TRUE if the operation was successful, FALSE if not. If an attempt is made to delete a key that does not exist, and the IndicateNotExisting flag is not set to TRUE, the StructDelete returns TRUE.

Syntax:

```
StructDelete(Structure, Key [, IndicateNotExisiting])
```

Example: The following example deletes the name key from a user structure:

```
#StructDelete(user, name)#
```

See also: StructClear, StructKeyExists, StructIsEmpty

StructFind, StructFindNoCase

Description: The StructFind and StructFindNoCase functions search through a structure to find the key that matches the specified search text. If a matching key is found, the value in that key is returned; if no match is found, an empty value is returned. StructFind performs a case-sensitive search and StructFindNoCase performs a non–case-sensitive search. Both functions take two parameters: the first is the structure to be searched and the second is the key to search for.

Syntax:

```
StructFind(Structure, Key)

StructFindNoCase(Structure, Key)
```

Example: The following example returns the username stored in a user structure:

```
User name is #StructFindNoCase(user, first_name)
➥# #StructFindNoCase(user, last_name)#
```

StructInsert

Description: StructInsert inserts an item into a structure. StructInsert takes four parameters: the structure, the name of the key to be inserted, the value, and an optional flag that specifies whether a key may be overwritten or not. StructInsert returns TRUE if the operation was successful, FALSE if not. Values can be overwritten unless AllowOverwrite is set to FALSE.

Syntax:

```
StructInsert(Structure, Key, Value [, AllowOverwrite])
```

Example: The following example inserts a key named `first_name` into a `user` structure:

```
#StructInsert(user, "first_name", "Ben")#
```

See also: StructDelete

StructIsEmpty

Description: `StructIsEmpty` checks to see if a structure has data. `StructIsEmpty` takes a single parameter: the structure to be checked. `StructIsEmpty` returns TRUE if the array is empty, FALSE if not.

Syntax:

```
StructIsEmpty(Structure)
```

Example: The following example reports whether a structure is empty:

```
<CFOUTPUT>Strucure empty: #YesNoFormat(StructIsEmpty(Users))#</CFOUTPUT>
```

See also: StructClear, StructCount, StructKeyExists

StructKeyExists

Description: `StructKeyExists` checks to see if a structure contains a specific key. `StructKeyExists` takes two parameters: the structure to be checked and the key to look for. `StructKeyExists` returns TRUE if the key exists, FALSE if not.

Syntax:

```
StructKeyExists(Structure, Key)
```

Example: The following checks to see if a key named `first_name` exists:

```
<CFIF StructKeyExists(user, "first_name")>
```

See also: StructCount, StructIsEmpty

StructNew

Description: `StructNew` creates a new structure. `StructNew` takes no parameters and returns the structure itself.

Syntax:

```
StructNew()
```

Example: The following example creates a simple structure:

```
<CFSET Orders=StructNew()>
```

Query Manipulation Functions

ColdFusion uses queries to return sets of data. Most queries are created with the `<CFQUERY>` tag, but other tags (`<CFPOP>` and `<CFLDAP>`) also return data in queries. ColdFusion also allows you to programmatically create your own queries using the QueryNew function and set query values using QuerySetCell.

> **N O T E** ColdFusion *queries* are essentially arrays with named columns. You may therefore use any of the array functions with queries. ▨

IsQuery

Description: IsQuery checks to see if a variable is a valid ColdFusion query. IsQuery takes a single parameter: the variable to be checked. IsQuery returns TRUE if the variable is a query, FALSE if not.

Syntax:

```
IsQuery (Query)
```

Example: The following example checks to see if a variable named Users is a query:

```
<CFIF IsQuery(Users)>
```

 IsQuery is particularly useful within custom tags that expect queries as parameters. IsQuery can be used to check that a valid value was passed before any processing occurs.

QueryAddRow

Description: QueryAddRow adds a row to an existing ColdFusion query. QueryAddRow takes two parameters: the query to add a row to and an optional number of rows to add. If the number of rows is omitted, the default number of 1 is used.

Syntax:

```
QueryAddRow(Query [, Number])
```

Example: The following example creates a new query called Users and adds 10 rows to it:

```
<CFSET Users = QueryNew("FirstName, LastName")>
<CFSET temp = QueryAddRow(Users, 10)>
```

See also: QueryNew, QuerySetCell

QueryNew

Description: QueryNew creates a new ColdFusion query. QueryNew takes a single parameter, a comma-delimited list of columns for the new query. QueryNew returns the newly created query.

Syntax:

```
QueryNew(Columns)
```

Example: The following example creates a new query called Users and adds 10 rows to it:

```
<CFSET Users = QueryNew("FirstName, LastName")>
<CFSET temp = QueryAddRow(Users, 10)>
```

See also: QueryAddRow, QuerySetCell

QuerySetCell

Description: QuerySetCell is used to set the values of specific cells in a table. QuerySetCell takes four parameters: the query name, the column name, the value, and an optional row number. If the row number is omitted, the cell in the last query row is set.

Syntax:

```
QuerySetCell(Query, Column, Value [, Row])
```

Example: The following example sets the FirstName column in the third row to the value Ben:

```
<CFSET temp = QuerySetCell(Users, "FirstName", "Ben", 3)>
```

> **NOTE** Query cells can also be set using the <CFSET> tag treating the query as a two-dimensional array. ■

See also: QueryAddRow, QueryNew

Security Functions

ColdFusion supports advanced security contexts that let you create complete security systems, which secure your applications. Security is managed and maintained using the ColdFusion Administrator. Once security is established, you can make a call to the <CFAUTHENTICATE> tag in order to return security information. Use these security functions to interact with that security information.

IsAuthenticated

Description: IsAuthenticated checks to see if a user has been authenticated with the <CFAUTHENTICATE> tag. IsAuthenticated takes two parameters: the user to be checked and the security context to be checked against. IsAuthenticate returns TRUE if the user has been authenticated, FALSE if not.

Syntax:

```
IsAuthenticated(User, Context)
```

Example: The following example checks to see if a user has been authenticated as an administrator:

```
<CFIF IsAuthenticated("#user#", "administrator")
```

N O T E To use this function, advanced security must be enabled in the ColdFusion Administrator and security contexts must already have been defined. ▓

See also: IsAuthorized

IsAuthorized

Description: IsAuthorized checks to see if a user is authorized to perform specific actions. IsAuthorized takes three parameters: the resource type to be checked, the resource to be checked, and an optional action. IsAuthorized returns TRUE if the action is authorized, FALSE if not. Table B.11 lists the valid resource types.

Syntax:

```
IsAuthorized(ResourceType, ResourceName [, Action])
```

Example: The following example checks to see if a user has been authenticated as an administrator:

Table B.11   Resource Types

Type
Application
CFML
DSN
File
Object

Example: The following example checks to see if a user is authorized to use a specific data source:

```
<CFIF IsAuthorized(DSN, "A2Z")
```

N O T E To use this function, advanced security must be enabled in the ColdFusion Administrator and security contexts must already have been defined. ▓

See also: IsAuthenticated

System Functions

The ColdFusion system functions allow you to perform manipulation of file paths, create temporary files, and verify file existence.

DirectoryExists

Description: DirectoryExists checks for the existence of a specified directory and returns either TRUE or FALSE. DirectoryExists takes a single parameter: the name of the directory to check for. The directory name cannot be a relative path, but must be specified as a fully qualified path.

Syntax:

```
DirectoryExists(Directory)
```

Example: The following example checks for the existence of a directory, creating it if it does not exist:

```
<CFIF DirectoryExists("#directory#") IS "No">
 <CFFILE ACTION="CREATE" DIRECTORY="#directory#">
</CFIF>
```

See also: FileExists

ExpandPath

Description: ExpandPath converts a path relative to the Web server document root into a fully qualified path. ExpandPath takes a single parameter: the path to be converted.

Syntax:

```
ExpandPath(Path)
```

Example: The following example returns the full path of the server's default document:

```
#ExpandPath("index.cfm")#
```

See also: GetTemplatePath

FileExists

Description: FileExists checks for the existence of a specified file and returns either TRUE or FALSE. FileExists takes a single parameter: the name of the file to check for. The filename cannot be a relative path, but must be specified as a fully qualified path.

Syntax:

```
FileExists(File)
```

Example: The following example checks for the existence of an image file before using it in an IMG tag:

```
<CFIF FileExists("C:\root\images\logo.gif")>
 <IMG SRC="/images/logo.gif">
</CFIF>
```

 TIP Use the ExpandPath function so you don't have to hard code the filename passed to the FileExists function; use ExpandPath to convert the relative path to an actual filename.

See also: DirectoryExists

GetDirectoryFromPath

Description: GetDirectoryFromPath extracts the drive and directory (with a trailing backslash) from a fully specified path. GetDirectoryFromPath takes a single parameter: the path to be evaluated.

Syntax:

GetDirectoryFromPath(Path)

Example: The following example returns the directory portion of a current template's full file path:

#GetDirectoryFromPath(GetTemplatePath())#

See also: GetFileFromPath

GetFileFromPath

Description: GetFileFromPath extracts the filename from a fully specified path. GetFileFromPath takes a single parameter: the path to be evaluated.

Syntax:

GetFileFromPath(Path)

Example: The following example returns the filename portion of a temporary file:

#GetFileFromPath(GetTempFile(GetTempDirectory(), "CF"))#

See also: GetDirectoryFromPath

GetTempDirectory

Description: GetTempDirectory returns the full path of the Windows temporary directory with a trailing backslash. GetTempDirectory takes no parameters.

Syntax:

GetTempDirectory()

Example: The following example returns the name of a temporary file beginning with the letters CF in the Windows temporary directory:

#GetTempFile(GetTempDirectory(), "CF")#

See also: GetTempFile

GetTempFile

Description: GetTempFile returns the full path to a temporary file for use by your application. The returned filename is guaranteed to be unique. GetTempFile takes two parameters: the first is the directory where you'd like the temporary file created, and the second is a filename prefix of up to three characters. You cannot omit the prefix, but you may pass an empty string ("").

Syntax:

```
GetTempFile(Directory, Prefix)
```

Example: The following example returns the name of a temporary file beginning with the letters CF in the Windows temporary directory:

```
#GetTempFile(GetTempDirectory(), "CF")#
```

 T I P   To create a temporary file in the Windows temporary directory, pass the GetTempDirectory function as the directory parameter.

See also: GetTempDirectory

GetTemplatePath

Description: GetTemplatePath returns the fully qualified path of the base template being processed. GetTemplatePath takes no parameters.

Syntax:

```
GetTemplatePath()
```

Example: The following example returns the full path of the base template being processed:

```
Processing: #GetTemplatePath()#
```

N O T E   GetTemplatePath returns the path of the base template being processed. If you are using GetTemplatePath in a template that is being included in a second template, the path of that second template is returned. ▪

Client Variable Manipulation Functions

Client variables allow you to store client information so that it is available between sessions. Client variables can be accessed just like any other ColdFusion variables; standard variable access tool such as <CFSET> can therefore be used to set variables. In addition, these functions provide special variable manipulation capabilities.

For more information about client variables and how they are used, see Chapter 26, "Web Application Framework."

DeleteClientVariable

Description: DeleteClientVariable deletes the client variable whose name is passed as a parameter. Unlike other ColdFusion variables, client variables persist over time and must be deleted with this function. DeleteClientVariable takes a single parameter: the name of the variable to delete. DeleteClientVariable returns TRUE if the variable was deleted, FALSE if it was not.

Syntax:

```
DeleteClientVariable(Variable)
```

Example: The following example deletes a variable named login_name and sets a local variable with the function return value:

```
<CFSET DeleteSuccessful = DeleteClientVariable("login_name")>
```

GetClientVariablesList

Description: GetClientVariablesList returns a comma-delimited list of the read-write client variables available to the template. The standard read-only system client variables, listed in Table B.12, are not returned. GetClientVariablesList takes no parameters.

Syntax:

```
GetClientVariablesList()
```

Table B.12   Read-Only Client Variables

Variable	Description
CFID	Unique ID assigned to this client.
CFToken	Unique security token used to verify the authenticity of a CFID value.
URLToken	Text to append to URLs; contains both CFID and CFToken. (Appended automatically to <CFLOCATION> URLs.)

Example: The following example retrieves the entire list of read-write client variables:

```
#ListLen(GetClientVariablesList())#
➥read-write client variables are currently active
```

TIP The list of variables returned by the GetClientVariablesList function is comma delimited, which makes it very suitable for processing with the ColdFusion list functions.

Expression Evaluation Functions

ColdFusion allows you to perform *dynamic expression evaluation*. This is an advanced technique that allows you to build and evaluate expressions on-the-fly.

Dynamic expression evaluations are performed on string expressions. A string expression is just that—a string that contains an expression. The string "1+2" contains an expression that, when evaluated, returns 3. String expressions can be as simple or as complex as needed.

DE

Description: DE stands for delay evaluation. This function is designed for use with the IIF and Evaluate functions. It takes a string as a parameter and returns the same string enclosed within quotation marks; all double quotation marks are escaped. This allows you to pass a string to IIf and Evalaute without them being evaluated.

Syntax:

```
DE(String)
```

Example: The following example uses DE to ensure that the string "A" is evaluated, instead of the variable "A".

```
#Evaluate(DE("A"))#
```

Evaluate

Description: Evaluate is used to evaluate string expressions. Evaluate takes one or more string expressions as parameters and evaluates them from left to right.

Syntax:

```
Evaluate(String1, …)
```

Example: The following example evaluates the variable "A":

```
#Evalutate("A")#
```

IIf

Description: IIf evaluates a Boolean condition and evaluates one of two expressions depending on the results of that evaluation. If the Boolean condition returns TRUE, the first expression is evaluated; if the condition returns FALSE, the second expression is evaluated.

Syntax:

```
IIF(Boolean condition, Expression if TRUE, Expression if FALSE)
```

Example: The following example determines if #cnt# has a value of 1; it evaluates "A" if it does, "B" if it does not:

```
#IIf("#cnt# IS 1", "A", "B")#
```

SetVariable

Description: SetVariable sets a specified variable to a passed value.

Syntax:

```
SetVariable(Variable, Value)
```

Example: The following example sets variable #cnt# to the value returned by the passed expression:

```
#SetVariable(#cnt#, "A")#
```

Bit and Set Manipulation Functions

ColdFusion provides a complete set of bit manipulation functions for use by advanced developers only. These functions allow you to manipulate the individual bits within a 32-bit integer.

The complete set of bit manipulation functions is listed in Table B.13. The descriptions for each function are given in the C/C++ syntax.

N O T E   Any start, length, or position parameters passed to the bit manipulation functions must be in the range of 0 to 31.

Table B.13   ColdFusion Bit and Set Manipulation Functions

Function	Description
BitAnd(x, y)	x and y
BitMaskClear(x, start, length)	x with length bits starting from start cleared
BitMaskRead(x, start, length)	The value of the length bits starting from start
BitMaskSet(x, mask, start, length)	x with mask occupying the length bits starting from start
BitNot(x)	x
BitOr(x, y)	x | y
BitSHLN(x, n)	x << n
BitSHRN(x, n)	x >> n
BitXor(x, y)	x^y

Miscellaneous Functions

These miscellaneous functions are some of the most important ones; are you are likely to find yourself using them repeatedly.

GetBaseTagData

Description: GetBaseTagData is used within subtags. It returns an object containing data from a specified ancestor tag. GetBaseTagData takes two parameters: the name of the tag whose data you want returned and an optional instance number. If no instance is specified, the default value of 1 is used.

Syntax:

```
GetBaseTagData(Tag [, InstanceNumber])
```

Example: The following example retrieves the data in a caller <CFHTTP> tag:

```
#GetBaseTagData(CFHTTP)#
```

Not all tags contain data (for example, the <CFIF> tag). Passing a tag that contains no data to the GetBaseTagData function causes an exception to be thrown. ▪

See also: GetBaseTagList

GetBaseTagList

Description: GetBaseTagList is used within subtags. It returns a comma-delimited list of base tag names. The returned list is in calling order, with the parent tag listed first.

Syntax:

```
GetBaseTagList()
```

Example: The following example displays the top level calling tag:

```
<CFOUTPUT>The top level tag is #ListFirst(GetBaseTagList())#</CFOUTPUT>
```

See also: GetBaseTagData

GetTickCount

Description: GetTickCount performs timing tests with millisecond accuracy. The value that is returned by GetTickCount is of no use other than to compare it to the results of another GetTickCount call to check time spans.

Syntax:

```
GetTickCount()
```

Example: The following example tests how long a code block takes to execute:

```
<CFSET count1=GetTickCount()>
...
<CFSET count2=GetTickCount()>
<CFSET duration=count2-count1>
<CFOUTPUT>Code took #duration# milliseconds to execute</CFOUTPUT>
```

IsBoolean

Description: IsBoolean determines whether a value can be converted to a Boolean value. (Boolean values have two states only, ON and OFF or TRUE and FALSE.) IsBoolean takes a single parameter: the number, string, or expression to evaluate. When evaluating numbers, IsBoolean treats 0 as FALSE, and any non-zero value as TRUE.

Syntax:

```
IsBoolean(Value)
```

Example: The following example checks to see if a value can be safely converted into a Boolean value before passing it to a formatting function:

```
<CFIF IsBoolean(status) IS "Yes">
 #YesNoFormat(status)#
</CFIF>
```

See also: YesNoFormat

IsDebugMode

Description: IsDebugMode checks to see if a page is being sent back to the user in debug mode. IsDebugMode returns TRUE if debug mode is on, FALSE if not. IsDebugMode takes no parameters.

Syntax:

```
IsDebugMode()
```

Example: The following code writes debug data to a log file if in debug mode:

```
<CFIF IsDebugMode()>
 <CFFILE ACTION= APPEND" FILE="log.txt" OUTPUT="#debug_info#">
</CFIF>
```

N O T E IsDebugMode() allows you to leave debugging code when writing your applications; they are not processed at runtime unless debug mode is enabled. ■

IsDefined

Description: IsDefined determines whether a specified variable exists. IsDefined returns TRUE if the specified variable exists, FALSE if not. IsDefined takes a single parameter: the variable to check for. This parameter can be passed as a fully qualified variable, with a preceding variable type designator. The variable name must be enclosed in quotation marks; otherwise ColdFusion checks to see if the contents of the variable exist rather than the variable itself.

Syntax:

```
IsDefined(Parameter)
```

Example: The following example checks to see if a variable of any type named USER_ID exists:

```
<CFIF IsDefined("USER_ID")>
```

The next example checks to see if a CGI variable named USER_ID exists, and ignores variables of other types:

```
<CFIF IsDefined("CGI.USER_ID") >
```

N O T E IsDefined is a little more complicated to use than ParameterExists, but it does allow you to dynamically evaluate and redirect expressions. ■

See also: Evaluate, IsSimpleValue, ParameterExists

IsNumeric

Description: IsNumeric checks to see if a specified value is numeric. IsNumeric takes a single parameter: the value to be evaluated.

Syntax:

IsNumeric(Value)

Example: The following example checks to ensure that a user entered a valid age (numeric characters only):

```
<CFIF IsNumeric(age) IS "No">
 You entered an invalid age!
</CFIF>
```

N O T E   Use the LSIsNumeric function for international number support. ▓

See also: InputBaseN, LSIsNumeric, Val

IsSimpleValue

Description: IsSimpleValue checks to see if a value is a string, number, TRUE/FALSE value, or DATE/TIME value. IsSimpleValue takes a single parameter: the value to be checked. IsSimpleValue returns TRUE if the value is a simple value, FALSE if not.

Syntax:

IsSimpleValue(Value)

Example: The following example checks to see that a description field is a simple value:

```
<CFIF IsSimpleValue(Description)>
```

See also: Evaluate, IsDefined, ParameterExists

ParameterExists

Description: ParameterExists checks to see if a specified variable exists. ParameterExists returns TRUE if the specified variable exists, FALSE if not. ParameterExists takes a single parameter: the variable to check for. This parameter may be passed as a fully qualified variable, with a preceding variable type designator. Do not enclose the variable name in quotation marks.

Syntax:

ParameterExists(Parameter)

Example: The following example checks to see if a variable of any type named USER_ID exists:

```
<CFIF ParameterExists(USER_ID) IS "Yes">
```

App

B

The next example checks to see if a CGI variable named USER_ID exists, and ignores variables of other types:

```
<CFIF ParameterExists(CGI.USER_ID) IS "Yes">
```

N O T E   One of the most important uses of the ParameterExists function is creating dynamic
SQL statements using the <CFSQL> tag. ■

See also: Evaluate, IsDefined, IsSimpleValue

PreserveSingleQuotes

Description: PreserveSingleQuotes instructs ColdFusion to not escape single quotation marks contained in values derived from dynamic parameters. PreserveSingleQuotes takes a single parameter: the string to be preserved.

Syntax:

```
PreserveSingleQuotes(String)
```

Example: The following example uses PreserveSingleQuotes to ensure that a dynamic parameter in a SQL statement is included correctly:

```
SELECT * FROM Customers
WHERE CustomerName IN ( #PreserveSingleQuotes(CustNames)#)
```

QuotedValueList, ValueList

Description: QuotedValueList and ValueList drive one query with the results of another. Both functions take a single parameter—the name of a query column—and return a list of all the values in that column. QuotedValueList returns a list of values that are each enclosed within quotation marks and separated by commas. ValueList returns the list separated by commas, but not enclosed in quotation marks.

Syntax:

```
QuotedValueList(Column)
```

```
ValueList(Column)
```

Example: The following example ensures that a dynamic parameter in a SQL statement is included correctly:

```
SELECT * FROM Customers
WHERE CustomerName IN ( #PreserveSingleQuotes(CustNames)#)
```

N O T E   The QuotedValueList and ValueList functions are typically only used when
constructing dynamic SQL statements. ■

   The values returned by QuotedValueList and ValueList are both in the standard ColdFusion list format, and can therefore be manipulated by the list functions.

TIP As a general rule, you should always try to combine both the queries into a single SQL statement unless you need to manipulate the values in the list. The time it takes to process one combined SQL statement is far less than the time it takes to process two simpler statements.

URLEncodedValue

Description: URLEncodedValue encodes a string in a format that can be safely used within URLs. URLs may not contain spaces or any non-alphanumeric characters. The URLEncodedValue function replaces spaces with a plus sign; non-alphanumeric characters are replaced with equivalent hexadecimal escape sequences. URLEncodedValue takes a single parameter—the string to be encoded—and returns the encoded string.

Syntax:

```
URLEncodedValue(String)
```

NOTE ColdFusion automatically decodes all URL parameters that are passed to a template.

Example: The following example creates an URL with a name parameter that can safely include any characters:

```
<A HREF="details.cfm?name=#URLEncodedFormat(name)#">Details</A>
```

Verity Search Language Reference

This appendix describes each of the search operators that can be passed to Verity in the CRITE-RIA parameter of a CFSEARCH tag. Refer to Chapter 29, "Full-Text Searching with Verity," for details on incorporating Verity into your ColdFusion applications.

This is not meant to be an exhaustive reference. You should consult your ColdFusion documentation for each operator's precise definition and syntax. Verity's Web site is also a good resource for information regarding the syntax and impact of the search operators discussed in this appendix. There are many FAQs (frequently asked questions) and examples of search syntax in action. Just keep in mind that Verity's search functionality is not a ColdFusion-only thing. You will find references to features that are not exposed to you as a ColdFusion developer. Verity's Web site can be found at http://www.verity.com/.

Using Angle Brackets Around Operators

With the exception of AND, OR, and NOT, you must use angle brackets around all Verity operators. This tells Verity that you're interested in actually using the NEAR operator, for example, rather than just trying to search for the word *near* in your document. The following line is not searching for the word *near*:

```
CRITERIA="Sick <NEAR> Days"
```

Again, AND, OR, and NOT do not need the angle brackets—the idea is they will be used very often, and people infrequently need to search for the actual words *and*, *or*, or *not* in their documents. The following two lines are equivalent:

```
CRITERIA="Sick AND Days"
CRITERIA="Sick <AND> Days"
```

Operators Are Not Case Sensitive

Verity search operators are not case sensitive, even when the search itself may be case sensitive. Therefore, these two statements are also equivalent:

```
CRITERIA="Sick <NEAR> Days"
CRITERIA="Sick <near> Days"
```

Using Prefix Instead of Infix Notation

All Verity operators except for the evidence operators (STEM, WILDCARD, and WORD) can be specified using something called *prefix notation*.

For instance, suppose that you have several search words on which you want to use the NEAR operator. Instead of sticking <NEAR> between each word, you can just specify NEAR once and then put the list of words in parentheses. The following two lines are equivalent:

```
CRITERIA="sick <NEAR> days <NEAR> illness"
CRITERIA="<NEAR>(sick,days,illness)"
```

Searching for Special Characters as Literals

Special characters—most obviously, the < and > characters—have special meaning for Verity. If you want to actually search for these characters, you need to use a backslash (\) to "escape" each special character. For example, if you want to search for documents that contain <TABLE>, you need to do it like this:

```
CRITERIA="\<TABLE\>"
```

Understanding Concept Operators

Verity's *concept operators* are used when you are specifying more than one search word or search element. The Concept Operator tells Verity whether you mean that all of the words/elements must be present in the document for it to count as a match, or if any one word/element makes the document count as a match. The concept operators include AND and OR.

The AND operator indicates that all of the search words/elements must be present in a document for the document to count as a match. Some examples:

```
CRITERIA="sick AND days AND illness"
CRITERIA="sick <AND> days <AND> illness"
CRITERIA="AND (sick,days,illness)"
```

 Remember that unlike most other operators, AND does not need angle brackets around it.

The OR operator indicates that a document counts as a match as soon as any of the search words/elements are present in the document. Some examples:

```
CRITERIA="sick OR days OR illness"
CRITERIA="sick <OR> days <OR> illness"
CRITERIA="OR (sick,days,illness)"
```

 Remember that unlike the majority of operators, OR does not need angle brackets around it.

Understanding Evidence Operators

Verity's *evidence operators* control whether Verity "steps in" and searches for words that are slightly different from the search words you actually specify.

Remember that unlike other operators, evidence operators cannot be used with prefix notation. Instead, they must be specified with infix notation—that is, they must be inserted between each word of a set. See the example for STEM, which follows.

Evidence operators include STEM, WILDCARD, and WORD.

The STEM operator tells Verity to expand the search to include grammatical variations of the search words you specify. In other words, Verity takes each word and finds its root, then searches for all the common variations of that root. If the search were for *permitting*, Verity would take it upon itself to also search for *permit* and *permitted*. Some examples:

```
CRITERIA="<STEM> permitting"
CRITERIA="AND (<STEM> permitting, <STEM> smoke)"
```

The WILDCARD operator tells Verity that the search words contain wildcards that should be considered while the search is occurring. Note that two of the wildcard characters—the question mark and the asterisk—are automatically assumed to be wildcard characters, even if you don't specify the WILDCARD operator. The other wildcard characters will only behave as such if the WILDCARD operator is used. The following statements are examples:

```
CRITERIA="smok*"
CRITERIA="smok?"
CRITERIA="<WILDCARD>smok*"
CRITERIA="<WILDCARD>'smok{ed,ing}'"
```

Table C.1 summarizes the possible operators for a wildcard value.

Table C.1   Verity Wildcards

Wildcard	Purpose
*	Like the % wildcard in SQL, * stands in for any number of characters (including 0).
	A search for Fu* would find *Fusion, Fugazi,* and *Fuchsia.*
?	Just as in SQL, ? stands in for any single character. More precise—and thus generally less helpful—than the * wildcard. A search for ?ar?et would find both *carpet* and *target,* but not *Learjet.*
{ }	Allows you to specify a number of possible word fragments, separated by commas. A search for {gr,frag,deodor}rant would find documents that contained *grant, fragrant,* or *deodorant.*
[ ]	Like { }, except brackets stand in for only one character at a time. A search for f[eao]ster would find documents that contained *fester, faster,* or *Foster.*
-	Allows you to place a range of characters within square brackets. Searching for A[C-H]50993 is the same as searching for A[DEFGH]50993.

If you use any wildcard other than ? or *, you must use either single or double quotation marks around the actual wildcard pattern. I recommend that you use single quotation marks around the wildcard pattern, since the criteria parameter as a whole should be within double quotation marks.

The WORD operator tells Verity to perform a simple word search, without any wildcarding or stemming. Including a WORD operator is a good way to suppress Verity's default use of the STEM operator; it is also effective if you didn't want the ? in a search for Hello? to be treated as a wildcard character. Some examples:

```
CRITERIA="<WORD>smoke"
CRITERIA="<WROD>Hello?"
```

Understanding Proximity Operators

Verity's *proximity operators* are used to specify how close together search words must be to each other within a document in order for that document to count as a match. For example, if you were looking for rules about where smoking is permitted, you might only want documents that have the words *smoking* and *permitted* sitting pretty close to one another within the actual text. A document that has the word *smoking* at the beginning and the word *permitted* way at the end would probably not interest you. The proximity operators include NEAR, NEAR/N, PARAGRAPH, and SENTENCE.

The NEAR operator specifies that you are most interested in documents where the search words are closest to one another. All documents where the words are within 1,000 words of each other are considered "found," but the closer together the words, the higher the document's score, which means it will be up at the top of the list. An example:

```
CRITERIA="smoking <NEAR> permitted"
```

The NEAR/N operator is just like NEAR, except that you get to specify how close together the words have to be to qualify as a match. Documents are still ranked based on the closeness of the words. In reality, NEAR is just shorthand for NEAR/1000. Some examples of the NEAR/N operator are as follows:

```
CRITERIA="smoking <NEAR/3> permitted"
CRITERIA="<NEAR/3>(smoking,permitted)"
```

The PARAGRAPH and SENTENCE operators specify that the words need to be in the same paragraph or sentence, respectively. Sometimes using these is better than NEAR or NEAR/N because you know that the words are related in some way having to do with their actual linguistic context, rather than their physical proximity to one another. Some examples are as follows:

```
CRITERIA="smoking <paragraph> permitted"
CRITERIA="<SENTENCE> (smoking,permitted)"
```

Understanding Relational Operators

Verity's relational operators allow you to search for words within specific document fields, such as the title of the document or a custom field. Searches that use these operators are not ranked by relevance. The relational operators include the following:

- CONTAINS
- MATCHES
- STARTS
- ENDS
- SUBSTRING
- =, <, >, <=, and >=

App
C

Table C.2 summarizes the document fields available for use with Relational Operators.

Table C.2 Document Fields Available for Use with Relational Operators

Field	Explanation
CF_TITLE	The filename of the document if the collection is based on normal documents, or whatever table column you specified for TITLE if the collection is based on database data.
CF_CUSTOM1	Whatever table column you specified for CUSTOM1, if any, if your collection is based on database data.
CF_CUSTOM2	Whatever table column you specified for CUSTOM2, if any, if your collection is based on database data.
CF_KEY	The filename of the document if the collection is based on normal documents, or whatever table column you specified for KEY if the collection is based on database data. You use relational operators with this field if the user already knows the unique ID for the record that you wanted, like a knowledge base article number.
CF_URL	The URL path to the document, as defined when you indexed the collection.

The CONTAINS operator finds documents where a specific field contains the exact word(s) you specify, like using the WORD operator on a specific field. If you specify more than one word, the words must appear in the correct order for the document to be considered a match. Some examples:

```
CRITERIA="CF_TITLE <CONTAINS> smoking"
CRITERIA="CF_TITLE <CONTAINS>'smoking,policy'"
```

The MATCHES operator finds documents where the entirety of a specific field is exactly what you specify. The field is looked at as a whole, not as individual words. A search for *Smoking Policy* in the CF_TITLE field would only match documents where the title was literally *Smoking Policy*, verbatim. This feature is probably most useful with custom fields, if the custom field holds nothing more than some kind of rating, category code, or the like. Here are some examples:

```
CRITERIA="CF_TITLE <MATCHES>'Smoking Policy'"
CRITERIA="CF_CUSTOM1 <MATCHES> Policies"
```

The STARTS operator finds documents where a specific field starts with the characters you specify, such as this:

```
CRITERIA="CF_TITLE <STARTS> smok"
```

The ENDS operator finds documents where a specific field ends with the characters you specify, such as:

```
CRITERIA="CF_TITLE <ENDS> olicy"
```

The SUBSTRING operator finds documents where a specific field contains any portion of what you specify. Unlike CONTAINS, this matches incomplete words. Here is an example:

```
CRITERIA="CF_TITLE <SUBSTRING> smok"
```

The =, <, >, <=, and >= operators perform arithmetic comparisons on numeric and date values stored in specific fields. These are probably only useful with custom fields, if the table columns you specified for the custom fields held only numeric or date values. Note that these operators don't need angle brackets around them. The following are some examples:

```
CRITERIA="CF_CUSTOM1 = 5"
CRITERIA="CF_CUSTOM2 >= 1990"
CRITERIA="CF_CUSTOM2 < #DateFormat(Form.SearchDate, 'yyyy-mm-dd')
➥#"Understanding Search Modifiers
```

Verity's search modifiers cause the search engine to behave slightly differently than it would otherwise. The search modifiers include:

- CASE
- MANY
- NOT
- ORDER

The CASE modifier forces Verity to perform a case-sensitive search, even if the search words are all lowercase or all uppercase. Here are some examples:

```
CRITERIA="<CASE>smoking"
CRITERIA="AND(<CASE>smoking,<CASE>policy)"
```

Verity will often run case-sensitive searches even if the CASE operator is not used.

The MANY operator ranks documents based on the density of search words or search elements found in a document. It is automatically in effect whenever the search type is SIMPLE and cannot be used with the concept operators AND, OR, and ACCRUE. The following are some examples:

```
CRITERIA="<MANY>(smoking,policy)"
CRITERIA="<MANY> smoking"
```

The NOT modifier causes Verity to eliminate documents that are found by the search word(s), such as:

```
CRITERIA="NOT smoking"
CRITERIA="smoking NOT policy"
CRITERIA="NOT(smoking,days)"
CRITERIA="<NOT>(smoking,days)"
```

Note that if you want to find documents that contained *not smoking*, you need to indicate this to Verity by using quotation marks:

```
CRITERIA="'not smoking'"
CRITERIA="AND('not',smoking)"
CRITERIA="AND(""not"",smoking)"
```

When used with a PARAGRAPH, SENTENCE, or NEAR/N operator, the ORDER modifier indicates that your search words must be found in the document—in the order that you specified them—for the document to be considered a match. The following is an example:

```
CRITERIA="<ORDER><PARAGRAPH>(smoking,policy)"
```

Understanding Score Operators

Every time Verity finds a document, it assigns the document a "score" that represents how closely the document matches the search criteria. The score is always somewhere from 0 to 1, where 1 is a perfect match and 0 is a perfectly miserable match. In most cases, Verity orders the search results in score order, with the highest scores at the top.

Score operators tell Verity to compute this score differently than it would normally. To a certain extent, this allows you to control the order of the documents in the result set. The score operators include the following:

- YESNO
- COMPLEMENT
- PRODUCT
- SUM

The YESNO operator forces the score for any match to be 1, no matter what. In other words, all documents that are relevant at all are equally relevant. The records will not appear in any particular order—even though Verity is trying to rank the search results by relevance—because sorting by a bunch of 1s doesn't really do anything. Here is an example:

```
CRITERIA="YESNO(policy)"
```

The COMPLEMENT operator is kind of strange. With this operator, the score is subtracted from 1 before it's returned to you. A closely-matching document that would ordinarily get a score of .97 would now get a score of only .03. If Verity is ranking records by relevance, using COMPLEMENT makes the search results appear in reverse order (best matches last instead of first). Unfortunately, this also means that a score of 0 now has a score of 1, which means that all documents that didn't match at all will be returned—and returned first.

If for some bizarre reason you only wanted documents that were completely unrelated to smoking—ranked by irrelevance—you could use this:

```
CRITERIA="<COMPLEMENT>smoking"
```

The PRODUCT operator causes Verity to calculate the score for the document by multiplying the scores for each search word found. The net effect is that relevant documents appear to be even more relevant, and less relevant documents are even less relevant. This operator may cause fewer documents to be found. The following is an example:

```
CRITERIA="<PRODUCT>smoking"
```

The SUM operator causes Verity to calculate the score for the document by adding the scores for each search word found, up to a maximum document score of 1. The net effect is that more documents appear to get perfect scores. Here is an example:

```
CRITERIA="<SUM>smoking"
```

Index

Read This Before Opening Software